Structural analysis in the social sciences 5

Governance of the American Economy

Structural Analysis in the Social Sciences

Mark Granovetter, editor

Advisory Board:

Peter Blau	Linton Freeman	Franz Pappi
Ronald Brieger	Maureen Hallinan	Everett Rogers
Ronald Burt	Nan Lin	Charles Tilly
Randall Collins	J. Clyde Mitchell	Barry Wellman
Claude Fisher	Nicholas Mullins	Harrison White

Other books in the series:

Mark S. Mizruchi and Michael Schwartz, eds., *Intercorporate Relations: The Structural Analysis of Business*

Barry Wellman and S. D. Berkowitz, eds., *Social Structures: A Network Approach*

Ronald L. Breiger, ed., *Social Mobility and Social Structure*

David Knoke, *Political Networks: The Structural Perspective*

The series *Structural Analysis in the Social Sciences* presents approaches that explain social behavior and institutions by reference to *relations* among such concrete social entities as persons and organizations. This contrasts with at least four other popular strategies: (1) reductionist attempts to explain by a focus on individuals alone; (2) explanations stressing the causal primacy of such abstract concepts as ideas, values, mental harmonies, and cognitive maps (thus, "structuralism" on the Continent should be distinguished from structural analysis in the present sense); (3) technological and material determinism; (4) explanations using "variables" as the main analytic concepts (as in the "structural equation" models that dominated much of the sociology of the 1970s), where "structure" is that connecting variables rather than actual social entities.

The "social network" approach is an important example of the strategy of structural analysis; the series also draws on social science theory and research that is not framed explicitly in network terms, but stresses the importance of relations rather than the atomization of reductionism or the determinism of ideas, technology, or material conditions. Though the structural perspective has become extremely popular and influential in all the social sciences, it does not have a coherent identity, and no series yet pulls together such work under a single rubric. By bringing the achievements of structurally oriented scholars to a wider public, the *Structural Analysis* series hopes to encourage the use of this very fruitful approach.

Mark Granovetter

Governance of
the American Economy

Edited by

John L. Campbell
Department of Sociology
Harvard University

J. Rogers Hollingsworth
Departments of History and Sociology
University of Wisconsin–Madison

Leon N. Lindberg
Department of Political Science
University of Wisconsin–Madison

CAMBRIDGE
UNIVERSITY PRESS

Published by the Press Syndicate of the University of Cambridge
The Pitt Building, Trumpington Street, Cambridge CB2
40 West 20th Street, New York, NY 10011-4211, USA
10 Stamford Road, Oakleigh, Melborne 3166, Australia

© Cambridge University Press 1991

First published 1991
Reprinted 1994

Printed in the United States of America

Library of Congress Cataloging-in-Publication Data available
A catalogue record for this book is available from the British Library.

ISBN 0-521-40257-3 hardback
ISBN 0-521-40827-X paperback

CONTENTS

LIST OF FIGURES

LIST OF TABLES

LIST OF CONTRIBUTORS

Patricia Arnold is Assistant Professor of Business and Accounting at the University of Wisconsin–Milwaukee. She has served on the faculty of the Department of Health Policy and Management at the Harvard School of Public Health. Her work has been concerned principally with examining the social, economic, and organizational consequences of accounting policy choice and the role of accounting in adjudicating distributions of wealth within nonmarket-contexts. Her dissertation, entitled *Capital Costs, Accounting Choice and Multihospital Systems,* focuses on the health sector. Her current research examines the effects of accounting policy in other regulated industries in the United States, and internationally through multinational transfer pricing practices.

Kenneth Bickers is Assistant Professor of Political Science at Rice University, Houston, Texas. His research is concerned principally with the evolution of American regulatory and social policy. He is currently writing with Robert Stein a volume to be entitled *Whither the Great Society: The Evolution of Domestic Public Policy, 1965–1990.* His dissertation, *The Politics of Regulatory Design,* explored the various institutional methods used in regulating the telecommunications industry in the United States.

John Campbell, one of the editors of this volume, is Assistant Professor of Sociology at Harvard University. He is author of *Collapse of an Industry: Nuclear Power and the Contradictions of U.S. Policy* (Cornell University Press, 1988), which examines how political and economic institutions influenced industrial and regulatory policy and performance in the U.S., French, Swedish, and West German commercial nuclear energy sectors. He is currently conducting an historical analysis of twentieth-century reforms in personal and corporate income tax policies in the United States to determine the conditions under which state autonomy varies in advanced capitalist democracies. He is also continuing his work on economic governance.

J. Rogers Hollingsworth, one of the editors of this volume, is Professor of Sociology and History and Chairperson of the Program in Comparative History at the University of Wisconsin–Madison. He has written numerous books and articles about the coordination of various sectors of the American economy, and he is presently engaged in a cross-national study of the governance of capitalist economies. His most recent book (with Jerald Hage and Robert Hanneman) is *State Intervention* *in Medical Care: Consequences for Britain, France, Sweden, and the United States, 1890–1970* (Cornell University Press, 1990).

Robert D. Kennedy, Jr., is Senior Fellow for Socioeconomic Analysis with The Madison Institute in Madison, Wisconsin. He has written about and drafted successful legislation on new approaches to economic development in Wisconsin. His current research and writing concerns emergent paradigms of economy and political economy, and political economic trends in the twenty-first century.

Leon Lindberg, one of the editors of this volume, is Professor of Political Science at the University of Wisconsin–Madison. He has published widely on comparative and international political economy, including *The Politics of Inflation and Economic Stagnation* (Brookings Institution, 1985), *The Energy Syndrome* (Lexington, 1977), *Stress and Contradiction in Modern Capitalism* (Lexington, 1975), and *Europe's Would-Be Polity* (Prentice-Hall, 1970). He is currently working on a study of "Capital Movements, Financial Services, and the Politics of Monetary Policy in the European Community."

John Portz is Assistant Professor of Political Science at Northeastern University in Boston. His chapter in this volume on the meatpacking industry is an extension of research on government responses to industrial plant closing and economic change. His analysis of plant closing responses by American governments, along with three case studies, is published as *The Politics of Plant Closings* (University Press of Kansas, 1990). His current research interests cover state and local economic policies, particularly as they pertain to targeting government assistance to new and mature industries.

Christoph Scherrer is Assistant Professor at the John F. Kennedy Institute, Free University of Berlin. He received his Ph.D. at the University of Frankfurt with a work entitled *Ruptures in the U.S. Regime of Accumulation,* which will be published by Edition Sigma, Berlin. He is currently working on a study about "National, Transnational, and Global Forms of Regulation of the American Hegemonic System," directed by Professor Elmar Altvater.

Brigitte Young is Visiting Professor at the John F. Kennedy Institute, Free University of Berlin, and Assistant Professor of Political Science at Wesleyan University. She was also a Social Science Research Council postdoctoral fellow in the Berlin Program for Advanced German and European Studies at the Free University of Berlin. She has written on problems of agriculture in the Soviet Union, the United States, and Germany. Her dissertation focused on agrarian reproduction and the institutions that regulate such processes in Germany and the United States. She is currently studying the role of the state in developing agrarian institutions during German fascism and the "New Deal" era. Her publications include *Prospects for Soviet Grain Production* (Westview Press, 1983), and "Does the American Dairy Industry Fit the Meso-Corporatist Model?" in *Political Studies* (1990).

PREFACE

This volume reports the findings of a project on the Governance of the American Economy convened at the University of Wisconsin–Madison by J. Rogers Hollingsworth and Leon N. Lindberg. The purpose of the project was to understand the forces producing major changes in the structure of the institutions of governance – or control – in individual sectors and in the production process more generally. We were interested in recording the variety of the institutional conditions of economic exchange in the American economy and how these are transformed through time. We felt a need to thereby correct some common misperceptions about the institutional characteristics of the American economy and about the relations between the state and the economy in the United States.

Initial concepts and theoretical orientations for the project were developed in a seminar cotaught by Hollingsworth and Lindberg in the Fall of 1984. These were formalized in their paper, "The Governance of the American Economy: The Role of Markets, Clans, Hierarchies, and Associative Behavior" (1985), and a paper by Lindberg, "Political Economy, Economic Governance, and the Coordination of Economic Activities" (1986). On the basis of these ideas, a Workshop on the Governance of the American Economy, consisting primarily of graduate students at the University of Wisconsin–Madison (many of whom had been in the seminar) met regularly from the Fall of 1984 until the Summer of 1986. Each graduate student participant tried to analyze the history of a particular sector of the American economy with the conceptual apparatus provided. The conceptual and theoretical ideas were then revised and refined as we collectively learned more about the technological, economic, and sociopolitical characteristics of each sector. The Workshop thus engaged in an iterative process in which conceptual and deductive analyses interacted with "thick description" as each sectoral study evolved in a series of drafts.

The vagaries of writing dissertations, taking first jobs, divergent schedules, and competing commitments of the editors after 1986 slowed the process of final review and revision of the sector case studies and the preparation of the concluding chapters, which try to tease patterns and regularities from the very rich "stories" the case studies tell. It is in the final chapters that we provide a more general analysis of the historical evolution of governance arrangements and the role of the state in constituting sectors and organizing economic activity.

We see this volume contributing to the revival of institutional analysis in political science, sociology, and economic and business history, which seeks to provide a corrective for the neglect of institutions in conventional economic analysis. In this tradition, economic and political institutions are analyzed in terms of their own dynamics, "economic rationality" is seen as historically contingent, and institutional arrangements not only shape agent behaviors, but can become themselves important "factors of production." We have sought to confront this style of analysis with a variety of more or less revisionist, but still "neoclassical," literatures within economics that claim to take institutions seriously, in particular, transaction-cost theory, the "new economic history," and property rights theory.

Our acknowledgments are numerous. Most particularly, we owe special thanks to our contributors, whose criticisms of early conceptualizations and efforts at theorizing greatly improved the end product. Jerald Hage, Donald N. McCloskey, Philippe Schmitter, and Wolfgang Streeck came to Madison during the project and served as consultants. The following colleagues commented on parts of the manuscript or discussed their ideas with us in ways that contributed much to the development of the project: John A. Hall, Elaine Backman, Peter Hall, Michael Allen, Gregory Hooks, Ivan Szelenyi, Mark Granovetter, Peter Katzenstein, Graham Wilson, John Witte, Peter Eisinger, Thomas Moore, Gerhard Lehmbruch, Howard Aldrich, Daniel Bromley, William Coleman, Fred Block, Stephan Haggard, Steve Brint, Helen Mitner, William Alonso, Peter Marsden, Alfred D. Chandler, Oliver Williamson, Bjorn Wittrock, Tom Burns, and Fritz Scharpf. Marc Schneiberg and Mark Eisner wrote memoranda for members of our project and attended many of our workshops. For manuscript preparation, we are grateful to Beatrice Lindberg, Ellen Jane Hollingsworth, Alice Mellian, Cheri Minton, Nancy Williamson, and Lory Dance.

Although this project was not supported by a large research grant, the editors received financial support for crucial tasks and for time to reflect and write. Campbell acknowledges the financial support of the Clark Fund and the Department of Sociology, Harvard University. Hollingsworth acknowledges financial support from the Graduate Research Committee of the University of Wisconsin and the Ford Foundation. Lindberg acknowledges financial support from the Graduate Research Committee of the University of Wisconsin and gives special thanks to the Wissenschafts-Kolleg zu Berlin and the Swedish Collegium for Advanced Study in the Social Sciences, where he was a Visiting Fellow in January to July 1985 and January to July 1987, respectively.

The Editors

Part I

Conceptual and historical foundations

1

ECONOMIC GOVERNANCE AND THE ANALYSIS OF STRUCTURAL CHANGE IN THE AMERICAN ECONOMY

Leon N. Lindberg
Department of Political Science, University of Wisconsin–Madison

John L. Campbell
Department of Sociology, Harvard University

J. Rogers Hollingsworth
Department of History, University of Wisconsin–Madison

The institutions that govern economic activity in the United States have changed dramatically since the late nineteenth century and continue to do so as politicians, business leaders, and others scramble to cope with sluggish productivity, rapid technological change, volatile markets, increasing international competition, trade deficits, and a host of other problems that plague the economy. This book explains how and why these transformations in governance, the political and economic processes that coordinate activity among economic actors, occurred in different industries and industrial sectors. Although we seek to understand the dynamics of the U.S. economy, we also address questions about the governance of modern capitalist economies in general by focusing on the emergence and rearrangement of several common institutional forms of governance, or governance mechanisms, which include markets, bureaucratic hierarchies, associations, and informal networks. We add further breadth to the analysis by discussing the unique role that the state plays in the governance transformation process.[1]

Of course, social scientists have adopted a wide-ranging set of theoretical positions to explain transformations in governance. Those following Adam Smith, John Stuart Mill, and the neoclassical economic tradition adopted

---

1 As a result, this study provides a substantial empirical and theoretical *complement* to the vast, normatively oriented literature, which suggests that a variety of institutional changes are necessary to solve the U.S. economy's recent problems. Much of this literature fails to appreciate not only the conditions under which various institutional alternatives are likely to emerge, but also that some institutional arrangements may be better suited than others to rectify different types of economic problems in different types of industries and sectors – an issue to which we give serious attention. For a sampling of this literature, see

a *utilitarian* view and suggested that governance transformations occur when rationally calculating economic actors see that alternative forms of governance offer more profitable ways of doing business than those already in place (e.g., Williamson 1975, 1985, 1986). Others followed an *organizational* approach, reminiscent of Max Weber, and suggested that a broader set of motivations and organizational goals, such as a sense of community and reciprocity, also influence governance transformations (e.g., Granovetter 1985). Borrowing from the *evolutionary* traditions of Auguste Comte, Emile Durkheim, and Herbert Spencer, some observers maintained that more efficient organizational forms emerged to govern economic activity through a natural selection process, where the institutional forms best suited to prevailing environmental conditions are most likely to survive (e.g., Hannan and Freeman 1977; Nelson and Winter 1982). A fourth group, influenced by Karl Marx as well as Weber, developed a *political economy* approach that argued that struggles over power transformed governance (e.g., Schmitter and Lehmbruch 1979; Berger 1981; Perrow 1981).

This book is located at the intersection of these debates and strives to move them forward by offering a new approach to the analysis of governance transformations. It does this by pursuing several more specific theoretical objectives. First, it offers a *new conceptual scheme* that we hope will build bridges in a fragmented and scattered literature about economic governance. Second, it provides an *empirical analysis* of the causal models that other scholars have offered previously to explain or predict the conditions under which different forms of governance emerge. Third, because we find that many of these models, especially those that are based on explanations about economic efficiency, offer causal predictions that are not always supported by our data, we argue that the search for universal generalizations with which to predict governance transformations is futile and that there are no universal or immutable logics in the governance of capitalist societies. Instead, we embrace the broadly neo-Weberian position that one can only hope to find and explain *historically specific* patterns and sequences of transformation. Fourth, we theorize the *process* by which governance transformations occur – something that has not been done in most of the literatures that are dedicated to predicting specific types of transformations with causal models. Through a critical synthesis of these models, we argue that transformations occur as actors select new sets of governance mechanisms in ways that are constrained economically, politically, institutionally, technologically, and culturally in complex ways, and that the choices actors make bear heavily on future constraints and choices.

Thurow (1980), Gilder (1981), *Business Week Team* (1982), Bowles et al. (1983), Reich (1983), Dolbeare (1984), and Adams and Brock (1986).

Fifth, whereas most theoretical traditions neglect or understate the importance of the state as it constitutes the institutional arrangement of economic sectors, we theorize the role of *state actors* and especially *state structures* in shaping the selection of new governance regimes. Finally, we believe that this book contributes to the debate about the origins and causes of the *productivity problems* of the contemporary U.S. economy and the prospects for solving them. Our findings are particularly relevant to those who argue that productivity problems stem from organizational weaknesses in the U.S. production system because our analysis illuminates how these organizational problems developed in the first place.

We begin to address these issues in this chapter by clarifying our assumptions about the nature of governance, particularly insofar as they differ from the prevailing neoclassical economic paradigm. We argue that it is not just the search for economic efficiency, but also struggles over strategic control and power within economic exchange that provide the principal dynamic for governance transformations. Furthermore, drawing on the idea that governance is largely a matter of social control, we provide a typology of governance mechanisms that are commonly found in advanced capitalist economies. We also discuss briefly the state's role in economic governance and why we consider it to be significantly different than the governance mechanisms we identify and, therefore, worthy of separate consideration. Finally, we offer a brief description of the governance transformation process for heuristic purposes. As such, this chapter provides a conceptual framework within which to analyze specific governance transformations that have occurred in the U.S. economy.[2]

THE NATURE OF GOVERNANCE

Unit of analysis

Governance is a phenomenon that is best conceptualized at the level of industries and industrial sectors. In contrast to neoclassical models that focus on the behavior of discrete market actors, we view each industry as

2 This chapter is signed by the editors but is in a profound sense a collaborative product of a dialogue with all the authors in this volume and with several other participants in the Workshop on the Governance of the American Economy, which met regularly in Madison at the University of Wisconsin from the Fall of 1984 to the Summer of 1986. Many of these individuals also provided detailed critiques of earlier drafts of this chapter. Memoranda prepared and presented to the workshop by Ken Bickers and Marc Schneiberg proved particularly useful in advancing the conceptual and theoretical work. In addition, special thanks for their comments go to Michael Allen, Howard Aldrich, William Coleman, Gerald Hage, Gerhard Lehmbruch, Marc Eisner, Philippe Schmitter, Marc Schneiberg, and Graham Wilson.

a matrix of interdependent social exchange relationships, or transactions, that must occur among organizations, either individually or collectively, in order for them to develop, produce, and market goods or services. Thus, governance is an extremely complex phenomenon. Transactions occur within a sector among a wide range of interdependent actors, including producers and suppliers of raw materials, researchers, manufacturers, distributors, and many others, who must routinely solve various problems, such as raising capital, setting wages, standardizing products, and establishing prices in order for economic activity to continue. Complicating matters further, there are several types of governance mechanisms that groups of actors may adopt to help them solve these problems. If we tried to specify all the actors, all their problems, and all the governance mechanisms they employed, analyzing governance in a sector would become an overwhelming task. One need only recognize that a matrix representing the relationships among all possible combinations of actors and problem areas would involve scores of cells. However, because our major concern in this book is with understanding the *transformations* in governance mechanisms historically, we have simplified matters by focusing only on governance mechanisms when they fail, encounter serious legitimacy problems, and when actors search for and devise alternative means of governing their relationships. By narrowing our attention to these moments when new arrangements of governance mechanisms emerge, the analysis becomes much more manageable.

Interests and rationality

Rather than assuming that economic behavior is always self-interested or rational in the sense that people select the most efficient course of action in order to maximize their utilities or wealth, we recognize that people may also be content merely to satisfy their needs. Furthermore, they will do so not just within the limits of bounded rationality, where actors make intendedly rational choices based only on the incomplete information available to them (e.g., Simon 1961), but also within those of *contingent* rationality, where the political, economic, ideological, and other institutional conditions prevalent at the moment constrain the range of choices available in the first place. Indeed, a variety of values or ideologies, including but not limited to opportunism and avariciousness, motivates economic activity and is conditioned by all of these contingencies, not just markets.[3]

---

3 For further discussion of contingent rationality, see Peter Hall (1986: 34–7) who, for example, argues that we cannot derive the rationality of economic actors from the market a priori because the institutional structure of markets and, therefore, market rationality is historically specific.

Significance of nonmarket forms of governance

Our approach to the study of governance is also different from neoclassical economics because, as noted earlier, rather than focusing almost exclusively on markets, we are concerned with shifts to alternative forms of governance. We agree that autonomous organizational actors often coordinate their transactions through markets, where hard contracts specify the terms of exchange, such as price, quality, wages, and conditions of work. However, market contracting does not always ensure that the interests of all parties to a transaction are sufficiently served. Market uncertainties may be so severe that actors believe that they do not have enough information with which to act. Economic risks may be so difficult to assess that parties to exchange find it very hard to develop acceptable contracts. In short, markets may fail to provide for the kinds of transactions that actors desire, in part because economic reality often differs from neoclassical assumptions about pure competition, uninhibited entry and exit from the market, the availability of accurate information, and the like.

Under these circumstances, actors seek alternative forms of governance rather than permitting exchange relationships to fracture under what Oliver Williamson (1985: 3) called the hammer of unassisted market contracting.[4] Collective action, for instance, a common phenomenon in industries despite the presence of Mancur Olson's (1965) free-rider problem, emerged in the U.S. textile industry during the early 1900s in an effort to stabilize production levels and prices when manufacturers, relying on markets to coordinate their activities, failed to do so (Galambos 1966). Indeed, alternative forms of governance warrant attention in their own right because it is their presence, as common elements of economic life, that undermines many of the neoclassical assumptions about how markets work in the first place. The presence of huge corporate bureaucracies, which limit some actors' access to markets and market information, is a common example (e.g., Galbraith 1967).

Power and equilibrium

We view production and exchange as systems of power, manifested through market and nonmarket governance mechanisms, an assumption that implies that economic activity does not necessarily tend toward equilibrium, equal exchange, or efficiency, but often involves institutionally determined, asymmetrical, and shifting exchange advantages. Hence, the institutional

---

4 See Alt and Chrystal (1983: 175–83) for a review of the vast literature on market failure. It is interesting that although even the most conservative neoclassical economists acknowledge that the problems of market failure may lead to alternative forms of economic governance, they persist in paying only scant attention to these alternatives (e.g., Friedman 1962: Chap. 2).

distribution of power, not just prices, regulates economic exchange. Furthermore, although governance mechanisms and their arrangement evolve over time, there is nothing natural or inherent about that evolution. Instead, the history of governance transformations is guided by actors searching in cooperative and conflictive ways for what they believe are the best available options. We will argue that governance transformations are likely to occur when actors, who are unable to manage problems of interdependence to their satisfaction within the existing arrangement of governance mechanisms, search for institutional alternatives in contingently rational ways. In sum, our framework forces a basic shift in the analysis of economic exchange processes, particularly away from the neoclassical economic tradition that emphasizes rational economic man, commodities, prices, and perfect or imperfect markets to one that focuses on organizational actors with complex motivations, their interdependencies, and the qualitatively different types of transactions in which they engage – phenomena that vary historically within and across industries.[5]

DYNAMICS OF CHANGE WITHIN THE GOVERNANCE FRAMEWORK

Despite the vast literature on nonmarket forms of governance, discussed in what follows, there is often a failure to theorize how economic performance and governance processes cause different governance mechanisms to develop, on the one hand, and how the relative influence of different governance mechanisms is determined historically, on the other. For example, it is not enough to assert that all economic action is embedded in networks of informal social relations (e.g., Granovetter 1985) and that such networks, rather than the largely fictitious pure market, account for whatever observable order exists in an industry. To do so neglects the important tasks of identifying different degrees and qualities of embeddedness, specifying different kinds of networks, explaining how they developed, and determining how effectively they moderate different types of exchanges. Similarly, it is not enough to know how private organizations or the state makes decisions, that work and exchange relations are hierarchically controlled, or that capitalists monitor each other's behavior through networks. We must also determine the origins and performance capacities of these different forms of governance.

For these reasons, we have been particularly interested in the recent literature on industrial economics, especially those variants that recognize that institutions play important, but often neglected, roles in shaping eco-

---

5 Our assumptions about the functioning of economic systems are similar to those of institutional rather than neoclassical economics. For an elaboration and comparison of institutionalist and neoclassical assumptions, see Stevenson (1987).

nomic performance within and between industries, sectors, and entire political–economic systems. Specifically, we are drawn to the work of Williamson (1975, 1985, 1986) and Douglass North (1981), who have used transaction-cost theory to develop models that seek to explain transformations in the institutional coordination of economic exchange. This may seem ironic because the transaction-cost approach is steeped in neoclassical assumptions, many of which we do not accept.[6] However, for reasons that follow, this approach provides useful starting points for addressing the issues with which we are concerned.

Williamson argued that corporate hierarchies emerge to coordinate economic transactions when the costs of conducting such exchanges through the market become prohibitive. That is, when actors feel that the financial costs of engaging in and monitoring transactions become too uncertain, because transaction-specific investments are great and it is difficult within the limits of bounded rationality to control an exchange partner's opportunism, they will develop hierarchically integrated, corporate organizations to supplant the market as the primary forum for exchange. Despite its problems (see note 6 before), transaction-cost theory offers the important insight that when actors can no longer efficiently consummate transactions through either the market or, we would add, another form of governance, at least to their satisfaction, they will try to develop other more efficient governance mechanisms. Furthermore, it suggests the need for a general theory of governance transformation that specifies a dynamic for change, accepts that there are different forms of governance, and recognizes that each may play an important role in coordinating economic activity.[7]

Yet to argue that transaction-cost inefficiencies are the sole cause of governance transformations is an excessively narrow view. First, when institutional arrangements undermine the efficient allocation of resources and information for *any* reason, not just because transaction costs are high, actors may begin to look for alternative arrangements that will improve efficiency.[8] For example, because labor is too expensive, managers in an

6 For extended criticisms, with which we are sympathetic, of the assumptions and other aspects of transaction-cost economics, see Ouchi (1977, 1980), Perrow (1981, 1986: Chap. 7), Johanson and Mattsson (1987), Robbins (1987), Hodgson (1988), and Lazerson (1988).
7 Williamson and other transaction-cost theorists generally assume that governance transformations begin with *market* failures. Although this is one possibility, we will argue for a more general theory of *governance* failure where transformations may also occur in response to the inability of nonmarket governance mechanisms to satisfactorily coordinate economic activity. To do otherwise requires that we accept the neoclassical assumption that markets are the ever-present starting point for the development of alternative governance arrangements, an assumption that has been rejected based on the historical record (e.g., Polanyi 1944; Lazonick 1986), but which has permeated transaction-cost theory (e.g., Williamson 1986: 143). See Robbins (1987) for an elaboration on the empirical and theoretical problems this presents.
8 Efficiency in this sense is a function of a firm, industry, or economy's input–output ratio,

industry may switch from a union-based, hierarchical system of obtaining labor, where the (transaction) costs of monitoring labor are low, to a market-based system with higher monitoring costs in the belief that a net saving in resources will be achieved through the realization of lower wages. Second, transaction-cost theory and orthodox economics in general ignore the *strategic* causes of governance transformations. That is, in addition to simply acquiring the resources and information they need at the lowest possible cost, actors may also be concerned with *controlling the terms of exchange* under which they make these acquisitions – a strategic concern insofar as power, rather than just the ability to procure resources, is at stake. In this sense, the arrangement of governance mechanisms is undesirable and worth changing from an actor's point of view if it systematically restricts the actor's control over the terms of exchange relative to that of the exchange partner. Thus, when strategic problems become intolerable for enough actors, the legitimacy of the prevailing set of governance mechanisms suffers, and they may press for governance transformations. If workers, for instance, labor for low wages under dangerous working conditions, they may decide to unionize and establish collective bargaining with management in an effort to control more closely the terms under which they exchange their labor. As a result, an alternative form of governance replaces the traditional labor market.[9] In sum, governance transformations are likely to occur not only when actors are unable to efficiently get the resources and information they want through exchange, but also when they cannot control satisfactorily the terms of exchange under which they attempt to obtain these resources and information in the first place.[10] However, knowing that all sorts of ineffi-

---

and is consistent with the neoclassical tradition. Optimum efficiency is reached when the output is maximized relative to a given set of inputs (or input costs) and markets clear. For example, firms obtain the production factors they need at lowest cost and sell the commodities they produce. Therefore, transaction-cost efficiency is a special type of the more general neoclassical notion of efficiency. For a critical discussion of these definitions of efficiency from an institutional economics perspective, see Stevenson (1987).

9 Failure to recognize the importance of strategic causes of governance transformations is linked to, and perhaps derived from, other problems with the transaction-cost and neoclassical economic perspectives. First, as Stevenson (1987) suggested, representatives of these schools fail to ask the important *normative* questions – how and in whose interest are the standards of efficiency judged and established? – questions which, when posed, would force them to recognize that definitions of efficiency are not always universally accepted and, thus, that there may be additional reasons why actors try to change governance arrangements. Second, as Perrow (1981) argued, adherents to these traditions usually fail to accept the fact that power and class conflict often play important roles in the development of nonmarket governance arrangements, phenomena that are often the result of inequalities in strategic control.

10 We have been influenced here by Zald's (1970) classic discussion of the political and economic aspects of organizational activity, where organizational politics and economics center on problems of the control and exchange of resources, respectively, within and between organizations.

ciencies and strategic considerations trigger interests in governance transformations tells us very little about how transformations actually occur and why governance assumes particular institutional forms.

Although North (1981) adopts the same transaction-cost perspective that Williamson does and, as others have noted (e.g., Robbins 1987), suffers from many of the same theoretical problems as a result, he makes several additional points. The institutions that coordinate economic activity are, in effect, property rights structures (we would call them governance mechanisms) that are comprised of systems of rules, procedures, and norms that define ownership and control of the means of production, govern transactions, and determine the efficiency with which resources and information are allocated. Furthermore, although property rights structures vary historically and are determined in part by the efforts of transacting parties to increase the efficiency of their exchanges, they are also determined by actors within the state who are trying to maximize their revenues and maintain the support of their constituents.[11]

North's analysis is helpful not only because he unbundles the concept of property rights by identifying three dimensions with which we can differentiate among property rights structures, or governance mechanisms, but also because he recognizes that *political* forces and, thus, the state play crucial roles in establishing property rights, an idea that implies that governance transformations often involve conflict, rather than a smooth evolution to more efficient exchange processes.[12] This also follows from his suggestion that property rights structures are the institutionalized systems of power and control that actors design to reproduce exchange relations so as to help them obtain systematically greater access to resources and information than others. In short, property rights structures are the institutional arrangements that determine not only the efficiency of economic activity, broadly speaking, but the strategic control of this activity as well. Hence, when actors from the state and civil society try to transform property rights, they necessarily engage in struggles over power and control. Furthermore, these struggles determine directly the various *institutional forms* of property rights structures that emerge and the degree to which they are efficient and strategically acceptable for different actors. As a result, these struggles constitute the central dynamic of governance transformations and largely determine which governance mechanisms emerge.

This is not to ignore the important effects that a variety of other factors has in sparking the search for alternative governance mechanisms. For example, problems may arise among actors due to the changing physical

11 North's theory of the state is steeped in neoclassical economic assumptions, such as the maximizing interests of state actors. Although we agree that a theory of the state is important in understanding the transformation of economic governance, as will become apparent in what follows, we do not embrace his version of that theory.
12 For an early attempt to develop these ideas, see Commons (1924).

or technological characteristics of the production and marketing process. In industries where markets become very large and require complex delivery schedules and specialized marketing services, producers may become vulnerable to wholesale and retail marketers who, by virtue of these changes in market structure, have gained more control over the exchange process. In other cases, suppliers of specialized parts or scarce natural resources may use their position of control over exchange to raise prices, restrict access to resources, and incite their customers to seek alternative forms of governance, by organizing consumer cooperatives as a means of counterbalancing the power of producers. North (1981) stresses the significance of such factors as these in the transformation of property rights structures and argues that different property rights structures tend to systematically produce inefficiencies in different ways. Indeed, all of the economic problems mentioned earlier with which actors must often contend, such as adjusting prices, standardizing products, and raising capital, are often the concrete manifestations of the general inefficiencies that may occur within an industry's property rights, or governance, structure. Hence, an analysis of economic governance should determine not only which governance mechanisms tend to develop in response to different strategic concerns or inefficiencies, but also which concerns and inefficiencies tend to occur as a result of the structure and dynamics of different types of governance mechanisms. Yet we must remember that although efforts to transform governance may stem from problems such as these, struggles for power and control will usually determine the outcome.

By critically employing these insights, we can begin to see the causal links between economic performance, governance processes, and the development of different combinations of governance mechanisms. Specifically, we are now in a position to do the following: distinguish systematically among different types of governance mechanisms according, in part, to the qualitative differences in their rules, procedures, and normative guidelines – dimensions that North has identified; recognize the important role the state plays in the governance transformation process; and recognize that the problems of political and economic performance and control are often the driving forces behind governance transformations. We will discuss each of these in order.

A TYPOLOGY OF GOVERNANCE MECHANISMS

There is a vast and very eclectic literature about many forms of governance, including markets, bureaucratic hierarchies, associations, and different types of networks, that expands the relatively narrow, market-oriented vision of neoclassical economics by providing points of departure for the consideration of how other organizational forms help govern economic activity.[13] Yet this literature remains largely fragmented and unintegrated, perhaps due to the intense academic specialization of the social sciences, but also because scholars have failed to specify the significant organizational dimensions that differentiate among types of governance mechanisms. This fragmentation has hampered the development of a more comprehensive understanding of economic governance that addresses *simultaneously* the wide array of governance mechanisms and the relationships that exist between them.[14] In an effort to remedy this problem, we have constructed a typology of governance mechanisms that integrates the previous research and provides the core concepts that guide this study. We also hope that it will help improve communication across different specialties in several social science disciplines. Bear in mind, however, that because we are concerned in this volume with the organization of production, this typology is intended primarily to describe the types of exchanges that occur among actors *within* the production process. Thus, the discussion that follows does not dwell at length on the relationships between manufacturers of finished products and the general consumer.

The theoretical dimensions that define our typology identify two of the most important questions one can ask about social control systems. First, is economic activity coordinated within a formal organization or through more informal relationships among economic actors? Second, do the institutions that coordinate economic activity involve interactions among a relatively small number of rather autonomous actors or a larger group, engaged in some form of collective enterprise?

The first dimension of our typology, degree of formal integration, is a continuum that embodies the distinction between *formal* and *informal* types of organizations (see Table 1.1) This is perhaps the most common distinction found in the literature on forms of economic coordination and control. For example, political economists differentiate between exchange and authority systems (e.g., Lindblom 1977), transaction-cost economists discuss markets and hierarchies (e.g., Williamson 1975), and organization theorists

13 For introductions to this literature, see, for example, Pfeffer and Salancik (1978), White (1981), Granovetter (1985), and Perrow (1986), on markets, networks, and hierarchies; Offe and Wiesenthal (1985) and Streeck and Schmitter (1985) on associations; and Aldrich (1979), Mintz and Schwartz (1985), and Pfeffer (1987) on less formally organized collective organizations. These literatures receive more thorough attention in Chapter 11. See McCloskey (1986) and deVille (1987) for discussions about the neoclassical tradition's obsession with the study of markets.

14 The need for such integration is indicated, for example, by the widespread attention that Williamson's work has received, which, we suspect, stems in part from his attempt to develop an analysis that links different types of governance mechanisms through a typology, on the one hand, and offers a theoretical explanation about the conditions under which each type emerges, on the other. As a result, his work appeals to a very broad, interdisciplinary audience that includes those interested in studying markets, hierarchies, and certain intermediate forms of governance, either alone or in combination.

Table 1.1. *A typology of governance mechanisms*

Degree of formal integration	Range of interaction	
	Bilateral	Multilateral
Low: No discrete organizational structure	*Markets* • Self-liquidating sales • Spot-market contracts	*Monitoring* • Extensive corporate interlocks for information sharing • Market-sharing agreements • Dominant-firm pricing
Moderate: Linked autonomous, but interdependent actors	*Obligational networks* • Follow-on weapons contracts • Long-term subcontracting • Franchise contracts • Inside contracting • Limited corporate interlocks to stabilize resource and capital flows • Small hierarchies • Joint ventures	*Promotional networks* • Action sets • R&D alliances • Coalitions • Interorganizational clans
High: Bureaucratic administrative control structure	*Hierarchies* • Vertical and horizontal integration • Conglomerate • Job-control union contracts	*Associations* • Trade association • Employer association • Producer cooperative • Unions

compare social choice and bureaucratic control systems (e.g., Weber 1978: 63–211). In the pure case of informal organization, there is no formal structural provision for a division of labor among organizations, and organizations attempt to control each other's behavior through dispersed, arms-length interactions, where each offers benefits to induce exchange and each is at liberty to accept or refuse those inducements from one exchange to the next. In the pure case of formal organization, on the other hand, actors coordinate behavior by command through a bureaucratic hierarchy. They use rewards and penalties that are institutionalized within a single organizational structure, such as those described by Alfred Chandler (1977) in his discussion of the visible hand of management. Hence, the element of coercion is not dispersed into innumerable arms-length exchanges, as it is in the informal case, but is hierarchically centralized.

The literature in transaction-cost economics and interorganizational relations has identified and theorized an intermediate form of coordination that seems to possess sufficiently distinctive organizational properties to warrant inclusion as a separate category, standing between thoroughly informal and formal types of governance mechanisms (e.g., Powell 1987). Williamson (1985) wrote about relational contracting, Mark Granovetter (1985) and Robert Eccles (1981) discussed the quasifirm, Arthur Stinchcombe (1985) described the contractually created small hierarchy, and others elaborated the concept of network control (e.g., Benson 1975; Pfeffer and Salancik 1978; Aldrich 1979). In all these cases, constituent organizations are neither integrated into a single, formal organization nor autonomously arranged to the extent that each is completely free to refuse or accept the inducements of others. Instead, independent organizations are loosely joined to each other by relatively long-term commitments that are sufficient to ensure some degree of stability and some capacity to cooperate and collaborate with each other through repeated exchanges.

The second dimension in our typology, range of interaction, distinguishes between governance mechanisms according to the degree to which organizations engage in exchanges that involve several or just a few members of the sector at a time. Again, we are referring to a continuum where exchange at one extreme is *bilateral* because it involves only two organizations, but at the other extreme is completely *multilateral* insofar as it involves all the organizations from the sector. Toward the bilateral extreme, actors are engaged in more individualistically oriented behavior and are less deliberately concerned with the well-being of the sector as a whole. Toward the multilateral extreme, actors use inducements to engage organizations in collective behavior and arrive at definitions of common sectoral interests.

While recognizing the dilemmas of large-group collective action, especially the free-rider and prisoner's dilemma problems that are stressed by economists (e.g., Olson 1965; Elster 1978), political scientists and sociologists have shown that collective action, in the form of voting, social movements, and voluntary associations, altruism and self-sacrifice, and obedience to rules, laws, and customs that are embedded in social relations are an important part of economic and political life, and that these phenomena play an important role in obtaining stability and social control. Yet the markets and hierarchies literature completely ignores collective action. Such action is also the kind of behavior that the neoclassical paradigm is least capable of handling and, thus, neglects systematically. We hope that this dimension of our typology will convince others to extend the discussion of governance beyond the bounds of much traditional economic theory.[15]

---

15 For further discussion of this point, see Etzioni (1988). The degree to which scholars continue to ignore collective forms of governance is sometimes remarkable. Some who have spent years studying networks, an important form of governance in its own right, still insist that markets and hierarchies are the primary forms of economic governance

The two dimensions that form our typology refer to *structural* characteristics of governance. Of course, there are many additional dimensions that one could choose with which to differentiate among types of governance. Many typologies could be devised. We recognize this, but focus on these two structural dimensions because they have been very important in much of the literature on economic governance. Yet we also understand that the *processes* that characterize different governance mechanisms are important and that these processes vary, depending largely on where the governance mechanism is located along our two structural dimensions. The discussion that follows focuses on both structure and process and is summarized later in the chapter in Table 1.2.

From our two structural dimensions, we derive a typology of six ideal types of governance mechanisms, each identified by a particular organizational form. For example, in the pure market case informally organized actors pursue their individual interests through numerous bilateral exchanges. In contrast, formally organized groups of actors, pursuing their collective interests through comprehensive multilateral exchanges, guide activity through associations. However, following North (1981), each governance mechanism also involves a unique set of processes or operating principles, by which governance is achieved. On the one hand, each is characterized by certain *types of rules* that define the terms of exchange between economic actors. On the other hand, to understand fully how different governance mechanisms operate, we must also recognize that each consists of different means for obtaining compliance to these rules of exchange. First, each involves a unique set of procedures that actors use for enforcing compliance when actors deviate from the rules, something necessary particularly in situations where actors would otherwise exercise opportunistic behavior, such as cheating on exchange agreements or shirking on contracts. Second, each involves a unique set of norms or ideologies that helps to reduce the costs of enforcement. Because no enforcement system can completely eliminate opportunism, these normative arrangements further minimize such behavior, thereby providing additional assurance that exchange relations will not break down. In short, each governance mechanism is associated with different means and combinations of *coercion* and *consent* for obtaining compliance to its rules of exchange. Because of these variations, actors have different capacities for handling different kinds of transactions, interdependencies, and uncertainties, depending on which governance mechanisms they have organized. Let us first consider these processes insofar as they characterize the three types of governance mechanisms that fall toward the bilateral end of the horizontal continuum.

(e.g., Burt 1988: 390–1). We hope that this typology and, indeed, this entire volume will help to temper that view.

Markets

Many theorists have criticized neoclassical economics for failing to recognize that markets are more than general systems of exchange linking buyers and sellers (e.g., Hall 1986: Chap. 2; Lazonick 1986). As Peter Hall (1986: 46) argued, markets are also institutions with particular organizational configurations that structure the relations between economic actors in significant ways. Following these criticisms, our definition of markets is much more specific institutionally than that of the neoclassical tradition.

The type of contracting that takes place during an exchange is important to understanding what is unique about a market. Actors conducting market exchanges engage in decentralized, arms-length bargaining where the rules of exchange are specified typically through what Williamson (1985: 70; 1986: Chap. 7) called classical contracting. The parties are informally organized and remain autonomous. Each presses its own interests vigorously, and contracting is relatively comprehensive (e.g., Williamson and Ouchi 1981: 361). That is, actors clearly specify performances and prices through contracts that, when fulfilled, are self-liquidating and require no further interaction among the parties involved, such as in spot-market contracts. Furthermore, the identities of the parties involved do not affect the terms of the exchange. Sellers agree simply to trade with the highest bidder regardless of who it is. Actors narrowly prescribe remedies for breach of contract so that if one exchange partner violates the agreement, the consequences will be predictable from the beginning and will not be open-ended (e.g., Telser and Higinbotham 1977: 997; Macneil 1978: 864; Williamson 1985: 69).[16] Finally, and in sharp contrast to corporate hierarchies, there is no mechanism for the planned coordination of the activities of individual economic actors (e.g., Powell 1987).

Coercion is a particularly important means of obtaining compliance in markets and typically involves a variety of legal and economic sanctions, such as fines levied in response to contract violations (e.g., Daems 1980: 205). Ultimately, actors will resolve their contractual disputes through litigation. Prices also serve an important coercive role in coordinating economic activity in markets (e.g., Ouchi 1980: 137–9), at least insofar as they discourage inefficient behavior. However, parties to market contracting often consent voluntarily to abide by the rules of market exchange to some degree because they accept norms of private appropriation, financial reward to self-interested behavior, and the legitimacy of free-market exchange as an

---

16 In fact, Williamson (1986: 114, 1985: 75–6) suggests that although classical contracts are the purest form of market contracting, neoclassical contracts, which involve more long-term agreements subject to arbitration, rather than litigation, during contract disputes, represent a modified version of the market form of governance. We recognize that there are variations on the classical contract form that are also found in markets. However, we emphasize the classical contract here to sharpen the distinctions in the typology.

efficient and self-stabilizing coordination measure (e.g., Weber 1958; North 1981: 52–4), although these ideologies are less influential in obtaining compliance to market exchanges than are more coercive measures.[17] Finally, market alternatives play an important role in ensuring that actors voluntarily uphold their commitments to one another. Opportunistic actors, who do not abide by their contractual agreements, run the risk of losing their trading partners to others in the future (Williamson 1985: 74).

Of course, market exchange may assume different forms. For example, competitive markets have large numbers of buyers and sellers, and supply and demand very much shape prices. Oligopolistic markets tend to exist where a few firms produce most of the output in an industry, and where these firms exercise considerable influence over prices and quantities produced. In a monopoly market, there is only one seller of a good or service, and the monopolistic firm has much greater control over prices and quantities. Similarly, a monopsony market exists when there is a single purchaser of goods and services. The point is that bilateral exchanges, based on classical contracting, may occur in all of these.

Obligational networks

Between market contracting and hierarchical control systems lies a wide variety of interorganizational arrangements and contracting practices that offers much more flexibility in relationships, performance, prices, and surveillance than markets, and yet works to some extent like hierarchies even though the actors retain their organizational autonomy. In order to ensure relatively permanent access to the critical resources or information upon which they depend, actors often participate in obligational networks, a form of governance where the rules of exchange are often characterized by what Williamson (1985: 75–6; 1986: 114–16) called obligational contracting. These contracts involve a closer identification of interests among the actors than under strict market arrangements because each wants to stabilize and maintain the exchange relationship over time. Similarly, because actors are seeking stability in changing environments, these agreements are less precisely specified and much more flexible than market contracts. Furthermore, they often entail periodic redefinitions of the obligations among parties and are more open-ended and continuous than self-

---

17 There has been substantial debate about the degree to which such ideologies are important for ensuring that capitalist market relations continue to operate efficiently. However, most participants in the debate agree that ideology is less important than more coercive means of obtaining compliance to the terms of market exchange (e.g., Abercrombie et al. 1980; Bottomore 1980). Even Weber (1958: 183), who argued that materialist explanations for the development and operation of capitalist market economies needed to be balanced with a theory of ideology, suggested that the latter should complement, not replace, the former.

liquidating market contracts. In contrast to corporate hierarchies, however, actors participating in obligational networks do not consolidate their exchange relationships within a single bureaucratic organization. As a result, these arrangements offer many advantages when compared to either markets or hierarchies in dealing with uncertainty, asset specificity, and transactions requiring teamwork and small-numbers bargaining. For example, they may include flexible incentive systems, methods for adjusting costs, quantities, and prices, such as open-ended escalator clauses, and complex arrangements for privately resolving disputes and making binding decisions (e.g., Stinchcombe 1985; Williamson 1985, 1986).

There are many examples of obligational networks based on such contracts, including follow-on agreements negotiated between the U.S. Department of Defense and weapons manufacturers, long-term subcontracting relationships, franchise contracting in the automobile and fast food industries, and some joint ventures.[18] In many respects, inside contracting is another example where a company hires another firm or a group of individuals to perform a specific task on either a piece-rate or fixed-price basis, and provides the subcontractors with the necessary plant, equipment, and materials (e.g., Buttrick 1952; Eccles 1981: 344–7; Williamson 1985: 156–7). We would also categorize as obligational networks interlocking corporate directorates that organizations establish to stabilize the exchange of important resources among themselves (e.g., Pfeffer 1972; Allen 1974; Pfeffer and Salancik 1978). Although interlocks are not obligational contracts, actors often establish them for many of the same reasons. Of particular importance are networks based on interlocking directorates where corporations and financial organizations interlock with one another to coordinate and secure the flow of capital over time (e.g., Knowles 1973; Mintz and Schwartz 1985). An example would be the efforts of J. P. Morgan and Company in the early part of the twentieth century to provide capital to many large manufacturing and transportation firms in exchange for key positions on the firm's board of directors.

What all of these examples have in common is that actors avoid many of the costs of hierarchies while they maintain control through interlocks, or what Stinchcombe (1985) called small hierarchies, systems of interor-

18 Our typology of governance mechanisms helps distinguish more precisely among different forms of interorganizational arrangements that are often referred to by the same name, such as joint ventures. In fact, there are various types of joint ventures (e.g., Pfeffer and Nowak 1976). Those that coordinate the flow of resources and information among a limited number of firms in order to serve their individual, or nonindustrywide, interests exemplify what we call an obligational network. Those that serve to reduce excessive competition or facilitate cooperation among firms throughout an industry for the industry's collective well-being are examples of the promotional network (discussed in what follows) in our framework. Such distinctions are important because different types of joint ventures, as distinguished in the typology, have different governance capacities and characteristics.

ganizational authority and administration that are organized contractually, not bureaucratically. These arrangements may be especially desirable when organizations seek to establish relatively long-term exchange relationships, but want to minimize their loss of organizational autonomy, something that would happen, for instance, through the creation of a more formal, vertically integrated hierarchy (e.g., Cook 1977: 74–5).[19] Such networks provide flexible ways of reducing the uncertainties associated particularly with an asymmetrical distribution of resources or power, although they may also institutionalize more egalitarian relationships among autonomous organizations, such as the joint venture where Toyota and General Motors agreed to produce cars together in the United States.

In addition to the explicit contractual arrangements that coerce participants to comply with the terms of exchange associated with obligational networks, the need for critical resources itself helps ensure that organizations will cooperate with each other over the long term once they have established such networks (e.g., Williamson 1986: 115). It follows that the more dependent an actor is on his exchange partner for critical resources and information, the more difficult it will be for that actor to get away with violating the agreement and dissolving the relationship. For example, obligational networks involving financial institutions tend to last only as long as firms are heavily dependent on financial institutions for their capital. As firms become more solvent, they may use other institutional mechanisms as instruments for their capital needs.[20] The more symmetrical the exchange, the more difficult it will be for either party to successfully violate the agreement.

However, before coercion becomes necessary, actors often consent willingly to abide by obligational agreements. Personal relations within the business community often help informally mediate exchanges and generate standards of behavior between firms (Granovetter 1985). One reason for establishing interlocks in the first place is to develop personal liaisons between corporations that depend on each other for key resources (Allen 1974). Furthermore, many firms voluntarily uphold their exchange commitments, even in the absence of formal contracts, precisely to preserve the exchange network over the long term (MacCaulay 1963).[21] There are clear advantages to doing this. For instance, by continuing to deal with each other over time,

19 These exchange networks may be either symmetrical or asymmetrical. For an extensive comparison of different types of symmetrical and asymmetrical networks, see Laumann and Marsden (1982).

20 For further examples of the coercive nature of resource dependence in obligational networks, see McCraw and O'Brien's (1986: 81–2) discussion of the Toyota automobile company's ability to terminate its obligational relationships with parts subcontractors, and Mintz and Schwartz's (1985: 35–40) discussion of the ability of banks to dominate their relationships with creditors.

21 See Gottfredson and White (1981: 482) for further discussion about the importance of maintaining reputation and long-term relationships as a consensual alternative to contractual coercion in networks.

buyers and sellers develop a stable and trusting relationship that may permit them to reduce their transaction costs because elaborate bidding procedures and costly new contracts are not necessary each time a different transaction occurs. A classic example is the relationship between general and subcontractors in the construction industry (e.g., Eccles 1981). By developing a continuing relationship, the general contractor does not have to resort to soliciting bids from a large number of subcontractors for each new project, and both parties increase the potential for a trusting relationship. In addition, because of the development over time of good communication between them, they are more likely to produce higher-quality products than would be the case if they had a less stable relationship.[22]

Hierarchies

In many industries, actors build formal administrative and bureaucratic command systems within a single organization to replace market contracting among autonomous exchange partners as the means by which they coordinate the flow of personnel, capital, and goods through the production and distribution processes. Some scholars have suggested that by increasing administrative control through corporate hierarchies, managers can improve productive efficiency, reduce transaction costs, maximize the gains of joint team production, and control the opportunism inherent in exchange relations (e.g., Coase 1937; Alchian and Demsetz 1972; Williamson 1975), although others disagree (e.g., Marglin 1974; K. Stone 1981; Perrow 1986). Regardless of the suspected benefits, hierarchies as a type of governance have a number of formal elements, including labor contracts, that subject employees to the authority of employers, fiduciary relations embodied in boards of directors as trustees or representatives of stockholders, legal arrangements establishing centralized decision-making authority and incentive systems, standard operating procedures providing for the routine governance of activities, and hierarchically controlled meetings for authoritatively resolving internal disputes (Stinchcombe 1985). Managers of hierarchies typically express rules of exchange as administrative commands.

One of the most common forms of hierarchy is the vertically integrated firm in which production technologies, such as mass assembly or continuous process production, are tightly connected. The firm transforms materials in a rigid but serial relationship so that the output of one task is the input of the next. These firms develop through backward or forward integration by absorbing suppliers or distributors, respectively, within a single corporate

---

22 We are not suggesting that harmony and cooperation always characterize obligational networks nor that organizations necessarily join these networks on a completely voluntary basis. Often, the opposite is true (e.g., Aldrich 1979: 267; Zeitz 1980; Mizruchi 1982: 41). The point is that both coercive and consensual means of obtaining compliance to the terms of exchange may be at work.

organization (e.g., Chandler 1966, 1977). A second form of hierarchy is the conglomerate firm, where managers concentrate and direct cash flows to what they perceive as being productive divisions within the firm, thereby simulating a capital market within a bureaucratic organization (e.g., Williamson 1975, 1985). Finally, we consider the very large, often horizontally integrated, firm to be another example of corporate hierarchy because even if these firms are engaged in producing only a single product and are not co-ordinating producers and processors or processors and distributors within one company, they often share one characteristic with vertically integrated and conglomerate companies: they all tend to coordinate the relationship between labor and capital within the firm by means of internal labor markets, job ladders, collective bargaining, and other bureaucratic systems designed to induce workers to accept the goals of the firm. These mechanisms are much different from spot-market contracts and individual wage bargains that coordinate the labor–capital relationship outside firms. Thus, at least in terms of labor relations, all of these firms possess hierarchical qualities (e.g., Williamson 1975: Chap. 4; 1986: 118–21).

To coordinate the activity of workers, organizational divisions, and sub-sidiaries, managers of corporate hierarchies rely on various coercive ca-pacities, including rules, supervisory procedures, and administrative sanctions, typical of bureaucratic organizations (e.g., Weber 1978: 956–1005). Insofar as formerly independent organizations are concerned, these capacities rest in part on the firm's legal ownership and administrative control over other organizations as a result of merger. In terms of labor, this coercive power of ownership and control translates ultimately into the legal right of managers to supervise and fire workers, at least as long as they do not violate collective-bargaining agreements or other contractual provisions that might apply (Daems 1980: 205–6).

However, managers also obtain hierarchial control by more consensual means, including what Weber (1978: 215–23) called legal–rational author-ity, a system of legitimacy whereby subordinates accept the legal, rule-based authority of their superiors and agree to be governed by them accordingly. For example, believing in the legitimacy of collective-bargaining agree-ments and other rules governing their interactions with management helps convince labor to consent to the dictates of supervisors, although the hope of sharing in the rewards of their company's success may be an equally impor-tant means of obtaining labor's consent (e.g., Cohen and Rogers 1983: 54–60). Consensus to governance through hierarchy may also be achieved through recognition that this form of governance may be the most efficient way to administer transactions (Hurst 1982: 107–8; Perrow 1986: 4), reduce transaction costs (Williamson 1975), and achieve economies of scale and planning (Galbraith 1967: Chap. 7; Chandler 1980; North 1981: Chap. 4).

Let us now consider the three governance mechanisms that fall toward the multilateral side of the horizontal continuum of our typology. In each case, many organizations collectively share resources and information, and interorganizational coordination is based, at least in part, on strategic incentives, common interests, and appeals to solidaristic values. As a result, these types of governance mechanisms tend to produce collective goods. Of course, we distinguish among three types by the degree to which actors engage in multilateral interactions through formal or informal organizations.

Monitoring

Of those forms of collective action that coordinate economic exchanges among organizations, monitoring most closely corresponds to the market as an informal and potentially unstable form of control. This form of governance is primarily dedicated to the collection and sharing of information as a collective good. To the extent that there are identifiable rules of exchange in monitoring, actors abide by mutual understandings that are often tacit in nature. Examples include what Harrison White (1981) referred to as mutual monitoring, Michael Useem's (1984) business scanning interlocking directorates, informal price-setting and market-sharing agreements, such as the famous Gary dinners and dominant-firm pricing strategies in the steel and other industries, and the communities of interest or elite networks that figure prominently in some of the neo-Marxist and other power-structure literature (e.g., Domhoff 1974, 1983: Chap. 3; Dye 1976). The latter are informal structures of control, which researchers *impute* from corporate interlocks or multiple board of director memberships (e.g., Mizruchi 1982; Useem 1984), whereby corporate actors tend to forge a capacity to represent capitalist class interests vis-à-vis corporations, the business community, and state policy makers. In contrast to those interlocks that we have identified as examples of obligational networks, which are largely bilateral in nature, occur among pairs or small cliques of firms, and serve to coordinate the buying and selling of products, the borrowing of money, the operation of some joint ventures, and the coordination of other specific exchanges, interlocks of the monitoring type are much more diffuse and include members from a greater number and wider spectrum of firms. They help corporate leaders identify problems concerning large numbers of companies, and facilitate the search for general solutions to these problems (e.g., Useem 1984: 41).[23]

Although the consequences of interlocking directorates are often difficult to specify with rigor, interlocks among the same or closely related

23 Thus, our typology allows us to distinguish among types of interlocking directorate networks, much as it helps us differentiate among types of joint ventures (see note 17). Indeed, Useem (1984: 43–5) argued that most interlocks are not of the obligational variety discussed earlier, where actors try to coopt or directly influence corporate policy, but are of the monitoring type. See Mintz and Schwartz (1985: 128–33) for an alternative opinion and a thorough discussion of different types of interlocks.

industries have occasionally discouraged expansion and diversification into competitive areas, and sometimes into the development of new fields of business. Whether intended or not, interlocks among buyers and sellers of relatively equal strength have provided channels of intercorporate communication, blunted the rivalry of each, and undermined the competitive position of opposing interests. For example, interlocks among groups of petrochemical companies during the 1960s apparently helped facilitate the development of similar product lines within the group (Knowles 1973: 36–41).

Although interlocking directorates have been a means of enhancing communication and stability among buyers and sellers, the dominant-firm pricing strategy has been a means of promoting price stability among competitors in single industries. Whereas the monitoring type of interlocking directorate tends to be based on common role positions and socialization patterns (e.g., Useem 1984), the dominant-firm pricing strategy results from the ability of one firm to impose its will on others. The dominant firm in an industry permits other competitors to sell as much output as they wish at whatever prices it sets. Competitors have no incentive to initiate price cuts because they know that the dominant firm has the ability to win a price war, at least as long as it is able to retain its cost advantages. Indeed, the dominant firm occasionally begins a price war to remind competitors of the need for price stability. However, when the dominant firm becomes no more efficient than its rivals, it gradually loses its position of power and either another firm assumes leadership over pricing structures or actors search for another form of governance (Scherer 1970: 164–6, 216–19; Lamoreaux 1985).

In general, actors engaged in monitoring based on corporate interlocks or sociability ties have few coercive means of obtaining compliance among the membership because there are almost no explicit rules or enforcement arrangements, other than perhaps peer pressure, to guard against opportunism and free-rider problems. Dominant-firm pricing is an exception to the extent that firms recognize the dominant company's capacity to coercively enforce price stability. More often, however, governance through monitoring rests primarily on the members' willingness to consent voluntarily to cooperate with each other – a consensus that is very fragile because it is based on little more than the lowest common denominators of social background, culture, socialization experiences, or political and economic interests. For example, industry leaders organized the dinner club meetings of the midnineteenth-century U.S. textile industry to fix prices informally through voluntary gentlemen's agreements, a very unstable and short-lived arrangement precisely because there were no coercive mechanisms for enforcement (Galambos 1966). In short, these networks depend heavily on a strong dose of what Albert Hirschman (1970) called loyalty to the group.

Promotional networks

Some networks among economic actors in an industry constitute what Howard Aldrich (1979; Aldrich and Whetten 1981) called action sets, observable and relatively stable groups of organizations formed into a temporary alliance or coalition for a common purpose. Actors create these networks, occasionally with the participation or initiative of state agencies, when managing organizational interdependencies is essential for the effectiveness of the industry as a whole. In contrast to monitoring, where the rules of exchange are tacitly recognized, actors in promotional networks *explicitly* negotiate and define these rules, although they do not necessarily specify them in contracts or other formal agreements. Furthermore, in contrast to obligational networks, where only a few members of the sector are involved and where members of the network are concerned only with their group's particular self-centered interests, many actors constitute promotional networks and do so, in part, to promote the collective interests of all, or at least a large segment, of the sector's members. They do this by negotiating common definitions of interest and rankings of their collective priorities through complex decision-making processes. Hence, the relationships among actors found in promotional networks tend to be more stable than those in market types of governance, where buyers and sellers are constantly changing. However, this stability is not hierarchically imposed within a corporation. Instead, shared norms, attitudes of trust, considerable knowledge about one another, and respect for each other's interests stabilize the relationships among actors.

Promotional networks typically bring together diverse actors from different parts of the production or service delivery chain for the purpose of the common promotion of a product, including the organization of research and development, the diffusion of information, and lobbying the state. For example, long-standing collaborations among federal and state governments, land grant colleges, extension services, and agribusinesses have played an important role for decades in guiding agricultural research and development in the United States (e.g., Hightower 1978). More recently, members of the U.S. semiconductor industry agreed to work together to develop and share more advanced production techniques by creating the Semiconductor Manufacturing Technology Institute (e.g., Sanger 1987), an arrangement with a more formal organizational structure than monitoring arrangements, but less so than the associations we describe later, particularly insofar as members retain their organizational autonomy. These networks are often more capable of achieving production flexibility, confronting technical change more effectively, and adapting quickly to volatile markets than corporate hierarchies (e.g., Porter 1986; Ernst 1987; Gordon 1987; Hollingsworth 1987; Powell 1987). Furthermore, by participating in promotional networks, actors have the potential of developing a common language and outlook regarding technical matters, rules of contracting, and the standardization of processes, products, and routines (Johanson and Mattsson 1987). The more exchange partners adapt to one another in these ways, the more trust evolves, which may offer stability and additional benefits, such as lower transaction costs. Finally, and in contrast to market governance, but similar to obligational networks, actors who participate in promotional networks are able to enter into open-ended and less precisely specified contingency contracts with much greater ease.

The coercive capacities available to members of promotional networks are limited and rest on peer pressure and the ability to organize selective access to collective goods. Policing deviance and enforcing compliance to group goals are particularly difficult because these coalitions have only an informal organizational structure and often no staff (e.g., Warren 1967). Hence, participation is largely voluntary and rests on the common values and interests among members, discussed earlier (e.g., Aldrich 1979: 317). In this sense, promotional networks are much like an interorganizational version of what William Ouchi (1977, 1980, 1984) called a clan, where normative mechanisms, negotiation, and socialization within the group coordinate relationships and control opportunism over relatively long periods of time. However, these are not clans in the anthropological sense, but are networks of suppliers and customers who, as a result of solidaristic values, establish, develop, and maintain lasting relationships with one another. In contrast to some types of obligational networks, such as a bank's informal control over its debtors through interlocking directorates, promotional networks also resemble Ouchi's clans to the extent that, although members may have different roles, they are all of relatively equal stature within the group. No member enjoys great superiority – another reason why compliance to the terms of exchange within the group rests primarily on consensus rather than coercion.[24]

Associations

Associations are distinctive forms of multilateral governance in that they involve structured negotiations among organizations that mutually recognize each others' status and entitlements and that seek to create formal organizations with charters, bylaws, and procedures in order to implement

---

24 For further discussion of the importance of relative equality among members of clans, see Durkheim (1933: 175–6), a source that Ouchi (1980: 132) draws from in deriving his concept of the clan. Also note that our attempt to typologize three types of networks (obligational, monitoring, and promotional), as distinct from each other and from associations, improves upon the otherwise very helpful literature on interorganizational relations that tends not to make these distinctions, but rather lumps these different forms of governance into very broad and homogeneous categories. For example, see the reviews by Aldrich and Whetten (1981) and Cummings (1984).

relatively stable and formal agreements in pursuit of some common interests (Schmitter and Streeck 1981; Streeck and Schmitter 1985). As such, the rules governing exchange within an association are typically formally organized membership agreements. Whereas markets, corporate hierarchies, and informal networks tend to coordinate economic activity among different types of actors, associations typically coordinate actors engaged in the same or similar kinds of activities, such as manufacturers or distributors within an industry, although they may also incorporate other actors more vertically. Associations vary in the degree to which their staffs are able to develop autonomy from members in order to pursue long-term strategies for the management of the industry's problems, particularly those involving the stabilization of relationships with the state, labor, or other forces in the industry's environment.

Associations are generally more important in coordinating economic activity in Europe than in the United States. Most significantly, in Europe, large numbers of firms and their corresponding sectors are often linked together through peak associations. Although U.S. business associations are usually more narrowly focused, they often collect data for their members about production levels and prices, conduct research, develop product-development projects, promote the standardization of products, develop codes of fair competition, develop common strategies toward public policies, and carry out negotiations with state agencies on behalf of the industry or some part of it. In the case of employers' associations, they negotiate industrywide labor–management agreements. On the other hand, producer cooperatives negotiate collective dealer–supplier exchanges. In some industries, associations occasionally exercise substantial influence by playing pivotal roles in both the enactment and implementation of public policies for the industry (e.g., Galambos 1966; Himmelberg 1976; Staber and Aldrich 1983: 163).

Despite the possibility that workers may be less well equipped to organize than capitalists (Offe and Wiesenthal 1985), scholars have produced much more literature on trade unions and other forms of collective action by labor. However, we still have very limited systematic knowledge about variation in the structure and function of working-class organizations over time and across economic sectors, and even less on the way that working-class and capitalist business associations affect each other. However, interest associations, whether on the part of labor or capital, are very active in mediating the conflicts that occur between both sides. For example, trade unions attempt to confront a wide range of problems that exist between labor and capital, including wage negotiations, working conditions and job specifications, and working hours. They also occasionally participate in decisions about employment levels, investment strategies, pricing policy, and pension fund accumulation. Thus, labor organizations are another important example of associations in our typology.

The capacity of trade associations to coordinate transactions in a sector depends often on the capacity of the organization to control opportunism and free riding via peer pressure (e.g., Whitney 1934: 42) and, more important, the coercive ability to restrict access to the information, status, and other collective goods the association provides for its members (Naylor 1921; Schmitter and Streeck 1981; Williamson and Ouchi 1981: 361–3; Streeck and Schmitter 1985). Associations usually enjoy a state-sanctioned capacity to provide these selective, solidaristic goods to members (Streeck 1983; Schmitter 1984), an important asset without which it becomes difficult for them to transcend the individual preferences of members who may contribute substantial resources to the association (Staber and Aldrich 1983: 165). In addition, the threat of state intervention into sectoral affairs often provides the association with leverage for obtaining cooperation among the membership insofar as members, faced with the choice of self-regulation or state regulation, generally prefer to avoid political meddling (Pfeffer and Salancik 1978: 177; Schmitter 1984: 16). However, grants of authority from the state (Schmitter 1984: 37), the socialization of members to the association's goals (e.g., Naylor 1921: 18; Foth 1930: 120), and the recognition of common interests, particularly in times of crisis (e.g., Warner, Unwalla, and Trimm 1967: 324; Pfeffer and Salancik 1978: 177) also serve as means of obtaining membership consent and augmenting the association's ability to govern.[25] As a result, associations often confront a contradictory situation, where, on the one hand, their staffs may need to coerce members into cooperating toward collective goals, but, on the other, must do so at the risk of driving members away because membership is ultimately voluntary (Streeck 1983: 278).[26]

Summary

Our descriptions of these six governance mechanisms represent *ideal types,* conceptual abstractions of what these governance mechanisms look like in their pure forms. Of course, not every empirical example perfectly fits these descriptions. With that in mind, we have summarized in Table 1.2

---

25 It is not clear from the literature to what extent utilitarian or more normative and affective incentives are necessary for the development and maintenance of economic associations (cf., Olson 1965; Moe 1980: Chaps. 7–8; Knoke and Wright-Isak 1982: 234). However, there is substantial evidence that for voluntary associations in general, not just economic ones, the latter incentives are often as important as the former (e.g., Warren 1967; Knoke 1981, 1985; Knoke and Wood 1981: Chap. 3; Knoke and Prensky 1984).

26 Because the threat that members will exit is higher in voluntary associations than it is for large, oligopolistic business firms (Hirschman 1970: Chap. 9), we would expect that the forms of coercion associations employ would usually be milder than those that corporate hierarchies use. For discussions of the important effect the threat of exit has in constraining associational behavior in general, see Warner et al. (1967: 301), Aldrich (1979: 224–5), Moe (1980: 75), and Knoke (1981).

Table 1.2. *Governance mechanism structures, rules of exchange, and means of compliance*

Governance mechanism	Organizational structure	Rules of exchange	Means of compliance to terms of exchange	
			Coercion	Consent
Market	• Informal • Bilateral exchange	• Classical contracting	• Legal and economic sanctions • Litigation • Contractual bonds • Prices	• Norms of private appropriation • Legitimacy of the free, self-stabilizing market • Market alternatives
Obligational network	• Moderately informal • Bilateral exchange	• Obligational contracting	• Contractual bonds • Resource dependence	• Personal relations • Interest in long-term stability
Hierarchy	• Formal • Bilateral exchange	• Administrative command	• Bureaucracy • Corporate rules • Administrative sanctions	• Legal–rational authority • Belief in efficiency
Monitoring	• Informal • Multilateral exchange	• Tacit agreements • Mutual understandings	• Peer pressure	• Common background, culture, interests, socialization • Group loyalty
Promotional network	• Moderately informal • Multilateral exchange	• Informal or formal explicitly stated agreements	• Peer pressure • Selective access to collective goods	• Common socialization, interests • Group loyalty • Sense of community • Trust
Association	• Formal • Multilateral exchange	• Formally organized membership agreements	• Peer pressure • Selective access to collective goods • Threat of state intervention	• Common socialization, interests • Grant of authority from the state

the organizational structure, the type of exchange rules, and the coercive and consensual means of obtaining compliance to the terms of exchange that are typical of each governance mechanism. Thus, where Table 1.1 represented simply the structural features of these six types of governance mechanisms, Table 1.2 offers an expanded version of the typology that includes its procedural elements as well.

It is important to recognize that some of these governance mechanisms appear to have particularly important relationships with the state, at least insofar as the state helps them obtain compliance to the terms of exchange. For example, the ability of markets to function effectively depends in part on the ability and willingness of state actors to enforce contracts and punish those who would violate the terms of exchange specified therein. The ability of business associations to muster support and cooperation among their members often rests on the threat of state intervention and grants of authority or other resources from the political authorities. State agencies may participate in promotional networks, such as the land grant college complex, described earlier. Indeed, because the state plays an especially unique and wide-ranging role in the governance process, it deserves special attention.

THE STATE AND GOVERNANCE MECHANISMS

What is the role of the state in our analytic framework? Should the state, or state regulation through its hierarchical controls and coercive capacities, be conceptualized as another governance mechanism comparable to the market, hierarchy, networks, or association? At certain stages of this project, we have taken that position (e.g., Hollingsworth and Lindberg 1985; Lindberg 1985). However, we now think that it is more appropriate to conceptualize and theorize the state in its own terms.

This is not to obscure the fact that state agencies or officials are frequently important actors in the production and exchange processes of a sector. Indeed, exchanges both between the state and other economic actors, and within the state, between its frequently uncoordinated actors and agencies, often play very important roles in sectoral governance and governance transformations, most obviously when state agencies are either sole or joint owners and operators within a sector. The case studies that follow make the importance of the state abundantly clear, even in the United States, where it ostensibly plays a much less prominent role in the economy than is generally the case in modern capitalism.

However, the state is theoretically and substantively distinct from our six governance mechanisms for several reasons. For example, different parts of the state apparatus provide arenas through which groups, whose participation in governance is not already institutionalized, may participate. In this capacity, the state serves as a gatekeeper to outsiders. The courts are a common gate-keeping mechanism that determine what effects, if any, outsiders, such as consumer and environmental groups, have on sectoral governance. Public regulatory proceedings and political referenda do much the same thing (e.g., Friedland, Piven, and Alford 1977; Wolfe 1977; North 1981: 21; Skowronek 1982).

Furthermore, the state may deliberately facilitate or inhibit production and exchange and, thus, the development of different forms of governance, by allocating resources and information. For example, it may offer subsidies or other financial incentives to encourage the formation of promotional networks in a sector, as was the case in the fledgling computer industry during the 1950s when the federal government helped orchestrate the industry's development of common programming languages by threatening that it would only purchase equipment from those manufacturers who participated in the network (e.g., Brock 1975). Often only the state is in a position to do this, particularly insofar as the manipulation of fiscal and monetary policies, whose effects span economic sectors, is concerned. Similarly, only the state can define and enforce property rights, policy tools whose use is often instrumental in altering governance, as we have seen. Indeed, different parts of the state apparatus often regulate specific markets, networks, corporate hierarchies, or associations, and may contribute to their formation in the first place, through the manipulation of constitutional, antitrust, labor, environmental, contract, and other laws that establish the parameters of exchange and ownership. By passing antitrust legislation, for instance, Congress made it very difficult for corporations to set prices collectively and thereby prevented individual firms from interfering with the price negotiations a competitor conducted with a customer. The development of various forms of multilateral exchange suffered as a result.

There are other unique and important ways in which the state influences governance, which we discuss in detail in Chapter 12. For now, the important point is that the state assumes a privileged conceptual position in this study because it is capable of influencing governance in many complex ways, most of which are not available to organizations in civil society. One of the things that is so fascinating about the state is that although its agencies can behave like other organizational actors in an industry, participating directly in production and exchange relations, other actors cannot behave like the state because they cannot serve as gatekeepers, allocate resources and information, influence and structure property rights, or affect governance and governance transformations in other ways as does the state.

A SIMPLE DESCRIPTION OF THE TRANSFORMATION PROCESS

Historical case studies follow this chapter and identify the arrangements of governance mechanisms that have succeeded each other over time in eight industries in the U.S. economy. They focus particularly on the political, economic, technological, and other structural conditions that contributed to these transformations as well as the perceptions, preferences, and struggles of the actors involved. The authors of these studies were guided by, and in several cases sought to test, propositions about the conditions under which governance mechanisms tend to emerge, succeed, and fail. However, they also shared a common conceptual framework, the governance-mechanism typology, and used a simple model of the governance transformation process to help organize the histories about which they wrote. This model is a heuristic device and is not intended to capture the complex subtleties of the transformation process. Indeed, one of the purposes of constructing these case studies was to provide data to help us develop later a more sophisticated model, a task to which we turn in Chapters 11 and 12.

In developing the simple model, we recognized that governance mechanisms do not exist in isolation, but occur together in various combinations, or *governance regimes,* in different industries and at different times in history. Furthermore, at any time, actors tend to organize themselves, adopt rules of exchange, and utilize means of compliance that are typical of one governance mechanism more than another. In this sense, we speak of some governance mechanisms as being *dominant* relative to others within a governance regime.[27] For example, when an industry's actors respond primarily to fluctuations in supply, demand, prices, and classical contracting agreements, the market is the dominant governance mechanism. Under these circumstances, if insufficient demand is the problem, competing firms might engage in short-term, individual strategies, such as price cutting. On the other hand, if firms adopted a more multilateral, cooperative strategy with long-term horizons, such as industrywide production quotas, collectively arranged through a formal organization, then an association would be dominant.

Furthermore, we recognized that governance transformations require some initial *pressure for change,* and suspected that these pressures, as suggested earlier, often stem from economic inefficiencies, such as problems in setting prices, standardizing products, establishing production levels, and raising capital, or from actors' strategic concerns about their inability to control the terms of exchange. Yet despite the presence of these and other pressures, we knew that governance transformations do not develop automatically. Instead, actors perceive pressures for change and

---

27 Because each industry is composed of different exchanges among different kinds of actors, certain governance mechanisms are likely to exert greater influence over some exchanges than over others. Actors may prefer to organize the exchange of technical information through promotional networks, but may arrange the exchange of raw materials through corporate hierarchies. Indeed, as noted before, we expect that different governance mechanisms and governance regimes will have different capacities for handling different kinds of exchanges and problems.

then initiate a *search process,* where they select new strategies for coping with these pressures and struggle to institutionalize their strategies as a *new governance regime.* Our notion of the search process was much broader than that of Richard Nelson and Sidney Winter (1982), from whom we borrowed the term. Whereas Nelson and Winter conceived of the search as a process that occurs within organizations, we believed that it is also very much an interorganizational exercise. Furthermore, we knew that actors do not have free choice to select any governance regime they want because there are a variety of factors that constrain their search. For example, we believed that the existing governance regime tends to limit the power of different actors and, thus, their ability to create the governance regime they may prefer. Similarly, we anticipated that the state's ability or willingness to ratify, legitimate, or otherwise help generate public acceptance for a proposed governance regime limits or expands the options available to actors during their search, and influences the stability of the new regime once it emerges. The rigidities of antitrust law and the dogged persistence of state agencies to enforce it, for instance, certainly constrain the ability of actors to search for collective solutions to their governance problems. In any case, we needed to know how all of these factors influence the development of new governance regimes.

The processes depicted in this model are evolutionary, not only because problems produced under an initial governance regime often trigger a search process and the creation of a new regime, but also because the search and, thus, the range of possible alternatives from which actors may choose are limited by the governance regime that already exists. Yet because some actors may succeed in blocking change, it is possible that a transformation will not occur even though the current governance regime is rather inefficient or strategically undesirable in the eyes of some actors for managing important exchanges. Hence, governance transformations may be either rapid or slow and emerge in some cases only after earlier attempts at change have failed. Similarly, because the search process does not necessarily produce governance innovations that are more efficient or satisfying to the parties concerned than those previously in place, the model does not imply that the "best" industrial practice necessarily emerges or even that there is one best practice under a given set of circumstances. Indeed, even when a new governance regime has emerged, it may be far from perfectly functional or efficient.

OUTLINE OF THE VOLUME AND A METHODOLOGICAL NOTE

What follows in Chapter 2 is an historical overview of the kinds of governance transformations that have been typical in the U.S. economy during the late nineteenth and twentieth centuries. This provides a backdrop against which to cast detailed case studies of the transformations that have occurred in the telecommunications, commercial nuclear energy, dairy, meatpacking, steel, railroad, automobile, and hospital sectors, stories that constitute Chapters 3 through 10 and comprise the empirical heart of this project. We return to more theoretical concerns in Chapter 11, where, in light of our case studies, we examine the current debates about the causes of governance transformations, and where we refine the governance transformation model, sketched before. Similarly, Chapter 12 is devoted to a discussion of the state's role in the governance transformation process.

Our task in this project is to understand why specific types of transformations take place over time from one governance regime to another. The extent to which different governance mechanisms operate and are dominant cannot easily be determined quantitatively. Thus, our method is to describe, through the construction of qualitative historical case studies, governance transformations in eight sectors.[28] However, this is more than simple storytelling. First, in selecting sectors to study, we chose those that have varied significantly on a number of critical variables. For example, we have selected sectors that differ in such characteristics as firm size, the degree of capital and labor intensity, and the degree of concentration and competitiveness. We have also picked sectors that vary in the degree to which their products and production technologies are complex and in the speed with which this technology has changed. We have also selected sectors that are both old and new, some having been born during the nineteenth century and others during the midtwentieth century. Second, because shifts in governance occur several times in each of our case studies, we are able to compare over two dozen examples of governance transformations, thereby giving us ample opportunity for generalizing theoretically from the data. Third, although these studies are thick with historical description, they are all informed and guided by the conceptual framework that we have developed in this chapter. Indeed, we have tried to pursue the ideal of the case study method, as described by Benjamin Ward (1972: 180), giving an account of an interrelated and complex set of phenomena in which factual historical material and theories of human behavior are mixed and inform each other. As a result, although we do not aspire to develop *universal* generalizations, we do seek, as a result of our largely inductive analysis of specific case studies, to develop generalizations about regularities that hold across similar historical circumstances.

---

28 For further discussion of the importance of such a methodology in social science research, see Ward (1972), Lawrence Stone (1981: 74–96) and McCloskey (1986).

THE LOGIC OF COORDINATING AMERICAN MANUFACTURING SECTORS[1]

J. Rogers Hollingsworth
Department of History, University of Wisconsin-Madison

The previous chapter assumes that in order to comprehend how a particular industrial sector is governed or coordinated at any moment in time, we must first understand the historical process from which the sector evolved. Each governance arrangement is both historically conditioned and contingent. Although this project has as its goal to illuminate variation in the governance of industrial sectors – both across industries and over time within a single industry – we must recognize that there are broad parameters within which this variation takes place in a nation's history. In other words, there are broad styles of governance that are distinct within specific historical epochs in each nation's history. Chapters 3 through 10 focus on transformations of governance structures of particular industries in American history, but this chapter defines the broad parameters within which the governance of various sectors has taken place over time in American society.

Because institutional arrangements emerge over long periods of time, this chapter focuses attention only on the coordination of manufacturing sectors in the American economy during the period since 1870. Due to space limitations, the chapter devotes very little attention to sectors in agriculture, service, or transportation except insofar as they impinge on manufacturing. In many respects, the coordination and governance of American manufacturing during this time frame falls within two distinct periods: 1870 to 1950, and 1950 to the present. Both periods experienced basic transformations in the coordination and governance of the nation's economy.

1 In writing this chapter, I very much appreciate the assistance of Leon Lindberg. He and John Campbell provided very useful comments on an earlier draft. In addition, I have very much profited from stimulating conversations with the following: Masahiko Aoki, Ken Bickers, Alfred D. Chandler, Jurgen Feick, Philip Genschel, Wyn Grant, Jerald Hage, Robert Hanneman, Hal Hansen, Rob Kennedy, Diane Lindstrom, Tom McCraw, Renate Mayntz, Richard Nelson, Yoshi Okada, Charles Sabel, Fritz Scharpf, Christoph Scherrer, Philippe C. Schmitter, Volker Schneider, Marc Schneiberg, Wolfgang Streeck, David Teece, Raymund Werle, Oliver Williamson, and Eric Wright. But the person who did more than anyone else to sharpen my views about the issues developed here is Ellen Jane Hollingsworth.

A complex explanation is required in order to understand the emergence of various governance arrangements during these two periods, for there are a host of contextual and interacting variables that shaped transformations in the governance of American manufacturing sectors. There are organizational- or firm-level variables. There are country-specific characteristics: the size of the country (both in terms of space and population); the degree of complexity of the national economy; the degree to which firms are embedded either in a rich or impoverished network of institutional arrangements (e.g., highly developed trade associations, capital markets, training institutions for the development of broad skills for the workforce); and the society's belief system, which gives rise to rules and normative constraints for the governance of particular sectors. There are variables that are sector-specific: the degree of competitiveness of specific industries; their level of capital intensity; the size of the sector measured by the numbers of firms and employees; and the degree to which consumer tastes are diversified or homogeneous. Transformations are also influenced by variables about the sector's product, especially its level of technological complexity and the rate of technological change, as well as by variables that influence the costs of transactions, e.g., the degree of uncertainty among actors engaged in transactions, the degree of asset specificity involved in transactions, and the degree of trust among transacting partners. Of course, the age of a sector influences its flexibility for change. New industries generally have greater capacities to undergo structural change than older industries that have highly institutionalized arrangements. Very importantly, there is the industrial relations system of a sector. It not only reflects the way that relations between capital and labor are constrained within an industry, but it may influence the way that relations among other actors are coordinated. And finally – but perhaps most importantly of all – there is the role of the state. The state defines property rights and the conditions under which each of the six types of governance arrangements may exist. Without the state, there can be no capitalist economy.

The goal of this chapter is to discover the logic by which broad parameters of governance existed during these two periods of American history. It was the interaction of all of these contextual variables that established a logic for the governance of American manufacturing sectors. However, there was nothing deterministic in the way these variables interacted. Rather, governance arrangements in each period were shaped as a result of an historical configuration of interdependent, very complex, loosely structured relationships. Because the models to be discussed involve dialectical, complex feedback relationships and mutual interaction among elements, it would be impossible to test the arguments with econometric tools or simulation strategies. There are other reasons as well for this. First, there is no single dependent variable that this chapter sets out to explain. There are six types of governance arrangements, each having its own logic.

Second, we are still in the early stages of theory construction about the emergence of governance arrangements in capitalist economies. And in most scientific disciplines, advance in the early stages proceeds through description. Rich theorizing can only occur at a later stage.

There is no universal and immutable logic involved in the governance of capitalist societies. Firms make decisions in response to a large number of variables that are interactive with one another. And although nothing is deterministic, there are in the histories of individual countries decision-making styles and strategic policy choices that emerge again and again. And it is as a result of such a logic of decision making that certain options tend to be chosen in specific time frames in various countries and others are rarely chosen. It is the distinctive interaction of a large number of interdependent elements that forms what Max Weber (1978) labeled as historical individuals (Sorge and Streeck 1988; Scharpf 1989). It is in the tradition of this type of scholarship that this chapter is written. It is an effort to discover the complex pattern by which numerous complex elements interacted during two periods of American history.

THE COORDINATION OF THE AMERICAN ECONOMY, 1870–1950

Prior to the Civil War, the United States was predominantly an agrarian society, in which most firms were small businesses owned by a single individual. Most industrial production took place in small shops, with goods purchased by merchants or commission men who then moved goods into streams of commerce. As a result of the communication and transportation revolution, which led to declining transportation rates, many firms during the post–Civil War era were able to extend the geographical area over which they marketed their products. Because of the large market area in which they operated and the introduction of new machinery, firms in numerous industries were able to increase their output, to utilize economies of scale and scope, and to undersell smaller and less efficient firms. After a couple of decades of expanding markets and impressive profits, firms in numerous industries were faced with a classic problem in the history of capitalism: intense price competition, "saturated" markets, idle plants, accumulating inventories, severe price declines, and the threat of bankruptcy. It was the effort to cope with these problems that resulted in a fundamental transformation in the coordination of the American economy during the late nineteenth and early twentieth centuries – though there was considerable variation in the way that industrial sectors responded to these problems.

Firms in some industries reacted to overcapacity by producing more differentiated products – turning out high-quality products and attempting to establish a good reputation for their brands.[2] For firms in most manufacturing sectors, the basic strategy for relieving the downward pressure on prices was to search for some means of stabilizing prices and/or restricting the output of mass-produced, standardized products.

Coordination among firms in the same industry

During the late nineteenth century, some of the most severe price competition occurred in industries that were very capital-intensive, that had high fixed costs, that were involved in the output of standardized products and in which no single firm had a clear-cut advantage over the rest, e.g., coal, metal and paper products, railroads (Warren and Pearson 1932, 1933; Lamoreaux 1985). In these sectors, firms increased their output as prices fell, causing prices to fall even more. It was in response to this type of syndrome that firms attempted to limit output and stabilize prices with a variety of collusive arrangements.

Collective action, in the form of pooling agreements or cartels (Cell Six), has been a classic device in capitalist economies for regulating output and prices. Before the Civil War, pooling agreements or cartels had rarely existed in American society and had occurred primarily in local or regional markets, but in the late nineteenth century, they became increasingly common. At first, firms entered into rather simple and informal agreements to stabilize prices and to lower production levels. When these failed to be effective, more formal arrangements such as trade associations emerged. By the end of the century, associative behavior had become quite common in a variety of industrial sectors: mechanical industries, such as lumber, flooring, furniture, shoes, and other leather products; refining and chemically oriented industries, such as petroleum, rubber footwear, paint, explosives, paper, and glass; industries engaged in mining, the fabricating of metals, and in most types of hardware (Schneiberg and Hollingsworth 1989). According to Chandler (1977: 317), "No industry appears to have been immune. Only in textiles, apparel, publishing, and printing were the number of trade associations small" (Dewing 1914; Ripley 1916; Burns

---

2 This is the same strategy that some firms employed in response to problems of overcapacity during the 1930s and 1980s. During each of these periods, this kind of strategy did little to contribute to an overall transformation of the sectoral structure. It is mentioned here simply because it is a logical reaction to the problem of overcapacity that capitalist economies periodically face. Such a strategy permits firms to increase earnings with high margins per item rather than with volume production, to maintain output during recessions, and to avoid the cheapening of the firms' image by engaging in price reduction (Warren and Pearson 1932, 1933; U.S. Bureau of the Census, 1960: 115). A few of the industries in which firms successfully pursued this strategy during the late nineteenth century were producers of high-quality writing paper, aged bourbon and rye, high-quality lubricants, and specialty metals (Dewing 1914: 51–2; Williamson and Daum 1959: 274, 464–5, 684–7; Lamoreaux 1985: 16–27).

1936; Williamson and Daum 1959; Galambos 1966; Becker 1971; Lamoreaux 1985).

Even though cartel-type trade associations became quite pervasive, they generally failed to stabilize output and prices. Cheating invariably occurred, as members would secretly cut prices, increase output, falsify reports, and/ or leave the cartel. In most industries, a number of firms failed to join. Even when cartels met with initial success, this simply provided incentives for other firms to enter the industry, thus destablizing prices again.

There were two major reasons why cartel-type arrangements of collective behavior were less successful in the United States than in several other capitalist countries at the same time. First, there was the size of the country. In contrast to Europe, most American industries had many more firms, and the larger the number of firms, the more difficult it was to organize and regulate them. Because of the large size of the country, there was more uneven industrial development among regions in the United States than was the case in smaller countries. In general, the larger the country and the more uneven the regional development, the greater the diversity of interests among firms. And the greater the heterogeneity of interests among firms in the same industry, the more difficult it was for collective strategy via cartels to be effective.

Another major reason for the ineffectiveness of cartel-type arrangements was that American courts and legislatures declared them to be illegal. The courts had long refused to enforce private contracts that were in restraint of trade or that were designed to develop monopolies. Then in the 1880s, in response to the development of cartel-type arrangements, a number of states passed antimonopoly laws, and in 1890, Congress passed the Sherman Antitrust Act. Congress has since expanded this legislation, clearly making cartel-type arrangements a violation of federal law. Important reasons why the Americans historically have taken antitrust considerations far more seriously than most European countries are the large size of the country, the uneven regional development, and the low dependence of the country on foreign trade. Had the United States been a small country with relatively few firms in each industry and heavily dependent on foreign trade, no doubt there would have been greater homogeneity of interests and a greater tendency among firms and the state to promote interfirm cooperation at the industry level in order to assist domestic firms in having a competitive advantage in international markets.

Even though state and federal governments have effectively limited the capacity of trade associations to fix prices and to limit production, it is important to emphasize that trade associations have been important institutions for the coordination of the American economy throughout the twentieth century, though never as densely developed as in a number of European countries. Indeed, during the First World War, the American government encouraged the development of trade associations so that it could more effectively coordinate the war economy. Moreover, Congress passed the National Industrial Recovery Act in 1933, which attempted to organize all manufacturing sectors in order to regulate prices and production – though the Supreme Court later held this legislation to be unconstitutional.

Even if American trade associations have not generally operated to limit production and to fix prices, they have since the turn of the century provided many coordinating functions for their members: gathering information about product markets, advertising products, conducting research, aggregating and articulating member interests, establishing codes of fair competition, developing industry standards, sharing information about production costs and industry output. These functions have been more important in industries in which firms have been too small to carry out most of these activities for themselves – competitive industries (e.g., textiles, apparel, shoes) – than in oligopolistic industries (e.g., automobile, steel, copper). Because of the large size of the country, the large number of firms eligible to join associations, and the heterogeneity of interests among firms in the same industry, business associations in the United States have been somewhat less developed and, therefore, have tended to have less autonomy, fewer resources, and less capacity to govern their members than in those smaller countries in which sectors have had fewer firms and the firms have had more homogeneous interests within the same industry.

The unintended effects of antitrust legislation

There were not only numerous cartels in Europe at the turn of the twentieth century, but the courts tended to enforce them (Cornish 1979). But in America, antitrust law was complex and dense. Ironically, the absence of effective antitrust law in Europe had the effect of perpetuating relatively small family firms, whereas in America, the evolution of antitrust law had the unintended consequence of accelerating the development of large-scale corporations or hierarchical arrangements.

In other words, antitrust law facilitated the transformation of a number of industrial sectors in the American economy. In the United States, the courts firmly ruled that "loose combinations" – e.g., "gentlemen's" agreements, pools, and other types of cartels – were illegal under the Sherman Antitrust Act. However, firms could not be held to be in violation of the Sherman Act simply because of their size and market share. Thus, "tight combinations" – even if their purpose was to lower output and to raise prices – would not automatically be held in violation of law. Before the courts would rule that consolidations and "tight combinations" were illegal, the government had to build a case based on the evidence of customers and competitors that the firm had engaged in abusive, restrictive, and/or predatory behavior. In order to prosecute firms under the Sherman Act successfully, the government had to demonstrate that a company had acted with the "intent to restrain trade" and that as a result of this "intent," it had already succeeded or would succeed in the future in obtaining monopoly power. By acting reasonably toward one's competitors – by adopting a live-and-let-live posture toward rivals – firms were permitted to do those things within a "tight combination" that were illegal under a "loose combination" or cartel-type arrangement. This over time became known as the "rule of reason." For many years, conviction under the Sherman Act required the testimony of competitors or customers in order to demonstrate "intent." It was in this context that Justice McKenna wrote that there could be no restraint of trade as long as there were no complaints (*U.S. v. U.S. Steel et al.*, 251 US 451). This kind of live-and-let-live policy meant that as long as firms did not engage in such "unfair" business practices as exclusive dealing contracts, railroad rebates, and other cartel-type arrangements, tight consolidations involving horizontal and vertical mergers were acceptable, legal forms of behavior (Lamoreaux 1985). Thus, the implementation of the Sherman Act encouraged firms to abolish their previous practices of restraining their competitors through loose combination and to pursue internal strategies (e.g., hierarchical arrangements) to enhance their market position and to stabilize their industries. Even though many Congressmen voted for the Sherman Act because they wanted to maintain a very decentralized, competitive American economy, a long-term consequence of the Act was to facilitate the development of horizontal and vertical integration in numerous industries and to enhance concentration of the American economy. In short, the American state in its antitrust policies unintentionally transformed the governance of many manufacturing sectors of the American economy to hierarchical-type arrangements (Thorelli 1955; Letwin 1965; Bork 1978; Fox and Halverson 1979; McCurdy 1979; Pratt 1980; Lamoreaux 1985).

The emergence of hierarchies via horizontal integration

Once it was widely understood that contracts establishing loose combinations were illegal, firms resorted to a strategy of merger, and it is in this context that the extensive merger movement of the late nineteenth and early twentieth centuries occurred. Horizontal mergers occurred with great frequency in industries that were capital-intensive, employed strategies of mass production, had undergone rapid expansion prior to the depression of the 1890s, and experienced severe price competition. However, many of the consolidations failed, for they succeeded only when tight integration resulted in economies of scale, led to lower labor costs, or raised barriers to entry in the industry. Thus, horizontal consolidations tended to succeed in industries engaged in high-volume, large-batch, or continuous-process production strategies, in industries that were capital-intensive, were high energy consuming, and had large mass markets. These included firms in the following industries: food processing, oil, chemicals, primary metals, paper, and consumer durables (e.g., sewing machines, office machines, agricultural machinery, electrical equipment, elevators, and other forms of standardized machinery). Consolidations that had no cost advantage over their competitors tended to fail. Indeed, the failure rate was especially high in the following industries: textiles, apparel, leather, shoes, furniture, printing, and publishing. Significantly, these were industries in which there were diversified consumer tastes and in which it was relatively easy for new firms to enter.

In the long run, cost advantages over competitors tended to lie in becoming vertically integrated. Whereas horizontal mergers were a form of transformation that addressed interdependencies among firms in the same industry, strategies of vertical integration represented a transformation by which firms confronted their interdependencies with actors on whom they had a dependency relationship, e.g., the relations processors had with producers, distributors, transportation firms, etc. (Galambos 1966; Chandler 1977).

The emergence of hierarchies via vertical integration

The strategy of backward integration. There were two basic motives for American firms to employ strategies of vertical integration. The first was to reduce the level of uncertainty about the availability of raw materials and transport facilities by engaging in backward integration, and to attain an outlet for their products by a strategy of forward integration. The second was to enhance their market share by erecting barriers to new competition. From the available historical evidence, it is often difficult to measure the relative importance of each of these motivations, though there was a clear logic to whether firms engaged in forward and/or backward forms of integration, and an understanding of this logic is important to understand the transformation that occurred in the coordination of manufacturing sectors in the first part of the twentieth century.

In general, American firms resorted to strategies of vertical integration because of the inability of markets to coordinate technologically separable production functions. More specifically, backward forms of integration tended to occur when processors had relatively few sources of suppliers for resources on which they were heavily dependent, it was difficult for firms to write contracts for supply far into the future, the technology involving the production process was relatively stable, and the product was in a relatively mature stage of the life cycle. Thus, food processing and tobacco industries tended not to engage in backward forms of integration, for they had large numbers of suppliers, no one of which was capable of producing enough to shape prices. In industries where there were large numbers of producers engaged in nonrecurring transactions with processors and there was little uncertainty in the minds of processors about the availability of resources in the future, coordination among actors tended to be coordinated by market transactions rather than within a firm. On the other hand, backward forms of vertical integration were quite common in the oil refining, steel, aluminum, and copper industries – industries in which processing firms believed that they might be vulnerable to having their sources of supply cut off or that they might have to pay monopoly prices.

Where firms were engaged in recurring transactions with other firms for the use of highly specific forms of assets, vertical integration was also a preferred strategy as a means of avoiding monopolistic pricing. Hence, the following industries tended either to develop their own railway cars or their own transportation facilities in order to reduce uncertainty and transacting costs with transportation firms: oil, chemical, coal, steel, automobile, meat processing. On the other hand, if transportation did not require unusual types of facilities for shipping, firms did not vertically integrate into the transportation industry (Chandler 1962, 1977; Williamson 1975, 1985; Hennart 1982; Lamoreaux 1985).

However, there was also often an offensive dimension to backward forms of vertical integration. Firms in some industries bought up raw materials in order to limit their competitors' access to materials. In the steel, copper, aluminum, and newsprint industries, a small number of firms gradually gained control of vital ore deposits and timber, thus removing the possibility for other domestic producers to compete. Where there was a threat of competition from abroad, firms in these industries often lobbied for tariff barriers (Schroeder 1953; Bain 1956; Smith 1970; Parsons and Ray 1975; Fell 1979).

Research and development also tended increasingly to become vertically integrated in the twentieth century. During the nineteenth century, American manufacturing firms had obtained most of their R&D in standalone research organizations. One such organization was Thomas Edison's laboratory in Menlo Park, New Jersey, and in it he developed the light bulb and many other products (Friedel and Israel 1986). Vertically integrated in-house research became increasingly common, for it was exceedingly difficult for firms to write satisfactory contracts for specifying research on new products that were not yet developed. In short, firms feared that by contracting out research and development, they might lose their proprietary interests to opportunistic contractors. Hence, proprietary considerations were served by tight integration (Teece 1988). However, firms also used in-house research as a means of restricting competition. For example, American Telephone and Telegraph, General Electric, Westinghouse, and numerous other firms used their laboratories to develop patents as a strategy of keeping substitute goods from being developed by their competitors and as a means of enhancing and maintaining market share with similar strategies (Passer 1953; Noble 1977; Reich 1977, 1980).

The main consideration here is that the consolidations that took place during the late nineteenth and early twentieth centuries could keep their dominance over time only by developing some edge over their competitors. These were obtained not only with economies of speed and appropriate management of horizontal consolidations, but, where appropriate, firms erected barriers to entry by backward forms of integration, and for a number of years, their superior competitive position could be altered only if other firms duplicated the firm's vertically integrated structure.

The strategy of forward integration. In contrast to the relationship between producers and processors, the logic that transformed the relationship between processors (manufacturers) and distributors was much more complex. The critical consideration involved the role that wholesalers and retailers exerted on the purchase decisions of consumers and the ability of the retailer to influence the purchase decision of consumers, which depended very much on the nature of the product.

Most relationships between manufacturers and retailers involving low-priced consumer goods have been coordinated by simple market transactions. Such products (e.g., food, matches, cigarettes) tended to have low unit prices and were bought very frequently. Because consumers did not invest much time and energy in searching for these products, manufacturers attempted to differentiate their product by creating brand images through advertising. If the manufacturer were successful in creating a brand image, the retailer had little leverage in dealing with the manufacturer, who had to exert very little effort to convince distributors to market the product. In such circumstances, the relationship between manufacturers and distributors was coordinated by market-type transactions. On the other hand, the less able the manufacturer was in differentiating the product through advertising, the more the manufacturer was dependent on the distributor. The manufacturer then had an incentive to control the distribution process either by authorizing exclusive dealerships, franchising, or integrating forward into retailing.

American manufacturers have often integrated forward into distribution when they have introduced new complex consumer durable products. In such situations, not only has the public been unaware of the product, but also the normal retail establishments have frequently lacked knowledge about how to operate and to service the product. In general, the more complex the product, and the less sophisticated the buyer, the greater the incentive for forward forms of vertical integration (Hennart 1982: 86). Thus, in the sewing machine, office equipment, and farm implement industries, manufacturers moved from a market form of coordinating distribution to forward integration to provide not only proper demonstration of their products, but also such ancillary services as repairs and credit. Companies such as Singer Manufacturing Company, IBM, Honeywell, and Xerox are only a few manufacturers of complex consumer durables that still maintain their own retail outlets (Jack 1957; Wilkins 1970; Hennart 1982).

On the other hand, manufacturers of consumer durables have long resorted to franchising when coordinating manufacturing and retailing has led to high management costs. When sales have required detailed knowledge of local conditions, manufacturers have found that central direction is inefficient. For example, automobile manufacturers have found that automobile trade-ins vary so much in condition that it is necessary for local retailers to have considerable autonomy to make decisions about prices. Thus, auto and truck manufacturers have tended to market their products through franchised dealers (Caves and Murphy 1976; Hennart 1982).

In general, when variations in local conditions are considerable, franchising (Cell Two) has become the preferred strategy over vertical integration. For example, manufacturers of beverage syrups such as Seven-Up and Coca Cola decided very early to grant franchises to independent local bottlers, for successful wholeselling of soft drinks required in-depth knowledge and close monitoring of the local reselling outlets (Caves and Murphy 1976: 582; Hennart 1982).

Monitoring networks

The strategy of price leadership. Even after corporate hierarchies were established by horizontal and vertical forms of integration, it was still possible for firms to engage in ruinous price competition with one another. Thus, many such firms still wished to engage in some form of industrywide or collective strategy of stabilizing prices. Though it was illegal to fix prices with cartel-type arrangements, oligopolistic-type hierarchies frequently engaged in an alternative form of collective price setting: price leadership, or what is frequently called the dominant-firm strategy. In our typology, this form of collective behavior is called a monitoring network. Price leadership existed when the price of the goods in an industry was announced by one firm – usually the largest – and the rest of the firms in an oligopolistically structured industry responded by adopting essentially the same prices. When one firm was much larger than others in the industry, it usually had the most interest in preventing price cutting. It generally had the most capacity to prevent price reductions, as it tended to have the greatest amount of financial resources and unused productive capacity. Moreover, in order to achieve price stability, smaller firms were willing for the largest firm to set industry prices.

The sectors in which price leadership occurred most frequently prior to

1950 were steel, copper, petroleum, agricultural implements, anthracite coal, newsprint, fertilizer, industrial alcohol, cement, and the refining of sugar and corn products. Whereas dominant-firm pricing tended to stabilize prices in industries in the short term, in the long run, price leadership was somewhat unstable: the leader's proportion of market share in the industry tended to decline, the differentials among size of firms diminished somewhat, and the leadership tended to decay as a result of competition from other industries or from foreign competitors in the same industry. Because price leadership stabilized the industry in the short term, firms tended not to have high incentives to innovate or to adopt new technologies. Hence, in the long run, firms adopting price leadership as a strategy tended to decline in efficiency. In this respect, it is interesting to note that while these industries used dominant-firm pricing to their advantage prior to and after World War II, Japanese firms in some of these same industries fiercely engaged in price competition within Japan after the War, and this is a consideration of importance in understanding why Japanese firms were so efficient and successful once they eventually entered the American markets. In short, the Japanese strategy suggests that corporate hierarchies without collective forms of price leadership tend to lead to intensive competitiveness among firms over prices, but high levels of innovativeness and efficiency over the long run (Burns 1936: 76–145; Stigler 1968: 108–12; Scherer 1980: 232–6; Lamoreaux 1985: 120–58).

Sources of capital and the emergence of corporate interlocks. To understand how important the source of capital potentially is in the coordination of industrial sectors, one need simply to think comparatively. In Japan and Germany, where industrialization occurred somewhat late and where mass markets have always been much smaller than in the United States, large firms before the Second World War were quite dependent on outside financiers for capital – the large banks in Germany and the major financial groups (e.g., *Zaibatsu*) in Japan. Historically, it was quite common for Japanese and German firms to rely on one or two major banks for capital. Not only did those banks closely monitor the firms' operations, but banks often held equity in the firms – making the bank–firm relationship quite tight. In Japan, there were extensive cross-company forms of stock ownership. These patterns in both countries are important reasons why Japanese and German firms were able to forsake short-term profit maximization in favor of a strategy of long-term goals. In the United States, where the equity markets have been much more developed, however, American managers of large firms have been much less dependent on commercial banks for financing. Indeed, during part of the twentieth century, the proportion of industrial funds contributed by commercial bank loans to American firms has been among the lowest in the world (Ackroyd et al. 1988; Oliver and Wilkinson 1988).

The capital markets developed earlier and became more important in the development of capital-intensive industries in the United States because it was an earlier industrializer. Substantial profits generated from textiles and sailing ships were available for investment purposes in the late nineteenth and early twentieth centuries. Specifically, it was the investment banking houses in the United States that served as the intermediary between those in need of capital and those having capital to invest, and without this intermediary to monitor investments and corporate practices, many large-scale hierarchical-type arrangements could not have emerged in the United States during the late nineteenth and early twentieth centuries.

For example, American investment banks not only channeled investment capital into American industry during the late nineteenth and early twentieth centuries, but they also imposed themselves on the boards of directors of numerous firms in order to convince investors that their investments were being carefully monitored and were relatively safe. The role of a few investment banks was so great in transforming the American railroad industry during the late nineteenth century that they could determine which railroads would grow and which would not, which areas of the country would have railroad expansion, and how many railroads would be established between major cities (Moody 1904; Navin and Sears 1955; Chandler 1956; Carosso 1970; Kotz 1978). The most powerful investment bank was J. P. Morgan and Company, which had access to vast amounts of capital because of its close financial ties with various New York commercial banks and insurance companies. With its power to provide capital and promote consolidations, the House of Morgan and its financial associates by 1912 exercised control through a system of interlocking directorships over a dozen major railroad systems, several of the nation's largest urban transportation systems, United States Steel, International Harvester, General Electric, American Telephone and Telegraph, and Western Union. In addition, Kuhn, Loeb and Company and the Rockefellers, through their control of the National City Bank, also exercised control over a number of companies – among which were Westinghouse Electric, Standard Oil, the Union Pacific Railroad, and Amalgamated Copper – predecessor of Anaconda Copper (U.S. Congress, House Banking and Currency Committee 1913; Kotz 1978).

By channeling investment capital into these various industries, these investment banks played an important role in transforming and stabilizing the railway, steel, copper, telephone, oil, and electric products industries during the late nineteenth and early twentieth centuries. Firms within these industries may have become large-scale hierarchies, but they were embedded in a well-established monitoring network that was extremely important as a governance mechanism. Without the monitoring and discipline exercised by these investment banks, these hierarchies would not have emerged when they did and in the same form. Moreover, without the key role played by investment banks in promoting mergers in the late nineteenth and twentieth centuries, these industries would have been much more unstable. But after 1912, the role of investment banks as a monitoring institution for these industries declined. Thus, for several reasons, there was a further transformation in the coordination of these industries.

State policy was the most important reason for the declining role of investment banking in governing these industries. For example, the Clayton Antitrust Act of 1914 made interlocking directorships among large banks and trusts illegal. Moreover, it forbade a corporation to acquire the stock of another if the acquisition reduced competition in the industry. In the longer term, the Clayton Act tended to reduce the ability of investment banks and firms to carry out a long-term strategy of promoting a community of interests among firms either in the same or in complementary industries – as was the case with the *Zaibatsu* and later the *Keiretsu* in Japan, or with the relationship between banks and large firms in Germany. In addition, the American government in 1933 forced a sharp separation between commercial and investment banking. From that point on, investment banks lost much of their access to capital and had diminished capacity to regulate or govern nonfinancial corporations. The net result was that both types of banks lost much of their control over the modern American corporation.

As a consequence, American nonfinancial corporations became dependent on liquid financial markets for raising capital rather than on the kinds of stable networks that Morgan and other financial banking houses had established at the turn of the century. Increasingly, corporate managers became dependent on the whims and strategies of stockholders and bond owners. When owners of American securities have thought that their investment was not properly managed – as reflected by price earnings ratios, current dividends or interest on the value of the bonds – they have tended to sell their assets. Since American management during the past half century has been evaluated more and more by the current selling price of the stocks and bonds of the company that they manage, the American corporate structure has increasingly been embedded in an institutional arrangement that places strong incentives on management to maximize short-term considerations at the expense of engaging in long-term strategy. In what follows, we observe how this process has placed constraints on the type of transformations that have occurred at subsequent points in time.

Industrial relations and hierarchical coordination

The way in which relations between employees and employers are coordinated is of fundamental importance in shaping the performance of a capitalist economy. Moreover, the type of coordination between labor and capital places limits on the type of transformation that can occur in an industry. In the United States, there has been considerable variation in the way that labor–management relations have been coordinated, not only over the last century and a half, but among different sectors of the economy. For example, during the 1870s and 1880s, inside contracting ("subcontracting") was a common form of employee/employer relations in the iron, steel, and construction industries. Under this system, the owners of a firm generally provided floor space, machinery, raw materials, and capital, and the work was carried out by inside contractors who hired their own employees, supervised the work process, and received a piece rate from the firm. Under this system, the owners of the dominant firm had little technical knowledge about the work process and limited their involvement to negotiating contracts with inside contractors, inspecting the flow of products, and assuming responsibility for final sales. Contractors exercised considerable autonomy in determining when to work, how much to work, and how the work would be done. However, as Braverman points out, this type of subcontracting was plagued by problems of irregularity of production, loss of materials in transit, embezzlement, slowness of manufacture, lack of uniformity, and uncertainty about product quality. But most of all, firms were limited in their inability to change the processes of production (Braverman 1974: 60–1. See also Buttrick 1952; Stone 1974; Williamson 1975, 1985). In other industries, work was organized very differently. There were artisans who worked as regular employees in a single firm, e.g., shoemakers, wagon, bicycle, and furniture makers. They tended to be highly skilled and were very much in control of the work process.

During the late nineteenth century, the communication and transportation revolution permitted firms to expand the size of their markets if they could only produce more. And it was the expansion of the market that transformed the system of production in many industrial sectors to one of mass production. Through the 1950s, the model of mass production became the undisputed means of enhancing industrial efficiency in numerous sectors of the American economy. For about a century, industrial economists assumed that the most efficient means of reducing costs was by employing economies of scale and a standardized system of production. Mass production became the basic strategy for expanding markets, and expanding markets became the means of minimizing costs.

Firms engaged in mass production followed a distinctive logic. They employed a particular form of industrial relations, used specific types of machinery, and related in particular ways to other firms in the manufacturing process. Mass producers took seriously Adam Smith's prescription that the most efficient way of organizing a factory was to routinize and differentiate workers' tasks down to the smallest detail. The key to breaking down manufacturing into even more detailed operations was to employ specific-purpose machinery for each manufacturing task along an assembly line. In much neoliberal thinking about mass production, employment was viewed as an impersonal economic-exchange relationship, and machines (when profitable) could easily be substituted for workers. Whatever labor was needed to work on assembly lines could be hired or dismissed on short notice. As machinery became more and more specialized, the skill and autonomy of individual workers often declined – though the process of "de-skilling" varied from industry to industry. As employees became increasingly "de-skilled," one worker could easily be exchanged for another. Management had little incentive to engage in long-term contracts with workers or to invest in the skills of employees.

Prior to 1960, mass-production strategies were dominant among (1) mass producers of low-priced, semiperishable packaged products, relying on large-batch and continuous-process technology, e.g., cigarettes, breakfast cereals, canned foods, and soaps; (2) processors of perishable products for regional and national markets, e.g., meat packing and processing firms; (3) manufacturers of mass-produced consumer durables that used continuous-process technology, e.g., sewing machines, automobiles, office equipment, and farm implements; (4) makers of high-margin production goods that were technologically complex but standardized, e.g., elevators and pumps; and (5) other industries that were capital-intensive, high energy consuming, and relied on continuous large-batch production technology for mass markets, e.g., chemicals, oil refining, glass, paper, and rubber products (Hollingsworth and Lindberg 1985).

Despite the fact that standardized mass production was the dominant technological paradigm for a number of decades, there were always industries that were organized differently. In short, there was considerable diversity in production strategies among firms and industrial sectors. Standardized mass production always demanded the existence of industries organized along completely opposite principles. For example, the special-purpose machines necessary for mass production could not be mass produced but had to be custom made. Therefore, it was always necessary that there be a sizeable work force having broad and flexible skills with the capability of continually redesigning, reorganizing, and reproducing special-purpose machines. In other words, industrial dualism was always a logical necessity even when standardized production was the dominant technology (Piore 1980).

Mass production and the "de-skilling" associated with it was also inappropriate in industries if processes of production were labor-intensive and low in energy consumption and if the markets for the products were quite heterogeneous. Examples included firms involved in lumber products, printing and publishing, and residential construction. In these industries, craft-based work was dominant, and it was essentially incompatible with systems of mass production, and thus continued. With craft work, each product was relatively unique, requiring considerable worker autonomy. Hence, craft-type activities took place in settings involving long-term stable contracts, often resulting in what Eccles (1981) has called the "quasi-firm" and that is analogous to obligational networks in the typology presented in Chapter 1.

By 1950, numerous manufacturing sectors of the American economy were tightly integrated into a system of mass production, in which the whole was greater than the sum of the parts. This form of production was dependent on stable and relatively defined but very large markets for products that were usually low in their technological complexity and relatively slow in their rate of technological change. Hierarchical governance structures (Cell Three) were particularly well suited for mass production and distribution. When the transaction costs of working with external suppliers and distributors became high, firms frequently resorted to vertically integrated structures and performed diverse functions in house. Such a system was complemented and supported by public-sector mass education, which provided a labor force with the basic training in reading, writing, and discipline to work on assembly lines. The capital markets were sufficiently well developed to provide the capital the standardized system of production required. Because the American model of coordinating mass production with hierarchical institutional arrangements was widely thought to be the undisputed means of enhancing industrial efficiency, many observers believed through the 1950s that the hierarchical form of mass production was the direction in which manufacturing sectors were converging both within and across countries.

THE UNITED STATES ECONOMY SINCE 1950: THE TRANSFORMATION FROM HIERARCHIES TO NETWORKS

As suggested earlier, many of America's industrial firms had succeeded with a hierarchical form of coordination because the barriers to entry were too high for effective competition from other firms – both domestic and foreign – in the same industry. But the day of reckoning was to come. Following the Second World War, various European and Japanese manufacturers adopted the latest technology in industry after industry at a time when transportation costs were declining and markets for high-quality consumer goods – as distinct from standardized products – were expanding. Moreover, manufacturers in Japan, Germany, and several other countries had never become as committed to the hierarchical form of standardized mass production as had manufacturers in many sectors of the American economy. Indeed, those countries had a very different form of coordinating manufacturing sectors – coordination forms geared to flexible forms of production, such as obligational networks based on subcontracting coalitions, strategic alliances rather than hierarchies based on vertical integration, and collective forms of governance.

In Japan, Germany, and other countries where industrialization occurred later and where markets were smaller, forms of coordination that were less hierarchical but more network in nature had long been common. These forms of coordination were more effective in coping with their environment than hierarchical-type arrangements once markets became unstable and consumers increasingly demanded products based on technologies that were highly complex and changing very rapidly. In other words, hierarchical forms of coordinating industrial production are quite effective when markets are quite stable, consumer tastes are relatively homogeneous, and the technology is not highly complex and is slow to change. But when markets are less stable, consumer tastes are more heterogeneous, and the technology of products is complex and fast changing, various types of obligational networks tend to be more appropriate for coordinating economic transactions among various types of actors.

During the 1950s and 1960s, the managers of most American manufacturing firms were unaware that obligational networks, as more efficient organizational forms, would eventually challenge firms in many older American industries, e.g., automobiles, steel, and consumer electronics. Nor were they highly conscious that in newer American industries in which the technology was highly complex and changing very rapidly – pharmaceuticals and other biotech industries, aerospace, and computer-related industries – various types of obligational networks were becoming a dominant form of coordination. But astute observers were noting that as the demand for more flexible forms of production increased, obligational networks provided flexibility in coordination far more so than hierarchically oriented strategies in vertically integrated firms (which in an earlier era had been engaged in producing standardized products).

Following the first world oil crisis of the 1970s, many American manufacturers who had been engaged in producing standardized products found themselves in the position of having products for which there was little demand, and yet their rigid system of production meant that they had little capacity to produce the products that were in demand. Once again, the teachings of Adam Smith were instructive: standardized production and an increasing division of labor were limited by the size of the market, but now markets were shrinking as they became increasingly saturated, volatile, and/or unstable.

Many American firms engaged in producing standardized products responded to saturated markets and the decline in profits simply by trying to reduce costs. Some froze or rolled back their employees' wages. Others took advantage of the declining costs of transportation and communication by shifting production to low-wage areas at home (e.g., the meat processing industry) and/or abroad (as in the auto industry). Most reduced their labor force and introduced new forms of automated equipment. Many firms and their trade associations – especially in the shoe, textile, steel, and automobile industries – pressured Washington for protection against foreign competitors. However, these were only temporary expedients, for it became increasingly evident that standardized systems of production were incompatible with volatile and unstable markets. Even when the market demand for certain goods remained relatively stable, less developed countries with lower wage rates were able to copy standardized products and sell them in the United States at lower prices. Hence, American mass producers increasingly faced severe price competition and losses.

Eventually, it became increasingly obvious that a different coordinating strategy was needed in many manufacturing sectors of advanced capitalist societies. And the question was whether industries in the United States, historically coordinated predominantly by hierarchical strategies, could shift to a mix of more flexible and less hierarchical coordinating strategies employed by their foreign competitors. The need for different forms of coordination did not, of course, extend to all industries. Standardized production strategies associated with hierarchical forms of coordination continued to be effective in industries where the technology was not very complex and rapidly changing, consumer tastes were relatively homogeneous, and markets were relatively stable.

The coordinating form that was slowly emerging in numerous manufacturing sectors was one involving flexible forms of production, with coordination based on a variety of networks. This was not an entirely new paradigm in the United States, but it had long been subordinate to the mass-production perspective. However, a flexible system of production involves vastly different views of labor–management relations, levels of skills and work tasks, and relations among producers, processors, and distributors. Whereas standardized production was characterized by an increasing hierarchically imposed division of labor, flexible systems of production require work forces with broad levels of skills, employees who have "learned to learn" about new technologies and can easily shift from one work task to another, and who can work closely and cooperatively with other employees and management. Labor relations must be structured so that people of various ranks engage in meaningful consultation with one another, rather than constantly responding to commands. Whereas many firms that earlier had engaged in mass production tended to pursue hierarchical strategies of vertical integration in order to lower transaction costs (Williamson 1975, 1985; Chandler 1977), manufacturing firms producing products with rapidly changing technologies reduce transaction costs by relying on long-term stable networks with their suppliers and distributors. The historic strengths of vertical production in the auto, aircraft, steel, consumer electronics, and many other industries are increasingly perceived to have enormous costs in a world in which markets are volatile and the technology is increasingly complex and changing. The older, more hierarchically vertically integrated firms have increasingly become saddled with structural inertia, slow response time, inability to develop in-house components with complex technologies and high production costs.

How widespread have flexible systems of production become across manufacturing sectors of the American economy and why have flexible forms of production become more pervasive in some sectors than in others? Unfortunately, it is difficult to determine the extent to which firms and sectors are moving in the direction of a flexible system of production. From the exterior of firms, it is often difficult to code production systems. Public and private statistics are often unreliable sources for understanding the internal labor markets of firms and the kinds of relationships that exist among producers, processors, and distributors. Even so, there is a great deal of qualitative and quantitative data, as well as in-depth studies of firms and industries, that make it possible to assess the pervasiveness of flexible forms of production. To understand why firms in some sectors have adopted flexible methods of production more than others, the analysis must be sensitive to the following variables: the degree of and nature of international competitiveness; the level of technological complexity and rate of technological change of the products; the degree to which other types of production arrangements had already become highly institutionalized within the sector; whether the industry has a long or a short history; and the potential of firms in an industry to engage in collective behavior.

For purposes of this discussion, a flexible system of production is simply the inverse of mass production. It is the production of goods by means of general-purpose resources rather than vice versa, a system of production that can quickly adapt to different market demands. Thus, firms that are embedded in obligational networks and that have flexible strategies of production have enhanced potential to be competitive in volatile environments, for they can make an ever changing range of goods to appeal to specialized tastes with customized designs (Piore and Sabel 1984; Sabel and Zeitlin 1985; Kristensen 1986: Streeck 1987b).

Markets for many products are changing with great speed, and in such sectors, it is less appropriate for firms to invest in product-specific machines and workers with a capability of doing only one thing. Production systems are closely linked to and conditioned by technology. For example, the emergence of microelectronic circuitry in numerous industries has done much to revolutionize systems of production. In short, the flexibility of microelectronic circuitry now permits firms to produce a variety of products in production runs of variable sizes. Because employees and general-purpose machines can be used for many different purposes in a flexible production system, manufacturing must be coordinated in ways that permit its various parts to be combined and recombined; and the extent of flexibility is measured by the ease with which suppliers, machinery, and workers can be rearranged for different tasks (Kristensen 1986: 38). However, flexible producers require a work force with high levels of skills, workers who can make changes on their own, with less hierarchical work supervision than under a mass-production system. Because of the need to shift production strategies quickly, management must be able to depend on employees to assume initiative, to integrate conception of tasks with execution, and to make specific deductions from general directives. Moreover, firms engaged in flexible systems of production tend to be less vertically integrated than firms engaged in mass production, and to be in close technical contact with other firms. Thus, firms operating in environments with volatile markets must adopt strategies that rely on highly skilled work forces operating with minimal supervision, general-purpose machinery, and flexible network forms of coordination with other producers.

As a result of microelectronic production technology, mass producers have been able to improve the quality and diversity of their products and to reduce the size of their production runs. At the same time, many craft-oriented firms have been able to increase their production volume without sacrificing their quality standards. And in the process, such large and small firms increasingly compete in terms of quality as well as price (Sorge and Streeck 1988).[3]

As flexible production systems become more pervasive, there is a tendency for mass markets to be divided into specialized segments, for consumers in more affluent environments to demand more customized and/or diversified products, and for firms to be smaller than would be the case with a mass-production system. Even in capital-intensive industries, product diversification and small-batch production are becoming very common. Flexible minimills are taking over an increasing share of the steel industry from the integrated mills. Large chemical companies have found it necessary to become increasingly flexible in order to produce more specialty products in small volume. Automobile factories increasingly produce thousands of varieties of cars in small batches. Thus, manufacturing firms with flexible production systems must develop a wide range of options for coping with demand shifts, material shortages, foreign competition, and other types of disruptions. Whereas firms engaged in mass production historically had a tendency to respond to market disruptions by lowering prices, re-

---

3 In writing this chapter, I am very indebted to the stimulating essays by Charles Sable (1982, 1987a, 1987b). However, I do have profound differences with Sable. Whereas he sees the introduction of microelectronic technology as introducing a new industrial divide in which small producers will become increasingly dominant, my perception of capitalist development is less utopian. My chapter assumes that very large firms in many industries will also adopt microelectronic circuity technology and will over the long term compete very successfully against small firms. In short, there is likely to be great variability across industries, with large firms dominating some industries (e.g., automobiles) and small firms doing very well in others (see the criticisms of Sable's perspectives in the essays in Hyman and Streeck, 1988).

ducing the scale of operations, and discharging employees and reducing wages, firms with flexible systems of production have tended to respond by developing new market niches and new products. And the emphasis on new products tends to contribute to more expert skills among management, workers, and subcontractors (Sabel 1987b; Lazerson 1988), thus increasing the demand for ever more products.

Even if there is an ideal typical form of industrial organization that we may label as a flexible production system, there is no single pattern of flexible production. However, there are several strategies of coordinating flexible systems of production that are becoming quite common. Consistent with the typology in Chapter 1, the coordinating form that is becoming increasingly pervasive in advanced capitalist societies is the obligational network.

Obligational networks

Obligational networks assume autonomy of linked firms working in an interdependent fashion. There are several forms of relationships subsumed under the term obligational networks: (1) subcontracting among firms; (2) cooperative contracting among small firms; and (3) strategic alliances and joint ventures among large and small firms, both at the nation-state and global level. *Although it is possible analytically to differentiate these various forms of coordination, they often overlap and are integrated in practice.* All of these forms of obligational networks involve actors in pursuit of the interests of individual firms. In other words, this form of coordination is not part of an effort to govern collectively an entire industry, though obligational relationships function most effectively when they are embedded in a rich set of promotional networks.

Subcontracting among firms. Increasingly, highly capital-intensive manufacturing firms producing products that have technologies that are complex and rapidly changing are engaging in long-term stable relationships with other firms. One type of relationship that is becoming quite common can be labeled as subcontracting. In contrast to vertical integration strategies for mass, standardized production, large firms in many manufacturing sectors are increasingly attempting to base their production process on many smaller-scale suppliers. Examples are found in the automobile, consumer and durable electronic goods, metal products, aircraft, aerospace, and computer industries. Because the American automobile industry has historically been more vertically integrated than many of its foreign competitors (e.g., the Japanese), it has been somewhat slow to "dis-integrate vertically," but even in the American automobile industry, the trend is toward long-term stable relationships among subcontractors rather than the construction of components in house. Such subcontracting provides the opportunity to move away from mass standardized production and to develop more diversified, higher-quality systems of production (see the automobile chapter in this volume, Chapter 7).

In most of these industries, there is usually a hierarchy of firms – the very large corporation at the top and a number of smaller firms under its influence. By relying on subcontracting, larger firms are able to reduce the amount of capital that they must invest, to change quickly the technology upon which their production is based, and to produce a variety of goods in small and medium batches using many kinds of materials and components. In general, the more complex the firm's technology and the better skilled the firm's labor force, the more autonomous the subcontracting firm. On the other hand, subcontracting is not very common in certain industries: furniture, food processing, petroleum, coal, ceramics, and stone products industries, where the technology is not very complex and rapidly changing.

The industrial relations system of industries is increasingly the key to a diversified quality system of production, to more obligatory network types of coordination. To attain diversification, and high-quality production, firms must have a labor force with very flexible and broad job skills. But in order to maintain such a labor force, medium- and long-term manpower planning and training are necessary (Hyman and Streeck 1988).

In order to stay at the cutting edge of technology, large and small firms are becoming increasingly interdependent. Just as large firms increasingly have broadly trained workers in order to remain competitive in world markets, so also have subcontractors had to train their workers according to flexible principles. This has become feasible as relationships among firms have become long-term and stable. Arms-length contracting based on short-term market pricing is not conducive to investing in the long-term training of a highly skilled work force.

Increasingly, large firms in the auto, aircraft, aerospace, computer, and other industries must provide capital, marketing, and research services to their suppliers. As products become more complex and change rapidly, many large firms no longer know exactly how to produce their products. To keep up with changes in the market, large and small firms must learn from one another about new markets and new technologies. To facilitate this, middle-level management increasingly moves back and forth between suppliers and final assemblers. Meantime, price considerations have become less important in shaping the relationships among suppliers and customers (Sabel 1987a, 1987b; Hyman and Streeck 1988).

As subcontractors work with complex technology, they increasingly attempt to develop long-term stable relationships with several companies, reducing their dependence on a single large firm. In some sectors, smaller firms not only have increased the number of buyers to which they sell, but also have diversified into several product lines. Through diversification, firms protect themselves in the event of a downturn in the market for a single product, and they become immune from "strong arm" tactics that could be exerted from a single customer. It is not uncommon for firms that make dies and molds for auto assemblers, as well as parts for aircraft assemblers, to make tractor parts as well as specialty machinery for electronics and computer industries.

The key to high-quality product diversification is technology based on a highly and broadly trained labor force using microelectronic machinery. This strategy has increasingly shifted competition away from a focus on prices to greater concern with product quality and other considerations of work-force capability to meet rapidly changing demands.

Although it is popular today to minimize the role of technology in dictating the strategies of firms and the governance arrangements dominant in particular industries, advances in semiconductor and computer technology since the 1970s have made it possible to develop a generation of machine tools that can easily adapt to new tasks and products. Before these advances in computerized technology, firms generally had to obtain new equipment whenever they produced different products. For firms engaged in mass production, it generally meant replacing the machinery. By relying on microelectronic technology, firms can put their manufacturing equipment to new uses simply by reprogramming the machinery. Because microelectronic technologies have almost limitless uses in a vast array of industrial sectors, firms can more easily shift into different product lines – assuming they have broadly trained workers.

Computerized technology alone cannot assure the emergence of flexible production systems and the existence of a broadly trained labor force. Indeed, firms engaged in standardized production often use computer-based technologies for rather rigid purposes. In many American industries, the paradigm of mass production is declining more rapidly than a new paradigm of flexible, diversified quality production is being institutionalized. Ideally, before a production system based on an obligatory form of networks can be highly effective, firms must be intricately embedded into an institutionalized infrastructure that provides for training of labor, extensive links with research institutes and business associations, cooperation with local governments and various types of credit institutions – in short in a system of promotional networks. Moreover, firms must have a willingness to cooperate and have trusting relationships with their competitors, suppliers, and customers. However, the degree to which firms are embedded into these two types of networks varies greatly across industries (Piore and Sabel 1984; Sorge and Streeck 1988; Herrigel 1989).

Even if this type of industrial coordination becomes increasingly more common, it will not completely replace hierarchical processes of standardized production. Flexible production processes require standardized production processes. For example, Herrigel (1989) has demonstrated that industrial sectors employing flexible, diversified, and high-quality forms of production are dependent on the mass production of flexible machines. Moreover, the customization of many products is based on the standardized production of component parts. Thus, it is still uncertain how widespread the diffusion of a flexible system of production will be across sectors of advance capitalist societies.

The study of firms employing a strategy of diversified quality production and engaging in long-term relations with firms in several industries poses difficult problems for sectoral analysis, for as firms become increasingly flexible in their production capabilities, they tend to engage in more and more product diversification. But as firms move into multiple product lines, the boundaries among sectors become increasingly blurred. Of course, product diversification within firms is not new, as the histories of the chemical and other industries demonstrate (Chandler 1962). But more recently, the pace of diversification is accelerating. Textile firms are producing medical supplies, optical-fiber materials, and print distributing boards; transport machinery makers have shifted to the general machinery sector and are producing motors and industrial machinery; chemical firms are moving into applied areas of biotechnology and are producing medical supplies and enzyme products, print distributing boards, electromagnetic materials, resins related to electronic products, carbon and optical fibers, as well as videotapes. Food manufacturers are moving into the service sector, particularly into the restaurant business; steel manufacturers are making electromagnetic products. On the other hand, there has been much less diversification in petroleum, paper and pulp, and rubber industries.

Cooperative (relational) contracting among small firms. In this institutional form, firms are small and skill-intensive. Each small shop specializes in one phase in the chain of production, but is engaged in long-term stable relations with other firms in the same community or region. These relationships are open-ended and continuous, with relationships being periodically redefined. This form of production is especially common in the industrial areas of Italy, in Smaland in southern Sweden, in the western part of Denmark, and in different regions of Japan. What is remarkable is the similarity in the structure and process of these small firms whether they exist in Japan or in Western Europe. In general, they rely heavily on microelectronic tools and extremely well-trained labor to produce high-quality shoes, silverware and cutlery, ceramics, textiles, apparel, agricultural implements, special machines, electronic musical instruments, and well-designed furniture. As each shop tends to engage in only one task in a complex chain of production, the long-term stable relationship among firms is similar to the following model: $A + B + C + D + E + F$. Thus, in the shoe industry, one firm makes the sole and another the heel, another cuts and sews the leather, etc. Cooperative contracting is based on high interdependence, with each actor completely dependent on every other for its survival. This type of production is labeled "cooperative contracting" rather than "subcontracting," though the final product of all of these firms may ultimately go to a large distributor as some form of subcontracting.

There is increasing evidence that in these industries this type of cooperative arrangement leads to higher levels of productivity than an hierarchical-type arrangement. At one time, the United States mass produced shoes, cutlery, and many other products in which this coordinating form exists, but because of their impoverished institutional environment, American firms in these industries have lacked the capacity to be transformed from a coordinating system based on hierarchical forms of mass production to one of cooperative contracting. And lacking the capacity to develop this form of coordination, American firms in these industries either are declining or have already died – though firms in these industries perform extremely well in some advanced capitalist societies. Why is this the case?

Cooperative contracting tends to flourish in those regions that historically had strong artisan traditions and where there had also been a tradition of small firms engaging in strong collective action, e.g., where highly institutionalized promotional networks exist. However, the United States either never had a strong artisan tradition in these industries – or if the tradition ever existed – it succumbed long ago to hierarchical forms of mass production. Moreover, the tradition of antitrust legislation, the strong ethnocultural cleavages in American society, the large size of the country, and heterogeneity of interests among firms in the same industry have placed severe constraints on the ability of firms in these industries to develop the kind of institutionalized networks for sustaining effective collective actions. In other words, cooperative contracting among small firms can be effective only if they are embedded in an environment consisting of a highly institutionalized set of promotional networks.

With cooperative contracting, each firm is dependent on a collectivity of firms – cooperative pacts and local associations in order to regulate their relations – to carry out a multiplicity of tasks in separate work settings that in the United States was historically more likely to have been carried out in a large factory. Elsewhere, small firms in these industries even join together to reduce all kinds of overhead costs – rent, insurance, accounting – and it is not uncommon that they borrow machinery from one another. Through negotiations conducted by their business associations, they often receive special subsidies from local, regional, and national governments. Moreover, they are embedded in a set of long-term stable networks with specialized banks, credit associations, and government lending agencies. Efficiencies are achieved by rapid responses to market needs because of the flexible organizational structure of the entire system (Sabel 1987b; Friedman 1988; Lazerson 1988).

Although declines in business cycles or in specific markets can injure all the firms engaged in this kind of relationship, when these conditions occur, firms cooperate in the development of new products. Because it is not easy to shift to different product markets, firms share in the costs of continual training and retraining their workers and the acquisition of new machinery. Indeed, cooperative production among potential competitors helps producers to prevent downward price competition and wage squeezing. Familiarity breeds cooperation and a willingness to share risks (Sabel 1987b; Lazerson 1988).

The survival of this kind of relationship depends on the intensity of group solidarity among firms. The stronger their sense of collectivity, the more successful they are in regulating the relations between owners of firms and their employees. Strong group solidarity permits small firms to resist high wage demands and profit pressures from large distributors. Otherwise, firms might lay off workers, reduce wages, move elsewhere, or close down.

Though this type of cooperative contracting is pervasive among small firms in Japan, Italy, and elsewhere, it would be a mistake to assume that this form of production is common across all manufacturing sectors in which small firms exist in large numbers. For example, the cooperative contract model is much less common in the production of printing, pencils, and food products – in short, in industries in which the skill levels have remained quite low and the technology of production has remained standardized and slow to change.

Strategic alliances and joint ventures among firms. Firms in a number of industries that historically conducted transactions with either a corporate strategy of vertical integration or in market-type transactions are presently conducting these transactions through obligational networks, specific forms of which are here called joint ventures. These are also forms of obligational networks and are becoming increasingly common in advanced capitalist societies.

These relationships are of a different order from the cooperative contracting and subcontracting discussed before. In the language of agency theory, firms in this type of relationship are both principals and agents: risk takers who allocate tasks and share in the gains or losses of the final product (Powell 1988). These relationships have the potential to be long-term and durable, much more flexible than the type of hierarchical arrangements that historically characterized firms specializing in standardized production.

In an era when the rate of technological change was relatively slow, production processes in an industry relatively standardized, and production runs quite long, vertical integration was an appropriate strategy for firms that faced high uncertainties and small numbers in their relationships with either suppliers or distributors. However, there have always been costs to integrating interdependent relationships within one firm. For example, there is high potential for bureaucratic rigidities to develop in vertically integrated firms. Moreover, it becomes increasingly inefficient for firms to produce everything in house when technology is very complex and changes very rapidly.

Historically, some companies developed special long-term relationships with firms in other countries in order to gain market access or to transfer technology through licensing agreements. In more recent years, however, joint ventures among firms have become more varied in goal and scope, e.g., the search for economies of scale, the need for market access, the sharing of risks, the need to have access to technology, and to pool know-how. Moreover, the frequency of these relationships has increased, especially in industries involving high-cost products with complex and rapidly changing technologies. Like mergers, strategic alliances and joint ventures offer benefits quickly, but without the necessity of giving up much of one's independence. Unfortunately, our knowledge about the conditions under which strategic alliances emerge – at both the empirical and theoretical level – is still quite limited.

In general, joint ventures function best when the various actors are embedded in a highly institutionalized set of promotional networks that facilitate trust and cooperation. However, the American political economy has a strong neoliberal tradition with networks designed to promote cooperation among actors in the same industry being poorly developed, especially in more traditional industries. But as the next section argues, cooperative and collective forms of networks have been better developed in newer industries where the technology is more complex and changing more rapidly.

The importance of multilateral and collective action

Hierarchical forms of governance are based on the assumption that in order to reduce uncertainty among actors, relationships must be coordinated within a firm. Markets tend to generate fierce competition among like actors, and through such competition, actors attempt to eliminate their competitors. But in advance capitalist societies, when obligational networks become more pervasive as a governance form, different forms of behavior become manifest.

Due to high research-and-development costs, rapid change in products, and volatile markets, it is no longer possible, in many industries, to coordinate as many things in house as was possible during the age of mass standardization. Markets and hierarchies can work best when firms are embedded in an impoverished institutional environment. But for obligational networks to operate efficiently, they must be embedded in an institutional environment that is highly developed with institutions that promote cooperation between processors and suppliers and even among their competitors, an environment that facilitates the exchange of information among competitors as well as among suppliers and producers. Firms must also be embedded in an environment that develops rich, broad, and flexible skills for the work force. In short, advanced capitalist societies require cooperative relations and collective resources far in excess to what is needed for markets and hierarchies to function effectively and in excess of what single firms can develop for themselves (Streeck 1987a, 1988). These collective arrangements are displayed in the right-hand column of the typology, Table 1.1, in Chapter 1.

Highly effective sharing of information and cooperation among various actors requires all of the following: collective action on the part of competitors, rich training centers – whether within vocational schools, universities, or other institutions – and institutions willing to provide financing on a long-term basis. In other words, obligational networks function best when they are embedded in an institutional environment with rich multilateral or collective dimensions that provide these conditions.

Of course, a number of American industries have long been coordinated by obligational networks that have also been firmly embedded in an institutional environment of promotional networks. In the American case, some of the most effective promotional networks have involved cooperative relations among university-based firms, commercial firms in the same industry, and the state and federal governments. For example, American agriculture owes much of its twentieth-century success to the way that agricultural producers have been embedded in a rich institutional environment that has provided cooperative activity among producers, the dissemination by the state of university-based knowledge to agricultural scientists, and financial assistance from a number of public and quasipublic institutions. Another sector with a long history of being embedded in promotional networks is the American chemical industry. Since the turn of the century, chemical firms have been extensively involved in promotional networks that have consisted of university-based scientists and, from time to time, the federal government. It is no exaggeration to argue that those countries that have lacked promotional networks involving rich university resources for the training of chemists and for the conduct of nonproprietary research have failed to develop a successful chemical industry.[4]

The key actor in promoting multilateral activity among producers in American society has generally been the American state. Significantly, the American state has rarely taken the lead in developing promotional networks among manufacturing firms that historically were coordinated primarily by markets and/or hierarchies. Rather, the American state has been most active during the past half century in developing promotional net-

4 I am indebted to Richard Nelson of Columbia University for this observation.

works for manufacturing firms that have addressed the military and health-related needs of the society. For example, the following are some of the products and technologies derived from firms coordinated by obligational networks that were firmly embedded in an environment (e.g., promotional networks) involving cooperative relations with university-based scientists and engineers, the state – especially the military – and other firms – both suppliers and competitors: commercial aircraft, semiconductors, integrated circuits, computers, nuclear power, microwave telecommunications, new materials such as high-strength steel alloys, fiber-reinforced plastics, titanium, and new methods of fabricating metals such as numerical-controlled machine tools. Without obligational networks embedded in promotional networks involving multilateral relations with universities, various agencies and departments of the federal government, and numerous business firms, these technologies and products could not have occurred in the United States at the time they did (Nelson 1982; Landau and Rosenberg 1986).

The importance of obligational networks being embedded in an environment with rich promotional networks is that it links together organizations having different knowledge bases. This kind of coordination is not possible within a single hierarchy, as no firm has had the capacity to incorporate all the knowledge and resources to develop any one of the technologies and products listed before. Nor could a single firm linked with its suppliers in an obligational network have developed these products. They could be developed only because obligational networks were embedded in an environment with highly developed promotional networks. In this context, the Agency for Science and Research reported in 1985 that 20% of the firms it surveyed were linked with other firms, universities, and government laboratories through networks involving joint research projects, commissioned research, or other forms of information exchange – and it predicted that in 1990, there would be 26% (Aoki 1988).

Thus, advances in electronics have required extensive communication networks involving physicists as well as engineers in electronics and material science. Even though American firms are highly sensitive to antitrust issues, the American government has increasingly realized the importance of cooperative research among competing firms and in recent years has relaxed its enforcement practices in certain industries. This has facilitated rich collaboration among firms in the semiconductor industry through the Semiconductor Industry Association and the American Electronics Association, both of which have research programs in conjunction with various American universities. In the pharmaceutical industry, promotional networks have been extensive in linking together experts in industry, government laboratories, and land universities in the fields of pharmacology, biochemistry, immunology, molecular and cell biology.

Because of the flexibility of obligational and promotional networks as well as the flexibility of the external labor market, and because venture capital markets have been quite well developed in the United States, it has been relatively easy – by world standards – for entrepreneurial-oriented American researchers and engineers to develop their own firms in order to commercialize new products. This has been especially common in information-based industries in and around Silicon Valley, California, as well as in the biomedical, biochemical, and artificial-intelligence-related industries throughout the United States.

With a cross-national perspective, it is apparent that this type of institutional arrangement has performed extremely well in American society in advancing knowledge at the frontiers of science and in the development of new products derived from basic science. Americans have been particularly successful in the development of new products that have many kinds of military and health-related applications. However, the American R&D system has been less successful in improving upon older and new products for commercial markets. For example, when one observes the Japanese system of research and development, one quickly becomes aware that the American system of networking facilitates creativity in developing new products, but it has its shortcomings in improving on existing products. Though the Japanese are much weaker in basic science, have not succeeded in developing radically new products, and are somewhat deficient in entrepreneurial leadership, they have concentrated on establishing very close communication among researchers and engineers with production and marketing personnel involved in existing product technologies. Japanese firms are also increasingly embedded in networks involving university-based scientists and engineers – but established networks are closely linked with established production facilities, whereas in the United States, manufacturing networks tend not to involve production personnel – or else the production activity is only at the periphery of the network. In Japan, R&D and production personnel frequently move back and forth among production sites, research laboratories, and engineering departments. Americans are socialized in their educational system to make scientific discoveries and to develop new products. In contrast, the Japanese are socialized to be highly attentive to detail and to improve upon existing products. Whereas the Americans excel in horizontal communication across organizations in the development of new products, the Japanese excel in establishing horizontal feedback types of communication "from marketing to production and production to redesign" (Aoki 1988: 247). In other words, the Japanese emphasis is clearly on the production phases of the industrial process, whereas the Americans have tended to be less creative in this area. And this difference in where networks focus their energies in the two countries does much to explain why the Japanese have over the long run been so successful in commercially producing and marketing products that the Americans first developed.

Similarly in Europe, producers of more traditional products (automobiles, ceramics, textiles, furniture, machine tools, shoes) are embedded in a rich infrastructure consisting of training institutes, business associations, and local and regional governments (Schmitter and Streeck 1981; Piore and Sabel 1984). And it is from this cooperative environment that diversified high-quality production has emerged in these European industries. One reason why American firms in these industries have not been highly competitive in recent decades – at least internationally – is because of the weakness of obligational networks embedded in a rich institutional environment of promotional networks.

Finally, there is one other aspect of American obligational networks in high-tech industries that deserves mention. Because of the flexible external labor market in the United States, it is very difficult for American firms to keep knowledge proprietary. The moving of personnel from one organization to another undoubtedly facilitates communication, creativity, and the development of new products. But it also tends to limit the ability of individual firms to focus all of their talents on the long-term development of particular products once they come into existence, whereas the rigid external labor market in Japan and Germany permits firms in these countries to focus enormous energy on the improvement and refinement of products.

This brief comparison of networking in the Japanese, European, and American environments suggests that despite the utility of our concept of obligational networks, there are different types of obligational networks, and they may be concentrated primarily at the research-and-development stage of new products or at the production stages or both, and they may or may not be deeply embedded in a set of promotional networks. All of this variation in national arrangements leads to different performance consequences following from the emphasis of the network.

CONCLUDING OBSERVATIONS

Historically, there has been much greater variability in the coordination of manufacturing sectors in the United States than in Japan, Germany, or the smaller democracies of Europe. The greater variability in the American case results from several factors, chief among them: (1) The United States has a very complex economy, much more complex than any other advanced capitalist society, with many more manufacturing sectors to be coordinated. (2) The United States is much larger – both in space and population – than any other advanced capitalist country, with very heterogeneous sectors. And because there is considerable heterogeneity of interests within sectors, it has historically been more difficult for firms to engage in collective action, to develop effective associative structures for the governance of their sectors. If there are large numbers of firms in industries but weak associative structures – as in the United States – there is more variability in the coordination of industries than in countries that have extremely well-developed systems of associations. (3) Because the United States became a highly industrialized society much earlier than most other capitalist societies, it has a mixture of earlier forms of coordination and new forms of coordination that have emerged since the Second World War. (4) More than in most countries, there are sectors at many different stages of the product life cycle – and variation in product life cycle leads to differences in coordinating styles. Some sectors are always growing or declining more rapidly than others. Because the United States industrialized relatively early and over a long period of time, because of the American tendency to be inventive in the development of new industries, and because of the complexity of the American economy, there tend to be more industries at different stages of the life cycle than is the case in most countries. In American history, there have been institutional forms for the coordination and governance of multiple economic sectors at different points in time. Thus, batches of sectors – branches of the economy – have similar competitive and cooperative arrangements. But some of the variability in governance of different branches of the economy occurs because industries developed and coordinating arrangements emerged at different times. In other words, part of the variation in the coordination of the same industries across countries results because institutional arrangements for coordinating specific industries developed at different times.

Taking a long-term perspective on the governance mechanisms used in American manufacturing, one sees truly effective forms of coordination of a collective nature for only brief periods. Monitoring as a form of coordination has been relatively uncommon, and promotional networks have been even less conspicuous, but most prominent in manufacturing industries that address the military and health needs of the society and that involve products that are very costly and with complex and rapidly changing technologies.

In contrast to most advanced capitalist countries, the distinctive feature of collective governance in the American case is its weakness of associative institutional arrangements (Galambos 1966; Hawley 1966; Schmitter and Streeck 1981; Hollingsworth and Lindberg 1985; Schneiberg and Hollingsworth 1989). A variable of considerable importance in shaping the associative structure of an industry is the degree to which the country has historically been dependent on foreign trade. Political elites in countries heavily dependent on foreign trade encourage firms to develop strong associational structures in order to cooperate in competing internationally, whereas countries less dependent on foreign trade tend to be less tolerant of associations, seeing them as institutions that retard change and grant monopolistic status to firms. It is in this context that antitrust legislation emerged more strongly in the United States than in most other capitalist societies. And, in recent years, as foreign trade has become more important in the overall American economy, there is evidence that the rigidity of antitrust enforcement is being moderated.

Countries with strong associative structures tend to have firms that co-operate not only with competitors, but also with suppliers and distributors in long-term stable networks (Schneiberg and Hollingsworth 1989). On the other hand, where associations are more weakly structured – as in the United States – coordination through markets and hierarchies has histor-ically been more pervasive. In the past forty years, however, there has been very substantial decline in the importance of the hierarchical form of coordination. Obligational networks, in numerous varieties, have become more prominent. Through joint ventures and strategic alliances, they may offer the prospect of economic coordination at a global level, especially when markets are volatile and technology is unstable (Porter 1986).

In assessing the relative roles of corporate hierarchies and networks in the United States, several points should be noted. First, since stable, ho-mogeneous markets remain for many products that have technologies with low levels of complexity, hierarchical forms of coordination remain in many industries. "Dis-integration" may be occurring, but hierarchical forms of coordination are still widespread in American manufacturing. Paper prod-ucts, breakfast cereals, soft drinks, bug sprays, floor wax, deodorants, soaps, shaving cream, and hundreds of other products remain, symbolic of the familiar hierarchical form of corporate America. The mass markets to which these products are directed seem quite stable and unsaturated, ready for products manufactured by semiskilled workers and distributed by general-purpose firms.

Second, the ability of the United States to move rapidly toward more network forms of coordination is drastically limited by prevailing practices of industrial relations. The type of industrial relations that facilitates di-versified and high-quality production strategies is one in which workers have broad levels of skills and some form of assurance that they will not be dismissed from their jobs. Indeed, job security or other arrangements that assure long-term employment tend to be necessary for employers to have sufficient incentives to make long-term investments in developing the skills of their workers. And this type of incentive and skill system has become much more widespread in Japan, West Germany, and Sweden than in the United States (Aoki 1988; Hyman and Streeck 1988). In the United States, manufacturing employment has tended to be much more job-specific, workers have been less broadly trained, internal labor markets have been more rigid, and employers have had much less incentive to invest in their workers' skill development. Because the United States has a very flexible external job market, it is much easier for American workers to leave jobs for other firms than is the case in countries where workers have long-term job security. This also provides disincentives for American employers to invest in worker training. Firms with semiskilled work forces have little capacity to be substantially involved in flexible production arrangements coordinated by obligational networks.

Third, the associational system of a country influences both its industrial relations system and its ability to engage in obligational networks. Where there is a well-developed associational system, firms have greater capacity to enter into collective agreements with their competitors so as not to poach one another's workers, in effect creating more rigid external labor markets. But this in turn encourages firms to develop more flexible internal labor markets, to invest in the skills of their employees, to develop more flexible forms of production and more pervasive forms of obligational networks, and to produce higher-quality products. Thus, countries with firms tightly integrated into highly institutionalized systems of business associations (e.g., Japan and Germany) have rather rigid external labor markets but flexible internal labor markets, whereas countries (the United States) with weak associative structures tend to have more flexible external labor markets but more rigid internal labor markets.

Fourth, the capital markets in the United States have placed constraints on the development of broad employee skills. The kinds of capital markets that have emerged in the United States have encouraged firms to engage in short-term maximization of profits. On the other hand, large firms in Japan and Germany have relied more on bank loans and/or cross-firm ownership as a major source of capital because of the lack of a well-developed bond and stock market such as that which developed in the United States (Zysman 1983; Aoki 1988). The short-term profit horizon of many American corporations has been very much due to their high dependency on very liquid equity markets, combined with the fact that American banks have been disinclined to provide long-term, low-interest loans. This kind of emphasis on a short-term horizon has placed constraints on the development of long-term stable relations between employers and their employees – a prerequisite for a highly skilled and broadly trained work force.

Fifth, as technology in sectors of advanced capitalist societies becomes increasingly complex, changes more rapidly, and becomes more expensive, actors in these sectors are increasingly finding that obligational networks are an effective form of coordinating and transacting with each other. But to maximize their effectiveness as governance arrangements, obligational networks need to be embedded in a rich institutional environment involving various forms of collective behavior. However, American firms with obligational networks as a major form of coordination are very weakly embedded in institutional arrangements of a collective nature. On the other hand, their Japanese and German competitors not only rely on obligational networks as a dominant form of coordination, but they are embedded in a rich institutional environment (Aoki 1988; Hyman and Streeck 1988). And it is for this reason that they are likely to continue outperforming their American competitors.

On the other hand, there is some convergence in the coordinating styles of American firms with those in Japan and West Germany. Indeed, the term "Japanization" has become increasingly common – a term used to describe the attempts by non-Japanese firms to emulate Japanese practices and to describe the process and impact of Japanese direct investment in the United States. In recent years, Japanese manufacturers have gradually increased their presence in the United States for a variety of reasons: the upward valuation of the yen, the threat of protectionism, the competition of new industrializing countries, and a response to their competitive struggle against rivals in Japan. Eight Japanese auto makers have either completed or are in the process of making plans to produce cars in North America. Even the large American automakers now purchase large quantities of their parts from Japanese component manufacturers. Most Japanese manufacturers that have located in the United States originally had considerable skepticism about the capability of American suppliers to provide quality products. However, there is increasing evidence that slowly – though often with great pain – American firms are succeeding in meeting Japanese requirements, and are thus entering into long-term, stable relationships – e.g., obligational networks – with Japanese firms. In many instances, this interaction with Japanese firms is having a major effect in changing management and production styles of American firms. Meantime, some Japanese component manufacturers are also locating in the United States. However, the Japanese emphasis on long-term, stable relationships among firms, long-term employment within firms, heavy emphasis on providing workers with broad skills, and a reward system based on seniority has not become dominant within many manufacturing sectors of the American economy. Nevertheless, diversified quality production practices and obligational network forms of coordination are becoming somewhat infectious in the United States, especially in those industries in which the Japanese are highly successful.

As one would expect, these practices have been far more successful in Japanese owned and managed firms than in American owned and managed firms (Oliver and Wilkinson 1988: 132–4). In response to Japanese competition, American management has often engaged in cost-cutting elements of just-in-time and total quality principles (see Chapter 7 on the automobile industry in this volume). Because American manufacturing firms remain embedded in a culture in which the business horizons are of a short-term nature, however, they have not engaged in extensive investments in the education and training of their employees. And this poses a fundamental problem for American owned firms, for as long as they are situated in an environment with flexible external labor markets, employers are fearful that if they make long-term investments in their workers, other firms may hire them away. With the business associative structure and various aspects of promotional networks very weak in older industries, it is very difficult to develop and implement a new set of rules that will facilitate the implementation of the kind of internal and external labor markets that are essential for high-level performance among firms engaged in obligational networks.

On the other hand, there are American firms that are excellently managed, that do have flexible internal labor markets, that invest in the long-term development of their employees, that make serious efforts to engage in systems of diversified quality production, and that are intricately linked into both obligational and promotional networks. For the most part, these are firms in industries that are relatively new, in which the technology is quite complex and changes very rapidly, and in which the product technology is heavily based on principles of basic science. Examples include firms in computer or computer-related, biotechnology, aerospace, and numerous defense-related industries. Most firms in these sectors never had an industrial relations system that was heavily dominated by a system of standardized mass production. These industries have tended to be very research- and growth-oriented, and because of the profitability of their firms, layoffs of employees – by American standards – have been less common. As a result, firms in these sectors have been willing to invest in their employees' future, and, in turn, employees have tended to develop strong loyalties toward their company.

Despite the revolution in communications and transportation and increased competitiveness in the world's economy, there remains considerable variation in the way that manufacturing sectors are coordinated in the United States. Much of this variation is due to political, social, and economic institutional arrangements that emerged at earlier moments in time and that have acquired considerable legitimacy. Because the legacy of the past very much influences the way that sectors are coordinated in the contemporary world, and because these traditional institutional arrangements are so intertwined, governance and coordinating mechanisms are likely to diverge among American manufacturing sectors long into the future.

Even so, it should now be quite apparent to the reader that many sectors of the American economy emerged from a market-oriented form of coordination to what has popularly been called Fordist in the late nineteenth and early twentieth century. However, due largely to international competition and changes in technology, a transformation to a post-Fordist system has been slowly emerging. The Fordist system was heavily based on the principles of mass standardized production, whereas the post-Fordist is shaped by the principles of diversified quality production. Empirically, the two types of production do not exist in pure form, but there are a

Table 2.1. *A typology of Fordist system of mass production and post-Fordist system of diversified quality production*

Variables	Fordist system	Post-Fordist system
Size and nature of the market	Large homogeneous markets, with competition based very much on price	Smaller markets; more heterogeneous tastes with competition based very much on quality
Technology of the product	Stable and slow to change; not highly complex. Products produced in large volume	Rapidly changing and highly complex. Products produced in small batches
Organizational characteristics of firms		
Chain of production	Tendency for production to be vertically integrated	Vertical disintegration, with various types of obligational networks linking various actors together. Subcontracting, cooperative contracting among small firms, joint ventures, and strategic alliances are common
Work skills	Narrowly defined and very specific in nature	Well-trained, highly flexible, and broadly skilled work force
Labor–management relations	Low trust between labor and management. Poor communication but hierarchical in nature	High degree of trust
Internal labor market	Rigid	Flexible
Centralization	Very hierarchical and semiauthoritarian	Decentralized, consensual, and participatory-type organization
Production equipment	Product-specific machines	General-purpose machines
Work security	Relatively poor security except due to considerable class conflict	Long-term employment, relatively high job security
Investment in work skills by firm	Low	High

Table 2.1 (*continued*)

Variables	Fordist system	Post-Fordist system
Conception of property rights	High degree of consciousness of property rights	Lower level of consciousness of property rights
Environmental structures:		
Relationship with other firms	Highly conflictual, rather impoverished institutional environment	Highly cooperative relationships with suppliers, customers, and competitors in a very rich institutional environment
Collective action with competitors	Trade associations poorly developed and where existent are lacking in power to discipline members	Trade associations highly developed with capacity to govern industry and to discipline members
Modes of capital formation	Capital markets well developed; equities are highly liquid, frequently traded	Capital markets are less well developed, strong bank–firm links, extensive cross-firm ownership, long-term ownership of equities
Antitrust legislation	Designed to weaken cartels and various forms of collective action	More tolerant of various forms of collective action
Institutional training facilities	Public education emphasizing very low levels of skills	Greater likelihood of strong apprenticeship programs linking vocational schools and firms

number of interacting contextual variables that give rise to these types, and Table 2.1 describes the variation of these variables in the two types. And it is these variables on which much of the preceding analysis has been based. As the analysis has demonstrated, however, elements of these two types often exist side by side during the same period in a nation's history – but generally one type is more dominant than the other and there is often strong tension between the two types in the history of any single sector.

Part II

Empirical studies of governance transformations in the United States

3

TRANSFORMATIONS IN THE GOVERNANCE OF THE AMERICAN TELECOMMUNICATIONS INDUSTRY

Kenneth N. Bickers

Department of Political Science, Rice University

As many commentators have noted, public policy in the United States traditionally has favored a market-oriented economic system (Fainsod, Gordon, and Palamountain 1959; Hurst 1982). Market competition, however, has proven to be an unstable mechanism for coordinating interactions in the telecommunications industry. From the time of the telegraph and later the telephone, the telecommunications industry has been at the center of efforts to institute nonmarket governance arrangements. Nonmarket alternatives that have been adopted include obligational networks, promotional networks, and hierarchical controls.

The recent court-ordered breakup of the Bell System marks an effort to reintroduce markets as a primary means of governing transactions in the industry. It is still too soon to know if this experiment will prove successful. Nevertheless, the controversies surrounding the current attempt to institute market coordination are revealing. The experimentation with alternative governance regimes over the past 150 years makes this industry a useful laboratory to study the evolution of governance.

The model employed here for analyzing the evolution of governance builds on the framework presented in Chapter 1. In schematic form, this framework posited that transformations from one governance regime to another occur when a governance regime experiences pressures for change, which, in turn, spark a search process for a more adequate regime. As before, it is assumed here that actors search opportunistically for governance regimes that are advantageous to their interests (Williamson 1985). This implies that actors with different interests often prefer the creation of governance regimes with different arrangements of governance mechanisms, and that conflict, rather than cooperation, often characterizes the search process. Hence, actors with different resources are differentially capable of influencing the choice of governance regimes in a sector.

In the telecommunications industry, industry actors historically have possessed vastly different resources. A small number of firms (the Bell System and Western Union) have been able to exercise significant control over the regimes that have emerged. Put simply, the "votes" of the various industry actors have not counted equally in the selection of governance regimes.

When we focus on the pattern of experimentation in the telecommunications industry, two types of factors appear to be crucial in circumscribing the set of governance arrangements that are likely to emerge from the opportunistic behaviors of industry actors. The first is that a potential governance regime must be compatible with the underlying technologies in an industry. This does not mean that each technology *necessitates* one and only one regime (Williamson 1985: 86–9). It does mean, however, that the characteristics of a technology are likely to be compatible with some, but not all, regimes. That is to say, the system of incentives and sanctions implicit in a governance regime may be more or less suited to the problems posed by a particular technology. These incompatibilities delimit the set of feasible governance arrangements (Bickers 1988).

The second factor similarly constrains the set of governance arrangements that can be institutionalized. A system of governance must possess political legitimacy for it to be viable as a mechanism of social coordination and control. In practice, of course, political legitimacy is not unidimensional. At least three dimensions can be identified, each of which functions as a hurdle that a potential governance regime must clear. First, a regime must be consistent with extant legal principles. Conflict with legal norms is likely to invite legal sanctions. For example, in most American industries, an attempt to use associations to coordinate prices would run afoul of the antitrust laws. Second, a regime must meet minimal standards of fairness. Failure to meet such standards is likely to result in organized opposition from groups demanding that the offending governance regime be dismantled. Finally, the regime is likely to face problems if it requires policies that upset the balance of power within the state. A change in the state's internal balance of power can be produced, for example, when a governance regime requires the creation of new regulatory capacities. This may provoke conflicts that reduce the support of public authorities for the regime.

The relationship between these factors can be represented visually. Figure 3.1 depicts the universe of choices over which opportunistically behaving actors will search for a new governance regime. Some governance arrangements are technologically compatible; others are politically legitimate. Instability will prevail, however, until a winning coalition of actors is able to find a regime that is both technologically compatible and politically legitimate. This intersection of governance arrangements is the set of feasible choices for the governance of the sector. The selection of a governance regime from the set results in a "satisficing" outcome, and thus terminates the search process. Another search process may, of course, occur if this equilibrium is disturbed by a change, for example, in technology or in the political environment.

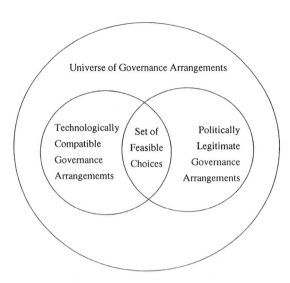

Figure 3.1 Spatial representation of the search process over a set of governance arrangements.

This model is used to analyze the evolution of governance in the telecommunications industry. It usefully highlights the range of alternatives and patterns of behavior in each of the periods in which the industry's governance regime has broken down and a search for an alternative has occurred. The first of these occurred in the period after 1840, and was completed by the early 1890s. The second period began in 1894 and came to a close in 1956 with the legitimization of a noncompetitive system of governance. The third period began in the late 1950s, and, as of the mid–1980s, has yet to reach a final resolution.

PERIOD ONE, 1840–94

From 1840 to 1876, when the telephone was invented, the telegraph offered the only form of telecommunications. During this period, relationships among telegraph carriers and their customers were coordinated by a market-based governance regime, but this proved to be an unstable system of governance. Carriers continually tried to gain monopoly control over the message traffic in local territories, in part because the telegraph required a huge investment of fixed capital to tie distant communities into an integrated network. Hence, rather than conforming to the image of a classic self-equilibrating market, the industry tended toward coordination by private hierarchies. This tendency, however, produced enormous conflict.

Monopolization by private hierarchies

The attempts to construct monopolistic hierarchies in the telegraph industry took two main forms (this discussion of the telegraph industry relies extensively on Brock 1981: 55–88). Carriers sought to win monopoly status for themselves by trying to obtain exclusive property rights to the telegraph. If successful in this legal strategy, a carrier could enjoy the sole rights to the telegraph apparatus. This was one way carriers could try to institute a governance regime that advantaged them, while solving the problem of political legitimacy. The basic stumbling block was the availability of telegraphic methods covered under different patents. Nevertheless, throughout the middle 1800s, carriers litigated their competing patent claims in the courts hoping to win exclusive control of the technology. None, however, was successful.

A second strategy pursued by some of the carriers was premised on unequal resource endowments. During the 1850s and 1860s, a number of carriers sought to be first to construct a nationwide telegraph system. The rationale was simple. By having a nationwide network and refusing to interconnect with geographically limited carriers, a larger company could reduce the value of a smaller company's services and drive it from business. Western Union, which was then controlled by the Vanderbilt family, used this strategy with success. It was able to force its last competitors to merge with it within a year after the end of the Civil War. Its success was short-lived, however. By the time the telephone entered the picture in the late 1870s, Western Union faced a serious competitive threat in Jay Gould's Atlantic and Pacific Telegraph Company.

The telephone soon became a pawn in the struggle between these two forces. In the years immediately after its invention by Alexander Graham Bell in 1876, the telephone was still too crude to threaten the telegraph. It was capable, however, of providing a valuable complementary service by connecting customers to the local telegraph office. Thus, it offered a competitive opportunity for telegraph companies (Garnet 1985: 11).

Apparently failing to appreciate this potential, Western Union refused an offer by Bell and his backers in 1877 to turn over their patents to Western Union for $100,000 (Danielian 1974: 40). By 1878, however, Western Union reversed course. It purchased another inventor's patent for a method of transmitting speech. It set up a telephone subsidiary, which quickly began constructing exchanges across the country.

Likewise, Gould responded by buying telephone companies that had been franchised by the Bell company. He also employed other tactics designed to weaken the Vanderbilts' hold over the business (Stehman 1967: 13–15).

Squeezed from both sides by companies with vastly superior resources, the Bell company initiated a strategy of rapid expansion, technical development to improve quality, and patent litigation with Western Union over their competing patent claims. Of more significance for Bell, Gould's attacks on Western Union apparently were having an effect. In 1879, Western Union agreed to a generous out-of-court settlement with Bell that was designed to prevent Gould from gaining an upper hand in the telegraph business. Western Union agreed to recognize the priority of Bell's patents and to sell all its telephone properties and patents to the Bell company. In exchange, Bell agreed to give all telegraph messages it collected to Western Union and to pay Western Union 20% of Bell's license fees for 17 years (Danielian 1974: 42).

This division of the telecommunications industry made Bell, for the first time, a major player. The telephone properties sold to Bell by Western Union amounted to 56,000 telephones in 55 cities, dwarfing Bell's preagreement system (Bornholz and Evans 1983: 9). The agreement was good for Western Union, as well. By giving it the corner on telegraph messages called in by customers, the agreement thwarted Gould's threat to the Vanderbilts' telegraph empire. Indeed, it marked the end of Gould's company as a serious competitor in the telegraph industry.

Hierarchical governance

Although the settlement gave Bell the opportunity to control the commercial exploitation of the telephone, the company still faced the task of transforming itself from "a relatively flimsy community of interests based on the original Bell patents" into a corporate form that could govern the affairs of the telephone industry (quote from Louis Galambos's introduction to Garnet 1985). To accomplish this, the Bell company moved swiftly on two fronts: creation of hierarchical controls over the industry and legitimization of its monopoly status.

The Bell company's early attempts to devise a corporate structure had been fairly haphazard.[1] The Bell partners, pressured by Western Union's move into the telephone business, had chosen to license local companies to build and operate exchanges. In terms of the governance typology developed in Chapter 1, this was an obligational network. This network shifted much of the risk, as well as the need for cash, to local entrepreneurs, who put up the capital and turned over a portion of their stock to the Bell company for the privilege of using its patents and renting its phones. But it also left these companies virtually autonomous from the Bell company. One of the first moves of the Bell company was thus to gain control over

---

1 The chronic shortage of capital led Bell and his backers to solicit the participation of a number of wealthy Boston merchants and financiers. These new partners soon voted themselves in control of the patents and the Bell licensing company, forcing Alexander Bell out of the telephone business in 1878. Henceforth, when I speak of Bell or the Bell company, I am referring to the Bell System holding company or the Bell System as a whole.

these companies (the following discussion relies extensively on U.S. Federal Communications Commission 1938; Stehman 1967; Danielian 1974; Garnet 1985).

Immediately taking over the property of the operating companies to subsume them into a single hierarchical system of governance would have been enormously expensive and taxing on the managerial skills of the Bell company. Instead Bell chose to strengthen gradually its control over the existing obligational network. Through this process, a governance regime, dominated by hierarchy, gradually emerged.

A key element in this process was the new license contracts that Bell required its operating companies to sign. Under the new contracts, the Bell company gave exclusive rights to the licensee to use Bell patents and to operate within a specified territory. Operating companies were prohibited, however, from interconnecting with independent companies or from participating in any business not licensed by the parent company. The right to build and operate long-distance service between operating companies was reserved to the parent company. The operating company was required to raise its own capital, but was to surrender 30% or more of its stock to the parent company. Over time, the percentage of stock owned by the parent company was increased to 100%.

The Bell company also undertook to strengthen its hierarchical controls by integrating vertically into the manufacturing end of the telephone business. This allowed Bell to bring some order to the industry by standardizing the equipment used by the operating companies. Previously, Bell had simply licensed various electrical companies to manufacture its telephone equipment. To gain control of these arrangements, Bell purchased Western Union's telephone equipment manufacturing subsidiary, Western Electric, and in 1882 began consolidating manufacturing operations into it (Smith 1985).

The final element of Bell's corporate reorganization strategy was to begin developing a long-distance network to tie the country into an integrated system. The construction of a long-distance system was viewed as a key barrier to entry against potential competitors. Theodore Vail, Bell's operating manager, later said: "What we wanted to do was get possession of the field in such a way that, patent or no patent, we could control it" (Brooks 1975: 83). For this purpose, the American Telephone and Telegraph Company was incorporated as a wholly owned subsidiary of the Bell company, to finance and construct this network. Construction of the long-distance system initially was hampered by the technical limitations of telephone transmission. Nevertheless, by the end of 1893, AT&T had created a network connecting most of the major cities from Boston to Milwaukee (Stehman 1967: 32–5).

The Bell company's strategy to make its monopoly control politically legitimate entailed the construction of an impregnable patent wall around the company. The goal was to secure exclusive property rights to the telephone technology. It embarked on a twofold plan: (1) obtain patents on all parts of the telephone technology, and (2) contest the right of any new entrants to provide telephone service.

The first element of this strategy involved the creation of an engineering department – the forerunner of Bell Labs – to do research and experimentation on the telephone and to evaluate outside inventions for their relevance to the telephone business. The idea was to stake out legal claims on all refinements to the technology (Danielian 1974: 95–6).

The second element of the strategy involved lawyers rather than engineers. Between 1877 and 1893, the Bell System filed over 600 suits for patent infringement against entrants into the industry. Most promptly went out of business when a suit was filed (U.S. Federal Communications Commission 1938: 125). The issue of Bell's property rights reached the U.S. Supreme Court when five suits were combined to decide if Bell's original patents should give the company exclusive control of the telephone apparatus. The issue was settled in Bell's favor in 1888 when the court by a 4 to 3 vote upheld the Bell patents in their entirety, in essence making Bell's patent monopoly *de jure* rather than merely *de facto* (126 U.S. Reports 1).

This ruling definitively sanctioned the legitimacy of the Bell System's monopoly over the telephone industry. The court's decision turned on the issue of who owned the property rights to the telephone technology. It also settled the nation's communications policy, by effectively delegating to the Bell company the responsibility for making the key decisions about the country's telephone system. The ruling thus settled the question of what governance regime would prevail in the industry – at least until the original Bell patents expired in 1894. As we will see, this hierarchically dominated governance regime broke down quickly once Bell lost the protection of its original patents.

PERIOD TWO, 1894–1956

In 1894, the industry entered a second period in which the issue of how it was to be governed was very much an open question. The event that precipitated this search process was the expiration of the original Bell patents, which stripped the Bell company's monopoly of its legal sanction and exposed two festering inadequacies in the existing governance regime. First, there was no provision for how to maintain or manage an integrated network once Bell no longer enjoyed a patent monopoly. Bell's ability to exercise control over the nation's telephone system had been completely contingent on its patent rights. Second, there was no institutional mechanism for addressing such problems as the reasonableness of telephone rates or the adequacy of service offerings because all the key policy issues in the sector were delegated to a private monopoly.

The reemergence of marketlike competition

Not surprisingly, the extant governance regime splintered when the patents expired. As a result, the sort of conflict-ridden market-based governance that had characterized the telegraph industry a half century before quickly reemerged. The opportunistic behavior of diverse actors led to a new round of efforts to adopt a new governance regime.

The Bell company apparently had grown complacent about satisfying consumer wants and about expanding into new areas during the years it had enjoyed the protection of its original patents (Stehman 1967: 292; Gabel 1969: 343–4). Thus, hundreds of independents surged into the telephone business after 1894, establishing exchanges in rural and smaller urban areas, which Bell had largely ignored, and in areas where Bell offered unsatisfactory service.[2] Bell fought hard to suppress this competition and to reestablish its hierarchical controls over the industry.

It first tried to get its patent monopoly extended. Although Bell won a controversial case that might have extended its patent monopoly until 1908, the patent was construed so narrowly in a subsequent case that it was of no use in preserving its patent monopoly (U.S. Federal Communications Commission 1938: 131–3). Bell wielded its patent weapon by filing dozens of infringement suits against the electrical manufacturers that were supplying the independents with telephone equipment (Danielian 1974: 98).

Bell also responded to the surge of competitors by utilizing other tactics that had characterized the period of market competition in the mid–1800s, for instance, by expanding its facilities, selectively slashing its rates to drive out potential competitors, and refusing to allow competing exchanges to connect to its long-distance network (U.S. Federal Communications Commission 1938: 133–6). The refusal to allow interconnections was potentially crippling to independents because Bell controlled the only extensive long-distance system. This became increasingly lethal as Bell introduced new technologies (e.g., the Pupin coil in 1900) that greatly extended the working range of the telephone (see Brock 1981: 118–19).

The associational movement

One of the major effects of Bell's competitive strategies was to encourage the independents to find a governance regime that would allow them to

2 To illustrate, in 1894, independent telephone companies formed 87 exchanges, constituting a total of 15,000 telephones and a combined 5% market share. The pace of new entry was explosive. By 1902, 4,000 independent exchanges controlled a 44% market share (U.S. Federal Communications Commission 1938: Table 31).

compete with Bell as a united front. Their solution was to try to form associations.

This effort was initiated in 1897 when representatives of many of the independent exchanges met to form the National Association of Independent Telephone Exchanges (Stehman 1967: 56). Although this association had some success as a forum for representatives of the independent companies to express their opposition to the Bell System, it failed to become a viable governance mechanism. To be sure, some long-distance toll lines were constructed among adjacent exchanges by newly formed regional associations (MacMeal 1934). But the association failed to establish an opposition exchange in Chicago, the linchpin of its strategy; failed to establish an independent long-distance system to connect the country's major cities; and thus failed to develop an independent integrated network covering the midwest, let alone the entire nation.

The limitations of the associations were vividly apparent in their inability to stop individual independents from dealing with the Bell System. For instance, in 1911, the national association desired a resolution of the competition with Bell that would maintain the integrity of the independents. Yet when talks were held between the national association and representatives of the Bell–Morgan network to discuss the consolidation of the entire industry at once rather than through individual buyouts, the negotiations broke down due to disputes among the independents (MacMeal 1934: 183–7; U.S. Federal Communications Commission 1938: 129, 136).

These failures appear to have been caused by a combination of two factors. First, the associations never were able to obtain compliance for their policies from the independent exchanges. The associations simply did not possess the sanctions to prevent companies from acting opportunistically when that suited their individual purposes. Second, the associations never obtained the necessary political legitimacy to function as effective trade associations. Indeed, the antitrust laws were hostile to such combinations. The associations were thus greatly impaired. They gradually devolved into mere promotional networks: interest groups, whose major task was to voice the collective interests of independents before Congress and regulatory bodies.

The Morgan–Bell obligational network

While the associations were being reduced to the status of promotional networks, an effort to eliminate market competition by establishing an obligational network was proving far more successful. This network, initially composed of financial elites and the Bell company, eventually controlled most of the industry's disparate actors. It was able to overcome, at least for a time, the problems of compliance and legitimacy that undermined the associational movement.

The genesis of this obligational network was the period of intense competition following the expiration of Bell's original patents (Brooks 1975). Competition had so drained the Bell System of capital that it was vulnerable to a takeover. In 1906, Bell's directors reluctantly agreed to make a sizeable bond offering through J. P. Morgan and his associates, who used this as leverage to install their own management team over the Bell System. Theodore Vail, the chief executive installed by the Morgan interests, shared Morgan's desire to consolidate the nation's telecommunications industry into an integrated whole. He was also knowledgeable about the telephone business, having been a top executive with Bell in its early years.

This network moved on several fronts to realize the goal of industrywide control. The first was to ensure that no new form of communication developed outside Bell's control. To do this, they increased dramatically the research-and-development effort of the Bell system. The R&D function was broadened beyond evaluation and acquisition of patents to encompass research into all telecommunications-related technologies, whether Bell intended to use them or not. The idea was to create a defensive patent wall around Bell's major fields (Brock 1981: 161–5).

Second, the network set out to capture the telegraph business. With Morgan's backing, Bell offered in 1909 to purchase 30% of Western Union's stock at a 13% premium over its market price, but with the condition that control of the company be turned over to Bell. Its stockholders consented. Vail was made president of Western Union as well as AT&T, and seven common directors were selected, thereby allowing the two companies to be operated as one (Brock 1981: 152–3).

The third move by the Morgan–Bell network to control the industry was to end the strategy of dealing with the independents through head-to-head competition. Instead, the network began buying up independents. Various tactics were used in this acquisition drive: sometimes exchanges adjacent to a target exchange would be allowed to connect with the Bell System and then their connections with the target exchange would be cut, isolating it and forcing its owners to sell; sometimes agents of Morgan were used to cloud the true identity of the buyers so that the owners did not realize their properties were being sold to the Bell System; sometimes the owners were offered such a good deal that they would not refuse; and sometimes rate competition was used to exhaust their resources and force a sale (MacMeal 1934).

Although these tactics evoked resentment and challenges to the network's legitimacy, they were nevertheless successful in altering the complexion of the industry. For example, from 1907 to 1920, the Bell System nearly tripled the number of its telephones, increasing its market share from 49 to 62% (U.S. Federal Communications Commission 1938: Table 32). The result was a significant reduction in the level of competition between the Bell System and the independents.

Ironically, the Morgan–Bell obligational network disintegrated just as competition was declining, but not because of challenges to its legitimacy. Instead, its downfall was due apparently to its inability to maintain the compliance of its major subordinate member, the Bell company. With Morgan's death in 1913, and Vail's in 1920, the network lost actors who had been instrumental in its successful operation. More importantly perhaps, following World War I, the Bell company began offering stocks directly to the public rather than indirectly through the Morgan bank. Hence, Bell no longer needed investment bankers to raise its capital. This meant that it was in a position where it could refuse to comply with the preferences of the Morgan interests (Stehman 1967).

With these changes, the ties that held the obligational network together came apart. In its place emerged an industry dominated by the Bell System, and ringed by a host of smaller carriers. It was a governance regime composed of largely noncompeting, but constantly interacting, corporate hierarchies.

The role of the state

As mentioned before, the actions of the Morgan–Bell obligational network evoked a torrent of opposition that directly challenged the political legitimacy of Bell's emerging monopoly. But unlike in the preceding century, there was no straightforward solution to the political legitimacy issue. Then, the decision of the Supreme Court had settled the political legitimacy issue by granting the Bell System exclusive property rights to the telephone technology. In the second period, no patent was sweeping enough to be so construed. As a result, a different sort of resolution had to be found.

During the years after the formation of the Morgan–Bell network, the legitimacy issue was sufficiently acute that a host of actors began to call for the government to break up, regulate, or nationalize the Bell System. There was little consensus, however, about which of these would be most effective or appropriate. Each implied a very different role for the state to play in the governance of the sector. Ultimately, all three were experimented with before a regulatory solution was finally institutionalized.

The antitrust solution. The solution favored by many of the independent companies was to have the courts dismember the Bell System under the antitrust laws or at least to prohibit it from acquiring additional independent properties. This sort of policy appears to have been attractive to many independents because they believed that the Bell System's growing monopoly was the product of unfair methods of competition (MacMeal 1934: 181–202). Their hope was that the antitrust laws would be used to police the industry to maintain a more level playing field.

In the first fifteen years of this century, antitrust suits were filed in a number of states by independent companies to stop the completion of acquisitions or to seek court protection for the rights of independent companies to connect with other exchanges (MacMeal 1934: 181–202).[3] Requests also were made to the U.S. Attorney General asking for the federal government to break up the Bell System. In 1913, in response to these complaints, the Attorney General and the Bell company negotiated a compromise agreement, known as the Kingsbury commitment, whereby Bell promised to refrain from acquiring directly competing exchanges, allow interconnections with independents, and divest its Western Union interests (Stehman 1967: 152–4; Danielian 1974: 76–7).

By forcing the divestiture of Western Union, the agreement dismembered a piece of the Morgan–Bell obligational network and prevented the Bell System from consummating its control of the nation's telecommunications network. The most important aspect of the agreement, however, was that it established a framework within which consolidations of independent exchanges into the Bell System would not invite antitrust suits by the Department of Justice. Indeed, the negotiation of this framework represented a rejection of antitrust law as an appropriate policy for the telephone industry.

In 1917, antitrust was further watered down by the Justice Department, which reinterpreted the Kingsbury commitment to allow Bell to purchase the properties of direct competitors, as long as an equal number of telephones were sold to independents (Brock 1981: 156–7). This permitted the reorganization of exchanges into geographical monopolies. The practical effect was to reduce the incentive to compete. This can be seen in the fact that by 1920, 84% of independent telephones were allowed to interconnect with the Bell System, whereas only 27% had been allowed to do so in 1907. In 1922, the Kingsbury commitment was reinterpreted to allow Bell to purchase virtually any independent properties it desired (*Telephony* 1922a, 1922b). In the period from 1922 to 1934, Bell purchased nine times more telephones than it sold, for a net gain of over 854,000 telephones and an 80% share of the nation's telephones (U.S. Federal Communications Commission 1938: 156).

The decline of competition, however, re-created a problem that had existed during the period of Bell's patent monopoly; that is, it removed the main institutional mechanism for arriving at rates that were perceived to be reasonable. Hence, there were demands for an alternative policy response by the state.

The regulatory solution. As this suggests, these antitrust responses did not end dissatisfaction with the state of affairs in the telephone industry. Even

---

3 These complaints were also heard by many of the state legislatures, with the result that by 1919, thirty-four states had enacted laws that provided for compulsory connection between telephone companies (U.S. Federal Communications Commission 1938: 137).

as the antitrust policy was being first implemented, many people argued that such a policy was incapable of addressing the industry's key problems. The argument was that the industry did not possess the characteristics of a true competitive market, but looked more like the railroads. On this view, the government should play a corrective role by compensating for the deficiencies of the market. The government would thus have responsibility to ensure that corporate decisions on such issues as rate levels, entry, and exit were consistent with the public interest.

In the years after 1907, this view was adopted in most of the states, which established telephone regulatory commissions modeled on the Interstate Commerce Commission. These commissions, however, were handicapped in their efforts to set telephone rates due to Bell's organizational complexity (U.S. Federal Communications Commission 1938). Consequently, demands that the federal government assume these responsibilities were soon being voiced.

Indeed, after Theodore Vail was installed as chairman of the Bell System in 1907, he began calling for such regulation. His position was that federal controls would be less disruptive than nationalization, which he feared was a real possibility. He argued that if competition were incapable of arriving at reasonable rates, federal rate and entry regulation would be preferable:

It is not believed that there is any serious objection to such control, provided it is independent, intelligent, considerate, thorough and just, recognizing, as does the Interstate Commerce Commission in its report recently issued, that capital is entitled to its fair return, and good management or enterprise to its reward. (American Telephone and Telegraph 1907: 17–18)

Vail was not alone. Many progressive reformers also were demanding that federal controls be instituted. In 1910, after several tries, progressives in Congress managed to attach to a pending bill a provision that would give authority to the Interstate Commerce Commission (ICC) to regulate interstate telephone and telegraph service on the same basis as the railroads (Bickers 1988: 88–103).

This tactic, however, backfired. The main purpose of the bill was to clarify the ICC's authority over the railroad industry. The unintended result was to enmesh the commission in a controversy over its proper relationship to the courts that apparently made the ICC reluctant to enter any new regulatory areas. The commission did not utilize its new authority to regulate telecommunications rates, and only in a few trivial instances did it agree to investigate alleged problems in the industry. Quite simply, this attempt at reform failed to place the telecommunications industry under effective national rate and entry controls (Bickers 1988: 88–103).

The government control solution. There were those, however, who believed that the appropriate government response to the situation in the industry was neither an antitrust policy nor rate and entry regulation. The alternative they favored was a government control policy. On this view, the state should nationalize the industry and manage it as a public enterprise, perhaps as part of the Postal Service. Advocates of this position tended to see the European experience with national Post, Telephone, and Telegraph services as the best solution to the problems confronting the American telecommunications industry (Bickers 1988: 133–46).

This position found a natural champion in successive Postmasters General during the years leading up to World War I, but few supporters in Congress. However, World War I provided an opportunity for proponents of government control to seek the nationalization of the industry. Statements made during Congressional hearings on the measure indicate that many members of Congress believed that the proposal to take control of the telecommunications systems was not directly related to the war effort, but was the first step in a permanent policy (Stehman 1967: 177). Nevertheless, few Congressmen wanted to deny the President powers that he claimed were crucial to the war effort (Bickers 1988: 146–50).

Cast as a war emergency, the measure was passed in the summer of 1918. President Wilson immediately assumed control of the telegraph and telephone systems and placed them under the supervision of the Postmaster General, who promised to improve services while lowering costs (Danielian 1974: 249). Yet despite the fact that communications systems were under government control in most industrialized nations, taking over the system in the United States was no simple task.

Because there was no civil service with the administrative capacities to manage such a vast network, the Postmaster General had little choice but to order the officers and employees of the telegraph and telephone companies to continue to perform their jobs, under the same terms of employment. But even though practical control of the industry remained in the hands of the carriers, the government assumed the risks and responsibilities for operating the telecommunications system (including guaranteeing regular stock dividends and interest on all debts) (Danielian 1974: 249–51).

Not surprisingly, industry officials, in their new capacities as government employees, moved quickly to persuade the Postmaster General to raise rates. Ultimately, they succeeded in winning rate increases of almost $50 million a year, including the institution of a service connection charge, which the Bell System had been trying to initiate for years without success (Danielian 1974: 254–69). Rate authorities in the states, however, objected. They appealed to the courts to block the increases from taking effect. The states argued that the Postmaster General lacked authority to determine intrastate rates. The Supreme Court disagreed. On June 2, 1919, it held that the communication companies were engaged in the internal administration of a federal agency; thus no state had constitutional power to interfere with their management or rates (Stehman 1967: 179; Danielian 1974: 260–4).

Nine days after this ruling was handed down, an angry Congress passed a joint resolution requiring the telegraph and telephone systems to be returned to private control, effective almost immediately (Danielian 1974: 267–8). Even the sponsor of the original resolution recanted, saying, "I owe it to my people and to Congress to apologize for my resolution if government control means increase in rates" (Danielian 1974: 269–70). In short, the rapid rate increases eroded completely whatever political legitimacy the experiment in government control had ever possessed.

The legitimation of hierarchical governance

With the disintegration of the Morgan–Bell network and the decline of competition, the kinds of problems confronting the industry underwent a subtle shift. They centered increasingly on the kinds of controls that should be imposed on noncompeting, but interacting, corporate hierarchies. After World War I, two issues came to dominate the politics in the sector.

The first involved the question of how intercarrier relations should be managed. Due to the system of governance in the industry, transactions among actors were based on negotiated agreements and administered relationships, not arms-length market exchanges. Carriers, however, brought unequal resources to these negotiated relationships. This was evident, for example, in conflicts over the separation of long-distance toll revenues between the Bell System and the independents. Because the independents relied on Bell's long-distance network to transmit most long-distance calls going to or from their customers, Bell could dictate the division of toll revenues with independent exchanges. The independents argued that the Bell System shared less revenues for calls passed between independent exchanges than for calls between Bell exchanges (U.S. Federal Communications Commission 1938: 143–4).

The second issue revolved around the fairness of the rates charged by carriers. Because rate levels were determined through corporate decision-making processes rather than through a mechanism such as market competition, subscribers and state regulators alike found it difficult to know whether or not rates were reasonable. In the words of one state commissioner,

Even if the State had the money, the interstate feature of the matter, the ramifications of the holding companies, the complications brought about by the manufacturing companies which sell to the telephone companies, makes it an impossibility for the State commission to get anywhere so far as results are concerned in a telephone-rate investigation. (Paul Walker, before the House Committee on Interstate and Foreign Commerce: U.S. House of Representatives 1934c)

Put simply, the existing governance regime in the industry made such appraisals problematic. What was lacking was a yardstick or procedure that could be used to judge the acceptability of rate schedules.

These issues raised basic questions about the legitimacy of the industry's governance regime. Although a number of years passed without significant progress, the Depression provided an opportunity for reform. This effort was initiated by New Deal reformers who wanted to overhaul the economic role of the federal government. They viewed telecommunications as a close cousin of broadcasting, in much the same way that earlier reform efforts had viewed it as a relative, respectively, of a competitive market, the railroads, and the Postal Service. (See, for example, the letter from W. M. W. Splawn to the Committee on Interstate and Foreign Commerce: U.S. House of Representatives 1934a: v). They argued that a single regulatory body was needed to provide unified control over the whole communications industry (see U.S. House of Representatives 1934b: 6–11).

Based on such recommendations, President Franklin D. Roosevelt urged Congress to create an independent communications commission (U.S. Senate 1934). The commission was to serve as an impartial panel to hear the presentation and rebuttal of evidence by interested parties before making policy decisions or adjudicating conflicts. The idea, at least initially, was to create an administrative mechanism that would produce outcomes in the public interest, in a way analogous to the invisible hand of a competitive market.

With the active support of broadcasters, state telephone regulators, and the telecommunications unions, and over the protests (contrary to capture theories of regulation) of the big telecommunications companies, both houses of Congress passed versions of the President's proposal (Bickers 1988: 164–9). By the summer of 1934, the differences had been worked out, and the Communications Act signed into law (Cushman 1941: 321–2).

The creation of the Federal Communications Commission (FCC) represented an important, if only partial, solution to the problems besetting the industry. The federal government assumed responsibility for, among other things, regulating entry, exit, rates, and service offerings of telecommunications carriers. The commission could thus begin to deal with issues arising from the interconnections of carriers and the setting of rates. Consequently, the establishment of the FCC removed one source of potential challenges to the legitimacy of the industry's governance regime. This was perhaps its signal accomplishment.

Yet the commission did not live up to expectations. A perception that the Bell System was able to evade the FCC's regulatory efforts festered for several years without resolution (see National Association of Railroad and Utility Commissioners 1950). In early 1949, the Antitrust Section filed suit against the Bell System, asking for the separation of regulated monopoly services from unregulated equipment supply, the divestiture of Western Electric from the Bell System, and the breakup of Western Electric into three companies. The goal was to create the conditions for markets to determine equipment prices (*U.S. v. Western Electric et al.* 1949). Underlying this was the view that market competition was a more appropriate mechanism than hierarchical controls for ensuring reasonable equipment prices (U.S. House of Representatives 1958: 1796–7).

The ensuing antitrust suit dragged on until 1956. Bell sought to exploit its role as a major defense contractor to get the suit dismissed or delayed indefinitely. This succeeded insofar as Bell and the Justice Department eventually agreed to a consent decree that contained none of the structural relief sought in the original complaint. In return, Bell agreed to two provisions that at the time were not seen to be important: (1) AT&T and the Bell operating companies were restricted to the provision of regulated services, and Western Electric was largely restrained from selling equipment for unregulated businesses; (2) all patents under Bell's control were to be licensed to others upon reasonable request (U.S. House of Representatives 1958: 2252–4).

The upshot, of course, was that the pricing problems that had long frustrated state and federal regulatory commissions were left unresolved. Yet despite the failure to create the conditions for a market-driven equipment sector, the antitrust settlement altered the governance regime in the industry in nontrivial ways.

In the first place, by requiring that Bell license its patents upon request, it lost the protection of its formidable patent wall. It was no longer protected from the entry of new competitors by its property rights to key technologies, but instead was protected by regulatory decisions preventing potential competitors from entering the industry. The result was an increase in Bell's stake in the decisions of its regulators.

Second, the provision restricting Western Electric from participating in unregulated sectors had a similar, if ultimately more dramatic, effect. Although the provision had little immediate impact, its long-term effect was to prevent the company from entering new sectors outside the FCC's jurisdiction (cf., Brock 1981). This served to tie the legitimacy of the industry's governance regime to the extant regulatory scheme.

The 1956 consent decree marked the culmination of the second period in the development of the industry. It preserved the noncompetitive, hierarchically based governance regime that had evolved during the first decades of the century. This was legitimized, however, by making the Bell System highly dependent on the regulatory process. The consent decree thus represented the capstone of a long period of evolution. It also set the stage for a third period of change.

A key effect of the Bell System's increased dependence on regulatory authorities was a corresponding increase in its vulnerability to adverse regulatory decisions. This became apparent as new telecommunications-related technologies emerged in the post–War period. Established carriers, led by the Bell System, contested the right of new entrants to exploit the new technologies. The result was a contagion of political controversies, and significant changes in the industry's governance regime. This process of change has yet to fully unfold.

Technological innovations

In the post–War period, controversy has revolved around three types of technological changes: the introduction of new modes of long-distance transmission, innovations in terminal equipment (i.e., equipment attached to the network at the customer's premises), and the integration of computers into corporate telecommunications systems.

New modes of long-distance communication. The first new long-distance technology to challenge the extant regulatory system in the post–War period was microwave radio. Coaxial cables (which Bell was beginning to install) and microwave radio were capable of carrying voice as well as video traffic; but many heavy users of telecommunications services preferred microwave because it used towers at 20- to 30-mile intervals and did not require rights-of-way, public easements, or huge fixed investments (see Brock 1981: 198–202). The television networks, for instance, saw microwave as a more efficient means of transmitting television programs to and from local stations.

The problem for the FCC was how to deal with the new technology. Initially, the FCC responded by granting experimental licenses for microwave systems, choosing to wait until more experience was gained with the technology before approving permanent licenses and frequency allocations. Several companies, including AT&T, obtained approval for experimental systems (U.S. Department of Justice 1980: 90–107). By the late 1940s, the FCC adopted the position that, although noncommon carriers (e.g., General Electric and IBM) could construct temporary systems, only common carriers (e.g., Bell and Western Union) had the right to operate such systems on a permanent basis (Brock 1981: 183).

This ruling barred direct competition with Bell in the long-distance area, but did not prevent completely the development of microwave systems by noncommon carriers. Permission was given for microwave systems to be built to import television programs into areas where regular broadcast service was infeasible; and many right-of-way companies, such as railroad and pipeline firms, built systems to serve their internal communication needs (U.S. Department of Justice 1980: 101–7).

The operation of these systems in geographic areas near Bell-owned systems indicated to the commission and others that microwave frequencies were less scarce than originally thought. As a consequence, the FCC reopened the issue of microwave licensing in 1956 in what became known as its *Above 890* proceedings. In 1959, the commission ruled that sufficient frequencies existed to allow both common carriers and private users to operate microwave systems. However, noncommon carriers were not granted the right to interconnect with common carriers or to share microwave channels (U.S. Federal Communications Commission 1959). *Above 890* was nonetheless a potential threat to Bell's dominance.

This became apparent when an upstart company, named Microwave Communications, Inc., tried to offer microwave services. In 1963, it requested authorization as a common carrier to construct a microwave system between St. Louis and Chicago in order to provide businesses with intra-corporate service on a more flexible basis and at lower prices than was then available from AT&T. From 1963 until 1971, the case wound its way through the corridors of the regulatory process and the courts. Bell, along with other established carriers, utilized every possible regulatory procedure to question and delay the MCI application. Eventually, however, MCI prevailed.[4]

Dissatisfaction with the performance of the regulatory process in the MCI case was widespread. Two main charges were leveled. The first was that the process unfairly benefited established carriers, who could (legally) use it to stymie the entrance of a new company into the industry. This was a major factor influencing at least one commissioner to support the MCI application (Brock 1981: 212). The second charge was that the resulting focus on claim and counterclaim diverted attention from broader policy issues (U.S. Federal Communications Commission 1969: 971–6).

In response to these concerns – and to the flood of applications that the FCC received following its MCI ruling – the commission opened a broad inquiry to address the policy issues involved in permitting competition in the provision of specialized microwave services (U.S. Federal Communications Commission 1970b: 327). Bell argued against competition, on the grounds that limited-service carriers would syphon profitable routes away from full-service carriers and leave the latter with unprofitable markets. Favoring competition was a coalition of major users of telecommunications services, possible entrants into the specialized services market, and suppliers of electronic equipment (Brock 1981: 214; Schiller 1982: 41–8).

The decision in this proceeding placed the commission behind a policy

4 For a different interpretation of the actions taken by the established carriers, see *U.S. v. AT&T et al.* (1980: 581–90).

of unrestricted entry for specialized microwave carriers. The retreat from a hierarchically based governance regime was self-conscious. The commissioners said, "We concede that AT&T has served the nation well and are confident that it will continue to make every effort to do so." But they went on to say:

[T]here is a public need and demand for the proposed facilities and services and for new and diverse sources of supply, competition in the specialized communications field is reasonably feasible, there are grounds for a reasonable expectation that new entry will have some beneficial effects, and there is no reason to anticipate that new entry would have any adverse impact on service to the public by existing carriers such as to outweigh the considerations supporting new entry. (U.S. Federal Communications Commission 1971b: 906, 912, 920)

With this, the FCC shifted the industry toward a regime in which market competition once again would play a role. It also created a highly unstable regulatory situation. Essentially, the commission decided not to accommodate microwave within the existing, hierarchical governance regime, but failed to resolve the problems of technological compatibility or political legitimacy that were raised by the attempt to move to a new regime. For example, it required that the full-service carriers make facilities available for local distribution of the new services, but rejected Bell's requests for guidelines specifying the terms and conditions under which interconnection with local facilities should be granted. Similarly, the commission recognized that such competition probably would require changes in Bell's pricing methods, but chose to address issues of pricing another day (U.S. Federal Communications Commission 1970b: 349, 1971b: 914–17).

Throughout the 1970s, the commission grappled with the problem of reconciling market forces with the hierarchical controls of the established carriers. At base, this was a debate over how, if at all, competition should be regulated, and thereby legitimized, by the government. The outcome was a messy institutional hybridization in which the FCC maintained traditional controls over rate setting and entry/exit with respect to established carriers, but allowed market forces to govern the behavior of new providers of telecommunications services. However, before discussing this outcome, it is useful first to describe the problems raised by other technological changes.

Terminal equipment innovations. Another set of technological changes occurred in the area of terminal equipment, that is, the equipment connected to phone lines at the customer's premises, such as telephone sets and switching units that route calls to particular offices within a company. Innovations in these technologies created demands that users be permitted to connect specialized terminal equipment into the network. These, in turn, sparked a debate over the obligations of common carriers to allow customers to connect their own equipment to the network.

From its inception, the FCC had taken the position that the carriers possessed the right to determine what equipment could be attached to the telephone system, on the grounds that they were best able to determine whether or not attachment of a piece of equipment might harm the network. In 1956, this right was rejected by the courts in a case involving a cuplike device known as a Hush-A-Phone. The major issue in the case was the trade-off between the likelihood of harm to the telephone network versus the private benefits that might accrue from the attachment of user-supplied equipment. The court ruled that Bell's restrictions against the attachment of customer-supplied equipment were unlawful if attachment were "privately beneficial without being publicly detrimental" (*Hush-A-Phone v. U.S. and FCC* 1956).

This ruling had the potential of opening a new competitive sector within the industry. Its immediate result, however, was not so auspicious. Contrary to instructions, Bell did not file new rules with the FCC that incorporated the "private benefit without public harm" test. Instead, it added a caveat to its existing rules to permit the attachment of devices such as the Hush-A-Phone, while continuing to prohibit the attachment of other types of devices.

In the 1960s, the question of the lawfulness of Bell's restrictions reemerged. Carter Electronics Corporation made a device, called the Carterfone, that translated voice signals from the telephone network into radio signals for retransmission on mobile radiotelephone systems. On the request of the Carter Corporation, the commission opened a proceeding to determine whether attachment of the device should be permitted. In 1968, the commission concluded that Bell's restrictions violated the court's ruling in the Hush-A-Phone case (U.S. Federal Communications Commission 1968). This decision effectively opened the way for a shift to market-based governance in the terminal equipment sector.

It also opened a pandora's box of regulatory problems for the commission. The FCC was faced with the problem of adapting its traditional regulatory controls to cope with the influx of interest claimants into the industry. Complicating the situation was the fact that the Bell System dominated the industry. It was in a position where it could exploit its control of the nation's network to place competitors at a great disadvantage. This potential soon became reality.

Bell's response to the Carterfone decision was to ignore the request that it specify technical standards to be met by non-Bell equipment. Instead, it required that such equipment be attached to the telephone network only through a Bell-supplied connecting device. Hence, it could thwart the entry of competitors simply by moving slowly to provide them with connecting devices. It also was able to charge rates for the connecting devices that sharply increased the effective price of competitive equipment.[5]

Bell's competitors appealed to the FCC for help. In 1975, the FCC ruled that the connecting-device requirement was unfairly discriminatory since only customers using non-Bell equipment were required to use such devices (even when Bell and non-Bell products were essentially identical). The FCC held that a registration and certification program should instead be instituted (see Brock 1981: 247). This decision marked the formal adoption of the view that the terminal equipment sector could and should be allowed to operate via a market mechanism. Prices and product offerings in the terminal-equipment sector would be determined through arms-length market processes, not regulatory proceedings. The registration and certification program constituted a recognition, however, of the need to prevent market-driven behaviors from undermining the integrity of the nation's telecommunications network. Yet the effect of the ruling was to exacerbate the conflicts in the industry.

The convergence of computers and telecommunications. Simultaneous with the changes in the terminal-equipment area, the commission was forced to grapple with a related set of technological innovations. With rapid advancements in computers during the 1960s, many businesses became interested in linking data-processing technologies into their corporate telecommunications systems. Makers of computer equipment, such as IBM, General Electric, Westinghouse, and Sperry Rand (now Unisys), stood to gain greatly if their customers were allowed to attach computer equipment into the telecommunications network. But for the commission, this convergence of technologies posed a quandary.

At the heart of the quandary was the question of what role the Bell System should (and could) play in offering data-processing services. The basic problem was the 1956 antitrust settlement. The terms of the settlement prevented the Bell operating companies or AT&T Long Lines from packaging computer services with their basic telecommunications services, since computing was not subject to rate and entry regulation. It also prevented Western Electric from supplying computer equipment to non-Bell companies. Thus, the Bell System had little to gain by encouraging the linkage of data-processing equipment into its network, and much to lose.

The initial foray by the commission into the issue began in 1966. Its first inquiry, which came to be called Computer I, involved representatives from a wide range of the country's largest enterprises. Although few problems were resolved, the inquiry did identify the major issues (U.S. Federal

5 For contrasting interpretations of Bell's post-Carterfone tariffs, see *U.S. v. AT&T et al.* (1980: 1141–379, 1099–103).

Communications Commission 1970a), which boiled down to two: (1) Should common carriers be permitted to market data processing services, and if so, what sorts of safeguards should be imposed to keep them from engaging in anticompetitive or discriminatory practices? And (2) should computer firms be allowed to engage in the transmission of information, and if so, should they be subjected to the full range of common-carrier obligations and restrictions?

After five years of hearings, the commission in 1971 adopted a so-called definitional approach (U.S. Federal Communications Commission 1971a). The commission identified a continuum, with telecommunications at one end and data processing at the other. In between, two hybrid categories were delineated: hybrid communications (communications with incidental data processing), and hybrid data processing (data processing with incidental communications). The two communications categories were to continue to be subject to the commission's traditional regulatory scheme. The two data-processing categories would not be regulated.

The problem was that the line between the two hybrid categories was impossible to define clearly. Demands for changes in the commission's regulatory approach to the technological convergence thus continued to be voiced.[6] Nonetheless, a growing number of corporations began to experiment with interlinked computer–telecommunications systems. Computer I had signaled the commission's reluctance to assert jurisdiction over data-processing services – even when such services incorporated some communications functions. Also, the commission's actions in other proceedings had encouraged the entrance of a host of companies offering a wide array of new services.

By 1976, the commission publicly acknowledged that its first approach had proven inadequate, and initiated a second computer inquiry (U.S. Federal Communications Commission 1976, 1977b). This attracted even more attention from business interests than the first one.[7] Initially, the commission proposed an adjustment to its definitional strategy in which the boundary between hybrid communications and hybrid data processing would be clarified (U.S. Federal Communications Commission 1977b, 1979). The commission soon recognized that the convergence of the two

6 See, for example, the dispute over the meaning of the categories where data-processing capacities were distributed among various sites within the communications network rather than in a central computing center, in U.S. Federal Communications Commission (1977a) and *IBM v. FCC* (1978).

7 Approximately eighty business firms and associations participated in the proceeding. These included a host of computer electronics equipment suppliers, a wide range of telecommunications-dependent enterprises (e.g., banks, finance companies, oil exploration firms, news wire services), and communications carriers of all sorts (e.g., AT&T and other traditional common carriers, and satellite carriers, telegraph and facsimile carriers, and specialized carriers such as MCI). See U.S. Federal Communications Commission (1980b) and Schiller (1982: 56–70).

technologies was such that no "enduring line of demarcation" could be drawn between them. Thus, in 1980, it rejected a pure definitional approach and adopted a new strategy (U.S. Federal Communications Commission 1980a, 1980b).

The FCC's new approach was premised on the view that market competition was capable of coordinating entry, exit, and prices of combined data-processing and communications services. It thus distinguished between basic transmission services traditionally offered by common carriers and so-called enhanced services. It held that basic transmission services would continue to be regulated as common-carrier offerings; enhanced services would not be treated as common-carrier offerings. It also held that AT&T and GTE could offer unregulated enhanced services and customer-premise equipment through fully separate subsidiaries. Its rationale was that structural separation would protect ratepayers from unfairly subsidizing a carrier's competitive services, while permitting market forces to determine the reasonableness of prices in the emergent data-services sector (U.S. Federal Communications Commission 1980a, 1980b).

The key to this strategy was that the commission interpreted the Communications Act to allow Bell to offer unregulated services and equipment through a separate subsidiary. This would give Bell the market discretion that it had been demanding. Corporate telecommunications users would also get what many of them had been demanding, that is, that Bell be free to "efficiently and economically provide all the data communications services that will be necessary to meet future needs" (William Saxton, president of DataComm User Inc., before Subcommittee on Communications: U.S. House of Representatives 1976: 730). Computer makers, however, filed suit, charging that the interpretation violated the Communications Act (*Computer & Communications Ass'n. v. FCC et al.* 1981).

The FCC's inclusion of Bell in this "structural approach" required a novel interpretation of the 1956 antitrust consent decree. According to FCC Chair Richard Wiley, the FCC's reasoning was that AT&T was not precluded under the decree from offering unregulated enhanced services because such services were subject to FCC regulation, even though it no longer intended to exercise that power (Wiley 1981: 57).

The aftermath of this ruling was a shift of conflict into the courts. The Department of Justice filed a suit in the District Court of New Jersey, where the 1956 antitrust agreement had been filed, challenging the FCC's decision to allow Bell to enter an unregulated sector. As we will see, this was only one manifestation of a growing debate over the legitimacy of using market-based governance in the telecommunications industry. It is, therefore, useful to focus directly on the legitimacy issue before further discussing this case.

The legitimacy issue

As we have seen, hierarchical controls gradually, if fitfully, were displaced and supplemented by market forces in each of the previous sectors. In this process, the FCC was forced to try to balance interests in network integration and pricing fairness against demands for new services. Inevitably, however, questions were raised about the legitimacy of the transformations in these sectors.

Congressional challenges. Because of its dependence on the regulatory process, Bell's position was threatened by FCC rulings allowing new entrants into key sectors of the industry. Therefore, it is not surprising that it repeatedly challenged the drift toward market competition. It was unable, however, to reverse the FCC's procompetitive policies. Hence, in the mid–1970s, Bell initiated an effort to persuade Congress to roll the clock back to the middle of the century.

For this purpose, Bell brought together representatives of the independent telephone associations and companies. This group drafted a bill that was introduced in 1976 as the Consumer Communications Reform Act, but more commonly was known as the "Bell bill" (see Derthick and Quirk 1985: 175–96). The strategy turned on the hope that Congress would view market competition as inappropriate in the telecommunications industry.

Central to the bill were two goals: (1) stopping "duplication" of the services offered by established carriers; and (2) inhibiting noncommon carriers from supplying terminal equipment to telecommunications users by transferring regulatory jurisdiction over terminal equipment to the state commissions, whose concern typically has been with controlling local telephone rates and avoiding "creamskimming."

This initiative was ineptly pursued, however. First, the president of AT&T, John DeButts, threatened that rates for basic residential service would be raised sharply if Congress refused to reverse the FCC's procompetitive policies. Then, rather than accept compromise when committee leaders expressed concerns with the bill, AT&T tried to do an end run around them. Bell, then, initiated an effort to line up support to take the bill directly to the floor. One hundred seventy-five House and seventeen Senate cosponsors were signed. This backfired when the leadership in both houses quashed the effort (von Auw 1983; Derthick and Quirk 1985).

These political miscalculations ended the possibility that Congress might reverse the commission's policy drift. For the next five years, bills much less favorable to Bell were seriously debated in Congress. Although AT&T managed to prevent any from passing, it was unable to muster enough support to get a bill of its own passed. In part, this was because the incident contributed to the creation of an increasingly organized promotional network, composed of Bell's competitors as well as business groups that were major users of telecommunications services. This network took an active role in subsequent Congressional committee debates on the changes that should be made in the industry's governance. The result was the creation of a persistent legislative stalemate (Schiller 1982: 66–70; Derthick and Quirk 1985: 136–9, 193–4).

Court challenges. Bell and the other established carriers were not the only actors that raised challenges to the legitimacy of the industry's governance regime. As it turns out, a more significant challenge to its legitimacy was an antitrust suit initiated in 1974 by the Department of Justice. According to one source, the antitrust suit was precipitated by frustration among government authorities and Bell's competitors with Bell's anticompetitive actions and evasions of FCC rulings (*Business Week* 1974: 68–70). The aim of the suit was the creation of the conditions for market competition to serve as the major governance mechanism in the industry. It was thus a direct challenge to the legitimacy of the hierarchical system of governance that had characterized the industry since the 1920s.

The Justice Department alleged that Bell's dominance across all sectors of the industry gave it the incentive and opportunity to use its monopoly in each area to maintain a monopoly in each of the other areas (U.S. Department of Justice 1980: 4–5). Justice asserted that the settlement of the 1949 antitrust case had failed to stop Bell from engaging in unreasonable restraints of trade in the long-distance and equipment markets (*U.S. v. AT&T et al.* 1982: 139, note 18). The remedy that the Justice Department sought was the divestiture of Western Electric and the Bell operating companies from AT&T, and the breakup of Western Electric (*U.S. v. AT&T et al.* 1974).

For several years the suit languished. Following the assignment of the case in 1978 to Judge Harold Greene's court, the suit moved forward rapidly. Greene managed to bring it to trial by the end of Carter's term. The case was a massive venture, lasting into the first two years of Reagan's, with a break to let Congress try (unavailingly) to resolve the issues raised by the case. Early in 1982, however, the government and Bell reached an out-of-court agreement. An opinion by Judge Green on a Bell motion for dismissal foreshadowed clearly that Bell was likely to lose (*U.S. v. AT&T et al.* 1981). The proposed settlement involved a complex double play of legal maneuvers. The Justice Department offered to drop its appeal of the FCC's Computer II ruling, if AT&T would agree to a settlement of the 1974 antitrust suit. In brief, the proposal was that AT&T would agree to give up its local exchange monopoly service by divesting the twenty-two Bell operating companies; in return, AT&T would gain the right to compete in unregulated markets.

The Justice Department and AT&T, therefore, filed a joint request with the New Jersey court asking that their agreement be accepted as a modification of the 1956 consent decree that had forbidden Bell from entering unregulated markets. They also asked that jurisdiction for the modified consent decree be transferred to Greene's court. The parties then asked Greene to dismiss the 1974 antitrust suit (*U.S. v. AT&T et al.* 1982: 140–3).

These legal maneuvers hit a snag, however. Although the New Jersey court agreed to the plan, Greene refused to dismiss the 1974 antitrust suit, insisting that the request be lodged with the court, pending appropriate public interest review. He reversed the New Jersey court's decision to view the proposed settlement as a modification of the 1956 agreement. Greene then consolidated the 1949 and 1974 antitrust cases into one action and ordered that extensive public interest proceedings be initiated with respect to the proposed settlement (*U.S. v. AT&T et al.* 1982).

Although a full explication of the terms of the settlement finally approved by Judge Greene need not detain us here, it is important to note its key implications. The first is that the noncompetitive, hierarchical system of governance that had emerged in period two was partially replaced by one in which market forces were given much wider scope. In several sectors of the industry (e.g., terminal-equipment and so-called enhanced services), markets were legitimized as a primary mechanism for economic coordination. In other sectors (e.g., local telephone service), traditional hierarchical controls were to remain dominant.

The second point to note is that the final settlement permitted judicial scrutiny and enforcement beyond the date on which the agreement was approved by the court, and established a "complaint and response" procedure to enable interested third parties to contest failures to comply with the settlement. These provisions gave the court authority to oversee the relations between AT&T and the divested Bell companies, as well as the terms under which they might enter telecommunications (and other) sectors. Consequently, the court assumed a continuing role in defining the extent to which market competition would be considered legitimate as a mode of governance (*U.S. v. AT&T et al.* 1982).

The continuing jurisdiction of Greene's court is significant inasmuch as the antitrust agreement left unspecified the exact conditions under which AT&T, Western Electric, and the divested Bell operating companies should be allowed to participate in various sectors. This question has been at the heart of most of the conflicts in the industry since the breakup of the Bell System. The FCC and the court have squared off repeatedly over it. For example, an ongoing dispute has been whether or not to permit the divested Bell operating companies to offer data processing and other information services within their geographic monopolies. The FCC has argued that these companies should be given almost unlimited discretion to enter these sectors (U.S. Federal Communications Commission 1986). The court has denied them this freedom on the grounds that the divested Bell companies, like AT&T prior to the breakup, would then be in a position to use their local monopolies to cross-subsidize competitive services or to deny equal access to competitors (*U.S. v. Western Electric Company, Inc. et al.* 1987:2).

This type of intragovernmental skirmishing over the direction of the industry has occurred frequently since the breakup. One consequence has been confusion over the discretion and obligations possessed by different carriers. For example, in 1985, the commission decided to open a broad inquiry into the impact of the divestiture on its Computer II structure by initiating a third computer inquiry. As a result of Computer III, the FCC lifted its earlier structural separation requirements on AT&T. The commission, however, refused to broach the question of how to ensure the interconnection of AT&T supplied equipment with equipment supplied by AT&T's competitors – an issue in which the court inevitably would become involved (U.S. Federal Communications Commission 1985). Yet the question of interconnection among competing systems is unlikely to go away. In the postdivestiture environment, the industry will be divided among many opportunistically acting firms.

Epilogue

The final word in this period of the industry's evolution has yet to be written. All three of the perennial issues highlighted before remain open.

First, the breakup of the Bell System has exacerbated the disagreements among carriers, suppliers, and customers over the governance regime that should prevail in the industry. These actors are not equally advantaged by the existing regime. For instance, the long-distance carriers (AT&T, MCI, Sprint, etc.) are arguing among themselves over what constitutes "fair competition" given the overwhelming market power of AT&T in the long-distance market. Likewise, the so-called Baby Bells (the former Bell operating companies) argue that they should be permitted to offer information services and long-distance services in addition to their local monopoly services, but are opposed by companies that fear the Baby Bells might use their local monopolies to unfairly stymie competition in these markets (*U.S. v. Western Electric Company, Inc. et al.* 1987). Opportunistic maneuvering over the selection of governance regimes is, thus, likely to continue.

Second, the issue of the compatibility of the industry's underlying technologies with various governance regimes is also unresolved, mainly because the technologies are in a state of flux. Innovation in the long-distance, terminal-equipment, and data-processing sectors has been occurring nonstop over the past three decades. If rapid technological changes continue, it may be difficult to establish a stable governance regime in the industry.

Finally, the legitimacy of the current balance between market governance and hierarchical governance is the key issue in the ongoing disputes between the FCC and the court. How this issue is resolved will depend in part on the willingness of Congress and the President to alter the existing political equation, either by supporting FCC's withdrawal from active oversight or by supporting the court's policy of requiring a distinction between competitive sectors and hierarchically coordinated, regulated sectors. The former option will probably result in renewed movement toward hierarchy by the major industry actors.

The uncertainty in each of these issues areas suggests that this phase in the industry's evolution may continue for some time to come. In the interim, we may see an increased use of markets in some sectors (e.g., telecommunications equipment supply) and decreased use of markets in others (e.g., long-distance services). Much will depend, however, on the actions of industry actors, the compatibility of these governance mechanisms with underlying communications technologies, and the responses of public authorities as they confront the question of what constitutes a legitimate governance regime for the industry. Until these issues are resolved, the industry will continue to undergo its current search process.

CONCLUSIONS

In conclusion, a number of observations can be made about the evolution of governance in this industry. First, the model outlined at the outset of the chapter usefully highlights key aspects of the changes in the industry. Another finding, however, is that there appears to be an important asymmetry in the transformation of governance. This asymmetrical property is the different degree of difficulty involved in establishing a new governance regime as opposed to that involved in undermining an existing system.

In the episodes discussed, a change in any one of three factors was sufficient to bring down the existing governance regime: (1) changes in the legal or political status of the industry's governance arrangements; (2) alterations in the industry's technological characteristics; or (3) a rise in the opportunistic behaviors of industry actors. For example, the first type of change was responsible for the breakdown of hierarchical coordination in 1894; the expiration of the basic Bell patents stripped the extant governance regime of its legal sanction. The second type of change, in the form of developments in long-distance and terminal-equipment technologies, was key to the demise of the regime that had emerged in the first half of this century. The third type of change was paramount in the failure of the Morgan–Bell obligational network to sustain itself after World War I.

By contrast, the establishment of a new governance regime required the satisfactory resolution of all three problems. In each episode, the test of a potential governance regime was that it withstand the opportunistic behaviors of industry actors, and also be compatible with extant legal–political conditions and the technological characteristics of the industry. Only when a regime was found that successfully addressed all of these problems was it able to persist for a significant period of time.

Also important to observe is the range of roles played by the state in the transformation of governance in this sector. At the most general level, the state has provided a system of authoritative rules that circumscribe private actions. These rules include such basic legal categories as property, patent, tort, antitrust, and contract law. By defining legal liabilities and freedoms, these laws determine what categories of actors can participate within a sector, and under what conditions. Thus, for example, a firm with the patent rights to a technology (such as the basic telephone patents in the late nineteenth century) possesses the freedom to exploit the technology, or not, as it sees fit; that is, it has the legal right to exercise control over the development and use of the technology. A firm that does not possess such patent rights leaves itself liable to prosecution and damages for improper use of the technology. Through these authoritative rules, the state establishes the limits of what is to be considered legitimate. By prohibiting categories of behavior, the state exerts a powerful influence on the type of governance that might be used in a sector.

These legal categories, however, are not the product of natural forces, nor are they immune from change. They are products of decision-making institutions within the state. Hence, the authoritative rules that circumscribe the selection of governance regimes must themselves be viewed as subject to political conflict and contestation. This is especially apparent, for instance, in the case of the Federal Communications Commission in its rulings permitting greater competition in the long-distance and equipment markets. It may be less apparent, but is no less present, in the case of the courts in their rulings in the 1949 and 1956 AT&T antitrust suits. In making such decisions, public officials, and the institutions of which they are part, establish the legal categories that influence the selection of governance regimes. Viewed from this perspective, authoritative rules are not distinct from the specific decisions of public officials. The specific decisions give content to general rules, permitting them to be interpreted and applied to classes of actors and actions.

At the most specific level, state actors sometimes play a role in the selection of governance regimes similar to that played by private actors. Public officials (as in the case, for instance, of the Postmaster General in the years leading up to U.S. participation in World War I) may seek opportunistically to alter the regime in a sector so to advance their own interests. Such actors may have certain advantages over private actors to the extent that they are better positioned to press their case with other government officials. Yet, in some cases private actors may have as much access to the decision-making processes of the government as any set of public officials. Certainly, AT&T was for many years able to utilize its connections with the state to thwart serious threats to its hierarchical control of the industry, as it demonstrated in the final settlement of the 1949 antitrust suit against it. Thus, the main difference between public and private actors may simply be one of resources and political acumen, rather than any fundamental difference in the status of one or the other.

By way of conclusion, this chapter suggests some issues that deserve further attention. One is that we know much less than we might want about the role of technological change in the transformation of governance arrangements. For instance, one might conclude from Bell's behavior, both in the early years of the century and in the post–War years, that it sought to control the rate and direction of technological change so as to protect its position of preeminence in the governance of the telecommunications industry. This may mean that there is an important *political* component to technological change, in addition to its scientific and economic components. Furthermore, it would appear from this chapter that technological changes tend to undermine most dramatically nonmarket forms of governance. Technological changes appear to place corporate hierarchies under enormous stress. For example, in the late nineteenth century, only the patent laws protected Bell from the gales of competition. Governance regimes may vary in their susceptibility to the destructive impact of technological changes; some may actually be favored by such changes.

A final issue that this chapter raises is whether or not different governance mechanisms vary in their ability to withstand the opportunistic behaviors of private actors. It may well be that a key difference among various governance arrangements is how adaptive they are to heightened opportunism. This chapter suggests that there is considerable variation on this score, with markets and hierarchies at one end of the spectrum and associations and networks at the other. Clearly, a broader sample and more systematic analysis are necessary to resolve this issue about the relative resilience of sectoral institutions.

CONTRADICTIONS OF GOVERNANCE IN THE NUCLEAR ENERGY SECTOR

John L. Campbell

Department of Sociology, Harvard University

People advocating the development of nuclear power in the United States used to predict that one day the commercial nuclear energy sector would produce electricity so economically that it would be too cheap to meter. Today, so many problems plague nuclear power that in some places, nuclear plants under construction and nearly complete are too expensive to finish even though hundreds of millions of dollars have already been invested in them. This chapter explains how the problems that caused the dramatic rise and fall of commercial nuclear power in the United States led to the transformation of the sector's governance regimes, and, conversely, how different regimes contributed to development of these problems in the first place.[1]

GOVERNANCE MECHANISMS AND SECTORAL COORDINATION

Organizational theorists have recently suggested that scarcities in *resources,* including capital, labor, and raw materials, and in *information* about competitors, suppliers, products, markets, technology, and government regulations lead to governance transformations (e.g., Lawrence and Dyer 1983). Although most of these scholars have not attempted to explain the *origins* of these scarcities, other observers have argued that they stem from the organizational characteristics of the sector's firms, such as their size and capital intensity, and certain characteristics of the sector's products and production technologies, including the rate of technological change and levels of technological sophistication. Furthermore, they have suggested that these characteristics help to determine which governance mechanisms become dominant in a sector (e.g., Hollingsworth and Lindberg 1985).[2]

1 I would like to thank Michael Allen, Tom Moore, and the authors in this volume for their comments on earlier drafts. Portions of this chapter were published previously as "Corporations, Collective Organization, and the State: Industry Response to the Accident at Three Mile Island," *Social Science Quarterly* 70(3): 650–66, adapted by permission of the University of Texas Press.

2 As noted in Chapter 1, a governance mechanism is dominant when its decision-making

Yet apart from these variables, there are other, more institutional, dynamics for change that stem from the *structure of the governance regime* itself. As discussed in Chapter 1, because different governance mechanisms tend to constrain the decision-making criteria and activities of actors in different ways, it is possible that these criteria and activities may contradict each other when actors organize themselves simultaneously through two or more governance mechanisms, as they usually do. For example, short-term price signals from the market may contradict an association's attempt to convince its members to collaborate in long-range planning. When this happens, it may confound the coordination of sectoral activities and governance problems will develop. Resources and information may not be distributed efficiently to those who want them. Under these conditions the sector experiences what Douglass North (1981) called an inefficient property rights structure – a situation where the rules, procedures, and norms governing transactions do not facilitate the desired distribution of resources and information. These problems may lead to a transformation of the governance regime as actors within the sector try to renew effective coordination.[3] This is a significant modification of early ideas about economic governance that suggested that we should view governance mechanisms as potentially complementary control systems coordinating economic activity together in efficient ways (e.g., Lindberg 1985).

Furthermore, contradictions within *individual governance mechanisms* may lead to a transformation of governance regimes. There is a rich literature suggesting that the institutional structures of economic markets (e.g., Baran and Sweezy 1966; Musgrave and Musgrave 1973; Williamson 1975; Chandler and Daems 1980; Williamson and Ouchi 1981), corporate hierarchies (e.g., Perrow 1981: 375; Piore and Sabel 1984), and the state (e.g., O'Connor 1973; Brittan 1975; Crozier, Huntington, and Watanuki 1975; Offe 1975) tend to undermine their own efficient operation and lead to their own transformation as well as the transformation of the overall governance regime. For example, Oliver Williamson (1975) argued that when excessive transaction costs develop in markets, corporate hierarchies replace the market as the dominant coordinating mechanism. Others ar-

logic is the principle logic guiding decision making throughout the sector. When actors use two governance mechanisms to help coordinate sectoral activity, the logic of the dominant one takes precedence over the other. For example, if the market dominates, actors respond primarily to price signals. If an association dominates, interests in long-term collective responsibility guide most sectoral activity.

3 Others have made similar arguments in different contexts. For example, Benson (1982: 161–5) argued that policy sectors are always generating new rule systems that may contradict the old ones. Policy crises and fundamental changes in rule systems may follow, depending on the balance of organizational forces involved. See Van de Ven and Astley (1981) and Streeck and Schmitter (1985: 7) for further discussions of this point with respect to interorganizational analysis and economic coordination, respectively.

gued that associations and promotional networks are also organized in ways that tend occasionally to undermine their own capacities for effectively coordinating sectoral activity (e.g., Foth 1930: 5–17; Williamson and Ouchi 1981: 351; Schmitter 1984: 18).

This chapter shows how contradictions between and within governance mechanisms created problems *directly* that led actors in the nuclear energy sector to search for solutions to their problems and, occasionally, new governance regimes. These problems often appeared as resource and information scarcities caused by breakdowns in exchange relations. In addition, governance regimes influenced governance transformations *indirectly* by limiting the number of options available to actors as they searched for remedies to their problems. Similarly, although other factors, particularly problems associated with nuclear reactor technology, created critical resource and information problems, governance mechanisms played important roles in mediating the extent to which these problems precipitated governance transformations. Hence, this chapter also demonstrates that we cannot fully understand the impact of technology on the governance process without a complementary analysis of the sector's governance regime. Finally, we pay special attention to the role of the state in this case because it exhibited a variety of important contradictions itself that substantially influenced the governance process.

THE COMMERCIAL NUCLEAR ENERGY SECTOR

The commercial nuclear energy sector includes several major sets of exchange partners (see Figure 4.1). First, in the so-called front end of the fuel cycle, private companies mine, mill, and fabricate uranium into fuel that electric utility companies buy to power their nuclear plants. Prior to fabrication, the federal government enriches the fuel through a chemical process that concentrates the uranium. Second, reactor manufacturers sell the nuclear portion of the power plant, which includes the reactor itself, to the utility. Utilities purchase many of the nonnuclear components from various suppliers and hire an architect-engineering firm to oversee construction, unless the utility chooses to do so itself. Third, in the back end of the fuel cycle, the utility hires a private reprocessing company, if available, to relieve it of its used fuel – material that is highly radioactive and toxic – and to chemically separate the uranium and plutonium from other waste products so that these useful elements may be recycled as fresh fuel. Reprocessors then turn the remaining waste over to the federal government for final disposal. If reprocessing is not available, utilities give their waste directly to the federal government for disposal.

Fourth, to finance all of this, utilities must raise capital from a set of

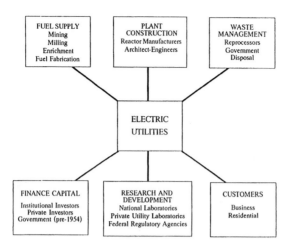

Figure 4.1   Primary commercial nuclear sector exchange relations.

actors that include institutional and individual investors, and utility customers, to the extent that revenues finance nuclear construction. As discussed in what follows, the federal government provided some financing until 1954. Fifth, utilities obtain research-and-development services and other technical information from federal regulatory agencies, often by way of the government's national laboratory system, as well as from various private research organizations. Finally, utilities sell their electricity to residential and business customers. A patchwork of government agencies, primarily at the federal and state level, regulates all six sets of these exchange relationships. The problems plaguing the U.S. nuclear sector involved government regulation, the back end of the fuel cycle, and the sale, construction, and operation of nuclear plants.

We can conveniently divide the history of the nuclear sector into three periods, corresponding to the important transformations of its governance regimes. The first period was a time when the sector developed and began to commercialize nuclear technology for use by the electric utility industry, a task that was not accomplished until primary responsibility for coordinating the sector's activities shifted from the state to the private sector. The second period was one of industrial expansion and sudden contraction, marked by increased political opposition to nuclear power, and a fragmentation of the state's authority over the sector that provided new opportunities for antinuclear groups to penetrate the policy process in ways that helped to undermine the sector's growth. During the final period, promotional networks and industry associations assumed important responsibilities for regulating activity throughout the sector.

STATE DOMINANCE AND THE SECTOR'S
DEVELOPMENT, 1946–63

The First Governance Regime

The 1946 Atomic Energy Act allowed the U.S. Atomic Energy Commission (AEC) and the congressional Joint Committee on Atomic Energy (JCAE) to dominate the development of nuclear power (e.g., Battelle Memorial Institute 1978: 101; Clarke 1985). The Act granted the AEC a monopoly over all nuclear technology, patents, and materials (Green and Rosenthal 1963: Chap. 1; Clarke 1985), and made the JCAE, overseer of all AEC activity, the most autonomous congressional committee ever created by allowing it to serve as both its own legislative and conference committees (Green and Rosenthal 1963; Nader and Abbotts 1979: 275). The JCAE demonstrated its ability to manipulate Congress as it successfully defended the AEC from would-be budget cutters several times during the early 1950s (Thomas 1956: Chaps. 5–6; Green and Rosenthal 1963: Chap. 1).

The AEC assumed primary responsibility for shaping the sector's governance regime. It restricted corporate access to nuclear technology by granting research contracts to only a handful of large corporations during the late 1940s and early 1950s, primarily those that had been involved with nuclear energy during World War II (Allardice and Trapnell 1974; Del Sesto 1979: 49).[4] Through its use of contracts, the AEC also created promotional networks with corporations and universities. The most important were the national laboratories, run for the AEC by a few corporations, such as Union Carbide and du Pont, and universities whose job it was to develop the technology, disseminate information about it to the private sector, and provide technical advice to the Commission (Allen 1977: 67). Despite the AEC's contractual dominance, the laboratories had considerable autonomy and independence in framing their research programs, especially projects involving commercial reactor technologies (Orlans 1967: 136). The AEC also created other promotional networks of university and private sector scientists, such as the Advisory Committee on Reactor Safeguards, which advised the agency about reactor safety matters (Metzger 1972: 30), and the General Advisory Committee, which helped the AEC develop research policy (Thomas 1956: Chaps. 2–3). Much of this activity was an attempt by the government to create a commercial market for nuclear power.[5]

---

4 The AEC played this gatekeeping role effectively. Through 1963, over half of all the AEC's contract funds went to just five corporations, General Electric, Union Carbide, Bendix, Sandia, and du Pont, and the Universities of Chicago and California (Orlans, 1967: Chap. 2).

5 The JCAE and AEC were also interested in developing nuclear technology for military purposes (e.g., Bupp and Derian 1978: 30–6; Clarke 1985). They became particularly

Trade and professional associations such as the Atomic Industrial Forum, the nuclear sector's trade association established in 1953, were active, but relatively unimportant in terms of sectoral governance. The membership of the Atomic Industrial Forum included reactor manufacturers, architect-engineering firms, uranium companies, and utilities interested in developing the technology. The Forum spent most of its time conducting policy studies and offering advice to the AEC, not coordinating economic activity (Orlans 1967: Chap. 11). Similarly, the Edison Electric Institute, the electric utility industry's trade association, was only important during this period insofar as it participated in critical debates in the mid–1950s about the extent to which the government should own and operate its own commercial nuclear plants.

Sectoral problems

Information scarcities posed formidable barriers to commercialization of the technology. Plant performance, reliability, and costs for the construction and operation of nuclear plants were unknown because the technology was underdeveloped and it was not clear which designs were feasible, either commercially or technically (Dawson 1976; Perry et al. 1977). The absence of full-scale support industries like waste management and fuel fabrication exacerbated these uncertainties. Utilities refused to buy nuclear plants until these problems were solved. The relative abundance, low cost, and safety of conventional coal-fired and oil-fired electricity generating plants made the development of a market for nuclear power even more difficult (Perry et al. 1977: 217; Clarke 1985).

There were also serious resource scarcities. In 1951, the AEC organized study groups, a form of promotional network, involving representatives from industry, the scientific community, and its own staff to analyze the impediments to commercialization. They found that research, development, and commercialization costs were higher than private corporations were willing to bear. The study groups were especially worried that reactors would be so expensive that utilities could not afford to buy them (Novick 1976: 40; Allen 1977: Chap. 3). Increasing these financial concerns, one of the national laboratories published a study in 1957 estimating that a serious reactor accident could cause $7 billion in property damage. The insurance industry and the utilities refused to shoulder that financial risk alone (Battelle Memorial Institute 1978: 113; Nader and Abbotts 1979: 27).

interested in the technology's commercial possibilities after 1953 when the Eisenhower Administration sought a commercial nuclear program to enhance national prestige, when the utility industry developed an interest in alternative energy sources, and when General Electric and Westinghouse Corporation became interested in the technology's potential profitability (Dawson 1976: Chap. 3; Allen 1977: 14–30).

The search process

The AEC tried to solve the problem of resource scarcities by subsidizing the sector's initial development. It offered discovery incentives and price supports to stimulate uranium exploration and mining, spent billions of dollars building uranium enrichment plants, and provided enrichment subsidies for the utilities. AEC officials agreed to buy reprocessed plutonium back from the utilities at attractive, fixed prices to reduce the utilities' fuel costs (Battelle Memorial Institute 1978: 103–27). Finally, the AEC provided technology and radioactive waste from its weapons program to stimulate the development of a waste reprocessing industry – an attempt to reduce utility operating costs through fuel recycling. The AEC also planned that reprocessing would be the first step in its waste disposal program (Campbell 1987b). The federal government spent over $18 billion between 1950 and 1977 in subsidies and incentives such as these to stimulate commercialization (Battelle Memorial Institute 1978: 103).

The JCAE solved the insurance problem in 1957 by pushing the Price–Anderson Act through Congress. This legislation limited a utility's liability in the event of a nuclear accident to $60 million. The federal government would pay the remaining damage claims, but only up to an additional $500 million. Beyond this amount neither the government nor industry could be held liable. The Act also created an indemnification program that subsidized about $10 million of the utility industry's nuclear insurance costs annually (Battelle Memorial Institute 1978: 117; Nader and Abbotts 1979: 227–9).

The AEC tried to resolve some of the sector's information scarcity problems by forming promotional networks, such as the national laboratory system. The AEC's Power Reactor Demonstration Program was another example where the agency solicited proposals between 1955 and 1962 from various utility and corporate groups interested in exploring the technical and commercial possibilities of different nuclear reactor designs. The government sponsored several groups that tested and developed these designs, identified the most promising ones, and shared the knowledge gained among all participants of the program (e.g., Perry et al. 1977). The AEC paid for most of the construction and fuel to reduce research-and-development costs for the corporations involved. The government's commitment to these and other similar programs was so great that AEC budgets for civilian reactor development soared from $18.9 million in 1954 to $102.3 million in 1961. The AEC spent over $768 million by 1963 on civilian reactor development (Dawson 1976: 80).

Because the AEC monopolized nuclear technology and material, there was tremendous uncertainty about the role corporations would play in the sector's development and governance. After heavy lobbying by the Edison Electric Institute, reactor manufacturers, including General Electric and

Westinghouse, and other interested corporations, Congress clarified the situation by enacting the 1954 Atomic Energy Act. The legislature designed the law to promote commercialization in the private sector by allowing corporations to own the technology and patent rights to it, and by prohibiting the AEC from building its own reactors for the purpose of selling electricity (Dawson 1976: Chap. 3; Allen 1977: 35–7). This was a legislative milestone because it reduced the AEC's authority and created the *possibility* of transforming the balance of power within the sector's governance regime. The corporations could now assume a much more dominant governance role, if they wanted.

However, the utilities remained skeptical about the profitability of nuclear power and continued to refuse to buy nuclear plants. The JCAE feared that the United States might lose the commercial market to other countries if it did not speed up commercialization. As a result, the JCAE introduced the Gore–Holifield bill in 1956 to permit and fund the construction of six government-owned commercial nuclear plants. Seventy-five utilities, the Edison Electric Institute, reactor manufacturers, the National Association of Manufacturers, and even the AEC, opposed the legislation, arguing that the government should not be allowed to build and operate reactors that would compete with the private utilities (Green and Rosenthal 1963: 153–8). Although Republicans defeated the bill in a vicious political battle in the House of Representatives, the JCAE continued trying through 1958 to persuade Congress to adopt similar legislation. Congress continued to refuse. However, the fear of such "creeping socialism" eventually helped convince utilities to begin building nuclear plants anyway (Dawson 1976: 122; Novick 1976: 40; Clarke 1985).

Reactor manufacturers helped spark commercialization in 1963 by reducing dramatically the utilities' concerns about inadequate resources and information. General Electric, and then Westinghouse, agreed to sell entire nuclear plants to utilities at guaranteed fixed prices without any help from the government. This was the manufacturers' way of signaling that the technology was perfected enough to ensure that the costs of building nuclear plants were under control. The utilities were convinced and bought thirteen of these so-called turn-key plants over the next three years (Bupp and Derian 1978). Commercial nuclear power had finally come of age.[6]

A technology emerges

The light-water reactor emerged from all the reactor technologies under consideration as the sector's cornerstone. It was selected because it ap-

---

6 As it turned out, neither plant designs nor the costs of building them had been stabilized. As a result, General Electric and Westinghouse lost an estimated $75 million per turn-key plant and stopped offering to build plants at guaranteed prices in 1966 (Del Sesto 1979: 90).

pealed to the dominant groups within the sector, *not* because it was necessarily the best technology for producing electricity for commercial purposes. By 1958, the JCAE decided that commercialization of the light-water reactor should be achieved as quickly as possible (U.S. Joint Committee on Atomic Energy 1958: 1; Dawson 1976: 101). This reactor concept was the most technologically mature at the time because the government had spent an enormous amount of money developing it as a propulsion system for the Navy's submarines (Dawson 1976: 46; Allen 1977: 65). Other promising designs never received comparable federal funding and were not developed enough to overcome the light-water reactor's head start (U.S. Atomic Energy Commission 1967: 3; U.S. Office of Technology Assessment 1975: 97). As a result, even though the reactor was one of the *least* promising designs in terms of fuel efficiency and safety, the JCAE supported it because it was available (Perry et al. 1977: 6–8).[7]

However, the 1954 Atomic Energy Act left the final choice of a commercial design to the private sector. General Electric and Westinghouse knew the light-water technology because they had developed it for the military. They also had the resources and reputation to sustain its development commercially. So in addition to its political advantage, the light-water concept had an economic edge over the others because these companies were prepared to market it aggressively (Arthur D. Little Inc. 1968: Chap. 4). In the end, sectoral actors chose the light-water reactor for commercialization because manufacturers recognized its lucrative potential and because it was technologically available at a time when the government was hurrying to promote the commercialization of nuclear power (Dawson 1976: 267).

The shifting public–private balance

The resource and information problems of this development period stemmed more from the absence of a full-blown nuclear sector with mature products, markets, and industries than from either the contradictions within and among the sector's governance mechanisms, or a breakdown in exchange relations. This is not surprising since the sector, and most of its governance mechanisms and exchange relations, was just forming. Never-

---

7 At the time, many observers questioned how safe the light-water reactor was for commercial purposes. The AEC felt that other reactor concepts were potentially safer and urged the JCAE not to overlook them (U.S. Joint Committee on Atomic Energy 1958: 47–66). A Westinghouse executive reported later that his company was also uncertain about the reactor's safety (Hertsgaard 1983: 33). Indeed, David Lilienthal, the AEC's first chairperson, eventually regretted that rigorous safety comparisons were never performed as part of the selection process that chose the light-water reactor (Lilienthal 1980: 17). Within the international community, the British quickly recognized the light-water reactor's safety limitations in comparison to other designs (Burn 1967: 20).

theless, the governance regime that did exist set limits on the search for solutions to the fledgling sector's problems. Although the government dominated the search process, nuclear corporations had significant influence too. For example, the utilities' resistance to adopting nuclear technology forced the JCAE to threaten to build government-owned plants. This part of the search involved intense political struggle among corporate and state actors as to whether nuclear power should be publicly or privately controlled.

The government's attempt to solve the sector's initial problems and create exchange relations, particularly through the development of a commercial market, involved the deliberate formation and transformation of the governance regime. One example was the AEC's effort to form promotional networks for research and development. Another was passage of the 1954 Atomic Energy Act, legislation advocated by corporations and trade associations, and designed to give corporations a more important role in sectoral governance. Yet that was not enough. Although the Act changed the limits within which the search for the commercialization of nuclear power could be conducted, the governance regime itself was not fully transformed until the JCAE's threats of building government-owned plants and the reactor manufacturers' turn-key offers finally established a commercial market for nuclear plants. Only then was the government able to shed some of its responsibility for developing the sector.

Throughout this period the state played two important, yet conceptually distinct, roles. On the one hand, the AEC allocated vast amounts of resources and information to the sector by contracting with various private actors, providing subsidies, and fostering the development of promotional networks. On the other hand, the government also manipulated property rights. The JCAE threatened government ownership, a threat that helped force the utilities to adopt nuclear technology. Furthermore, Congress set specific rules (the atomic energy legislation) within which all of the sector's actors had to operate. The government's plan to commercialize nuclear technology worked in part because both roles were consistent with each other and with this plan. Such consistency was often conspicuously absent after 1963 – a condition that created serious dilemmas for the sector. Furthermore, after 1963, the sector felt the state's influence in a third way, through the impact of more general legislative parameters that constrained the efforts of corporations seeking solutions to many new problems.

MARKET AND CORPORATE DOMINANCE, 1963–79

The second governance regime

Markets and corporations had become the dominant governance mechanisms in the nuclear sector by 1963 as commercialization began to blossom.

Led by General Electric and Westinghouse, four reactor manufacturers sold all the light-water reactors in the United States (U.S. Nuclear Regulatory Commission 1980). About a dozen architect-engineering firms were available to build the nonnuclear portion of the plant. Four corporations offered waste reprocessing services by 1969. Several huge, vertically integrated energy companies came to control the front end of the fuel cycle (Nader and Abbotts 1979: 267–8; Barkenbus 1984a: 3). As a result, competition among corporations in a variety of markets guided most of the sector's activities during the 1960s.

Although the 1954 Atomic Energy Act had substantially reduced the state's authority over the nuclear sector, the government continued to exert significant influence over sectoral activity, primarily through regulation and other property rights policies. That influence, however, was fragmented among several agencies, sometimes at different levels of government, with different and occasionally contradictory policy priorities. The AEC was responsible for promoting nuclear power and for ensuring that operation of the technology did not endanger the public health – two roles that eventually conflicted with each other. State-level public utility commissions controlled the rates electric utility companies charged their customers. At a more general level, environmental and antitrust legislation, bodies of law not designed specifically with the nuclear sector in mind, had important effects on the sector's governance and performance.

Actors arranged in promotional networks, particularly the national laboratory system, continued to provide research support for the AEC, as did some corporations. However, now that the government believed commercialization had been achieved, Congress and federal regulators restricted this research primarily to reactor safety insofar as the light-water reactor was concerned (Shaw 1968: 178). The government recognized that cooperative projects, such as the Power Reactor Demonstration Program, were no longer necessary and abandoned them. The Atomic Industrial Forum continued to collect and disseminate information on a wide variety of topics of concern to its members and the government. The Edison Electric Institute spent most of its time lobbying on issues other than those related to nuclear power (Mills and Mills 1983).

Sectoral problems

Ironically, the sector's tremendous success and its governance regime created new resource scarcities. The market for nuclear plants boomed as utilities ordered 197 plants between 1966 and 1974. They had ordered only 27 plants before then (U.S. Nuclear Regulatory Commission 1980). However, severe materials and labor shortages began to develop because of the sudden increase in orders (Lester 1970; U.S. Joint Committee on Atomic Energy 1974: 67). More important were the capital shortages that materialized. Reactor manufacturers competed for sales by offering utilities progressively larger reactors and promising that increased sizes would pay off through increased economies of scale. During this so-called nuclear horsepower race between 1965 and 1974, reactors nearly doubled in size (Bupp and Derian 1978: 73). Yet economies of scale did not follow, often because the costs of building nuclear plants climbed dramatically. The average cost for a nuclear plant skyrocketed 50% over original estimates just between 1966 and 1968 (Arthur D. Little Inc. 1968: 23). Nevertheless, although nuclear plants were more expensive than conventional generating plants, utilities continued to buy them, in part, because the formula public utility commissions used to set electricity rates rewarded utilities for capital investment, as long as capital was available at low cost (Willrich 1975: 24; Dieckamp 1979: 246).[8] Between 1967 and 1972, the amount of the utilities' capital invested in construction work in progress rose from 8.3 to 18.2% of their total net investment – an increase of $12.2 billion (U.S. General Accounting Office 1980a: 18). Much of this investment was for nuclear projects because nuclear's share of all the steam-generated electricity capacity ordered increased about 8.5% annually and reached a total of 68% of all the capacity ordered in 1972 (Campbell 1986: 712). Tying up so much money in construction work in progress created a severe earnings squeeze for utilities since most public utility commissions did not allow these investments to earn a return until the plant was actually operating, something that could take a decade or more for nuclear plants (Gandara 1977: 95; U.S. General Accounting Office 1980a: 3, 1980b: 15; U.S. Congressional Budget Office 1982: 6). Although utilities sought rate increases to cover their construction costs and reduce their cash flow problems, beginning in 1969, consumer opposition prevented public utility commissions from granting more than about 60% of the increases utilities requested (U.S. Senate 1974: 196, 310; Gandara 1977: 33; U.S. House of Representatives 1981a: 229).

The sector's success and governance regime also generated information scarcities insofar as the regulatory environment became less predictable. First, as utilities rushed to join the nuclear bandwagon, they swamped the AEC with applications for construction permits and operating licenses. Licensing times grew longer and more uncertain due to the backlog (U.S. Nuclear Regulatory Commission 1980: 14–17, 1981a: 39–41). Furthermore,

8 The public utility commission determines the rate a utility company may charge its customers for electricity. Once the rate is set, a utility company can increase the absolute amount of revenue it collects from its customers by expanding the size of its rate base, its total capital investment, because the revenue it is allowed to collect is a function of its operating costs plus the quantity of the rate base multiplied by the rate the utility commission sets. Under these regulatory conditions, unless capital is prohibitively expensive, the utility has an incentive to increase the size of its rate base (Averch and Johnson 1962; Westfield 1965).

the dramatic increases in reactor size, and a Supreme Court decision in 1971 that required utilities planning nuclear plants to comply with the 1969 National Environmental Policy Act, created a wave of additional regulatory requirements, including detailed environmental impact reviews (U.S. Atomic Energy Commission 1973; Komanoff 1981; Barkenbus 1984a; U.S. Office of Technology Assessment 1984: 121–4). Second, the AEC found itself on the horns of a dilemma that led to a massive legitimation crisis. The Advisory Committee on Reactor Safeguards and some of the national laboratories warned the AEC that the larger plants utilities were planning were more dangerous than previous models and that current reactor safety systems needed to be tested in order to verify that they would work properly on the new plants. However, the AEC believed that the sector's recent commercial success would be jeopardized if utilities had to wait to build plants while the agency tested and perhaps changed current safety criteria. Under intense pressure from the JCAE, reactor manufacturers, utilities, and some AEC administrators, the AEC chose to continue licensing despite the absence of recommended technical data. Scientists at the national laboratories leaked the story to the public, thereby discrediting the agency and unleashing a storm of public protest, sudden changes in these safety criteria, and new regulatory uncertainty (Campbell 1987a).

The AEC's legitimation crisis galvanized antinuclear opposition that had been developing for years over a variety of issues (Nelkin and Fallows 1978: 285). In 1973, Ralph Nader and other environmentalists sued the AEC in an attempt to shut down two-thirds of the nation's nuclear reactors because, according to the plaintiffs, the plants had inadequate safety systems. Antinuclear groups also planned further suits and a massive lobbying campaign in Congress against the sector (Barfield 1973). Nuclear critics convinced Congress and 28 state legislatures by late 1975 to consider stopping nuclear expansion until safety problems were solved (*Energy User's Reports* 1974; Burn 1978: 91). Nuclear critics intervened in reactor licensing and construction permit reviews, causing significant delays (Cohen 1979). By 1978, 45% of the public polled opposed the construction of nuclear plants near their homes – an increase of 28% in five years (Rankin, Nealey, and Melber 1981: 30). All of this led to more stringent regulatory requirements and licensing delays that helped make nuclear plants more expensive to build (e.g., Montgomery and Quirk 1978).[9]

Although largely unrelated to the AEC's legitimation difficulties, the reprocessing industry died, leaving utilities nowhere to send their radioactive waste. Competition had driven two reprocessing corporations from the market by 1972. Another company tried to improve its competitive

---

9 See Campbell (1988: Chap. 5) for further discussion about the relationships between antinuclear opposition, regulatory delays, and rising nuclear plant costs.

position by closing its reprocessing plant temporarily for modifications. The idea was to expand the plant and achieve significant economies of scale. However, the expansion required a new construction permit from the AEC and, therefore, public hearings. Environmentalists and company workers participated in these hearings and convinced the AEC to impose new environmental and safety requirements on the plant. As a result, the company abandoned the project, arguing that these and other changes the AEC required were too expensive. The last reprocessor left the market shortly after the Carter Administration suspended reprocessing indefinitely in 1977 in response to political groups who were concerned that reprocessing increased the possibilities of nuclear weapons proliferation by isolating plutonium, an essential weapons material, from other nuclear wastes (Campbell 1987b). Competition and the government's accessible policy process contributed significantly to the industry's demise. By 1978, storage for nuclear waste at reactor sites was filling up and utilities were beginning to worry that they would have to shut down their plants if something was not done soon to relieve the problem (Beckjord 1978: 16).

The search process

Corporations pioneered attempts to reduce many of these information and resource problems. For example, General Electric and Westinghouse decided to standardize a few of their reactor designs and asked the AEC in the late 1960s to approve these designs *before* they were sold to utilities. They planned that any utility could buy a preapproved, standardized reactor and avoid much of the AEC licensing review. In addition to speeding licensing, reactor manufacturers argued that standardization would reduce costs and materials shortages by enabling them to stockpile inventories of expensive components (Gartman 1968; Arnold and Grain 1972). The AEC rejected the proposal at first, arguing that plant designs had been changing too quickly due to the nuclear horsepower race and, as a result, were not refined enough to warrant eliminating design reviews for each plant (Ward 1977). However, manufacturers, architect-engineers, and utilities continued to press the AEC. The agency finally issued a standardization policy in 1972 to relieve its licensing logjam and to ease the financial problems the sector was beginning to experience (U.S. Atomic Energy Commission 1972, 1974: C–1). Officials accepted the preapproval scheme, promising to minimize future regulatory changes and speed up the licensing process for plants participating in the program (U.S. Atomic Energy Commission 1973: 92). The AEC also put a 1,300-megawatt ceiling on the size of all new reactors to end the nuclear horsepower race.

However, market competition severely limited attempts to standardize reactors. General Electric built a boiling-water reactor while its three competitors sold pressurized-water designs.[10] A more effective standardization program would have required the industry to adopt a single design. Of course, such a policy would force at least one reactor manufacturer, and perhaps three out of four, to leave the market (U.S. Office of Technology Assessment 1981: 68). None would have left voluntarily, and the government lacked the power to force a restructuring of the reactor manufacturing industry. After all, the AEC's mandate under the 1954 Act was to promote, not reduce, competition. Certainly, antitrust law would have presented additional legal obstacles to such an industrywide reorganization. As a result, not just one, but a variety of reactors continued to be available, depending on how many designs manufacturers submitted for pre-approval.[11]

Antitrust law also undermined efforts to standardize the nonnuclear portion of the plant. Before granting final preapproval for a plant design, the AEC required architect-engineers to submit blueprints so detailed as to virtually specify the brand name of certain components. Utilities feared that using a preapproved plan would eliminate competitive bidding on these components and leave the excluded component manufacturers little choice but to file antitrust suits against the utility companies involved (U.S. Senate 1978: 377). In addition, the utilities worried that limiting competition among these suppliers would lead to monopoly pricing and more expensive components (U.S. Office of Technology Assessment 1981: 304). As a result, most utilities refused to buy preapproved designs for the nonnuclear side of their plants. Different government policies, embodied in antitrust law and the AEC's standardization program, contradicted each other and prevented standardization from succeeding.

The competitive structure of capital markets helped constrain the utilities' search for a way to solve their capital shortage problem. Having failed to get much rate relief from the public utility commissions, utilities turned to the capital markets for additional financing. However, they had trouble competing with other industries. The utilities' earnings-to-investment ratios started to deteriorate in 1967 primarily because of their cash flow problems (U.S. Office of Technology Assessment 1984: 48). Raising capital through the sale of stocks and bonds, investing it in more construction, but not

---

10 Boiling- and pressurized-water reactors are variations of the basic light-water reactor concept. Boiling-water reactors permit water circulating in the reactor to boil and convert to steam in the reactor itself. Pressurized-water reactors do not allow water to boil in the reactor, but transfer the heat from the first cooling system through a heat exchanger to a second system that is allowed to boil and be converted to steam.

11 The French have been able to achieve a more complete level of standardization because the institutional constraints are different in that country. There is only one reactor manufacturer in France, so design competition is not a problem. Furthermore, the nationalized electric utility company is a state monopsony that has successfully demanded standardization (e.g., Lucas 1979: 88–9; Tanguy 1980). As a result, the French produce only a few different sizes of pressurized-water reactors.

being allowed to earn an immediate return on it by utility commissions only made matters worse. Eventually, the nuclear utilities' stock and bond ratings declined to a point where it became extremely difficult and expensive for them to raise more capital. In 1965, only 11% of the nation's major electric utilities held bond ratings at or below Moody's low Baa rating, one that discouraged investments in these utility companies. However, by 1975, half of the nation's utilities held that rating or one that was worse. Utility bond yields nearly doubled between 1965 and 1970, reflecting a rapid decline in their market strength (U.S. Department of Energy 1983a: 21). By 1967, utility debt was less attractive than most other industrial investment possibilities (Stich 1971: 21). The situation was most severe for utilities with the largest nuclear investments (Neese 1982). The same was true for stocks. In 1967, the average price-to-earnings ratio for utility stock, a measure of the amount of money investors were willing to pay for it, slipped below the average for most other industrial offerings (Stich 1971: 23; U.S. Department of Energy 1983a: 23). By 1972, the situation had deteriorated to a point beyond which many institutional investors were legally prohibited from further investment in these utility stocks (U.S. Department of Energy 1983a: 21).

To deal with the problem, some utilities formed joint ventures, long-term contractual agreements whereby a small group of companies agreed to purchase one or more plants together and share the electricity, as well as whatever costs and responsibilities were associated with it. Over 40% of the nuclear projects utilities initiated between 1970 and 1974 were joint ventures designed as a mechanism for utilities to pool their capital and finance nuclear construction cooperatively. Utilities organized only 28% of all their nuclear construction in this way between 1965 and 1969 (Perry et al. 1977: 39). Despite these efforts to share capital, the priorities of utility companies started shifting in 1972 away from expanding generating capacity and toward minimizing capital investments (Gandara 1977: 34; S. M. Stoller Corporation 1980: 21; U.S. House of Representatives 1981a: 80; U.S. Department of Energy 1983a: 25). Significantly, although utilities ordered a record thirty-two new nuclear plants in 1972, another more ominous trend developed as some began *canceling* orders for nuclear plants. They canceled seven that year. The short-term profit-maximizing logic of the capital market, coupled with utility commissions that were hesitant to grant full rate requests, contradicted the utilities long-term nuclear investment plans. The sector inched closer toward the brink of disaster.

The OPEC oil embargo in 1973–4 contributed to the move away from nuclear power by encouraging a national energy conservation drive that cut deeply into the demand for electricity. In 1974, the nation's electricity consumption declined for the first time ever – a dramatic switch from the 7% annual growth rates of the previous 15 years (U.S. General Accounting

Office 1981: 4). Consumption began growing again within a year, but never reached the old rate. In addition to aggravating the utilities' earnings squeeze by reducing revenues, the shortfall in electricity demand created an excess in generating capacity that further undermined the utilities' construction plans (U.S. Federal Energy Administration 1974: 3.3–3.6; Studness 1980: 54). Public service commissions, facing stiff consumer pressure, continued to deny utilities full rate relief (Gormley 1983: 96). So despite the brief surge in reactor ordering following the OPEC embargo, excess generating capacity, the drop in electricity consumption, and continuing capital shortages led to a rash of cancelations for all types of steam-generated electricity power plants. However, 75% of the generating capacity canceled between 1974 and 1981 was nuclear (U.S. Department of Energy 1983a: 5, 1983b: 4). Eventually, the bottom fell out of the nuclear market altogether. Utilities only ordered fifteen nuclear plants after 1974 and none after 1978 (U.S. Nuclear Regulatory Commission 1980).

The OPEC crisis and its effects did not cause the reactor market's decay, but they did exacerbate it. The decline in electricity demand growth rates and excess generating capacity do not explain the cancelation of seven nuclear plants in 1972 – before the OPEC embargo. Nor do they explain why utilities canceled nuclear capacity at an enormously higher rate than fossil-fueled plants. The governance regime that constrained so severely the options of utilities, trying to finance nuclear projects, explains both phenomena.[12] Recognizing that public utility commissions had played a key role in this drama, the federal government urged them to grant rate increases and allow capital sunk in construction work in progress to earn a return. However, utility commissions had legal autonomy in such matters and refused to cooperate (U.S. General Accounting Office 1980a, 1981).

In an attempt to cope with the problem of flagging regulatory legitimacy, Congress replaced the AEC in 1975, giving the Nuclear Regulatory Commission (NRC) responsibility for safety regulation and the Energy Research and Development Administration (ERDA) responsibility for energy development (Mazuzan and Trask 1979). This reorganization was an attempt to separate institutionally the AEC's two contradictory responsibilities, regulation and promotion. Furthermore, the newly elected Democratic majority in Congress replaced the JCAE in 1977 with twenty-eight new congressional committees and subcommittees, thereby fragmenting the state's authority further and providing antinuclear groups with even greater access to the policy process than had been available earlier through the courts, licensing procedures, and state-level politics (Bupp 1979; Barkenbus 1984b). Congress did this because it was concerned that members of

---

12 Utilities frequently used declining electricity demand as an excuse for dropping nuclear orders when the more important reason was insufficient finance capital (U.S. Senate 1974: 16; U.S. Department of Energy 1983a: 17).

the JCAE did not fully understand the technology, had worked too closely with the nuclear corporations, and that the committee was suffering from a terrible public image. The decision to abolish the JCAE was significant insofar as the new committees that replaced it were, at least occasionally, more critical of the sector's activities than the JCAE had been (Ford 1982: 226–7). However, despite the government's efforts to regain legitimacy, antinuclear groups around the country continued to struggle against the sector and public support for nuclear power continued to decline (Rankin et al. 1981: 30). In response, the Atomic Industrial Forum increased its public relations budget to $1.4 million in 1975, initiated a massive publicity campaign to promote nuclear power, and organized pronuclear campaigns to defeat antinuclear referenda in several states (Gyorgy 1979: 68; Hertsgaard 1983: 71). Nuclear supporters routinely outspent antinuclear groups two to one in referenda campaigns (Wasserman 1979: 59).

The federal government began trying more seriously to solve the waste management problem, doubling its waste management budget between 1974 and 1976 (U.S. Department of Energy 1981: 52). ERDA planned at first to store waste temporarily, but dropped the idea when the Environmental Protection Agency, the Council on Environmental Quality, and other environmental groups, including the Sierra Club, protested, fearing that such a facility might become a de facto permanent storage repository (U.S. General Accounting Office 1977). The situation deteriorated further in 1976 as several states started banning the long-term storage or disposal of high-level radioactive waste within their borders. California and a few others prohibited the construction of new nuclear plants until there was a federal waste management program in place (U.S. Nuclear Regulatory Commission 1981b, 1982b; Atomic Industrial Forum 1982). The Department of Energy proposed another temporary storage plan in 1977, but it became clear that antinuclear and environmentalist groups would try to block it (U.S. House of Representatives 1977: 102–13). The Carter Administration made a similar recommendation in 1979 (Interagency Review Group 1979: 62). Despite these efforts, the problem remained unsolved.

The effect of technology on governance transformations

The light-water reactor technology contributed to sectoral problems. Although dangerous accidents were possible in all kinds of reactors, they were especially troublesome in the light-water variety, particularly for failures in the reactor cooling system (Hendrie 1976: 673). This danger was the technical issue around which the AEC's legitimation crisis and subsequent reorganization revolved.

However, this is not to say that technology *caused* either the AEC's legitimation crisis or the agency's reorganization. The light-water reactor only provided the technical *possibility* for the legitimation crisis. Actors' decisions, as influenced by the prevailing governance regime, played a more determinant role. First, AEC administrators felt that nuclear power would only be a commercial success if it could survive in the marketplace. They worried that regulatory delays associated with the development of new safety criteria would undermine the technology's market appeal. As a result, they refused to take a more cautious approach to the safety issue. Second, as noted before, the earlier governance regime, in place from 1946 to 1963, had an important influence on the decision to adopt the light-water technology, rather than a safer one, in the first place. We have seen that in both cases the market-based interests of corporate actors constrained government decision making. Hence, the effect reactor technology problems had on governance between 1963 and 1979 highlights the market's dominance within the sector's governance regime, and the regime's dominance over technological factors insofar as governance transformations were concerned.

The contradictions of governance

Contradictions developed *between* governance mechanisms during this period in ways that undermined the efficient distribution of resources and information within the sector. For example, contradictions developed between short-term price signals in several markets, on the one hand, and the interests the government, actors organized in promotional networks, and corporations had in planning solutions to the sector's problems, on the other. The market's logic often prevailed and constrained the search process. For example, competition undermined the standardization effort and attempts by the AEC and various corporations to resolve labor, materials, and capital scarcities by reducing plant costs and regulatory uncertainties. Competition with other industries in the capital markets helped prevent the utilities from solving their capital scarcity problem and achieving the long-range financial stability required to sustain the nuclear expansion. Competition within the reprocessing industry helped eliminate reprocessing as an outlet for the utilities' nuclear wastes. Finally, tensions between actors in promotional networks, particularly the national laboratories, and the government contributed to the AEC's legitimation crisis and the attendant information problems that flowed from it.

The state's role was especially important during this period inasmuch as the contradictions *within* agencies specifically dealing with nuclear power generated serious problems of sectoral governance. The AEC's dual mandate, promoting the industry while guarding the public safety, contributed to the agency's legitimation crisis and one of the few governance transformations during this period. The public utility commissions were responsible for protecting the utilities' economic well-being, but also for ensuring that utilities did not charge their customers excessively high rates.

Most commissions straddled the fence, granting only partial rate increases when requested. As a result, they contributed to the utilities' earnings squeeze and capital crisis. In both cases, these contradictions appeared as part of the state's role in establishing and enforcing the specific rules within which other actors operated.

However, contradictions also appeared within the state between the policies and policy processes of *specific* nuclear agencies, on the one hand, and those of a more *general* nature, on the other. These contradictions helped constrain the search for solutions to the sector's problems. General antitrust policy helped undermine the sector's standardization program. The requirements of the National Environmental Policy Act, as interpreted by the Supreme Court in 1971, helped subvert the sector's efforts to reduce nuclear plant licensing times. Furthermore, the state's fragmented, decentralized, and increasingly accessible organization exacerbated these difficulties as environmentalists and antinuclear groups pressed their demands on policy makers through a variety of arenas, such as the courts and legislatures at all levels of government – forums generally available to many interest groups, not just those concerned with nuclear power. Such political accessibility also provided opportunities for these groups to undermine the search for solutions to problems, such as utility financing and the absence of a nuclear waste disposal facility.

SELF-REGULATION BY ASSOCIATIONS AND NETWORKS, 1979–87

The third governance regime

Although the number of joint ventures in which utilities engaged had increased, the governance regime had not changed substantially between 1963 and 1979. Markets and corporations continued to be the dominant governance mechanisms that constrained sectoral behavior in ways that perpetuated the absence of new nuclear orders as well as the cancellations of old ones. The state continued to exert its influence in a variety of ways, primarily through NRC and public utility commission regulation, but it seemed that there was still nothing state actors could do to convince utilities to start buying nuclear plants again. In fact, the most significant institutional change was the abolition of the AEC and JCAE, transformations that provided antinuclear groups with greater access to the policy process and a stronger role in sectoral governance, on the one hand, and that undermined the sector's congressional support, on the other, but that did not alter the balance among governance mechanisms per se. Actors who operated through networks and associations continued to exert only limited influence by comparison. However, this would soon change.

On March 28, 1979, a reactor at Three Mile Island in Pennsylvania suffered the worst commercial nuclear accident in U.S. history. Corporations throughout the sector recognized that another accident like this would bury commercial nuclear power forever in the United States (Hertsgaard 1983: 186). In response, they mobilized through associations and promotional networks to counterbalance the self-interested logic of individual corporations and competitive markets, bilateral forms of governance, and to coordinate more effectively sectoral activity. They moved quickly to restore public confidence in nuclear power, to improve the technology's quality, safety, and operating efficiency, and to solve a new insurance problem discovered after the accident. Despite their efforts, utilities canceled another forty-eight nuclear plants between 1979 and 1982, 82% of all the generating capacity that was dropped during these years and a clear indication that markets and corporations were still the dominant governance mechanisms (Catalano 1982; U.S. Department of Energy 1983a: 5, 1983b: 4). The state's influence over sectoral affairs increased as the NRC suspended plant licensing for about a year and issued a barrage of new regulations that were intended to improve plant safety.

Sectoral problems

Resource scarcities flourished. The accident made Wall Street investors even more skeptical about the profitability of nuclear investments than they had been earlier. The immediate damage to the Three Mile Island plant was estimated at $1.6 billion, not including personal liability claims or the cost of buying replacement power to compensate for the burned out reactor (U.S. Nuclear Regulatory Commission 1982b: 1–3). As a result, bond ratings for nuclear utilities dropped again, making it even more difficult and expensive for them to raise capital for nuclear projects (Hertsgaard 1983: 148). Insurance problems exacerbated the nuclear utilities' financial woes. The Three Mile Island plant had carried $300 million in property insurance, the maximum amount available and the amount commonly accepted as adequate by the sector. It was apparent that utilities were grossly underinsured, but additional coverage was not available.

The accident also caused, increased, and revealed serious information scarcities and other problems. First, the NRC's new regulatory requirements created severe licensing delays. As a result, plant and operating costs increased further and standardization became even more elusive (Komanoff 1981; Barkenbus 1984a: A–2; Szalay 1984: 300; U.S. Office of Technology Assessment 1984: 124). Second, investigations revealed that several of the technical problems that caused the accident had happened earlier at other plants. Utilities had reported these problems as they occurred to the NRC, but regulators had not disseminated that information effectively to utilities even though the agency had a system that was supposed to do that (Ford 1981; U.S. Office of Technology Assessment

1984: 121). Third, studies also reported that the quality of management, construction, and operation of nuclear plants by some utilities was unacceptable (Barkenbus 1984a: 5–6). Finally, new legitimation problems developed. Polls showed that public opposition to nuclear power increased significantly after the accident (Rankin et al. 1984). Antinuclear groups staged rallies around the country and two government investigations raised doubts publicly about the NRC's ability to regulate effectively (e.g., President's Commission on the Accident at Three Mile Island 1979; U.S. Nuclear Regulatory Commission Special Inquiry Group 1980). Forty-three legal suits were pending against the NRC by 1981. Most of these objected to the agency's regulations and procedures, indicating that it was not just the legitimacy of nuclear corporations and utilities that was suffering, but also that of the NRC (Barkenbus 1984a: B–7).

Unrelated to the accident, the Supreme Court ruled in 1983 that any public utility commission could refuse to grant permission for a utility to build a nuclear plant if the utility could not determine accurately the costs of radioactive waste management. Because, in the absence of permanent waste disposal facilities, no one knew what these costs would be, the ruling posed a massive obstacle to the rejuvenation of a market for nuclear plants. Even before then, Wall Street investors were reticent about investing in nuclear utilities because of the waste problem (U.S. House of Representatives 1980: 117). This uncertainty suddenly assumed new proportions that exacerbated the capital shortage problem.

The search process

Within two weeks of the accident, the Edison Electric Institute, other utility associations, and the Atomic Industrial Forum established the Three Mile Island Ad Hoc Oversight Committee, a promotional network of utility executives and other sector leaders organized to solve the problems that the accident had exposed. In turn, the Oversight Committee created a promotional network of public relations personnel from several utilities in 1979 called the U.S. Committee for Energy Awareness to renew the sector's legitimacy. Using advertising as its primary tool the Committee for Energy Awareness tried to convince the business community and the public that the sector would strive to operate more safely and that America needed nuclear power to reduce its dependence on foreign oil (Hertsgaard 1983: 187–90; Mills and Mills 1983: 27–30). By 1983, the Committee had a $27 million annual operating budget, four times the estimated budgets of all antinuclear organizations combined (U.S. Office of Technology Assessment 1984: 214). In addition, the Atomic Industrial Forum spent $2.2 million a year keeping the press, opinion leaders, and the sector abreast of events and information it considered important (Mills and Mills 1983).

The Oversight Committee created the Institute for Nuclear Power Operations (INPO), an association of all nuclear utilities and some suppliers, to correct problems in utility operation, management, construction, and quality-assurance practices. INPO began inspecting plants regularly and recommending improvements to the utility's management. INPO relied on executives from other utilities and members of its own staff to persuade management to comply with these recommendations for the sector's sake. This peer pressure appears to have been effective in most cases (e.g., Cook 1986: 54), but, if it fails, INPO has said that it is prepared to ask insurance companies to *force* the utility to comply by threatening to raise the utility's premiums or by considering a reduction in its insurance coverage (Barkenbus 1984a: 11).[13] INPO also tried to improve the sector's safety and operation by establishing a computerized communication network called "nuclear notepad" that disseminated information about important technical and managerial problems discovered by its members. This self-regulation scheme was intended to improve the spotty performances of individual utilities, correct the deficiencies in the NRC's information-sharing system, and elevate the industry's operating standards overall so as to prevent another major reactor accident (U.S. Office of Technology Assessment 1984: 130–4).

The utilities and INPO searched for ways to improve the sector's performance through more research. INPO formed a monitoring arrangement with the NRC, through a formal "memorandum of understanding," where they coordinated research efforts and exchanged information with each other (Barkenbus 1984a: 10–11; U.S. Office of Technology Assessment 1984: 130). The utilities established the Nuclear Safety Analysis Center to study the technical aspects of the accident and other safety matters. The Safety Center soon developed a system for evaluating technical problems occurring at individual plants and reporting that information through channels, including the nuclear notepad, to other plant operators, if necessary, something the NRC had failed to do effectively before Three Mile Island. The Electric Power Research Institute, a research organization formed by the electric utilities in 1973 to conduct long-term, mostly nonnuclear, research that was too expensive for the companies to perform individually, supervised the Safety Center's activities (Walsh 1973; Starr 1983). The Safety Center worked closely with INPO and was a member of the NRC and INPO monitoring agreement (U.S. Office of Technology Assessment 1984: 130–4). Both INPO and the Safety Center seemed to be serious

---

13 Whether INPO will ask insurers to do this is unclear. According to a former vice president at INPO interviewed for this study, although INPO says it is prepared to report serious problems to insurers, it had not done so by 1983, despite the reluctance of a few utilities to adopt INPO recommendations. On the other hand, Nuclear Electric Insurance Limited, one of the principal insurance providers for the sector, has access to INPO's plant inspection reports if it chooses to use it.

attempts to solve the sector's new problems. Their budgets for 1980 were $11 million and $7.5 million, respectively (*EPRI Journal* 1979a, 1979b).

The sector tried to cope with problems associated with the NRC's response to the accident in two ways. According to one NRC staff member, interviewed for this study, reactor manufacturers, utilities, and architect-engineers recognized that regulatory changes were inevitable after the accident and consulted almost daily on an individual basis with the NRC in an effort to convince the agency to implement these changes on a schedule compatible with the utilities' needs. The Atomic Industrial Forum and the reactor manufacturers also lobbied the NRC and the Reagan Administration to speed up licensing (Szalay 1984: 300). Apparently, it worked. Congress discovered in 1981 that the NRC was trying so hard to increase the pace of licensing that the agency was neglecting several important safety projects (U.S. House of Representatives 1981b).

The waste problem continued to stymie the sector's resurgence. After trying for nearly three years, Congress passed legislation in 1982 with a strong push from the American Nuclear Energy Council, the Atomic Industrial Forum's lobbying arm, directing the Department of Energy to develop waste management facilities. However, to muster enough support to ensure passage of the bill, Congress created an institutional opportunity for political stalemate by granting any state or Indian reservation, designated as a potential waste disposal site, the opportunity to veto that selection (Barlett and Steele 1985: Chap. 5). The Reagan Administration tried to help generate a solution to the waste problem by lifting Carter's reprocessing ban and offering the nation's military waste to anyone interested in building a reprocessing plant. However, the Edison Electric Institute and the American Nuclear Energy Council vehemently opposed the plan, fearing that any affiliation with the nuclear weapons program would only hurt the sector's already tarnished image (Hertsgaard 1983: 242–3). To date, nobody has accepted the administration's offer.

The sector also tried to reduce resource scarcities. The utilities organized an insurance pool in 1973, Nuclear Mutual Limited, to supplement the property insurance utilities had traditionally purchased from a consortium of insurance companies. They formed another pool in 1978, Nuclear Electric Insurance Limited, to provide insurance for replacement power if an accident knocked out a reactor. Both were incorporated associations. When the sector discovered the problem of insufficient insurance after the accident, the new pools and the utilities' traditional insurance sources offered substantially expanded coverage. By 1982, nuclear utilities could buy $740 million in property insurance and $187 million in replacement power insurance per site, a figure still well below the estimated damages suffered at Three Mile Island, but much higher than had been available previously (U.S. Nuclear Regulatory Commission 1982b).

In addition to lobbying Wall Street, some utilities, struggling with the finance problem, persuaded their public utility commissions to grant larger rate increases and allow some capital invested in nuclear construction work in progress to earn a return. They argued that this was necessary to avoid "rate shock," a single massive rate increase, when the plant finally began to operate. Nevertheless, eight state legislatures prohibited their utility commissions from granting the latter request. The depreciation allowances and investment tax credits offered by the 1981 Economic Recovery Act also helped reduce capital shortages, making investment in utilities somewhat more attractive (U.S. Office of Technology Assessment 1984: 50–6), but not enough to stimulate nuclear ordering, at least as of this writing.

The effect of technology on governance transformations

Although the accident sparked this governance transformation, it would be a mistake to argue that the technological problems involved were the only cause of the ensuing changes in governance. The accident was only possible in a plant based on the light-water reactor technology – a technology selected because of the governance regime that was in place during the 1950s and early 1960s. Furthermore, the NRC and the utilities failed to recognize and respond to warnings earlier at other plants that such an accident could occur. Hence, although problems associated with the light-water reactor did cause the accident in an immediate sense and, therefore, contributed to the manifestation of several new problems with which the sector had to cope, the sector's governance regime played an even greater role, just as they had during the AEC's legitimation crisis. In short, the accident and the governance transformations that followed were more the result of problems with the sector's governance regime than they were the result of a technology failure per se.

The contradictions of governance

For the first time since the early years of the sector's development, the governance regime began to assume a more multilateral character, shifting substantially as actors began to organize new associations, promotional networks, and monitoring agreements in a major effort to help better coordinate sectoral activity. Working through associations and promotional networks, actors tried desperately to rejuvenate the sector's legitimacy by mounting public relations, lobbying, and advertising campaigns. They also assumed greater responsibility for managing the sector's business practices by trying to improve utility management, construction, and safety procedures, by providing more insurance coverage, by pushing for nuclear waste management legislation, and by coordinating research and regulation with the NRC. Three Mile Island had triggered a crisis and then a search process that stressed the sector's fundamental, collective interest in long-term survival, rather than the more particularistic, short-sighted interests of its individual members that tended to prevail during the previous period, and that were institutionalized in a governance regime that was dominated by bilateral governance mechanisms. As a result, actors mobilized through multilateral forms of governance that assumed a more important role in coordinating the exchange of critical resources and information.

However, contradictions emerged again between and within governance mechanisms that constrained the ability of actors to search successfully for solutions to their problems. For example, one former INPO executive told me that his organization had never been completely effective in improving utility performance because it was a voluntary organization and did not have the coercive tools necessary to force utilities to comply with its recommendations when peer pressure failed. Furthermore, despite attempts by corporations, associations, and actors who were organized through networks to control the regulatory situation, the NRC promulgated a wave of new regulations that contributed to increased licensing delays and plant costs (Komanoff 1981). On the other hand, through their ties with the NRC, corporations convinced the agency to pull its regulatory punch enough so that it neglected some of its safety research programs. Once again the state seemed to be torn between guarding the public's safety and ensuring the viability of the nuclear sector. Nevertheless, despite the sector's creative efforts to revive itself through a variety of innovative, private, self-regulatory governance mechanisms, utilities continued to refuse to buy nuclear plants.

Conflicting interests between different levels of government continued to undermine the search for solutions to older problems. The Department of Energy has, as yet, been unable to choose a permanent waste disposal site because state-level governments have threatened to use their veto power in addition to filing suits, passing laws, and using a variety of other general institutional opportunities to prevent their states from being selected. Much of this opposition stems from suspicions as to whether the Department of Energy is trying to pick sites that are geologically sound or just politically expedient (Campbell 1988: Chap. 7). As noted before, in some cases, state legislatures also forbade public utility commissions from allowing utilities to charge their customers for construction work in progress, thereby helping to perpetuate the utilities' capital shortage problem. Ironically, the absence of a market for nuclear plants continued to be the sector's most fundamental problem during the 1980s, just as it had been thirty years earlier.

DISCUSSION

We saw earlier that some theorists of economic governance argued that problems of resource and information scarcity cause changes in the institutional means for coordinating sectoral activity. Yet they often failed to explain what causes these problems in the first place. Others tried to provide an explanation by attributing resource and information problems to changes in product and production technologies, and to changes in characteristics of the firm. Building on these insights, I have shown that the contradictory tendencies of governance mechanisms, both individually and in combination, also cause resource and information scarcity problems that eventually lead to governance transformations.

However, the presence of institutional contradictions and sectoral problems are not sufficient conditions for a governance transformation. Transformations only occurred in the nuclear sector when actors deliberately tried to change these arrangements through search processes. They often did this after recognizing that a transformation was vital to the sector's long-term survival. In the 1950s, the government and corporations realized that a market for reactor technology would not materialize automatically, even though there was a product that was apparently ready for commercialization, and that there would not be a nuclear sector unless they deliberately created such a market. In the 1980s, members of the sector's trade associations saw that unless they moved to rejuvenate the sector's legitimacy and improve operations after Three Mile Island, there was a good chance that the sector would never recover from its ordering hiatus. On the other hand, although serious problems developed between 1963 and 1979, actors did not perceive them as being a fundamental threat to the sector's existence. Hence, they did not try to transform the governance regime in any *fundamental* way, that is, by altering the relations of relative dominance among governance mechanisms. Instead, actors searched for solutions within the *existing* governance regime. For example, they reorganized the AEC, an important institutional change, but not one that altered appreciably the governance regime. As a result, in addition to the structural preconditions I have described, it appears that the perception of a fundamental crisis, a major threat to the sector's overall viability, is also necessary to trigger a major transformation of governance, at least in this sector. Of course, it is possible that even when some of the actors involved see a crisis and try to change the governance regime they will be unsuccessful if others are powerful enough to block the attempt. This happened in 1956 when utilities, their trade association, and others defeated the JCAE's bid to pass legislation that would have allowed the government to build its own nuclear plants, thereby renewing the state's dominance within the sector.

It is interesting that every time actors perceived a fundamental sectoral crisis they began to rely more on governance mechanisms with the institutional capacity for long-term, sectorwide planning. State agencies with a high degree of autonomy dominated governance during the first period and were primarily responsible for the major shift to a market- and corporate-dominated sector. After the accident at Three Mile Island, actors began to use associations, promotional networks, and other multilateral arrangements more often, although the market and corporations continued to be the most dominant forces. This supports those who argued that associational (e.g., Miles 1982; Willmott 1985) and state (e.g., Habermas 1973; Wolfe 1977) activities increase in response to sectoral crises. After all, actors have greater potential to plan and coordinate activity in terms of the sector's long-term, collective interests if they use the state and multilateral forms of governance, such as associations and promotional networks, than if they rely exclusively on bilateral forms, specifically markets and corporations (e.g., Streeck and Schmitter 1985).

However, it is still not clear why actors used associations, rather than the state, to come to the sector's rescue after the accident. The answer is that influential members of nuclear corporations, associations, and other private groups believed that the NRC was incapable of managing the sector's new problems effectively. Indeed, the accident proved that the NRC had not been able to ensure the sector's safe and efficient operation in the first place.[14] Furthermore, the NRC faced its own severe legitimation problems and was in no position to help renew the legitimacy of the sector as a whole. In short, state officials had been unable to secure the political and economic stability that theorists have recognized as necessary for an economic sector's continued viability (e.g., O'Connor 1973; Offe 1975). Associations tried to fill that role by undertaking public relations and advertising campaigns to restore sectoral legitimacy, and by creating new organizations to improve safety and economic efficiency. This suggests that when states are relatively incapacitated during times of sectoral crisis, associations or other forms of multilateral industrial organizations may rise to the occasion and assume a greater share of these regulatory responsibilities.

Those who study corporatism argued that associational behavior is often an attempt by the private sector to avoid state intervention (Schmitter 1984; Streeck and Schmitter 1985). They also argued that if the state is sufficiently weak and fragmented, it is unable to foster, sanction, and legitimize associations as central actors in the governance process. The growth of associational governance will be stunted as a result (Salisbury 1979). However, associational activity developed more extensively in the

---

14 Representatives from the Atomic Industrial Forum, the Electric Power Research Institute, INPO, the Nuclear Safety Analysis Center, and the Three Mile Island Ad Hoc Oversight Committee, who helped establish and organize INPO and the Nuclear Safety Analysis Center, testified before Congress and reported to me during interviews that they realized after the accident that government regulation was insufficient to ensure plant safety and successful operation, and that the private sector must assume an active self-regulating role as a result (U.S. House of Representatives 1979a: 17; 1979b: 13; U.S. Senate 1979: 280).

nuclear sector after 1979 precisely because the state was *incapable* of conferring legitimacy on the sector when it was especially necessary. Furthermore, in this case, associational behavior was not the private sector's response to a potentially strong and active state, as corporatist theories suggest, but was the private sector's attempt to cope with problems it felt the state could *not* fix. Contrary to corporatist theory, in this case, the weak nature of the state actually facilitated the elevation of associations to a more prominent position within the governance regime. Indeed, actors who were instrumental in establishing INPO and the Nuclear Safety Analysis Center told how they recognized that increased NRC regulation was inevitable after the accident and that they could do little, if anything, to alter it through such organizations. Instead, we have seen that their concern and motivation for establishing these organizations was in part that the NRC did not have the technical or managerial capability to prevent another accident and the financial consequences it would entail. Apparently, the state's effect in encouraging the formation of associational behavior may be more complex than corporatist theory has recognized. During times of sectoral crisis, it is possible for associations to become important governance mechanisms even though the state does not deliberately encourage their activity.[15]

As noted in Chapter 1, the state plays a unique, multidimensional role in economic governance, often influencing the governance process in several conceptually and institutionally distinct ways. The history of the nuclear sector supports that argument. Policies developed in political arenas specifically designed to deal with the nuclear sector and policies developed in other state arenas with a more general focus had important and often contradictory effects on governance in the sector. For example, general antitrust legislation set important limits on the AEC's standardization effort, a program targeted specifically at the nuclear sector.[16]

However, the institutional organization of the state also had another very important effect on governance. The state's fragmented and decentralized organization provided political groups, previously excluded from the governance process, opportunities to participate. This often occurred in an escalating pattern. When nuclear critics could not influence governance satisfactorily through political channels dedicated just to nuclear policy, they turned to institutional means at a more general level. For example, when antinuclear groups could not convince the AEC through licensing hearings and other regulatory forums to toughen reactor safety system requirements enough to meet their standards, they resorted to court

---

15 For further discussion and defense of this argument, see Campbell (1989).

16 See Benson (1982) for a discussion about the importance of studying how general political and economic rule systems intersect more sector-specific ones with significant consequences for sectoral governance.

suits and congressional lobbying (Campbell 1988: Chap. 5). Although antinuclear and other grassroots political groups are not considered to be governance mechanisms in this study, they did have considerable influence insofar as they contributed to the development of governance problems and limited the options available to sectoral actors searching for solutions. Hence, the state played a unique role relative to the governance mechanisms that were described in Chapter 1, not only because its effects on the governance process originated from a variety of different institutional locations, but also because it served as a gatekeeper, regulating the access of outside political groups to the governance process. Indeed, to the extent that this pattern occurs in other economic sectors, the state has a very special role in the governance process.

THE STATIST EVOLUTION OF RAIL GOVERNANCE IN THE UNITED STATES, 1830–1986

Robert Dawson Kennedy, Jr.
The Madison Institute

As American capitalism's oldest major enterprise, the 155-year-old railroad industry offers a special opportunity for theorists to test hypotheses of governance and state intervention on a wide range of governance trans-formations. The history of railroad governance includes some of the earliest American developments of governance mechanisms, such as associations and corporate integration, as well as different forms of state intervention. It also provides an opportunity to examine long-term trends in an industry's governance transformations.

This chapter uses the existing literature to offer a new analysis of rail gov-ernance. The distinct characteristics of the rail industry, including the steep-ness of its capital and technical requirements, led from a state-sanctioned, but relatively free-market governance regime to others that were progres-sively less private and less market-controlled. Triggered at each critical junc-ture by recurrent performance crises, this evolution proceeded in five stages, moving from what I call private capitalist governance through two stages of negative state intervention to positive, or proactive, state intervention, and finally to the more recent attempts to reverse state intervention. Two factors have been most critical in driving this evolutionary process toward state-dominated governance. The first has been the special "density" and mobili-zation of competing class and intraclass interests. The mobilization of small shippers and rail workers created governance problems that could not be solved by any private institution. The second factor has been the state itself. Once it became an important part of the governance process, the institu-tional requirements and capacity of the state regarding the railroads increas-ingly exerted independent pressures for solutions to rail governance crises that involved the state (see Kennedy 1985).

THE SPECIAL NATURE OF THE RAILROAD INDUSTRY

Before explaining this history, it is worth noting the unique technical, capital, labor, operational, and coordination characteristics of the railroad industry. None of these things can be considered causes per se for the development of particular governance regimes. For example, the industry's need for standard, safe rail car couplings at the end of the nineteenth century did not of itself require the solution of state intervention instead of some action on the part of private rail associations. Yet this and other nature-of-the-industry requirements did define the context within which dynamic factors such as the mobilization of interest groups and economic crises interacted to produce governance transformations.

Density of interests and transactions in the railroad industry

The railroad industry is relatively unique in having been intimately involved for almost a century with most of the U.S. population and their economic interests. Indeed, the railroads at one time employed enough workers to play a critical role in the development of U.S. labor relations in general. Likewise, it played such an important role in the early development of most segments of American business that it is often described as the motor for U.S. industrial development. As I argue later, this uniquely high density of business and labor interests predisposed the railroad industry, contingent upon the mobilization of the interests involved, to state intervention as a means of solving its governance dilemmas. In short, if any industry was going to require the attention of the state, then if would surely have been the rail industry.

Because the rail industry is comprised of relations and transactions between groups of actors with so many often contradictory interests, it is not surprising that most analyses have tended to concentrate on one of these relations, or even a particular transaction within a relation, to the relative exclusion of others. Kolko (1965), for example, concentrates on certain interventions regarding price regulations for freight shippers, but spends little or no time deciphering antitrust or labor regulations. This piecemeal approach has resulted in various contradictory conclusions regarding the character and etiology of rail governance transformations. This chapter makes a special effort to include all major industry transactions, improving the possibility of constructing a truly comprehensive analysis of the evolution of rail governance.

The analysis that follows pays special attention to the governance of transactions that occurs between rail companies and a variety of other actors in the industry. These relationships are illustrated in Figure 5.1, and include transactions between rail companies and (1) other rail companies in the same service region and nationally; (2) customers, such as passengers and large and small freight shippers, including farmers; (3) rail workers; (4) finance agencies, such as banks; (5) equipment and energy suppliers, including manufacturers of fixed and rolling equipment, and coal suppliers; and (6) other carriers, such as canals, steamships lines, truckers, airlines, and buses.

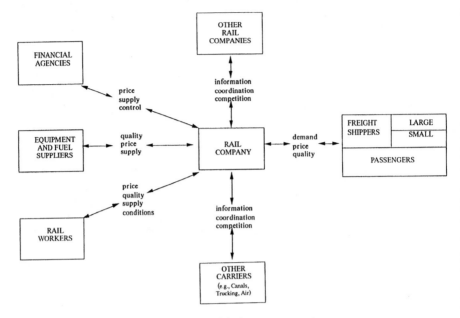

Figure 5.1   Railroad industry transactions.

Unique industry requirements

Due to its unique characteristics, the railroad industry confronted special governance problems. First, the industry had enormous capital requirements. This feature made it a dominant competitor for public as well as private monies, and made it vulnerable to dominance by financial institutions as well as the state during times of performance crises. A high level of capital investment created a strong incentive to ensure that there was enough demand to keep service running at full capacity. During its history, the industry used many ploys, including standardization and the purchases of coal companies, steamship and canal boat lines, to secure the necessary volume of freight traffic.

Second, although railroads were the largest and most dispersed companies of their time, they were also labor-intensive, especially during construction. As Alfred Chandler (1965: 129) observes, the relative scarcity of labor gave workers considerable power, which was further enhanced by the industry's need for relatively skilled operators. This situation, in combination with the industry's high fixed costs, made the railroads significantly vulnerable to strikes by key workers. In short, the nature of the industry facilitated the organization of rail workers. As a result, rail worker mobilization became one of the dominant influences on rail governance.

Third, the railroad industry had state-of-the-art technical requirements, especially during the first fifty to sixty years of its development. The railroads were the first to tackle such problems as designing standard, reliable, and safe couplings between heavy moving vehicles. Similarly, the development of increasingly more powerful, efficient, and reliable locomotives and the construction of thousands of bridges and tunnels, capable of handling the demands of rail traffic, required the solution of technical and engineering problems of a type and on a scale that surpassed any confronting industry up to that time.

Fourth, as a consequence of both its scale and its long-distance through-traffic capacity, that is, the potential to transport freight and passengers over long distances by transferring them from one line to another, the railroad industry had unprecedented coordination requirements. In part, this organizational problem had technical implications. For instance, to take advantage of its through-traffic capabilities, the industry needed to standardize the gauge of its rails and rolling stock, and in order to provide efficiency and safety, it was necessary to discover some way to overcome the obstacles created by the diverse ownership of different sections of the nation's rail network. Beyond this, the industry needed to organize among its operational units to minimize competition, increase the smooth flow of information and traffic signals, standardize freight rates, and much more. Chandler (1965) discusses many of these points and their implications for the development of corporate hierarchies that arose to deal with the management requirements of the complex and dispersed operations within individual rail companies. These organizational requirements of scale and through traffic also had implications for intercompany governing institutions.

The state context in the early years

Although British and other European rail companies had to accept national regulations to get their charters and rights-of-way in the early 1800s, this was not the case in the United States. Although the U.S. government provided huge land grants to help capitalize much of the rail industry in relatively unsettled western, midwestern, and southern territories, these subsidies came without strings attached (e.g., Haney 1910; Savage 1959; Bagwell 1970; Carson 1971). That is, although the state provided the foundation for a free market through such things as the protection of property rights, mechanisms for the chartering and legal disposition of corporations as well as specific subsidies and other supports for a few private accumulation projects with infrastructural value, it did not attempt to govern pricing, investment practices, or the coordination of different interests concerned with the industry. In short, the state at this time did not move beyond what I would call environmental governance, and, as Carson (1971: 20) remarks, in most respects, the rail industry was on its own with respect to governance at its inception.

State governments did try to intervene by passing and attempting to enforce rail regulations. However, the decentralized, federal structure of the U.S. state allowed the rail industry to escape the fetters of state regulation until the early twentieth century. As the first industry to have big corporations, the railroads were singularly capable of executing ferocious campaigns to defeat legislation at the level of individual state governments. Moreover, when statutes, such as the granger laws, were passed by some states, the interstate nature of rail operation made these restrictions largely ineffective because the rail companies could not be prevented from boycotting the offending state in some fashion or otherwise subjecting the state to unbearable service discriminations.

In the end, the crazy-quilt patchwork of regulations imposed by different states made coherent rail governance, and often the efficient operation of through traffic, generally impossible (e.g., Meyer 1903; Benson 1955; Miller 1971). This state-structured predicament was fairly unique to the United States. In Britain, where the state was more centralized, all interventions affecting rails necessarily came from Parliament. Regulations began there at the inception of the industry, were completed twenty years before they were in the United States, and were more effective as well (e.g., Jagtani 1924; Alderman 1973: 32–43; Aldcroft 1974: 31–52; Bagwell 1974: 177, 503–4).

STAGE ONE: THE EVOLUTION OF PRIVATE CAPITALIST GOVERNANCE, 1830–84

In the first stage of rail governance, rail companies attempted to escape the dangers and instability of the market by formally organizing the relations between various parts of their industry according to their own private capitalist requirements. This period was characterized by the rise of industry administrative and rail professionals' associations, rate pooling, and the drive to concentrate via horizontal rail mergers and the purchase of other carriers as well as major freight sources, such as coal companies. (Table 5.1 summarizes the major features of this and the other four stages in the overall analysis of the evolution of rail governance.) Ultimately, this process was interrupted at the turn of the century by the mobilization of other interests and the consequent actions of the state.

Associations and promotional networks

Although they remained active throughout the history of U.S. railroads, associations and, to an extent, promotional networks are perhaps most noteworthy for the *transitional* role they seem to have played in the transformation of rail governance. Relatively easy to create, these multilateral forms of governance were among the first governance mechanisms in evi-

Table 5.1. *Summary sketch of five-stage evolution of rail governance*

Stage	Dates	Dominant characteristic	Dominant governance problem	Factors behind specific governance innovation	Governance innovation
Stage one	1830–86	State-sanctioned private/capitalist governance	• Through-traffic coordination • Initial investment • Old carrier competition	• Rail company and capitalist hegemony	• Phase one and two corporate integration • Associations: professionals, intercompany • Corporate integration of other carriers and traffic sources
Stage two	1887–1919	Negative state governance	• Small shipper and rail worker problems • Excess capacity	• Mobilization of small shippers, antimonopoly forces, and rail workers	• Negative federal regulations • Employer associations
Stage three	1920–65	Negative state governance stalemate	• Market contraction from new carrier competition • Negative governance • Excess capacity	• Stronger but incomplete state or rail company power • New carriers	• Inconsequential reregulating and emergency loans
Stage four	1966–75	Proactive state	• Insolvency • Excess capacity • Uncoordinated governance policies	• Downwardly sticky state mechanisms	• Proactive state: DOT, takeovers (Amtrak, Conrail)
Stage five	1976–86	Attempted return to private governance	• Excess capacity • Restricted market reaction options	• State takeover of worst performers • Remobilization of capitalists	• Partial deregulation and possible reprivatization

dence in the rail industry. They were often the industry's first response to any governance problem, but were also unable to permanently solve any of these more difficult problems. For the most part, they gave way to other governance mechanisms, particularly corporate hierarchies, and to various forms of state intervention.

It is useful to identify three groups of these multilateral arrangements: so-called railroad company associations, including pools, peak or interrail company umbrella associations, and associations of railroad professionals. As opposed to rail professionals associations, rail company associations were by definition more powerful organizations since they were established specifically to coordinate problems between different companies. Although our information about the earliest of these associations is very poor, it seems that from at least the Civil War, when through traffic became a goal, administrative pools were being utilized to coordinate traffic when rail cars, owned by one company, needed to pass over tracks that were owned by other companies. However, these pools do not seem to have been anything more than working agreements between companies (Clark 1966: 3) and, thus, resemble a form of promotional network, rather than associations per se. Moreover, McPhearson (1912) writes that most rail companies were actually quite indisposed to the idea of pooling rolling stock and sharing track use. Ultimately, it took an act of Congress in 1866, expressly allowing, although not compelling, these practices to spur them into regular use. In fairly short order, these administrative pools were apparently replaced by separate through-line companies in the later 1860s, which coordinated the shipping of freight over different company lines (McPhearson 1912: 162–4; Cochran 1965: 167–8). Hence, administrative pools seem to have been transitional coordination devices that were eventually replaced by mechanisms with more legitimate status, such as legal corporate entities.

Similarly, what are sometimes referred to as the first rate associations seen after the Civil War were not really much more than loose and invariably very ephemeral agreements between competing companies. Among the different types of these loose agreements traffic pools were apparently more definite arrangements, dealing in a relatively formal way with the division of traffic and revenues (Campbell 1938: 17; Ripley 1920: 575–606; Cochran 1965: 167). Rail historians do not classify any of these arrangements prior to 1870 as associations in any recognizable institutional sense. In 1870, a pool was founded to divide passenger traffic among companies servicing the Chicago/Omaha route, and "by the middle eighties pools were regarded as the normal means of regulating competition" (Cochran 1965: 168). As extralegal arrangements, however, they were unenforceable and thus very short-lived, typically lasting only one to three years, and not reaching their full associational form until the next stage in the industry's history. Even then, the rail companies sought to replace these formal associations via mergers with their own permanent intercorporate hierarchies.

An equally important development took place with the establishment of the first interrail company umbrella organization, which eventually became the American Railroad Association (ARA). Founded in 1873 as the General Time Convention (GTC), this body of over 100 rail companies met on a fairly regular basis to coordinate scheduling, signaling, and the different aspects of through-traffic connections. Their first major act during this stage was to establish the Interline Uniform Time Tables in 1874 (Clark 1966: 4, 204–6). In the second stage of the industry's history, the role played by the GTC and its successor the ARA would continue to be important.

Rail professionals' associations were organizations of skilled and managerial-level employees of the rail companies who were organized according to a specific skill or function that did not formally represent their particular employers, the rail companies. As Table 5.2 indicates, some were founded relatively early and were perhaps the first devices for coordinating between many different rail operations. Corporate mergers were certainly getting started during this same time, but it would not be until late in the 1800s that they would unite numerous rail operations, especially those from different regions. Moreover, the industry's peak associations, the GTC and its successor the ARA, were not yet developed enough to deal with many specific issues, leaving them to the rail professionals associations, especially in the first two stages of rail history.

Although it is difficult to know anything definitive about the start of these organizations, the timing of their establishment relative to prevalent governance problems suggests a great deal. Most of the first associations established in this stage between 1855 and 1884 (AAPTO, AAPTA, AABTM, GPCER) were expressly involved with the coordination of through traffic. It is reasonable to hypothesize then that these groups were formed precisely in order to surmount the difficulties posed by diverse rail company ownership for long-distance travel. Other associations (MCBA, RMWAA, ATSS, ARBBA, ABA, NRAA), which were established and active a bit later, between 1883 and 1894, focused on the various technical and hardware requirements of the industry. The timing of the establishment of these associations coincides precisely with the era during which such issues as the development of safe car couplings, uniform gauge, safe braking procedures and devices, and stronger bridges were part of the public agenda. Clark (1966: 122–4) writes, for instance, that the reason for the founding of the Master Car Builders Association (MCBA) in 1869, which became most active in the 1870s and 1880s, was to promote the development of a standard and safe automatic coupling device. The pin-type coupling device, then in use, claimed hundreds of rail worker lives every year.

Table 5.2. *Chronological listing of rail industry nontraffic associations, 1855–1946*

Founding date	Initials	Name of association
1855	AAPTO	American Association of Passenger Traffic Officers
1869	MCBA	Master Car Builders Association
1872	AATPA	American Association of Travelling Passenger Agents
1873	GTC	General Time Convention
1882	AABTM	American Association of Baggage Traffic Managers
1883	RMWA	Roadmasters & Maintenance of Way Association of America
1884	GPCER	General Passenger Committee–Eastern Railroads (Cos.)
1891	ATSS	Association of Track and Structure Suppliers
	ARA	Association of American Railroads (from GTC and other railroads)
	ARBBA	American Railway Bridge & Building Association
1892	RFOOA	Railway Fuel & Operating Officers Association
1893	ABA	Air Brake Association
1894	NRAA	National Railway Appliances Association
1896	AARS	American Association of Railroad Superintendents
1899	RSMA	Railway Supply Manufacturers Association
	AREA	American Railway Engineering Association
	ARDA	American Railway Development Association
1900	TCRPA	Trans-Continenal Raiload (Cos.) Passenger Association
1901	CDOA	Car Department Officers Association
	AARDCO	Association of American Dining Car Officers
1905	LMOA	Locomotive Maintenance Officers Association
1906	RSCSA	Railway Signal and Communications Suppliers Association
1908	RWA	Railway Wheel Association
	RBA	Railway Business Association
1911	RSBA	Rail Steel Bar Association
1913	ASRA	American Shortline Railroad Association
1914	AAPRM	American Association of Passenger Rate Men
1915	ARCI	American Railway Car Institute
1919	RTA	Railway Tie Association
1931	RSA	Railway Supply Association
1946	ARCEA	American Railway Car Export Association

Source: Encyclopedia of Associations 1946: 213–16.

The new device that they proposed eventually became the device the industry agreed to employ. The same story could be repeated for the most part with respect to the Air Brake Association (ABA). Similarly, the timing of the foundation of the American Railway Bridge and Building Association is exactly in line with the era of terrible rail accidents due to bridge collapses. In short, the sketchy evidence that is available seems to confirm the idea that these rail professionals' associations were the first attempts to transcend the fragmentation of the rail industry on certain key technical issues.

Early interrail company corporate integration

In dissecting the history of mergers and rail company buyouts of other corporate entities, it becomes clear that corporate integration in the rail industry happened in a phased, or evolutionary way. The first phase, stretching from roughly the Civil War to the late 1870s, was dominated by end-to-end mergers between rail companies. In the second phase those companies which had been successful in creating a trunk line through end-to-end mergers made lateral purchases of smaller feeder lines and shorter parallel carriers. In the third phase, occurring later during the second major historical stage, discussed later, these large trunk-line empires struggled to purchase each other in an effort to create regionally integrated railways. This third phase of regional integration, still in evidence as of 1986, was largely forestalled by federal antitrust regulations since the turn of the century.

During the earliest period of rail history, there were hundreds of companies, each with anywhere from 10 to 100 miles of track as well as different gauges and types of rolling stock (Ripley 1920: 456–7). These first rail companies fulfilled very ad hoc transportation needs, for example, to carry freight, such as coal, relatively short distances from a mine to a canal or ocean port, or to its actual end-use market in some town. Over time, however, rail companies and businesses that gained experience with rail transportation began to focus on the long-haul potential of this new carrier for many different cargoes. Accordingly, rail companies were forced to recognize that changing from one car to another every time cargo came to another company's line was a considerable obstacle to the development of a railway transportation system (e.g., McPhearson 1912: 161–2). This problem became especially visible during the Civil War as the Union, and to an extent the Confederacy, sought to move troops, war materials, and later mail as quickly as possible over long distances.

As mentioned earlier, with the permission granted to them by specific federal legislation, the railroads tried to deal with this problem by establishing administrative pools. Eventually, these pools were replaced by separate through-line companies, but even this solution was not totally satisfactory. At best, these through-line companies could smooth arrangements between very separate and often incongruent operations.

The ultimate answer to the problem was the end-to-end integration of these different lines into single companies (e.g., Campbell 1938: 12; Cochran 1965: 168). Just as important, of course, this integration was also the basis for further profit making and expansion in the industry. Campbell (1938: 13–17) records the first solely owned through connection between Chicago and Philadelphia as being established by the Pennsylvania Railroad in 1870. This was the dominant type of integration within the industry until the late 1870s, when the process was relatively complete (e.g., Carson 1971: 26–7), and when enough small lines had been brought together to allow through traffic in most parts of the United States (Ripley 1920: 413–90).

At the end of this first phase of rail concentration, the surviving through-line rail companies needed to expand laterally in a second phase of concentration. At first, this meant simply buying all of the smaller spurs, shorter parallel lines, and, preliminary to that, all the lateral connecting routes in between. However, having done this, rail companies, some of which were now in possession of 3,000 to over 10,000 route miles, were left in the position of defining – or invading – the traffic boundaries between themselves and an adjacent rail company that was itself similarly expanding (e.g., Ripley 1920: 456–7; Campbell 1938: 12–15; Carson 1971: 26–7).

In short, within the second phase of rail consolidation, the rail industry began to be characterized by dozens of *duopolies*. In turn, this triggered the famous rate wars between rival rail empires, signaled by the aggrandizing activities of the robber barons. But this is where the story of consolidation must temporarily end. As described later, although invasive, horizontal consolidations did take place, they were severely interrupted and complicated by the arrival of a new governing force, the state, via antitrust regulations after 1887 and 1890.

Rail company purchases of competitors and freight suppliers

During this period, rail companies did not just buy other rail companies. Indeed, although this was one way to ensure or expand traffic for profitable operation, it was not the only way. Given the absence of any restraints, it is hardly surprising that during this same period, they turned to buying the sources of demand for their services. Again, what is indicated here is the connection between the accumulation requirements of the rail industry and the specific technical demands of rail companies that are located in a particular spatial arrangement.

The most celebrated case of this is to be found in the northeast, where the rail companies that transported primarily coal began buying coal lands and mining companies during the Civil War (e.g., Ripley 1920: 534–46). These purchases served the dual purpose of securing sufficient regular demand for rail service and providing increased profits because any railroad with a monopoly over the transportation of a mine's output was thereby in a position to buy that mining operation cheaply. The purchase of coal lands was largely completed by the early 1870s, at least in this region (Bogen

1927). It was just one example of the general practice by rail companies of buying the mineral rights to land. Especially in the west, midwest, and south, rail companies got a head start in this practice from the land giveaways of the federal government to rail companies that were constructing routes in these relatively uninhabited areas. A vast portion of U.S. mineral rights is still owned by the rail companies.

Similarly, in order to ensure regular demand for service, other railroads used a slightly different approach. Along the east coast, railroads during the 1860s began buying the steamship lines that operated out of ports where their rail lines had connections. This was especially the case in southern New England with the New Haven Railroad and it appears to have been the normal state of affairs in the east by 1880. Although it might appear that the railroads were motivated by an interest in buying out their competition, this was probably not the case. Steamship lines were simply not very successful competitors with rail lines once north–south rail routes were in place. The railroads were not only faster, but they were also capable of moving directly and more precisely between any two inland destinations. Thus, rail company purchases of steamship lines served largely to secure a new source of freight traffic, especially that which depended upon the oceangoing ships, originating from east coast ports (e.g., Taylor 1970).

The actions on the part of the rail companies to insulate themselves from intercarrier competition are more clearly illustrated by their response to canals. It was not as simple a matter as buying the canals, as these were owned by the individual states and, in some cases, municipalities. Instead, beginning with the first decade following the Civil War, the rail companies bought the boat lines that used the canals. Most of these operated in the Great Lakes region. Within a couple of decades, the rail companies owned almost all of the carriers that worked the canals (Moulton 1912: 82–5).

However critical all of these various corporate integrations between rail companies or other carriers and freight suppliers were to the rail industry, they nonetheless did not end the rail companies' exposure to the vagaries of the market. First, since many of these companies, such as those owning coal mines, were dependent primarily upon one commodity, they suffered market contractions just as that commodity did. Moreover, as noted earlier, their considerable fixed costs made them particularly vulnerable to any downturns in traffic. Second, although a far cry from the earlier chaos of diverse ownership, the rail industry was still very divided after the first two phases of concentration, and, if anything, was more competitive and in need of corporate integration than ever before.

Conclusions: Halfway to private rail governance

Between the 1830s and the mid–1880s, the rail companies and other private actors had been largely responsible for governing their industry. With the state playing only a minimal or "environmental" role, private actors had started to build capitalist institutions to insulate rail companies, to some degree, from the vagaries of the marketplace. Indeed, by 1887, rail companies had managed to subdue partly the volatility of both carrier competition and demand for their services by purchasing coal mines, and coastal steam and canal boat lines. Through the development of multilateral governance mechanisms, including a peak association, they had also started working on the larger regional and national coordination problems that confronted their industry. Finally, they had moved through two phases of corporate concentration, having reached the point of "duopolistic competition," and were ready to complete the project of integration into large regional monopolies. However, this was a project that they would never complete because small shippers and rail workers would seize the initiative for shaping the industry's governance regime and would strive to increase the state's role in rail governance.

STAGE TWO: ANTIRAIL MOBILIZATION AND NEGATIVE REGULATION, 1885–1919

In the second stage of rail governance, associations continued to play a significant role, but state intervention developed in two phases, first in a pro-forma fashion and later in a more substantive way, in reaction to the mobilization of two class groups: small shippers, including farmers, and rail workers. The end of this period was punctuated by the wartime seizure in 1918 of the rail industry by the state after the rail companies, in contrast with their British counterparts, had failed to solve their governance problems when given the chance in 1917. In retrospect, this event was just one indication that new federal regulations had undermined the capacity of private actors to continue to develop a governance regime that was capable of solving the industry's governance problems.

The maturation and limits of associational governance

As Table 5.2 shows, the vast majority of the rail professionals' associations were founded between 1885 and the First World War. Given the paucity of available data, we can only presume with Clark (1966: 4) that they continued to help standardize equipment and procedures. On the other hand, it is during this period that we discover their limits as well as new reasons for these associations to exist. Consider again the Master Car Builders Association (MCBA), which, as noted earlier, had been founded in 1869 to propose a new and safer automatic coupler. Despite its efforts, it was never the institutional instrument for establishing its device as the industry's standard. Instead, it worked only to influence other associations to take action, especially the American Society of Railroad Suppliers (ASRS), which was founded in 1881 and represented 242 companies. Eventually, the ASRS, spurred by the MCBA and acting probably in the interests of stabilizing and expanding the market for the products of its member firms, did recommend in the later 1880s to the GTC that the MCBA coupler design and air brakes become standard equipment on U.S. rails (Clark 1966: 204–6).

Far more critical during this time were the rail company associations and the associations of companies that supplied rail equipment. The decisions made by these associations, of course, could be translated directly into practice by the represented companies. The GTC/ARA, for instance, established standard times across the country in 1883, and in 1886 created a standard telegraphic network (Clark 1966: 204–6). The other types of trade associations between companies (e.g., NRAA, RSMA, RWA, RSBA) expressly dealt with the problems of sharing information and developing standards for the manufacture and marketing of railway equipment.

Although more capable of coordinating the industry with regard to these matters than other associations, company associations nevertheless fell short with respect to most of the critical issues facing the industry. The GTC had the power to effect a relatively industrywide implementation of the automatic coupler and the air brake. As it turned out, however, after having renamed itself and absorbed more companies to become the American Railroad Association (ARA), it responded to the request of the ASRS by recommending against any new standard equipment regarding the coupler and air brake in 1892. It took the Railroad Safety Appliance Act of 1893 to require these safety devices as standard equipment. Thus, despite twenty-four years of extremely energetic actions, associative behavior, whether between companies or rail professionals, ultimately failed to solve these critical problems. Eventually, as state intervention increased, the functions of rail companies associations, like those of the rail professional associations, began to revolve around the state's role in governance. Notably, the ARA became the major lobbying arm of the railroad companies.

During this stage, rail professionals' associations also appear to have been critical in implementing state policy. Although secondary data is virtually non-existent, it is clear that the Air Brake Association (ABA), established in 1893, could not have been involved in the promotion of the air brake since it was not established until the same year that air brakes were mandated by law. On the other hand, it would have been useful for the purpose of agreeing on the details regarding the installation and manufacture of that device. The Railway Accounting Officers Association (RAOA), founded in 1888, probably played a similar role. It would be difficult to imagine that this association was not a direct response to the Interstate Commerce Act of 1887, which suddenly required rail companies to report their financial situation in a standard way.

Beginning in 1889 with the creation of the Interstate Commerce Railway Association by the western roads, the industry turned to more formally and thoroughly structured traffic associations as a way to control rate competition. This particular association even had a commission presided over by a former Interstate Commerce Commissioner. The same concept was introduced in the east in 1892, starting with a traffic agreement between two rival railroad empires, the Pennsylvania and the Central. None of these associations lasted very long. Nevertheless, the industry continued establishing traffic associations for at least the next decade. The other form of company association that came into existence during this period was the rail company employer association. Although it is probable that in many cases the other types of rail company associations were used informally for developing united responses to rail worker actions, these new associations were explicitly established for that purpose. The General Managers Association (GMA), for instance, was founded in 1886 by twenty-four companies with connections in Chicago to deal with a recent upsurge in worker actions. The GMA was later instrumental in crushing the Pullman Strike in 1894 by calling successfully upon the Governor and the President to move in troops. This rise in employer-oriented associations seems to have been a relatively general phenomenon during this period (McNaughton 1954: 248–9; Rayback 1966: 201–9).

In general, then, it appears that associations had a very limited governance capability. They effectively governed only certain, less conflictive industry transactions. Associations had the capacity for solving dilemmas when the required change in a given transaction did not competitively disadvantage any individual firm involved. Thus, associations proved adequate for coordinating the installation of a general telegraph system and the response to certain labor actions. However, even when companies had no reason to fear a competitive disadvantage, associations sometimes proved unsuccessful if the value of the investment in an industrywide improvement was relatively indirect or less than immediate. Thus, associations were not able to bring about the production and implementation of uniform equipment standards. For instance, because it represented a short-term cost and not an immediate profit for individual rail companies, state intervention was required to bring the automatic safety coupler into general use. This was so despite the acknowledgment by industry associations that the coupler was necessary for the safe and efficient functioning of the industry as a whole as well as for stabilizing the market for equipment manufacturers. Where a transaction involved direct conflict between companies, such as with respect to prices and market shares, associational governance proved to be totally inadequate.

State intervention and the supplanting of private governance

Much has been written about state intervention in the form of rail regulations and what it means. Kolko (1965), for instance, wrote a brilliantly crafted critique of the tendency of many historians to ignore issues of class conflict and, thus, to see regulations as serving the public interest. He argued that rail regulations were a direct response to the rail companies' interests, and that the ICC was "captured" by the railroads and served to provide them with the market stability they required to continue their capitalist accumulation. In apparent reaction to Kolko, the economist Martin (1971) vehemently argues the opposite. Differing a bit with Kolko, Freitag (1985) has argued that these regulations responded within a class struggle setting and served capital more generally via the so-called relative autonomy of the state. Frietag's renewed emphasis on class struggle in a sense recalls a traditional school of thought that stressed class struggles for state reforms. Benson (1955), for instance, argued that these regulations were a response to the antimonopoly organizing taking place during this period among small business interests. Similarly, Chandler (1965: 185–9) sees the dissatisfaction of farmers as well as rail labor as responsible for creating a conflict within the industry that only the state had the power to resolve. Most labor historians have long argued that specific labor regulations are contingent on the balance of mobilization or class struggle (e.g., Uhl 1954; Raybeck 1966; Eggert 1967). Finally, mainstream historians responding to the Kolko–Martin debate continue to argue that these regulations primarily served the public welfare (e.g., Hoogenboom and Hoogenboom 1976).

Sanders (1982) argues with regard to rate and antitrust regulations that the best explanation of rail regulatory history requires a more complex analysis than any of those found thus far in the literature. The same could be said for rail regulations in general, including those dealing with rail workers. It is my contention that the rise of state intervention in the rail industry was a response to the failure of private capitalist governance mechanisms to solve the industry's governance problems. On the other hand, I would also argue that these regulations interrupted the evolution of a private capitalist governance regime and failed to satisfy the interests of rail companies and other capitalists in further capital accumulation until other new carriers accepted state actions that discriminated against the rails. Finally, the rise of small shippers and worker mobilization thwarted the rail companies' designs for a purely private capitalist governance regime. In conjunction with the development of state institutions, endowed with progressively greater interventionist capacities, these antirail company mobilizations ultimately forced the railroads to accept more state intervention as a means of solving the governance crises of the period. Although the rail companies would later try to capture the state's regulatory institutions, it is clear, as Sanders (1982) argues, that the concept of capture is inadequate for describing the complex and often contradictory relationship between ICC actions, new Congressional regulations, and rail company interests.

WHY THE STATE INTERVENED IN RAIL GOVERNANCE

No one, it seems, disputes the idea that private rail governance was in a state of severe dysfunction characterized by excess capacity by the end of the nineteenth century. Kolko (1965) correctly identifies this as a result of excess competition between often adjacent rail company miniempires for the same traffic. In short, by the late 1800s, the rail industry needed to find some way to reduce, if not end, the competition between rail companies, and, as Kolko argues, this was one reason for the regulatory events that followed for the next half century. On the other hand, the need to deal with disruptive and wasteful competition cannot be understood as a reason for the *particular* resolution that eventually took place in the form of state intervention. In addition to state intervention, a number of responses to this problem could have been implemented, including traffic associations and mergers. However, as suggested later, the state limited these options.

The disruption of pooling and intercorporate integration

The first rail company solution for the competition problem, traffic associations or pooling, was effectively excluded as a solution for two reasons. First, as Kolko (1965: Chaps. 1–3) and Chandler (1965: 160–1) point out, the agreements on which these traffic associations and pools were based in Stage One constantly fell apart since they were merely voluntary. To be sure, in Stage Two, more sophisticated versions of associations did better, especially those arranged between 1888 and 1890 by J. S. Morgan and later by his son J. Pierpoint Morgan, who owned considerable rail stock in different companies. Even so, these proved to be impermanent affairs. Second, the only conceivable solution to the traffic association problem, a solution recognized and fought for by Morgan and others, was blocked by the state's unwillingness to go along with rail company designs. In order to get traffic associations to be effective, the rail companies needed them to be legally recognized so that pooling arrangements were enforceable in court. Congress refused repeatedly to do this. Further, the Supreme Court's decision to dissolve the Trans-Missouri Association in 1898 essentially dissolved all existing associations, including those painstakingly es-

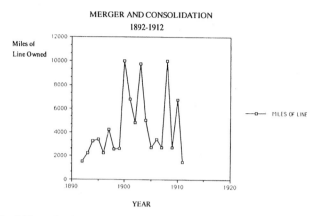

MERGER AND CONSOLIDATION
1892-1912

Figure 5.2   Miles of rail line merged, 1892–1912. (Source: Adapted from Ripley 1920, p. 490.)

tablished by Morgan. This decision marked the beginning of a new resolve on the part of the state to enforce the antipooling and rate association stipulations of the 1887 Interstate Commerce Act (Carson 1971: 29–34). Despite their pointed efforts in Congress over the next two decades, the rail companies did not gain legal status for pooling until the Transportation Act of 1920.

As Figures 5.2 and 5.3 indicate, from the very beginning of Stage Two, there was much consolidation simultaneous with the efforts by the Morgans and others to create functional versions of pooling. However, after the pooling option was effectively excluded in 1898, the rail companies' response was to turn with still greater vigor to intercorporate mergers. As Carson (1971: 35–7, 46) reports, within a month of the Trans-Missouri decision, one-eighth of the mileage of American railroads came under the control of other railroads through mergers, leases, stock control, and other devices. However, because of the dramatic rise of antirail company mobilization, examined in what follows, this governance option soon encountered the state's opposition.

As suggested earlier, by the time Stage Two began in 1887, the railroad industry was set to move from a disunited system of numerous, unstable duopolies between rival companies to what might be referred to as "Phase Three Consolidation," that is, stable, regional monopolies. At the same time, as a part of the Interstate Commerce Act of 1887 as well as the Anti-Trust Act of 1890, mergers that reduced rail competition had been specifically prohibited. However, because the state did not have enforcement powers, neither of these bills actually managed to stop the rail companies from accomplishing at least some intercorporate concentrating; they did as much as they could without attracting too much state and public attention. The state's impotence regarding antitrust statutes began to change

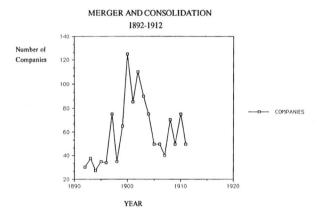

MERGER AND CONSOLIDATION
1892-1912

Figure 5.3   Number of rail companies merged, 1892–1912. (Source: Adapted from Ripley, 1920, p. 490.)

shortly after the antipooling decision of the Supreme Court in 1898. In 1904, the Supreme Court dissolved the newly arranged Northern Securities merger. This decision stopped several larger mergers in the east and dramatically reduced progress with respect to the larger (Phase Three) regional consolidations that sought to end competition between major railroad companies (Carson 1971: 49). Keeler (1983: 36) marks the effective end of anticompetitive mergers as 1909, when the Supreme Court blocked the Burlington–Great Northern Pacific Merger.

After 1909, larger regional mergers, such as that merging the New England and Union Pacific Railroads, were often attempted, only to be dissolved by the Justice Department (Ripley 1920: 462). Moreover, in the midst of the general campaign during the next decade on the part of rail companies for the right to some form of rail industry integration, Congress passed the Clayton Act in 1914. This measure reaffirmed the fact that the Antitrust Act applied to the railroads in all its aspects. From 1904 to at least the 1940s, and despite the formal relaxations of some aspects of antitrust regulations that occurred in later stages, the courts would continue to dissolve and the Congress would continue to prohibit rail company merger moves (e.g., Sharfman 1936: Chaps. 3–4; Armitage 1969: 48; Martin 1971: 194–318; Hoogenboom and Hoogenboom 1976: 171).

Unfortunately, thorough statistics of rail consolidation trends since the nineteenth century have not been compiled in a way that distinguishes between types of mergers. However, the effects of the state's rejection of the rail companies' consolidation plans are indicated in trends regarding the number of U.S. companies and their market shares, as shown in Table 5.3 In other countries during this same time, trends were very different,

Table 5.3. *Number of operating railways, 1890–1979*

Date	Total	Over 1,000 miles	Date	Total	Over 1,000 miles
1867	—	1	1933	700	53
1877	—	11	1934	678	50
1877	—	28	1935	661	50
1890	1,013	40	1936	641	46
1891	991	41	1937	631	46
1892	1,002	43	1938	611	46
1893	1,034	42	1939	600	45
1894	1,043	44	1940	574	45
1895	1,104	42	1941	559	45
1896	1,111	44	1942	543	45
1897	1,158	44	1943	534	45
1898	1,192	44	1944	524	45
1899	1,206	44	1945	517	45
1900	1,224	48	1946	513	43
1901	1,213	49	1947	502	42
1902	1,219	51	1948	485	42
1903	1,281	50	1949	481	42
1904	1,314	48	1950	471	43
1905	1,380	49	1951	42	42
1906	1,491	50	1952	454	43
1907	1,564	51	1953	448	43
1908	1,323	52	1954	443	43
1909	1,316	53	1955	441	43
1910	1,306	54	1956	422	42
1911	1,312	56	1957	415	40
1912	1,298	58	1958	412	40
1913	1,296	57	1959	411	40
1914	1,297	58	1960	407	39
1915	1,260	55	1962	395	38
1916	1,216	56	1963	395	38
1917	1,168	56	1964	380	36
1918	1,131	54	1965	372	36
1919	1,111	54	1966	375	36
1920	1,085	55	1967	370	34
1921	1,058	55	1966	360	31
1922	1,041	54	1969	361	32
1923	1,023	54	1970	351	30
1924	995	53	1971	341	30
1925	947	53	1972	332	29
1926	929	53	1973	331	29
1927	880	53	1974	341	29
1928	849	54	1975	340	29
1929	809	55	1976	314	26
1930	775	54	1977	320	27
1931	749	54	1978	59	27
1932	709	53	1979	63	26

Sources: Moody's Transportation Manual 1950: a3, 1980: a4; Ripley 1920: 458.

since mergers were not discouraged, but often encouraged. In Britain, for example, the Railways Act of 1921 mandated the amalgamation of the British rail system into four regional operations (e.g., Armitage 1969). By contrast, in the United States, the number of operating companies remained extremely high, having only slightly decreased by the time Congress created Conrail in 1978. Furthermore, the number of companies operating over 1,000 miles increased quickly from the mid–1800s, but quickly leveled off after the first decade of 1900s.

Were stock control manipulations themselves an adequate solution to the excess competition problem faced by the rail companies? To be sure, a stock arrangement could suffice for coordinating some of the more external relations (including financial manipulations) between companies. The rail industry was active in this regard during Stage Two (e.g., Chandler 1965: 88–94), but no trust could create an internally unified operation with all of the attendant efficiencies in day-to-day administration as well as reductions in labor, plant, and equipment requirements. The voting trusts were limited to terms of perhaps five years (Chandler 1965: 90) and were only as stable as the syndicate of financiers that put them together. Furthermore, stock ownership deals by themselves amounted to financial agreements between two operations that were themselves still separate, often containing jealous or hostile staffs. Agreements could still fall apart if one of the two parties felt cheated or for other reasons did something disruptive with their stock. Indeed, if stock manipulations had been adequate, the Morgans would not themselves have used stock manipulations between 1888 and 1900 to force consolidations between companies (e.g., Campbell 1938). Nor would rail companies have persisted for the next three-quarters of a century in trying to reverse the state's opposition to mergers, which intended to reduce rivalries between adjacent operations.

Rail company interests and rate regulations

With the associative and other intercorporate governance options effectively excluded by the state, the option that then remained was state intervention. As mentioned earlier, Kolko (1965) argues that the form of intervention that eventually occurred, rate regulation, was in the rail companies' interest. That is, regulations were the answer to the rail companies' need to stabilize rail competition. To buttress this argument, he cites various company statements supporting particular regulatory legislations. Nevertheless, it seems unlikely that rail regulations can actually be explained in terms of the rail company interests. First, as just discussed, the rail companies were very active during the regulatory period 1887–1915, as well as later, in advocating other legislative measures, such as enforcing pooling and permitting anticompetitive mergers. Without fail, the state opposed the rail companies' designs for these legislative proposals. Second, others, writing after Kolko, have shown that the rail companies actually opposed the same regulations he says that they favored (e.g., Harbenson 1967; Hoogenboom and Hoogenboom 1976). Using statistical information others have maintained that rate regulations had clearly deleterious effects on rail investments and performance (e.g., Martin 1971). Third, it is not at all clear how rate regulation was capable of solving the big problem that resulted from excess competition for the rail industry: excess capacity. Certainly, rate regulations had the potential to reduce a rail company's incentive to build still more track adjacent to another company's route. However, by the turn of the century, this was no longer a problem. Most routes where excess capacity was an issue were already overbuilt. The only solution to that problem was to reduce capacity. And although corporate combination provided incentives for reducing capacity via the combining of redundant plant, equipment, work forces, and track in the case that duplicate service existed solely for competitive purposes, none of these was set into motion by merely regulating rates.

Antirail company interests

The key to why the state intervened lies with the failure of the rail companies to satisfy the governance crisis regarding the rail companies' transactions with two other parts of the industry. First, the rail companies failed to govern satisfactorily rates, service to freight customers, and the competition between rail companies for these customers. Second, they failed to deal effectively with labor. In both these cases, rail companies had a preferred solution and were developing it – corporate integration and rail company associations. Yet it also seems clear that this preferred solution was defeated by the rising mobilization of rail workers and small shippers. That is, as a result of strikes and the chaos of contradictory state and local regulations, a crisis developed that was unsolvable via private capitalist means.

During Stage Two, the interests of freight customers, including small shippers, and rail workers could be summarized as follows:

Freight customers. Rail company relations with large shippers were perhaps relatively satisfactory from the viewpoint of rail companies and large shippers. However, relations with the smaller shippers, such as farmers and small town manufacturers, were bad enough that these groups began working hard in the 1870s to restrict the rail companies in numerous ways (Sanders 1982: 23–6). Although large shippers, also the major accumulators of the era, received discounts, rebates, and special services, small shippers did not. Moreover, especially if they were located on a less-traveled spur or line, small shippers were forced to subsidize the special deals that rail companies offered to large shippers via both discriminatory prices and services (Tarbell 1936; Wiebe 1962). In fact, it is clear that the railroads' special deals were a major factor in the monopolization of other industries such as oil, tobacco, meat cutting, and lumber. This rail/monopoly connection was openly decried by smaller business concerns (e.g., Wiebe 1962: 53–4).

In the end, the character of rail regulations that were produced eventually between 1887 and 1915 conformed to the list of demands made by farmers regarding the kind of state intervention they desired (Chandler 1965: 188–9). In addition, the vote on the 1886 "Reagan Bill," which first proposed interstate rail regulations, conformed to the regional distribution of interests on the railroad regulation question. As Sanders (1982: 24) observes, votes on rail regulation since the Reagan Bill in 1886 have tended to be divided between the big "core" cities in the northeast, dominated by pro-railroad, large industrial interests, and the small towns or rural areas of the "periphery," which vote for restrictive rail regulations.

Rail workers. If small shippers throughout the rural and urban United States were very dissatisfied with the current governance regime, so too were rail workers. Their reasons were relatively simple. Rail workers suffered low wages, working days of 12 hours or longer, and working conditions that were responsible for the deaths of thousands of workers every year (Eggert 1967). Moreover, recourse via collective bargaining had been only partially successful, given the drastic moves against them by rail companies and their employer associations in 1877 and again in 1894 during the Pullman Strike. Thus, workers eventually turned to the "political field" (Bonnett 1956: 422). Simultaneously, as Chandler (1965: 131) suggests, the rail companies discovered that they could no longer deal by themselves with the higher level of labor–management strife that was becoming a regular feature of the industry.

Antirail mobilization and negative regulation

The effects of both rail worker and shipper mobilization in the political field can plausibly be divided into two phases. Phase One regulations consist of the preliminary, less-substantive legislative measures passed from 1885 to roughly 1903. Phase Two regulations consist of the later legislation up to World War I, which all regulatory historians agree was significantly different, and which amounted to substantive reforms from the viewpoint of rail workers and small shippers.

Phase One regulations. Phase One regulations, affecting small shipper interests, included the Interstate Commerce Act of 1887, the Sherman Antitrust Act of 1890, and the Elkins Act of 1903. For rail workers, Phase

One regulations included the so-called Hungarian Scab Act of 1885, the Railroad Relations Act of 1888, the Rail Safety Appliance Act of 1893, and the Erdman "No Yellow Dog" Act of 1898. Although this legislation generally did not resolve the concerns raised by small shippers or rail workers, it did nevertheless legitimate the mobilization of these two class groups. In the case of small shippers, who had been fighting for three decades at the level of individual states, these acts at least formally acknowledged their contentions as just and prosecutable under law. Second, it moved their agenda for the first time to the national level and admitted them as regular participants into the governance decision-making process regarding relations between themselves and the rail companies. All of this corresponds to developments in other countries. In Britain, the Railway and Canal Act of 1888 gave small shippers what was called locus standi, a place of standing or the legal right to be represented. Similarly, small shippers in the United States now had mechanisms, however unwieldy at first, through which they could press their claims. Whatever else they might accomplish after that, small shippers clearly had to get to this point first. Moreover, these mechanisms would be strengthened in the first decades of the twentieth century.

It is apparent that the timing of these locus standi regulations in the United States corresponds to developments in the organizing and actions of small business interests. The literature makes it clear that both small shipper mobilization as part of the small business, antimonopoly movement, as well as rail worker mobilization (along with much of the rest of the American working class), peaked during the period preceding the legislation until World War I, that is, from 1870 to 1917 (e.g., Boyle 1935; Benson 1955; Boyer and Morais; 1955; Wiebe 1962).

At the local level, farmers were active in granges and other associations. As congressional hearing reports would testify, for the next thirty years, small shippers mobilized against the railroads at the federal level through associations, such as the Anti-Monopoly League, and in individual states via state and local chambers of commerce. This period was in general, as Schmitter and Brandt (1979: 42–3) report, characterized by the rise of associational behavior among businesses. Notably, small business interests and antitrust politics seem to have dominated the early National Association of Manufacturers, which was founded in 1895. After a power struggle at the national meeting in 1902, however, small business and antirail interests apparently lost their hegemony in the new organization to larger corporate interests, aligned with the railroads (Steigerwalt 1964; Schmitter and Brandt 1979). Actually, it is possible that by the time it occurred, this loss was not really a disaster for antirail interests. By the turn of the century, the antimonopoly fight was popular enough such that to get elected, virtually every candidate in an electoral campaign, whether Democrat or Republican, needed to promise to trim both the power of the monopolies in general and the railroads in particular (e.g., Tarbell 1936: 74–9, 91, 203–17; Benson 1955; Wiebe 1962: 13–14; Steigerwalt 1964: 86–90).

In a more striking fashion, parallel events were occurring in the case of rail workers, whose movement established much of the foundation for the U.S. labor movement. Indeed, no one disputes the observation that since the 1870s, rail workers had grown increasingly strong and successful in starting organizations and carrying out strikes. Burtt (1963: 117), among others, characterizes the later 1800s in the rail industry as a "great rush to join the unions." Nor is it difficult to connect the passage of specific labor reforms with specific actions on the part of rail workers (e.g., Boyle 1935; McNaughton 1954; Boyer and Morais 1955; Bonnet, 1956; Rayback 1966: 269–70).

However, with the exception of the later Safety Act, none of the rail worker Acts passed by Congress directly improved the workers' lot. Rather, these acts served to undergird rail worker organizational efforts in an important way. The Scab Act of 1885 was really an acknowledgment of the rights of rail unions to enforce a union shop and contracts negotiated therein. The same is true of the Labor Act and Erdman Act, which came later. None of these mandated negotiations between the rail companies and the unions, but they did allow and encourage them. The Erdman Act, passed in 1898, provided for an arbitration process. Although not used very much until later, so-called Erdman arbitration boards were eventually used sixty-one times between 1906 and 1913 (Chandler 1965: 132). The Erdman Act also prohibited rail companies from using one of the weapons they had previously employed to stop unions. Rail companies were forbidden from making a promise not to join a rail union a condition of employment. In short, as in the case of small shippers, before rail workers got any substantive reforms, they fought for and achieved their niche in the governance process. Undoubtedly, this niche was never totally secure. However, with the handlehold it provided, they could then redirect their energies from establishing basic organizational rights to other issues on their agenda.

Phase Two regulations. The second set of rail regulations occurred at roughly the same time for both rail workers and small shippers. In the case of shippers, there is considerable controversy in the literature concerning the effects of these regulations on governance. However, in the case of rail labor regulations, there are no controversies. The state clearly interfered with the companies' transactions with rail workers and this interference was, in turn, expressly and actively opposed by the rail companies. Time and again, the rail companies and other capitalists demonstrated that the state input they desired regarding their labor problem was protection from union monopolies over hiring as well as the use of state and federal troops to break strikes. In fact, troops were used numerous times, as in

1894 in order to crush the Pullman Strike after the GMA requested their employment from the President. However, in 1913, rail worker unions were successful in Congress in gaining the Newlands Act, which created a railway board of mediation, and the Adamson Act of 1916, which provided for the eight-hour day on the railroads. Finally, during its wartime takeover of the railroads, the newly legitimized bargaining mechanisms, which had become increasingly common before that time, were fully established as standard operating procedure for the industry. Moreover, under the state's wing during World War I, rail workers received dramatic wage increases (e.g., Godfrey 1974: 108–32).

All of this bought a critical measure of labor peace for rail and other capitalists, preserving the general conditions for accumulation. Moreover, none of these rail labor regulations forced the rail companies to surrender their ultimate advantage to their work force. However, the retention of this ultimate advantage was bought only at the price of both granting rail workers substantive concessions and setting them up with a state-secured mechanism that would enable them to later (in Stage Three) secure concessions unusual for a contracting industry.

Considerably more controversy exists with respect to the effectiveness of rate regulations. Even so, there is some consensus among historians that rail regulations generally, and rate regulations specifically, started to show some teeth after the turn of the century, especially after the Supreme Court decision in 1904 to stop the Northern Securities merger. Even Carson (1971: 48–9), who broadly supports Kolko's capitalist state thesis, implies as much when he argues that in 1906, the ICC "clearly did not yet act as the manager of American railroads." He nonetheless finds that during this period, the ICC grew in its powers and that the courts ceased being protectors of the railroads. However, I would go further than this.

When the ICC was established in 1887, it was ineffective insofar as it lacked various specific enablements and powers of enforcement. Nevertheless, most students of the ICC and rail regulations agree that, whether or not it used it, the ICC did finally gain the power it required to govern freight–rail relations with the passage of the Hepburn and Mann–Elkins acts. The Hepburn Act of 1906 expanded the size of the ICC, explicitly outlawed rail investments in other carriers, and provided for maximum rates. The Mann–Elkins Act in 1910 gave the ICC the power to suspend proposed rate increases and put the burden of proof on the rail companies in the case of rate complaints.

The issue confronting historians regarding the period after passage of the Mann–Elkins Act is then whether or not the rail companies managed to capture the state mechanisms that were created to regulate them. It appears that capture did not occur. At the very least, the rail companies did not succeed as measured against their own rate increase agenda. Until World War II, the railroads periodically asked for general rate increases only to have them denied in celebrated cases (e.g., Armitage 1969: 48; Martin 1971: 194–318; Hoogenboom and Hoogenboom 1976: 171). Moreover, the poor and volatile economic performance of the railroads for the rest of the century indicates that the rail companies were not getting what they wanted from regulators.

Conclusions: State disruption of evolving private governance

Although the regulatory interventions of Stage Two clearly responded to the rail governance crises of the time, they did so in a very particular way. Rather than facilitate or allow the express governance interests of the rail companies to prevail, the state chose to become a "negative regulator, interfering with private decision-making" (Carson 1971: 93). Thus, whether or not the state was ultimately restrictive of capitalist interests, by 1919, it was the key managing agent – if not yet in a positive sense – within the larger regime of rail governance. Perhaps more importantly, it would remain thereafter integrally involved in governance.

Indeed, it is clear that by the end of Stage Two, after three decades of federal attempts to regulate the railroads, the industry was far from effectively governed. Highlighting this is the famous failure of the industry to manage itself sufficiently within the existing governance regime to keep the railroads in private hands during World War I. As Godfrey (1974) notes, by 1918, when President Wilson took over the rails, even the most conservative observers were calling for state seizure, yet at the same time in Britain, private governance was working despite an even greater crisis regarding car and labor shortages. The critical difference between the two situations was simple. In Britain, the regional amalgamation and, thus, unified coordination of the private rail system was virtually complete; in the United States, this was far from the case (e.g., Armitage 1969; Bagwell 1970, 1974).

STAGE THREE: STATE-ENFORCED GOVERNANCE DEADLOCK, 1920–65

Although Stages One and Two are defined by diverse, dramatic shifts in rail governance, Stage Three is most striking for what did not happen during that period. Despite the fact that the unions suffered a severe, general decline in mobilization, and despite the passing of the heyday of small business mobilization, rail governance did not turn back to a significantly more private, capitalist track. Stage Three did witness performance crises, which in turn triggered flurries of contradictory legislation. However, as a result of the particular institutional nature and increasingly independent powers of state actors, established earlier to help govern rail relations, the overall extent and even the type of "negative" state regulation changed little until 1966, when the Department of Transportation was created.

Rail worker mobilization and regulations

By 1919, as World War I was ending, the country was very much wrapped up in the so-called railroad question. The rail brotherhoods were at the pinnacle of their strength and as radical as they had ever been. Very confident after their gains during the time when the rails were under the state's wing, they organized a massive campaign to enact the Plumb Plan, which called for the unification of the rails under government ownership and worker management. Debated for months in congressional hearings, it was part of a larger drive for state takeover supported by Senator "Fighting" Bob La Follette, the Director General of the wartime Railroad Administration McAdoo, and his successor Hines (U.S. House of Representatives 1919; *Labor,* 1919: passim; Kerr 1968: 160–221).

However, although in countries such as Britain, labor would climb to greater power in the decade following the war, in the United States, the armistice ushered in an era of anticommunist hysteria and red-baiting. All of this came crashing down on the heads of rail workers. At one point in the Congressional Hearings on the rail question, Congressman Sanders read a paragraph " . . . that all forests, mines and waterways having national importance should be declared national properties. . . . " He then asked the brotherhoods' attorney, Glenn Plumb, if he agreed with this doctrine. After Mr. Plumb's affirmative response, Sanders revealed that he was reading from the new Soviet constitution (U.S. House of Representatives 1919: 694–5). As *The New York Times* (1919: 10) asserted the next day, this was the end of the Plumb Plan, and I would add the golden era of rail worker mobilization. Over the next few years, the rail unions suffered such setbacks as wage cuts, the disaster of the failed 1922 Shopmen's Strike, and the gradual loss of more than half of their numbers over the years as their industry contracted. In short, rail workers were put completely on the defensive after 1919 (e.g., Uhl 1954: 60–3).

Given the demise of labor, one would have expected the railroad companies to have gained more than they actually did. However, although the dramatic decline of the rail industry during the Depression and after World War II made much of the rail work force redundant, the rail unions were able to limit their losses and maintain their wage levels fairly effectively. That is, although the extent of rail worker redundancy, decried by the use of such terms as featherbedding, was no doubt exaggerated, it is nonetheless clear that rail workers were able to keep many obsolete jobs intact – much to the consternation of the rail companies. Moreover, although the Railway Labor Act of 1926 forbade rail worker strikes, rail workers were still able to gain special protections for themselves, such as the Railroad

Retirement Act of 1936, which provided redundant, Depression-era rail workers with an unprecedented pension, significantly better than social security. Similarly, in 1938, the Railroad Unemployment Act provided them with unemployment benefits significantly better than that which was available via the federal unemployment compensation program. Or again, in 1940, via the "Washington Agreement," rail workers who were forced to take less desirable jobs were given monetary compensation to make up the difference for five years (McNaughton 1954: 125). Finally, as part of the legislation creating Amtrak and Conrail, redundant workers were given a $250,000 lump-sum settlement (e.g., Saunders 1978: 83–5, 308–9).

Why were the rail unions still relatively successful? In large part, the answer is to be found in a stipulation included with the 1926 Railway Labor Act that the President appoint an emergency board to negotiate labor–management disputes that could not otherwise be resolved privately. Although rail unions at the time generally counted this Act as a big loss – given its stricture against strikes – it did give the relatively weak rail unions a place to fight for their interests when they would otherwise have lost almost everything. These emergency boards were utilized in 1935, 1937, 1943, 1946, 1948, and 1950. Notably, the creation of emergency boards preceded and resulted in the Acts of 1936 and 1938 (see generally, McNaughton 1954: 124–32; Uhl 1954: 63–81). In short, governance of the critical transactions between companies and workers relating to price and conditions of labor continued to be governed essentially by the "negative regulations" of the state. Moreover, the particular state institutions responsible for this governance proved to be downwardly sticky in the sense that they endured and were no less invasive despite the demise of the once strong worker mobilization that had earlier put them there.

Rate, antitrust, and abandonment regulations

During this stage, small shippers clearly lost the offensive to the rail companies, who set themselves during this period to the task of capturing the ICC and Congress. However, it is difficult to find evidence that the rail companies actually succeeded. Until the 1970s, small shipper interests appear to have been able to muster enough electoral power to prevent any wholesale reversals of those regulations that served their interests (Sanders 1982: 23–50). Thus, just as with rail labor regulations, regulations concerning rates, abandonments, and consolidation changed only very slowly in favor of rail company interests, falling short of any wholesale change. Rather, according to Hoogenboom and Hoogenboom (1976), the state, particularly the ICC, enacted "discriminations balancing discriminations" that made regulations more complex and specific, and extended the regulatory sphere to other carriers.

Ultimately, according to Sanders (1982: 33), "[g]iven its political imperatives to protect agriculture, the South, the small shipper, and communities that would be greatly harmed by rail abandonments, the ICC did what it could to keep the railroads solvent." However, it was not able to do enough. As opposed to Britain, where adequate returns were effectively guaranteed through the regulatory mechanisms and net incomes were relatively steady (e.g., Mitchell 1971 [1962: 4 and 5]: 226–7), U.S. railroad income was volatile and passed through many periods of deficits and bankruptcy. Periods of deep deficits and bankruptcies occurred, especially in the 1930s, the late 1940s, the late 1950s and, of course, the late 1960s, when the Penn Central merger and later Amtrak and Conrail materialized (e.g., Mitchell 1971 [1962: 4 and 5]: 226–7; *Moody's* 1985: a4). In short, with respect to the ultimate criteria of industry success, income, the U.S. state failed to provide adequate governance regarding rail rates, consolidations, and abandonments.

With the Transportation Act of 1920, the rail companies finally gained the right to pool traffic. Additionally, the Act directed the ICC to allow mergers and create a consolidated system of regional railroad corporations. Thus, at first glance, the Act of 1920 would seem to fit the rail companies' legislative agenda quite precisely. However, there were a number of strings attached to all of these new directives that canceled out their potential with respect to the rail companies' hoped-for return to a more private, capitalist governance path. First, the "recapture clause" of the 1920 Act required rail company profits over 6% to be handed over to the weaker roads via a special fund. Second, the powers of the ICC were not reduced but widened and reinforced, especially in the case of abandonments and extensions. In disputes over these matters, local municipalities and shippers had rights of participation that gave them the upper hand and made these procedures lengthy and difficult for the rail companies (e.g., Hoogenboom and Hoogenboom 1976: 111). Although ICC figures show that it granted a majority of the abandonments applied for by the rail companies, this does not mean that rail management simply what it needed in this regard. Rather, between 1920 and 1976, the ICC did not usually approve abandonments unless practically all shippers and local governments along a line accepted them. This and the long and costly procedures involved in pursuing abandonments discouraged railroads from pursuing abandonments unless they were confident of approval (Keeler 1983: 39).

The ICC was also reluctant to come up with its own mandated plan for a consolidated national rail system – potentially the biggest change in rail governance up to that point. The plan that was finally delivered in 1929 was poorly received by the companies because it attempted, as directed by Congress, to preserve rather than reduce competition. Furthermore, because the ICC failed to press the point, nothing happened. Similarly, although the ICC was empowered to allow mergers in ad hoc cases, this was only as long as it did not reduce competition within the rail industry

for a particular region (e.g., Pegrum 1963; Locklin 1966: 225–38; Hoogenboom and Hoogenboom 1976).

Thus, the Act of 1920 did not effectively settle the long-standing problems of competition, surplus capacity, and divided administration. By contrast with the British state's regional unification of the British rail system
in 1921, the American state did not provide for a coherent governance of
the rail industry along either private capitalist or statist lines. Toward the
end of this stage during the 1960s, some consolidation did occur (see Table
5.3), but relative to the need for more unification and consolidation, as
understood in the industry, few mergers were allowed – not enough to
allow for coherent governance of the industry (e.g., Hoogenboom and
Hoogenboom 1976: esp. 47; Keeler 1983). In a recent treatment of the
issue, Keeler (1983: 36) notes that "many railroad mergers occurred in the
nineteenth century before the passage of the Sherman Anti-Trust Act in
1889, but relatively few between 1909, when the Burlington–Great Northern Pacific merger was blocked, and 1956." He goes on to observe that
although the number of ICC-permitted mergers increased after 1956, these
were of a special variety. The ICC did not allow or encourage mergers
that decreased competition between relatively strong rival empires. Rather,
seeking to keep track from being abandoned, the ICC permitted and, thus,
companies applied for mergers protecting extremely weak roads that would
otherwise have been forced to abandon their service. In short, and perhaps
ironically, the ICC tended to encourage mergers that ensured the continued
existence of what to the rail companies epitomized their problem of excess
capacity. In those situations where monopolies would have supplanted real
competition and allowed for potentially great savings in capacity, the ICC
failed to act or denied the merger, such as the case reviewed by Keeler
(1983: 36–8), the proposed Union Pacific–Rock Island merger, which was
held up for over ten years from the mid–1960s until Conrail was finally
created and the case was dropped.

All of this was quite clear to the rail companies, and they tried different
approaches to circumvent the obstacles that blocked the mergers that they
desired. In the midst of the Depression, the rail companies pressed Congress for the right to create larger corporate administrative entities via
holding companies, only to have those devices prohibited via the Emergency Act of 1933. Governance of relations between rail companies or
segments of the industry were kept in a dysfunctional condition throughout
the next few decades. Despite all of the rail companies' efforts to continue
down the road to what I have called "Phase Three Consolidation," as late
as 1959, Nelson (1959: 315–61) could still write that "the possibilities of
cost reduction through elimination of overlapping . . . services should be
explored and more widely used by the railroads. . . . Recently the railroads
have shown increased interest in mergers and coordinated use of facilities
allowing certain facilities to be abandoned or converted to other uses."

Rates, the other aspect of rail company transactions with freight customers, were the focus of constant struggle, but little effective change occurred in Stage Three, particularly insofar as less state intervention was concerned. After 1920, the ICC remained the effective arbitrator of rates. It set maximum rates and during the Depression, to prevent destructive competition, it was required to set minimum rates on an ad hoc basis, but often generally as well. As such, it largely supplanted the traffic-dividing function of pools that had finally been permitted in 1920.

Although not an adequate characterization of the relationship between the ICC and the rail companies, it is true that in some respects, the ICC was increasingly captured by the rail companies it regulated. With the "fair-return-on-fair-value" stipulation of the 1920 Act, rail companies were able to gain a number of rate increases and were allowed to collectively propose rate changes. However, it is possible as well to find numerous times during the 1930s when the ICC forcefully resisted rail company rate demands (e.g., Hoogenboom and Hoogenboom 1976: 171). Moreover, the ICC generally kept rates for agricultural products low (Sanders 1982: 35). Still, by 1976, when Congress was ready to enact certain railroad deregulations, the railroads were opposed and committed to defending existing rate regulations (e.g., Derthick and Quirk 1985: 14–16; Weaver 1985: 53–61).

How can this opposition to deregulation be explained if it were not in fact true that the rail companies had captured the ICC? The best answer to this question is that proposed first by Nelson (1959) and more recently by Sanders (1982) and Derthick and Quirk (1985). Having been more or less captured themselves by regulations, the railroads sought to capture other carriers with the same restrictions so as to not be disadvantaged. From the beginning of Stage Two, the railroads were effectively handicapped by the state in their competition with airlines and trucking. Clearly, this was and remains the case in view of the government's discriminating policies during the twentieth century regarding subsidies to carriers. While during Stage Two airlines were supplied with free airports and air traffic controllers and other workers, and while trucking received subsidized highways, the railroads were on their own. Additionally, the railroads were disadvantaged in setting their rates and designing their services. As Nelson (1959: 115) puts it:

It cannot be overlooked that the pronounced shifts of traffic and revenues from the railroads in recent years (1945–1959) have occurred under a scheme of regulatory control that affects rates and services of the railroads to a far greater extent than those of highway and water carriers; and that has tended to establish a parity of rates between rail and regulated truckers, *thus emphasizing competition rather than rate and cost competition.* (My emphasis)

In particular, Nelson and others cite evidence pointing out that the ICC's restrictions on minimum rates prevented the railroads from effectively gaining or maintaining traffic in competition with other carriers. Still, it is clear that at least later they opposed deregulating these same restrictions. This is not surprising. Given the railroad companies' failure to end state restrictions on maximum rates, they had every incentive to cling tenaciously to those restrictions that set minimum rates, while seeking simultaneously to ensure that other carriers operated under the same restrictions (e.g., Sanders 1982: 34; Derthick and Quirk 1985: 14–16).

Conclusions: The failure of negative regulation

By the close of Stage Three, the state's negative form of regulation was clearly inadequate. On the one hand, it had managed to protect the interests of workers, small businesses, and communities somewhat more than they were protected in other industries such as the steel industry. On the other hand, by 1965, the state's protection of these interests was being undermined by the one thing that the state's regulations had never adequately addressed, that is, keeping the industry solvent. Despite the gradual relaxations of the state's restrictions on rate setting, abandonments, and consolidations between 1920 and 1965, these relaxations were simply too little too late.

In a nutshell, the state's role in governance during Stage Three continued to be negative and grew more and more contradictory in form. The rail companies had remobilized sufficiently since the turn of the century to prevent the state from increasing its role in the industry. Nevertheless, because state mechanisms proved to be downwardly sticky, the rail companies were not able to shift responsibility for governing key aspects of the industry back into more private hands. In short, the stalemate between the state and the rail companies denied either side the latitude for applying the kind of coherent, "positive" solution of their own that might have solved the industry's problem of insolvency. Although the state continued to protect small business and rail worker interests, it did not have the power to take over the rails so as to keep them running. Concurrently, although the rail companies managed to stop the state from taking even more proactive measures, they were denied the usual tools businesses employ to reorganize themselves and maintain solvency, such as disinvestment, abandonment of weak roads, and regional corporate integration. In the next stage, this stalemate was broken when the state finally gained the chance to act proactively.

STAGE FOUR: THE PROACTIVE STATE AND GOVERNANCE, 1966–75

Starting with the establishment of the Department of Transportation (DOT) in 1966, the fourth stage of rail governance was characterized by a wave of more substantive, positive state interventions, including the state's takeover of national passenger rail via Amtrak and freight rail in the northeast via Conrail. In many ways, the dramatic governance transformation that occurred between 1966 and 1975 came like the sudden shift that occurs periodically along a geological fault line after the buildup of innumerable small, unreleased pressures – themselves resulting from all the smaller subterranean shifts that have already occurred. Indeed, the rather sudden spurt of state activity signaled by the creation of the DOT was in fact the product of factors that had been developing since the turn of the century. Locked into a mix of state regulation and corporate governance, which had failed to solve the industry's recurrent performance crises during all of this time, and with the mounting pressure of the need to coordinate an increasingly complex, nonrail transportation system, things clearly needed to change. They could conceivably have moved either back to a more private capitalist governance regime or toward one with an even greater role for the state. That is, the proactive, or positive, state interventions of 1966–75 were not inevitably given (e.g., Weaver 1985: 123).

The final performance crisis trigger

By 1966, although rail workers were bitterly dissatisfied with their lot, and while abandonments were causing many small shippers to lose their only transportation links with their markets, neither of these groups were sufficiently mobilized to create the huge stalemates that powered earlier governance transformations. Rather, the creation of DOT and the state takeovers that came later were precipitated by the growing failure of the railroads to find a way to maintain sufficient income in the face of numerous changes in the transportation sector and the inadequacy of state regulation.

The story of the changes in the transportation sector since 1920 is relatively well known. With the growth of the automobile industry, passenger traffic on the rails was greatly curtailed. Moreover, much of the passenger traffic that remained, especially rush-hour commuter service, was sporadic and, thus, frequently left labor and equipment idle. In addition, the growth of trucking helped reduce freight traffic on the rails to about half of what it had traditionally been after 1920 (e.g., Nelson 1959; Locklin 1966; Lyon 1968; Keeler 1983). Although aggregate national traffic recovered a bit with World War II and remained fairly level for years afterwards, in fact traffic fell off dramatically in the east and parts of the midwest while some western roads gained some new tonnage as a result of increased mining and the development of other economic activity (e.g., *Moody's,* 1980: a10; Weaver 1985: 98). With the large ratio of fixed costs in the industry, those roads that suffered stagnant or reduced traffic slipped increasingly into bankruptcy and/or abandonment.

The result of these trends and the state's restrictions on abandonments and noncompetitive mergers, as observed earlier, was an increasingly volatile income history and a deteriorating industry reinvestment situation. Over time, without the capital to cover necessary reinvestments in the industry, the condition of both rolling and fixed equipment had deteriorated to the point that trains were obligated to operate at low speeds, further undercutting their competitiveness. Moreover, because of the ICC's abandonment policies, by the middle of the 1960s, the industry had thousands of miles of freight traffic and passenger routes that earned no net income at all.

The late 1960s' failures of the Pennsylvania and New York Central railroads and their merger, the Penn Central, were not surprising. Rail problems in the northeast surpassed those that ravaged the industry generally. As opposed to traffic sectors transporting freight such as coal, railroads in the northeast carried relatively small batches of many different types of products of a higher value. This made traffic in the northeast especially vulnerable to truck competition. Furthermore, since it served the most densely populated parts of the country, it was also saddled with larger obligations regarding the generally unprofitable passenger traffic (Salsbury 1982: 32–3). In summary, a merger between the two rival companies linking the northeast with Chicago was long overdue. However, by the time it finally occurred in 1968, each of the rivals was too bankrupt to properly handle the considerable expense and operational dislocation that went along with a merger.

Writers have accused the managers of Penn Central of poor administration and dangerous stock manipulations (Saunders 1978; Roberts 1980). Indeed, Salsbury (1982) shows that the new corporation operated according to a sort of blind faith in the inherently increased efficiency of mergers and probably erred in ignoring the cautions voiced by the Penn Central's vice president in charge of finance, David C. Bevan. On the other hand, it may have been that a merger solution for an operation such as the Penn Central's might have simply been too little too late. In this regard, Keeler (1983: 49–61) makes the point that the economies of scale that accrue from a merger cannot be expected to be high in the case of a highly dense, multiproduct freight operation such as the Penn Central's. In short, although Salsbury's case against the corporation's management is valid, it is probable that the margin of error for successfully managing the Penn Central was very small given the burden of problems under which it operated. The miles of unprofitable track and the unprofitable passenger rail obligations that weighed down on the Penn Central pointed out the need for a larger solution, one that entailed changes in the way the industry as a whole was governed. In the end, although the merger apparently allowed many investors to get rich, it failed to revive the rail system in the northeast, and the new corporation was soon bankrupt. Two years after the merger was announced, the Penn Central was a problem laying at the doorstep of Congress.

No matter how important the crisis of the Penn Central was at the end of the 1960s, it could only trigger and not determine the events that followed. American industrial history is replete with examples of bankruptcies in major parts of an industry that do not necessarily lead to state takeovers. (See Chapters 6 and 7 on steel and automobiles, respectively, in this volume.) Whether in the form of loan guarantees as in 1958 or a special consolidation and subsidy package as in the case of the later Milwaukee Road Restructuring Act of 1979, alternative solutions clearly existed and were actively proposed for the rail industry. However, none was used. Rather, Congress was persuaded in 1970 to create the national passenger railroad corporation, today called Amtrak. This state-controlled corporation with a presidentially appointed board of directors operates a much reduced system that unburdened all rail companies in the country from the strain of carrying unprofitable or less-profitable passenger service. Furthermore, to deal with the rest of the bankrupt northeast region, in 1973, the state created Conrail, another state-run corporation, which ran freight service in the northeast. What is especially interesting regarding Amtrak and Conrail is that the call for a state takeover did not come from the unions, the rail companies, the passengers' groups, or the shippers. Instead, the initiative and the major force behind this wholesale jump in the state's involvement in rail governance came from the state itself. As they had been doing since their defeats after World War I, the rail unions adopted a defensive posture and simply supported any measure as long as it dealt reasonably well with their wage and job security issues. Passenger groups and shipper representatives acted similarly. Rail companies, meanwhile, had already succeeded in their drive to ensure passage of a subsidy bill being pushed by the chair of the Senate Transportation Subcommittee, Senator Vance Hartke. This bill would have covered 80% of the losses reported by the companies for their passenger lines. It was the newly created DOT under Secretary Volpe that fought a celebrated battle against the Nixon White House for the Amtrak and Conrail measures that eventually won in Congress (e.g., Saunders 1978: 308–9; Weaver 1985: 87–100).

The events of 1966 to 1975 indicate the independent effects that the state's growing institutional capacities were having on the process of governance transformation. Once in place, state agencies, charged with some aspect of governance, tended to call for further state intervention. For example, between World War I and 1966, every coordinating agency and study commission charged with recommending changes in rail governance recommended some form of a DOT (e.g., Dearing and Owen 1949: 440–8; Davis 1970; Mertins 1972). Most of the study commissions were filled partly from the ranks of the ICC, people well in touch with the problems of rail governance in their time. In part, their interest in creating a DOT stemmed from a desire to end the administrative confusion created by the fragmentation of state authority over the industry among the Department of Commerce, the ICC, and other smaller agencies, such as the Bureau of Public Roads, the Civil Aeronautics Board, and the Army (Pegrum, 1963: 501). Similarly, all three of the federal agencies that had ever been charged with the coordination of the railroads, the wartime Railroad Administration, the short-lived Federal Rail Coordinater Office during the 1930s, and the DOT itself, called for some form of federal–state ownership (Latham 1959: 86–103; Lyon 1968: 140–7; Armitage 1969: 93–5). This behavior is still the predominant pattern regarding state agencies involved with the railroads.

STAGE FIVE: THE STRUGGLE TO REVERSE THE PROACTIVE STATE, 1976–86

Stage Five has been distinguished from previous stages by efforts to reduce state involvement in rail governance. Thus, this stage has witnessed significant deregulations and efforts to reverse the state takeovers that occurred in Stage Four. Although the story of this stage is hardly over, events thus far indicate, first, that all state actions are contingent upon the relative balance of mobilization of capitalist and other class groups, and, second, that the state does not easily give up its proactive role in an industry's governance once that role is institutionalized.

Almost immediately after the creations of Amtrak and Conrail, Congress began deliberations on a deregulatory measure that was finally signed into law in 1976. The Railroad Revitalization and Regulatory Reform (4R) Act allowed greater latitude to rail companies regarding competitive minimum prices, shortened the hearing process regarding mergers, and stipulated that with ICC review, companies could abandon lines that were not making a profit. Further deregulations were enacted with the "Staggers Act" in 1980 as well as with various smaller measures that allowed Conrail to abandon more track and lay off more workers. Meanwhile, the Republican Administration of Ronald Reagan and his Secretary of Transportation Elizabeth Dole succeeded in privatizing Conrail and fought with Congress in an attempt to strangle Amtrak by cutting off its subsidies.

Although this reduction of state involvement is significant, the state's role in governance has not been reversed completely. First, all of the deregulatory acts passed so far have been coupled with provisions for subsidizing Amtrak and Conrail as well as various private lines operating outside the northeast (e.g., Keeler 1983: 33–5). Second, although Congress relaxed some ICC requirements regarding abandonments, mergers, and rates, it has continued to stress the same concerns as before and has not changed the size, prerogatives, or overall responsibilities of state agencies such as the DOT and ICC for governance. Moreover, numerous reregulations regarding rates for such things as "recyclables," coal for certain municipalities, Atlantic ports, and seasonal rates were included along with the deregulatory stipulations of the Staggers Act of 1980. Primarily, the Acts of 1976 and 1980 directed these state agencies to make sure their rulings and directives allowed for the health of the rail industry. However, who is to say that the current rewriting of rail regulations will not itself become a straightjacket for the industry, as was the case with past regulations?

Notable as well are the forces from within the state that often stymied Reagan's drive to unburden the state of Conrail and Amtrak. Congress balked repeatedly at the President's proposal to end Amtrak subsidies. Moreover, along with Congressional opposition, the Justice Department's Antitrust Division opposed the sale of Conrail to Norfolk Southern as first proposed by the DOT (Williams 1985). Indeed, the events of the past few years have testified to the institutional dynamic of state structures themselves. Even Stephen Crane, appointed by Reagan as Conrail's chief executive officer to ultimately dismantle Conrail, acted in accordance with a state-institutionalist dynamic. He was at various times the strongest force in opposition to the sale of Conrail to Norfolk Southern, and hired lobbyists and publicity relations and media consultants to wage this battle (Williams 1985).

Nevertheless, there were during this period significant moves to reverse the state's role in governance. Why? First, the creation of Amtrak and Conrail made the concern and, therefore, the regulating of private monopolies and destructive rate rivalries a bit of a moot point for a large – and formerly the most problematic – part of the national rail system. This change of affairs permitted Congress to move on to a new agenda regarding regulation. It is interesting in this regard that significant deregulations also followed in the case of the nationalization of Canadian railways (Weaver 1985) as well as after the establishment of a Ministry of Transportation and the state amalgamation of the railroads in Britain in 1920.

But who were the deregulators? Shippers by and large fought deregulation, and the labor unions were at best very apprehensive, fearing even more job losses through abandonments and service reductions. Indeed, current events signal a virtual end to the historic mobilization of the rail worker unions, and to a lesser degree small shipper and business interests, which earlier ushered in the regulations that grew to characterize so much of U.S. industrial governance.

It is also clear that the rail companies themselves did not initiate deregulation. The 4R Act in 1976 had little to offer them because, although it ended common minimum rate requirements between carriers, it did not release them from maximum rate regulations. It was only after the 4R Act was passed that the rail companies formed an association called Transportation by Rail for Agricultural and Industrial Needs (TRAIN) and enthusiastically pressed for deregulation. This organization was particularly active regarding the Staggers Act in 1980, and this time the rail companies got more maximum rate deregulation (Derthick and Quirk 1985: 15–16; Weaver 1985: 48–57).

Thus, while the rail companies began to support the deregulation drive once the ball was rolling and it appeared that it would go far enough to help them, the instigators of the current emphasis on reversing the state's role in governance are not to be found within the industry. The record shows, in fact, that the pressure for the first deregulatory measure seems to have come from a more general disposition to deregulate, as crystallized in President Ford's requirement that Congress accept deregulation as a quid pro quo for more subsidies to Conrail (Weaver 1985: 53). Indeed, the current upsurge of moves to reverse the state's role in rail governance corresponds closely to the general drive for deregulation in many major industries during the period as chronicled by Derthick and Quirk (1985). In turn, this general deregulatory drive was unmistakably a consequence of the recent mobilization of conservative capitalists as heralded by the Reagan Presidency.

In coming years it may be that a continued resurgence of capitalist mobilization will succeed in moving the state out of its role as governor of the nation's rails. Given current advances in rail technology as well as in energy and mining, railroads have started to become profitable again. For many of the past few years, Conrail has shown very respectable profits. On the other hand, although rail companies and perhaps capitalists generally are in a better position than earlier to reverse state involvement in rail governance, we simply have not yet witnessed any sort of wholesale movement back toward private capitalist governance. The private sector will probably never be interested in buying Amtrak, the nation's unprofitable passenger service.

Moreover, though weaker than before, shipper constituencies were able to mount considerable opposition in Congress to the monopoly that would have been created had Conrail been sold, as Reagan's Transportation Secretary wished, to Norfolk Southern. In short, state institutions that help govern railroads have for the most part proven to be remarkably sticky in the downward direction.

Forecasting future governance transformations in any industry is a risky business. However, technological developments such as new high-speed rail technologies are changing long-standing nature-of-the-industry requirements for the railroad industry in many important ways. Moreover, growing energy and environmental concerns as well as increasingly intractable automobile and airport congestion problems are converging to make railroads a more competitive transportation choice relative to the very carrier systems whose ascendance so recently triggered the railroad's recurrent performance crises. In short, it is probable that the next two decades will see new rail initiatives and even, perhaps, the rejuvenation of American railroading. President Bush's new Transportation Secretary is widely reported to be interested in new large-scale high-speed rail projects to deal with short- and intermediate-distance intercity travel. To the extent that these intercity rail links promise to be profitable, conservatives are likely to want to make them private initiatives. This does not, however, mean that the state is sure to relinquish its now well-institutionalized proactive role with respect to rail governance. Rather, the state is likely to be heavily involved in capitalizing and regulating any new private intercity rail links. Moreover, the state will probably create a number of publicly owned railroads, including federal- and state-owned high-speed intercity rail links as well as state- and municipally owned light rail and commuter rail systems.

It would not be surprising if the state introduced a new stage of American railroading in partnership with the private sector. World market forces remain the dominant dynamic within which governance systems must operate. Nonetheless, the world marketplace is changing. Among other things, the United States is now competing on a relatively level playing field with nations that take for granted the importance of proactive state intervention in their own economies. Even in the United States, capitalist policy analysts are showing signs of moving from a Reagan-style conservative antistate stance to one that presumes increased state involvement, albeit on behalf of capitalist profitability (e.g., Phillips 1983). In short, if the history of railroad policy is any guide to general trends, capitalist countries like the United States could very well experience a persistent and even increased involvement of the state in industrial governance in the future.

CONCLUSIONS

Some connections can be made between the specific phenomenon of the history of rail governance transformations and some of the theoretical issues under consideration in this book.

Nature-of-industry problems

The special technical, organizational, marketing, and financial requirements specific to the rail industry constituted the fundamental set of problems around which all other governance issues for the industry revolved. In the beginning, especially during Stage One, the straightforward problems, such as coordination and equipment standardization for long-haul transportation, sufficient startup capital, and sufficient traffic given fixed capital costs, were predominant. In later stages, these and related problems were joined or complicated by other developments. This is especially true regarding the mobilizations of different antirail company interests that opposed earlier rail company moves to solve these problems and govern themselves. However, although these underlying nature-of-industry problems were eventually created pressures for change, they never determined the specific outcomes of a governance transformation. For example, long-haul coordination could have been accomplished by any of the following solutions: corporate concentration of industry, which in fact occurred to an extent, state-sanctioned associational coordination, state regulations, or state ownership of an integrated system. Similarly, the industry's huge capital requirements were at different times dealt with by such diverse solutions as state grants, increased dependency on financial institutions, and stock watering.

Performance crisis as trigger

Every governance transformation experienced by the rail industry was triggered by some sort of critical breakdown of the industry's performance as it affected transactions between the rail companies and some other part of the industry. Whatever the cause, in the case of the rail companies as well as shippers, these performance crises generally took the form of earnings losses. For rail workers, breakdowns regarding their working conditions were as important as those affecting their earnings. In no case, however, did a performance crisis per se define the specific outcome of any transformation. In the Depression, the worst performance collapse in rail company history triggered the development of a conglomeration of ineffective reregulations and a new, temporary federal advising office, but in 1958, rail company losses triggered guaranteed loans, and in 1968, they led to state ownership. As suggested in what follows, the outcome of a particular governance transformation as well as whether or not a particular performance crisis was significant enough to trigger a governance transformation in the first place depended largely upon other factors.

Interest density and mobilization

First, the railroad industry's high interest density meant that resolutions of its governance crises tended to require state intervention. That is, because they involved such a large number of different interests relative to the size of the general population, when governance disputes occurred, they tended to overwhelm the organizational capacities of any private interests, including the rail companies, to resolve them. Second, the outcome of a particular governance transformation was contingent in part on the relative mobilization of these interests. The importance of the mobilization variable is especially apparent in Stages One, Two, and Five. In Stage One, the mobilization of the rail companies and capital stood essentially unchallenged and the largely private governance outcomes and capital-supporting actions of the state reflected this. In Stage Two, the antirail company mobilizations of workers and small shippers were sufficient to force the state to intervene via negative regulations to protect some of their interests. The current attempt to reverse the state's proactive role in rail governance corresponds closely with the recent mobilization of conservative, capitalist elements in the United States, culminating in the Reagan Presidency. In contrast, Stages Three and Four are not easily explained with the mobilization variable. During these stages, the level of rail worker and small shipper mobilization clearly declined, but the industry failed to adopt a governance regime that involved less state intervention, as the rail companies desired. This can be explained with reference to the following variable.

Institutional capacity of the state

Once created, the state mechanisms that partly governed the rail industry were not simply neutral instruments waiting to be captured or destroyed by the most ascendant interests. These interests from 1920 to the present, rail companies and capital generally, did not accomplish their agenda regarding the freedom to combine, to abandon tracks, and to secure the rates they wanted. Instead, state mechanisms acquired a downward stickiness and dynamic of their own. Emergency labor–management dispute boards requiring presidential intervention and ICC mechanisms for deciding mergers and abandonments tended to lock rail worker, community, and small shipper interests, respectively, into the governance decision-making process. Thus, compromises were forced on rail capitalists despite the fact that the levels of mobilization of these interests were greatly diminished. Finally, once established, state mechanisms continued to rationalize the industry in terms that presumed the continued and ever increasing involvement of the state in the governance of the rail industry. That is, the state tended to propose more elaborate and invasive forms of state intervention.

Sequential logic of governance transformations

The history of rail governance transformations evolved in five relatively distinct stages, each of which makes sense to an extent only in light of the stages that preceded it. First, each stage demonstrated the limitations of various governance options in ways that eliminated them as choices for the next search process. Second, each stage created mechanisms that acquired their own institutional dynamic and that had a certain downward stickiness, such that they were difficult to abandon or take apart. Third, the mobilizations of different interests, affecting the level of state involvement,

Table 5.4. *Trajectory and limitations of governance mechanisms and state interventions utilized in rail govenance*

Type of governance mechanism	Limitations
Intercompany/employer associations	Limited to implementation and proposals
State-sanctioned company and traffic associations	Limited to intercompany transactions not involving income competition
Corporate integration	Cannot unify diverse companies' capacity, equipment, and staff

Type of state intervention	Limitations
Individual negative state regulations	Cannot resolve interstate conflicts
Locus standi, negative national regulations	Cannot solve rail company solvency problems
Enforceable negative national regulations	Cannot ensure profitable rail company performance
Proactive state	Theoretically unlimited except by underlying market regime

tended for their own reasons to develop in a progressive fashion. Fourth, once antirail forces gained an institutional foothold within the governance regime, such as the first "locus standi" regulations of Stage Two, this contributed to the capacity of these actors to gain further influence over rail governance. Fifth, governance mechanisms at one time affected the industry's later economic performance, thus leading to further transformations.

Tendency toward nonmarket governance

Established interests in the industry sought above all to decrease the exposure of their transactions to market forces. For example, governance of rates and the supply of traffic tended to become dominated by mechanisms and forms of state intervention that were organized to provide a relatively permanent suspension of market forces. Moreover, the historical development of these mechanisms and forms of intervention became progressively stronger in the sense that they increasingly reduced the influence of market forces in industry governance.

As summarized in Table 5.4, the trajectory of weakest to strongest governance mechanisms moved from professional associations, intercompany associations, traffic associations, state-sanctioned traffic associations, to corporate integration. For state intervention, the trajectory developed from negative regulations at the level of individual state governments, to formal and then enforceable negative regulations at the federal level, to proactive state intervention through the DOT.

The tendency of governance in the industry to evolve in the direction of stronger institutions seems partly a function of the limitations of the less-institutionalized mechanisms. Table 5.4 summarizes what the record indicates regarding the rail industry. Clearly, associational governance was not capable of providing lasting solutions to rail governance problems, at least relative to such solutions as corporate combination and state intervention. Again and again, on rate issues and long-haul coordination issues, associational governance was forced to give way to corporate combination. On the other hand, even the strongest private form of governance, corporate combination, was incapable of dealing with the governance crisis created by the mobilization of rail workers. For these intra- and interclass struggles, governance in the rail industry required state intervention.

None of this implies that an evolution toward the increasing domination of the state over rail governance cannot be reversed, or that it applies generally to all U.S. industries. The tendency of an industry's governance regime to evolve in a statist direction remains circumscribed for the foreseeable future by the market forces and the larger capitalist system that still dominates the national and international economy.

6

GOVERNANCE OF THE STEEL INDUSTRY: WHAT CAUSED THE DISINTEGRATION OF THE OLIGOPOLY?

Christoph Scherrer
John F. Kennedy Institute, Free University of Berlin

For generations, the U.S. steel industry has been a prototypical oligopoly. It has been the subject of innumerable antitrust investigations by Congress, the courts, and economists. Its leaders have taken pride in having overcome the "chaotic" nature of competitive markets, thus maintaining remarkably stable steel prices. In contrast, we now read in the trade press of price rebates that exceed 25% of the list price. Advocates of protectionism blame imports for the industry's loss of price-setting power.

Students of the U.S. steel industry show us that there are now in fact two steel industries, one that tries to cling to oligopolistic practices, and one that is highly competitive (Barnett and Schorsch 1983; Acs 1984; Barnett and Crandall 1986). The latter, the so-called minimills sector, is credited with having captured more than 20% of the domestic steel market, and this sector is expected to continue to thrive. In the future, it is believed, the minimills will alter the structure of the U.S. steel industry permanently.

The deterioration in the competitive position of American integrated steel makers and the subsequent disintegration of the oligopoly is frequently attributed to the oligopoly structure itself (e.g., Borrus 1982; Barnett and Schorsch 1983; Acs 1984). This popular thesis often ascribes the crisis in the U.S. integrated steel industry to subjective factors, such as management's refusal to abandon its oligopolistic behavior. Management, of course, rejects this contention and blames factors outside its control, such as slow market growth, U.S. and foreign government steel policies, and labor, among others (American Iron and Steel Institute 1980). The product life cycle thesis, that the decline in the U.S. steel industry was inevitable (e.g., Kurth 1979; Markusen 1985), supports this view.

However, there are problems with these arguments. For example, both approaches tend to focus only on industry-specific factors, when others may also be involved. Furthermore, most academic studies of the steel industry that focus on structure do not distinguish clearly between the factors that underlie a particular structure and the structure itself. Oligopolistic structure is commonly conceptualized in an idealized fashion; that is, it is thought of as the product of choice and is judged accordingly on normative grounds. As is shown in this chapter, many features of the steel oligopoly were deeply rooted in the unique characteristics of the steel production process and could not be disposed of at will. Compounding the analytical problems is the rather loose use of the term oligopoly. Although its effect is evident, that is, price rigidity, its working mechanisms are often clouded by suspicions of evil intentions on the part of big business.

To remedy these shortcomings, this study uses a disaggregated approach to the structural changes in the industry. With the help of the typology of governance mechanisms, discussed in Chapter 1, the constituent elements of the former oligopolistic structure are defined and identified. This allows tracing changes in the structure of the steel industry more precisely. It should also help us discover which aspects of the oligopolistic structure impeded the process of adaptation and to what extent governance mechanisms could have been changed to facilitate this process.

A governance approach to the industry's structure reveals that the governance mechanisms in the oligopoly were an appropriate response to the industry's main problem, cutthroat competition due to immense outlays of capital. Although the need for price stability can be deduced from the imperatives of economies of scale, the emergence of particular governance mechanisms was contingent on a variety of factors, the national economic and legal framework being of greatest importance. The basic challenges to this structure originated in macroeconomic and political developments that were outside the control of the original participants of the oligopoly, and thus they failed to require that new competition conform to the rules of the game.

Structural rigidities facilitated the rise of new competitors, but a more flexible response was ruled out precisely by the large capital outlays and low capital mobility that caused the rigidities in the first place. Low capital mobility proved especially decisive with regard to labor. Thus, although it will be shown that a number of governance mechanisms compounded the problems of the industry, seeming to confirm many academic studies on the steel industry, it will also become evident that these elements of the oligopoly were not subject to managerial decisions, thereby giving credibility to managements' contentions that such forces were outside their control.

However, could some of the serious impediments to adaptation have been overcome by state intervention? I question the common notion that the lack of a European-style steel policy is predominantly the result of sociopolitical structures peculiar to the United States (Dyson 1983). Instead, I argue that the major obstacles to a corporatist style of crisis management rested in the specific structural conditions of the U.S. steel industry. Again the emphasis is on the problems that arise from the high capital requirements of integrated steel production.

Accordingly, I start with a description of the steel industry's governance mechanisms and the way they functioned before large-scale import penetration of the U.S. market began. This is followed by an inquiry into the causes of the new competition that disrupted the structure of the oligopoly. Next I explore the extent to which particular governance mechanisms have impeded the process of adaptation to the new competitive environment. I then offer an analysis of the reasons why the American steel industry preferred trade protection rather than a European-style tripartite management of its adjustment crisis. Finally, a discussion of this chapter's main findings is combined with a look at current trends in the evolution of governance in the domestic steel industry.

THE ELEMENTS OF OLIGOPOLY

In the period preceding the arrival of large quantities of foreign steel in the U.S. market and the rise of the minimills, the structure of the domestic steel industry looked very much like a textbook definition of an oligopoly. A few, highly vertically integrated firms organized most of the steel production and dominated the market. But why had the market been replaced as the dominant governance mechanism? It is argued that the steel industry's production process required market stability. However, although the need for stability clearly results from the imperatives of economies of scale, the means to achieve it appear to be contingent.

The spatial organization of steel production that has historically been most efficient has been the concentration of blast furnaces, steel converters, and rolling mills in one location. This geographical integration has been further enhanced by such energy-saving devices as the use of blast furnace gases for energy in all stages of the production process. Thus, a precondition for success in the steel market was lowered production costs through maximum integration in this production chain (Chandler 1977: 258–9; U.S. Office of Technology Assessment 1980: 187).

But not only benefits were associated with spatial concentration and economies of scale. First, the indivisibility and durability of plant and equipment made it impossible for the producer to plan growth to keep in step with expanding markets (Steindl 1976: 10). Furthermore, the demand for steel proved to be extremely cyclical. Therefore, the steel producers frequently found themselves with problems of excess capacity. In neoclassical analysis, the adjustment of supply to shifts in demand happens either through price changes or by changing numbers of competitors. For various reasons, the steel producers struggled to avoid these mechanisms.

One reason was that the price elasticity of demand for steel is relatively low (MacPhee 1974: 58). Consequently, potential sales increases do not compensate for the loss of revenue from price reductions. In addition, with fixed costs representing a rather high percentage of total costs, competitive pricing in periods of slack demand could trigger a devastating price war. As long as the variable production costs (current expenses) are met, the continuation of production is preferable to a shutdown, although depreciation of the fixed capital incurs huge losses. The propensity to continue operations despite a decline in demand is further strengthened by the high costs that are associated with the shutdown and startup of a blast furnace (Stocking 1954: 25).

What mechanisms were available to avoid the negative consequences of market competition? The industry experimented with various governance mechanisms. Historically, the use of promotional networks, such as pools or cartels, has accompanied the trend toward horizontal mergers. In the United States, cartels lacked legal sanctions, so their stability depended on the intelligence and good faith of their members. Successive failures among the cartels stimulated horizontal mergers and takeovers that culminated in the formation of the United States Steel Corporation (U.S. Steel) in 1901, with control of more than 65% of American steel production (Hogan 1970/1971: 480). With U.S. Steel's inception, a means for stability was found that no longer had to rely on pool agreements or further capital concentration. Two elements formed the basis of the new and rather stable governance regime in the steel industry. First, U.S. Steel's tremendous financial resources, its modern equipment (at least at the turn of the century), and its control over a large portion of the steel industry's raw material resources had put it in such a strong position that its competitors could in no conceivable way win a price war. Second, the willingness of U.S. Steel to allow its competitors a disproportionate share of market growth (by the 1960s, its market share had declined to about 25%; Adams and Mueller 1982: 80) removed the incentive for competitors to challenge it in the marketplace through price cuts or in court with antitrust action.[1]

This "friendly competition" strategy can be explained partly by U.S. Steel's conscious determination to avoid a court-ordered breakup. Contrary to the fate of Standard Oil and American Tobacco, whose aggressive behavior had won them many enemies among their competitors, U.S. Steel secured a favorable ruling from the Supreme Court that rested partly on the friendly testimony of competitors (Adams 1954: 151). But it can also be argued that U.S. Steel wanted to sustain above-average profits by growing at a slower rate than the market, thus reaping the benefits of a higher rate of capacity utilization (Piore and Sabel 1984: 56).

By the time U.S. Steel had lost its hegemony, though it remained the strongest and largest steel producer in the United States, eight other companies, who together supplied about 75% of the steel for domestic consumption (U.S. Federal Trade Commission 1977: 53), had formed a tight oligopoly. This group of companies, so-called "Big Steel," were among twenty-three *integrated* firms that by 1964 owned about 98% of the U.S. pig iron capacity and about 93% of its steel capacity. The remaining 7%

---

1 For a discussion of dominant-firm strategies, see Lamoreaux (1985).

of the country's steel capacity was shared by sixty-six *semiintegrated* companies.[2] Additionally, some 124 *nonintegrated* steel companies were in the business of finishing steel (Weiss 1967: 140). The *integrated* companies combined the production steps at least from the preparation of coal and ore to the rolling of semifinished steel. They also sold considerable quantities of semifinished steel to the *nonintegrated* sector. The *semiintegrated* mills relied on outside suppliers for pig iron and scrap. They often specialized in the production of stainless and high-alloy tool steels that did not require large production facilities (Weiss 1967: 142).

The distinctive feature of Big Steel was a high degree of vertical integration. The mechanism of corporate hierarchy governed the production process of steel well beyond the melting of steel, which accounts for only about 10% of the whole process as well as of its costs (Barnett and Schorsch 1983: 114).

Upstream, in the production steps prior to the melting of steel, most of the major steel companies owned sources of raw material. Coal and iron ore were supplied predominantly by captive mines, though the degree of self-sufficiency varied from company to company (Hogan 1970/1971: 1485). Only marginal amounts of raw material, besides scrap, were purchased under short-term market agreements (U.S. Federal Trade Commission 1977: 37). Big Steel also exercised a high degree of control over the transport for its supplies of ore (Hogan 1970/1971: 1495).

The motives for Big Steel to control upstream resources were largely defensive and not rooted in economies-of-scale considerations (Chandler 1977: 363). On the one hand, these investments protected the steel companies against the opportunistic behavior of a small number of mining firms, an especially important consideration because of the volatility of steel demand. On the other hand, corporate control over raw material resources made entry extremely expensive because it forced a prospective entrant to make heavy capital investments in exploration for iron ore (Lamoreaux 1985: 145–7).

Downstream, in all the production steps after the primary rolling of steel, the Big Steel companies produced almost all makes and grades of steel. They also controlled some of the steel-consuming companies, especially in steel wire, but also construction companies and ship yards (Scheuerman 1975: 341). In addition, the producers owned some of the largest steel service centers in the country (Patton 1985: 37).[3]

---

2 Historically, the term "Big Steel" was used for the United States Steel Company (U.S. Steel) and "Little Steel" referred to the other major integrated companies: Bethlehem Steel Corp., National Steel Corp., Republic Steel Corp., Jones and Laughlin Steel Corp., Armco Inc., Inland Steel Corp., and Youngstown Sheet and Tube Corp.

3 The steel service centers are the principal means for distributing steel to the small customer. They allow the mills to take advantage of economies of scale in production, while keeping the small customer supplied with timely deliveries of specific products.

Forward integration not only ensured the viability of existing mill locations, but also reduced the degree of competition among the steel producers.[4] It provided for a captive market for some of the companies' output. Similar effects resulted from long-term contracts with some of the industry's largest customers.[5]

This centralization of control was complemented by open communication between the steel producers. Engineering societies, such as the American Institute of Mining, Metallurgical, and Petroleum Engineers, and the Association of Iron and Steel Engineers, provided for a constant exchange among the steel engineers on technical aspects of steelmaking. Independent trade and technical publications, such as *Iron Age, 33 Metals, Blast Furnace and Steel Plant Engineer,* and *American Metal Market,* further facilitated the free flow of information that, together with patent agreements, prevented the development of any significant technological advantage for one firm (Christiansen 1982: 77; Lynn 1982: 131). Thus, production cost differences were kept to a minimum.

Though not voluntarily instituted, the practice of multiemployer bargaining also helped equalize production costs.[6] The twelve largest steel producers formed a multiemployer bargaining unit that negotiated the labor contract, usually for a period of three years, with the United Steelworkers of America (USWA) on behalf of its participating members (Hogan 1970/ 1971: 1633). Because 92% of total national ingot capacity was organized by the USWA, other companies usually followed these collective bargaining agreements (Stieber 1960). As in the automobile industry (see Chapter 7 on automobiles in this volume), these had a distinct "job control focus," further reinforcing interfirm wage equality. The rigid classification of jobs

4 On the attempts to preserve investment at geographically unfavorable locations, see Stocking (1954: 60) and Warren (1973: 203).
5 In some instances, relations with large steel consumers have extended beyond the regular purchase of steel. In the early 1950s, General Motors helped finance new equipment at two mills because it was afraid of a steel shortage. The specific condition for the payback of these loans was repayment on the basis of tonnage shipped to GM (U.S. Senate 1956: 366).
6 The relationship between capital concentration and unionization of the industry is quite intriguing. In the beginning, concentration led to the demise of craft control. In the famous Homestead Strike of 1893, Andrew Carnegie used his vast resources and political power to crush the union of skilled steelworkers. In the aftermath of the Homestead massacre, the industry mechanized quickly, further undermining the position of skilled labor. By 1909, the union had been driven out of the industry. Their hard line in the unsuccessful steel strike of 1919 again illustrated the power of the steel bosses (Brody 1960). When in 1937 the steelworkers were finally able to challenge the corporations, the union won bargaining rights for almost half of the industry's work force through gaining a contract with U.S. Steel. Other companies were able to hold out against the union, often with violent means. However, after a court ordered the reinstatement of 7,000 union members at Republic in 1940, the USWA was able to organize the rest of the industry very quickly (McColloch 1987).

and the elimination of merit in the determination of individual paychecks allowed for the adoption of a uniform wage scale throughout the industry (Tilove 1948). In addition, the seniority system provided for the smooth adjustment of employment to output, reducing the pressure to cut prices during periods of weak demand.

An important role in regulating competition among the steel companies was performed by the industry's trade association, the American Iron and Steel Institute (AISI). Beyond fulfilling the ordinary tasks of trade associations, such as overseeing government activities, organizing trade fairs, and collecting statistics, AISI was engaged in grading steel qualities. Together with publication of the list prices for U.S. Steel, the grading activity made for easy comparison of prices on standard products. At one time (in the period of multiple basing-point pricing), the industry's trade journal, *Iron Age,* collaborated by publishing the latest freight rates as well (Adams 1954: 162).[7]

In conjunction with mutual collective bargaining, joint subsidiaries (Fusfeld 1958), and interlocking directorates (Scheuerman 1975), AISI provided the institutional framework for a network among the chief executives of the major steel companies. The industry's leaders were known for their common culture of business practices, which one observer has called the industry's "finely-honed *esprit de corps*" (Scherer 1970: 210). Having its origin in the famous Gary dinners of 1907 through 1911, this corpsgeist, or collective corporate spirit, was still prevalent in the 1960s (e.g., Cordtz 1967).[8]

Although governance mechanisms such as the corporate hierarchy represented institutional forms for providing stability, this management network, a form of monitoring, added the personal element that was necessary for price collusion. In cases such as special orders for individual customers, where virtually infinite gradations in finish, temper, etc., made price comparisons difficult, management even resorted to illegal activity, such as covert meetings, where they agreed on uniform standards (Scherer 1970: 159).

The foremost effect of this interplay of different governance mechanisms was the practice of "administered pricing" (Adelman 1961). At regular intervals, usually after contract negotiations, U.S. Steel announced across-the-board price increases. After 1958, U.S. Steel's price leadership was replaced by a "barometric" price-leadership system. The companies now

7 It was abandoned in 1948 after a successful antitrust case against another basing-point system in the cement industry. In its simplest form, this system meant that the industry sold at the Pittsburgh price plus freight from Pittsburgh regardless of where the steel was delivered from. For more details, see Stocking (1954).
8 On the initiative of Judge Gary, who was the president of U.S. Steel, the industry's leaders met, in Gary's own words, to "tell one to the others of all the circumstances surrounding [their] particular business" (Hogan 1970/1971: 533).

took turns announcing price increases for a limited number of products (Weiss 1971: 175).

The practice of "oligopolistic cooperation" (Munkirs and Sturgeon 1985) effectively suppressed the potential influence of demand fluctuations on the price structure. Changes in demand were not even reflected in noticeable deviations from list prices (Crandall 1981: 31). This permitted producers to avoid outright losses unless output fell below 40% of capacity. The temptation to engage in price cutting once demand became soft was therefore reduced (Scherer 1970: 197).

Another factor that accounts for this arrangement is to be found in the fact that similar or functionally equivalent structures and institutions were also existent in other industries at that time. In conjunction with a Keynesian state that stabilized overall demand and guaranteed the development of credit money, stability in the core industries allowed for a high level of consumption that was congruent with the potentials of mass production. In particular, the post–War invention of linking wages and productivity through industrywide collective bargaining created a new level of mass consumption. In addition to linking demand to the rate of growth in productivity, the establishment of a social safety net made possible increased individual consumption of durable goods (Aglietta 1979: 155–61; Piore and Sabel 1984: 79–84). The two commodities that typified the new consumption norm, the suburban home and the automobile, had a profound impact on the steel industry.[9] The greatly increased demand for sheet steel used in automobiles and home appliances filled the vacuum left by declining military orders (Hogan 1970/1971: 1443). The contractualization of wages and the establishment of privately funded welfare programs, however, assumed that the major firms would be able to control their prices relatively independently of fluctuations in demand. As the case of steel has shown, high barriers to entry through extensive vertical integration and close collaboration between the autonomous firms provided the required stability.

THE EMERGENCE OF NEW COMPETITION

In the late 1960s, competitors outside the old oligopoly began to challenge the price-setting power of Big Steel. Foreign steel mills expanded their market share in the United States from 4.7% in 1960 (Hogan 1972: 49) to 26.4% in 1984 (American Iron and Steel Institute, *Annual Statistical Yearbooks*). At the same time, the minimills emerged as a whole new sector in the domestic steel industry. Its market share rose from 3% in 1960 to around 21% in 1985 (Barnett and Crandall 1986: 102). Furthermore, other materials, such as aluminum, found widespread application at the expense

---

9 For the intriguing relationship between these two commodities and the increased intensity of labor at the workplace, see Aglietta (1979: 158).

of steel. According to scholarly literature on the crisis in steel, the integrated producers were unable or unwilling to meet the new competition from foreign producers and minimills.[10] Most scholars challenge the contention of many steel industry leaders, trade union officials, and politicians that state subsidies caused the import problem. They concede that some of the weaker competitors in the world market received substantial government subsidies, but argue that the major competitive advantages for foreign steel were attributable to superior technology and lower overall costs.

Since these arguments are well developed with regard to the strength of some foreign producers and domestic minimills, the present analysis touches only briefly on cost comparisons. Instead, the analysis focuses on an area that has been neglected so far – the socioeconomic interdependence between the rise of foreign producers and the minimills, on the one hand, and the stagnation of the domestic mills, on the other.

The growth path of foreign mills

As a basic industry in the period of reconstruction after World War II, the European steel industry received a great deal of governmental attention. However, the real growth of foreign steel capacity was attributable to the unfolding of a mass-consumption market, particularly the rapid increase in demand for automobiles and other steel-intensive durable goods, which provided an El Dorado for the steel producers. Fast market growth made it easy to maintain high operating rates while lowering unit costs and, thus, increasing profitability. Boosted profits and cash flow fostered the construction of new plants and the adoption of the latest technology. Competitiveness was further enhanced by the resulting reduction in labor requirements (Barnett and Schorsch 1983: 143).

The United States' contribution to the so-called European and Japanese economic miracles was due less to the much heralded "Marshall Plan" than to the inauguration of a new system of international relations, especially a new system of monetary rules and institutions. The Bretton Woods agreement on fixed exchange rates created the stability necessary for an orderly growth in trade. The simultaneous introduction of the dollar as the major international currency allowed the United States to pursue expansionary economic policies without being subjected to the normal balance-of-payment restraints. Furthermore, while keeping the dollar overvalued after the mid–1950s, the United States stimulated capital exports to and commodity imports from the emerging countries. The capital exports facilitated the diffusion of superior U.S. management and production techniques,

10 For example, see Crandall (1981), Borrus (1982), Barnett and Schorsch (1983), and Acs (1984).

thus furthering growth within the United States, while domestic expansion within emerging countries, together with a high trade dollar, provided an external stimulus for those economies (Altvater, Hoffman, and Semmler 1980; Aglietta 1982).

Although the overall productivity of German and Japanese steel works did not reach the American level before the 1970s (U.S. Federal Trade Commission 1977: 476; Marcus and Kirsis 1981), unit labor costs, that is, wage costs per ton, were less in both countries from the 1950s onward. The lower wage bill far outweighed the shortcomings in productivity. While in 1969 the average Japanese steel mill lagged by 35% in labor productivity, its wage costs per hour were only about 30% of the U.S. level (Marcus and Kirsis 1981).

It was not only lower labor costs that favored the foreign producers, but also lower capital costs. For the period from 1964 to 1967, the cost for adding one ton of integrated steel capacity was only $85 in Japan, but $399 in the United States (Thorn 1975: 8). More recent studies suggest that the Japanese enjoyed a 28 to 41% cost advantage in the late 1970s (Barnett 1977). Those lower capital costs encouraged the installation of modern equipment and thus facilitated growth in productivity.

Some of the higher increases in productivity in both Japan and in West Germany stem from their adaptive labor relations systems (Christiansen 1982: 203). Although efforts to quantify the effects of different labor–management relations in steel by comparing West Germany with the United States were rather unsuccessful (Naples 1981; Christiansen 1982: 139), the rich literature on industrial relations in the international auto industry does suggest that the lack of job control in the labor contracts of both countries has had a positive effect on productivity (see Chapter 7 on automobiles in this volume).

Finally, a drastic decline in ocean freight rates benefitted foreign producers in two ways. First, it lowered their raw material costs, and, second, it facilitated exports to distant markets (U.S. Council on Wage and Price Stability 1977: 71; Crandall 1981: 23).

After the first oil price hikes in the early 1970s, international competition intensified. Post–War expansion for many countries was coming to an end; growth rates declined and the market for consumer durables became saturated. The emergence of excess capacity in the steel industry led to a very precarious situation. As explained earlier, with fixed costs representing a rather high percentage of total costs, producers were tempted to engage in price battles on the basis of incremental costs. Such a price war would have forced out the producers with the highest costs. For national security reasons and in order to avoid the social and political consequences of mass layoffs, the national governments propped up their weakest steel mills with subsidies and arranged for the establishment of a European cartel. Countermeasures were taken. For example, the granting of subsidies was tied to the willingness to reduce capacity (Woolcock, Hart, and van der Ven 1985: 34). However, the consequence of this governmental intervention was continued excess capacity (Barnett and Schorsch 1983: 47). Therefore, the rationale for seeking export opportunities remained. The case of Japan differs in that the extraordinarily favorable competitive position of its steel industry encouraged privately funded expansion of capacity even in the latter half of the 1970s. By the 1980s, the steel recession had also caught up with the Japanese producers, as some Asian and Latin American countries had started to develop their own steel industries with even lower production costs (Hogan 1984: 153–82). Originally planned for their own growing demand for steel, the new steelworks had been forced to seek markets abroad. The austerity measures invoked by the international debt crisis had stifled internal growth (Hurtienne 1985: 34–64).

While the international austerity regime drove the foreign steel producers into an export strategy, the attempt by the Reagan Administration to regain the United States' old hegemonic position directed the export flows to the United States (Schubert 1985: 72). The fast appreciation of the dollar against most currencies in the early 1980s made almost every foreign producer cost competitive with the domestic mills.

The rise of the minimills

As a relatively new sector in the steel industry, the minimills deserve some detailed attention. A comprehensive definition of minimills was given by Barnett and Schorsch (1983). They distinguish between minimills and integrated mills along three dimensions. First, minimills produce carbon steel by melting scrap in electric furnaces. This *technology* eliminates the need for the coke ovens and blast furnaces found in integrated plants. Second, they have generally been located in smaller regional *markets,* endowed with local sources of scrap and isolated by transportation costs from competition with other producers or scrap purchasers. Finally, they concentrate on relatively simple, low-value commodity *products* such as wire rod, concrete reinforcing bar, and merchant-quality bars and shapes (Barnett and Schorsch 1983: 85).

In 1988, this description fit about thirty-two companies in the United States with fifty-one works and a net capacity of 21 million tons (*Iron and Steelmaking* 1988: 18–36), up from about 4 million tons in 1960 (*The New York Times* 1984a). The minimills' competitive edge also translated into higher-than-average profit rates. Between 1970 and 1979, the annual average net return on assets for a sample of minimills was 7.17%, that is, almost twice as high as for the integrated steel industry, which showed an average of 3.74% (Wyman 1980: 4). The lead taken by the minimills continued through the recession of 1981–3, when some minimills managed to remain profitable in spite of a drop in the capacity utilization rate to below 50% (Schorsch 1984: 31). How can their success be explained?

Technology accounts for much of the mini's success. Their use of the electric furnace in combination with continuous casting results in substantial capital and labor savings. The capital costs per ton of steel shipment capacity varied for several minimills between $154 and $320 in 1978 and 1979, and estimates for integrated carbon-steel plants on greenfield sites ranged from $956 to $1,514 and for roundouts of existing facilities from $520 to $880 (U.S. Office of Technology Assessment 1980: 315). Part of this great difference is due to a different product mix, but capital costs per ton of wire rods, the typical minimill product, were still twice as high in the integrated steel works (Barnett and Schorsch 1983: 175). This also translates into lower labor requirements. By 1980, a minimill far outdistanced its integrated counterpart in the production of wire rod; instead of 6.45 man-hours per ton (MHPT), they required only 3.51 MHPT (Barnett and Schorsch 1983: 119). The causes for this difference in productivity were mainly to be found in the lack of primary processes, but also in the advantages of specialization and higher capacity utilization.

To compensate for the lack of economies of scale, minimills specialize in a limited range of products. Most of the mills produce mainly rebars and rounds, and may roll one or more products. Few companies offer more than five different steel makes. The specialization reduces downtime for tool adjustment, requires less operating skills, and saves on sales and engineering staff (for details, see Scherrer 1988b: 1188–9).

In sum, minimills enjoy the best of two worlds: their technology allows for high labor savings, thus increasing their capital–labor ratio, and yet their capital unit costs are much lower in absolute terms than are those of integrated works. These advantages, together with lower hourly wages and more freedom to discipline workers (Scherrer 1988b: 1188–9), enabled minimills to produce a ton of wire rod for $284 compared with $393 at an integrated steel work (Barnett and Schorsch 1983: 95).

However, these technologically induced cost advantages did not emerge overnight. In fact, in 1958, labor productivity in minimills compared unfavorably with integrated wire rod production and only slowly did minimills gain their current lead (Barnett and Schorsch 1983: 119). For the full development of the technological potential of minimill steelmaking, the minimills had to have time to develop as a viable alternative to integrated steel mills. Although incremental progress in technology reinforced the viability of the minimills step by step, their success was also critically dependent on "environmental" factors.

The growth path of minimills. The emergence of the minimills in the United States appears to be closely related to the migration of U.S. industry to the Sunbelt, where capacity expanded most dynamically.[11] This relation, however, is not coincidental, because minimills were well suited to the sociopolitical climate of the south. Lacking a tradition of mass-production industries, the south was governed by a set of social regulations that differed markedly from those in the north or in Europe. As a result of the federalist structure of the state and an implicit understanding with northern industrialists, southern politicians were able to exempt their states from many social provisions of the New Deal legacy (Piven and Cloward 1972). The resulting availability of a large and docile labor pool, a low level of taxation, and high responsiveness to infrastructure requirements made the south attractive for northern capital in the 1960s.

Unlike many manufacturing industries (Bluestone and Harrison 1982), the integrated steel mills, for a variety of reasons, did not capitalize on the advantages the south offered. Slow market growth in the United States did not warrant the addition of new integrated capacity, and the southern boom did not require sheet steel, for which integrated technology is best suited. Furthermore, the indivisibility of the integrated production process forestalled any dispersion of parts of the production process to the south. Finally, it would have been impossible to avoid unionization.[12]

This inability of the integrated producers to take part in the migration to the Sunbelt opened up opportunities for steelmaking on the basis of the new technology and organizational principles of the minimill. There were three reasons for this development. First, the low capital requirements of minimills allowed outsiders/foreigners to invest in minimill steelmaking capacity at little risk. Without exposure to domestic unionized steel workers, they were in a better position to organize the labor process according to their own perceptions. Second, locating steel mills close to a regional market, as was now possible with the minimills, minimized transportation costs, thus protecting them from their competitors in the north. Geographical mobility also allowed managers of minimills to select locations with weak labor markets and to threaten to relocate in the event of unacceptable labor demands (maximizing management authority).[13] Third, the minimills'

11 Although in the 1960s, the first minimills tended to be located in the traditional steel regions, in the 1970s, more than 50% of all minimill capacity growth took place in the south and only 29% in the northeast, central, and mid-Atlantic regions. In the 1980s, this share increased to 70% whereby the south central region became the favorite location (calculated on the basis of *Iron and Steelmaking* [1987] and Barnett and Crandall [1986: 8]).

12 The automobile industry had opened many subsidiary plants to make auto parts in the south, though with limited success. Their vulnerability to the pressure of the union in their old locations prevented them from making full use of the subordinate position of labor in the south. In fact, by the end of the 1970s, the UAW had succeeded in organizing almost all of Ford, Chrysler, and General Motor's southern plants (Katz 1985: 123).

13 Nucor had built its plants in nonurban areas on the theory that people there would be more willing to work hard and less willing to unionize (Sease 1981). About 40% of the

product lines met the specific steel requirements of the booming construction industry in the south, for example, concrete reinforcing bars and light structural steel.

In comparison, the conditions of the north were less favorable for the development of minimills. In the absence of lower labor costs and higher labor discipline as well as lower transportation costs, the other advantages of minimills were clearly outweighted by the integrated mills' economies of scale. Nevertheless, the availability of inexpensive scrap also allowed for the existence of northern minimills.

Minimill expansion under the umbrella of the major mills. While the South provided the sociopolitical framework for the minimills to expand, their rise also depended on developments in the integrated sector. Scrap is the main feedstock of electric furnace operations and the most costly input item of electrically produced steel (at least 50%, Hersch 1984: 101), so electric furnace capacity can expand only if enough inexpensive scrap is available. With the transition from open hearth furnaces, which can use a scrap charge of more than 50%, to the basic oxygen furnace, for which slightly over 30% has been the average (Wyman 1980: 19), more scrap became available. The loss of a significant part of the domestic market to imported steel products added another new supply of scrap. The net result was that scrap prices remained relatively low (Wyman 1980: 14–19). Minimills were in a better position than integrated mills to capitalize on the decline in scrap prices. They were able to locate in areas where scrap was in abundant supply and therefore available at even lower prices (Marcus and Kirsis 1984: 4–9).

Another source of minimill growth directly related to the integrated mills was the oligopolistic pricing policy in steel. Substantial price increases by the Big Steel producers during the 1950s made entry into the market very attractive to minimill producers (Barnett and Schorsch 1983: 84). When the pricing rigidities of Big Steel weakened at the end of the 1960s, import quotas were imposed to maintain the general price levels (Hufbauer, Berliner, and Elliott 1986: 158). Because the foreign producers reacted with a shift to higher-priced items and with a substantial increase in prices for wire rods (Hogan 1972: 59), the minimills became the principal beneficiaries of the integrated firms' push for protectionism. After the implementation of the Trigger Price Mechanism in 1977, minimills were again able to expand their market share at the expense of imports (Scherrer 1988a: 479).[14]

minimills are organized by the USWA, and even in the unionized minimills, average compensation, including benefits, tends to be some 25% lower than in the integrated mills (Scherrer 1988b).

14 In the first two years after the enactment of the initial VRA, the import share of the minimill markets declined drastically from about 25% to about 14% (Barnett and Schorsch

Finally, the minimills may have profited from the lack of a cohesive national steel policy. Public support for the modernization of the steel industry would certainly have gone to the integrated mills, where the political power of some of the largest U.S. corporations combined with the strength of a highly organized industrial union, as well as with the local and state governments whose tax base depended on the steel industry.[15] Naturally, reinvigoration of the integrated mills with public money would have strengthened their competitive position. Furthermore, the introduction of antipollution laws placed a heavier burden on the integrated sector, where coke ovens and blast furnaces were the major sources of pollution (Barnett and Schorsch 1983: 250). Therefore, the United States apparently followed unintentionally a strategy that fostered the growth of a new, highly efficient way of steel making.

A comparison with Europe seems to support this argument. The growth of the very efficient minimills in Italy, the so-called Bresciani, has been retarded by the Eurofer cartel that allocates production quotas on past production volume (Eisenhammer and Rhodes 1986: 452). In Germany, the minimill pioneer Korf blamed his bankruptcy in 1983 on the quota system and the tight alliances between the integrated producers and the major West German banks (Engert and Wolf 1983: 12–17).

In sum, three aspects of the minimill's successes stand out. First, the lack of national cohesiveness, as exemplified by the north–south dichotomy and by the absence of an explicit industrial policy, provided the sociopolitical framework for minimill expansion. Second, minimill growth was clearly encouraged by developments in the integrated mills: the declining demand for scrap, the original oligopolistic price policy, and the ability of the integrated producers to obtain import restrictions. Finally, favorable production and market conditions held out prospects for higher profits that encouraged the flow of capital into minimills. In turn, these investments allowed the use of improved technology, which reduced costs and boosted profits for the next round of investments, thus creating a cycle of continuing growth.

RESTRAINTS ON THE INTEGRATED MILLS

In order to combat the onslaught of foreign competitors successfully, the Big Steel companies needed to become low-cost producers themselves. Since the Japanese mills represented the most efficient practice in sheet production, and since the latest minimill constructions epitomized the best

---

1983: 89), while at the same time, the total market shares of foreign producers were reduced from 16.7 to 13.8%.

15 The absence of minimill representation in the Steel Tripartite Advisory Committee (U.S. Department of Labor 1980) suggests their minor role in any steel policy deliberations.

practice in production of small bars and rods, Big Steel had to follow the Japanese and the minimill examples, respectively. These goals have not been achieved. Big Steel neither came close to the economies of scale, state-of-the-art technology, and efficient labor use of Japanese mills nor managed minimills successfully.[16] For this failure, most of the scholarly literature points to the oligopolistic structure of the industry. Borrus puts it most drastically: "... the industry's oligopolistic structure, ... was to become a singular structural barrier to the industry's ability to respond to foreign competition in the 1960's" (1982: 71).

In this section, I explore the extent to which the governance mechanisms specific to the oligopolistic period caused Big Steel's loss of competitiveness. Contrary to Borrus and others, the empirical evidence presented does not completely support the argument that the industry's governance regime is at fault. Although the structure of the governance regime had effects, the analysis argues that other conditions to which actors responded, not all of them industry-specific, were more important.

A common argument blames the generally insensitive, utilitylike, administered price policy for the failure of Big Steel to remain competitive. Walter Adams and Joel Dirlam trace this rigid price behavior to the imperatives of corporate hierarchies as the primary mechanisms coordinating the production process (1964: 628). They demonstrate that for wire rods, which were the major import of the early years, the domestic integrated mills had to maintain their prices, since they competed with the nonintegrated mills in the market for finished wire products. Since the nonintegrated mills purchased wire rods at the integrated mills, a price reduction in these items would have allowed the nonintegrated wire producers to lower their prices, thus depressing the prices of finished wire products. However, the rigid price argument confuses the effect with its cause. Given the overall higher production costs of domestic mills vis-à-vis their foreign competitors, a more aggressive price policy would have halted imports only temporarily.[17] In fact, as prices of steel products became more and more

---

16 Some modern Japanese steelworks have an annual capacity of up to 17.6 million short tons (Old et al. 1981: 31; as converted from metric tons), whereas the largest U.S. mill complex, Inland's East Chicago works, has a capacity of 6.1 million tons (Stone and Michaelis 1985: 48). Of Japan's steel output in 1984, 89.1% was continuously cast and none was produced with the outdated open hearth furnaces, while for the United States the numbers are 39.6 and 9%, respectively (*Iron and Steelmaking* 1985: 2–4). For the superiority of Japanese mills, see Barnett and Schorsch (1983: 51–65).

It is also worth noting that in the past, several of the integrated producers have considered the possibility of constructing a minimill or acquiring an existing one. In fact, Armco built one minimill and bought a second, but apparently without much success because it soon sold these facilities. As for now, none of the major integrated producers operates a minimill (Barnett and Schorsch 1983: 85; Hogan 1984: 111).

17 A statement by Wallace from U.S. Steel illustrates both arguments: "If we decided we had to meet the West German price, we would be forced to reduce our entire price

responsive to market conditions (Crandall 1981: 32), imports continued to gain market shares.

Nevertheless, the vertical structure of Big Steel did contribute to higher production costs. With iron ore available on the world market, the traditional comparative cost advantage of the United States was eroded. Despite these new cost relationships, the Big Steel companies continued to use their own ores (Barnett and Schorsch 1983: 304). The reason for this may be found in the massive amounts of capital sunk into unsalable property that made it extremely costly to abandon iron mines. Furthermore, according to U.S. Steel's Chief Economist, interviewed for this study, and corporate documents, although the domestic producers were in the forefront of worldwide iron ore prospecting, the expropriation of U.S. Steel's subsidiary in Venezuela in 1974 had convinced Big Steel that they must invest in mines that were not vulnerable to political pressures (United States Steel Corporation 1976).

Although the expropriation of the Orinoco mine put a halt to the multinationalization of Big Steel's mining activities, steel production remained a domestic affair because of its importance to the national security and also because of its key role for industrial strategies that precluded major direct investment by U.S. firms in foreign companies.[18] Furthermore, in contrast to the automobile industry, the very nature of the integrated steelmaking process ruled out geographic fragmentation.[19] This lack of multinationalization made the domestic producers extremely vulnerable to exchange rate policies (Walter 1982). The industry suffered from an overvalued dollar during their modernization campaign in the 1960s (until the fall of the fixed exchange-rate regime in 1971) and again in the 1980s.

Whatever the benefits of a multinational strategy would have been, there is strong evidence that the steel industry's capital immobility impeded its effort to transform its labor relations. Unlike many manufacturing companies, the steel industry could not exert the "rational tyranny of capital mobility" (Burawoy and Smith 1985: 150) over its work force. For reasons explained earlier, they were not able to follow a southern strategy.

The relative strength of labor vis-à-vis steel management is highlighted by the fact that the United Steelworkers of America (USWA) were able to keep their real hourly wage increasing until 1977 and to maintain that

structure in the United States. And they could still go lower. Spot cuts would be in conflict with our marketing methods and would completely disrupt our distribution system" (quoted in McManus 1967: 77). See also Howell et al. (1988: 499, note 15).

18 Starting in 1961, USS invested in foreign steel companies on a small scale, some of which were later discontinued (Hogan 1970/1971: 168).

19 Only very recently, attempts have been made to import semifinished slabs for further treatment in the United States. In these cases, it has been argued that the costs of modernizing the melting facilities outweigh the loss of efficiency due to the separation of part of the production process (Roderick 1983).

level until 1982. In the meantime, average real hourly earnings had declined for overall manufacturing, so that the traditional premium paid to steel-workers rose from about 40% in 1970 to 75% in 1982 (Barnett and Schorsch 1983: 68). These increases also exceeded productivity gains, so that unit labor costs rose by about 30% from 1970 until 1977 (calculated on the basis of data from AISI's *Annual Statistical Yearbooks*).

It has become fashionable to accuse steel management of having taken a soft stand against labor. Nothing could be further from the truth. In fact, when foreign competition was rising on the horizon, Big Steel immediately recognized the danger (Greer 1977: 72) and sought to increase productivity by abolishing rank-and-file control over local work practices (Betheil 1978: 3). The resulting 116-day strike of 1959 ended in a standoff (Adelman 1961: 34). Foreign companies, however, used the strike to increase their presence in the U.S. market. Their market share surged from 1.7 million net tons in 1958 to 4.4 million tons in 1959 (Crandall 1981: 22). Not surprisingly, management became concerned with keeping the industry strike-free, es-pecially when labor militancy was on the rise in the late 1960s (Cooper 1967: 113). Finally, in 1973, management succeeded in negotiating a so-called "Experimental Negotiating Agreement" (ENA) that limited the union's right to strike. Since the United Steelworkers had adamantly op-posed giving up the right to strike in the past, the industry granted attractive wage increases in return.[20] At the next contract negotiations, in 1977, despite changed economic conditions, management felt it had to maintain the level of wage increases to keep the cooperative leadership of the United Steelworkers in power. This was because there was a radical challenge within the union that threatened to overthrow them (Crandall 1981: 38).

The immense amounts of capital required in the integrated steel sector caused not only the geographical immobility that increased the bargaining power of the union, but also had a profound effect on the industry's ability to modernize. Restrained by slow market growth, the steel firms were not able to build completely new steel works with optimum new technology and plant layout. Because of the exorbitantly high investment costs of a so-called greenfield expansion, the industry chose the so-called brownfield modernization, arguing that "an investment leading to better utilization of existing plant is . . . preferable to one bringing into existence new plant working at a low utilization factor" (Leckie and Morris 1968: 452).[21] While saving considerable money, the industry obtained only suboptimal effi-ciency gains.[22] The brownfield modernization was, in any event, haphazard,

20 For a critical account of the USWA's internal conflicts, see Betheil (1978). For the USWA's official view, see Abel (1976).
21 Crandall (1981: 84) estimated for 1978 that the operating-cost savings of a new mill in comparison to "current practice" would amount to $60 a ton, and capital charges would increase by about $131 a ton.
22 The capital-cost estimates for new shipments capacity at an integrated carbon-steel plant

and often resulted in bottlenecks that made the new installations of little benefit (Rosegger 1980: 157).

Although the industry chose the less-costly route of brownfield modernization (with the exception of Bethlehem's new Burns Harbor works), it was not able to complete its great modernization drive of 1964 to 1968, that is, the introduction of the basic oxygen furnace and modern rolling mill techniques, which were intended to combat foreign intrusion into the domestic market (Hogan 1970/1971: 1543, 1583). The capital investments proved to be so expensive that a growing gap appeared between the invested capital, on the one hand, and productivity improvement, on the other. Although the investments led to a skyrocketing capital–labor ratio, stagnating steel demand depressed operating rates (capacity utilization) and, therefore, limited the potential productivity gains (Barnett and Schorsch 1983: 147). Furthermore, the growing foreign competition restricted the previous practice of passing on increased costs to the consumer. The result was a noticeable decline in profitability of Big Steel (U.S. Office of Technology Assessment 1980: 120–1; Scherrer 1988a: 215). Consequently, the industry discontinued the modernization drive. Capital productivity (employment costs, interest charges, taxes, and net income/net fixed assets) then grew strongly as the technological gap between Big Steel and its foreign competitors widened (Scherrer 1988a: 231–4).

It has been argued that the disappointing gains in productivity were partly due to poor management choices when modernization programs were considered in the 1950s. Instead of experimenting with the new labor-saving basic oxygen furnace (BOF), the industry took a conservative stance and expanded capacity on the now obsolete open-hearth technology, a decision from which they have never recovered. This lethargy on the part of management has been blamed on the oligopolistic structure of the steel industry (Adams and Dirlam 1966), but the debate sparked by this argument has come to rather inconclusive results.[23] Most convincing is the case-study approach of Lynn (1982), which compares the adoption of the BOF among several Japanese and American steel firms. In addition to technical factors and governmental attitude, and contrary to some ideas about a lack of competition, Lynn finds that the failure of American producers to adopt the BOF was in fact attributable to the relationship between steel producers and their equipment suppliers, as well as insufficient monitoring of foreign technological developments. Whereas in Japan the steel mills did most of the equipment engineering themselves, their U.S. counterparts relied heavily on autonomous engineering firms, of which the largest, Koppers, had

---

range from $520 to $880 for a brownfield, and from $956 to $1,514 for a greenfield modernization, as expressed in 1978 dollars per ton of capacity (U.S. Office of Technology Assessment 1980: 315).

23 The participants in this debate were, among others, Dilley and McBride (1967), Maddala and Knight (1967), McAdams (1967), Ault (1973), Huettner (1974), and Sumrall (1978).

turned down the opportunity to be the general licensee for BOF technology in the United States. Koppers' heavy investment in open-hearth technology probably provided for little incentive to adopt new technologies (Lynn 1982: 187). Although the U.S. steel industry enjoys the benefits of a well-developed network for the dissemination of engineering information, the limited international scope of the information isolated the industry from foreign discoveries (Lynn 1982: 132). In contrast to the oligopolistic pricing case, the integrated producers apparently extended their corporate hierarchy insufficiently for the rapid adoption of new mill technology.

Nevertheless, the overriding problem for the modernization of the U.S. steel industry appears to be the high cost of capital during periods of slow market growth. As Lynn tells us, even some Japanese firms had invested in open-hearth capacity at a time when the superiority of the BOF had been clearly established (Lynn 1982: 106–10). Yet the phenomenal growth of steel demand in Japan soon diminished the effect of those mistakes, while the U.S. integrated producers were haunted for years by their misjudgments.

In addition, many of the previous arguments probably help to explain why the integrated mills were unable to move into the minimill sector. First, capital spent on minimill capacity would have imperiled investment in existing facilities. Since the integrated mills had been operating considerably below capacity for most of the previous decade, the construction of minimills would have been directly at their expense. In the early 1970s, however, integrated firms spent substantial sums on modernizing their existing facilities that competed directly with the minimills. These investments proved to be failures, as demonstrated by the large wire-rod mill of U.S. Steel in South Chicago, which had to be closed within a decade due to a lack of cost competitiveness (Barnett and Schorsch 1983: 95). Although some investment opportunities existed, the wrong choices were made. At last, this is one clear instance of management failure, probably due to the bureaucratic corporate culture. Second, there is every reason to believe that the integrated companies would not have succeeded in excluding the union from their minimill ventures or that they could have bargained for a more favorable contract. Without the benefits of management control on the shop floor, these minimills would have been less competitive.

THE OPPOSITION TO INDUSTRIAL POLICY

Once it has been shown that the steel industry was not capable of becoming more competitive by itself, the question arises whether state intervention might have helped. The first industry-specific supports were the Voluntary Restraint Agreements (VRA) of 1968. Since then, import restrictions have remained in place with only a few exceptions, the most recent being the imposition of import restrictions by the Reagan Administration in 1984

(Woolcock et al. 1985). Government support in the form of guaranteed loans for the modernization of facilities amounted to about $500 million during the Carter Administration (U.S. General Accounting Office 1981: 6–8). In 1981, steel producers were exempted from timely compliance to air-pollution standards (Vogel 1984). In addition, the antitrust laws have been enforced in a more lenient way since 1984, as evidenced by the LTV–Republic merger, although the Department of Justice successfully intervened against the proposed merger between U.S. Steel and National (Hogan 1984: 30–2). The Justice Department liberalized its merger guidelines in 1982 (Williamson 1986: 114–19), which encouraged the steel companies to undertake joint ventures and multiparty bargaining with suppliers (*The New York Times* 1984b). In 1981 and 1986, Big Steel was granted specific exemptions from tax regulations, which saved it more than a billion dollars (Roderick 1984: 142; U.S. Congressional Budget Office 1987: 15–20).

This ensemble of government supports for the ailing steel industry has been criticized for its haphazard nature and especially for its heavy reliance on international trade policies (e.g., U.S. Office of Technology Assessment 1980; Borrus 1982; Gray, Pagel, and Walter 1982; Walters 1982; Barnett and Schorsch 1983; Acs 1984). Almost unanimously, although for different reasons, import restrictions have been branded as ineffectual.[24] Given such a poor track record for protectionism, why was a more aggressive industrial policy not pursued?

Generally, American management of industrial crises is interpreted in terms of existing sociopolitical structures peculiar to the United States (Cohen and Meltzer 1982; Dyson 1983). The riotous pluralism of public life in the United States to which Shonfield (1965) referred has been seen as responsible for the lack of a coherent public policy for industries in crisis. Although this interpretation possesses considerable explanatory power, the case of the steel industry raises further questions. When the Carter Administration provided for a tripartite policy committee to draft a rescue package for the steel industry, many of the proposals that went beyond the implementation of import restrictions met with resistance from steel management.[25] The leaders of the industry were especially opposed to any kind of state subsidy and many of them even criticized the Loan Guarantee Program.[26] Why did the managers of Big Steel not emulate their

---

24 The supporters of protectionism blame the failure on the presumably insufficient degree of protection. The opponents claim that the import restrictions have only delayed the necessary adjustments.

25 According to one of the organizers of the Steel Tripartite Advisory Committee, interviewed for this study, Big Steel was even reluctant to participate in the discussions of the Committee.

26 Of the Big Steel companies, only Jones and Laughlin (LTV) took advantage of that program. Many of the others started law suits against the granting of loan guarantees (U.S. General Accounting Office 1981: 6–8).

European colleagues' practice of requesting state subsidies for modernization?

There is, of course, an explanation that leads back to the pluralist argument. Anticipating the difficulties of obtaining government funds, steel management might have opted for the easier road of protectionism. Although steel consumers supposedly paid $1 billion a year more than they would have paid without trade restrictions (Crandall 1981: 139), it appears highly unlikely that the industry could have obtained that amount from the taxpayers in the form of subsidies. However, under President Reagan, it was possible to receive this amount in the form of tax breaks, as mentioned earlier.

Furthermore, the relationship between the industry and the state has traditionally been rather adversarial, at least on the surface. Particular tension arose from two aspects of state intervention. First, the antitrust laws impeded further concentration. In 1958, Bethlehem Steel and Youngstown Sheet & Tube were frustrated in their attempt to merge by a court decision that upheld the Justice Department's opposition (Hogan 1970/ 1971: 1692). Second, as the authors of a Federal Trade Commission study wrote, "the U.S. Government has directed more of its price control effort at the steel industry during the last quarter-century than at any other industry" (U.S. Federal Trade Commission 1977: 251). On other issues, however, the relationship between the industry and the government seems to have been friendlier. A month after the famous Kennedy–Blough confrontation (McConnell 1963), Roger Blough, Chairman of U.S. Steel, was appointed to chair a committee that advised President Kennedy on economic matters, especially in the area of taxation, and policies consonant with his views were subsequently enacted (Blough 1975: 49).

In sum, both arguments are not very convincing. For a better understanding of this crisis management, the specific conditions of the steel industry need to be taken into account. As shown earlier, the capital-intensive nature of integrated steel technology requires secure guarantees against price wars in times of low capacity utilization. Hence, it is no surprise that the European steel industry not only received public support for modernization, but also operated under a system of production quotas and import restrictions (Hogan 1983: 201). Thus, regardless of public funds, the U.S. steel industry still had to rely on some sort of trade protection.[27]

A more significant reason, however, was steel management's drive for altered labor relations. Their past strategy of cooptation had not delivered the expected results; real wages continued to rise, while shop-floor unionism prevented major reductions of manpower levels. President Carter's attempt to draft a coherent rescue package for the steel industry, however,

27 Even such staunch critics of Big Steel as Barnett and Schorsch (1983: 286) concede the need for countervailing duties on imports.

continued the "cooperative" strategy. As indicated by its name, the Steel Tripartite Advisory Committee was designed to solve the steel crisis by a combined effort of the USWA, AISI, and certain state agencies. Labor's participation in this neocorporatist arrangement meant that management would have had to continue to show consideration for the workers' interests, that is, maintenance of high employment at accustomed pay levels. This would have perpetuated precisely what management perceived to be its main problem. Furthermore, the distribution of subsidies through the tripartite committee would have politicized management's investment decisions. As the case of the Youngstown plant closures between 1977 and 1979 suggests, workers and their communities would have tried to exercise strong political pressure to use the federal funds to keep their particular steel work open (Lynd 1984). Independent of American businessmen's general dislike for any infringements on their authority (Vogel 1978), steel management had to avoid such a public debate because it ran directly counter to its retrenchment strategy.

Ironically, the strongest supporters of this protectionist strategy were the steelworkers themselves. Not strong enough to impose their industrial policy concepts on the representatives of government and industry, they settled for protectionism as the easiest way to protect their jobs (Scherrer 1987).

As the Chrysler case suggests, any plan for corporatist crisis management would also have called the industry's diversification strategy into question.[28] Although few of the investments into nonsteel-related industries proved to be very successful, they provided the companies with added bargaining strength vis-à-vis the union.[29] Less dependent on their steel activities and, therefore, less vulnerable in case of strikes, the companies were able to use the severe recession of 1982 through 1983 to pursue aggressively a new confrontational labor-relations policy (Scherrer 1987).

Aided by the examples of other industries and by a sympathetic government, in 1983, the management of Big Steel succeeded in extracting considerable wage concessions ($1.4 billion) from a work force whose jobs were disappearing under the combined impact of a severe recession and increasing levels of import penetration.[30] Management was able to cash in

---

28 Chrysler was forced to sell most of its operations that were not auto-related (U.S. Public Law 1980: 1327).

29 In 1985, steel operations provided only 55% of total sales for the member companies of the AISI, down from 72% in 1979 (calculated on the basis of AISI data). Acs (1984: 139) argues that "despite its many acquisitions, the steel industry remains relatively unprofitable." However, Bethlehem's "steel only strategy has yet to yield a profit" (*The New York Times* 1985).

30 The extracting of major labor concessions started in the automobile industry in 1979 and spread throughout the unionized industries (Slaughter 1983). Similarly, steel wage em-

on its Experimental Negotiating Agreement investment. Because of the previously prevailing spirit of social partnership and the lack of strike experience, steelworkers were in a rather powerless position. After 1983, not only was the historic wage trend broken, but management used, and continues to use, its new strength to redefine labor relations. At many plants, the two main principles of shop-floor unionism, the grievance procedure and the seniority principle, were undermined either by labor–management participation teams or by unilaterally imposed new work rules (Scherrer 1988a: 390–445).

From management's point of view, the strategy of opposing an "industrial policy" was a success. The historic wage trend had been reversed and productivity rose by a phenomenal 7.3% annually from 1981 to 1988 (U.S. Bureau of Labor Statistics, n.d.), while spending on capital investments was cut in half (Scherrer 1988a: 508). In 1986, however, it seemed that this strategy would falter, when the second largest domestic steel producer, LTV, had to seek protection under Chapter 11 of the bankruptcy code and when USX was threatened by a hostile takeover bid while it engaged in a bitter showdown with the USWA. In this situation, a change in attitude toward government bailouts occurred (*Business Week* 1986: 25). However, further bankruptcies were averted by (1) the Reagan VRAs, which started to show their effect at the end of 1985, (2) the decline of the dollar starting in autumn of 1985, (3) the continuation of the debt-driven recovery of the U.S. economy, and (4) the six-month lockout and strike at USX, which enabled the other steel mills to serve its customers (Stundza 1988). USX was also able to recruit its main banks' support against the takeover bid (*Business Week* 1987: 26). By 1987, the steel mills had become profitable again and cost competitive with the foreign producers at the current exchange rate. Furthermore, they could boast a higher level of labor productivity than the Japanese mills thanks to their higher degree of capacity utilization (U.S. International Trade Commission 1987). This feat was achieved without any commitments to the government, labor or other special interests. Although not without risks, the private crisis management had strengthened management's autonomy in decision making.

However, problems remain in addition to the devastating impact of this strategy on steelworkers and their communities. On the average, domestic mill equipment has remained less modern than abroad, the mills have become almost completely dependent on foreign technology, and in the next recession, the public will probably have to absorb even higher costs (Scherrer 1988a: 515–19). Already in 1987, the Pension Benefit Guaranty Corporation, the public insurance company for private pension plans, had

---

ployment dropped from 291,483 in 1980 to 168,852 in 1983 (American Iron and Steel Institute, *Annual Statistical Yearbook* 1985: 22).

to take charge of $3 billion in steel-related pension liabilities (U.S. International Trade Commission 1987: 29–31).

OUTLOOK AND DISCUSSION

In the course of the last twenty years, despite added import restrictions, the domestic steel industry has moved from oligopolistic practices to competition. What is the effect of this new competitive climate on the governance regime of the American steel industry? Some changes in the mid–1980s indicate a tendency toward convergence of the Big Steel form of governance mechanisms with that of the minimills.

Integrated capacity became more concentrated through mergers and failures, while at the same time some new corporate hierarchies were formed as spinoffs from the established corporations.[31] While the integrated mills imported increasing quantities of semifinished steel (from 155 tons in 1980 to 2.4 million tons in 1985, according to AISI data from various years), minimills expanded their control over sources of scrap, their major raw material input.[32] As the integrated mills dropped some product lines (Hogan 1984: 111), minimills began to expand considerably their product lines (Barnett and Schorsch 1983: 85).

The movement of some integrated companies toward extensive diversification corresponded to the status of many minimills as divisions of conglomerates (Hersch 1984: 109). And the joint ventures of foreign companies with domestic integrated producers, as well as foreign direct investments in established integrated mills (Tony 1987), made this sector almost as international in terms of ownership as the minimills (Hersch 1984: 109).

After the industry's multiemployer bargaining unit had been disbanded in 1985, labor relations became similar in both sectors. For example, Bethlehem Steel succeeded in revamping its bar, rod, and wire division along minimill concepts. Work rules were eased, and wages were cut and tied to performance. The movement toward labor–management participation teams gathered momentum (Hoerr 1988).

Under the pressure of competition from steel mills in industrializing countries, a number of minimills joined the protectionist lobby and formed their own association in 1988, the Steel Manufacturers Association (McManus 1989: 22–4). The disintegration of the industry has left its mark on AISI. Differences surfaced among its members on such policy issues as

---

31 LTV combined Jones and Laughlin, Youngstown Sheet and Tube, and Republic. Weirton Steel was divested by National and Gulf States by Republic.
32 In 1982, when it appeared that scrap would soon be in short supply, minimill companies rushed out to buy scrap companies (*American Metal Market* 1984; Hersch 1984: 101).

granting loan guarantees and importing semifinished steel (U.S. Senate 1983: 54). Furthermore, a number of large companies, such as LTV and Wheeling Pittsburgh, filed for bankruptcy under Chapter 11 and dropped out of AISI. Nevertheless, AISI became involved in a new type of activity. On a small scale, it initiated joint ventures in research and development among its member companies (U.S. Congressional Budget Office 1987: 25–31).

Overcapacity, the typical ailment of the steel industry, developed as minimill capacity exploded. No longer protected by the major mills' price umbrella, the minimills experienced the stiff winds of competition in their pursuit of new market niches in the mid–1980s (Scherrer 1988b). The success of the Reagan VRAs, the devaluation of the dollar, slight increases in demand, and new technological developments again improved the prospects of minimill expansion at the end of the 1980s (McManus 1989).

In sum, the old governance regime, which protected the industry from cutthroat competition, gave way to a combination of limited government market regulation and individual survival strategies. However, this new regime does not appear to be stable and lasting. The achievement of both the minimills and the integrated mills, that is, international cost competitiveness, has been based on short-term profit maximization, and has been achieved through substandard wages and working conditions as well as the neglect of R&D and manpower training. Although it is far from certain that the VRAs will be phased out by 1992, as the Bush Administration has announced (*The New York Times* 1989: 1), if trade protection is removed, then further transformations in the steel industry's governance regime can be expected.[33] This instability must also be seen in the context of the current contradictions in the world economy that must be resolved before a new worldwide phase of prosperity develops (Altvater 1987).

Although attempts to insulate the steel industry from volatile market forces will continue, the last twenty years of the domestic steel industry clearly support the classroom wisdom that oligopoly attracts market entrance. On a macrolevel, three main reasons for this have been identified. First, the unfolding of a mass-consumption market abroad allowed foreign steel companies to match the traditional economies of scale of American companies and, as a result, close the previous productivity gap. Second, the political–economic climate in the south nurtured the growth of a mode of steelmaking that could effectively carve a niche in the existing domestic market. Third, the end of post–War economic growth in the United States

---

33 For an analysis of the compatibility of the different strategies that are pursued in the steel industry regarding labor power control, labor relations, and the production paradigm, on the one hand, and the industrial relations regime as well as macroeconomic policy, on the other, see Scherrer (1989).

caused a slowdown in the growth of domestic steel demand and thereby limited severely the integrated producers' ability to modernize their production facilities.

The integrated steel mills failed in their effort to shield their oligopoly from these new challenges. Their traditional governance regime had been developed in response to the dangers of cutthroat competition among steel producers who operated on similar organizational and technological principles within a single market. They did this effectively for many decades. Yet the system of price collusion broke down in the early 1980s when the erosion of market shares was accompanied by disparities among the Big Steel companies in strategy and production costs. Oligopolistic pricing practices may have survived for so long because the mechanisms that made price collusion possible also had a profound impact on the government. State support for the continued suppression of market forces had been effectively solicited by both the industry's trade association and organized labor. In the end, however, import barriers turned out to be inadequate and were no help against the emerging minimills.

The alternative to these efforts of maintaining the status quo would have been to adapt to the new competitive environment. As noted earlier, this raises the question of whether the existing governance regime impeded speedy adaptation. Contrary to previous studies, this analysis cautions against overemphasizing the impact of the oligopoly structure on the ability of Big Steel to adjust to its changing environment. Instead, I have argued that three other factors were primarily responsible. First, the unique properties of the steel production process constrained Big Steel's adaptability. In particular, vast amounts of capital were required to maximize economies of scale and became immobile as they were invested in massive integrated mills. The development of an alternative technology for certain steel products with lower capital requirements compounded the problems of those companies that operated with the old technology. Second, the relative strength of the steelworkers in the integrated mills, derived in part from the low capital mobility of these plants, prevented the imposition of lower wages and other work requirements that were comparable to world market standards. This in turn facilitated the retrenchment strategy of the steel companies. In conjunction with the general political weakness of organized labor in the United States, the steelworkers' shop-floor strength convinced managers to oppose a neocorporatist style of crisis management in favor of a private form of crisis regulation. Additionally, the union's inability to organize all steelworkers helped to undermine the previous oligopolistic arrangement. Third, the peculiar fragmentation of the U.S. state contributed to the dissolution of the formerly tight steel oligopoly insofar as it encouraged the growth of the minimills and discouraged the formation of a cohesive national steel policy.

GOVERNANCE OF THE AUTOMOBILE INDUSTRY: THE TRANSFORMATION OF LABOR AND SUPPLIER RELATIONS

Christoph Scherrer
John F. Kennedy Institute, Free University of Berlin

Until the 1970s the U.S. automobile industry was largely insulated from global competition.[1] Its products, like those of most domestic manufacturers, were designed according to the specific demands and characteristics of the domestic market. Exports were seen as a bonus to normal business operations and, therefore, did not require special attention (Wilkins and Hill 1964: 376). Instead, foreign markets were served primarily by the domestic producers' foreign subsidiaries with largely autonomous product developments. During the last decade, however, the domestic supremacy of the three major U.S. manufacturers, the so-called Big Three, General Motors, Ford, and Chrysler, was challenged. Starting in the small car market, foreign producers were able to capture ever-increasing market shares. Since the mid–1980s, the investment in domestic assembling facilities by some foreign auto makers has meant that not even import restrictions or manipulations of the value of the U.S. dollar are effective tools for insulating the Big Three's U.S. operations from foreign competition. Domestic automobile production has become permanently integrated into global circuits of competition.

The initial difficulties faced by the U.S. automobile industry in adjusting to this new competitive environment became the subject of public debate. As Lawrence and Dyer (1983: 17) pointedly remarked, "[i]n a crisis of such magnitude, there is plenty of blame to go around, and there has been no shortage of critics (inside and outside the industry) offering opinions as to what went wrong." In the meantime, the Big Three have managed a spectacular comeback, but doubts about their competitiveness remain. This skepticism is nurtured by the continuing successs of foreign imports, which captured a record market share in 1987. Because the Big Three have spent enormous sums on retooling their production facilities, the rising tide of imports seems to vindicate those who have argued that attaining

---

1 This chapter is a much revised version of a working paper published by the Free University of Berlin (Scherrer 1986). I would like to acknowledge my debt to the Institute fur Sozialwissenschaftliche Forschung in Munich, which has provided the funding for the research on supplier relations. A somewhat more detailed discussion of the supplier relations has been published in German (Scherrer 1989).

parity with foreign producers involves more than realigning the product line and implementing state-of-the-art technology (Abernathy 1982: 3). More specifically, a number of academic studies have suggested that the industry's past industrial structure was a major barrier to swift adaptation to new conditions of competition.[2]

The analytic approach to economic governance, adopted in this volume, is well suited for investigating these claims. It allows a more precise identification of the structural impediments to smooth adaptation inasmuch as economic coordination is differentiated into six major types of governance mechanisms. Accordingly, the analysis in this chapter is guided by three questions. Which governance mechanisms did industry actors perceive as being inadequate for coping with the industry's new competitive conditions? To what extent did they transform the industry's governance regime as a result? What were the restrictions that prevented them from changing the industry's governance regime in more profound or fundamental ways?

While it can be shown that certain governance mechanisms generated competitive disadvantages for domestic auto manufacturers, in contrast to arguments offered by others (e.g., White 1982a; Lawrence and Dyer 1983; Salter, Webber, and Dyer 1985), it is doubtful that these manufacturers could have adopted at an earlier time a new governance regime that would have improved the industry's international competitiveness. Indeed, this chapter suggests that a governance transformation in favor of more flexible production and exchange relations that could have responded more quickly and perhaps more effectively to foreign competition was possible only in the context of the internationalization process, and that the industry's competitive crisis was a primary condition for these changes.

The chapter begins with a brief description of the governance regime that existed prior to the deep crisis of the domestic producers in the early 1980s. Second, the main causes and the macroeconomic background of the industry's competitive problem are discussed. Because many macroeconomic developments that affected basic manufacturing are presented in Chapter 6 on the steel industry in this volume, only those aspects that differentiate the automobile industry from the steel industry are highlighted. Next, the major governance transformations that have occurred in the automobile industry since the crisis are analyzed in two case studies. The first case pertains to the problems of organizing production through corporate hierarchies. Changes in technology, industrial relations, and other factors encouraged a reduction of vertical integration in favor of an expansion of market relations and obligational networks in the coordination of parts production. The second case addresses the attempts to replace contractual and adversarial labor relations with more informal and con-

---

2 For example, see U.S. House of Representatives (1980: 59), Abernathy et al. (1981: 13–24), Altshuler et al. (1984: 171–5), and Dyer et al. (1987).

sensual relations. In addition to explaining what happened specifically in the automobile industry, this discussion also sheds light on the problem of explaining governance transformations in general.

GOVERNANCE BEFORE THE 1980s

The automobile industry began at the turn of the century with many little machine shops employing skilled workers, some of whom were union members. This structure changed rapidly with the onset of mass production, ushered in by the famed Model T of Henry Ford in 1908. Through the introduction of the assembly line and the principles of Taylorism, that is, strict separation of planning and execution within the labor process as well as an extreme division of labor, drastic increases in labor productivity were achieved that made the automobile accessible to the middle classes. The predominant use of unskilled labor, relatively high wages, such as the Five Dollar Day, and an aggressive open-shop campaign kept the huge auto factories basically union-free. After World War I, market leadership, originally enjoyed by Ford due to its superior production technology, passed on to General Motors (GM), which was created by a number of mergers, financed by Wall Street and the du Pont family. Its new marketing strategy of differentiation ("a car for every purse and purpose") proved to be superior to Ford's exploitation of the economies of scale of one model. Productivity increases remained impressive: 7.6% per automobile from 1919 to 1929 (Scherrer 1988: 127). During the depression of the 1930s, the Big Three consolidated their grip on the market, and their market share rose from 59% in 1927 to 87.5% in 1933 (Katz 1977: 59). Furthermore, the Depression galvanized workers' dissatisfaction with the authoritarian factory regime. By 1937, the United Automobile Workers (UAW) had overcome the bitter resistance of GM management, which had relied on police power and its own spy system to undermine the unionization effort. The UAW's victory was overdetermined by the workers' shrewd militancy (sit-down strikes), a change in the balance of political power (the governor of Michigan refused to use troops against sit-down strikers in Flint and President Roosevelt called on management to negotiate), and the interest of GM in stable labor relations. Ford held out longer, but had to give in with the onset of World War II. Thus, before the war began, the governance regime was in place that would guide the industry during much of the post–War era.[3]

This regime was dominated by corporate hierarchies. General Motors,

3 On the beginnings of the industry and its marketing strategies, see Katz (1977) and Epstein (1972/1928). The introduction of new methods of work organization and non-union labor relations are discussed in Hounshell (1984: 263–301) and Gartman (1986). The story of the UAW has been told by many. A good account can be found in Jefferys (1986) and Fine (1969).

the country's largest manufacturing firm, held a market share throughout this period that hovered between 40 and 52%. Ford accounted for between 22 and 31% of total new car registrations, and Chrysler's share fluctuated between 22 and 10% (U.S. House of Representatives 1980: 5). GM's strategy and multidivisional organization not only won widespread acclaim among business administrators, but was also adopted by its major competitors (Lawrence and Dyer 1983: 31).[4] They all offered a family line of automobiles and trucks, directed foreign subsidiaries, and operated multiple plants. Their corporate control extended far back into the production of parts and forward into consumer credit institutions.[5] The degree of vertical integration corresponded to sales volume; that is, GM was the most thoroughly integrated, as discussed in what follows. In turn, market coordination by means of price signals was restricted during this period insofar as competition among the major automakers was not price-based. Indeed, price differences among firms on comparable models were insignificant. Instead, GM played the role of a price leader, a form of monitoring, and competition on the basis of style and marketing was more pronounced than on technology and manufacturing. The propensity of car buyers to develop brand loyalties further reduced the allocative effectiveness of price signals (Lanzillotti 1971: 270, 274). In contrast, despite the extensive regulation of the production chain through corporate hierarchies, the multitude of parts that went into an automobile allowed for a viable supplier industry of about 2,500 firms, and the market ruled most of the relationships between outside suppliers and assemblers – a phenomenon that we explore in greater detail later in the first case study.

The conditions of employment for the industry's blue collar work force were not stipulated by the market, but by collectively bargained contracts. The UAW and a few other unions had organized all of the Big Three's hourly workers and most of the hourly work force at the outside suppliers plants. The collective bargaining agreements were negotiated on a company-by-company basis and usually lasted for three years. These contracts not only determined the hourly wage rate, but also contained detailed rules concerning the allocation of labor in the production process. Nor did pure market forces rule the employment conditions of white collar workers, although they were hired on the basis of individual contracts, because they could expect lifetime employment and fringe benefits in line with the UAW contract (Snyder 1973).

In addition to the union, other associations were found in the automobile

---

4 For a detailed discussion on the strategy and structure of GM, see Chandler (1964), Drucker (1972) and Sloan (1972).

5 For about ten years, Ford and Chrysler were prevented by consent decrees with the Department of Justice from affiliating with finance companies. In contrast, GM successfully contested divestiture of GM Acceptance Corporation (Lanzillotti 1971: 297; Heaton 1982: 5).

industry. For example, the manufacturers were organized in the Motor Vehicle Manufacturers Association (MVMA), initially the American Manufacturers Association (AMA), which was mainly engaged in public and governmental relations.[6] However, the scarce literature on the activities of associations in the automobile industry suggests that they played only a minor role. The Big Three lobbied mainly through their own large public and governmental relations staffs.

Obligational networks developed between the manufacturers and their dealers. Dealers operated under a franchise system that granted them exclusive rights to sell a specific line of cars within a certain geographical location.[7] The importance of quality-oriented sales and service outlets for the producers, on the one hand, and the lopsided balance of power between manufacturer and dealer, on the other, created the need for some form of self-governing mediation.[8] In reaction to extensive lobbying of the National Automobile Dealers Association (NADA), GM was the first to establish a Dealer Relations Board in 1938. The four highest ranking officers of GM served as arbitrators in disputes between its sales organization and dealers (Drucker 1972: 105). Apparently, these corporate "judges" lost credibility with the dealers so that in 1956, in the wake of the Automobile Dealers Franchise Act, a retired United States district court judge was appointed as an impartial referee.[9] He heard and determined appeals by dealers concerning decisions that were made by a body of elected dealers at the divisional level (Sloan 1972: 351). Through the Motors Accounting Company, which audited the dealers accounting records, through Service Training Centers for training the dealers' personnel, and through its Motors Holding division, which financed the setup of dealerships, GM exerted

---

6 The AMA was especially active in regulatory issues. For example, in 1957, the auto companies, through the AMA, pledged themselves to foreswear participation in auto racing. Furthermore, they occasionally took refuge behind the AMA on the issue of automotive air pollution, and they set standards on safety developments through committees of the AMA (White 1971: 215–19, 231).

7 The manufacturers preferred independent dealers because, according to White (1971: 137) "the factory outlet system had three disadvantages: it required management personnel; it required money; and it offered no dilution of the risks of the automobile business." Since the acceptance of trade-ins made every sales transaction unique, standard procedures could not be used to provide the coordination needed for effective centralized decision making (Marx 1985: 474). The franchise agreement struck a balance between the rigidities of a company distribution system and opportunistic behavior of independent dealers, such as quality shading "by requiring franchisee investment in specific . . . assets that upon termination imply a capital loss penalty larger than can be obtained by the franchisee if he cheats" (Klein 1980: 359).

8 For a discussion of the possible areas of conflict between dealers and manufacturers, see Macauly (1966).

9 This Act provided legal remedies against unfaithful termination of a franchise (Lanzillotti 1971: 293).

further nonmarket control over its independent dealers (Sloan 1972: 335–8).

The industry was affected by several important state policies. First, the industry benefited tremendously from low taxes on gasoline, low taxes and fees on automobiles, the development of a magnificent system of generally toll-free superhighways, and federal support for suburbanization (U.S. House of Representatives 1980: 11). Second, beginning in the late 1960s, the industry was increasingly subjected to federal product regulation that covered safety, emission, and fuel-consumption standards (U.S. Office of Technology Assessment 1979: 305–9). Third, antitrust laws impeded joint research efforts and limited the degree of vertical integration. For example, in response to the National Highway and Motor Vehicle Safety Act of 1966, the industry sponsored joint research projects, but the Justice Department proceeded successfully on antitrust grounds against these promotional networks and their subsequent substitutes, such as cross-licensing agreements regarding auto emissions technology (White 1982b).

To summarize, within this amalgam of governance mechanisms and state policies, corporate hierarchies were clearly dominant. The tremendous power of these corporations structured most of the other relations. It was they who were most influential in determining the areas of competition, the form of supplier contracts, and the dealers' rights and duties. At times, the state intervened and limited their discretionary powers, but in general, the state's macroeconomic policies proved to be very conducive to the growth of the automobile manufacturers.

In contrast to what occurred in other manufacturing industries, such as steel (see Chapter 6 on steel in this volume), multilateral governance mechanisms played relatively minor roles in the auto industry. Price leading and unions were the only significant examples. Perhaps the small number of manufacturers and the brand loyalties of consumers did not necessitate major collective activities. Stability in terms of price and the relations among the economic agents was nevertheless comparable with that in steel. It also served the same purpose, to protect the large capital outlays for the achievement of ever increasing economies of scale against the volatility of the market.

THE NEW COMPETITIVE ENVIRONMENT

The crisis of the U.S. automobile industry became evident in the early 1980s when the second Mideast oil restriction was met with a deflationary policy of extremely high interest rates and an overvalued dollar. The major auto companies reported massive losses that were unprecedented in the history of U.S. business. However, the origins of this crisis can be traced back to the first oil price shock in the early 1970s, when a dramatic increase in the demand for small cars coincided with the closing of the productivity gap between U.S. and Japanese automakers.

Until the oil embargo of 1973–4, consumer preferences were surprisingly predictable. The annual face-lifting of autos was in essence little more than a sales incentive in a saturated market. The basic concept and mechanical components of automobiles remained much the same.[10] This product continuity allowed the manufacturers to perfect their system of standardized mass production (Abernathy 1978: 145). However, shocked by rising gasoline prices, consumers became suddenly interested in small and energy-efficient cars. For the sake of fuel efficiency, the Big Three had to switch to the production of four- and six-cylinder engines, scrapping much of their investment in highly automated V–8 engine-production facilities. To allow for sufficient space in the passenger section while drastically shrinking the overall length of the cars, the auto companies changed over to front-wheel-drive technology. Thus, the companies suddenly had to abandon their long-standing strategy of incremental improvements. Yet even after these revolutionary changes had been made, it was no longer possible to return to the old incremental strategy because volatile gas prices made consumer preferences difficult to predict, and the availability of competitively priced foreign cars no longer allowed Detroit to dictate what the consumer wanted. In short, the auto companies had to become much more flexible in their market response (Altshuler et al. 1984).

Although the success of foreign producers rested initially on their ability to provide inexpensive and fuel-efficient cars, by the late 1970s, their competitive lead derived increasingly from better workmanship and superior driving capabilities (U.S. House of Representatives 1980: 47). But while this product quality incurred high costs in Europe, Japanese producers managed to combine quality with substantially lower production costs. Japanese production costs were about 20 to 35%, or $1,300 to $2,200, less than they were in the United States (Flynn 1983).

These advantages are generally attributed to several factors. First, hourly *wage costs* in Japan were 40 to 60% less than what they were on average in the United States (Flynn 1983). Second, the Japanese developed a *new organization of the labor process,* based on a new division of labor, that combined the functions of production, quality inspection, and repair in one job. Considerable savings of indirect labor derived from these practices. In terms of work hours, the Japanese producers needed only between 40 and 85% of the labor required in the U.S. industry to produce a comparable product in the early 1980s (Flynn 1983). Third, according to MIT's

10 In large part, American automobiles only became longer (from 197.5 to 222.7 inches between 1950 and 1974), heavier (3,145 to 4,389 pounds), stronger (216.5 to 350 cubic inches), less fuel efficient (15.3 to 13.1 miles per gallon between 1940 and 1973), and more convenient (automatic transmission, air conditioning) (U.S. Office of Technology Assessment 1979: 304–7).

international automobile project, Japanese producers seemed to require much less plant and equipment per unit produced. These *lower capital costs* were mainly due to lower in-process inventories, which resulted from the invention of "just-in-time" production scheduling (Altshuler et al. 1984: 161). Fourth, the *general conditions of production* were such that Japan's lower wages and higher labor productivity were not achieved at the expense of labor peace, but were accompanied by lower levels of absenteeism and less frequent strike activities.[11] Fifth, *supplier relations* were important. Legally separate, but financially linked through minority stock holdings, hundreds of suppliers were clustered around the major assemblers. These industrial groups ensured a close operational coordination that increased flexibility and innovative capacities. Within these networks, the legal separation of the component producers allowed for wage differentiations, and close relations between the assemblers and financing sources facilitated strategic long-term planning (Altshuler et al. 1984: 147–51). All of these private arrangements seemed to be reinforced by a variety of government policies, such as manpower programs (e.g., Friedman 1983: 385).

Together with the unsaturated domestic demand for automobiles in Japan, these advantages resulted in a virtuous dynamic for Japanese automakers.[12] This dynamic not only provided the financial means to implement the latest technology, but also enabled Japanese producers to move from market followers to market definers within many automobile classes. In contrast, the loss of market shares by the Big Three in the United States caused low levels of capacity utilization that limited their potential productivity gains as well as their financial resources to modernize their production capacities. To overcome this vicious circle, however, the domestic producers would have to radically alter their production and organizational techniques.

CASE STUDIES

Since the early 1980s, new governance mechanisms have emerged in the U.S. automobile industry that address some of the areas in which domestic producers suffer a comparative disadvantage: supplier relations and production organization, and labor relations. The causes, the context, and the form of these transformations in governance are the subjects of the following case studies. The first case analyzes the Big Three's three-dimensional plan to reorganize parts sourcing – a plan that is designed to reduce their level of vertical integration, reduce the number of outside suppliers

---

11 For a critical discussion of the post–War industrial relations system in Japan and the defeat of independent unions at Toyota, see Shirai (1983).

12 By 1980, there were 203 automobiles per 1,000 persons in Japan versus 537 in the United States (Altshuler et al. 1984: 108).

with which they have to deal, and allow them to reformulate their relationships with these suppliers. These efforts have resulted in an increased role for associations and networks in the coordination of the production process. The second case deals with transformations in labor relations.

THE TRANSFORMATION OF SUPPLIER RELATIONS

In the early years of the auto industry, the majority of car makers were actually only assemblers of parts (Katz 1977: 253). In the 1920s, the major producers began manufacturing components in house on an increasing scale, either through acquisitions of already established parts manufacturers or through internal development. In the post–War period, the remaining automobile producers had achieved a high level of vertical integration. In 1963, about 78% of most parts shipments originated from plants owned by these vehicle manufacturers (Nelson 1978: 25).[13] The industry's leader, GM, has historically bought only 10 to 15% of standard components outside and produced the rest in house. Ford used outside suppliers for 40 to 50% of its parts requirements, and Chrysler used them for about 70% of their parts (Scherrer 1989: 212). When measured on the basis of the Adelman index, the ratio of value added to sales, the industry's vertical integration was only at or below the average for all manufacturing.[14] The Adelman index, however, does not capture the multitude of processes and components that go into an automobile (Chrysler used to employ 70,000 different parts).

Reasons for vertical integration

Extensive vertical integration occurred for several reasons, which have been detailed at length elsewhere, and only require brief review here.[15] First, similar to the control over natural resources in the steel industry (see Chapter 6 on steel in this volume), ownership of the capital-intensive production of auto bodies and engines deterred market entrance. Of course, these obstacles were reinforced by coordinating the relationship between assemblers and dealers through obligational networks whose existence meant that would-be competitors would encounter prohibitively high costs in establishing a distribution system for their products (White 1971: 54–76). Second, the assemblers repeatedly forced their dealers to take on more cars than the market could bear. Thus, costs of carrying inventory

13 This figure does not include electrical items, pistons, piston rings, springs, carburetors, valves, and lamp bulbs.
14 In 1978, the ratio was 48.5% for GM, 39.0 for Ford, and 33.2 for Chrysler, compared with 43.1% for all manufacturing in 1976 (White 1982a: 414). For 1955, the ratio was 40% for GM, 35 for Ford, and 30 for Chrysler (Katz 1977: 254).
15 The various lines of interpretation are well documented in Helper (1987).

were shifted to the dealers and a stable market outlet for manufacturers was secured (White 1971: 150). Third, and most important in terms of assembler–supplier relations, integration protected an assembler from what Williamson (1985) called the "opportunistic" behavior of suppliers, such as unreliable delivery, price gouging, and the secret transfer of strategic technology to competitors.[16] The automobile manufacturers required a secure planning horizon because the benefits of economies of scale depended on long and uninterrupted production runs. Concerns about unpredictable stoppages of production due to labor disputes at supplier companies motivated the auto companies to expand their vertical integration over suppliers in the 1950s (Katz 1977: 263).

The integration of different production steps presupposed, however, the command of large financial resources. Until the 1920s, this money was provided by banks or capital markets (except in the case of Ford). Later, the success of oligopolistic market control guaranteed auto companies a better than average rate of return, thereby enabling them to use their own funds for vertical expansion (Scherrer 1988: 194–9). Therefore, oligopolistic market control and vertical integration were closely intertwined.

Further, vertical integration was impeded by antitrust laws and the volatility of demand. In the 1950s and 1960s, the Justice Department forced the auto companies to divest of holdings in a number of parts suppliers (White 1971: 278–80; Dyer, Salter, and Webber 1987: 48). To ensure a continuous utilization of their own plants, the auto companies preferred to let suppliers provide for additional capacity in times of excess demand (Katz 1977: 255).

Traditional relations with suppliers

The assembler's relations with *outside* suppliers, that is, those who were not already vertically integrated with the automakers, was governed in most cases by arms-length market relations. Reflecting the multitude of automotive parts, the assemblers were served by about 2,500 suppliers. In addition, they purchased parts from thousands of other companies that were not primarily auto parts producers. Among the primary suppliers, some companies belonged to the Fortune 500 and were technological leaders in their field. However, the overwhelming majority were small- or medium-sized companies, of which many were extremely dependent on the assemblers (Helper 1987: Chap. IV).

Safeguarding against opportunistic behavior, purchasing agents of major assembly facilities kept two or more suppliers for the delivery of *identical*

---

16 Although I find this term of heuristic value, Williamson's transaction-cost theory cannot adequately explain the governance of the production process in the automobile industry, as I have suggested elsewhere (Scherrer 1986: 14–16).

parts, a practice called multiple sourcing. In many cases, about a dozen suppliers produced *similar* parts. Most supply arrangements were under semiannual or annual blanket orders, where suppliers were awarded contracts without exact specification of the amounts to be delivered. Usually, contracts were awarded to the lowest qualified bidder. This competitive bidding procedure allowed prices to be the primary criteria in buying decisions. Nevertheless, for a number of parts, the auto companies relied on both in-house production and outside sourcing. This practice, which is called partial or tapered integration, provided for additional competitive pressure on the suppliers (White 1971: 80–3).

In order to keep enough suppliers, the assemblers instituted policies that reduced the barriers to entry for would-be suppliers. First, individual suppliers received detailed blueprints of the part they were supposed to make. The supplier could thus save on engineering personnel. Second, each supplier obtained orders for only a few parts, a practice that reduced overhead costs for the supplier. Third, in many instances, the auto firms provided suppliers with tooling, thereby reducing capital requirements. These practices applied mainly to the procurement of low-tech products (Helper 1987: Chap. IV, 18–19).

It is worth mentioning that assemblers extended a greater commitment to about 1% of their suppliers (one-third by dollar volume of purchases). These were firms that produced more complex parts, such as brakes or steering wheels. Although written contracts were almost always for only one year at a time, implicit rules of reciprocity governed the relationship between these sophisticated suppliers and the auto companies. On the one hand, suppliers felt obliged to take extraordinary measures to avoid shutting down an assembly plant. On the other hand, the assembler had an obligation to provide for enough work, if it had asked a supplier to build a plant to supply a particular part (Helper 1987: Chap. IV, 43–5). However, these obligational networks did not represent a balance of power. The power of the assemblers was manifest in their ability to force suppliers to license their technology of new products or processes to their competing suppliers (Cole and Yakushiji 1984: 166).

In contrast to the small- and medium-sized suppliers, the large or sophisticated ones were in constant communication with the engineering departments of the assemblers. However, communications were mainly limited to fine-tuning the engineering effort. Only in very rare cases did suppliers and assemblers cooperate in the initial design of a product. Also, when quality problems arose, the parties tended to focus on assigning blame for defects, not on fixing the problem. Communications were not much better between assemblers and their in-house suppliers (Helper 1987: Chap. IV, 63–9).

The low level of technical cooperation fits into the predominant production paradigm. Since the core configuration of the automobile remained basically unchanged, strategies of rationalization concentrated on incremental, process-oriented innovations. These could be achieved within a hierarchical structure, whereby different components or portions of the production process were developed in functionally divided departments (or suppliers) with little horizontal communication (Abernathy 1978). From the assemblers' perspective, this so-called Fordist organization of the supply chain proved to be quite efficient. (For a more general discussion of Fordism, see Chapter 2 in this volume.) Their productivity increases were above average and they consistently earned a higher return on investment than either their suppliers or the average manufacturing firm in the United States (U.S. Department of Commerce 1985: 149).

The vision of the 1980s

In the early 1980s, the Big Three announced that they would substantially reduce their vertical integration, and by 1985, about 47% of their parts were bought from outside suppliers – a substantial increase from the early 1960s. Further reductions in vertical integration with respect to suppliers was anticipated by 1990 as assemblers continued to cultivate markets for parts. GM increased its third-party sourcing from about 15 to 30% and planned to buy 80% of the parts (not value!) for its new Saturn car from outside suppliers. At the same time, the Big Three have planned to drop 20% of their direct suppliers, that is, those who ship directly to the auto assembly plants. In 1982, for example, GM announced that it would soon cut the number of its suppliers in half (Scherrer 1989: 217).

The apparent contradiction between an increase in out-sourcing and a reduction in the number of suppliers can be explained in light of the push for *modular assembly*, a process whereby the supplier engages in the subassembly of car sections, such as instrument panels and suspension systems, so that fewer and larger sections of a car are joined together in the assembly plants of the vehicle manufacturers. The result is a pyramid of assemblers, the top of which is occupied by a few large companies that deliver the subassembled modules to the final assembly process. These companies are supplied with the discrete parts by second-tier suppliers, which in turn may be served by even lower-tier suppliers. So far, seats and instrument panels remain the only true modules (Andrea, Everett, and Luria 1988: 5).[17] More progress has been made concerning purchasing agreements. However, assemblers increasingly source only from a single supplier under long-term arrangements. Nevertheless, single sourcing does not mean that the far-flung empires of the Big Three are served exclusively by one company for

---

17 The first three to five years were characterized largely by "a lot of loud talk," according to one Chrysler executive (Helper 1987: Chap. V, 60). See also Flynn and Cole (1988).

every part they purchase; this is true only for the individual assembly plant (Scherrer 1989: 218). In any case, these long-term single-sourcing arrangements illustrate that the trend to more market-based relations between assemblers and suppliers has been coupled with the development of obligational networks.

Another objective of the Big Three during the 1980s has been the introduction of just-in-time (JIT) production. As noted later, JIT is another form of obligational network. Its primary goal is to reduce inventory stocks through tight delivery schedules. Materials, parts, and components are scheduled to arrive at the point of assembly just before they are needed. In an interview for this study, a member of the Automotive Industry Action Group, an industry-sponsored research group, reported that about 10 to 15% of all suppliers had switched to JIT by 1988.

Assemblers also started to involve both inside and outside suppliers in the product-planning stage. An example, often cited as a successful attempt to overcome the traditional sequential approach to product development, is Ford's "Team Taurus," which brought together representatives from product planning, design and manufacturing engineering, and marketing, who, in close cooperation with suppliers, oversaw the whole development process of the Ford Taurus (Helper 1987: Chap. V, 26–32).

Finally, product and process engineering has been increasingly purchased from independent engineering firms. However, General Motors has tried especially hard to keep control over the technology that is involved in systemic rationalization through the acquisition of high-tech firms, such as the satellite producer, Hughes Aircraft, the data-processing specialist, Electronic Data Systems, and through joint ventures with the robot specialist, Fanuc (Scherrer 1989: 219–20).

Motives for change

The transformation in assembler–supplier relations from vertical integration to markets and obligational networks is motivated mainly by two objectives: immediate reduction of production costs, and efficient use of labor and capital throughout the entire production chain. The primary means for achieving the first objective is the exploitation of wage differentials. The second objective will be met by a systemic rationalization of all auto-related supply, production, and distribution processes.

Exploiting the wage differential. The decision to reduce vertical integration seems to be motivated primarily by the desire to save on wage costs. GM had already tried to exploit in the 1970s the lower wage levels and the "right-to-work" laws in the south for the labor-intensive production of parts. However, this so-called southern strategy provided only a brief period of relief because the UAW managed eventually to organize all of these new production sites (Katz 1985: 90). In contrast, outside suppliers were more successful in keeping the union out. Since the early 1970s, the UAW's ability to win certification elections in these plants has waned considerably.[18] At the same time, the wage differential between suppliers and assemblers increased. In 1963, the premium for vehicle assembly work was on the average about 12%, but it increased to 24% in 1974, and hit a record 48% in 1983 (Scherrer 1989: 221). Accordingly, it has become very attractive for assemblers to switch their procurement sources.

This hierarchy of wage rates is illustrated by the production of wiring harnesses. At GM's Packard Electric plant in Warren, Ohio, hourly compensation, including fringe benefits, amounted to $19.60 in 1983. Domestic nonunion competition paid about $6 per hour, and at GM's Mexican plants, hourly compensation did not exceed $2. After approximately 4,600 jobs had been eliminated in Warren and further jobs losses were threatened, the membership of the International Union of Electrical Workers Local 717 voted in 1984 for a two-tiered wage system. The contract guaranteed the current employees virtual lifetime income and job security, but new employees were entitled only to 55% of the base rate in the first year (Russo 1985).

The *Maquiladora* program is another attempt to exploit wage differentials through out-sourcing. Under this program, which allows custom-free exports of parts to Mexico and their reexport under a value-added tax scheme, the volume of imports from Mexico increased between 1982 and 1985 from $122 to $305 million. GM alone operated seventeen such plants along the Mexican border, employing about 24,000 workers (*UAW Research Bulletin* 1987: 14). However, low work intensity, political instability, high transportation costs, and quality problems limit the future growth prospects of these so-called in-bound plants. Furthermore, the *Maquiladora* strategy is not compatible with the just-in-time concept, which requires a highly dependable delivery schedule (Helper 1987: Chap. V, 50–1).

Besides the activities of the UAW, discussed later, thus far two factors have limited a drastic increase in out-sourcing. First, according to a UAW researcher interviewed for this study, wages paid by major suppliers with the technical capability to produce complex parts were roughly comparable to those at the Big Three. Second, many smaller suppliers lacked the financial resources necessary for modernizing and expanding their production facilities (Smith 1986).

These limits, however, do not apply to *foreign* sourcing. On an increasing scale, domestic producers scour the globe in search of new supply sources. In 1984, local content was about 95% and was expected to fall to 86% by

---

18 In 1983, only about 58% of the workers in the establishments surveyed by the Bureau of Labor Statistics were covered by a collective-bargaining agreement (Williams 1985: 40), down from between 80 and 84% in 1974 (U.S. Bureau of Labor Statistics 1976: 15).

1990 (Andrea, Hervey, and Luria 1986: 6).[19] Some of the foreign parts originate from subsidiaries of the major domestic producers. The reasons for these captive imports extend beyond cost differences resulting from lower wages. The benefits of economies of scale in combination with local content requirements seem to be equally important (Dohse and Jürgens 1985: 38). With respect to independent foreign producers, costs, quality considerations, and product characteristics are of great significance. When product quality is comparable, the Big Three have decided in favor of a foreign supplier only when cost savings of at least 15% could be achieved. Accounting for shipping and handling costs, the foreign production costs were then about 30 to 40% lower than in the United States (Hartley 1984: 29). Thus, the future prospects of markets for foreign sourcing are closely related to the dollar's exchange value.

The recent direct investment of foreign auto parts suppliers in the United States could reduce the current impediments to increased domestic outsourcing. These affiliates of multinational companies command ample financial resources and technical know-how. They also stand a better chance to remain union-free. From less than 20 plants in 1980, the number of Japanese supplier plants increased to 232 by 1989. Of these, 85 had already secured orders from the Big Three (Callahan 1989).

Systemic rationalization. The primary reason for introducing just-in-time production is to use capital more efficiently. Smaller buffer stocks, achieved through JIT, save on inventory carrying costs, on plant-size requirements, and on material-handling personnel. Inventory costs at Toyota amounted to only $42 per car, compared to GM's $577 in 1985 (*Automotive Industries* 1987b).[20] JIT also proves to be valuable in the quest for higher quality standards (Schonberger and Ansari 1984).

A representative from the Automotive Industry Action Group said that the introduction of JIT requires a new relationship between assembler and suppliers. On the one hand, the tightly scheduled continuous flow of parts calls for intense communication. JIT suppliers receive orders for volume, delivery time, and destination on a daily basis. This density of information exchange can be handled only by electronic data exchanges. On the other hand, JIT imposes substantial costs on outside suppliers and in-house suppliers. Without inventory buffers, a disruption of supply or late delivery may lead to the shutdown of the entire assembly process. Suppliers must, therefore, organize their own production accordingly. They either have to

19 From 1973 until 1984, parts imports have increased at an annual rate of 26% in U.S. dollars, except in Canada (U.S. Department of Commerce 1985: 70).
20 The information on the savings achieved so far through JIT seems to be rather unreliable. According to Aggarwal (1985: 9), GM has slashed annual inventory-related costs from $8 billion in 1980 to $2 billion in 1984. However, *Automotive Industries* (1987b) reports only a slight reduction in inventory costs per vehicle: $628 in 1981 and $612 in 1984.

carry the inventory the auto companies would have carried in the past or they have to adopt the JIT principle themselves. Furthermore, they have to minimize the risk of transportation disruptions by locating their production facilities or their warehouses in the vicinity of the assembly plants.

In order to meet these requirements, which in most cases involve substantial amounts of capital for the redesign of operations and for the installation of electronic data interchanges, the suppliers need a long-term commitment from their assemblers, and, as a result, often establish obligational networks with them. However, single sourcing and long-term contracts eliminate the traditional coercive powers of the assemblers. Thus, one would assume that the auto manufacturers would prefer to extend their hierarchical control over the production process. Yet this is not the case because the emergence of international competition has strengthened the bargaining power of the assemblers vis-à-vis their suppliers. How? First, it increased the numbers of component suppliers from which the domestic assemblers can order. Second, the U.S. parts suppliers' own precarious position in the world market made them more dependent on the Big Three. Nevertheless, international competition has not completely eliminated the exposure of the automakers to the opportunism of their domestic suppliers. Once the assemblers signed long-term contracts, they could not easily switch suppliers.[21] As a result, the Big Three have devised substitutes for the now absent disciplinary powers of the market. For example, the assemblers have become more sophisticated in their selection of suppliers. Besides price, the supplier's record on quality, dependability, and technical capability has now become a criterion in the selection process. Superiority in these areas can offset at least minor price differences (Flynn and Cole 1988: 102–3). Once the supplier is chosen, the assembler closely monitors its dependability and quality record. The winners of the various quality reward programs are more likely to receive new business in the future, have easier access to credit, and can impress new customers. At Ford, these incentives have been supplemented with a penalty system for defective parts (Scherrer 1989: 227).

Furthermore, the Big Three initiated groups and committees for the purpose of courting the active support of suppliers for their plans to transform the entire industry. The activities included huge conferences on the new shape of the industry, the establishment of a supplier council, and the creation of joint study groups, such as the Automotive Industry Action Group. The latter group, a promotional network that includes representatives of all car makers and many suppliers, has been responsible for developing the standards for electronic communication among the firms.

---

21 The assemblers insisted in most cases on an "inferior technology escape clause" that allowed them to cancel a contract ahead of time if another supplier offered a technologically more advanced product (Helper 1987: Chap. V, 15).

It has also assisted smaller suppliers in implementing information technologies (*American Machinist* 1989: 50–1).

The efforts of soliciting more engineering input from first-tier suppliers and of using a team approach for product development are primarily motivated by volatile consumer preferences, intensified competition, and new methods of manufacturing. As long as the basic configuration of the automobile remained unchanged, little coordination between the different departments was necessary. The successful management of radical changes in product and process technology requires a dense flow of information horizontally, which transcends traditional organizational boundaries.

The greater involvement of outside suppliers is also intended to keep open a variety of technological options. However, some representatives of the auto companies are worried that suppliers of complex systems might consider market entry themselves (see Helper 1987: Chap. V, 20). This may be one reason why the move toward the subassembly of parts through outside suppliers (modularization) has advanced farthest in the manufacturing of secondary components, such as seats and dashboards, while core components, such as engines and drivetrains, remain under control of the auto companies (Andrea, Everett, and Luria 1988). For example, General Motors expects to gain a strategic competitive advantage by controlling the development of key products and processes (Gooding 1987).

In sum, the activities discussed before constituted a multifaceted set of governance mechanisms, designed to overcome the inherent deficiencies of the traditional form of governing assembler–supplier relations. Vertical integration has been replaced in many cases by market-based transactions, that is, foreign sourcing, and obligational networks, that is, JIT and single sourcing. However, two points are worth mentioning. First, many of these obligational networks were characterized by an asymmetrical distribution of power in favor of the assemblers (see what follows) that was not unlike the traditional network ties between the manufacturers and their dealers. Second, the possibilities for closer collaboration depended on changes in antitrust enforcement. Although antitrust action had been brought in the past against certain practices between suppliers and assemblers (e.g., Nelson 1978), under the Reagan Administration, the Department of Justice became more lenient in enforcing antitrust rules, and began to encourage joint ventures and joint research-and-development activities.

The role of unions in the reorganization

The fate of the restructuring efforts rests to a large extent in the hands of the unions and their membership. In a number of ways, unions are able to influence the make-or-buy decisions discussed before. First, the union's strength has been a barrier to a further reduction in the degree of vertical integration. Out-sourcing became a top priority issue with the UAW. Although with uncertain success, the UAW has tried to curb this practice through its collective-bargaining agreements since 1982. One effort has consisted of a job bank that has protected all jobs lost because of out-sourcing. Workers in this bank have received retraining or new assignments. This measure, which aims only at making the decision to out-source more expensive, has been supplemented by local sourcing committees. Notified at least 60 days in advance of any contemplated out-sourcing decisions, these committees have had the right to propose alternatives that the corporation has to consider seriously (United Automobile Workers–General Motors 1984: 1–6). Because of this rather weak contract language, UAW workers have often found themselves faced with the choice of job loss or substantial concessions. At Ford and GM, these restrictions on out-sourcing were tightened in the 1987 contracts. The prospect of having to match these contract provisions may have contributed to the decision of Chrysler to sell its components division, Acustar. However, the UAW reacted swiftly by suspending its cooperation in joint programs and by preparing to strike. This show of strength prompted Chrysler to rescind its decision (Slaughter 1988).

The unions affect these governance transformations in a second way. The degree of out-sourcing also depends on the willingness of the union to narrow the differences between union and nonunion wage rates and working conditions. The Big Three have used out-sourcing as a threat to coerce workers to accept wage cuts and changes in local work practices (Katz 1985: 66). While the UAW has successfully resisted any pay cuts or lower wages for newly hired workers at the local level, it has encouraged those locals, which are threatened with plant closure, to bargain over local work rules and to participate in teamwork experiments (Katz 1985).

The interest of management in more cooperative labor relations also relates to JIT, since the absence of buffer stocks has made the production process very vulnerable to industrial action. A strike, even at a small supplier, has the potential of shutting down an entire assembly plant. The strategic position of individual supplier plants became evident in the Twins-burg incident of November 1983. Within two days after UAW Local 122 went on strike, four of Chrysler's eight assembly plants had to be closed down (*International Herald Tribune* 1983).[22] Furthermore, the geographical aspects of JIT production potentially strengthens organized labor. The requirement of proximity of supplier to assembler favors the traditional regions of the automotive parts industry and, thus, the old strongholds of the UAW. In recent years, new assembly plants were again built in these

---

22 Another case was the strike of the Canadian UAW branch in 1984. This nine-day walkout of about 36,000 workers caused the layoff of 40,965 workers at thirty GM plants in the United States (*The New York Times* 1984).

areas, especially in Michigan and Missouri, thereby reversing the trend of the 1970s (Conway 1987).

It is not difficult to imagine what this increased leverage for organized labor would have meant during the period of shop-floor militancy. In fact, labor's militancy was one of the reasons why automotive manufacturing became geographically more decentralized in the post–War period.[23] Today, management apparently rules out a resurgence of union militancy. Although the application of the JIT principle increases the bargaining power of the union, management holds most of the cards in current labor relations. If the UAW does not cooperate, the jobs of its members will be even more threatened by foreign imports. And although JIT offers many advantages to the auto producers, there are alternatives. The cost savings of JIT can be substituted by the international wage differentials, especially in relation to newly industrializing countries. In fact, even as the Big Three introduce JIT at their domestic plants, they increase their foreign sourcing of parts, or even of fully assembled cars (Jürgens 1986: 46). Nevertheless, the tighter language against out-sourcing in the last contracts in exchange for work-rule concessions may indicate a willingness on the part of the Big Three to give priority to improving the efficiency of their existing parts production over out-sourcing (e.g., *American Machinist* 1988: 73).

THE DEMISE OF JOB-CONTROL UNIONISM

A close look at the relationship between autoworkers and the auto companies reveals a complex interplay of governance mechanisms. The individual worker contracts through the labor market with the companies, but the content of the contract is stipulated by a collective-bargaining agreement. An association bargains for the conditions of employment on the worker's behalf. This association (i.e., the labor union) does not meet the employers in the marketplace, and it does not act as a labor agent who rents out labor power (though some craft unions function in a comparable fashion). Instead, the union represents the collective interests of those who are already employed. Therefore, it encounters its corporate adversary

---

23 While GM, as a conglomerate of different car manufacturers, has always been more decentralized, Ford's and Chrysler's plants were heavily concentrated in the Detroit area. Ford's River Rouge complex may even be called the grandfather of just-in-time production because it concentrated all aspects of Ford's auto production, from steelmaking to final assembly, in a single location. Lacking today's computer sophistication, the different production steps were, of course, not as finely tuned as in current JIT plants. At its peak, this huge complex employed 87,000 workers. It was also the home of the UAW Local 600, renowned for its militancy. Former Ford chairman, Philip Caldwell, speculated that the post–War decentralization was a deliberate strategy to keep the newly unionized workers as dispersed as possible (Scherrer 1989: 236).

within the corporate structure, unless its members are on strike. Within the limits of the collective-bargaining agreement, managers allocate work and determine the nature of the work process through their corporate hierarchies. Of course, the union's relationship with its members, as well as with employers, is regulated by the state (e.g., Wagner Act, Taft–Hartley Act, Landrum–Griffin Act). The state also governs many aspects of the employee–employer relationship directly, such as through health and safety regulations.

The specific form of industrial relations in the auto industry has been characterized by Piore (1982) as *job-control unionism*. In the voluntarist tradition of American industrial relations, the state regulates only marginally the content of collective-bargaining agreements. Moreover, the low level of social security provided by the state enlarges the scope of possible bargaining issues between the union and the employer. UAW contracts contain extensive provisions for health care, pensions, and supplemental unemployment benefits. Although management is free to make basic entrepreneurial and managerial decisions, their discretionary control over the allocation of labor and the conditions of employment was severely restricted by the three pillars of job-control unionism: detailed job classifications, a comprehensive seniority system, and legalistic conflict resolution (Katz 1985).[24]

The local collective-bargaining agreements contained detailed lists of *job classifications* that specified the individual tasks in production. For example, within the tool and die and maintenance departments, this codification of the division of labor among workers was accomplished by specification and demarcation among the different skilled trades. The allocation of workers to these specified jobs was governed by the *seniority system,* which regulated the lines of succession in regard to hiring, firing, and internal promotions according to the length of service (Köhler and Sengenberger 1983). Merit criteria, such as performance, qualifications, and conduct, were generally not used for the selection of workers. These rules were enforced by shop stewards, who represented their union members in the *grievance procedure.* The allocative powers of management were further restricted by rules on production standards (Herding 1980).

Through these collective-bargaining rules, management lost important means for rewarding and punishing workers. Greater work efforts could not be elicited through individual bonuses or through promotion, except to a position outside the bargaining unit, such as supervisor. Thus, man-

24 Job-control unionism should not be confused with *craft control* or *workers' control,* phenomena where skilled workers control the work process and the labor market, the latter through hiring halls (Jefferys 1986: 14). In contrast, under *job-control unionism,* workers have already lost this control over the labor process, and job controls, a characteristic of the more general phenomenon of Fordism, become increasingly important as the informal control of workers over the labor process is dismantled (Dohse et al. 1979: 143).

agement had to develop other forms of control. First among these was the incorporation of control into the labor process itself, such as through machine pacing. Second, more time-study personnel were employed and the industrial engineering departments gained influence. Third, the number of supervisors was drastically increased (Jefferys 1986: 129, 137, 154).

How was it possible that U.S. management, known for its tough image, accepted such encroachments on its authority? The rigid, codified division of work did not pose any major problems as long as the predominant production paradigm rested on an increasingly more detailed breakdown of tasks and long production runs (Doeringer and Piore 1971). In addition, from management's point of view, these protective rights of labor were preferable to the alternative of constant struggles on the shop floor. During unionization, for instance, workers in many companies attained a high level of control over production standards and other issues of work organization, and considered protest, wildcat strikes, and even sabotage as legitimate forms of resistance against any speedups (Gartman 1986: 263–91). Thus, the contractual limitations on management's power constituted a compromise insofar as labor agreed to limit this sort of activity. However, the concrete form of the compromise was subject to constant contention (Gersuny 1982).

The first attempts to move toward more cooperative labor relations can be traced back to the early 1970s, when, in response to the so-called blue collar blues (a general discontent among workers over their work, which led to problems, such as high rates of absenteeism and poor product quality), some auto companies started to experiment with quality circles and teamwork approaches. Predictably, framed as an issue of human work life improvement, these experiments drew little attention. Management's interest in them grew only when they could no longer deny the superiority of foreign production concepts. On the basis of comparable technology, foreign producers made more efficient use of labor power and achieved higher levels of workmanship. This was true for producers, such as those in Sweden and West Germany, who had to contend with a strong independent trade union, and was even more so for Japanese producers who enjoyed docile company unions. What they had in common was a more cooperative climate on the shop floor, more flexibility in manpower allocation, and a larger array of positive and negative incentives for eliciting superior work performance (Altshuler et al. 1984; Jürgens, Malsch, and Dohse 1989).

But even while Detroit acknowledged the importance of improved labor relations, it gave priority to technological solutions in its drive to regain its competitiveness in the early 1980s. In particular, GM expected to overcome its labor problems by reducing through automation the role of workers in the production process. However, once GM realized that this strategy did not yield significant productivity increases, in part because the work force was insufficiently trained to operate the automated equipment, management began to pay more attention to the organization of work and labor relations, much as Ford and Chrysler had done earlier (Katz 1988).[25]

In pursuing a transformation of job-control unionism, the Big Three struggled to decide how much they wanted to involve the UAW in this effort. After some unsuccessful attempts to unilaterally impose teamwork concepts in some plants, GM proposed in 1985 to set up a new division, called Saturn, and to manage it jointly with the union – a remarkably bold offer. The UAW accepted and signed a preliminary contract with GM that encompassed many features that were supposed to introduce more flexibility and cooperation into human-resource allocation. Job classifications were abolished, the different crafts were combined in two general classifications, and wages were tied to performance. Although the union retained the right to strike, it agreed to decision making based on consensus instead of formal bargaining. Therefore, GM's old hierarchy of bosses began to give way to management–union committees on all levels of decision making (Meyer 1986). In short, the organization of labor–management relations began to move in a less hierarchical, more cooperative direction.

However, the initial interest in Saturn waned as soon as the New United Motors Manufacturing Inc. (NUMMI) plant, a joint venture between Toyota and GM in Fremont, California, showed that the aim of better work performance could also be achieved by granting only small concessions to labor.[26] The Saturn project was announced with much media fanfare as a new beginning in small-car assembly in the United States. An annual production of 500,000 cars and a high degree of in-house sourcing was promised. Yet production projections were scaled down in 1988 to 150,000 midsized cars, and many parts were scheduled to be sourced from outside suppliers, especially from European subsidiaries located in the United States (Andrea et al. 1988: 9). NUMMI became the main model for new labor–management relations throughout the industry (Parker and Slaughter 1988).

The Saturn–NUMMI experience raises doubts about the long-term viability of flexible and participatory labor relations in the United States, which seem to be quite vulnerable to the vagaries of shifting balances of power between management and labor – something that is derived from the marginal status of unions in the U.S. political system (e.g., Erd and

25 Between 1979 and 1987, GM invested about 50% per auto more than it did between 1973 and 1978, and it spent 25% more than Ford and 40% more than Chrysler in relation to sales. However, despite these capital expenditures, GM did not gain an advantage in productivity over its rivals (Scherrer 1988: 506–7).
26 For a discussion of the NUMMI experience, see Parker and Slaughter (1988: 100–22).

Scherrer 1984: 83–7). The institutional relations between capital and labor, established in the United States during the 1930s, differ from those in Europe, and especially West Germany, by their high degree of decentralization and fragmentation. In contrast to its West European counterparts, U.S. capital has resisted many schemes for coordinating economic activity at the macrolevel. This is particularly evident in capital's reluctance to recognize that unions play a socially useful role, but also in the liberal antiinterventionist tradition of the state. As a result, unions in the United States have experienced only a relatively rudimentary institutionalization in the political system. Consequently, organized labor has been severely limited in responding with political mobilization to changed labor market conditions. Even under President Carter, the unions were no longer able to reverse the progressive weakening of their legal rights, which had been occurring as a result of judicial interpretations. Eventually, the battle for labor law reform was lost in 1978 (Ferguson and Rogers 1979). Thus, unions in the United States seem to enjoy only minimal legal protection against the attempts of employers to unilaterally cancel collective-bargaining agreements. Under these conditions, organized labor in the United States is not able to influence the restructuring of a particular industry through the state (Ross and Gourevitch 1984).

Because unions depend heavily on their shop-floor control for their power and legitimacy, changes in shop-floor relations may endanger the unions' survival. For example, if a union agrees to the broadening of job classifications and to a less-rigid enforcement of the lines of demarcation, its members may no longer feel protected by the union. Similarly, if workers' complaints are handled by team leaders, selected jointly or by the company, shop stewards may become dispensable in the eyes of union members. The same holds true for loosening the seniority system in exchange for more job security. In the absence of legally mandated codetermination structures, the union faces the risk that once cooperation has undermined its legitimacy, management will try to get rid of it all together (Mroczkowski 1984: 56). So far, even the legal status of the current teamwork practices has remained uncertain (Heckscher 1988: 134–6). In order to avoid these risks, unions will have to educate and mobilize their membership on a continuous basis (Parker and Slaughter 1988: 76). In sum, more participatory, less hierarchically governed labor relations seem to require some support from the state in order to ensure their stability. Yet the U.S. political system cannot do that very well and so denies the unions the institutional safeguards that are needed.

DISCUSSION AND OUTLOOK

Writers have expressed their concern that in its pursuit of short-term distributive gains, the automobile industry may put its competitiveness at risk in the long run (e.g., Altshuler et al. 1984; Helper 1987; Katz 1988). These apparently contradictory motives are evident in the new relationships that the Big Three have with suppliers and labor. For example, the assemblers' demands for substantial price cuts on parts would violate the much heralded new spirit of cooperation.[27] Also, many suppliers believed that JIT meant only a transfer of inventory costs at their expense (Helper 1987: Chap. V, 56). It is said that the assemblers have thereby fostered a certain amount of distrust concerning their intentions, which may harm their efforts to intensify cooperation with suppliers.

Some suppliers felt that the auto companies were not fully aware of the heightened information and coordination requirements for a systemic approach to sourcing. Furthermore, the harsh pricing conditions have impeded the modernization of the supplier plants. Many of the suppliers also lack engineering capabilities, but the auto companies have offered only limited technical assistance – much less, for example, than have aerospace companies or Japanese firms with plants in the United States (Helper 1987: Chap. V, 70; Flynn and Cole 1988: 110).

Conflicting motivations are also apparent with regard to labor. In its entirety, the story of the reorganization of labor relations in the auto industry has been described as one of halting beginnings followed by often disconnected experiments by firms and plants (Katz and Sabel 1985: 13). The reasons for the slowness of this transformation involved the pursuit of mutually incompatible cooperative and distributive modifications, and the repeated attempts to sidetrack the union. On the one hand, forced to act quickly by the severe recession of 1981–2, the auto companies tried to combine the introduction of more flexibility into human-resource allocation with a reduction in wage levels. Obviously, the strategy of taking dollars from the pockets of workers contradicted the attempts to elicit their co-operation for a more efficient design of the labor process (Altshuler et al. 1984: 281). On the other hand, in many cases, management tried to impose work-rule changes on union locals that were in a weak bargaining position because of threatened plant shutdowns. Cooperation elicited at gunpoint stands on weak ground, so it is not surprising that in a number of instances, workers stopped participating in quality programs when they learned of further layoffs.[28]

In sum, the two case studies of supplier and labor relations lend credence to the statement that "strategic confusion" exists in the U.S. auto industry. Yet the implicit claim that often conflicting objectives could have been balanced more harmoniously appears to be without sub-

---

27 For example, Ford demanded immediate price cuts of 2.5% and further cuts of 25% in the following five years (*Automotive Industries* 1987a).
28 For examples, see Parker (1985: 63–7) and Parker and Slaughter (1988). Slaughter (1983: 57–8) lists cases in which plants were closed despite extensive concessions.

stance. Given the intense competitive pressures and the lack of state support for less contractually oriented supplier and labor relations, the tendency of the industry to give priority to short-term gains comes as no surprise. Whereas the Big Three faced a stagnating and even declining market, the Japanese supplier and labor relations schemes were able to evolve under the favorable conditions of increasing demand. These favorable market prospects mitigated against any persistent opposition to the extreme asymmetry of power that marks the Japanese system of supplier and labor relations (Nomura 1987).

The discussion of the competitive disadvantages of the American automobile industry shows that its traditional governance regime is not compatible with the new competitive environment. This fact has been recognized by the executives of the auto companies. On their initiative, as the evidence presented in this chapter demonstrates, tremendous efforts are under way to transform the character of the relations among the main actors in the industry. Principally, the relationship between assemblers and suppliers, as well as that between employers and workers, is the focus of these endeavors. However, suppliers and workers are reluctant to follow the course laid out by management, especially because distributive issues are also at stake. Nevertheless, the possibility of global sourcing, the potentialities of new technology, and the eventuality of economic disaster if the necessary changes are not made force upon all actors the need to join together in the pursuit of higher productivity, better workmanship, and lower costs.

Such "cooperation in the context of competition" (Altshuler et al. 1984) is organized largely in ways that are independent of the political system. Privately established networks (e.g., joint committees, participation teams, action groups, and councils) represent the vehicles for change. They replace or supplement the more legalistic forms of economic coordination, such as corporate hierarchies and to an extent markets, that have been dominant traditionally in the auto industry. But despite the rhetoric of mutuality that accompanies these networks, they are marked by an asymmetry of power. Although the assemblers have to rely on the active cooperation of their suppliers and workers for the smooth operation of their production process, particularly insofar as JIT is concerned, these latter two groups can exert only a more-or-less self-defeating, obstructionist pressure; the ultimate authority rests with the assemblers through their unchallenged control over capital because, unless restrained by the state, they are free to source from abroad.

In its crisis intervention, the state has left management's prerogatives largely untouched. Local and state governments have scrambled to offer foreign and domestic automakers attractive deals. The federal government bargained for voluntary export restraints with Japan, granted tax relief, and temporarily relaxed its fuel-economy standards and its antitrust rules (Scherrer 1988: 339–54). A slight deviation from this pattern was illustrated by the loan guarantees for Chrysler. The Chrysler Corporation Loan Guarantee Act of 1979 placed the company under the supervision of an independent board, and required the sale of assets as well as concessions from Chrysler's banks, suppliers, and employees. Although the Act gave the government veto power over most management policies, the company still enjoyed considerable freedom in its investment and production decisions. Although the rescue was publicly justified as an attempt to save jobs, about half the jobs involved were lost (Reich and Donahue 1985: 5, 296). Under the Reagan Administration, no tripartite solutions were pursued.

Over all, several factors have caused and constrained, in varying degree, the transformation of governance in the auto industry.

1. *Market pressure and economic performance.* Market pressures, particularly the competitive challenge of foreign producers, accentuated by the oil price increases, helped to trigger the search for a new governance regime. This challenge required change if the Big Three were to avoid further losses of their market shares. It also provided a model of an alternative governance regime, although not the only one possible, and it forced reluctant actors, such as the unions, to participate in the transformation process.

2. *Technology.* The need to reduce labor costs and improve quality, and the need to meet the increasingly volatile demands of consumers sparked the drive toward automation and flexible production techniques, respectively. In this sense, innovations in technology were dependent, rather than independent, variables in this story. On the other hand, the development of new computer technologies created the possibility for closer communication among various actors in the industry, thereby facilitating the development of more sophisticated obligational and promotional networks.

3. *Levels of political mobilization.* The collective strength of autoworkers constituted an incentive for changing the governance of labor–management relations initially insofar as the development of contractual agreements and hierarchical control of labor by management was concerned. However, the ability of labor to mobilize also limited the options for change. In particular, the political weakness of the labor movement, and especially the UAW, precluded state intervention on labor's behalf and made workers wary of changes that might erode their shop-floor power.

4. *The state.* The U.S. government provided the space in which new governance regimes could emerge, such as by passing various pieces of labor legislation that facilitated the development of

unions and contractual bargaining over wages and benefits, and by loosening antitrust policies that created opportunities for new promotional networks to arise. Rarely, however, did the state deliberately mandate the creation of new governance mechanisms. Indeed, this did not even occur in the unprecedented Chrysler rescue.

5. *Prior governance regime.* The late and slow process of change revealed the considerable inertial weight of the existing governance regime. This was evident, for example, where management resorted to a command strategy, typical of hierarchical coordination, in trying to force work-rule changes on weak union locals through threats of plant closings. However ironic, this attempt to develop a more cooperative means of governing labor–management relations was embedded in the previously existing and more adversarial governance regime, and the potential for success was limited as a result.

In conclusion, the potential for less hierarchical and more cooperative forms of governance in the U.S. automobile industry seems to rest largely in the hands of the state. In the absence of legislation to support and institutionalize mechanisms of flexible adaption, voluntary programs, such as those discussed before, are subject to the shifting balance of power among the actors involved. Given their record of short-range planning, it remains to be seen whether automobile manufacturers can sustain a cooperative momentum over a long period of time. As we have seen, workers have reasons to be skeptical. As long as corporate managers retain complete control over investment decisions, the present shift in governance away from corporate hierarchies may turn out to be just a fad.

THE DAIRY INDUSTRY: FROM YEOMANRY TO THE INSTITUTIONALIZATION OF MULTILATERAL GOVERNANCE

Brigitte Young

John F. Kennedy Institute, Free University of Berlin, and Department of Political Science,
Wesleyan University

Dairying is one of the most regulated industries in the American economy. The main pillars of these regulations are the antitrust exemption, federal milk-marketing agreements, price supports, and import controls. Perhaps more importantly, the dairy industry is an interesting example of multilateral governance. Dairy producers organized collective-bargaining associations, such as the National Milk Producers Federation, and promotional networks in order to overcome market failures that were the result of the unequal power relationships between dairy producers and processors. In particular, the history of the National Milk Producers Federation illustrates how a trade association can acquire increased autonomy and the ability to govern an industry for over fifty years.

These multilateral forms of governance, which originated primarily in the midwest, were embedded within a specific "dairy culture," based on solidaristic values and shared norms of existing social collectives. The promotional networks brought together diverse actors from different parts of the agricultural system, such as dairy cooperatives, agricultural scientists at the land-grant universities, members of the state extension services, and the U.S. Department of Agriculture (USDA), for the purpose of designing rules in keeping with the specific needs of the dairy producers. The common bond between the leaders and the members of cooperative associations allowed the leadership to pursue long-term strategies for the management of the industry's overproduction and pricing problems.

This particular governance regime, resting on associations and promotional networks, was sanctioned by the state, yet it avoided direct state intervention. Dairy producers struggled for the recognition of cooperative bargaining associations and for the right to negotiate and enforce the terms of regulations. These findings contradict Skocpol and Finegold's (1982) thesis that the autonomy of state managers within the USDA accounted for the success of New Deal agricultural programs. In the dairy industry, state managers were unable to impose production controls against the will of the associations.

In this chapter, I analyze four specific time periods that were marked by governance transformations. I show how dairy producers were able to overcome the historic market failures of an atomistic market structure and institutionalize a governance regime that promoted the collective interests of the industry for decades. I conclude by explaining the challenges to the industry that have emerged since the beginning of the 1970s, and speculate about how these may affect the future of the dairy industry's traditional governance regime.

ATOMISTIC MARKET STRUCTURE BEFORE 1880

Specialized dairy farming was virtually unknown prior to 1850 (Pirtle 1926). Although the first importation of cattle dates back to the colonial period of 1611, dairying was not pursued as an economic activity until well over 200 years later (Pirtle 1926; Gates 1960). Essentially, the milk trade could not develop because of the absence of a transportation system for shipping milk to the cities, and the lack of sanitation in handling fluid milk (Pirtle 1926).

Until about 1880, milk production was not confined to rural areas alone. Although many small farmsteads produced fluid milk, cheese, and butter, and traded the small surpluses, some cows were also kept within city limits. Since yields of cows were rather low at that time, the city milk supply was inadequate to meet the demand of the town dwellers, thus surrounding areas had to make up the difference.

Colonial Boston provides a rather typical example of how most cities secured their milk supply. In 1742, Boston had 141 cows for a population approaching 16,500 (Friedman 1973: 198). Records of that period show that milk was part of the daily diet of most city dwellers. A 1749 Boston law suggests the importance of surrounding areas in supplying milk to the city, since certain ferryboats passing between Boston and Charleston were required to provide adequate space for the transportation of milk (Friedman 1973: 198). With regard to cheese and butter production, these items were regarded as luxuries, and there is little evidence that low-income families in Boston had frequent access to these food items (Friedman 1973).

However, the city milk system was plagued with problems. Eleven out of twelve milk samples taken in Boston during 1857 and 1858 contained from 15 to 47.5% water. The adulteration was largely the work of dealers, not farmers. According to the *New England Farmer* in 1858, when asked whether all dealers diluted their milk with water, one Cincinnati dealer reported that the best milk dealers never put water into their milk, but rather put milk into water (Gates 1960).

While, prior to 1814, the problem of milk quality was mostly related to added water or unsanitary handling of milk, after this time, the problem was exacerbated when many dairies became linked to the distillery business and city cows were fed the remnants of grain distilleries. Dairies linked to distilleries were called "slop-dairies," since they used the hot "slop" from the distilling process to feed the cows. Domestic distilleries had started to proliferate in the populous areas of the east, since the War of 1812 had resulted in the suspension of imported spirituous liquors from the West Indies. The eastern distilleries were initially very lucrative, but a large influx of whiskey from the American west in the 1820s and 1830s virtually destroyed their profits, except from the selling of "slop" to dairies. At the same time, dairymen in the city welcomed the availability of a new feed source. As a result of the increasing population pressures, dairymen were suffering an increasing shortage of feed for their cattle. In this way, a linkage developed among slop-dairies, the distilleries, and consumers of liquors and milk. Although the business was extremely profitable for the former two groups, for the latter, the relationship turned into a deadly game, as infants reared on this type of milk increasingly died from malnutrition (Hartley 1842).

About 500 slop-dairies operated in New York and Brooklyn around 1840. Fluid milk sold at varying prices, depending on the amount of adulteration. In most cities, vendors sold three quality grades of milk. As the price decreased from six cents to four cents, the amount of dilution increased (Hartley 1842). The slop-dairies survived for decades. As late as 1908, such operations still existed in Cincinnati (Roadhouse and Henderson 1941).

Laws began to be passed to control the milk supply to cities. Massachusetts became the first state to prohibit the adulteration of milk with water in 1856, but it was 1861 before an inspector was appointed to enforce these laws (Pirtle 1926). Other states soon followed suit to control milk supplies: New York in 1862, New Hampshire and Wisconsin in 1866, Rhode Island in 1867, Maine in 1869, and Virginia in 1872 (Gates 1960). In addition to state laws, many local ordinances were also passed to regulate the supply of milk (Roadhouse and Henderson 1941).

These early laws had virtually no impact on the sanitary conditions of the fluid-milk supply, since inspection of country dairies was not required until 1906 (Roadhouse and Henderson 1941). Hence, while the law forbade the sale of adulterated milk, the enforcement mechanisms were extremely lax. For example, in Washington, D.C., more than thirty years elapsed between the enactment of legislation in 1863 to protect the city's milk supply and the requiring of inspectors to visit dairy farms in 1895 (Pirtle 1926). Nor did existing health codes undermine the slop-dairies.

The final demise of the city milk system was largely due to increasing population pressures between 1850 and 1900 (Roadhouse and Henderson 1941), and the construction of the railroads in the 1850s (Gates 1960). The competition for scarce land gradually crowded out the dairies and forced them to relocate. In addition, changes occurred on both the demand and supply sides that altered the existing milk-marketing structure. The growing population centers created a large pool of wage earners with cash purchasing power. At the same time, the construction of railroads facilitated the retail business between the country and the city.

In summary, the market functioned essentially as the only coordinating mechanism in the fluid-milk trade prior to 1880. The system consisted of many small farmers selling milk directly to consumers, or to small dealers who peddled the milk from wagons to customers. Larger city dairies emerged after 1814, often operated and managed as part of the distillery business. The fluid-milk market during this period was dominated by small-scale competition. It was a highly competitive market, and essentially the seller could ask the price the market would bear. However, it was well to heed the warning, *caveat emptor*, in this period.

The state tried to intervene and regulate the quality of milk, but it did not have the enforcement mechanisms to control the multitudinous small dairy producers. To make health regulations effective, a very large number of inspectors would have been needed. Mandatory federal inspection of rural dairies was not inaugurated until 1906.

DEALER DOMINANCE, 1880–1915

The fluid-milk market witnessed a transformation from the earlier atomistic market structure, in which farmers sold milk directly to consumers or to salesmen, who then sold milk to consumers, to a system of greater market concentration, with many dairy farmers selling fluid milk to a few large dealers. However, remnants of the former atomistic, small-scale competition continued to operate during this period. In Boston, the market was divided between a few large dealers handling 75% of the total milk supply, and many small peddlers handling the remainder. In New York, the situation was similar, although the market was not as concentrated. Approximately 80 to 90% of the milk sold was handled by 125 dealers (Whitaker 1905: 35).

As pointed out in the previous section, the most influential factors in the transformation of the fluid-milk market were the rapid population increases in the cities and the development of the railroads. The total population in New York, Boston, Philadelphia, and Chicago increased sevenfold between 1850 and 1900 (Roadhouse and Henderson 1941). Since the farmer could not personally deliver the milk to the increasing number of city milk sheds, retail and wholesale outlets became important in the distribution network. Hence, a distinction began to emerge between production and distribution, and the role of the "contractor" or "dealer" gained in importance (Whitaker 1905).

The growth of the fluid-milk market also witnessed the rise of specialized dairy farms and regional specialization, in contrast to the previous system, in which dairy cows were part of any farmstead. By the late nineteenth century, dairying was increasingly perceived as an important commercial activity. This process was greatly aided by the introduction of new technologies. For example, although 70 miles was considered the outer limit for transporting milk to the cities in 1850, trains went as far as 250 miles in search of milk by 1879 (Sheldon 1907). This distance was made possible through the introduction of refrigerated cars in 1867, and even longer distances could be traversed once glass-lined refrigerated milk cars were introduced in 1924–5 (Pirtle 1926). Many other technical innovations that improved sanitation also facilitated long-distance hauling: can and bottle washers (1905), pasteurizing machines (1906), paper bottles (1906), glass-lined cooled tanks (1911), and bottling and capping machines (1910–15) (Pirtle 1926).

The new market structure for the supply of fluid milk differed markedly from city to city, but they all had in common that the dealers emerged as dominant actors in setting conditions for marketing the milk, oligopolistic behavior that was greatly resented by the dairy producers. A comparison of the systems of milk supply in Boston, New York, and Philadelphia in 1903 is useful as illustration.

The system in Boston was most unique, since milk was sold through contracts. Five contractors handled about 75% of the milk. The remaining milk was handled by small dealers. Market concentration in 1903 stood in marked contrast to 1880, when 700–800 wholesale dealers had operated in the city (Sheldon 1907). The contract arrangement worked as follows: The five large wholesale houses contracted for and bought the milk in the country, leased railroad milk cars, managed the transportation to the city, and sold most of their supplies to peddlers for retail distribution (Whitaker 1905). Initially, the contractors had restricted their operations to purely wholesale business, but they became increasingly involved in milk retailing, which allowed them to control the retail trade by eliminating the second middlemen.

The power of these five contractors to control the market was enormous. Although their business operations were technically separate, a common understanding nevertheless existed among these contractors. One person was in charge of three corporations; hence, three officials controlled virtually the entire fluid-milk market in Boston. Some of the contractors were not only involved in the fluid-milk trade, but also had butter and cheese factories in the country. Although these factories were independent of the milk business, in emergency situations, the contractors had access to additional milk (Witaker 1905).

There was a great deal of conflict with milk producers over the system of payment, which was determined by the dealers. The price of milk in the city of Boston was fixed, but the dealers discounted the price they paid to cover the costs of transportation and handling. The dealers leased the railroad milk cars and were responsible for managing transportation to the city and then determined the discount they would subtract to cover these transactions and the producer received payment in accordance with the dealer's calculations. Producers had no way of knowing the expense of handling the milk or of the cost of transportation (Whitaker 1905). In addition, much discontent occurred over the power of contractors to return spoiled milk. Essentially, the dealers functioned as prosecutor, judge, and jury, and there was no opportunity for the farmer to verify whether the milk had indeed arrived in a spoiled condition (Whitaker 1905).

The New York distribution system was not as heavily concentrated. Whereas in Boston, five dealers handled about 75% of the fluid-milk market, in New York, the five largest dealers handled one-third of that market. Milk was received from the farmers at 539 rural shipping stations, owned by the dealers, where it was prepared for shipment to the city. Hence, dealers functioned as receivers of milk at these rural shipping stations, as well as being wholesalers and retailers (Whitaker 1905).

Producer prices were established primarily through the New York Milk Exchange. Seventeen directors determined the price of milk, based on information supplied by producers and dealers in regard to supply, demand, and the cost of production. No advance contracts or price agreements were made by the Exchange. Prices were changed as the situation warranted. Producers greatly resented this method of price fixing to which they had little input. This animosity between dealers and producers strongly resembled that in the Boston system.

Although the Philadelphia milk-market structure was in many respects quite dissimilar to Boston and New York, producer resentment against dealers was as prevalent as in the other two systems. Whereas in Boston and New York, the supply came from a distance of between 40 and 400 miles, most of Philadelphia's milk supply came from nearby sources. In 1903, Philadelphia still reported having 5,000 cows within the city limits (Whitaker 1905).

However, the most significant difference was in the number, and the relationship between small and large dealers. In contrast to the markets in Boston and New York, which were dominated by a few large dealers, Philadelphia had mainly small dealers.[1] In 1903, the large dealers had not acquired the same market power they had in the other two markets, and thus the smallest dealer had privileges equal to those of the largest (Whitaker 1905). An explanation for the more equal power sharing among differently sized dealers can be found in the virtual absence of wholesalers. Practically no milk was sold by dealers to be resold again. The majority of the dealers bought their supply directly from the producers, and went to the train daily to get their shipment of milk. In addition, payment for

---

1 This market system of many small dealers did not survive for long. By 1929, the Philadelphia system was similar to those in Boston and New York. Over 85% of the milk was handled by four distributors; in contrast, producers numbered over 30,000 (Bartlett 1931).

transporting milk was made through a system of tickets that were attached to the milk cans. This system of issuing tickets for transporting milk had many advantages over the discount system in Boston, since the producer paid for the transportation directly to the railways.

Despite the more equal power relationship among the dealers, producer resentment against dealer dominance was as widely shared as in the other two city markets. The price paid to the producers was fixed in advance at the Philadelphia Milk Exchange. The members of the Exchange met once a month, and the price was set for the coming month, with little producer input (Whitaker 1905). Another point of contention between dealers and producers was the problem of seasonal production. Although various dealers and producers tried to devise methods to deal with the problem of seasonal surplus milk, it could not be resolved.

This survey of three fluid-milk-marketing systems reveals that there was no uniform distribution system in the various cities. However, it does demonstrate that by the turn of the century, dealers were dominant in the fluid-milk market (Spencer and Blanford 1973). This system produced an extremely unequal power relationship between the many small, atomistically organized farmers, on the one side, and the dealers who had virtual market control, on the other. Most importantly, the dealers had the power to set prices that the producers had to accept. The failure of the market to create greater equality between producers and distributors led to the mobilization of the dairy producers during the 1910s, and to the creation of the National Milk Producer Federation (NMPF) in 1916, which became the collective voice for the milk producers to gain legal recognition for producer cooperatives to bargain collectively with dealers.

Individually, dairy producers had no bargaining power. Withholding milk from the market as a weapon became effective only when producers agreed collectively to such a course of action. This was the case when the Dairymen's League, which supplied the region around New York, called a 14-day strike in 1916 and an 18-day strike in 1919, which greatly reduced the milk supply to the city. In both cases, the dealers had to pay the prices demanded by the producers (Bartlett 1931).

Increasingly, producers came to believe that only through collective action could they counter their individual weakness and wrest some market power from the large dealers. However, strict antitrust enforcement prevented milk producers from creating effective bargaining institutions until 1922. This was not the case for manufacturing cooperatives engaged in making cheese and butter, which were often protected by state law. For example, a statute to provide for associations of creameries had already been passed in Minnesota in 1897 (Nourse 1927). Hence, cheese-making and creamery associations emerged earlier than fluid-milk-marketing cooperatives. Cooperatives of dairy producers were relentlessly pursued by the courts on antitrust violations, because they were designed to bargain collectively over fluid-milk prices, and this was seen as a conspiracy in restraint of trade (Nourse 1927). On the other hand, creamery and cheese-making associations were formed as sales agencies to market dairy products collectively, not to try to influence the prices of these products (Guth 1981).

THE IMPORTANCE OF MULTILATERAL GOVERNANCE, 1915–33

Farmer militancy was not a new phenomenon. In the last century, the Granger Movement symbolized great agrarian discontent. The railroads were blamed for the depressed agricultural situation after the Civil War. Discrimination in transportation rates, as well as high freight rates to ship farm produce to market caused the organization to "spread like a prairie fire" in 1873 and 1874 (Key 1947: 23). The Grange proposed to regulate railroad corporations, which was viewed by the railroads as no less than a communist plot intended to subvert American institutions (Key 1947: 24). Although the resulting state laws regulating the railroads were not the most effective in dealing with the problem, the importance of the Granger Movement does not rest with the actual regulations. Rather, the Grange is important because the farmers appealed to the state to intervene and regulate institutions that were beyond their immediate control. As Fainsod et al. (1959: 251) noted, "Agrarian forces distrustful of central controls were compelled to invoke national power in order to come to grips with economic organizations that eluded local jurisdictions." The militancy of the Grange ebbed by 1880, but the Granger Movement had set an important precedent for future political activities of farmers (Key 1947).

Hence, when milk producers invoked the federal government after 1915 to help them gain market power vis-à-vis the dealers, it was not a step into virgin territory. On the other hand, dealers looked frequently to the Department of Justice to intervene against the emerging cooperative movement around 1915. The International Milk Dealers Association (IMDA), founded in 1908, was used primarily to lobby the Department of Justice to intervene "against the epidemic of milk strikes engineered by the constantly growing producers' organizations" (Guth 1981: 173–4). Thus, milk producers looked to the federal government for state sanction of cooperatives, and dealers implored the state to prohibit such organizations.

While producer discontent with dealer dominance had been a constant factor for some time, there were particular events in the 1910s that fueled the discontent further. In 1915, the European War increased inflationary pressures. Milk prices had barely risen between 1900 and 1914, but as grain prices and other input costs soared, dairy producers countered by organizing milk-bargaining organizations, which the dealers invariably refused to recognize. As a result, farmers engaged in extensive milk strikes. The action taken by the militant Chicago Milk Producers Association (CMPA) in 1916 was particularly important for future strategies of dairy farmers. A strike organized by the CMPA led to the capitulation of the dealers in 1916. The CMPA was recognized, and the dealers had to pay the higher milk prices. This success had an exhilarating effect on the dairy producers in other areas. By 1916, a wave of cooperative organizations had spread throughout the milk-producing areas. The largest of this type was the Dairymen's League of New York with a membership of 100,000 (Guth 1981).

The increasing success of the dairy producers in achieving higher milk prices brought forth new actors. In 1917, consumers, resenting the higher prices, joined the dealers in demanding state antitrust action. Consumer activism was not new in the milk market; historically, their complaints had focused most heavily on questions of product quality. Now they shifted to pricing concerns. The National Housewives League was a particularly potent consumer force, since it had organized successful bread protests only a few months earlier, in 1917 (Guth 1981).

A new challenge to antitrust legislation was added when the Chicago Milk Producers Association and the New York Dairymen's League created the National Milk Producers Federation (NMPF) in 1916 to coordinate market strategies that involved activities across state lines. Amidst rising milk prices, dealers and consumers petitioned the state and the federal Justice Department to intervene. As new milk strikes loomed in October 1917, and renewed consumer protests were on the horizon, the State of Wisconsin filed charges against the CMPA, and the Illinois Attorney General joined the suit some time later. Simultaneously, the federal Justice Department also prepared to intervene, but Herbert Hoover, as the Administrator of the U.S. Food Administration, used his influence with the federal Justice Department to have the charges dropped against the NMPF and the CMPA (Guth 1982).

It is difficult to explain Hoover's action. Guth has speculated that the looming milk strikes persuaded Hoover that a solution to the milk conflict could not be found in the legal arena. Rather, he believed that an administrative solution had to be negotiated between dealers and producers. Yet Hoover's position was ambiguous. He certainly did not initially favor recognizing the farmers' organizations. Inadvertently, Hoover's early stance against cooperatives changed the objective of the NMPF, which thenceforth became a lobbying instrument for the cooperative movement (Guth 1982). Hoover's position toward cooperatives changed by 1918, by which time he saw these institutions as the only bulwark against the demands of militant dairy producers. Hence, in his later tenure as Food Administrator, he not only recognized the cooperatives, but became an ardent supporter of such institutions (Guth 1981).

At first, the Food Administration was reluctant to intervene in the milk-market dispute, hoping that the parties involved could resolve the conflict among themselves. Intervention was restricted to encouraging the formation of federal commissions in Boston, New York, Chicago, and San Francisco to work on private settlements between producers, distributors, and consumers. These commissions were then superseded by producer-dealer conferences, which met with considerable success during 1918 (Guth 1981). Importantly, in some areas "two-price" plans were inaugurated for the first time, which paid farmers for milk in accordance with end use. This "two-tiered" pricing structure tried to address the seasonal surplus problem, which was such a contentious issue between distributors and producers. Although these innovations did not survive the 1920s, they reemerged in slightly altered forms as part of the Agricultural Adjustment Act (AAA) of the 1930s (Guth 1981).

With the end of the war in 1918, the Food Administration was disbanded. Once the protection of the Food Administration was gone, the dairy producers feared renewed antitrust attacks. In response, the Dairymen's League drafted a bill in 1918 that would have exempted cooperatives from the restraint of trade and monopoly provisions of the Sherman Act (Guth 1982). Already in 1914, farmers had received a partial exemption in the Clayton Act; however, this act exempted only financial nonstock-owning farm cooperatives from the Sherman Act (Odom 1985), and most dairy cooperatives relied on stocks for their financial existence. Starting in 1914, Congress passed an annual appropriations "rider" that prevented the Justice Department "from prosecuting farmers who cooperated and organized to obtain a fair and reasonable price for their product" (Odom 1985: 41). President Wilson, however, declared the provision null and void, and, hence, the marketing groups gained little through the congressional action (Guth 1982).

Finally, in 1922, the much embattled Volstead bill was passed by the Senate (Guth 1982). The Congress intended that the Capper–Volstead Act "[i]nstead of granting a class privilege, . . . aims to equalize existing privileges by changing the law applicable to the ordinary business corporations so the farmers can take advantage of it" (Williams et al. 1970: 337). The NMPF saw the Capper–Volstead Act as "one of the greatest victories ever won by farmers" (Guth 1982: 81). The exuberance of the NMPF is understandable given the fact that the federal Justice Department indicted the Dairymen's Cooperative Association while the final bill was debated in Congress (Guth 1982). However, there were also voices that presaged the consumer attacks of the 1970s. Senator Atlee Pomerence poignantly summarized his objection to the bill: "There is nothing in this bill to prevent a combination of men who are dealing in food products – and I refer to dairymen – from getting the most exorbitant prices, and doing so at the expense of the babes of the country" (Odom 1985: 40).

The fight for the Capper–Volstead Act was essentially carried out by the NMPF. After the bill was defeated in a conference committee in 1920, the

NMPF was especially adroit in consolidating the farm ranks by obtaining the support of the Farmers Union and the American Farm Bureau Federation (AFBF). In fact, only the united farm front established after 1920 convinced Congress to act and pass the bill in the subsequent Congress.

However, even the cooperatives proved no match for post–war economic problems. Agricultural prices fell as industrial prices rose during the 1920s. The Co-Operative Marketing Act of 1926 was a new attempt by Congress to help farmers bargain more effectively with middlemen (Fainsod et al. 1959). The problem with the Capper–Volstead Act and the Co-Operative Marketing Act was that neither contained mechanisms enabling cooperatives "to control output of members, or control production entry, or prevent free riders from selling at the cooperative-established price" (Odom 1985: 41). Although many farm groups championed direct government intervention in the form of the McNary–Haugen Bill, President Hoover strongly believed that the government's role should be restricted to improving the marketing of machinery (Fainsod et al. 1959).[2] In this, he was strongly supported by the Republican business establishment. The Republican Party saw the furtherance of the cooperatives as the "ultimate farm relief solution" (Guth 1977: 443). The 1928 Republican Platform expressed the party's position succinctly: "We favor, without putting the Government into business, the establishment of a Federal system of organization for cooperative and orderly marketing of farm products" (Porter and Johnson 1966: 285).

This promise was fulfilled with Hoover's inauguration. In 1929, the Agricultural Marketing Act was signed. A Farm Board was established with $500 million to stabilize output and prices of farm products. Loans were made to cooperatives to withhold surpluses from the market. Again, there was no mechanism to control production. And as prices declined, farmers increased their production in order to make up for the falling prices. As a result, the Board suffered huge losses (Fainsod et al. 1959).

With the onset of the Depression, the Board was unable to cope with the agricultural crisis. The milk cooperatives viciously competed for markets, often making individual deals with milk handlers. Price cutting was frequent in this chaotic market as dealers tried to bring in cheaper milk from the surrounding area. The situation was equally catastrophic in the butter and cheese markets, where prices reached a nadir as sales agencies for manufacturers were forced to find outlets at any price. In response,

2 The McNary–Haugen Bill envisioned a two-tiered pricing structure for agricultural products. "Its aim was to secure the world price plus tariff for the domestically consumed portions of export crops. Under this plan, a federal board would purchase enough agricultural products for sale abroad to raise domestic prices above world prices by the amount of the tariff duties. Losses in marketing surpluses abroad were to be covered by an equalization fee collected from the growers" (Fainsod et al. 1959: 132). The Bill was twice passed by Congress in 1927 and 1928, but President Coolidge vetoed the Bill on both occasions.

angry farmers in Wisconsin, Iowa, and Minnesota resorted to milk dumping and strikes. By 1933, chaos reigned in the industry (Guth 1980).

However, even though economic conditions proved formidable, the milk producers entered the 1930s with a well-established cooperative structure and the very powerful NMPF. The cooperatives and the NMPF had acquired considerable political expertise in forging coalitions with other farm groups, and in working with administrative and congressional offices. Furthermore, they had experimented with government-sponsored pricing mechanisms during the war and also with a regulated market. The acquired institutional structures and the concomitant experience from the war years served the industry extremely well in the struggle to achieve its program goals within the Agricultural Adjustment Administration during the 1930s.

The USDA was also engaged in institution building and had also acquired new expertise. Wartime regulations, as well as the economic crises of the 1920s, demanded new approaches to old problems. Before the U.S. Farm Administration was disbanded in 1918, it provided a great laboratory for experimenting with individual food product regulations, lessons which later could be applied to the Agricultural Adjustment Administration. Many new innovations were devised, often very crudely designed, but, again, often later reshaped into more sophisticated regulatory devices.

INSTITUTIONALIZATION OF MULTILATERAL GOVERNANCE, 1933–70s

What emerged in the 1920s was a system of small dairy cooperatives, which were nationally organized in the NMPF. These associations represented a distinctive form of multilateral governance of dairy producers. The stimulus for the creation of these institutions was the inability of the many individual dairy producers to gain market power vis-à-vis the dealers. Only the multilateral action of dairy producers could have reversed the unequal power relationship between producers and distributors in the milk markets, and control the free-rider problem among dairy producers. The highly decentralized and competitive nature of the dairy industry made the control of opportunism a particular problem, because individual dairy farmers, not organized in cooperatives, could reap the benefits of collective action without incurring the costs (Nourse, Davis, and Black 1937; Manchester 1983). Higher prices arranged by cooperatives invariably led to increased supplies, since nonmembers augmented their production, which depressed the price again. Without the coercive ability of associations to restrict access to collective goods, the dairy producers were unable to control prices and overproduction of individual dairy producers.

The state played an important role in sanctioning the capacity of these associations to coordinate transactions among dairy producers. As pointed out in the previous section, producer cooperatives could only bargain collectively once the Capper–Volstead Act of 1922 provided an exemption to the antitrust provisions of the Sherman Act.[3] Of course, this exemption was only needed because of the state's prior prohibition of trusts.

Associations, while sanctioned by the state, avoided direct state intervention. This particular mode of state action can perhaps be accounted for by the ambivalence that existed in the relationship between the state and the farmers. While the dairy farmers looked toward the state for protection, at the same time, they were distrustful of direct state intervention, and the state was equally reluctant to intervene directly in the production process. As a result, associations became the mutually agreed-upon mechanism to control the disequilibrium in the market. The state recognized and strengthened the cooperatives, but the formation and implementation of dairy policies was largely left to the milk-marketing associations.

Streeck and Schmitter (1985) have referred to this form of governance as "private interest government," or regulated self-regulation. In such a system, the state escapes direct intervention, and in addition, "[t]he same associations that negotiate the terms of regulation of their members' behavior, are charged as private governments with responsibility to enforce them" (Streeck and Schmitter 1985: 22). This accommodation within associational structures avoids the legitimacy problem encountered with direct state intervention, and is particularly well suited to counter the failures that arise in a market system.

What makes the institutional arrangement of the dairy industry particularly interesting is the emergence of a stable set of actors in the 1910s, which created an informal coalition for the common purpose of stabilizing the industry. Such a promotional network consisted of dairy cooperatives, agricultural scientists at the land-grant universities, members of the state extension services, and the USDA. These promotional networks brought together diverse actors from different parts of the agricultural system for the purpose of designing rules in keeping with the specific needs of the dairy producers, and it also enabled the actors to implement these regulations with relative ease. In turn, this assured greater compliance by the membership. Hence, the cooperative associations, however much they were facilitated and institutionalized by state authority, were rooted in the values and interest perceptions of existing social collectivities, as Streeck and Schmitter (1985: 27) would anticipate. In order to seek compliance from the members, the dominant actors in the dairy industry relied on some shared community norms that provided a common bond between the leaders and the members.

3 For a useful discussion on the different interpretations of the Capper–Volstead Act, see Guth (1982). Most farm groups claim that the Act exempts farmers from most, if not all, provisions of the Sherman and Clayton Acts. This interpretation is not shared by the Justice Department.

The stimulus for the emergence of these promotional networks in the dairy industry came from the midwest primarily because of a reinforcing combination of cultural, economic structure, and political–institutional factors. This complex set of institutional linkages evolved into a well-developed "dairy culture." This concept is similar to Dyson's industrial culture, which is defined as a "distinctive ideological, institutional, and cultural inheritance of societies and the impact of that inheritance on their capacity to manage industrial crises" (Dyson 1983: 35). Thus, a country's political tradition and industrial development are reflected within industrial cultures, which in turn find expression in institutional structures.

The "dairy culture" of the midwest – especially Wisconsin and Minnesota – has been shaped by immigration patterns, more specifically the influx of Nordic and German people who had some exposure to the idea of collective action within agricultural cooperatives in Europe. Important also are the historic land-tenure patterns and the availability of land. The midwest was more suitable for small-scale family farming than the arid west.

Also the establishment of a Wisconsin Agricultural School under the Land-Grant College System of 1862, and the subsequent authorization of the Extension Service offered Wisconsin's dairy farmers and the agricultural economists an opportunity to make the concern of dairying a central research focus within these institutions.[4] The existence of agricultural schools in the upper midwest, dedicated to the concerns of dairy farming and the educational outreach program of the extension service to the rural population, made it, in turn, attractive for many sons of dairy farmers to become agricultural economists. Because of their acquired expertise in dairying, many of these academician-farmers spent some of their lives in the USDA. These institutional structures embodied and reinforced a "dairy culture" that centered around small farming operations, their linkage to dairy cooperatives, and close concertation between the industry, government agencies, and the universities. The central mechanisms for coordination within the industry were based on appeals to solidaristic values, collective action, and the creation of collective goods. Of particular importance was the pursuit of long-term strategies for the management of the dairy industry's overproduction and pricing problems.

4 Government intervention in agriculture was extensive between 1860 and 1920. The most important interventions came in 1862 with the establishment of Land-Grant Colleges, authorized by the Morill Act. The USDA was created in that same year. The emphasis in both institutions was on education. In 1887, federal support for research was inaugurated in the Hatch Experiment Station Act, which provided federal matching support to state experiment stations. The stations were to be established in conjunction with the land grants (McCalla 1978). Finally, the Smith–Lever Act of 1914 created the cooperative agricultural partnership between federal and state extension services (Baker et al. 1963: 521). Federal involvement did not remain at the educational and research levels. In 1916, the Federal Farm Loan Act provided financial assistance to farmers, and federal and state health care codes date back to 1856.

While the establishment of cooperatives changed the dairy industry's governance regime, the associations in the 1920s did not have the regulatory capacity to pursue the long-term interests of the industry. This was no more evident than in the economic crisis of the 1930s. Only the enactment of the Agricultural Adjustment Act (AAA) of 1933, and its subsequent amendments, gave the dairy industry the necessary tools to control and regulate the industry. Federal marketing orders, dairy price supports, and import restrictions had the "combined effect of achieving a considerable degree of price stability, a concomitant reduction in market risk, and some upward effect on the price level for producer milk, at least in short-run periods of time" (Jacobson 1980: 156).

What seems to explain how a regionally based "dairy culture" and its associations came to predominate in the industry as a whole? By the 1920s, the NMPF had emerged as the dominant political representative for the dairy interests in the midwest and northeast. It functioned as the political channel to influence national dairy legislation. Nearly all the northeastern and midwestern fluid-milk associations and the large manufacturing sales agencies, such as Land O'Lakes Creameries, were members of the NMPF. With the onset of the Depression in the 1930s, it became clear that co-operatives did not have the necessary mechanism to secure the adhesion of all the producers within a given marketing area.

The incoming Democratic Administration shifted from the previous Republican reliance on cooperative marketing to a new strategy that endorsed production controls in order to combat the surplus problem. The enactment of the Agricultural Adjustment Act of 1933 symbolized the Democratic approach to the farm crisis. However, this shift in policy set off an intense struggle between the USDA and the dairy cooperatives. The membership of the NMPF was staunchly opposed to production controls, because the AAA did not provide assurances that the cooperatives had a role in the future administration of the new program. Although the dairy producers immediate complaint centered around the fear that production controls "would reduce volume, increase unit costs, and reduce overall returns" (Guth 1980: 3), their more important concern had to do with the fear that the USDA was planning to set up government-controlled cooperative agencies, and hence bypass the farmer organizations.[5] It is difficult to guess whether the fierce opposition to allotment plans would have materialized if Secretary of Agriculture Henry A. Wallace had incorporated the co-operatives in his plan. But the exclusion of the cooperative organizations from a role in the implementation of dairy policy turned the struggle over policy into a fight for the survival of these institutions.

Instead of production controls, the dairy cooperative leadership proposed a "double" program that relied on marketing agreements and "sta-

5 For details, see Guth (1980).

bilization" purchases of surplus dairy products. It was hoped that federal enforcement of marketing agreements would not only raise prices, but force producers and dealers in a market to accept the same cooperative bargaining technique. The marketing agreements were intended to eliminate the "free-rider" problem that had created such havoc in the previous period, because it allowed cooperatives to achieve control in the territory covered by the marketing orders.

The "double" program, worked out between the fluid-milk producers and the manufacturing dairy groups in 1933, made it possible for the more prosperous sector of the dairy industry, organized in cooperatives, to present a united front. Smaller dairy farmers, not organized in cooperatives, did not benefit from cooperative marketing, and these marginal producers united in protest organizations, such as the Farmers' Holiday Association and the Wisconsin Milk Pool, to protest the conservative, managerial orientation of cooperative leaders. Wallace was not unsympathetic to the view of these marginal dairy farmers, since he viewed cooperatives as an instrument of wealthy dairy farmers who dominated the NMPF. In response to the threat of militant new protests by the small dairy farmers in 1934, and Wallace's ousting of USDA members who had become identified with the program of the NMPF, the leadership of the NMPF concentrated on uniting its membership by calling a national meeting in Washington in 1934, and by forging a congressional alliance of 130 legislators that included both northeastern and midwestern Congressmen. The new House "Dairy Bloc" demanded that allotment programs be dropped and that the program of the NMPF be implemented.

To counter the increasing influence of the NMPF, various AAA administrators and county agents held regional meetings to entice midwestern farmers to accept the allotment plan, but they were unsuccessful. Although farmer opinion in the midwest was strongly divided, the NMPF fought a well-organized battle against allotment plans and was successful in persuading dairy farmers to defeat the Administration's policy. The victory of the cooperatives against the AAA was in no small part the result of the well-orchestrated strategy of the NMPF and its ability not only to unite its own members, but also to seek alliances with other farm groups and with congressional leaders. A common bond among these otherwise feuding actors was the desire to keep the marginal dairy farmers, organized in the Farmers' Holiday Association and the Wisconsin Milk Pool, from gaining converts to their more militant production-control schemes.

Aside from federal milk-marketing orders, price supports were established under a 1933 Executive Order that created the Commodity Credit Corporation (CCC). Under this program, the CCC has purchased butter, nonfat dry milk, and cheese at price levels that have enabled manufacturers to pay farmers the announced support price for milk in surplus production periods. The Agricultural Act of 1949 provided permanent authorization for the price-support program. It provided an underpinning for the entire price structure for milk sold by farmers to processors. The government's willingness to buy surplus milk products essentially set a floor under the price of fluid and manufactured milk (U.S. Department of Agriculture 1984). In calculating the support price, the midwest had again played a key role, since the Minnesota–Wisconsin price series is used as an indicator of the national supply–demand situation for manufacturing grade milk (Cropp and Cook 1977a, 1977b).

Price supports made it possible to raise domestic price levels above the world price. In order to keep out inexpensive foreign imports, domestic dairy markets had to be protected. As a result, import quotas were established in the Agricultural Adjustment Act of 1935 (Jacobson 1980).

The New Deal regulations vastly increased the importance of the cooperatives in the federal milk-marketing system. Cooperatives handle approximately 80% of milk produced in the United States. Within the forty-seven separately defined federal milk-order systems, the producers, through their cooperatives, vote on the minimum price of raw grade A milk that handlers are required to pay to dairy producers. The creation of a new milk-marketing order, or amendments to an existing order, requires approval of two-thirds (measured by either number of producers or production volume) of the producers selling milk in that marketing order. However, cooperatives may vote as a "bloc" for their members, which means that the cooperative is empowered to cast "the votes of all its members regardless of a minority position within the cooperative" (MacAvoy 1977: 7). Cooperatives also provide for the transfer of milk from the farm to the factory and are themselves often processors, producing cheese, butter, and other dairy products. Thus, the functions of dairy cooperatives extend far beyond the marketing of milk.

The argument so far is that the NMPF, a trade association grouping dairy coops that market milk, while also entering into the processing of dairy products and performing many standard functions of trade associations, played an important part in developing and in coordinating the implementation of federal dairy policy.[6] Today, the NMPF represents nearly all of the nation's several hundred marketing cooperatives (National Milk Producers Federation 1983). Its membership accounts for 75% of the milk produced in the United States. Because of the well-developed cooperative structure in the midwest, the regional representatives have played the leading role within the organization in resolving differences among cooperatives and in developing a consensus position for the industry. NMPF policies are developed through an elaborate process designed to encourage member participation and to tap professional expertise. Special committees and task forces investigate dairy-related issues and develop

6 Some of the following material has appeared in slightly altered form in Young et al. (1989).

proposals for legislative and regulatory interventions. These committees and task forces have involved a large network of dairy farmers, coop leaders, and agricultural experts in an almost constant process of considering the problems of the national governance of the dairy industry. Annual conventions, and more frequent Board of Executive Committee meetings are the form for debate and compromise. The NMPF dispenses information on marketing conditions and government regulations to its members, monitors trends in the dairy industry, and assists dairy coops in dairy promotion and public education programs. Its officers and committees have worked especially diligently to develop long-term perspectives on emerging industry problems through maintaining regular contacts among member coops, other farm organizations, and the federal government (Vander Schaaf 1985).

Due to the strong regional concentration of the dairy industry and the absence of competition emanating from other areas, the NMPF has been able to initiate, successfully defend and adapt, and actively participate in the implementation of a national dairy policy. It played a large role in drafting dairy legislation and attempted to coordinate the lobbying efforts of dairy coops. As an organization, the NMPF over the years developed a high degree of internal cohesion and authority among dairy cooperatives, and a high degree of involvement in government programs that is quite unusual among American trade associations.

The fact that the NMPF was able for nearly fifty years to maintain its cohesion and authority within the industry seems attributable to the leadership position maintained within the organization by representatives of the midwest and northeast and to the common interests of producers and coops in these regions – interests rooted not only in history, but in a relative homogeneity of size of firm. Their interests and perceptions coincided with those of an informal promotional network linking university researchers, state and local agricultural officials, and other state-level farm associations, and with key USDA officials and Congressional members.

Hence, a "structure of familiarity" permeated the public and private institutions that were engaged in New Deal agricultural policy making. In the dairy case, promotional networks were particularly pronounced, facilitated by the regional nature of the industry, and by the educational ties that connected the various institutions. "Characteristic career lines were beginning to carry individuals from the colleges to Experiment Stations, then into the Department of Agriculture, and perhaps finally back to the administrative positions in the colleges or in state agricultural programs" (Skocpol and Finegold 1982: 273).

The institutionalization of the dairy subsystem has to be seen as the capacity of dairy farmers to build "policy capable" institutions that were able to promote the collective interests of the dairy farmers organized within cooperatives. This finding contradicts Skocpol and Finegold's thesis that the autonomy of state managers within the AAA accounted for the success of the New Deal agricultural programs (Skocpol and Finegold 1982). In the dairy case, the state managers were unable to impose production controls against the well-organized NMPF. The ability of the NMPF to build coalitions with some members of the USDA, with Congressional members, farm groups, and the agricultural land-grant complex, has largely been responsible for the success of the dairy producers to develop and implement a set of regulatory mechanisms that has governed the industry for over fifty years. The development of these associations and promotional networks in the dairy industry did not occur, however, according to some grand plan. Rather, it developed out of a series of pragmatic adjustments to actual market failures in the industry.

THE BREAKDOWN OF MULTILATERAL GOVERNANCE

It has been the central argument of this chapter that the NMPF was able to shape dairy policies, because it was embedded within a traditional "dairy culture" that relied on informal promotional networks, stressing the importance of solidaristic values and multilateral action. However, in the 1970s and 1980s, actors, organized through the traditional governance mechanisms that had been successful previously in coordinating the industry, were unable to rise to the new challenge of imposing order on an industry that was radically changing. The emergence of new regional actors and the rise of large regional cooperatives came to create discord within the industry.

California has emerged as the second largest dairy producer in the nation. The increasing importance of California has meant that the NMPF has a limited capacity to mediate between the producers and the federal government, for California's dairy producers are integrated into a state milk program and, hence, their interest in the policy goals of the NMPF are secondary. More importantly, California's interest in expanding dairy production collided with the goals of the NMPF to reduce the national surplus production.

Dairy operations in California have become large, highly commercialized operations with substantial funding coming from outside investors. These dry-lot dairy operations are often owned and operated by nonfarm interests, having herds of as many as several thousand (Cook et al. 1978).

Dairying in California is mainly a business operation and is not linked to a traditional "farming ideology." Rather, many of the large California dairy enterprises, with their different operating procedures, their different factor costs, their different marketing structures, are more akin to corporate farming. Furthermore, there has been an increasing trend to integrate vertically forward as well as backward. Through forward integration, producer cooperatives also became engaged in operating processing plants, and there has also been a trend for large grocery chains to integrate backward into fluid-milk processing. Integrated supermarket chains in California process approximately 35% of the fluid milk; this compares to a national average of about 13 to 17% (Cook et al. 1978).

A second factor that has undermined the traditional governance regime, dominated by associations and promotional networks, has been the emergence of huge regional cooperatives. Historically, most cooperatives were relatively small and were members of the NMPF. Because of the strategic importance of the NMPF in the industry and because of the small size of the member cooperatives, the executives of NMPF were able to dominate the organization and to shape a national dairy policy acceptable to its members. By the 1970s, however, the membership structure of NMPF had changed. As the result of consolidation and mergers, several large cooperatives, such as American Milk Producers Inc., Dairymen Inc., and Mid-American Dairymen, Inc., were members of NMPF, but NMPF executives were no longer able to dominate the organization's political process. Increasingly, the large regional cooperatives have become quite autonomous, thus fragmenting the power of dairy cooperatives. As a result, many decisions affecting dairy producers were increasingly made by large regional cooperatives rather than by NMPF executives (Young, Lindberg, and Hollingsworth 1989). Thus, the NMPF has been placed in the weakened position of acting merely as a facilitator of decisions reached by the giant regional cooperatives.[7]

The large regional cooperatives not only have the organizational resources to compete with the NMPF, but they have usurped the organizational structure of the NMPF and have used it to further their aims. Increasingly, these huge regional cooperatives have gained a virtual monopoly on representation and, thus, have been successful in penetrating congressional committees and the executive branch of government, and in establishing clientele relationships with the Dairy Division of the USDA. This was no more evident than during the support-price deliberations in 1977, when the USDA called for large support-price increases that were opposed by the leadership of the NMPF. The trade associations feared that price increases were incongruent with the then existing market conditions and that they would result in a consumer backlash. However, the leadership of the NMPF was unable to stem the increasing influence of the large regional cooperatives in the political arena, and the USDA sided with the demand to increase the average milk support price from $9.50/cwt to more than $13/cwt (Jesse 1984). This price hike encouraged an unprecedented increase in dairy production. Since there was no increase in commercial consumption, nearly all of this increase in production was

7 Interview with John W. Siebert, University of California–Davis, on January 7, 1985.

purchased by the federal government. For example, in 1983, the CCC purchased the equivalent of over 12% of total milk marketed by U.S. farmers. In contrast, the amount of products removed from the market by the CCC over the 1966–79 period, before the recent expansion in milk production, averaged 3.3% of the milk marketed by U.S. farmers (U.S. Department of Agriculture 1984). Since dairy farmers have not been obligated to reduce production in order to obtain program benefits, they have continued to produce excess supplies, which are then sold to the federal government. Government support purchases rose to $2.6 billion for fiscal year 1983 from an already high point of $1.3 billion for fiscal year 1980. This contrasts starkly with the period 1976–9, during which average yearly CCC supported purchases were as low as $361 million. California has increasingly played an important role in the creation of this excess production. The state overwhelmingly leads the nation in CCC purchases of nonfat-dry milk, and is a close second in butter sales to the federal government (U.S. Department of Agriculture 1984). The resultant burden on the federal budget was considerable, and the huge dairy surpluses have become an issue of national concern (*Time* 1985: 66; *Washington Post National Weekly Edition* 1985: 23).

Until now the NMPF has been unable to develop a politically acceptable program that can eliminate the disequilibrium in the market. Increasingly, the concertation function of the NMPF has changed to lobbying activities with the single purpose of achieving short-term pecuniary gains for a selected group of large dairy operations instead of pursuing the collective interests of the industry as a whole. In retrospect, the capacity of the NMPF to enforce industrywide norms was rather tenuous, because it did not develop the ability to integrate diverse territorial interests, nor was it able to develop mechanisms to restrain the actions of the supercooperatives. As long as the industry was regionally based, and the cooperatives remained small in size, the NMPF was able to develop and enforce industrywide norms for nearly fifty years.

CONCLUSION

A remarkable governance regime developed in the dairy industry that had stabilized farm income, promoted productivity, and managed intraindustry conflict for nearly fifty years. At its center was the structure of cooperatives and its national association, the NMPF. These institutions were imbedded in a regional "dairy culture," based on solidaristic norms and a strong belief in multilateral action. The strength of the NMPF was at the same time its weakness. Its strength derived from the regional nature of the dairy industry, the promotional networks that facilitated intraindustry flexibility in achieving goal congruency, and the homogeneous size of the dairy producers. As the structure of the industry has changed, as California has challenged the economic hegemony of the midwestern dairy center, and as the creation of supercooperatives has upset the power balance within the NMPF leadership, the NMPF has been unable to govern the industry. The weakness of the NMPF stems from its inability to integrate the territorially heterogenous interests of the industry. Thus, the history of the NMPF is an interesting example of how a trade association may acquire increased autonomy and ability to govern an industry, but as the environment changes, the capacity of the association to enforce industrywide norms may decrease.

A governance transformation seems to be in the process, even though no clear alternative to the associations and promotional networks has emerged at this time. There is a distinct possibility that the present governance regime will be replaced by regionally diverse systems. In California, one likely outcome will be probably an enhanced trend toward corporate farming, that is, toward governance by corporate hierarchy. Federal tax and credit policies have already been pushing in these directions since the 1970s. But even outside of California, there has been a trend toward corporate hierarchies, not so much in terms of corporate farming, but in the increased vertical integration of cooperative associations. Dairy cooperatives, from Wisconsin, New York, Pennsylvania, to California, have become more fully integrated into nearly all stages and functions of milk production and marketing, up to processing for fluid milk and through the primary manufacturing for Grade B as well as surplus manufacturing for Grade A (Cook et al. 1978: 74). In addition, retail stores have increasingly integrated backward into milk processing.

The stimulus for the increased vertical integration has been the cooperatives' desire to extend their marketing share, but also extend their control over supply allocation between markets (MacAvoy 1977). As a result of the increased vertical integration in the dairy industry, the boundaries between the interests of the dairy producers and processors have become blurred.

Furthermore, the market may start to play an increasingly important role in agriculture. President Reagan, the Office of Budget and Management, the Justice Department, and the Federal Trade Commission have been strong advocates of eliminating price supports and restoring agriculture to the free market. This policy position toward the agricultural sector cannot be seen in isolation, but has to be interpreted as part of a larger national trend of deregulation. The drive to deregulate the airlines, trucking, the banking sector, and the railroads has opened the possibility of extricating the state from the dairy industry. Nevertheless, I would hypothesize that a possible deregulation of the dairy industry will not lead to more market coordination. If milk markets are not controlled by the collective action of cooperatives in federal milk-marketing orders, dairy producers will have to find some control mechanism in order to govern the markets. Since small autonomous actors have proven incapable of such a task, formal administrative and bureaucratic systems may have to coordinate the flow of goods through the production and distribution process. As pointed out, there is already increasing evidence that the industry is moving toward more vertical integration.

Aside from the possible formation of formal bureaucratic systems to control the exchange relationship between producers and processors in the dairy markets, the probability exists for the emergence of less-formal interorganizational arrangements. For example, the creation of obligational networks may allow actors to enter into obligational contracting that would preserve the organizational autonomy of the dairy producer, but at the same time assure market stability and maintain exchange relationships over time. In contrast to the present system of multilateral action in pursuit of a common pricing strategy, obligational networks may tie individual dairy producers to corporate entities. Their common resource dependency may suffice as a means for market control. Furthermore, dairy processors are equally interested in market stability because their increased factory capacity requires a steady supply of large quantities of milk without which they cannot achieve the advantages of economies of scale.

In conclusion, we may witness the transformation of a governance regime that has been based on state-sanctioned associations and promotional networks to one that is dominated by hierarchies and obligational networks. It is important to remember that market failures have historically provided the stimulus for dairy producers to find alternatives to market regulation, and hence a future reliance on the market may return the American dairy industry to an era of persistent agricultural crisis akin to those of the 1920s and 1930s (Lawrence and Dyer 1983). However, any transformation to a new governance regime may have the unintended consequence of destroying many small-scale and marginal dairy farmers because the increasing emphasis on competitiveness will favor large-scale operations.

9

ECONOMIC GOVERNANCE AND THE AMERICAN MEATPACKING INDUSTRY

John Portz
Department of Political Science, Northeastern University

In recent years, the meatpacking industry has received public attention as an industry in turmoil. Bankruptcies, corporate restructuring, labor strikes, internal labor conflict, and wage reductions are typical themes in news reports on the industry. Although these reports present images of an industry undergoing major change, they rarely explore the fundamental political and economic properties so essential to understanding that change. This research begins such an effort by analyzing the changing nature of economic governance in the industry.[1]

In presenting the history of governance transformations in the meatpacking industry, I employ the tools of analysis that were introduced in Chapter 1, particularly the heuristic model of the transformation process. In applying this framework, this chapter highlights markets and corporate hierarchy. Although other modes of governance have played a role, transitions to and from markets and corporate hierarchy have dominated the meatpacking industry. Thus, a central concern in this chapter is the conditions that facilitate transformations between these two forms of governance.

In tracing governance transformations, this study divides the history of meatpacking into three major time periods and follows a common format within each. First, each historical period begins with a discussion of economic changes and other pressures on the existing system of coordination. This discussion often highlights changing technology, but other factors are considered as well. Second, the search process is analyzed. The focus is on the role played by existing governance mechanisms and the state in successful or unsuccessful adaptations by economic actors to the new environment. And, third, the new governance regime is highlighted. This new regime becomes the starting point for the next time period. Before proceeding to the historical study, the next section briefly outlines the boundaries of the meatpacking industry.

---

1 The author acknowledges research funding provided by J. Rogers Hollingsworth during the early drafts of this chapter.

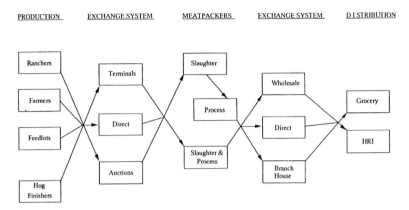

Figure 9.1   Transactions in the meatpacking industry.

BOUNDARIES AND TRANSACTIONS IN THE MEATPACKING INDUSTRY

The meatpacking industry has been and continues to be a major sector in the American economy. In past years, meatpacking ranked as one of America's premier industries. In 1914, for example, the slaughtering and meatpacking industry was the largest in the country as measured by its $1.67 billion in sales (U.S. Department of Commerce 1920). It surpassed the foundry and machine industries, the steel sectors, and the fledgling automobile makers. By 1986, meatpacking no longer held such a position, but it still ranked as one of America's largest industries with sales of $50 billion.

Most of those sales are composed of cattle and hog products. In 1983, for example, cattle and hogs constituted 92% of all livestock slaughtered in the red meat industry. The other specie in the industry – sheep and lamb – play a small part and are not considered in this study. Poultry, though not a part of the red meat industry, has become an important competitor and is referred to in discussions of more recent industry experiences.

As shown in Figure 9.1, the meatpacking industry includes economic activities of animal production, meatpacking, and product distribution. Although this study focuses on meatpackers and the adjoining exchange systems, both production and distribution enter the story. Also important for understanding transactions in this industry is the role played by organized labor and the state.

Production refers to raising animals for slaughter. Included in this category are small farmers and ranchers raising only a few hogs or cattle as well as large commercial cattle feedlots and hog finishers specializing in raising large numbers of livestock specifically for slaughter. At the other end of the production-to-distribution process are retailers that sell various meat products to the final consumer. The basic division among retail establishments is between sales by grocery markets and those by hotels, restaurants, and other food service institutions (HRI).

Between production and distribution are the meatpackers. Among meatpackers, an important distinction is made between slaughtering and processing. Whereas slaughtering involves the disassembly of an animal to yield a fresh meat or carcass product, processing entails additional manufacturing steps to make sausage and other prepared meats. As noted in Figure 9.1, some meatpacking firms both slaughter and process, either at the same plant or different plants, and other firms perform only one of these activities. Earlier in this century both activities were typically performed by the same firm, but in more recent years, specialization has become common.

Exchange systems play a central role in the history of the industry. Coordination through these channels is an important task for the various forms of governance. Whether through market transactions, corporate hierarchy, or other governance mechanisms, the allocation of resources to and from meatpackers is a critical economic process.

Between producers and meatpackers, three exchange systems are highlighted – terminals, auctions, and direct sales. Exchange through terminals, which was the dominant mechanism prior to 1960, involves the transportation of livestock by rail car or motor vehicle to large stockyards for sale and slaughter. Prices and other terms of exchange are typically set through negotiation between buyer and seller at the terminal. In contrast, auctions involve open competitive bidding among buyers for livestock assembled at the auction yard for inspection. Auctions have never been a dominant form of exchange, but they are often presented as the best forum for competitive price discovery. The third major exchange mechanism, direct sales, is the dominant form today. This involves a variety of forums in which packers or independent dealers purchase livestock through negotiations with producers at buying stations, packing plants, farms, or commercial feedlots.

The second major exchange system – between packers and distributors – involves sales of meat products to grocery and institutional outlets for final consumption. In this exchange, three forums are highlighted – branch houses, wholesalers and brokers, and direct sales to buyers. Branch houses, which were most important in the early twentieth century, are packer-owned distribution points located along rail lines in urban centers. Wholesalers and brokers typify a second form of exchange in which a middle person is responsible for meat sales. A third form of exchange, direct sales between packers and retailers, has become the dominant form of exchange in recent years.

This outline of exchange systems and major actors in the sector provides a brief overview of the boundaries and transactions in the industry. With this as background, we turn now to an historical analysis of the role of governance mechanisms in achieving economic coordination in the meatpacking industry. The next section provides the historical setting for subsequent analysis.

MARKET GOVERNANCE IN AN INFANT INDUSTRY

Prior to the 1880s, the meatpacking industry was dominated by the market. Characterized by historians as atomistic and unconcentrated, meatpacking was a small-scale venture with few barriers to entry. Between 1850 and 1890, the number of meatpacking establishments grew from 185 to 1120 as new operations opened their doors in cities around the country (U.S. Department of Commerce 1905). During this era, competition among meatpackers focused on local consumer markets.

The small-scale and competitive nature of the meatpacking industry was shaped in large part by the perishability of the product. As one historian noted, the meatpacking industry "was ruled by Mother Nature with a mighty invisible hand" (Yeager 1981: 1). Spoilage was the primary concern. Once an animal was slaughtered, to avoid spoilage, the resulting fresh meat was either consumed or preserved. If immediate consumption was desired, quick delivery to consumers over existing transportation networks meant only a small market area could be served.

As an alternative to immediate consumption, a variety of curing and salting methods was used to preserve the product. Preservation, however, was more acceptable to consumers in pork products than beef. Thus, it was common to transport live cattle to packing plants located near eastern population centers. Although meat products could then be quickly distributed after slaughter, the transportation of live animals was difficult, costly, and resulted in weight loss and deaths along the way.

In addition to product perishability, the early meatpacking industry was also shaped by existing and emerging modes of transportation. Cincinnati, with its ideal river location, became the earliest meatpacking center. Dubbed "Porkopolis," Cincinnati by 1854 had forty-one packing houses involved primarily in the preparation of pork products (Clemen 1923).

The expansion of railroads, however, changed dramatically the contours of the industry. Railroads, rather than steamships and overland trail drives, were used to transport live animals as well as meat products. With the development of a rail system in the midwest, Illinois became the new center of the industry. By 1862, Chicago packers slaughtered and packed 500,000 hogs, exceeding packer operations in Cincinnati. By 1864, there were fifty-eight packers in Chicago located along the numerous rail lines into the city (Clemen 1923). Chicago quickly became a central point for both departure of livestock headed east on rail cars as well as slaughtering and processing at local packing houses.

By the mid–1880s, meatpacking was showing signs of an established industry. As one historian noted, meatpacking was becoming "a well-organized industrial operation demanding technological improvements and systematic business organization" (Walsh 1982: 89). Mechanization was increasingly important in disassembly operations in the plant, and packers were expanding procurement and distribution channels. In this early stage of industry growth, the entrepreneur played a central role in adapting and responding to the changing nature of a largely market-oriented economy.

THE SEARCH FOR MARKET SHARE AND PROFITS: CORPORATE HIERARCHY AND ASSOCIATIONS, 1880–1920

Between the 1880s and 1920, the meatpacking industry changed from a largely market-governed sector to one of the largest oligopolistic industries in the United States. Five major packers – Swift, Armour, Morris, Cudahy, and Wilson – dominated the industry. By 1917, these five packers, known as the Big Five, controlled 81% of the interstate slaughter of cattle and 60% of interstate hog slaughter (Aduddell and Cain 1981a).[2] This transformation from market coordination to a governance regime relying upon corporate hierarchy and associations is the subject of this section.

Pressures for change

The meatpacking industry in the 1880s was experiencing rapid expansion. Entrepreneurs and those established in the new industry were continually searching for opportunities to increase sales and expand market share. Product improvement, wider sales distribution, and greater production efficiencies were among the means to reach those goals.

Refrigeration. As already noted, product perishability posed a major barrier to increasing sales and market share. From the 1860s on, meatpackers engaged in experiments to develop cold storage and other preservation techniques that would preserve fresh meat, principally beef, without curing and salting. If preservation of fresh beef could be ensured, new opportunities would open for packers, particularly those locating in the midwest near the supply of animals. Rather than ship a live animal, 60% of which was inedible, to the east coast, cattle could be slaughtered at midwest plants and fresh meat shipped to the east at a lower cost.

To meet this need, refrigerated rail cars became the ticket to success. As one historian of the period concluded, "the refrigerator car revolutionized the industry" (Yeager 1981: 233). It opened new marketing and

---

2 The Big Five became the Big Four in 1923 when Armour acquired Morris.

sales possibilities for meatpackers no longer restricted by the spoilage of fresh meat. By 1919, Swift & Co. was able to write:

The refrigerator car is one of the vehicles on which the packing industry has ridden to greatness. Before the advent of this type of carrier the packing house was a local institution. To-day it is an international concern. And its development is attributed to one factor – the refrigerator car. (U.S. Federal Trade Commission 1919: Part 1, 134)

The first refrigerator car was developed in 1868 during an era of "tinkerer – inventors" that made tentative, small-scale applications of the new technology. By the early 1870s, an expanding overseas market led to successful adaptation of refrigeration to steamship lines. The shipment of dressed beef to Great Britain, rather than live cattle, reduced shipping costs by over 80% and resulted in large packer profits (Yeager 1981). Although refrigerated shipments occasionally spoiled, the potential of the new technology was noted and adopted by many packers.

One of the first to recognize this potential was Gustavus Swift. Arriving in Chicago in 1875, Swift focused his efforts on improving refrigeration technology and identifying secure market outlets in the east. Using a refrigerator car that emphasized air circulation, Swift sent his first shipments to the east in 1877. By 1883, Swift had established forty-three branch houses in the east as distribution points for dressed beef. By this time, other industry leaders – Hammond, Morris, and Armour – were also utilizing refrigerator cars for dressed-beef shipments.

In developing and adapting this new technology, packers met considerable resistance from rail companies. The major rail companies, which owned most of the stock cars to transport live animals, were reluctant to build refrigerator cars for a yet-to-be-proven market that would only undermine their own interests in live animal shipments. Confronted with this resistance, Swift and the other large packers built and owned their own refrigerator cars, yet shipped over existing rail lines. Packer control of refrigerator cars used in the dressed-beef trade increased over the years. By 1917, the five largest packers owned 92% of the 16,875 refrigerator cars suitable for dressed beef shipments. In contrast, the rail companies continued to own 85% of the stock cars for live animal shipments (Federal Trade Commission 1919: Part 1).

Refrigerator cars opened new opportunities for meatpackers, but they also posed important costs. To increase sales through this new system, packers needed to invest in rail cars and preservation equipment as well as establish stable distribution outlets and construct new packing plants. Financial costs requisite for survival in the industry were increasing. For example, the average plant investment rose between 1869 and 1909 from $4,000 to $70,000 (Corey 1950). Indeed, the needs of the industry were changing. Refrigeration technology, rail cars, and storage facilities required considerable capital resources; a growing population and year-round consumption meant expanding markets and higher production levels; and limitations on the preservation of refrigerated beef required quick and reliable distribution outlets to handle large quantities over wide geographical areas.

Although the competitive and entrepreneurial strategies of market actors were important in initial efforts to meet this changing environment, the uncertain nature of market relationships also had negative consequences. Meatpackers wanted reliable and timely transactions in all phases of the process – from procurement of animals to distribution of products. Uncertainties and failures in delivery at any point undermined packer goals of increasing sales, expanding markets, and earning profits.

Public policy: Antitrust and meat inspection. In addition to changing technology, the governance regime during this period was also influenced by an expanding state role in economic and sectoral affairs. This role took two major forms – antitrust and meat inspection. In both roles, the state established important boundaries for the industry.

Of the two roles, antitrust action was the most significant for governance of the industry. As discussed in the next section, the search process by packers involved several strategies that were deemed by political authorities to be monopolistic and collusive. In fact, the passage of the Sherman Antitrust Act in 1890 was prompted, in part, by the Vest Report, which charged meatpackers with collusion in such practices as beef pricing (Aduddell 1971). The state's antitrust role was an effort to rekindle in the industry market standards deemed appropriate for a competitive economy. Throughout this period, the corporate strategies pursued by meatpackers to increase profits and market share were heavily influenced by this state policy.

The state also played a role in the area of meat inspection. In 1890 and 1891, the first federal meat inspection laws were passed, but applied principally to meat sold overseas. Unlike the negative response to antitrust action, packers accepted and, in some cases, encouraged the application of this inspection law as a means to help the export trade (Yeager 1981). After Upton Sinclair's study of Chicago meatpacking plants, additional legislation expanded the domain of federal inspection. As one historian argues, this expansion was supported by the larger packers as a way to remove competitive advantages realized by smaller packers who did not formerly submit to inspection (Kolko 1963). Although less significant than antitrust, public meat inspection nevertheless established standards of behavior applicable to meatpackers as they sought to expand in this growing industry.

The search process

In the midst of this changing setting, meatpackers pursued several strategies to realize a more adequate system of coordination. This search process by business firms involved both bilateral and multilateral efforts. On the bilateral side, corporate hierarchy in the form of stock ownership and vertical integration was most prominent. On the multilateral side, a variety of associative and less formal arrangements were attempted, albeit with less success. In these efforts, particularly those of a multilateral nature, the state played an important role in drawing and redrawing boundaries for new forms of governance.

Corporate hierarchy. The dominant governance mechanism that emerged through the search process was corporate hierarchy. Coordinating procurement of animals with production of meat products and distribution to consumers was imperative to increase sales. Corporate hierarchy through stock ownership and vertical integration was the means. Alfred Chandler's analysis is to the point: "The visible hand of management replaced the invisible hand of market forces where and when new technology and expanded markets permitted a historically unprecedented high volume and speed of materials through the processes of production and distribution" (Chandler 1977: 12).

In the procurement of animals, packers exercised influence through control of stockyards. By 1916, there were fifty terminal stockyards markets in the United States through which passed 90% of livestock purchased by the Big Five packers. Terminal stockyards provided an array of livestock services, such as weighing, watering, and feeding, as well as facilities for transacting the sale of animals. Many of the major meatpacking plants were located adjacent to stockyards.

Packer influence over the operations of terminal stockyards was exercised principally through stock ownership. In twenty-two of the fifty stockyard companies that operated the terminals, the Big Five, either singly or in combination, held controlling interest in the voting stock of the company. Through these twenty-two terminal yards passed 57% of all animals slaughtered. Packer minority interest in other stockyard companies covered an additional 28% of livestock transactions (U.S. Federal Trade Commission 1919: Part 3).

Through partial ownership, along with high volume purchases, the Big Five were in a position to guide activities at the terminals. They could control or influence loans made to producers or feeders as well as the distribution of information on current prices and transactions. As one livestock producer reported to the Federal Trade Commission, "I look at it this way. They (packers) own all the yards. From the time that my cattle arrive at the yards they are in the hands of the man that is eventually going to buy them for slaughter" (U.S. Federal Trade Commission 1919: Part 3, 87).

In the distribution of meat products, corporate hierarchy took the form of vertical integration through packer-owned branch houses. Rather than rely upon commission merchants and independent wholesalers, packers complemented their ownership of refrigerated rail cars with branch houses as distribution centers located on rail lines. The refrigerator car became the "supply house on wheels" as it delivered dressed beef and other food products to branch houses. Meat products at branch houses were placed in cold storage awaiting distribution or further processing prior to sale to retail outlets. By 1900, the Big Five had opened 544 branches, and by 1917, the number reached 1,120 (U.S. Federal Trade Commission 1919: Part 1).

In addition to branch houses, big packers established "peddler car" routes in less-populated areas. On these routes, a refrigerator car made assigned stops at small communities along the rail line. The peddler car was loaded at the packing plant according to orders secured by traveling salesmen. Routes varied considerably in length, but an average midwest route covered 200–250 miles and included twenty to thirty towns (U.S. Federal Trade Commission 1919: Part 4). By 1918, the Big Five packers operated over 1,200 routes reaching 38,000 towns. By 1916, peddler car routes and branch houses accounted for 60% of sales by the Big Five (U.S. Federal Trade Commission 1919: Part 1). This packer-owned distribution system built around the refrigerator car had become the dominant exchange mode.

Ownership of refrigerator cars and establishment of branch houses and peddler routes required significant capital outlays and set a premium on early entry to establish distribution outlets. For packers failing to meet those requirements, a local market niche was the alternative strategy, but even that was difficult to establish. As the Federal Trade Commission concluded, the consequence of big packer ownership of refrigerator cars and branch houses was "the practical disappearance of the local slaughtering plants" (U.S. Federal Trade Commission 1919: Part 4, 62). As one indication of this trend, although independent packers (outside the Big Five) slaughtered 27% of all animals, they made only 7% of branch house sales and 11% of peddler car sales (U.S. Federal Trade Commission 1919: Part 1). In an era of oligopoly, small packers were left with a shrinking local market.

Although corporate hierarchy extended forward to branch houses and backward to stockyards, the packers did not extend this system of control to include retail outlets or livestock production. On both ends of the production-to-distribution process, packers were facing large numbers of dispersed producers and retailers that possessed little market power. In 1920, there were over five million farms, of which 75–80% produced cattle or hogs for slaughter, while at the retail end there were over 310,000 grocery and meat outlets with a relatively small number under the umbrella of a chain operation (Aduddell 1971). As Williamson (1975; 1985) and others note, when firms confront such large numbers, there is little incentive for vertical integration. Both producers and retailers were essentially price takers in an environment heavily influenced by the big packers.

Although corporate hierarchy did not cover all stages of the production-distribution system, what did exist, particularly in the form of branch houses and peddler routes, provided important profit opportunities for packers in meat by-products and other food lines. Meatpackers, for example, often owned and operated tanneries and other related operations that utilized slaughtering by-products. Packers also became extensively involved in the distribution of such meat substitutes as eggs, cheese, and poultry, as well as a variety of other grocery, canned fruit, and vegetable products. In their study of the industry, the Federal Trade Commission found that Swift, Armour, Wilson, and Cudahy handled 49% of the nation's dressed poultry and 33% of shipped eggs (U.S. Federal Trade Commission 1919: Part 4). As one circular distributed by Morris & Co. to its branch house managers stated:

Our business has ceased to be exclusively a Beef and Pork business. We are the natural distributors of many other products and a Manager or Salesman can't hope to be a real success, unless he sells the full line. (U.S. Federal Trade Commission 1919: Part 4, 54)

By 1919, the Federal Trade Commission concluded that the big packers had "entrenched themselves in what may be called the strategic positions of control of food distribution" (U.S. Federal Trade Commission 1919: Part 1, 38).

Associations. Although ownership of branch houses and control over stock-yards was a critical part of the search process for a more adequate form of coordination, these bilateral or company-specific efforts did not stand alone. The big packers soon realized that price competition in purchasing livestock and selling meat products was counterproductive to steady expansion and stable profits. Although corporate hierarchy facilitated administrative control within the firm, it left each packer open to the competitive tactics of others. In an attempt to minimize competition in prices and marketing, packers turned to several multilateral efforts.

The common label given to the earliest schemes to achieve collective coordination was "pools." From 1886 to 1902, there were at least three identifiable pools in which several of the big packers combined to stabilize and control production, distribution, and prices. The two most successful pools, known as the Veeder Pools, covered most of the years from 1893 to 1902.[3] In the first Veeder Pool, the member packers adopted a uniform method of computing costs and margins that had the effect of standardizing

---

3 A major predecessor to the Veeder Pools was the Allerton Pool formed in 1886 by five major packers. This pool divided market shares in the northeastern United States and established a crude system of uniform profit margins and price lists (Yeager 1981).

profit margins on dressed beef. Each firm provided weekly statements detailing beef shipments and price margins. If shipments exceeded the allotment for that firm, a penalty was paid into a common fund; if shipments fell short, the firm received a check from the fund.

The pool was administered by attorney Henry Veeder and ten to fifteen office staff located in Chicago. Veeder was responsible for collecting and compiling information on beef shipments and price margins provided by the packers, mailing such information to all packers in the pool, and administering the "under" or "over" shipment payments. Every Tuesday, the chief executive officer from each firm met to discuss the data provided by Veeder and make decisions as to changes in firm allotments. In 1898, the second Veeder Pool raised the fines for shipments that exceeded allotments and hired a taskforce of auditors to verify reports and inspect each firm's books (U.S. Federal Trade Commission 1919: Part 2; Yeager 1981).

These pools represented an important effort to achieve associational governance. The member firms operated in a collective manner based on formally negotiated agreements. The members were guided by what Streeck and Schmitter (1985: 9) refer to in another context as "inter- and intraorganizational concertation" bound together by "mutual recognition of status and entitlements" as well as a basic desire for "satisficing interests."

However, an associational form of governance was difficult to sustain. Disruptive forces came from a number of quarters. For example, competition among members continued, particularly as each firm expanded its operations into new geographic areas. Disagreements and threats of withdrawal were common as each member asked for periodic reassessment of base calculations to reflect changing market strategies. In addition, competition from nonmembers proved disruptive. The second Veeder Pool, for example, was formed to include Schwarzschild and Sulzberger of New York (which became Wilson), a firm whose competitive actions had helped to undermine the first pool.

Although competitive rivalries might be overcome, success was heavily dependent upon legitimacy granted by state authorities. As Streeck and Schmitter (1985: 25) note, "associations can usually govern the interests of their members only with some kind of state facilitation and authorization." In this regard, the pools established by the packers clearly lacked legal status. Not only did the packer pools operate without state-sanctioned contracts, but they were seen as collusive. This position was established in 1890, prior to the first Veeder Pool, when a U.S. Senate investigation (the Vest Report) concluded that Armour, Swift, Morris, and Hammond had colluded in fixing prices of livestock and dividing the country into sales regions (Adudell 1971).

Although a 1905 government report by the Bureau of Corporations was more favorable to the packers, legal inquiries continued. In 1902, the U.S. Attorney General conducted an investigation of the packers' pool and charged the members with conspiracy and constraint of trade. An injunction was issued in 1903 and affirmed by the U.S. Supreme Court in 1905 (Aduddell and Cain 1981a). This led to the dismantling of the formal organization of the pools. The logic of associational governance was clearly in conflict with the antitrust standards that were guiding state policy.

Still, efforts to coordinate actions of the big packers did not end with the demise of the Veeder Pools. Drawing inspiration from the recent creation of U.S. Steel, the five largest packers signed preliminary contracts in 1902 to merge part of their assets into one holding company. When outside financing was withdrawn during the Panic of 1903, the proposal was scaled back and Armour, Swift, and Morris pursued a less-ambitious plan. These three packers combined recently acquired companies into the National Packing Company. National integrated the operations of the smaller merged firms, established a branch house system, and became a significant actor in the meatpacking business.

Most importantly, National provided a means for multilateral coordination. The three big packers split the stock of National and sent representatives from their respective firms to sit on National's board of directors. This provided a forum in which the "old goals of cartelization might be pursued legally" (Yeager 1981: 151). National Packing Company was an information clearinghouse for the three packers. Data on prices and shipments of the three packers could be shared and decisions made under the auspices of National. Livestock purchasing and product distribution by National were used to "even" market fluctuations. As one historian noted, National became a " 'half-way house' between pooling and complete merger" that institutionalized joint decision making, but did so "through the vehicle of an 'outside' company" (Yeager 1981: 154–5). This hybrid of corporate hierarchy and associational governance provided an important means of coordinating information among Swift, Armour, and Morris.

Although National provided a forum for associational coordination, it, like the earlier pools, was subject to state antitrust policies. In 1910, the directors of National were charged under the Sherman Act with collusion in buying livestock and various other monopolistic practices. Although the trial ended in 1912 with an acquittal, a civil suit was brought that same year. To avoid further legal battles, Morris, Armour, and Swift voluntarily dissolved National and split the company's stock (Yeager 1981).

A new governance regime

With refrigeration technology as a primary impetus, the first decades of the twentieth century witnessed the transformation of the meatpacking industry from a system of market coordination to corporate hierarchy and associational forms of governance. As one historian concluded, "The packers arrived at oligopoly through a strategy of vertical integration designed to solve problems of marketing a perishable product" (Yeager 1981: 235). Although a competitive market environment set the stage for this change, capital requirements and the need for coordination between procurement and distribution called for new governance tools. Hierarchy and association were the tools.

Corporate hierarchy was central. The visible hand of management took the place of market mechanisms to provide coordination in the industry. From stock ownership of terminal yards to ownership of branch houses, the big packers extended corporate control into procurement as well as distribution. From a transaction-cost perspective, the bounded rationality and opportunistic behavior of human actors, combined with the asset-specific nature of refrigerated rail cars, led packers to conclude that corporate hierarchy offered the best opportunity to stabilize the slaughtering and distribution process. Corporate hierarchy became the means to "economize on transactions by harmonizing interests and permitting a wider variety of sensitive incentive and control processes to be activated" (Williamson 1975: 104).

Associational governance, despite state resistance, also served an important role. As several historians have argued, the dissolution of the pools and National was not debilitating; the big packers were aware of each other's practices and no longer needed a formal structure for coordination. "They knew each other's current costs, and they knew the current demand and available supplies and adjusted their flows accordingly" (Chandler 1977: 401). A system of tacit coordination remained. As Chandler concluded, "price leadership without formal collusion became the standard practice" (ibid.).

DECLINING CONCENTRATION AND THE RISE OF MARKET GOVERNANCE, 1920–60

By 1920, the meatpacking industry was one of the largest oligopolistic industries in the country. The governance regime of corporate hierarchy, association, and tacit coordination had served well the big packers' interests in sales, profits, and market share. According to a government study, the Big Five controlled 94% of cattle slaughter and 81% of swine slaughter in the top twelve packing cities (U.S. Federal Trade Commission 1919: Part 1). However, this condition was soon to change. From 1920 to 1960, the meatpacking industry experienced a decline in concentration as new firms entered an increasingly market-coordinated industry. In this new environment, the "old" tools of corporate hierarchy and association would prove to be less adequate for big packers' efforts to hold a share of the market.

By 1960, corporate hierarchy, particularly in the form of vertical integration, played a less-prominent role as more firms competed in the industry.

Pressures for change

This transformation of the industry to a greater reliance on market governance had several driving forces. Two are noted here as being of particular importance, First, public policy in the form of government antitrust and other regulatory actions, and, second, changing technology, consumption, and an expanding highway system.

Public policy: Antitrust and regulation. In this time period, state authorities played an important role in shaping the industry. Highlighting this role was a continuation of federal antitrust investigations of the big packers. One of the most important of these investigations was begun in 1917 by the new Federal Trade Commission (FTC). Spurred by livestock producer claims of packer monopoly and unfair practices, the FTC focused its investigation on the vertical structure of the big packers' corporate power as well as collusive actions among the packers. Completing the study in 1919, the FTC concluded that the Big Five engaged in a variety of collusive and monopolistic practices:

It appears that five great packing concerns of the country – Swift, Armour, Morris, Cudahy, and Wilson – have attained such a dominant position that they control at will the market in which they buy their supplies, the market in which they sell their products, and hold the fortunes of their competitors in their hands. (U.S. Federal Trade Commission 1919: Part 1, 24)

The recommended solution by the FTC included government ownership of stockyards, rail stock cars, rail refrigerator cars, and branch houses. Public ownership would strike at the "root of the tree of monopoly" (U.S. Federal Trade Commission 1919: Part 1, 26).

Following the FTC report, the U.S. Attorney General sought an indictment against the packers for monopolistic and collusive practices. At the same time, at least five bills were introduced in Congress to regulate the industry. A common theme in legislative proposals was the comparison of meatpackers and stockyards to public utilities. A variety of regulatory strategies was suggested and several bills advocated public ownership of stockyards (Aduddell 1971). Faced with these attacks, the big packers pursued both legal and legislative avenues for more moderate changes.

To avoid court actions, the Big Five in February 1920 negotiated a consent agreement with the U.S. Attorney General. Under the "consent decree," the packers did not admit guilt, but did agree, among other terms, to sell their interests in public stockyards and disassociate themselves from the sale and distribution of 145 different commodities (Aduddell and Cain 1981a). The most important effect on the packers hierarchical control was the loss of control over terminal yards. Although packer influence at the livestock producer end was thereby reduced, the forward distribution system of branch houses remained intact. The vertically integrated system of the big packers was certainly threatened, but key elements would remain.

In the legislative arena, Congress passed a bill that was considerably less encompassing than the recommendations in the FTC report. Enacted in 1921 as the Packers and Stockyards Act, this legislation outlined a modest state regulatory role rather than public ownership. Under the act, all major stockyards were required to register with the federal government, maintain proper records, and report rates and charges. A new agency, the Packers and Stockyards Administration (P&SA), was created to enforce these regulations. The P&SA was also given responsibility to investigate and initiate discriminatory, collusive, and monopolistic charges against meatpackers. The P&SA could hold hearings and issue cease-and-desist orders against packers (Aduddell and Cain 1981a).

A pattern of antitrust action continued in succeeding years. Between 1920 and 1956, the P&SA filed a number of complaints of unfair trade practices and the Department of Justice charged the big packers twelve times with monopolistic or collusive behavior involving livestock purchases and product prices (Aduddell 1971). In addition, between 1948 and 1954, a Department of Justice investigation concluded with a recommendation to split the four largest packers into fourteen companies (Fowler 1961). Although the P&SA issued only three cease-and-desist orders and none of the other suits resulted in successful prosecutions, the big packers were under constant scrutiny for signs of collusive behavior.

Ironically, although the consent decree, the Packers and Stockyards Act, and antitrust action relied upon the state's authoritative sanction, a voluntary program, government grading of meats, may well have played a more significant role in transforming the industry. Although federal grading did not mandate change, as was attempted in antitrust action, it provided a key ingredient for market coordination – information.

Grading of meats, primarily beef, provided a measure of quality and a language for communication among buyers and sellers. Although some packers had been using their own private quality grades since early in the century, federal government grades (e.g., prime, choice, good) provided a universal classification that appealed to many independent packers and wholesalers–retailers reluctant to be tied to individual packer brands. Federal grades became a "common language" that facilitated sales by description rather than on-site inspection (Williams, DeLoach, and Engelman 1959).

Despite the benefits of grading, acceptance came slowly. Although the first federal grading program for beef carcasses began in 1927, by 1941 only 10% of commercial carcass production was graded under this voluntary program. However, after periods of mandatory grading during World War

II and the Korean War, the use of federal beef grades reached 51% by 1959 (Fowler 1961).

Although some packers, particularly the larger and more established ones, continued to use private grades as a means of identification and quality differentiation, federal grading provided a universal form of communication that expanded potential marketing channels and eased entry into the beef industry for many new packers selling fresh beef. In effect, state intervention in the form of beef grading played a role in supporting new market entrants and facilitating market competition.

Changes in technology, consumption, and transportation. In addition to public policy actions, changes in technology, meat consumption, and transportation constituted important pressures for change in the industry (Williams and Stout 1964). Better refrigeration equipment, both in packing plants and in transit, became available to a growing number of meatpackers. In addition, improved technology in slaughtering and processing was utilized by old and new packers alike. Electric cutting knives, mechanical hide pullers, power saws, and new processing techniques were becoming standard in the industry. New plants were built with the intention of improving the utilization of these tools and techniques. For new entrants in the industry, these technological advances offered important opportunities to match the capabilities of the old packers.

Technology also played a role in expanding meat consumption. The use of home refrigeration and home freezers increased the convenience and availability of fresh meat. By 1950, 86% of urban homes had electric refrigeration. This ability to store meat, when combined with a growing urban population, translated into increased beef consumption. Beef consumed per person increased from 55.5 pounds in 1921 to 85.2 pounds in 1960 (as measured in carcass-equivalent weight). In contrast, pork consumption per person increased over the same period only marginally from 64.8 to 65.3 pounds (Breimeyer 1961). A growing consumer market in beef meant sales opportunities for new packers.

Although advances in technology were significant, an equally significant change was the development of a highway system and motor truck transport. If rail lines were central to the big packers' earlier system of vertical integration, the highway system would be a major reason for its demise. Between 1920 and 1955, hard-surfaced road mileage increased over 800% while motor truck registrations increased over 500% (Aduddell 1971). Both highways and motor trucks facilitated diverse marketing strategies for new packers that lacked vertically integrated systems.

Opportunities from a highway system were evident at both ends of a new packer's operations. In the producer-to-packer exchange, trucks gradually replaced the railroad stock car as the primary mode of livestock transport. Whereas in 1920, 80% of livestock reached terminals by rail, by

1959, the same percentage of livestock reached public markets by motor vehicle (Fowler 1961; Aduddell 1971). Although the old rail terminal stock-yards initially defined the destination, the flexibility of motor transport offered possibilities for stockyard locations at alternative sites. By the 1950s, livestock producers and new packers had much greater flexibility to utilize a variety of different exchange points.

In the packer-to-distributor exchange, motor transport and the highway system offered even greater flexibility. Although branch houses could still be used, they were tied to rail lines that were of decreasing importance. Unlike refrigerator rail cars and branch houses, motor vehicles and the highway system were readily available to all entrants in the industry. Again, new opportunities for more flexible marketing provided seeds for change in the industry.

The search process

The changes just described marked a new environment for the meatpacking industry. Confronting this environment were not only the big packers, but a growing number of new entrants in the industry. In addition, organized labor began to play a more significant role. These actors became involved in a search process for a governance regime that would accommodate the new legal, technological, and structural changes in the industry.

Response by the big packers. The big packers faced this environment with a regime – corporate hierarchy and associational coordination – inherited from the previous period. Based on this system of coordination, the big packers' role in the search process took the form of resistance as well as accommodation to changes.

One of the clearest examples of resistance was opposition to implementation of the 1920 consent decree. Shortly after signing the decree, the big packers argued that enforcement by the judiciary exceeded legitimate court authority since antitrust law could not be applied when violations were not proven or admitted in court. Although this argument was dismissed by the courts, the packers continued to resist the decree by asking for modifications of restrictions on handling foods unrelated to meats. Here, also, the packers lost. In 1932, a ruling involving Swift & Co. finally forced the packers to comply with all the provisions of the decree (Aduddell and Cain 1981a). Still, the packers continued to seek relief, but even limited success did not come until 1975 (Aduddell and Cain 1981b).

A second example of resistance was the big packers' opposition, along with several newer national packers, to federal government grading of beef. As noted earlier, government grading provided an important means of communication among packers and wholesalers–retailers, but at the expense of the larger packers' private brands. As Table 9.1 indicates, the

276   *John Portz*

Table 9.1. *Use of government and packer grades (1955 survey)*

Type of firm	Number of firms	Type of grading in percent		
		Government	Packer	Ungraded
Packers				
National packers	6	27	50	23
Independent packers	42	77	2	21
Distributors				
Independent wholesale	53	78	1	21
Independent retail	183	69	18	13
Retail chains	28	94	5	1

Source: Williams et al. 1959.

use of government grading of beef varied considerably among those in the industry.

All six of the national packers in the survey preferred not to use government grades; five of the six advocated abolishment of the program. To these packers, government grading restricted the "legitimate merchandising opportunities of the packer" in a private enterprise economy (Williams et al. 1959). Government grades were used by these firms only when requested by purchasers. In contrast, most independent packers responded favorably to government grading, particularly if it eliminated the need to establish a private brand. Distributors were also favorable toward government grades; government grading helped ensure quality control, facilitated large-lot specification buying, and aided consumer identification.

In both examples of resistance, the big packers were unsuccessful. The consent decree continued and government grading soon became the norm in the industry. The tools of corporate hierarchy and association were inadequate for responding to these changes. The big packers lacked a truly effective means for coordinated action and access to policy-making circles that could alter the consent decree or the grading system. In attempting multilateral coordination to affect public policy, the packers were at their weakest.

Along with strategies of resistance, the big packers simultaneously pursued several paths of accommodation to the new environment, although change did not come easily. In one example, the big packers attempted to adapt their procurement and distribution systems to the new mode of highway transportation. In distribution, for example, Armour as early as 1917 had an extensive "autotruck" system that distributed meat products to towns in the south and west (U.S. Federal Trade Commission 1919: Part 1). By 1959, Armour had a fleet of 2,400 trucks and 260 tractor-trailer combinations engaged in procurement and distribution (Fowler 1961). In general, the other big packers followed suit.

However, this strategy came at a cost. The branch-house system on rail lines was only partially adaptable to the new environment. With distributors developing large-lot purchasing capabilities, direct sales increasingly utilized highways and bypassed the branch houses. Between 1929 and 1958, the number of packer branch houses declined 50%, whereas direct shipments and shipments through independent wholesalers increased (Aduddell and Cain 1981b). By 1963, branch houses handled only 14% of meat sales (U.S. National Commission on Food Marketing 1966). At the procurement end, the use of direct truck shipments to packing plants reduced the utility of terminal markets that had been so important in the packers' earlier system of vertical coordination. The big packers were attempting to adapt, but it required often difficult and costly changes in the existing system of coordination.

In another example, the big packers recognized the importance of adopting new methods and techniques in slaughtering and processing, but such productivity improvements also came at a cost. Many of the old multilevel plants of the big packers were not easily adapted to new slaughtering and processing methods. These plants had obsolete physical structures as well as large and older work forces that resulted in higher wage costs.

To accommodate the new methods and techniques, plant closings in one area, and, on occasion, new openings in another became increasingly common. Armour, for example, closed twenty-one plants between 1951 and 1965, while opening eight new ones in an effort to modernize its operations (Shultz and Weber 1966). Although such programs as the Armour Automation Fund for displaced workers attempted to minimize negative impacts, packer accommodation to a changing industry was costly and difficult, particularly for workers and their communities.

Along with efforts to adopt new production methods and utilize the highway system, the big packers also pursued a variety of other strategies to maintain profitability. Between 1930 and 1955, the Big Four acquired 227 firms in order to expand meat production as well as diversify into other product lines (Aduddell and Cain 1981b). As examples of product diversification, Wilson became an important manufacturer of sporting goods and Armour invested in pharmaceuticals.

Another strategy, less planned perhaps, was a relative decline in efforts to expand beef slaughtering and processing. Between 1920 and 1960, when per-capita beef consumption was growing, the Big Four concentration in commercial cattle slaughter dropped from 49.0 to 23.5% (Nelson 1985). The Big Four's vulnerability in the beef subsector was attributable, in part, to the ease of entry in this area. Beef slaughtering and processing required less sophisticated facilities than swine slaughter, pork curing, packaging, etc. Moreover, beef involved little product differentiation and could be federally graded, which increased its marketing potential with the growing supermarket business. All of these characteristics made fresh-beef operations the most likely target for new firms entering the industry (Aduddell and Cain 1981b). One such firm, Iowa Beef Processors, would become the new industry leader in the late 1970s.

New firms in the industry. While the big packers pursued various strategies of resistance and accommodation to the new environment, an increasing number of new firms took advantage of the changing setting. Although these new entrants often lacked the capital resources of the big packers, they were less burdened by the corporate hierarchy and older, poorly located plants that the big packers brought into this period. For new packers, this flexibility translated into local, regional, or even national market niches.

As noted earlier, such changes as government grading of beef and highway transportation offered important opportunities for new packers. Government grading provided a common language for communication on meat quality and sales, and highway transportation freed packers from the dominant role of rail lines. Both changes worked in the interests of new firms seeking a position in the industry. In brief, the role of new firms in the search process was to build and expand using the changes in the industry to their advantage.

Organized labor. In the various adaptive strategies used by meatpackers, particularly the larger firms, organized labor was becoming an increasingly important factor. As in the pre–1920 period, workers continued efforts to establish labor unions and negotiate wages and conditions of work.[4] For most of the years prior to World War II, meatpackers resisted unionization and collective bargaining. Highlighting this resistance was a nationwide strike in 1921 when the Big Five packers refused to negotiate with the union. Two years after the strike, the Amalgamated Meatcutters had declined in membership from 100,000 in the prestrike period to less than 10,000 (Corey 1950; U.S. Department of Labor 1952).

By 1943, another union, the United Packinghouse Workers of America (CIO affiliate), as well as a separate union at Swift, competed with the Amalgamated Meatcutters. During the war years, each of the unions

---

4 In the pre–1920 period, the major union in the meatpacking industry was the Amalgamated Meatcutters and Butcher Workmen. Formed in 1896 and affiliated with the American Federation of Labor the following year, the Amalgamated Meatcutters attempted to organize packinghouse workers and butchers under the umbrella of one union. In the face of business opposition, the union supported a national strike in 1904 that resulted in temporary union recognition. However, recognition was lost later that year and the membership in the union dwindled to approximately 7,500 by 1916. During World War I, a federally appointed administrator made an award that included an eight-hour day, overtime standards, and wage increases. With this support, membership in the union increased to approximately 100,000 by 1920, although meatpackers returned to resisting union recognition after the war emergency was over (Corey 1950; U.S. Department of Labor 1952).

sought, with government support, companywide contracts to replace individual plant contracts. First signed at Armour and Cudahy in 1941, companywide contracts extended to Swift and Morrell by 1950. By the early 1950s, union contracts covered over 70% of workers in the industry (U.S. Department of Labor 1952).

Although the Amalgamated Meatcutters and United Packinghouse Workers occasionally competed for membership, there was a growing effort to pool resources and conclude labor agreements that furthered the interests of all workers in the industry. Organized labor was moving toward an industrywide standard that would remove wages from competition. Rather than allowing individual firms and the market dictate wages and working conditions, organized labor turned to labor contracts. Through these contractual arrangements, workers accepted a hierarchical form of governance as the means to achieve wage growth; the meatpackers accepted the same as a means to stabilize the industry.

A return to market governance with big packer leadership

By 1960, big packer control was fading, but the top three – Armour, Swift, and Wilson – remained the dominant actors in the industry. Their position was tempered, however, by at least six other firms that marketed on a national basis as well as a growing number of smaller regional and local packers. The highway system, motor transport, beef grading, and other changes during this period supported new entrants, albeit under the influence of national packers, into an increasingly market-coordinated sector in which prices and competition played a key role.

Market coordination was evident in an industry that reached its largest size as measured by several dimensions. According to the 1963 Census of Manufacturers, 4,100 companies with 4,330 plants were engaged in meat slaughtering and processing. Both figures would be the highest in the history of the industry. Total employment also peaked at 271,500 in 1956. Although the ranking four-firm concentration ratios in cattle and hog slaughter would continue to decline, by 1960, 23% in cattle and 35% in hogs indicated a basically competitive industry (Nelson 1985). It was in this setting that such brand names as Oscar Mayer, Rath, Hormel, and Morrell won recognition.

At both ends of the production-distribution continuum, a mix of market-coordination settings was playing a role. In the producer-to-packer exchange, the dominant position of packer-controlled terminal markets was clearly gone. Whereas in 1920 approximately 85% of hogs and cattle bound for slaughter passed through terminal markets, by 1963 only 39% of cattle and 27% of hogs were acquired through terminals. Auction markets were still small, accounting for 18% of cattle and 15% of hogs. The dominant form of exchange was direct marketing. By taking advantage of the new highway system and increased producer size, 45% of cattle and 61% of hogs came from ranchers, farmers, and feedlot owners through direct purchases by packers (U.S. National Commission on Food Marketing 1966). In direct purchases, buyers and sellers relied primarily upon a process of negotiation or bidding to set prices and determine other terms of sale. Market transactions had replaced corporate control.

In the packer-to-distributor exchange, there were also major changes. In 1920, over 50% of meat products passed through packer-owned branch houses. By 1963, branch houses accounted for only 14% of packer meat distribution, 34% went through independent wholesalers and other merchants, and 51% was sold directly to retail stores and hotel, restaurant, and institutional purchasers (U.S. National Commission on Food Marketing 1966). In direct sale transactions, a competitive-bid process was often used with meat grades as the basis for product differentiation. Retail buyers typically avoided buying more than 25% of a product from one packer and periodically changed suppliers to encourage competitive bidding. Concluded one writer, these practices "had the result of creating relatively perfect markets for fresh meat products" (Aduddell 1971: 123). As with procurement, transactions were typically taking place in a market environment where terms of trade were negotiated among buyers and sellers. Again, the previously existing system of corporate hierarchy in the form of vertical integration (branch houses) was being replaced by a market-dominated governance regime.

By 1960, the meatpacking industry was assuming a new shape and form in which market governance played an increasingly important role. Although labor contracts represented a countertrend by removing wages from market fluctuations, the general pattern was toward greater reliance upon market relationships in most transactions. The advantages of administrative control and internal cost containment associated with corporate hierarchy, principally in the form of vertical integration, waned under changed conditions in the industry. New packers entered the business and relied increasingly upon market transactions to provide adequate supply of animals and distribution of products. The influence of the Big Four was still present, but their commanding position had weakened. Although the final symbol of their decline, the closing of the Chicago Union Stockyards, would not come for ten years, the big packers no longer commanded the industry.

MARKET GOVERNANCE UNDER STRAIN, 1960–85

This final time period is perhaps the most difficult to assess. Pressures for change and adaptation are certainly present, but they lack the sweeping influence that refrigeration and highway motor transport played in earlier periods. Furthermore, with market governance so influential, adaptations to competitive pressures have taken different paths as firms pursue strategies reflecting their own position and interests. In this period, we consider

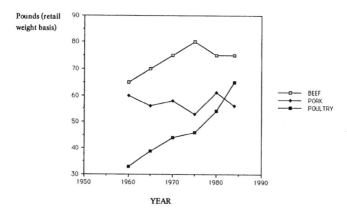

Figure 9.2 Beef, pork, and poultry consumption per capita, 1960–84. (Source: American Meat Institute 1985a.)

not only the role market governance plays in the search process, but also examples where packers seek alternative means to coordinate transactions in the industry.

Pressures for change

Between 1960 and 1985, the meatpacking industry was subject to several key pressures testing the existing system of coordination. Three important forces for change were particularly prominent – declining per-capita meat consumption, competitive pressures from a new meatpacking firm, and the changing nature of livestock production.

Declining meat consumption. One important pressure, most pronounced in the late 1970s and 1980s, was the relatively stagnant demand for red meat products. Beef consumption per capita increased into the late 1970s, but then declined rapidly; pork consumption on a per-capita basis changed very little throughout this period. As Figure 9.2 indicates, poultry became a possible substitute for red meat.

The stagnant nature of demand was also evident in the declining share of the consumer dollar spent on red meat. While average consumer expenditures on red meat (beef, veal, pork, and mutton) between 1955 and 1960 were 4.68% of disposable personal income, the comparable measure dipped to 3.16% between 1980 and 1985 (Breimeyer 1961; American Meat Institute 1985a). Red meat consumption, for a variety of reasons, was not providing an expanding consumer market. For an industry that relied on high-volume sales for economic success, this indicated hard times for many meatpackers as each attempted to secure a share of the market.

New competition: Iowa Beef Processors. In addition to the drop-off in consumer demand, competitive pressures on packers also came from a new firm in the industry – Iowa Beef Processors (IBP). Opening its first plant in Denison, Iowa, in 1961, within twenty years, IBP surpassed Armour as the industry sales leader. IBP's 1984 sales of $6.6 billion was twice that of the nearest competitor. IBP set new industry standards through its boxed beef production, plant locations, wages, and marketing strategies.

Boxed beef was the heart of IBP's competitive strategy. In boxed beef production, IBP cut beef carcasses into primal and subprimal sections at the packing plant rather than shipping beef carcasses to other facilities for cutting and fabrication. Primal and subprimal sections were then vacuum sealed, packed into boxes, and shipped directly to retail outlets for final cutting and consumer packaging. In comparison with whole-carcass shipments, boxed beef offered easier shipment, lower freight costs, shipment of less fat and bone, greater flexibility for product specification, and longer shelf life (Hayenga 1978). As one writer concluded, "the development and acceptance of boxed beef has been the most important change affecting the beef subsector since the mid–1960s" (Marion 1986: 131)

Although other packers experimented with similar production techniques, IBP perfected the vacuum-sealing technology and combined boxed beef production with a low-cost operating structure and aggressive marketing techniques. This low-cost structure was based on location of plants near cattle feedlots, an assembly-line slaughtering and boxed beef process, and low wages. IBP was one of the first major packers to establish wage levels below the master agreement contracts of the other national packers.

In procurement and sales, IBP was also very aggressive. As it grew in size, the company was characterized as "capturing" slaughter plants that provided carcasses for IBP's boxed beef production as well as retail outlets that became reliant on boxed beef. These slaughter plants and retail outlets adjusted work-force levels and production – sales patterns to fit IBP's boxed beef production. In so doing, they became "locked" into IBP's production and distribution system (U.S. House of Representatives 1979b).

By the mid–1970s, IBP was well established as the leader in the beef subsector. In 1975, it had seven plants located in the cattle production areas of Texas, Kansas, Nebraska, Minnesota, and Iowa (IBP 1975). With additional plant purchases in the Pacific Northwest, by 1977, the company accounted for 10% of federally inspected slaughter and was the largest boxed beef producer (IBP 1977). In the late 1970s and early 1980s, the company's intention to enter the pork subsector sent a chill through large pork packers. IBP's low-wage structure and aggressive marketing strategies signaled trouble to pork packers already mired in an economic recession.

Changes in the beef subsector. A third change that influenced the industry, primarily in the beef subsector, was the changing nature of livestock production. Since World War II, there was a trend toward consolidation of livestock production into large feedlots equipped for intensive feeding of nutrients, grains, and feed concentrates. By 1964, it was estimated that 56% of slaughtered cattle came from feedlots, and by 1984, the figure stood at 69% (U.S. National Commission on Food Marketing 1966; U.S. Department of Agriculture 1983).

What was particularly significant was the changing location of feedlots. Although Iowa ranked as the number one state in feedlot production in 1960, by 1984, it was passed by Texas, Nebraska, and Kansas (U.S. Department of Agriculture 1983). Locating feedlots near sources of grain supply meant cost efficiencies for producers. In response, a number of beef packers, such as IBP, constructed plants in these areas. Those beef packers that retained older facilities distant from feedlots faced the competitive pressures of trying to compensate for this advantage held by other packers.

The search process

Between 1960 and 1985, meatpackers pursued a variety of strategies in response to the pressures just outlined. Most of these strategies reflected bilateral forms of governance – markets, obligational networks, and hierarchy. Of the three, market-driven strategies dominated the search process. In addition, an example of associational coordination was also evident, although it was of a quite different nature than the packer pools attempted seventy years earlier.

Markets. In market-driven strategies, meatpackers pursued cost-reduction and profit-maximization strategies in a competitive industry guided by prices. Stagnant demand and competition from IBP led individual firms, including the big packers of earlier times, to seek lower cost levels through a number of adjustment strategies. Four strategies were characteristic: closing older plants, concentrating on one specie (cattle or hogs), reducing wages, and specializing in processing or slaughtering. Each strategy is briefly presented in what follows.

Although plant closings were not new in the industry, the 1970s and 1980s marked a wave of closings by firms trying to reduce capacity and costs. Typical closings involved older multistory facilities that were less adaptable to new slaughtering and processing techniques. In addition, older plants typically had older work forces with high wage and fringe-benefit structures and were often located near terminal and auction yards in urban areas rather than more convenient and less costly sites close to hog and cattle producers. Among packers reporting to the Packers and Stockyards Administration, there was a ten-year decline (1972–82) in cattle plants from 935 to 632 (32%) and in hog plants from 597 to 466 (22%) (Nelson 1985).

A second strategy was the decision by a number of firms to exit either the pork or beef subsector. In most cases, this involved an older, full-line packer reducing or terminating beef operations as the least-cost response to IBP's growing control of beef production. Older packers, with plants located away from new feedlots and subject to master agreement wages, claimed they could no longer compete with packers such as IBP in beef production.

Evidence supporting this strategy is reflected by a comparison of costs. In contrast to pork production, cattle packers operated with a much smaller gross margin within which operating costs were covered. In 1982, for example, cattle packers operated with a gross margin of 13.5% of the sales dollar, whereas hog packers had a comparable measure of 31.7%. Even though labor costs were higher in the hog subsector, the larger margin gave hog packers greater flexibility to maintain an acceptable earnings level (American Meat Institute 1985a).

Another market strategy that involved most firms in the industry was reduction of labor costs. Although labor costs (wages and benefits) in 1980 represented only 10% of total costs, they were approximately 50% of operating expenses (American Meat Institute 1985a).[5] Meatpackers, particularly the older packers, often identified labor as a key area for cost reductions. Such reductions were achieved partially through a decline in employment. Between 1960 and 1982, the number of production workers in the industry declined 15% (U.S. Department of Commerce 1963, 1982).

Equally important, labor-cost reductions were achieved through a sharp decline in wages as the master contract system was overturned. As already noted, master contracts between labor unions and the major packers had an important equalizing effect in the industry. A common wage standard removed basic labor costs from competition among packers. This system, however, was under increasing strain in the beef subsector as several companies paid wages below the industry standard. IBP, in particular, operated most of its plants as nonunion with wage levels below the industry standard; its major union plant in Dakota City, Nebraska, experienced work stoppages at the conclusion of nearly every labor contract.

By mid–1981, hourly wages in the beef subsector averaged $8.25 per hour and in pork production workers earned approximately $9.60 (United Food and Commercial Workers International Union 1981b). In December 1981, the labor contract with Armour set a new standard. This contract involved an extended wage freeze, but at a level of $10.69 per hour, primarily in pork production. This higher wage was accepted by several other companies, but interfirm wage differences were becoming increasingly pronounced. During the ensuing recession years and decline in consumption, the industry experienced a major labor–management confrontation as most

---

5 The major costs for meatpackers consist of livestock and other raw-material purchases. In 1980, this represented approximately 80% of the sales dollar. The balance consists of labor costs and other operating expenses (American Meat Institute 1985a).

packers, including Armour, significantly reduced wages through corporate spin-offs, bankruptcy proceedings, or other strategies. By 1985, wage levels in the industry ranged from $6.00 to $9.00 per hour (American Meat Institute 1985b). It was, as one magazine titled its article, "The Slaughter of Meatpacking Wages" (*Business Week* 1983).

During this period of wage reductions, the major union in the industry – the United Food and Commercial Workers International Union (UFCW) – sought to prevent wage reductions, but was left with a strategy of "controlled retrenchment" (United Food and Commercial Workers International Union 1984).[6] Unlike the World War II period, when state support facilitated the beginnings of a master contract system, during this period, the market rather than the state was providing the context. The union goal was to return the industry to a master contract system with a wage standard that would again remove wages from competition. In 1984, the union set $10 per hour as the bargaining goal.

A fourth market strategy realized cost reductions by a process of "disintegration" between slaughtering and processing. While historically many packers were involved in both activities, the higher value-added nature of processing led a number of packers to reduce slaughtering operations and concentrate on processing as the more profitable segment of the industry. By 1985, the slaughtering end of the industry had become a commodity business concentrated in a few companies and dependent upon high-volume sales.

This trend reflected the tight cost structure of operating a slaughtering plant. Between 1967 and 1984, in both pork and beef, the inflation-adjusted value-added for slaughtering operations actually decreased, while the value-added measure for processing increased (Nelson 1985). This, in combination with lower raw-materials costs for processors, meant greater opportunities in processing for cost adjustments and profits. As an indication of this opportunity, a recent survey found processors with an average net income on sales of 2.96% whereas packers that both slaughtered and processed had a comparable measure of 0.78% (American Meat Institute 1985b). As one corporate executive concluded:

The era of the generalist is past in the meat industry. This is the era of the specialist. The industry has developed into two distinct segments: those specializing in slaughter, breaking and boning; and those emphasizing the processing and marketing of high quality consumer products. (Cassens, Cook, and Kauffman 1984: 20)

---

6 The United Food and Commercial Workers Union (UFCW) became the primary union for the meatpacking industry in 1979 when the Amalgamated Meatcutters and Butcher Workmens Union merged with a retail clerks union to form the UFCW. This merger was preceded by the 1969 merger of the Amalgamated Meatcutters and Butcher Workmen with the Packinghouse Workers. By 1980, approximately 80% of production workers in the industry were unionized.

This trend toward "disintegration" is an important example where corporate hierarchy in the form of vertical integration was replaced by market-type transactions. The preference for market transactions reflected a recognition of production cost advantages in processing as well as reduced transaction costs between the two stages. Using Oliver Williamson's terminology, the "asset specificity" of slaughtered beef and hogs was low, meaning a packer did not have to make asset-specific investments that tied slaughtering and processing together in one firm (Williamson 1985). Instead, slaughtered meat could be purchased on the market from a firm that was likely to specialize in slaughtering. As Williamson recognized in his study, "market procurement has advantages in both scale economy and governance respects where optimal asset specificity is slight" (Williamson 1985: 93).

These four market-driven strategies – plant closings, specie specialization, labor-cost reductions, and specialization in processing – captured key elements in the search process. In each strategy, meatpackers were responding to competitive pressures with cost-reduction efforts based on market exchanges. Meatpackers were acting as autonomous units in an environment where prices played the central role in shaping the response.

Hierarchy. While adjustment strategies reflecting market governance were central during this period, coordination via conglomerate acquisition of meatpackers was also important. These acquisitions occurred in two waves. In the late 1960s and early 1970s, Esmark purchased Swift, Greyhound bought Armour, LTV acquired Wilson, General Host acquired Cudahy, and United Brands purchased Morrell. In the late 1970s and early 1980s, the trend continued as General Foods acquired Oscar Mayer, Occidental purchased Iowa Beef Processors, and Cargill acquired MBPXL Corporation. By 1985, nearly every major packer in the industry had been involved in a corporate merger.

The effect of these changes in corporate management varied among firms, but in many instances, they constituted an important change as corporate decision making moved to a new boardroom. The packers were no longer solely responsible for business strategies. The goals, assets, and liabilities of the parent company now entered the calculations.

Although this move toward hierarchy might have positive consequences for packers, as when capital availability is increased through the resources of the parent company, it can also have negative consequences. For example, the United Food and Commercial Workers International Union argued that the conglomerate acquisitions of Swift, Armour, and Wilson resulted in a "pattern of financial cash drain and asset stripping which competitively incapacitated these packers" (United Food and Commercial Workers International Union 1981a: 20). According to the UFCW, conglomerate control led to high management fees, high interest loan payments, tax write-offs on closed plants, and reductions in investments. Exemplifying this trend, the combined capital expenditures of Wilson, Swift, and Armour were only two-thirds of comparable expenditures by IBP. In short, the old packers were constrained by conglomerate control and "out-invested, out-managed, and out-competed" (United Food and Commercial Workers International Union 1981a: 25).

Examples in the industry. Recent experiences of the big packers highlight this search process involving corporate hierarchy via conglomerate acquisition and market-driven cost-reduction strategies. Armour, for example, reported closing forty facilities prior to 1983 in an effort to make its operations profitable. In 1983, after unsuccessful efforts to attain wage concessions, Greyhound, the corporate owner of Armour, sold all but two processing plants (Greyhound Corporation 1983). Twelve plants were closed, then reopened by another packer as nonunion facilities at wage levels of approximately $6 per hour.

Wilson followed a different path, but the end point was similar. In 1981 LTV, the corporate parent of Wilson, became dissatisfied with the "low profit margins and volatility of earnings" in the meat industry and established Wilson Foods as an independent company (LTV Corporation 1981). When financial problems continued, Wilson filed Chapter 11 bankruptcy and abrogated its labor contract. Wages were reduced from $10.69 to $6.50 and then raised to $8. Plant closings continued as Wilson attempted to reduce its slaughter operations and expand the sales of high-margin, value-added products.

The story at Swift provided another example of market strategies. Swift, under the corporate ownership of Esmark, was split in 1981 between slaughtering operations, which became Swift Independent, and processing plants that remained with Esmark. In this transition, a number of plants were closed while Swift Independent attempted to successfully position itself in fresh meat production. In subsequent years, Swift Independent, backed by favorable spin-off conditions from Esmark, purchased additional plants while reducing labor costs to build its fresh meat capacity.

Obligational networks. Corporate hierarchy and market-driven strategies were not the only bilateral strategies evident during the search process. A number of packers turned to a contractual arrangement known as formula pricing to stabilize transactions. While lacking the administrative coordination of corporate hierarchy, formula pricing used contractual arrangements to minimize fluctuations and uncertainties often found in market transactions.

Used most often in packer-to-distributor or slaughterer-to-processor exchanges, formula pricing involved a contract for product delivery at a future date and at a price based on market prices reported on the specified date.

Put differently, in formula pricing, a transaction was agreed to, but the price was left undetermined; it would be based on the market price at the time of delivery. As one academic observer noted, "In the truest sense of the word, formula pricing is trading on someone else's price" (Marion 1986: 73).

The use of formula pricing was common throughout this period. Based on data from 1964–5, a government study reported that 30 to 40% of transactions by beef and pork packers were made according to a formula price (U.S. National Commission on Food Marketing 1966: 57). More recent studies have found formula pricing to be used in 40 to 60% of fresh pork sales and 50% of beef carcass sales (American Meat Institute 1985c; Hayenga et al. 1985).

This use of formula pricing represented an obligational network in which economic actors used contractual bonds to avoid lengthy and contentious price negotiations as well as ensure product delivery at a specified time (U.S. House of Representatives 1978). The uncertain nature of open market transactions was avoided as firms used formula contracts to facilitate a stable relationship. As one commentator noted, "formula pricing facilitates long standing supplier–customer relationships, reducing the risk involved in shifting from supplier to supplier, or customer to customer" (Hayenga 1978: 22). In the language of transaction-cost analysis, formula contracts reduced uncertainty in transactions, attenuated opportunistic behavior, and compensated for the bounded rationality of human actors (see Williamson 1985).

Associations. While the search process in this time period was dominated by the bilateral strategies already outlined, multilateral efforts were also evident. One that deserves mention concerns industry associations. A number of national and regional associations provided a variety of services for meatpackers. These associations were concerned primarily with government relations, product development, research, promotion, advertising, and dissemination of general information. The American Meat Institute is generally regarded as the primary association of meatpackers and the National Livestock and Meat Board, particularly important in advertising and promotion, is supported primarily by livestock producers.

In response to the changes outlined earlier, particularly the decline in red meat consumption, industry associations played an active role in advertising and promoting meat products. Such slogans as "Beef is Strength" and "America, You're Leaning on Pork" highlighted various campaigns to improve the image of red meat products and encourage consumption. Also, in government relations, associations represented meatpackers on regulatory issues such as grading, inspection, and labeling.

However, in areas of potential competition between meatpackers, such as pricing strategies and production and labor costs, associations played a much smaller role. Trade associations might make tentative ventures into these areas, as in the American Meat Institute's 1985 study of meat pricing (America Meat Institute 1985c), but rarely would an association take a lead role in altering existing competitive practices. Competition was the norm in the industry. As one industry journal found in surveying beef-packer production costs, packers were unwilling to be specific in this area; as all packers agreed, a company's production costs are "highly proprietary, competitive, secret information" (*Meat Industry* 1981: 15).

Thus, the trade associations in the 1970s and 1980s represented a quite different form of multilateral behavior than the pools and mergers attempted seventy years earlier. The types of transactions subject to associational governance were of a much different and more limited nature. Although the American Meat Institute and other associations represented a highly formal structure for multilateral action, the early experiences with state antitrust actions were a reminder of the types of issues closed to associational action. Associational coordination in the recent period fits more closely the interest-group model of lobbying and public information than corporatist strategies to coordinate production and prices.

A new governance regime?

Each of the earlier time periods highlighted the emergence of a new dominant governance mechanism. In the current period, however, such a transformation has been less apparent; market governance still appears to dominate the industry. The recent "shake-out" in the industry, captured by the examples of Swift, Armour, and Wilson, was primarily market-driven. Plant closings, wage reductions, and other market strategies have set the pattern during this adjustment process.

Yet, market governance has come under stress. Formula pricing, for example, has become part of a larger debate on the adequacy of the pricing system in the industry. In the case of formula pricing, some industry observers argue that if enough transactions are formula priced, the resulting "thin" base of actual negotiated prices may not accurately reflect market conditions. Since prices are the major transmitters of information in a market economy, this practice could undermine a critical pillar of market governance. As one agricultural economist argues, "The central pricing issue and problem of the meat industry is formula pricing on a forward basis" (Williams in U.S. House of Representatives 1978: 3).

The concern over formula pricing has become part of a larger inquiry into the adequacy of price reporting and price information in the industry. In the last ten years, government and private-sector reports and congressional hearings have questioned the adequacy of price information and the general process of price discovery. In an industry that relies on voluntary price reporting, criticisms abound not only of formula pricing, but also of the market news systems that report prices on livestock and meat products (U.S. House of Representatives 1978). As a General Accounting Office report on pricing concluded, "the current beef marketing system functions largely in an information vacuum" (U.S. General Accounting Office 1978: 22).

Concern over the viability of a market system has also been raised with respect to the effects of corporate hierarchy on industry competition. The UFCW, for example, has characterized the industry as becoming increasingly monopolistic. The union notes that IBP and Excel Corporation control 35–40% of fat cattle slaughter and 60% of the nation's boxed beef. In the pork sector, twelve companies slaughter approximately 70% of federally inspected hogs (United Food and Commercial Workers International Union 1985). According to the union and others that support this position, the result is an industry increasingly subject to the dictates of large firms, such as IBP. As one congressman argued, "in certain areas conditions in the meat industry are ripe for large, predatory companies to almost invade a region and drive efficient competitors completely out of business" (U.S. House of Representatives, 1979a: 1).

However, others have reached a different assessment. In a study commissioned by the American Meat Institute, the conclusion was that "the meat packing industry is highly competitive on a national, regional, and state basis" (Schnittker Associates 1980). The study cites a number of reports and conducts its own analysis of the industry. In a recent USDA study, the industry is characterized as relatively competitive with national four-firm concentration ratios of 35% in cattle slaughter in 1982 and 36% in hogs. However, the study noted that at a regional or product (e.g., boxed beef) level, concentration ratios can be considerably higher (Nelson 1985).

In both areas of concern – price information and monopolization – the debate continues. Arguments can be made for either side, but the evidence does point to significant weaknesses or problems in a market economy. The practice of avoiding price negotiations and the exercise of corporate power represent dangers to a market governance. Both reflect an interest on the part of business firms to avoid the difficulties of the market. With these caveats, market governance still appears to best characterize the industry.

CONCLUSION

Although a number of governance mechanisms are discussed in this case study, markets and corporate hierarchy have occupied center stage. The earlier time period, from 1878 to 1920, traced the growth of corporate hierarchy, and the remainder of the study followed the path back toward markets. In the earlier transition, the packers' interests in sales and profits led to administrative control through vertical integration and stock ownership. In the later transformation, a new transportation system and expanding meat consumption facilitated diverse marketing strategies by a growing number of firms. Throughout this process, the industry witnessed periodic excursions into other forms of governance, including associations and obligational networks.

One theme that emerges from this history is the inherent dynamic in economic governance. Stability is not the norm. Whether the impetus for change comes from adaptations of new technologies, as with refrigeration and motor transport, or from the competitive strategies of new firms, as with IBP, governance regimes are constantly under stress and strain. The resulting transformation process is a contentious one involving winners and losers. However, the tools of victory for one transformation may become liabilities at a later time, as with refrigerated rail cars at the turn of the century. This dynamic highlights the important role history plays in understanding the nature of economic problems.

A second theme is the dominant role of bilateral forms of governance. Both markets and hierarchy are systems of coordination based on the self-interested actions of individual firms. Multilateral forms of governance that appeal to solidaristic values, such as associations, are more problematic in the industry and play a smaller role.

The importance of bilateral forms of coordination, and markets in particular, provides useful insights into the institutional dynamics of a market economy. Although markets represent the quintessential form of coordination in a capitalist economy and are heralded by policy makers as the appropriate basis for economic coordination, the institutional requisites of a market economy are not always understood and receive less-specific policy consideration. There often appears to be an underlying assumption that markets are self-supporting and self-perpetuating. However, as one agricultural economist noted, a market economy "has little innate capacity to provide for its own survival . . . it must be supported internally and defended externally" (U.S. House of Representatives 1978: 30). Recent debates over formula pricing, price information, and monopoly control exemplify this concern.

And, finally, this case study joins the others in this volume by highlighting the important role of the state. As in all industries, the state establishes important boundaries within which economic coordination takes place. In the meatpacking industry, the state played a major role through meat inspection, beef grading, and antitrust action.

However, unlike such industries as nuclear energy and railroads, which have a public utility nature, the state did not play a significant role as an economic actor in the meatpacking industry. The state provided important boundaries, but it rarely entered the economic arena as a major purchaser, supplier, or distributor of industry products. Yet, even as a boundary setter the task is significant. Concerns over the adequacy of existing price information have raised interest in an expanded state role to support this aspect of the market (see U.S. House of Representatives 1978, 1979c). To provide price information for the meatpacking industry would indeed be a formidable challenge. This issue reiterates the important role the state can play in the operation of the governance mechanisms analyzed in this volume.

THE INVISIBLE HAND IN HEALTHCARE: THE RISE OF FINANCIAL MARKETS IN THE U.S. HOSPITAL INDUSTRY

Patricia J. Arnold

School of Business Administration, University of Wisconsin–Milwaukee

The concepts of hospitals as a business enterprise and healthcare as an investment opportunity are relatively new and distinctively U.S. phenomena. As recently as 1960, the image of the community hospital operated as a voluntary service organization, rather than a business, to serve local physician and community needs, was fairly realistic. Today, healthcare in the United States can aptly be described as a commercial venture in which the hospital industry is an integral subsector. The community hospital has changed character. It is more likely to be either a member of a nonprofit multihospital system or managed by one of the large for-profit hospital conglomerates such as Hospital Corporation of America, Humana, Inc., or American Medical International. Whereas the majority of hospitals remain nonprofit institutions, most have undergone corporate reorganizations, spun off for-profit subsidiaries, integrated vertically through affiliations and joint ventures with physician groups or health maintenance organizations, or diversified into new markets and services to increase market share, obtain access to capital, and improve their competitive position in an increasingly market-oriented industry.

This case study examines the dynamics of change in the institutional structure of the hospital industry. A study of the pharmaceutical industry, the health insurance industry, or the medical profession could provide an equally interesting picture of governance within the U.S. health sector. The emphasis on the hospital industry will undoubtedly fail to highlight certain important aspects of the institutional arrangements governing economic activity in this sector, such as the development of health maintenance organizations in the insurance industry, or the role of state-sponsored research in the development of medical technology. On the other hand, emphasis on the hospital industry will highlight other aspects of sectoral governance that studies of these other industries might overlook. In particular, the case of the hospital industry draws attention to the critical governance issue of how capital investment in the infrastructure facilities of the healthcare system is coordinated and controlled.

Three central questions guide the organization of this chapter. First, do emerging organizational forms, such as multihospital systems and corporate hospital conglomerates, reflect changes in the economic governance of the hospital industry? Governance here is taken to mean the institutional arrangements through which basic economic decisions are made concerning the production and distribution of health services. The question then is whether the emergence of new organizational arrangements within the hospital industry reflects a shift in the locus of control over decisions about what healthcare services will be provided, by whom, and to whom? Second is the question of causality. Why did new organizational structures develop in the hospital industry in the 1970s and 1980s? Of specific concern is the adequacy of economic explanations for the rise of hospital organizations fashioned after the corporate model. Do economic explanations, such as economies of scale, technological imperatives, administrative or transaction-cost efficiencies adequately explain the growth of multihospital systems and investor-owned hospital-management companies? Likewise, do economic imperatives adequately explain the increasing reliance upon markets, with their promised efficiencies, as a mechanism for coordinating the production and distribution of hospital services in the United States? Finally, what role has the state played in shaping the institutional arrangements that govern economic activity in the hospital industry?

This chapter begins by presenting a history of the governance transformation that occurred in the hospital industry following the establishment of the federal Medicare health insurance program in 1965. The historical analysis suggests that the reorganization of the hospital industry reflects a change from multilateral forms of governance (monitoring, promotional networks, and associations) dominated by the medical profession to bilateral forms of governance (markets, obligational networks, and hierarchies). The transition to bilateral forms of governance is seen most dramatically in the emergence of financial markets as the predominate mechanism for allocating capital investment to the hospital industry. Next, and in light of the historical case of the U.S. hospital industry, I assess the adequacy of conventional economic explanations of organization change. The evidence presented shows that efficiency theories that ignore the role of the state in shaping the institutional arrangements at the sectoral level cannot explain the transitions that occurred in the hospital industry. In the third section of the chapter, I examine the role that the state played in influencing the institutional reorganization of the hospital industry. I also identify the limits that state actors faced as they tried, on the one hand, to effectively allocate resources to meet social demands for health services, while, on the other hand, enforcing the property rights of actors in the private sector to own and control hospitals.

GOVERNANCE OF THE HOSPITAL INDUSTRY

To understand the transformation that occurred in the U.S. hospital industry, it is necessary to examine the interorganizational relationships that

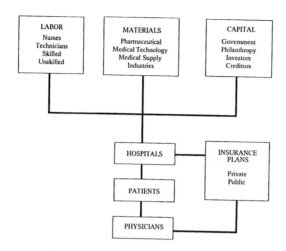

Figure 10.1 Economic transactions in the hospital sector.

govern the economic activity of hospitals. Figure 10.1 identifies the economic transactions that occur between hospitals and other economic agents in the health sector. Interorganizational transactions in the hospital industry are similar to those in other economic sectors in several ways. First, as in other industries, the production and distribution of hospital services require basic productive inputs (labor, materials, and capital) and an infrastructure for delivering and financing services. Hospitals employ nurses and other professional skilled and unskilled laborers, purchase equipment and supplies from the pharmaceutical and medical technology industries, and obtain capital from some mix of government sources, philanthropy, investors, or creditors. Second, as in other industries where technology is capital-intensive, hospitals serve as an organizational apparatus for accumulating capital to acquire the physical facilities, machinery, and equipment required for the practice of medicine. And, finally, as in other private-sector enterprises, hospitals finance their operations by charging patients for services.

Two of the exchange relationships depicted in Figure 10.1, however, are unique to the U.S. hospital industry. Private health insurance companies and public health insurance programs play a unique role by providing insurance mechanisms for financing hospital payments. The relationship between hospitals and physicians is also unique in the U.S. health system. Physicians admit and discharge patients, prescribe treatments, and direct hospital medical care, but most are not employees of the hospital. Historically, hospitals in the United States have granted privileges to private physicians to practice within the hospital. As independent practitioners, physicians use hospital facilities to treat their patients, but they set prices for their service independently and receive payment directly from patients and insurers, not from the hospital.

This section describes the institutional mechanisms used to coordinate exchanges between hospitals and their sources of capital and operating funds during two time periods. The event separating the periods is the establishment of the federal Medicare health insurance program for the aged in 1965, which made the state a major source of hospital payments. The periodization around 1965 reflects the concern of this chapter with analyzing the role of the state in shaping governance regimes. The focus on Medicare, rather than other instances of state regulation of the hospitals, follows Chandler's (1962: 385) argument that instances where the state has directly intervened in the market as a customer have had greater impact on the development of U.S. industry than other regulatory actions and public policy initiatives.

Governance in the pre-Medicare era

The historical development of U.S. hospitals has been described by Hollingsworth and Hollingsworth (1987) and Starr (1982). Hospitals originated in the nineteenth century as almshouses – charity institutions that provided custodial, rather than medical, care for the mentally ill, orphaned, disabled, and sick urban poor. The first hospitals specializing in treatment of the ill developed in the northeast in the second half of the nineteenth century. The impetus for their development came from physicians who wanted to both improve medical education and enhance their own prestige through institutional affiliations (Starr 1982: 152). Lacking funds to finance their own hospitals, physicians sought sponsorship from wealthy donors to fund hospitals through voluntary contributions. Although the early voluntary hospitals specialized in providing medical care, they remained welfare institutions serving primarily the poor who could not afford private care at home.

During the late nineteenth and early twentieth centuries, social, economic, and technological developments encouraged the growth of the modern hospital. These included an increasing popular belief in the efficacy of medical care, the professionalization of nursing, the discovery of anesthesia and improvements in surgical techniques and sanitation, and changes in demographic patterns and physician practice that shifted the location of healthcare delivery from the home to the hospital. With increasing public acceptance of modern medical practice, patients from the middle and upper classes began using hospitals and the hospitals began to rely more on patient payments, rather than private donations, to fund their operations.

This change in the method of financing hospital care altered the distribution of power and authority in hospitals. When hospitals depended on charity, trustees and benefactors exercised significant influence, but as private payment became a more important source of revenue, the power and authority of physicians increased. Starr (1982: 166), in fact, attributes the unique position of physicians as independent practitioners, rather than hospital employees, to both the consolidation of authority and legitimacy within the medical profession and the hospitals' economic dependence on physicians as a source of patient admissions.

The site of healthcare delivery eventually moved from the home to the hospital. Starr (1982: 148) describes this transformation of healthcare in the nineteenth century in Weberian terms as a "movement in social structure from 'communal' to 'associative relations'." Households gave up the function of providing care for the sick to physicians and hospitals. As a result, the delivery of healthcare became a service industry that relied on economic exchanges and associative relations paralleling those of business enterprises.

Although there was some regional variation in the development of hospitals during the first half of the twentieth century, private voluntary hospitals became the predominant form of hospital organization. Private voluntary hospitals are nonprofit organizations, but unlike public hospitals, they are private-sector enterprises, funded by private donations and payments for service, rather than tax dollars. The phenomenon of private voluntary hospitals has been attributed in part to the heterogeneity of the U.S. population (Hollingsworth and Hollingsworth 1987). Voluntary hospitals thrived particularly in the northeast and midwest where cohesive religious and ethnic groups provided capital to build hospitals for their own communities. Where the population was more homogenous or where communities lacked financial resources to build hospitals, municipal and for-profit hospitals were more common. By 1946, private voluntary and religious hospitals operated 64% of all hospital beds, and for-profit hospitals and public hospitals, respectively, owned only 8 and 28% (American Hospital Association 1975: 17–19).

The hospital system that developed in the first half of the twentieth century was decentralized and locally controlled. With the exception of some hospital chains owned by religious institutions, multihospital systems were non-existent. Funds for hospital construction was provided at the local level by donors, physicians, or municipalities. Power and control within the hospital industry was also decentralized. Voluntary hospitals were governed locally by boards of directors comprised of local physicians, whose authority to admit patients provided the operating revenues, and influential community members, whose leadership in fund-raising campaigns provided capital for expansion and renovations.

Federal funds for hospital expansion and renovation first became available in 1946 with the passage of the Hospital Survey and Construction Act, commonly known as the Hill–Burton Act. Hill–Burton is significant as one of the first instances of federal government intervention in the hospital industry. Although state governments had facilitated the consolidation of the medical profession by granting the medical associations control over licensing and medical education, the federal government was not active in the hospital industry before World War II. As a result of American Medical Association (AMA) opposition to any movement toward public health insurance, healthcare was defined as a private-sector venture.

The first federal initiatives in the health sector occurred in the 1940s, first, with support for medical research funded through the National Institute of Health (NIH), and, second, with support for hospital construction through the Hill–Burton program. Since both these programs were federal subsidies for private-sector activities, they did not pose a threat to local physician control, and consequently were not opposed by the AMA (Brown 1983: 12).

The Hill–Burton program, which provided direct grants for hospital construction, was intended to make capital available to build hospitals in geographic regions and rural areas were voluntarism had failed. Since Hill–Burton subsidized private voluntary as well as public hospitals, it further strengthened the position of the private sector in the hospital industry. For-profit hospitals, however, were excluded from eligibility for Hill–Burton funds. As a result of low profits and limited access to capital through either philanthropy or government subsidies, the number of for-profit hospital steadily declined from 1950 to 1965 (American Hospital Association 1975: 19).

During the Depression of the 1930s, private health insurance plans emerged to provide a mechanism for financing hospital payments. The impetus for the development of hospitalization insurance came from the hospital industry itself. When patient collections plummeted during the Depression, hospitals responded by lobbying through their trade associations for state governments to pass special legislation enabling the establishment of tax-exempt, insurance organizations, known as the Blue Cross Plans. The Blue Cross Plans differed from commercial insurance in several ways (Blue Cross and Blue Shield Association 1984). First, the Plans were organized as nonprofit, tax-exempt service organizations authorized by state legislation that exempted them from certain insurance regulations. Second, unlike commercial insurers who paid policyholders, Blue Cross Plans paid hospitals directly. The amounts and method of payment varied among Plans, and was negotiated on a local level between Blue Cross and the hospitals, who in most cases gave Blue Cross special terms and discounts.

Blue Cross was the industry-sponsored alternative to New Deal initiatives to implement a national health insurance program. The keystone of the Blue Cross system was local autonomy (Blue Cross and Blue Shield Association 1984: 4). Since Blue Cross Plans were organized on a regional level and maintained close and cordial relationships with local physicians and hospitals, they posed little threat to existing power structures.

In 1948, the Blue Cross Association was established as a national umbrella organization whose primary function was to coordinate insurance coverage for large national employers with offices in more than one region. On the national level, the Blue Cross Association was also closely linked to the hospital industry. Until 1972, Blue Cross and the American Hospital Association (AHA), the national trade association of hospitals, had interlocking directorates, and AHA held the franchise rights to authorize or withhold use of the Blue Cross insignia (Law 1974: 19).

The mechanisms that emerged in the first half of the twentieth century to coordinate economic activity in the hospital industry can be characterized as multilateral forms of governance. The rules of exchange between hospitals, physicians, Blue Cross insurers, and donors were based on mutual agreements involving various degrees of formal and informal structure. More than any other factor, the force that shaped these organizational arrangements was the cultural authority and collective political power of the medical profession.

Starr (1982: 25) has described the historical process through which the physicians rose to a position of sovereignty in American medicine by gaining control of the market for their services through professional licensing and by escaping the control of hierarchical organizations:

The rise of bureaucratic organizations represented two types of threats to the medical profession. First, organizations employing physicians and providing medical services might enter into competition with independent practitioners. And, second, organizations that provided facilities or financing for medical care, such as hospitals and insurance companies, might subject physicians to unfavorable terms of exchange and reduce their autonomy in fee setting and decision making. Doctors sought to eliminate entirely the first kind of organization – the free dispensary, the company or fraternal medical program, later the prepaid group practice plan – on the grounds that such arrangements were an unconscionable violation of their professional ethics. The second kind of organization – the hospitals and insurance companies – physicians attempted to shape to their own interests, particularly their interests in controlling their own work and setting their own prices.

Through collective political organization, the American Medical Association and the American Hospital Association were able not only to block national health insurance, but also to gain state backing for private insurance plans and federal funds to finance construction of private, voluntary hospitals. Hence, multilateral governance mechanisms served many of the functions normally associated with hierarchies. In particular, they provided physicians with access to capital-intensive medical facilities, equipment, and technology. At the same time, governance arrangements in the hospital and insurance industries enabled physicians to avoid control by bureaucratic hierarchies and maintain their professional autonomy.

Governance in the Medicare era

In 1965, Congress established the Medicare program, a federally funded insurance program to finance payment of healthcare services for the aged. The Medicare legislation stipulated that the government would contract for services with private hospitals and pay them for all "reasonable costs" incurred in providing care to Medicare patients. Direct state participation in the health sector as a major payor had a profound economic impact on the hospital industry.

Government insurance increased demand for hospital services by providing a means for the aged to access the healthcare system and reduced hospitals' financial risk by guaranteeing a stable source of operating revenue. Medicare also altered traditional mechanisms for financing capital investment in hospitals. Unlike Hill–Burton grants, which provided subsidies for nonprofit hospital construction, Medicare paid for capital costs by reimbursing both nonprofit and for-profit hospitals for interest and depreciation expenses. Finally, Medicare payment regimes introduced financial incentives that prompted hospitals to adopt strategies and organizational structures designed to maximize their Medicare revenues.

These changes in hospital financing initiated a shift from multilateral to bilateral forms of governance. The post-Medicare era saw the emergence of hierarchies, obligational networks, and markets as the hospital industry responded to the influx of state dollars. The following section traces the historical development of hierarchies, obligational networks, and markets in the hospital industry during the period 1965 to 1985 and examines the extent to which each came to play more dominant roles in the hospital industry's governance regime.

Hierarchies. Following the establishment of Medicare in 1965, the hospital industry underwent several organizational changes. The most visible was the rise of multihospital systems and large-scale, investor-owned hospital-management corporations, such as the Hospital Corporation of America, Humana, and American Medical International. Figure 10.2 illustrates the dramatic growth of multihospital systems after 1965 (American Hospital Association 1981, 1985). In 1940, there were only fifty multihospital systems in the country, and together they operated only about 200 hospitals. Most of these were small systems owned by religious institutions; none was investor-owned. By 1985, 249 multihospital systems controlled nearly 2,000 hospitals and 40% of the members of hospital chains were investor-owned (American Hospital Association 1985: 3–4).

Paralleling the development of multihospital systems, contract management emerged as a new form of hierarchical organizational control. As late as 1960, contract management was virtually unknown in the hospital industry. But by 1985, nearly one-fourth of the members of hospital chains

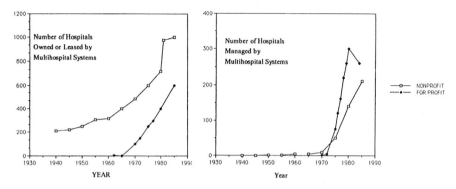

Figure 10.2 Growth of multihospital systems. (Source: American Hospital Association 1981, 1985.)

were operated under contract-management arrangements (American Hospital Association 1981, 1985: 3–5).

As Figure 10.2 shows, the growth of multihospital systems followed similar patterns in both nonprofit and for-profit hospitals. Consolidation and hierarchical control, however, was far more extensive in the for-profit sector. Throughout the late 1960s and 1970s, for-profit hospitals consolidated through a series of mergers and acquisitions that left three large hospital corporation in control of over two-thirds of the proprietary hospital market. Starkweather (1981: 6–7) describes the pattern of acquisition and merger in the for-profit sector between 1966 and 1981:

As late as the mid–1960s virtually all of the nation's proprietary hospitals were owned singly by individuals or small, privately held partnerships or corporations. Most owners were physicians. In the late 1960s, the great majority of these privately held hospitals were sold to larger stock corporations. These can be considered public corporations in that their financial issues were traded on the New York and other stock exchanges. . . . With the economic downturn of the early 1970s another phase of selling and buying occurred: many of the 25 to 30 stock corporations which had been formed in the 1960s to purchase and run hospitals were sold to a smaller number of the largest hospital corporations. . . . As of 1976, this consolidation had reached the point that five corporations . . . had acquired ownership of 60 percent of all investor-owned hospital beds. In 1978, the degree of concentration moved higher with the merger of two of these five corporations, American Medicorp and Humana. Then in 1981, the two largest of these, Hospital Corporation of America and Hospital Affiliates International, merged.

The development of hierarchies in the hospital industry took a new turn in the 1980s. New Medicare payment schemes designed to cut federal expenditures and increase competition within the insurance industry began to cut into hospital revenues and squeeze profits. In response, the large for-profit corporations curtailed expansion through horizontal integration and began to integrate vertically into the insurance business and to diversify into new markets and services (Alexander, Lewis, and Morrisey 1985). By 1985, centralization and corporate control were a fait accompli in the for-profit sector of the hospital industry. Hospital Corporation of America, Humana, and American Medical International owned the vast majority of proprietary hospitals, and were integrating forward into the insurance industry and diversifying into new lines of business including for-profit health maintenance organizations, home healthcare services, emergency medical centers and clinics (American Medical International 1985; Hospital Corporation of America 1985; Humana, Inc. 1985).

Although concentration was not extensive in the nonprofit hospital sector, nonprofits faced the same incentive structures as the for-profits and followed many of the same organizational strategies. As Medicare payment regulations tightened in the late 1970s and early 1980s, a wave of corporate reorganizations swept the industry (Tillet, Linklater, and Suchen 1982). Voluntary hospitals reorganized as subsidiaries of parent holding companies in order to increase Medicare reimbursement and shield endowment funds and outside revenue from government regulators. In the late 1980s, nonprofits followed the lead of for-profits and began to seek affiliations with local health maintenance organizations, nursing homes, and physicians group practices, forming small hierarchies, to serve as feeders for hospital admissions. Similarly, the profit incentives introduced by new Medicare payment schemes in 1983 encouraged nonprofits to aggressively market services, diversify into new lines of business, and expand the operations of for-profit subsidiaries. As nonprofit hospitals adopted business practices similar to those of the for-profits, the distinction between them blurred to the point where, in the late 1980s, they were threatened with the loss of their tax-exempt status (Herzlinger and Krasker 1987).

Bitter opposition from the medical profession drew much public attention to the growth of for-profit hospital conglomerates and the trend toward "corporate medicine" (Wohl 1984). Yet, on the whole, the hospital industry remained relatively decentralized. Although highly centralized, the for-profits hospitals owned only 14% of all hospitals in 1985 (American Hospital Association 1986). Most hospitals remained independent, voluntary institutions; only 20% of the nonprofits where controlled by multihospital systems in 1985 (American Hospital Association 1985: 6).

It is more appropriate to characterize the transformation that occurred in the nonprofit hospital industry in the 1970s and 1980s as "commercialization," rather than centralization. Independent, nonprofit hospitals assumed the modus operandi of commercial ventures as they struggled to capture resources in an increasingly competitive industry. Commercialization of the hospital industry became pervasive, but centralized corporate control was not a reality for the majority of hospitals in 1985.

Obligational Networks. New institutional arrangements were required to implement the Medicare program. In 1965, the Health Care Financing

Administration (HCFA) was established to oversee administration of the Medicare program and to translate broad legislative policy mandates into administrative regulations. An extensive bureaucracy was also created to provide hospitals with a mechanism to appeal denials of Medicare claims. Federal Medicare officials together with researchers and policy analysts from universities and state agencies formed a new core of state managers with a financial stake in the governance of the hospital industry.

Nonetheless, the new federal bureaucracy did not exercise centralized state control over the hospital industry. To the contrary, it merely provided the administrative apparatus through which the state contracted with existing private-sector institutions to deliver health services to Medicare recipients. The state, itself, provided no health services, but rather contracted for services with private hospitals and doctors. Even the routine functions of administering the federal insurance program, such as processing Medicare claims and auditing hospitals for compliance with Medicare regulations, were contracted out to Blue Cross, rather than provided by a federal bureaucracy.

Some advocates of Medicare had hoped that the implementation of federal health insurance for the aged would serve as an incremental step toward centralized state health planning and comprehensive national health insurance (Marmor 1970: 14). The most serious attempt at centralized state control was the enactment of the National Health Planning and Resource Development Act of 1974. The Health Planning Act set national health policy objectives and established an elaborate hierarchy of health planning organizations at the national, state, and local levels to implement national policy. State governments were directed to enact certificate-of-need programs that required hospitals to receive approval for major capital projects from local planning agencies. Medicare reimbursement could be denied for any capital project that did not receive planning agency approval.

In the 1980s, this effort to establish centralized state coordination of the hospital industry suffered drastic setbacks. The ideology of deregulation and free-market competition dominated executive health policy under the Reagan Administration. Budgetary cutbacks rendered state and local planning ineffective, and discussions of national health planning and comprehensive national health insurance disappeared from the political agenda.

Despite the demise of the national health planning structure, the Medicare bureaucracy continued to exercise authority over the hospital industry in the 1980s. In 1983, for example, Medicare abandoned cost-based payment and replaced it with a system of state-administered prices. The new Prospective Payment System represents a direct attempt by the state to structure financial incentives to encourage hospitals to reduce costs (Enthoven and Noll 1984).

By becoming a major purchaser of hospital services, the Medicare bureaucracy had gained some degree of economic control over the production and distribution of hospital service. But the role of the state in the governance of hospitals was limited in its control over the terms of Medicare contractual payments. The mechanism of state control, the power to allocate funds, did not extend beyond the Medicare program, which represented only a third of all hospital revenue. More importantly, since the terms of the Medicare contract applied equally to all hospitals, the state did not have power to selectively allocate resources within the industry.

In the absence of budgetary controls and a comprehensive national health insurance program, state coordination and control over the hospital industry was not achieved. Rather than an administrative hierarchy, as envisioned by the National Health Planning Act, Medicare created an obligational network – a set of long-term contractual relationships with the hospital and insurance industries that enabled the private sector to retain its autonomy.

Markets. The most substantive, albeit subtle, change in the hospital industry's governance regime during the period 1965 to 1985 was the shift toward market control. While public debate centered around concerns over "corporate" medicine and "socialized" medicine, economic control over hospital capital investment was relinquished to the financial markets.

Prior to the 1960s, the stock and bond markets were not important sources of hospital capital funds. Investor-owned hospital stock corporations were virtually non-existent, and voluntary hospitals obtained only 3 to 4% of their capital from the bond markets (Stambaugh 1967: 12). However, Medicare spending increased demand, provided a stable source of operating revenue, and guaranteed reimbursement of capital costs. These factors reduced the risk of investing in hospital stocks and bonds and created the conditions for the emergence of private capital accumulation in the hospital industry. At the same time, the two major sources of capital funds in the pre-Medicare period, philanthropy and Hill–Burton grants, declined in significance. The federal government began to phase out the Hill–Burton program after 1970, and hospital philanthropy declined in the wake of the perception that the welfare state had replace voluntarism. As a result, hospitals became dependent on the financial markets to secure capital funds to expand, renovate, and replace facilities. Table 10.1 shows the increase in the use of debt financing from 1965 to 1979 and the accompanying decline in government grants and philanthropy (Stambaugh 1967; Taddey and Gayer 1982).

Capital market funds and commercial debt financing were readily accessible to for-profit stock companies and to large multihospital systems. Independent, nonprofit hospitals, however, had to develop new institutional mechanisms to access the credit markets. The state actively facilitated the opening of credit markets to hospitals by providing Federal Housing Administration (FHA) mortgage guarantees, and by creating tax-exempt hospital bonding authorities. With encouragement from hospitals and in-

Table 10.1. *Changes in the source of capital financing for
hospital construction*

Source of financing	Percent of financing		
	1965	1973	1979
Tax-exempt bonds	13.7	20.9	49.3
Other debt	22.6	21.8	10.8
Total debt	36.3	42.7	60.1
Government grants	19.3	23.5	8.6
Philanthropy	28.4	10.4	6.2
Reserves	9.3	16.4	18.5
Miscellaneous	6.7	7.0	6.6
Total	100%	100%	100%

Sources: Percentages for 1965 are reported in Stambaugh (1967: 10). Percentages
for 1973 and 1978 are reported in Taddey and Gayer (1982: 12).

vestment bankers, several state governments created state hospital bonding
authorities in the 1970s. As state agencies, these bonding authorities provided a legal vehicle through which private voluntary hospitals could issue
tax-exempt bonds. Use of tax-exempt bond financing grew dramatically
from $262 million in 1971 to over $5 billion in 1981 (Kinkead 1984: 65).
By the 1980s, the bond markets provided the major source of hospital
capital financing.

Hospitals' reliance on capital markets was in part responsible for the
commercialization of the hospital industry. To ensure a continued source
of capital financing, hospitals had to demonstrate to stockholders, bankers,
and bond raters that they were sound business investments. The shift in
the source of hospital capital financing represented a critical change in the
locus of economic decision-making power. By 1985, the power to invest
in or withdraw capital funds from the hospital industry rested with the
financial lending institutions and capital markets. Since the market-based
structure of the U.S. financial system limited the states ability to selectively
allocate capital resources (Zysman 1983), financial market control meant
that decisions concerning the allocation of capital resources were made
according to the criteria of price and profitability, rather than national
needs and priorities. As Kennedy (1986) aptly puts it, "Wall Street" became the new health planning agency.

THE ECONOMICS OF INSTITUTIONAL CHANGE

It has become commonplace to explain the institutional changes that took
place in the U.S. hospital industry with functionalist economic arguments.

Articles in both the academic and popular press frequently begin with a description of the dramatic rise in the cost of hospital care and then proceed to explain organizational changes as a response to economic imperatives to reduce costs. Little is said of how power, authority, class, or ideology shape the governance of economic activity. The history of the hospital industry, however, indicated that economic theories that attribute organizational changes to economies of scale, technological imperatives, or administrative and transaction-cost efficiencies cannot explain the dynamics of institutional change. The growth of multihospital systems and contract-management companies provides two examples of cases where efficiency theories fail.

The growth of multihospital systems

Health economists have attempted to explain the growth of multihospital systems in terms of the economic benefits that theoretically accrue to large-scale organizations, such as economies of scale, and administrative and transaction-cost efficiencies. Efficiency theories, however, have not been supported empirically in the health economics literature. Although there is some evidence that membership in multihospital systems improved hospital bond ratings and borrowing capacity, there is little evidence of other economies of scale or efficiencies. In fact, studies have shown that multihospital systems tend to increase rather than decrease costs, particularly after mergers (Ermann and Gabel 1984).

These results should not be surprising given the historical context in which multihospital systems developed. From 1965 to 1983, cost-based Medicare payments constituted a major portion of hospital revenue. Table 10.2 shows the extent to which the revenues of the three largest for-profit hospital corporations came from cost-based payments. An industry that received a significant portion of its revenue from cost-based reimbursement had little incentive to minimize costs. Advantages of scale, if they existed, are more likely to have been associated with the ability of large institutions to both influence and profit from the increasing complexity of government regulations, rather than their ability to minimize costs (Starr 1982: 434).

The case of the merger of two of the largest for-profit multihospital systems provides an example of how the consolidation of the proprietary hospital sector increased, rather than reduced, hospital costs. In 1981, Hospital Corporation of America (HCA) purchased Hospital Affiliates International (HAI) for $425 million in cash and $190 million in stock. The HCA–HAI merger was one of the largest hospital mergers in history involving the acquisition of 55 hospitals, contracts to manage 102 hospitals and scores of nursing homes, medical office buildings, and other corporate entities.

Upon congressional request, the General Accounting Office (GAO) in-

Table 10.2. *Sources of revenue for Humana, Inc., Hospital Corporation of America (HCA), and American Medical International (AMI), 1977–84*

| | Percent of revenue | | |
	Humana, Inc.	Hospital Corporation of America	American Medical International
Cost-based revenue:			
• Medicare	40	38	45
• Medicaid	4	4	7
• Blue Cross	4	3	2
Total cost-based revenue	48	45	54
Other revenue	52	55	46
	100	100	100

Source: Corporate 10-K filings with the Securities and Exchange Commission (adapted from Arnold 1987: 22).

vestigated the effect of the HCA–HAI merger on hospital costs and Medicare payments. The investigators found that the merger increased net corporate expenses by $55 million dollars in the first year after the merger. The $55 million net increase was due to a $62.5 increase in interest expense, a $8.5 million increase in depreciation expense, and a $15.7 million decrease in administrative costs. Interest costs had increased by 300% because HCA borrowed the money to purchase HAI. Depreciation expenses had increased by more than 80% due solely to accounting methods HCA used to record the merger, which doubled the book value of HAI assets (U.S. General Accounting Office 1983a).

The General Accounting Office was not able to determine the extent to which these cost increases were passed on to patients and insurance companies in the form of higher charges. The investigators did, however, examine the impact of the merger on Medicare payments made to two HAI hospitals, and found that the merger increased Medicare payments by 28% in one hospital and 16% in the other. Although the GAO auditors questioned certain of HCA's accounting practices, the bulk of the increase in Medicare payments was not disputed. Both the increase in depreciation payments arising from accounting revaluations and the interest payments on debt that HCA incurred to finance the merger were legitimate reimbursable costs under the Medicare regulations in effect at the time of the HCA–HAI merger.

Following the General Accounting Office's report, Congress enacted legislation in 1984 that prohibited hospitals from receiving higher Medicare capital-cost payments as a result of mergers or acquisitions. The fact re-

mains, however, that between 1965 and 1984, Medicare regulations encouraged horizontal integration among for-profit hospitals by rewarding
consolidation with increased payments.

Hospital mergers may have produced long-term cost efficiencies, particularly in nonprofit hospitals, where mergers occurred more frequently between neighboring hospitals. Local mergers and regional multihospital
systems potentially reduce costs by eliminating excess capacity and duplication of services. The pattern of acquisition in the for-profit hospital
sector, however, crossed widely dispersed geographic regions, promising
little in the way of physical economics of scale (Starkweather 1981). Moreover, the case of the HCA–HAI merger was not unique. Medicare merger
and acquisition accounting regulations inflated national healthcare costs by
significantly increasing Medicare payments to for-profit hospitals that engaged in mergers and acquisitions (Arnold 1987).

The rise of contract management

Full-service contract management is an inside contracting arrangement in
which a hospital-management company takes responsibility for the day-to-
day management of a hospital, placing its own employees in chief executive
positions, while the hospital maintains legal ownership and control. Figure
10.2, discussed before, shows the dramatic rise of contract management
in the hospital industry in the late 1960s and 1970s. Throughout this period,
many of the largest for-profit hospital chains invested extensively in the
contract-management business. By the end of 1984, HCA alone held contracts to manage almost 200 hospitals and 25,000 hospital beds (Hospital
Corporation of America 1984: 15). As in the case of multihospital systems,
efficiency theories fail to explain the emergence of contract management.
The administrative history of the Medicare regulations indicates that rather
than creating cost efficiencies, contract management inflated hospital costs.

Prior to 1982, Medicare regulations were silent on the issue of reimbursing hospitals for the fees they paid to management companies. In the
absence of guidelines, any fees paid by a hospital to a management contractor were passed on and reimbursed by Medicare. In the late 1970s,
there was a growing concern within the Medicare bureaucracy about contract-management practices. In 1977 and again in 1980, HCFA issued proposals to establish regulatory guidelines for reimbursing management fees.

In June 1980, in a letter to the Administrator of HCFA, the General
Accounting Office presented the findings of an investigation of contract-
management fees. The letter (U.S. General Accounting Office 1980) provides what may be the only publicly available information about the fees
that hospitals paid to management companies. The GAO investigation
revealed a wide variation in fees, ranging from approximately $600 to
$4,500 per bed. In one case, the GAO auditors found that the management

company marked up its fees 500% over costs. They also found that management fees were frequently based on a percentage of revenues. Percentage-based fee structures were of particular concern because they created incentives for hospital contract managers to increase their fees by raising hospital charges and providing unnecessary services. As a result, the General Accounting Office recommended that percentage-based fees be prohibited and that guidelines be established for Medicare auditors to use in determining whether management fees were reasonable before they would be reimbursed (U.S. General Accounting Office 1980).

In March 1982, the Medicare regulations were amended to implement the first GAO recommendation (Health Care Financing Administration, *Medicare and Medicaid Guide*, para. 5995). The new regulation, however, provided an extremely vague guideline, the "Prudent Buyer" principle. Management fees could be reimbursed provided that hospitals acted as prudent buyers in purchasing contract-management service. The regulation encouraged, but did not require, competitive bidding as evidence of prudent purchasing. The GAO's recommendation to prohibit percentage-based fees was passed into law in 1982, but never implemented through regulations (*Medicare and Medicaid Guide,* para. 5995B).

Similar issues and controversies surrounded the use of limited-service contracts (U.S. General Accounting Office 1983b). Hospitals commonly contract for a wide range of in-house services, including laundry, food, data processing, maintenance, and clinical services. Industry surveys show that the use of limited-service contractors grew rapidly throughout the 1970s (*Modern Healthcare,* 1977–1985). In many cases, hospitals contracted with outside firms to operate whole departments, such as purchasing departments or respiratory therapy units. In the absence of Medicare regulations governing payment for contract fees, limited-service contracts contributed to inflation of hospital costs in the same fashion as full-service contracts. A General Accounting Office (U.S. General Accounting Office 1984a) audit of respiratory therapy contracts, for example, found that respiratory therapy costs were overstated by approximately 38% and that the majority of the contractors were paid on a percentage-of-revenue basis.

Inside contracting created information asymmetry within the Medicare payment system. When hospitals performed services in house, Medicare audited the books and reimbursed only the cost of services. When hospitals hired contractors to perform services, however, Medicare paid the contractors' fees with no knowledge of how fees related to costs.

Throughout most of Medicare's history, subcontractors' books were closed to Medicare auditors. In 1980, Congress passed legislation requiring that subcontractors' books and records be opened to Medicare auditors as necessary to verify the nature and cost of services furnished to Medicare. Interpretation of the language "as necessary" was controversial, and the law was not implemented in regulations for several years. When finally written in 1984, the regulations were extremely restrictive. It allowed auditors access to subcontractors books only in cases where there were written accusations and evidence of fraud, kickbacks, bribes, or other illegal activities (*Medicare and Medicaid Guide,* para. 7514G).

Contract management can, theoretically, introduce economies of scale. Large management-contracting firms, for example, can obtain purchase discounts on supplies and pharmaceuticals through volume purchasing. On the other hand, the administrative history of Medicare regulations suggests that contract management inflated hospital costs. Percentage-based fee structures increased costs by creating incentives for overutilization of services and higher charges. Furthermore, Medicare procurement and audit policies that did not require competitive bidding and kept subcontractor books and records closed both invited contracting abuses and provided contractors with the opportunity to charge exorbitant fees.

The long-term contractual relations between Medicare, hospitals, and subcontractors illustrate one of the most significant features of governance associated with obligational networks. These networks enabled contracting parties to maintain stable relationships without sacrificing their flexibility or autonomy. In the case of Medicare subcontractors, contracting served another function as well. Obligational networks created layers of separate legal entities that contracted indirectly with Medicare, but were not subject to either cost-based payment or audit. Since Medicare could not examine the books of subcontractors, obligational networking limited Medicare's access to information.

Transaction-cost theory would predict that such information asymmetry leads to the development of hierarchies (e.g., Williamson 1975). But state hierarchy did not replace obligational networks in the hospital industry. The selection of governance mechanisms depended more on the institutionalized distribution of power than on potential transaction-cost efficiencies. It may have been more cost efficient for Medicare to coordinate exchanges with contractors and subcontractors through a state hierarchy, but it would have been less profitable for the subcontractors. Obligational networks rather than hierarchies emerged in the hospital industry because of *political,* not economic, imperatives.

THE POLITICS OF INSTITUTIONAL CHANGE

State action has been a recurring theme throughout the development of the hospital industry. At the subnational level, the state helped shape governance by granting medical associations authority over licensing privileges and by enacting legislation that fostered the development of private insurance in the 1930s and tax-exempt bond financing in the 1970s. After World War II, state action on the national level further ensured the stability of private voluntary hospitals by providing federal funds for hospital construction. With the establishment of Medicare in 1965, however, the state for the first time became directly involved in an exchange relationship with hospitals as a major purchaser of hospitals services for the elderly.

This section examines two issues concerning the role of the state as a direct participant in exchanges with the private sector. First, why did the federal government intervene in the hospital industry when it did, and why did it do so in the form that it did? Second, what does the history of state involvement in the hospital industry tell us about the capacities and limits of the U.S. state to effectively coordinate economic activities at the sectoral level through direct intervention as a player in the market?

The politics of Medicare

The answer to the question of why the state intervened in the hospital industry in 1965 lies in the legislative history of the Medicare program. In his monograph, *Politics of Medicare,* Theodore Marmor (1970) described the political processes leading from the defeat of the Truman Administration's comprehensive national health insurance plan in 1949 to the passage of the Medicare legislation in 1965. Several conclusions emerge from Marmor's analysis of Medicare politics.

First, the fundamental issue underlying the long debate over national health insurance was the issue of income redistribution. As is characteristic of redistributive politics, the debates over national health insurance throughout the period from 1949 to 1965 polarized along ideological and class lines. The ideological conflict centered around the contest between socialism and big government versus voluntarism and local control. Marmor (1970: 112) further argued that the political debate divided according to class interests rather than special interests:

Medicare was one of those issues that separates "money-providing" and "service demanding groups" in society – a division that "cuts closer than any other along class lines". . . . The health industry's public opposition [to Medicare] was fused with that of almost every national, commercial, industrial and right-wing group in American politics. The united front of the "service-demander" was equally apparent in the Medicare fight. The ultimate consumers – the aged and their organizations – were overshadowed in the procession of "liberal," professional, labor, and service organizations championing their cause.

Second, Marmor shows that the Medicare legislation, although ostensibly a victory for proponents of national health insurance, was in reality a conservative compromise. The compromise began after the defeat of the Truman proposal for comprehensive health insurance in 1949. After 1949, state policy elites who favored national health insurance adopted a "strategy of incrementalism" (Marmor 1970: 14). By targeting hospitalization insurance for the aged and tying it to the Social Security program, rather than financial means, state policy managers hoped to make the first move toward national health insurance more palatable to a public that was ideologically resistant to any notion of welfare. As a result, the Medicare legislation as enacted in 1965 was markedly different than the health insurance programs adopted in other industrialized nations. The United States, for example, was the only country to target health insurance for the aged, whereas in other countries, national health insurance began with low-income workers and was later extended to higher-income groups. Thus, although state involvement in the hospital sector originated in class politics, the unusual form that public health insurance took in the United States was conditioned by ideological constraints and historically contingent political strategies.

North (1981) argues that political and ideological forces play a crucial role in establishing and maintaining property rights – the rules, procedures, and norms governing economic transactions. Such was the case with the Medicare legislation. As part of the conservative compromise that enabled the passage of Medicare, the legislation was structured to ensure that the private sector would continue to control the production and distribution of healthcare service. The Medicare legislation authorized use of a private-sector fiscal intermediary, Blue Cross, to administer the insurance program, rather than developing a state insurance bureaucracy. Medicare also established an elaborate judicial appeals system to protect hospitals from administrative dictates.

Most importantly, rather than establishing budgetary control over hospitals, Medicare opted to contract with the private sector and pay any "reasonable costs." Cost-based contractual payment was intended to limit state involvement to the role of a passive insurance underwriter. Although the architects of the Medicare program were aware of the potential inflationary effect of cost-based payment, incentive effects were given secondary consideration to the main purpose of cost-based contracting, which was to ensure that the state would remain "neutral" and not interfere with private-sector prerogatives to control the delivery of hospital services (Wolkstein 1968: 18).

The limits of state action

Despite the conservative nature of the Medicare legislation, Marmor (1970: 126) contended that the resulting "price inflation was not intended, even by those in the Johnson Administration who most understood that the bitter Medicare bill must be sweetened for its opponents in the health industry." Indeed many of the consequences of Medicare are seemingly unintended. Interest-group politics and capture theories of regulation (e.g., Stigler 1971; Peltzman 1976) cannot explain the boom that Medicare provided to the hospital industry. To the contrary, Marmors' analysis of the long process leading to the enactment of Medicare suggests that reformers within the state played a leading role in pushing for redistributive health legislation. Likewise, the network of state bureaucrats and policy intellectuals that formed to direct national health policy in the Medicare period typify the concept of independent state managers (Block 1980; Skocpol 1980). The major health policy reforms emanating from Washington during the 1970s and 1980s, such as the National Health Planning Act and the Medicare Prospective Payment System, did not reflect the interests of business in either intent or consequence.

Yet despite the efforts of relatively autonomous state managers to initiate social reforms and implement national health policies, the consequences of state involvement in the hospital sector turned out to be quite different from those they had intended. Rather than providing an incremental step toward national health insurance and centralized state coordination of the healthcare delivery system, Medicare led to the rise of large investor-owned hospitals, spiraling costs, commercialization, and market control.

The answer to the question of why the state failed to effectively coordinate economic activity in the hospital industry lies in structural factors, including both property rights structures and the institutional structure of the U.S. political and financial systems. The structure of property rights was a key determinant. Whereas public ownership of schools became an accepted norm, public ownership of hospitals did not. As the hospital system developed in the nineteenth and twentieth centuries, the medical profession, through its exercise of moral authority and collective political action, succeeded in defining healthcare as a private-sector venture. As a result, hospitals were organized as private voluntary enterprises. Later, when the state intervened to provide health insurance for the aged in 1965, the Medicare program was intentionally structured to reproduce the existing property rights structure and maintain private-sector ownership and control of the hospital industry.

Once private-sector rights to own and control hospitals were defined, political structures further constrained the state's ability to effectively intervene in the hospital industry. As Brown (1983: 21) stated, "the interplay between health policy and politics" can only be understood within the structural context of an extremely decentralized political system. Separation of authority both between and within federal, state, and local governments, and between the administrative, judicial, and legislative branches of government contributed to the failure of attempts to establish centralized state control of the hospital industry. Medicare administrative agencies and the courts, for example, frequently divided on issues raised in the Medicare appeals process.

The impact of fragmented authority is particularly evident in the lack of a coordinated capital-allocation policy. While national and local health planners attempted to implement national goals to reduce the number of hospital beds, Medicare and other national and subnational state authorities encouraged capital investment by reimbursing capital costs, establishing tax-exempt state bonding authorities, and granting federal loan guarantees.

Likewise, the structure of the U.S. financial system contributed to the inability of the state to effectively coordinate capital investment in the hospital industry. In his cross-national, comparative analysis of financial systems, John Zysman (1983) concluded that the institutional structure of a national financial system affects a state's ability to implement industrial policies. National financial structures can facilitate or limit the state's ability to selectively allocate capital funds and coordinate capital investment in industries. According to Zysman (1983: 18) credit-based financial systems in France and Japan facilitate state-led strategies for industrial change, whereas market-based financial systems in the United States and Great Britain encourage market-led industrial change. In U.S. capital markets, where capital entry and exit are determined by the prices of stocks and bonds, decisions about how capital is allocated to production rest with individual buyers and sellers. Such decentralization and capital mobility make state-led strategies for industrial change difficult to implement.

In the hospital sector, changes that were precipitated by the increased involvement of financial markets continually confounded state efforts to implement national health policies and control healthcare costs. In the 1970s, market forces limited the ability of national health planning agencies to control expansion and coordinate delivery of hospital services. Medicare spending attracted large-scale private capital investment to the industry. While health planners attempted to curtail unnecessary expansion, the stock markets readily provided funds for the growth of large-scale for-profit hospital corporations, and the bond markets provided capital for new construction and expansion of voluntary hospitals. By absorbing risk and uncertainty, Medicare spending created the conditions for accumulation, which drew capital investment to the hospital industry and, in the process, undermined the efforts of health planning agencies to effectively control or coordinate hospital expansion.

Similarly, market forces in the 1980s impaired the state's ability to control federal healthcare expenditures without jeopardizing public access to needed services. Cutbacks in Medicare spending in the 1980s made hospital investment riskier and raised concern that investors would move funds out of the hospital industry. Faced with declining revenues and a worried Wall Street, many hospitals began to abandon unprofitable operations, move into more lucrative markets and services areas, or turn away patients who were financially unable to pay. Public access to needed services could be ensured only by further state spending, subsidies to sole community hospitals, and costly tax breaks for investors.

In short, both the expansion of the hospital industry in the 1970s and

its commercialization in the 1980s were market-led, not state-led, strategies. Claus Offe (1975) argued that

> the basic prerogative of "free enterprise" is a negative one: the right not to produce
> unless production is at the same time accumulative. . . . The first and most important
> element in the definition of a capitalist state is thus: The state cannot "initiate"
> production within private enterprises that is thought to be "not" accumulative by
> the private accumulating units, and it cannot, conversely, "stop" production that
> is considered accumulative (profitable) by the accumulating units.

In the hospital industry, state welfare spending could initiate or stop production of hospital services only by making production more or less profitable. Medicare spending could prompt capital entry and exit, but the state
could not selectively allocate capital resources within the industry according
to national needs and priorities. In a market-controlled financial system,
health policy planners were unable either to direct investment away from
hospital services that were profitable but unneeded in the 1970s or to direct
capital investment to services that were needed but unprofitable in the
1980s.

The dynamics of change

Prior to 1965, the hospital industry was governed by relatively stable multilateral arrangements between physicians, private voluntary hospitals, and
private insurance. These forms of governance were shaped and bound
together by the economic power, political influence, and cultural authority
of the medical profession. In 1965, social and political pressures gave rise
to the Medicare insurance program and an influx of state dollars into the
hospital industry. As part of a political compromise, the Medicare legislation created an obligational network – a contractual arrangement between
the public and private sector that maintained private-sector ownership and
control over the production and distribution of hospital services. In the
process, however, Medicare spending changed the character of the private hospital industry by introducing financial incentives for hospitals and
investors that transformed the institutional structure of the hospital industry in a bilateral direction. State spending made the hospital industry
profitable and created the conditions for private accumulation that led to
growth and consolidation of large for-profit hospital corporations, contract-
management arrangements, and commercialization of the voluntary hospitals. Indeed, most of the changes in the institutional structure of the
hospital industry in the Medicare era can be traced to the strategic response
of hospitals, corporate managers, and capital markets to financial incentives
provided by Medicare payment schemes.

Physicians and their associations remained influential actors in the governance regime of the Medicare era, but their position of authority was

challenged by an array of new institutional actors with a financial stake in the hospital industry. For-profit hospital corporations, corporate-style non-profit hospitals, the Medicare bureaucracy, and the capital markets emerged as key influences and altered the institutional distribution of economic and political power within the industry that once was the private domain of physicians.

The capital markets became the predominant mechanism for coordinating capital investment in the hospital industry in the post–1965 period. State welfare spending made investment in hospitals profitable and private capital investment replaced philanthropy and government grants as the major source of hospital capital financing.

Markets, however, are a potentially unstable governance mechanism in a sector as politically charged as the health sector. Despite the free-market rhetoric that dominated executive health policy in the 1980s, the underlying social divisions that led to the adoption of Medicare in 1965 require continued state involvement to guarantee basic health services. Thus, the stability of existing governance mechanisms depends on large-scale state spending to ensure continued capital investment. But fiscal constraints pose limits on the state's ability to meet public demands for health services and investors' demands for profits. In short, the U.S. state in the 1980s faced the classic "fiscal crisis" (O'Connor 1973) arising from the attempt to meet social pressures for redistributive social programs while at the same time maintaining private-sector property rights to control the production and distribution of healthcare services. This tension makes existing mechanisms for coordinating economic activity in the hospital industry inherently unstable and politically volatile.

Part III

Theoretical evaluation of the empirical cases

11

THE EVOLUTION OF
GOVERNANCE REGIMES

John L. Campbell
Department of Sociology, Harvard University
Leon N. Lindberg
Department of Political Science, University of Wisconsin–Madison

Social scientists have produced a massive literature about transformations in the organization of economic activity from which we can identify five general theoretical traditions that seek to identify the key determinants of governance transformations. These enable us to specify more precisely the simple model of the governance transformation process that we presented at the end of Chapter 1. This model suggested that the transformation process occurs when pressures for change develop and cause actors to search within certain limits for an alternative combination of governance mechanisms, which we called a new governance regime. In this chapter, we describe these five theoretical traditions, or models, derive from them a new evolutionary model of governance transformation, and assess the new model in light of the evidence provided in our case studies.[1] Finally, we explore the implications of this analysis for debates about the long-term institutional development of advanced capitalism.

FIVE MODELS OF GOVERNANCE TRANSFORMATION

Economic efficiency

Economists typically attribute governance transformations to shifting economic conditions, including variations in the supply and price of production factors, fluctuations in demand, and other things that inhibit firms operating efficiently, that is, maximizing output with a given set of inputs. Within this tradition, it is assumed generally that governance through markets is the norm (e.g., Alchian and Demsetz 1972), but that alternative gover-

---

1 As is often the case in exercises, such as this, that seek to address debates between broad paradigms, rather than the nuances within them, the models that result appear to be neat and tidy, when in fact they actually conceal sharp disagreements and debates among those who subscribe to each one. Inevitably, this is the case here due to the sheer volume of literature that is involved, only a sampling of which is actually mentioned. However, we try to address some of the more important debates that exist within models in the text and footnotes wherever relevant.

nance mechanisms will develop when markets fail to operate efficiently. For example, actors may build corporate hierarchies when they perceive that market pricing has become an inefficient way of coordinating transactions (Coase 1937) or when they believe that economies of scale may be achieved (Scherer 1970: 81) – a goal that may also lead to the creation of obligational networks, such as joint ventures (e.g., Pfeffer and Salancik 1978: 153).[2] Oliver Williamson (1975, 1985) developed one of the most sophisticated explanations of governance transformations within this tradition. He argued that when the costs of conducting and monitoring transactions through the market become excessive, because they involve the recurrent exchange of products whose manufacture requires substantial investments in idiosyncratic factor inputs (high asset specificity) and, therefore, small numbers bargaining, actors will turn to alternative governance arrangements that reduce these transaction costs. When the frequency of exchange and level of idiosyncratic investments are high, he argued, actors will replace markets with hierarchies. When the frequency of exchange is high but the level of such investments is moderate, they will turn to less stable subcontracting relations among a few firms (Williamson 1985) – another example of an obligational network. In either case, the alternative to market contracting is an allegedly more efficient form of governance. Thus, unless noted otherwise, efficiency refers throughout this chapter to the capacity of transacting organizations within the production system to obtain the resources they need and information they need and to manufacture their products at the lowest possible cost.

In addition to arguing that economic inefficiencies create pressures for changing existing governance regimes, this tradition assumes that the most efficient form of governance eventually emerges. Hence, as discussed in Chapter 1, not only have others criticized this perspective for ignoring that market-based governance may be transcended for reasons unrelated to efficiency (e.g., Perrow 1986), but also for relying on a functional logic to explain which specific governance mechanisms finally emerge in different situations – a logic that is flawed insofar as it maintains that the most efficient mechanisms eventually develop simply because they are the most efficient (e.g., Robbins 1987). This difficulty reflects, and perhaps stems from, the fact that adherents to this tradition, such as Williamson, fail to incorporate into their analysis a rigorous account of the search process, wherein actors decide how to solve their economic and organizational problems.[3]

---

2 Criticisms of this view abound. For example, see Nelson and Winter (1982) and Hodgson (1988), who challenge the orthodox rational-choice model's neglect of the decision-making constraints that actors face that are posed by bounded rationality, organizational routines and inertia, political and legal frameworks, and other organizational and institutional obstacles.

3 For an attempt to infuse orthodox economic accounts of governance transformations with an organizational analysis of the search process, see Nelson and Winter (1982).

Technology development

At least since Marx argued that changes in the forces of production created the possibility for shifts from capitalism to socialism, observers of economic history have recognized that technological developments often contribute to governance transformations. Alfred Chandler (1977), for example, argued that the revolutions in transportation and communication technologies that occurred in the United States during the nineteenth century fostered rapid growth in markets, mass-production technologies, and, thus, the creation of modern industrial hierarchies with which capitalists could more efficiently stabilize and exploit these markets and technologies, respectively.[4] Following Chandler, others argued that mass-production technology tends to produce long hierarchies and bureaucracy, whereas craft-production technology often yields more subcontracting and short hierarchies, reminiscent of our obligational networks (e.g., Caves 1980; Stinchcombe 1983: 111–15; Piore and Sabel 1984).

Whereas the development of new technologies is generally viewed as a pressure for change that triggers a search for new governance arrangements, efficiency criteria are often offered to explain why one form of governance emerges from the search rather than another. This is an important parallel with economic arguments and is perhaps most obvious in Chandler's (1977) work, where he argued that hierarchies are most likely to develop in mass-production industries because they are the most efficient way to organize the scheduling and flow-through requirements of such production technologies. Similarly, he maintained that associations frequently preceded the emergence of corporate hierarchies, but were short-lived largely because they were unable to manage efficiently the problems associated with mass production and distribution (Chandler 1977: Chap. 4). Similarly, although recognizing the importance of political and other struggles around the creation of governance arrangements, and, therefore, offering a more multidimensional account than Chandler's, Michael Piore and Charles Sabel (1984) suggested that with the advent of computers and numerically controlled machines, we have the opportunity to create more decentralized, flexible economic institutions, akin to our obligational and promotional networks, that can adapt more effectively to the shorter product cycles and other instabilities of the late-twentieth-century world economy.[5]

---

4 Chandler's argument is not entirely removed from the economic tradition insofar as he argued that, with the advent of these technological breakthroughs, existing markets were unable to handle the scheduling and distribution problems associated with new mass-produced goods. Hence, he also incorporated a market-failure model into his analysis.
5 The linkage between technological and institutional developments, on the one hand, and efficiency, on the other, is deeply rooted in much of this literature, often penetrating to the definition itself. According to Arthur Stinchcombe (1983: 93), technology is not just gadgets, inventions, and other *things,* but rather patterns of activities that influence, or are

We are not suggesting that this literature succumbs to crude technological determinism. In fact, deliberate attempts are made often to avoid such pitfalls while establishing the causal links between changing technologies and institutions. At least passing reference to the important role of the state, class struggle, and other factors in determining institutional outcomes is common (e.g., Torstendahl 1984). Even Chandler (1977: Chap. 4) recognized that the replacement of federations and pools by corporate hierarchies during the late nineteenth century was premised in part on the lack of support from the state for these more collective forms of governance. Piore and Sabel (1984) recognized that technological change simply created the *opportunity* for governance transformations, and that political and other struggles would ultimately determine which technology and accompanying set of governance mechanisms actors would select.

Yet it is the effect of technological change that these scholars *theorized,* not these other influences.[6] Hence, the emphasis on the technological determinants of social organization is unmistakable, but also because this literature tends to pay much less attention to the processes whereby actors, responding to new technological possibilities, or pressures for change, actively search for alternative governance arrangements through which to realize these possibilities – a second parallel with the economic tradition, discussed before. Ann Markusen (1985), for example, developed a fascinating argument about how technological and product innovations typically drive an industry's profit cycle and, thus, transform its governance arrangements. She argued that the initial, unprofitable stages of innovation foster lots of small-firm subcontracting, or obligational networks, that give way first to intense market competition, as the innovation becomes very profitable, and then to corporate hierarchies, as weaker competitors exit the market and barriers to entry develop. Later, as new innovations cut into existing markets, profits sag and actors begin to deconstruct hierarchies and resort once again to subcontracting. Associations play a greater role in trying to prevent further industrial decline. However, she paid very little attention to the processes by which actors who face these technologically driven profit cycles decide which governance arrangements to adopt.[7] In-

thought to influence, the *effectiveness or efficiency* of the use of things for achieving certain goals – a definition that is reminiscent of Schumpeter's (1983) claim that economic development is largely the result of entrepreneurs who combine available resources in innovative ways.

6 Although Chandler, for example, recognized the state's role in undermining collective governance arrangements, his theoretical discussion does not address the state's role at all (e.g., Chandler 1977: 6–12, 484–90).

7 The presumption that technology is the primary, but certainly not the only, force behind governance transformations is clear insofar as a host of additional variables are discussed in this literature as modifying the effects of technology. For example, many who work within this tradition have recognized that the extent to which technological change leads to the replacement of markets with hierarchies is influenced by such things as product type,

deed, one of the most common criticism of Chandler's work is that he tended to neglect the struggles that occur over the selection of governance arrangements in different industries (e.g., Perrow 1981).

Power and control

In contrast to arguments about economic efficiency or technological change, a third tradition maintains that governance transformations occur when actors try to increase their power and control over each other and whatever resources and information they deem to be important for their economic survival and prosperity. For example, some have argued that firms build corporate hierarchies through horizontal mergers in order to reduce and control market competition (Scherer 1970: Chap. 4; Perrow 1981, 1986: Chap. 7), and through vertical integration to minimize the degree to which one firm depends on another for key resources (Aldrich 1979; Pfeffer 1987). They have also maintained that firms create corporate interlocks (monitoring), joint ventures (obligational networks), and more formally organized collective governance mechanisms (promotional networks and associations) to better manage various types of resource interdepencies (e.g., Pfeffer and Salancik, 1978: 152–7; Aldrich 1979: Chap. 12; Pfeffer 1987).[8] In this literature, power generally refers to the capacity of an organization to extract for itself valued resources, including wages or profits, and information in a system where other organizations seek to do the same thing for themselves, or to otherwise control the behavior of other organizations within the system (e.g., Perrow 1986: 259).

According to this tradition, because the desire to gain power and control, and to avoid becoming the object of another's power and control, is the critical impetus for change, it is easy to see that actors will struggle among themselves over the formation of new governance arrangements, particularly to the extent that governance transformations will institutionalize new power relationships. The frequent zero-sum nature of these relation-

---

the existence of already well-developed distribution systems, the availability of finance capital and skilled managerial talent, wage levels, the centralization of urban markets, state policy, and historical tradition. For further discussion of these issues, see Kurth (1979), Markusen (1985: Chap. 5), and the essays in Chandler and Daems (1980).

8 The resource-dependence school has also recognized that there are important modifying variables to consider. For example, Pfeffer's (1987) review of the literature indicated that if controlling competition was the goal, industries with many firms simply relied on the market to regulate competition, industries with a moderate number of firms employed extensive corporate interlocking, and industries with only a few firms relied on oligopolistic price leading. For further discussion of how the degree of organizational leadership, the level of organizational homogeneity, the use of positive and negative incentives, and ideology modify the relationship between resource dependence and governance transformation, see Aldrich (1979: 319–21). For criticisms of the resource-dependence school from within the power and control tradition, see Mintz and Schwartz (1985: Chap. 2).

ships means that one actor's gain in power will often come at the expense of another.[9] Hence, in addition to offering additional insights about what may constitute pressure for changing existing governance arrangements, this tradition creates a broader analytical space for understanding the search process itself than either the economic or technology traditions that tend to lapse into arguments that confuse efficiency with causality. This is not to say that the power and control position does not have problems of its own. Williamson (1981: 572–3), for example, charged that proponents of this tradition had not developed a precise, multidimensional definition of power that would permit researchers to determine when power did or, more importantly, did not influence organizational changes. Some of the more radical representatives of this tradition, who have suggested that power and control tend to accumulate in increasingly centralized organizational forms, have difficulty explaining why hierarchies are not found everywhere (Perrow 1986: 241). Nevertheless, the merits of this perspective are clear insofar as understanding the search process is concerned and how the balance of power among the actors involved helps determine the institutional outcomes of the search.

Culture

Karl Polanyi (1944: 46) argued that "man's economy, as a rule, is submerged in his social relationships." More recently, sociologists have reminded us of this by arguing that the determination of governance arrangements is due as much to cultural and ideological factors, including norms, values, levels of trust, and so on, as it is to economic or technological imperatives, or struggles over power. Michel Crozier (1964: 312) claimed that values and cultural trends influence the form of hierarchy that emerges in different countries, and that as these cultural attributes change, so does the nature of hierarchy. Cultural explanations of institutional structure have proliferated in the literature on organizations (Smircich 1983) and have proven useful in explaining the conditions under which actors organize themselves in obligational and promotional networks, rather than hierarchies, where Williamson would have predicted otherwise (e.g., Lazerson 1988). Mark Granovetter (1985: 503), for example, suggested that when the economic conditions exist for the development of transaction-cost problems, hierarchies are not likely to develop if there is an already well-established network of personal relations that mitigates against opportunism and malfeasance among economic actors. Thus, he maintained that both Williamson and Chandler had adopted "undersocialized" views of

---

9 This assumes that economic exchange rarely occurs between actors with equal power – a fundamental departure from theories that are rooted in the economic efficiency tradition, and a point stressed by others (e.g., Etzioni 1988: xii).

economic activity that neglected the importance of trust in economic transactions, particularly insofar as the creation of obligational networks is
concerned.[10] Others have shown that a common cultural background also
contributes to the development of certain forms of monitoring arrangements, such as class-based social clubs, through which economic and political activity may be coordinated tacitly (e.g., Domhoff 1974, 1983).

The point is not that representatives of this tradition believe that cultural arguments should replace entirely economic and other explanations
of governance transformation, but that they should complement them.
Geoffrey Hodgson (1988: 156), an ardent critic of orthodox economic
explanations of institutional change, including transaction-cost theories,
suggested that "the basis of [exchange] agreements is not simply the rational
calculation of abstract individuals with a view to their perceived costs and
benefits; it is a combination of both formal legislation and legitimation,
and inherited custom and tradition of a less formal kind." Yet the use of
culturally focused arguments has been criticized for failing to define precisely what is meant by culture (Smircich 1983) and for failing to clearly
specify the mechanisms that link cultural conditions with the development
of specific governance mechanisms. This later criticism has been especially
pronounced in studies that seek to determine how different national economic structures emerged in countries sharing similar cultural traditions
(e.g., Hamilton and Biggart 1988).[11] Indeed, this suggests that cultural
explanations also tend to overlook the search process through which culture
may affect governance transformations.

State policy

Hodgson's point that economic activity is embedded partially in a political
context is important and has been reiterated by others who have noted
that governance transformations are caused, at least occasionally, by shifts
in legislation and other state policies. Some have gone so far as to argue
that the primary source of governance transformations is the state itself,
such as those who have claimed that changes in the definition and enforce-

10 For further discussion of the important effects that trust and other relatively subjective
   factors play in the organization of economic activity through obligational and promotional
   networks, see Macaulay (1963), Ouchi (1977, 1980), Eccles (1981), and Lorenz (1988),
   all of whom contribute directly to the criticism of more orthodox economic explanations
   of these governance transformations. For further criticisms of Williamson's position from
   this point of view, see Johanson and Mattsson (1987), who argue that trust is institutionally
   based insofar as it develops through repeated exchanges.
11 Some do a better job of establishing these linkages than others. Compare, for example,
   Crozier's (1964: Chap. 8) rather vague discussion of the culturally based differences in
   French, U.S., and Soviet bureaucracy with Lazerson's (1988) excellent analysis of how
   cultural traditions contributed to the formation of extensive subcontracting networks in
   Italy.

ment of property rights policies by the state are the fundamental sources of the transaction-cost and other inefficiencies that Williamson and others believed to be so important in explaining the development of economic institutions (e.g., North 1981).[12] In contrast to these arguments that are sympathetic to economic efficiency models, some cross-national studies of economic development have suggested that politicians and state bureaucrats successfully promoted different governance arrangements in different countries in order to legitimize their political authority (Hamilton and Biggart 1988) and to compete more effectively with other nation-states in economic and geopolitical affairs (Weiss 1988). Of course, Polanyi (1944: 139–41) was among the first to suggest that the state was often directly responsible for governance transformations. He demonstrated that during the nineteenth century the British market system, allegedly the epitome of laissez-faire capitalism, developed, ironically, out of deliberate state action, and had to be supported by the state thereafter, or face self-destruction. Finally, a vast literature has shown that the state is often directly responsible for the development of associative forms of governance, primarily as a means of avoiding state intervention (e.g., Streeck 1983; Useem 1984: Chap. 6; Streeck and Schmitter 1985).

Not all of this literature views state policy and politics as the primary independent variables in governance transformations, the elements that are responsible for generating the central pressures for change. Others see them in a more indirect role, orchestrating the search process when other factors have already created pressures for change. For example, in an argument that is sympathetic to the power and control tradition as well as Piore and Sabel's technological arguments, Scott Lash and John Urry (1987) noted that advanced capitalism experienced an institutional disorganization during the 1970s and 1980s, triggered not by the state, but largely by the globalization of economic activity and transformation of national class structures. However, they showed that this led to the breakdown of class-based politics, the fragmentation of political struggle, and, as a result, the decline of corporatism, associative governance, and even the partial deconstruction of corporate hierarchies.

The literature about how the state affects governance transformations is vast enough to require a separate and more extensive treatment in Chapter 12. For now, it is sufficient to understand that political struggles within and around the state may play important roles in the governance transformation process, both in terms of creating pressures for change and constituting an important part of the search process.

---

12 For a review of this property rights school, see Bowles (1984), and for a critique, see Hodgson (1988: Chap. 7).

AN EVOLUTIONARY MODEL OF GOVERNANCE TRANSFORMATION

These five theoretical traditions each have distinctive strengths and weaknesses, thus suggesting that a more comprehensive approach is required for understanding governance transformations. However, we cannot develop such an approach simply through an eclectic addition of elements selected from each tradition because many of these are rooted in incompatible philosophical positions. Consequently, we must first expand upon the institutionalist assumptions, specified in Chapter 1, that we have made about rationality, and the relationship between human agency and institutional structure. This will help us fuse the useful elements of previous traditions into a more precise composite and evolutionary model of governance transformations.

The basic ontological premise that informs our evolutionary model is that although actors, including individuals, groups, and organizations, are subject to economic, technological, institutional, cultural, and other constraints, they are at the same time creative, active forces that can shape and reshape these constraints. In other words, these constraints generally limit the *range* of interests and opportunities available to actors, but they do not determine the *specific* interests and opportunities that actors select. Thus, rationality is contingent, as we discussed in Chapter 1, and there is some, but not unlimited, room for actors to select their goals and actions, a condition that creates the possibility that actors may occasionally interpret and react to their problems in new and unexpected ways. Conversely, although actors may process information, evaluate circumstances, and make purposeful decisions that reshape, intentionally or unintentionally, the constraints that they face, these constraints cannot be reduced to the interests and acts of *individual* actors. This is because their choices are somewhat limited in the first place, but also because these constraints, interests, and acts arise from the *interactions* that occur among actors. Indeed, as the preceding chapters demonstrate, actors produce, cooperate, exercise power, and struggle with each other frequently in situations where resources and power are distributed unequally.[13]

In Chapter 1, we suggested that governance regimes constrain production and exchange relationships among diverse economic actors and the state according to various types of rules and means of compliance. These regimes change over time as actors, whose range of choices is constrained in ways that we have just discussed, adjust to exogenous and endogenous forces. However, this process of governance transformation is rarely smooth. First,

---

13 For well-developed defenses of this ontological position, see Baumgartner et al. (1984, 1985), Giddens (1984), and Hodgson (1988).

as noted before, economic signals and technology are not usually decisive in determining specifically the direction of change or the outcomes of governance transformations. Second, because governance transformations involve significant changes in a governance regime's structure of rights, rules, and compliance procedures, these matters are of intense, often strategic, interest to most actors. As a result, prolonged processes of trial-and-error learning, negotiation and cooperation, and coercion and struggle occur over the structure of new governance regimes. We have referred to this as the search process.

The point is that the reciprocal effects between actors and social constraints, as well as the presence of contingent rationality and the search process, suggest the need for an evolutionary explanation of governance transformations, although one that is neither teleological nor functionalist. The elementary logic of such an explanation begins by recognizing that endogenous and exogenous forces episodically disrupt production and exchange. In response, actors search for solutions to these disruptions through a series of complex decisions in which economic, organizational, and political choices that were institutionalized in the most recent governance regime limit the options that are currently available to actors during the search. In turn, these actors institutionalize their choices in a new governance regime that constrains their future options. This process repeats itself, usually in a gradual manner, as new governance regimes evolve out of old ones, again and again, in the stepwise historical process that we have illustrated in Figure 11.1.[14]

The centerpiece of such an evolutionary view of sectoral development is what we have summarized heuristically as the search – a process whereby sectoral actors pursue their interests within a variety of constraints and eventually *select* a new governance regime by combining in intended and unintended ways their individual strategies for coping with the dilemmas of production and exchange. Indeed, the concept of *constrained selection* captures the essence of the search process as it embodies the reciprocal relationship between actor and constraint, or strategy and structure, as outlined before.

Our model of governance transformation as the selection of new governance regimes is summarized schematically in Figure 11.2 This figure represents the intricacies of one step of the evolutionary process depicted in Figure 11.1. Three sets of actors are linked to each other through complex relationships of dependence and interdependence. These include *producer organizations*, such as firms, *other organizations* that typically

---

14 Ikenberry (1988) develops a stepwise, evolutionary analysis of U.S. energy-policy regimes that illustrates the kind of developmental logic that we have in mind, although his analysis does not focus on institutional transformations per se. Evidence for this kind of logic supports our contention that in order to understand governance transformations, one must have an historical analysis of distinctive sectoral and national experiences that accounts for the contingent nature of structural change.

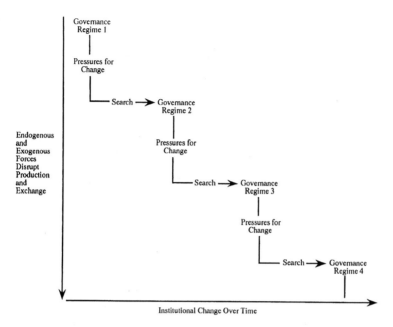

Figure 11.1   An evolutionary view of sectoral development.

respond reactively to producers, including suppliers, labor, financial institutions, public interest groups, and consumer groups, and the ensemble of *state organizations* that behave reactively, but also on the basis of their own interests. Governance transformations are usually initiated by producers, but occasionally by other organizations, who respond to new problems and opportunities that are created by changes in economic conditions and technology. In Chapter 1, we referred to these problems and opportunities as pressures for change. Of course, shifts in state policy, the efforts of actors to increase their power and control over exchange, and other factors may alter economic conditions and technology in the first place, or create pressures for change in their own right to which producers and other organizations may respond. However, if the state initiates a transformation, it does so in response to changes in domestic or international political–economic conditions.

Actors do not respond automatically to pressures for change in a knee-jerk fashion, but rather select the ones, if any, to which they will react. The state does the same thing insofar as changing political–economic conditions are concerned. Of course, some pressures for change may be more difficult to ignore than others, so the existing set of pressures constrains the choices that are initially available to actors. Furthermore, pressures for change are not always exogenous to the model. The institutional character of the existing governance regime or the specific actions of actors

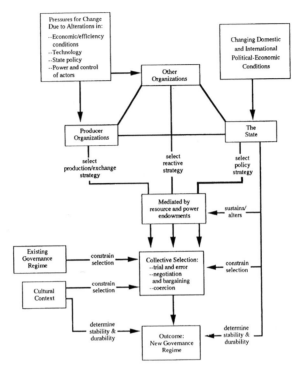

Figure 11.2   The selection of new governance regimes.

within the sector may contribute to the formation of these pressures. However, to avoid excessive complexity, we have not included these feedback loops in Figure 11.2.

For ease of presentation, we make two further simplifications. On the one hand, we tell the story, depicted in the model, from the producers' point of view. That is, the producers initiate change. On the other hand, we recognize that these three sets of actors should not be treated as mysterious black boxes. Producers, for example, have distinctive interests, organizational routines, time horizons, and performance standards through which they interpret the flow of information about economic and technological options (e.g., Nelson and Winter 1982). These develop within the context of previous governance regimes and represent the cumulative momentum and/or drag of earlier decisions about economic conditions, technology, and relationships with other groups and the state. In this sense, they constitute the producer organization's institutional memory. Of course other organizations, including the state, also have their own interests, routines, time frames, and standards. However, because this model focuses on interorganizational relations, we do not elaborate on this point further.

Three streams of action constitute the central dynamic of the selection process. First, producers initiate the search for a new governance regime, sometimes without realizing it, by selecting in an opportunistic manner new production and exchange strategies to optimize their interests on the basis of endogenously and exogenously produced problems and opportunities – strategies that they seek to implement by manipulating their own organizations and their relationships with other actors. Second, these efforts are constrained by the strategies of other economic organizations, reacting to producers. Finally, the state may pursue its own interests and strategies, such as maintaining its legitimacy in the face of public controversies, initiated by producer strategies, or dealing with international pressures from other states and economies, in ways that constrain the actions of producers and other organizations. The state may also become involved if producers or other actors mobilize politically to implement their strategies and achieve their interests.

The idea that one actor's strategy may constrain the implementation of another's strategy suggests an interactive process. Indeed, actors eventually select a new governance regime as these streams of action intermingle in complex ways. Trial-and-error learning as the result of spontaneous interaction may predominate in some instances, such as when actors learn how to coordinate their actions around emergent common conventions, incrementally discard unsuccessful strategies, or tacitly align themselves with especially powerful actors. In this sense, selection is very much a process of muddling through. In other cases, deliberate negotiations among organizations will take the place of, or supplement, trial and error. Contracts and legislative bargains that formally reflect the interests, institutional capacities, and relative bargaining power of different actors, including the state, can be important steps along the path to new governance regimes (e.g., Young 1989). Finally, selection may involve elements of coercion through political and economic struggle. For example, producers may exercise economic and organizational power to force labor or suppliers to accept a new governance regime. Recognizing that selection involves the intermingling of streams of action helps to highlight how our model departs from conventional rational-choice conceptions of transformation, and suggests that selection is in many ways a *collective* process.

Of course, these complex interaction processes are mediated initially by the resources and power with which actors are endowed insofar as the strategies selected by powerful actors are more likely to be implemented than those of weak ones. In addition, the institutional arrangements within the existing governance regime, such as systems of labor–management relations and finance, constrain the selection process to the extent that existing patterns of interaction usually embody a degree of institutional rigidity or inertia out of which it is difficult to break. For instance, when actors have already established promotional networks or associations in their sector and, thus, the capacity for selecting far-sighted, cooperative strategies, they can more easily devise new multilateral governance mechanisms than actors from a sector where short-sighted, bilateral mechanisms, such as markets, dominate the governance regime. Furthermore, the state constrains the selection process. The state's actions, such as defending or modifying property rights, sustains or alters the relative endowments of resources and power. Likewise, the procedural and legal principles that state actors choose to promulgate and enforce may temper the *use* of these endowments, and may constrain the types of interactions that occur during the selection process. So does the state's institutional structure, as we explain in Chapter 12. Similarly, cultural factors, including norms of fairness, justice, competition, and cooperation, either of a general or sector-specific nature, may constrain the use of power and resources.

The degree to which trial and error, negotiation and bargaining, or coercion prevail during the selection process determines, and is reflected by, the new governance regime that emerges, particularly insofar as the balance among bilateral and multilateral, and informal and formal mechanisms of coordination is concerned. However, the nature of the selection process also helps to determine the stability of the new governance regime. Presumably a regime that is imposed through coercion will be less stable, and perhaps less durable, than one that is crafted through cooperation. In this regard, stability and durability also depend critically on the ability and willingness of the state to ratify and help legitimate the regime. For example, if state actors provide political support, resources, and legal enforcement for a regime, its stability and durability are likely to be enhanced. The same will probably occur if the emergent regime is organized in ways that are consistent with the current cultural and normative context.

AN EMPIRICAL ASSESSMENT

We have outlined how five theoretical traditions attempt to explain governance transformations, and we have offered an evolutionary model that we argue helps to integrate these theoretical traditions. Our strategy of integration has been to suggest through what mechanisms the central, purportedly causal relationships that are offered by each tradition actually operate. Our model does this through a theory of action that is based on assumptions about the reciprocal effects of strategy and structure. That is, we recognize how various actors respond to changing conditions by selecting strategies, first, individually and then through complex collective processes, that eventually become institutionalized as new governance regimes, but in ways that are constrained by the already existing governance regime as well as other factors. Thus, the model implies that explanations of governance transformation cannot simply postulate dependent and independent variables, but must explain the mechanisms that link these variables – mechanisms through which causal factors actually enter into the evaluations and choices of actors. However, we also recognize that the variables in which we are interested, particularly economic and technological conditions, power, culture, and state policy, are loosely coupled in the sense that over time, the manner in which they affect actors and the transformation process varies under different internal and external conditions (e.g., Sorge and Streeck 1987). Let us now demonstrate *empirically* how our model helps to link the separate stories that these five theoretical traditions offer by considering in turn the central arguments of each theoretical school from the perspective of our model and case studies.

Economic efficiency

Our case studies revealed several examples of governance transformations that resulted from actors selecting production and exchange strategies that they believed would help improve economic efficiency. For example, manufacturers in the automobile sector created huge corporate hierarchies by extending their operations through vertical integration, both forward and backward, in order to achieve economies of scale. Indeed, General Motors experienced much greater demand for its products than American Motors and, as a result, became more vertically integrated due to the promise of greater economies of scale. In meatpacking during the late nineteenth and early twentieth centuries, vertical integration proceeded downstream from meatpackers into wholesale distribution. However, retailing was not subject to as much integration, and beef production upstream rarely became integrated with the large packing houses – a finding that supports Williamson's transaction-cost theory insofar as asset specificity was relatively low in beef production and retailing, but rather high elsewhere where special capital-intensive railroad refrigeration systems had to be built to transport slaughtered meat to distant markets. Similarly, a reduction in capital-intensive-specific assets after the Second World War, due to the development of readily available refrigerated trucking, lowered barriers to entry in meatpacking and contributed to vertical *dis*integration. Vertical disintegration also occurred during the 1960s and 1970s as corporations tried to improve their efficiency by reducing labor and production costs through plant closings in both sectors, and in the automobile sector through the development of precisely coordinated subcontracting schemes between parts suppliers and manufacturers, where parts were scheduled to arrive at the manufacturer just in time for assembly, thus minimizing inventory costs.

Nevertheless, it was often the case that even when interests in economic efficiency, through either promises of reduced transaction costs or improved economies of scale, helped spark the search for new governance regimes, there were additional forces that helped set the selection process in motion. After all, it was breakthroughs in transportation technologies that created the conditions under which vertical integration and then disintegration could be economically efficient in meatpacking. In automobiles, the development of new computerized information and production systems created the possibility for just-in-time scheduling. The economies of scale that actors hoped to achieve by building large integrated steel companies were only possible because of the capital-intensive nature of the technologies that were involved. Thus, as suggested earlier with respect to Chandler's work, the interconnection between economic efficiency and technology explanations of governance transformations is often very tight.

Equally important, however, there were times when actors selected hierarchies and other governance mechanisms for reasons completely *unrelated* to efficiency considerations. For example, in the hospital sector after 1965, companies began to integrate vertically through hospital-management corporations and later through diversification schemes, not because actors believed that this would reduce transaction costs or improve economies of scale, but because state policy rewarded them for doing so through larger Medicare payments. In fact, these hierarchies emerged in an environment where there were very few incentives to minimize costs at all because Medicare paid a patient's medical expenses on a cost basis – a situation, it turned out later, that actually led to a *decrease* in economic efficiency insofar as the creation of corporate hierarchies increased the organizational costs of providing healthcare.[15] Furthermore, when vertical disintegration occurred in our cases, it was not always due to the perception of private actors that markets or obligational networks had become a relatively more efficient governance alternative, but because state policy forced the transformation for political reasons, as happened when the federal government invoked antitrust law to break up both AT&T in the telecommunications sector in 1982 and some of the vertically integrated hierarchies in the meatpacking sector during the first half of the twentieth century. Indeed, many of the transformations that occurred in our cases do not appear to have been caused primarily by private actors searching for greater economic efficiency. Rather they stemmed from shifts in technological, political, and other conditions, elaborated in what follows.

It is worth mentioning that economy of scale or transaction-cost models were only helpful for understanding those transformations that resulted in the selection of *bilateral* forms of governance – mechanisms located on the left side of the typology of governance mechanisms that we presented in Chapter 1 (see Figure 1.1). Often these were related directly to the creation or undoing of corporate hierarchies. In addition to the examples already discussed, formula pricing, a type of obligational network, developed in the meatpacking sector, where, in response to the vertical disintegration that occurred after 1960, beef producers established flexible long-term contracts with packing houses well in advance of product exchange through

---

15 There is also evidence, as Hollingsworth suggests in Chapter 2, that some forms of monitoring, such as price leading, developed in the United States, although they tended to be relatively inefficient.

an agreement that allowed them to specify prices at a later date. They selected this form of governance to reduce the transaction costs associated with what would have been a constant series of price negotiations. Similarly, steel manufacturers sought long-term contracts with customers to stabilize demand, a necessary precaution taken to ensure that their expensive mills would run continuously and realize the economies of scale that they were designed to achieve. In contrast, when actors pursued *multilateral* forms of governance, they often did so to counteract what they believed was excessive price competition, a problem that is much different from those of efficiently obtaining production factors or manufacturing products that we have been discussing, and that are typically the focus of the economy-of-scale or transaction-cost literatures. Formally organized associations and pools emerged during the nineteenth and early twentieth centuries in steel, meatpacking, and railroads to reduce price-based competition. Steel companies also orchestrated explicit price-fixing agreements through the infamous Gary dinners, a promotional network, and actors in the meatpacking, steel, and automobile sectors pursued tacit price-leading strategies, a form of monitoring, at various times. All of these were attempts to extract greater profits from consumers and, therefore, illustrate governance transformations driven by the collective exercise of power, rather than the quest for greater efficiency.

Furthermore, although it appears that conventional economic efficiency models are helpful for identifying important pressures for change, at least in some cases, they are less useful for understanding how and why actors eventually selected one alternative governance mechanism, rather than another, to be dominant, particularly insofar as *multilateral* forms are concerned. We cannot, for example, understand why meatpackers first selected pools, then a holding company, and then the least formally organized multilateral form of all, price leading, to control cutthroat price competition between 1880 and 1920, or why price leading, rather than these other forms, finally succeeded in solving the problem unless we introduce a political analysis that includes a discussion of the struggles that erupted around the antitrust issue. Transaction-cost or economies-of-scale models are of little value here.

Perhaps we should not be too critical. After all, the economic-efficiency literature has been preoccupied with developing models to explain the conditions underlying the formation of bilateral, not multilateral, forms of governance (Etzioni 1988: 5; Schneiberg and Hollingsworth 1990).[16] This is ironic because orthodox economists have tried to apply their models to

---

16 Indeed, representatives of this tradition, such as Williamson, have often failed to recognize that multilateral forms of governance have been frequently an important institutional means of coordinating economic activity in the United States, as our case studies demonstrate.

many social phenomena that others consider to be beyond the traditional domain of economics, such as politics (e.g., Downs 1957) and the family (e.g., Becker 1976) – an exercise that some have condemned as a dangerous form of economic imperialism (e.g., Granovetter 1989; Swedberg 1989). However, orthodox economists have not done so in this case.[17] We must turn to other explanations if we are to understand the forces that precipitate searches for the full range of governance transformations that have occurred in the United States.

Technology development

Innovations in technology created possibilities for governance transformations in many of our case studies by providing actors with an opportunity to devise new strategies for production and exchange. In the extreme, these opportunities permitted actors, previously excluded from participating in the sector, a chance to carve out a niche for themselves. For example, we have seen that the increasing availability of relatively low-cost highway transportation reduced barriers to entry in the meatpacking industry and helped to foster market competition where an oligopoly had exercised control for decades, in part through its control over enormously expensive railroad distribution systems that were made possible in the first place by the development of railroads and refrigeration technology during the nineteenth century. The geographical expansion of milk distribution, due to improvements in railroads, refrigeration, and sanitation, established the possibility for transforming the dairy sector during the late 1800s from an economy of locally based milk markets into one where central distributors had a chance to develop, form oligopolies, and dominate the distribution system in urban areas. The development of microwave technologies during the 1950s and 1960s created the opportunity for independent firms to break into a telecommunications industry that had been monopolized by AT&T and its affiliates for nearly a century.

This is not to say that major technological breakthroughs automatically trigger governance transformations. As Piore and Sabel (1984) suggested, new technologies simply broaden the range of production and exchange strategies from which actors may select in organizing economic activity. In our cases, it was always an open question which option actors would eventually choose, and, once they had decided, it

---

17 Of course, beginning with Olson's (1965) path-breaking study, many economic theories have been offered to explain the collective action of individuals. Yet, we are not aware of any that explicitly try to understand the development of the types of *interorganizational institutions* that are located on the multilateral side of our governance mechanism typology. Knoke and his colleagues, however, appear to be moving in this direction (e.g., Knoke and Wood 1981; Knoke and Wright-Isak 1982).

often took a long time before the institutional effects of their decisions began to materialize. Although companies began trying to utilize microwave technologies, for instance, in the 1950s to penetrate AT&T's monopoly on telephone service, it was not until 1971, after years of litigation and regulatory haggling that culminated in an FCC decision to permit long-distance competitors to interconnect with the Bell System's local exchanges, that they began to establish competitive services for customers. Thus, new technology created the *possibility* for a governance transformation, but struggles over regulatory policy determined the final outcome. Similarly, in the nuclear sector, adoption of the lightwater reactor established the possibility for the kind of accident that occurred at Three Mile Island. In turn, the accident created the conditions that prompted actors to search for a new governance regime, one where they selected self-regulatory associations and promotional networks to improve the sector's performance and public image. Yet the accident was also due in part to mismanagement of the technology, that is, laxity in safety research and regulation, problems that stemmed from the already existing governance regime. Thus, a variety of factors, including state policy and the structure of governance itself, modifies the influence that technological developments have on the transformation process.

On the other hand, once the decision has been made to pursue and institutionalize one technology, rather than another, in a particular regime, the availability of alternative technologies and regimes tends to decrease as movement along the chosen path develops a momentum of its own out of which it is hard for actors to break (Dosi 1984: 85; Piore and Sabel 1984). Although most members of the nuclear sector recognized the benefits of standardizing reactor designs, this became virtually impossible to do after manufacturers and utility companies decided to commercialize two different versions of the light-water reactor and market them competitively. Elsewhere, massive capital investments by the big steel hierarchies in old brownfield sites during the 1950s and 1960s made it extremely difficult for them to abandon these traditional mill technologies in favor of new, more flexible minimills later, even though the minimills appeared to be a more appropriate technology for the shifting economic climate of the late-twentieth-century steel sector. As a result, it was not the old steel oligopoly that innovated with the minimill technology, but a new group of competitors that selected a more market-oriented governance regime. The point is that although dramatic changes in technology *expand* periodically the range of choices for organizing governance, once these choices have been made, actors tend to become locked into the technology and the governance regime in which it is embedded in ways that *constrain* future choices in an evolutionary manner, as discussed earlier.

Many of the technological developments that were described in the preceding chapters, including minimills, truck transport, and microwave communications, encouraged the selection of new production and exchange strategies that eventually led to major governance transformations. However, in light of the arguments reviewed earlier that suggest that technological change is often the driving force behind governance transformations, we need to explain why in some cases new developments in technology did *not* induce change, such as the hundreds of innovations that occurred in the telecommunications sector as a result of AT&T's extensive research-and-development efforts. Following Giovanni Dosi (1984), we can divide these technological innovations into two categories. The development of these steelmaking, transportation, and communication technologies are examples of *extraordinary* technological innovations because they were so revolutionary that they opened up a new range of production and exchange opportunities for actors, whereas the latter AT&T innovations are examples of *normal* innovations that merely refined already existing technologies and, therefore, did little to alter the range of strategic opportunities, unlike the development of microwave-transmission technology.

Not only does extraordinary innovation tend to create pressure for change, it appears to do so in ways that often foster market competition. The advent of microwave technology enabled actors to create competitive markets in telecommunications, as did trucking in meatpacking and minimills in steel. This is consistent with Dosi's (1984) prediction that when extraordinary innovation occurs, it tends to induce competition as many actors try to pursue the new technological path and take advantage of new commercial opportunities. However, he also suggested that once the new technology becomes firmly established, normal innovation becomes the typical pattern, and oligopoly tends to emerge as some firms begin to internalize the process of technology development, thereby constructing barriers to entry, a process that is similar to that which Markusen (1985) described, and that we summarized earlier. This was precisely the purpose of AT&T's research-and-development strategy, where the company spent tremendous sums of money to stay at the forefront of technological development in telecommunications, and patented its innovations to create barriers to entry that contributed to the development and reinforcement of its monopoly position. In fact, as this case suggests, actors may use normal innovation more generally as a strategy to stabilize the already existing governance regime. In the nuclear sector, a variety of normal safety innovations, such as those developed during the 1970s in response to the public outcry over inadequate emergency systems, appear to have been devised, at least in part, to stabilize a politically volatile situation that threatened to disrupt the current regime. Thus, extraordinary innovation tends to generate pressures for new governance regimes and normal innovation tends to help actors adjust to changes in their sector's political economic environment in ways that help them stabilize or reinforce already established regimes.[18]

Of course, it is difficult to determine *in advance* whether an innovation will be extraordinary or not. This problem was another reason why AT&T pursued its aggressive policy of developing and patenting as many innovations as it could. If the corporation discovered a potentially extraordinary innovation, AT&T's patent would prevent another firm from using the technology to challenge the existing monopoly. Thus, this is an example that also suggests that powerful actors, endowed with substantial resources, are often able to control the range of technologically determined strategies that are available to others.

In addition to these change-inducing and adjustment-inducing influences, technology also seems to provide certain background conditions that help us anticipate how different sectors are likely to be organized. Our cases indicate that actors in sectors that are based on expensive, mass-production or process technologies tend to form governance regimes that are dominated largely by hierarchies, such as occurred in railroads, steel, automobiles, and nuclear energy, a finding consistent with much of the literature (e.g., Chandler 1977; Caves 1980; Stinchcombe 1983), and discussed by Rogers Hollingsworth in Chapter 2. When the large capital requirements for adopting expensive technologies are not met easily by single firms, actors also appear to form obligational networks. Examples include the joint ventures among utility companies who sought to build nuclear plants together after investment capital became more expensive in the early 1970s, and the joint venture between the Bell System and the Morgan banking interests during the early 1900s that provided the capital Bell needed to buy out independent telephone operators, obtain telegraph technology, and initiate its research-and-development program. The Morgan–Bell network dissolved after the Bell company turned to public stock offerings as an alternative source of finance capital. However, when the new technologies involved are less expensive relative to the old ones, as they were in microwave communications and minimills, or when they are craft-based, as they were in dairying, which, until recently, was based on relatively

18 This argument is consistent with recent work in economics on long waves and macroeconomic development, where it is argued that fundamental breakthroughs in technology, such as the invention of the steam engine, the automobile and low-cost petroleum products, and, most recently, microelectronics have triggered long-term swings in economic performance. For reviews of this literature, see Freeman (1984, 1986). We do not address this literature here because it dwells on the relationships between technological innovation and macroeconomic performance, and gives only very limited attention to how technological innovation affects the institutional structure of the economy, although there are some exceptions (e.g., Perez 1986).

small farms, corporate hierarchies appear less likely to emerge than either market competition (steel, telecommunications) or perhaps multilateral forms of governance (dairy).

Finally, although an elaborate discussion is well beyond the scope of this chapter, our case studies shed some light on one of the fundamental disagreements about economic change that continues to rage between orthodox and institutional economics. The orthodox school treats the development of technology, as well as the possibilities and constraints it poses for the economy, as a phenomenon that is exogenous to the economic system and, therefore, as something that economists do not have to explain in order to develop a theory of economic change. Institutionalists maintain just the opposite: technological change is endogenous to the economy and requires explanation if we are to construct such a theory.[19] On the one hand, we have seen that some important technological innovations occurred outside of the sectors that were eventually affected. The development of truck transport, a technology that helped transform the meatpacking sector, had little to do with anyone connected directly with this sector. On the other hand, a vast proportion of the technology improvements that occurred in the telecommunications sector were the deliberate work of AT&T as part of its patent wall strategy. The selection and refinement of the light-water reactor as the nuclear sector's technological cornerstone was largely due to the military and political interests of Congress, and the financial interests of a few large manufacturers who already had a stake in this technology. In both cases, technological innovation did not spring magically from the heads of independent entrepreneurs as Markusen implies. Nor was it developed because it was believed to be the most administratively or technologically efficient way to proceed. Instead, these innovations were primarily the result of a search for greater political and/or economic power by actors who *already* played substantial roles in economic governance, and who sought to institutionally reinforce them through further techno-logical development. So, in addition to lending some support to the insti-tutionalist position on the origins of technological pressures for change, these examples also suggest the need for an analysis of struggles for power.[20]

Power and control

In addition to technological developments and problems of economic ef-ficiency, the interests of actors to increase or maintain their power over

19 For elaborations of this criticism of orthodox economics, see especially Hodgson (1988: 12–21), but also Elliott (1984) and Stevenson (1987).
20 For further discussion about how technology is developed to maintain or increase power, rather than efficiency, see David Noble (1977) and Katherine Stone (1981).

each other, and their control over critical resources and information often constituted pressures for change in many of our case studies. Steel manufacturers, for example, integrated backwards into coal mining during the 1800s to discourage others from entering the steel manufacturing business, as well as to guard against the opportunism of mining companies. In the dairy sector, milk distributors, seeking to augment their already considerable power to force prices on dairy farmers, established urban milk exchanges and monitoring networks through which they banded together to set the purchase price of milk without input from farmers. In telecommunications, the Bell company granted certain local companies exclusive rights to use its technology in specific geographical areas in exchange for which the companies relinquished eventually all of their stock to Bell and agreed not to interconnect with other independent operators. This was a deliberate attempt by Bell to increase its control over these firms, and a strategy that contributed to the eventual development of a single corporate hierarchy in the sector.

In response to offensive drives for power, such as these, actors often took defensive steps, selecting *reactive strategies* that led to the further transformation of governance. Most obviously, workers in the railroad, steel, meatpacking, and automobile sectors tried to counteract the power of large corporate hierarchies by creating unions. When they succeeded, union-based wage bargaining and long-term labor contracts replaced competitive labor markets as the mechanism for setting wages. In turn, corporations themselves occasionally banded together to deal with organized labor, as was the case in the steel sector, where they formed multiemployer bargaining groups to negotiate with the United Steelworkers. Similarly, dairy farmers formed cooperatives to deal from a position of collective strength with powerful milk distributors – a strategy to which distributors responded by creating their own associations. When AT&T tried to eliminate independent telephone companies by refusing to interconnect them with its long-distance lines during the late 1800s, the independents formed associations to counter these tactics. In the hospital sector, physicians fostered and supported such collective organizations as the American Hospital Association and the American Medical Association in order to defeat the movement for national health insurance, and to reinforce their own autonomy and control over the healthcare system. Finally, shippers who objected to the rate fixing of railroad companies formed associations to stop these practices. Indeed, in our case studies, when one group of actors sought to alter the balance of power or increase its control over resources through multilateral forms of governance, others who were threatened often responded in kind – an *evolutionary* process, noted by some sociologists (e.g., Aldrich 1979: 321; Useem 1984: Chap. 6; Offe and Wiesenthal 1985: 189), where strategic selections build upon each other in a serial fashion. As will be discussed shortly, the evolution of governance regimes in this manner is very much the result of an interactive process among different actors.

Two points are worth noting here. First, although we have seen that concerns about economic efficiency generated pressures for change in some cases, more often it was a concern about power and control that created this pressure, at least in part. This supports the position of scholars, such as Charles Perrow (1981, 1986), who argued that although efficiency considerations may lead occasionally to transformations, it is the desire of firms, and we would add other groups as well, to control markets, labor, and production that is most often the critical stimulus. Second, although much of this debate has been cast in terms of the conditions under which markets and hierarchies emerge, our data indicate that it is also relevant to the formation of multilateral forms of governance. In our cases, concerns with power and control triggered searches that led to the selection of multilateral forms of governance far more often than did concerns with economic efficiency. We have already reviewed several key examples where defensive reactions to power led to the creation of multilateral governance mechanisms, such as unions and associations.[21] Hence, it appears that analyses based on power are more useful generally than those based on efficiency, although not exclusively so, in explaining the development of pressures for change, regardless of whether the governance regime that emerges is dominated by multilateral or bilateral governance mechanisms.

Those who have argued for an analysis of governance transformations based on power, including Perrow, have focused on struggles among actors *within* sectors of the economy as the key source of pressures for change. Yet these are not the only conflicts over power that precipitate transformations, especially those leading to the formation of multilateral governance mechanisms. The same may occur when actors perceive that *outsiders* threaten their common interests. For example, foreign competition in the automobile sector led members to search for ways to improve their competitive position, particularly against the Japanese. Eventually, they selected promotional networks, including industry conferences and collaborative research and information exchanges among suppliers, manufacturers, and dealers. Similarly, in steel, the American Iron and Steel Institute organized industrywide research-and-development projects to help the sector compete more effectively against foreign imports. In meat-packing, as consumption of red meat declined nationally during the late 1970s and 1980s due to consumers turning to other products, such as poultry, trade associations assumed an increasingly important role in promoting

---

21 For further discussion about how associations often develop in response to market power, rather than considerations of economic efficiency, see Schneiberg and Hollingsworth (1990).

the sector's products. In all of these cases, threats of product substitution, either from foreign competition or other sectors, caused actors to realize and defend their common interests. This is consistent with those who have argued that multilateral forms of governance are more likely to appear when the primary interests of actors are homogenous (e.g., Aldrich 1979: 319–21), and when actors are bound up in relationships with each other that are marked by what Jeffrey Pfeffer (1987) called commensalistic interdependence – a structural relationship among organizations that is derived from their mutual dependence on the same resources. Indeed, what better way to sensitize actors within a sector to their common interests than to threaten, through foreign competition or product substitution, the most critical resource that they share: the total pool of available customers for the finished product.

What most distinguishes the power and control tradition from the economic-efficiency and technological-development models is that in addition to helping us understand the origins of pressures for change, the power and control view also provides insights about the selection process. As noted earlier, the relative resource and power endowments of actors *mediate* the selection process by affording more richly endowed actors with greater capacities to implement the governance mechanisms of their choice. For example, although the Carter White House selected a corporatist strategy to rejuvenate the ailing steel industry in the late 1970s, a scheme that would have led to a multilateral governance regime, large steel manufacturers and organized steelworkers opposed the plan, for different reasons, and were powerful enough politically to block the Carter initiative. Similarly, although independent telephone companies during the late 1800s organized associations in an attempt to counter the coercive tactics of AT&T, the associations were short-lived because AT&T had enough resources to undermine their effectiveness by buying out some of the members, and because the state invoked antitrust and other policies that further crippled their operation. Hence, the power and resources of other actors prevented the development of effective associative behavior among the independents. In railroads, the substantial political strength of farmers who were opposed to railroad pools and associations around the turn of the century contributed to the failure of these forms of governance, in part by helping to persuade federal officials that state, not private, railroad regulation was necessary. Finally, in telecommunications, the Bell company was able, through its possession of patents, to license technology to local companies for building and operating telephone exchanges during the late nineteenth century, thus establishing hundreds of obligational networks around the country that enabled the Bell System to shift much of the risk and capital costs in establishing local telephone service on to these smaller and less-powerful companies.

A second way in which the power and control tradition sheds light on the selection process is by focusing on the *interactive and collective dynamics* that are involved. We have already examined the evolutionary nature of the selection process insofar as one actor's strategic choice often induces another's strategic response. Through repeated interactions, such as these, actors collectively construct new governance regimes through power struggles and coercion. Sometimes, however, selection is more of a bargaining process, as was the case in the dairy sector when, during the early twentieth century, the Federal Food Administration orchestrated corporatist-style price bargaining between dairy cooperatives and distributors, a new multilateral form of governance. At other times, selection is at least partially a matter of trial and error, such as when meatpackers first formed pools, then a holding company, and, finally, tacit price-fixing schemes to eliminate excessive price competition, although in this case, state power was also operating to the extent that government officials challenged the legality of the pools and the holding company.

Richard Nelson and Sidney Winter (1982) and others who have advocated that economic-efficiency models be supplemented, if not replaced, with evolutionary models of economic change have started to recognize that power and control models are useful for explaining not only pressures for change, but also the selection process that results. They have done so by arguing that the search for new economic arrangements often involves conflict *within* firms among people who are responsible for choosing organizational options.[22] Yet, as we have demonstrated, this is not enough. We must push beyond such microlevel organizational analysis and explore how conflicts *among* firms and other organizations within and beyond sectoral borders determine new governance regimes.

Culture

Although there are relatively few examples in our case studies that provide insights about the effects that culture and ideology (i.e., general systems of beliefs, norms, and values) have on governance transformations, we do find some that suggest that these factors constrain the selection process, facilitating or inhibiting the formation of different types of governance mechanisms, and helping to determine how effective and stable a new governance regime will be once it emerges. For example, steel executives formed what Christoph Scherrer described in Chapter 6 on steel as a "corpsgeist," that is, cooperative attitudes and collective understanding,

---

22 Insofar as Nelson and Winter recognize that conflict within organizations may help determine the course of organizational change, it is somewhat surprising that they express reservations about including an analysis of power in their models (e.g., Nelson and Winter 1982: 44). See Foster (1987: Chap. 7) for a macroeconomic argument in favor of evolutionary models that is very sympathetic to Nelson and Winter, but that includes an explicit analysis of power.

through the Gary dinners between 1907 and 1911, much as meatpackers developed a cooperative ideology through earlier pools and holding companies. Later, actors in these sectors were able to establish monitoring arrangements, particularly price-leading schemes, that operated successfully for years because they had already developed, through these earlier promotional networks, a familiarity with each other's practices and a sense of cooperation – a collective consciousness about what was best for their sectors. In dairying, immigrant farmers brought to the midwest European ideals of collectivism and cooperation that helped to shape an early dairy culture. This served as the ideological foundation upon which they later built dairy cooperatives. During the 1910s, the development of a promotional network of farmers, cooperatives, agricultural extension agencies, and land-grant universities throughout the region reinforced and contributed further to the articulation of the sector's long-term collective goals, which, in turn, helped farmers to form associations of dairy cooperatives during the 1920s in response to a variety of economic problems. Furthermore, the Grange movement of the 1870s cultivated a collective militancy among midwestern farmers that also served dairymen who sought to found cooperatives and associations.

These cases stand in stark contrast to the railroad sector, where actors formed pools and associations to control cutthroat price competition, scheduling, and other collective economic problems, but where such multilateral governance failed in part because members could not resist the temptations of short-term, individual gains that could be won by betraying their collective commitments. These temptations might have been tempered had there been a stronger cooperative ideology among railroad executives. Yet, apparently there was not, even though the federal government passed legislation in 1866 that encouraged the formation of these multilateral forms of governance.

As noted earlier, Granovetter (1985) argued that actors are likely to create successful obligational networks instead of hierarchies, if transacting parties have well-established, trusting relationships with each other, thus reducing the need for actors to control opportunism and malfeasance with administrative controls. Our data suggest that we can extend his argument to multilateral forms of governance insofar as they may also serve as an alternative to hierarchy, if cultural and other conditions are right. Ironically, support for this proposition comes from the meatpacking and railroad sectors, two cases where hierarchies *replaced* pools and associations, but for different reasons. In meatpacking, where economic activity was embedded in a milieu of familiarity and cooperation, multilateral governance enabled actors to effectively control the difficulties associated with excessive market competition until the state forbade it, largely through antitrust policies. As a result, actors created hierarchies to resolve these sectoral problems. On the other hand, in railroads, although the state tried to promote these multilateral mechanisms, at least until the late nineteenth century, rampant individualism, the antithesis of a cooperative ideology, undermined the project. Given the differences in cultural context, had the state not interfered, multilateral governance might have succeeded in meat-packing; but without even stronger doses of political support, it was still probably doomed to failure in railroads. Thus, these cases substantiate the claim of Piore and Sabel (1984: 255–65), and others, that multilateral forms of governance generally require a sense of community, common background, or other ideological or cultural adhesives to sustain them.[23]

Yet these examples also suggest that culture and ideologies are not free-floating, but institutionally based systems of beliefs. The dairy culture, for instance, was nourished in the United States through an elaborate institutional network of private and public organizations. It seems, then, that William Domhoff (1974) was correct when he argued that the development of class consciousness, and we would add all consciousness that contributes to governance transformations, is facilitated by institutions that contribute to the production and reproduction of culture and ideology, an idea that has been echoed recently by other scholars from different theoretical traditions that are critical of orthodox economic models of transformation insofar as these models provide no room for cultural influences (e.g., Foster 1987; Etzioni 1988). The more important point, however, is that the effects of institutions and culture are reciprocal. That is, a current governance regime may facilitate the development of an ideological and cultural milieu that contributes to governance transformations later, as was the case when the dairy sector's promotional network supported a dairy culture that, in turn, helped foster the collective consciousness that was central to the formation of associations of dairy cooperatives. Unfortunately, our case studies do not provide enough data to pursue this point further.

Nevertheless, all of this sheds light on arguments that have been critical of culturally based explanations of governance transformations, such as those posed by Gary Hamilton and Nicole Biggart (1988), who argued that cultural explanations of institutional change in East Asian economies were unconvincing because, although the entire region's culture was fairly homogenous and static, the variations in governance regimes, both historically and cross-nationally, that emerged within the region after the Second World War were substantial. Their analysis was insightful in many ways. However, our data indicate that one must move very cautiously when

---

23 We are not claiming that such cultural support is always *sufficient* to foster and sustain multilateral forms of governance, just that it often appears to be necessary. We have already noted that there is a substantial body of literature that suggests that political support from the state is also usually important (e.g., Streeck and Schmitter 1985), as these cases illustrate. Similarly, Weiss (1988: 202) suggested that although culture may have some effect, the more important determinant in facilitating the development of networks is the state.

attributing a general set of cultural or ideological traits to regions or national economies, something that critics as well as proponents (e.g., Crozier 1964) of cultural explanations have often failed to do. Our cases reveal tremendous cultural and ideological variation across sectors within the U.S. economy. Furthermore, we have seen that these features tended to change, often in an evolutionary manner, as they did in steel, where a cooperative ideology developed gradually through repeated interactions among steel executives. In short, if one recognizes that culture is heterogeneous and dynamic at the sectoral level, then there may be a more significant role for cultural explanations in the analysis of governance transformations than critics have been willing to admit.[24]

However, we must also recognize that in our examples, cultural and ideological factors did not serve as pressures for change that triggered the selection process, as other factors did. Nor did they determine in any immediate or direct sense the new governance regimes that actors selected. This was largely a matter of the interactive selection processes that we described earlier. Instead, where they could be clearly identified, cultural factors served a much more subtle and indirect role insofar as they provided a social context within which the selection process occurred. In other words, they helped to define the *range* of available governance mechanisms from which actors might choose, and influenced the *probabilities* that actors would institutionalize their choices on a relatively permanent basis and use these mechanisms successfully. This latter point is an important one to the extent that emergent governance regimes that were clearly inconsistent with surrounding cultural and ideological parameters were often ineffective in helping actors solve the problems for which they devised new regimes. As a result, these regimes were short-lived. This is what happened in railroads, where associations proved to be only transitional forms of governance that preceded other more permanent ones because they conflicted with the politically dominant laissez-faire ideology of the time, expressed in antitrust policy. Of course, this raises again the issue of the state's role in the selection process.[25]

State policy

We have referred repeatedly to the many ways in which the state influenced governance transformations in our cases. Although we have reserved a thorough discussion of these influences until the next chapter, it is worth

24 Biggart seems to have recognized this point more recently and has tried to build a normative element into her analysis of the formation of different types of markets (e.g., Abolafia and Biggart 1989).

25 The state is very important in this regard because it both helps to define the politically dominant ideologies, and plays a very important role in ratifying, or refusing to ratify, new governance regimes. We defer further discussion of these issues until Chapter 12.

sketching, however briefly, the major aspects of the state's roles in order to highlight their complexity and to round out the preceding discussion.

Perhaps more than any of the other factors discussed here, the state is capable of influencing governance transformations throughout the entire transformation process. First, state actors may devise policy that creates *pressures for change* either intentionally or unintentionally. In the former category, we have seen how policy makers deliberately manipulated antitrust laws in the dairy, steel, railroad, meatpacking, and telecommunications sectors to either facilitate or break up corporate hierarchies, promotional networks, and associations. In the latter category, the passage of Medicare legislation helped to spawn indirectly the development of capital markets in the hospital sector.

A second way the state influences governance transformations is by facilitating the *selection* of a new governance regime once pressures for change have materialized. Sometimes state actors select policies specifically designed to solve problems for a sector, such as when federal regulators passed beef-grading regulations during the 1920s that increased the amount of information about beef quality that was available to consumers, thus helping inadvertently to create competitive markets in the meatpacking sector. At other times, the state sustains or alters the balance of power among actors, as was the case during the 1920s when the Federal Food Administration protected fledgling dairy cooperatives from antitrust prosecution, and orchestrated producer–distributor price bargaining throughout the sector. At other times, the state's influence is much more subtle as its legal principles and institutionalized procedures constrain the selections of other actors. In the automobile sector, for instance, right-to-work laws in the south helped to keep labor costs low for southern parts suppliers, a situation that encouraged automobile manufacturers, who were looking for ways to reduce costs during the 1970s and 1980s, to reduce the level of vertical integration in their operations by establishing just-in-time subcontracting arrangements with these suppliers. Finally, the state often helps to ratify and stabilize new governance regimes once they emerge. In telecommunications, for example, independent firms frequently challenged the Bell company's monopoly by asking the courts to determine whether Bell was entitled to control telephone technology through its patents. Judges generally sided with Bell, thereby legitimizing and further stabilizing the company's hierarchical domination within the sector.

Not only do our cases reveal that the state plays important roles throughout the transformation process, but that it does so with respect to the creation of all types of governance mechanisms. One of the most interesting of these involves the creation of markets. Much of the literature on governance transformations has focused on the conditions under which corporate hierarchies replace markets as the principal institution for coordinating transactions. A good deal of this literature implies that markets occur naturally or spontaneously, in the sense that actors do not deliberately plan or construct them in advance of actual transactions, and that the existence of markets precedes the development of hierarchies insofar as actors will begin to organize their activity through hierarchies only when extenuating circumstances arise that cause markets to breakdown.[26]

Yet our analysis of the state's role in governance transformations suggests that there is nothing natural or inevitable about the existence of markets, and that markets are not necessarily the precursors to all other forms of governance. Instead, we found that actors select and socially construct markets, just as they do other forms of governance. For example, although utility companies were reluctant to begin buying nuclear reactors for the commercial generation of electricity during the 1950s, Congress finally convinced them to do so by threatening to build government-owned nuclear plants that would compete with private utilities. In telecommunications, a series of regulatory rulings from the Federal Communications Commission and the courts between 1968 and 1982 led directly to the creation of competitive markets for long-distance telephone service where once there had been only the AT&T monopoly. Of course, we have already seen how state policy contributed to the formation of markets in meatpacking and hospitals. Brigitte Young suggests in Chapter 8 that the trend toward deregulation may help precipitate a shift away from associative forms of governance in the dairy sector toward an economy organized more through markets. In these examples, the state played an active role in helping to construct markets where there had never been commercial exchange to begin with (nuclear), or where alternative governance mechanisms had come to coordinate exchange (hospitals, meatpacking, telecommunications, dairy). Thus, we agree with Hodgson (1988: 210), who argued that "the onus is as much to explain the existence of the market as it is to explain the existence of the firm," and we would add other governance mechanisms as well. Indeed, as Polanyi (1944) suggested years ago, an analysis of the effects of state policy must be an integral part of these explanations, particularly insofar as they concern the social construction and maintenance of markets. Perhaps the reason why economists and others have tended to grant such a privileged status to markets in the first place is that they have systematically ignored the empirical effects of po-

---

26 For examples of those who create this impression, see Williamson (1975, 1985) and Chandler (1977). For recent criticisms, see Lazonick (1986) and Hodgson (1988: Chaps. 8–9). The most extreme form of this argument is perhaps that offered by Armen Alchian and Harold Demsetz (1972), who argued that, contrary to conventional wisdom, the firm does not settle issues through authority, fiat, or disciplinary actions in ways that are much different from the market. Hence, they suggest that the firm is actually a special sort of market, and tended to imply, therefore, that markets are everywhere.

litical and other social processes by which actors have selected markets historically – an omission that our case studies help to correct.[27]

To summarize briefly, we have demonstrated that the insights of all five theoretical views of governance transformation are valuable, although in different ways, for developing a more comprehensive, evolutionary model of the transformation process. We have done this by showing the extent to which each view is particularly relevant for explaining how the selection process proceeds at *different stages* of our evolutionary model. Most perspectives helped us to identify the origins of pressures for change. Theories that emphasize the importance of power and control, as well as the state, were especially useful for understanding how actors collectively produce new governance regimes by blending their individually selected strategies in complex ways. Those that stress cultural and political factors provided important clues for understanding how emergent regimes are stabilized and become durable. In addition, we have shown that the new evolutionary model conforms in many ways to the empirical stories of our case studies.

As a result, it is clear that exclusively economic arguments about governance transformation, including the so-called new institutionalism, offered by Williamson and his followers, are myopic to the point of reductionism. Without an analysis of politics, technology, culture, and other social factors, one cannot arrive at a solid theoretical understanding of the governance transformation process. Yet we are not trying to *replace* economic analyses of this phenomenon with other forms of social analysis. To do so would be to engage in the same sort of intellectual imperialism for which economists have recently been accused. Rather, we suggest that a far more eclectic approach is required, one that squares well in this regard with the socioeconomics that scholars have recently proposed, and one that refuses to reduce governance transformations to any narrowly focused category of variables.[28] However, it would be a mistake to simply search for an assortment of economic, political, technological, and other variables that seem to trigger transformations. Although insights may be gained from such an exercise, as Hollingsworth demonstrated in Chapter 2, we concur

27 Even those who seem to have fallen into the same trap as Alchian and Demsetz (1972), that is, suggesting that markets are more or less everywhere (see note 26), have, nevertheless, recognized recently that it is incorrect to argue that markets are naturally occurring phenomena. For example, Abolafia and Biggart (1989) suggest that such diverse forms of governance as the Chicago Board of Trade, Japanese business groups, and direct sales organizations, all of which they consider to be markets, were created deliberately through a complex variety of social forces, often including political struggle. Coase (1988: 8–9), an early proponent of transaction-cost economics, a school that often leaves the impression that markets are naturally occurring precursors to other forms of governance, has also recognized recently how political forces often play important roles in the deliberate planning and social construction of markets.

28 See, for example, Etzioni (1988). The danger with such an approach, as Etzioni (1988: 15–16) noted, is that breadth of focus is often achieved at the expense of depth.

with Nelson and Winter (1982), who argued that the key to understanding economic transformations is an analysis of the search process. Indeed, the evolutionary model we have developed gives pride of place to the processes through which actors select new governance regimes. Without such an analysis, governance transformations will appear to be knee-jerk reactions to various constellations of independent variables, and explanations will lack much appreciation or insight as to the causal mechanisms that are involved.

TRAJECTORIES OF CAPITALIST DEVELOPMENT

Our discussion of governance transformations bears directly on debates about the long-term institutional development of advanced capitalism. During the 1950s and 1960s, both liberals and Marxists argued, for different reasons, that the imperatives of economic and technological rationality were propelling all capitalist societies toward a common institutional structure, characterized by large firms, concentrated industries, and mass-production technology (e.g., Baran and Sweezy 1966; Galbraith 1967). Later, critics, who were concerned with explaining the presence of industries and parts of industries consisting more of craft-based production and small firms than of colossal corporate hierarchies, argued that these *convergence* theories had grossly overstated the case. They offered theories of *dualism* instead, which suggested, for example, that more traditionally organized sectors persisted because large modern firms often sought to avoid a variety of labor problems and restrictive regulations that were commonly associated with modernization, and because volatile market demand occasionally required the flexibility in production that more traditional institutional arrangements offered (e.g., Berger and Piore 1980; Goldthorpe 1984).[29]

The evidence reported before supports the dualism thesis to the extent that we have found some sectors, such as automobiles, telecommunications, steel, and meatpacking, that are hierarchically organized and highly concentrated, whereas others retain a more decentralized, traditional structure, such as dairying, where relatively small farms still conduct most production. We also find evidence for dualism insofar as parts of the production process *within* some sectors are organized increasingly in a rela-

---

29 Goldthorpe (1984: 317) suggested that one reason why proponents of convergence theory had neglected the importance of traditionally organized pockets of capitalism was that they were writing during the 1950s and 1960s, a period of economic prosperity that did not experience the problems associated with the stagflation of the 1970s – problems that gave rise to the dualist tendencies he documented. Hence, their perspective was limited historically. We would add that convergence theory also tended to pursue a relatively economistic analysis, much at odds with the multidimensional view offered here, and that this, for reasons developed in what follows, contributed to the shortcomings of which Goldthorpe and others spoke.

tively decentralized fashion. Subcontracting to small firms has been rejuvenated in automobile manufacturing, and minimills have developed in steel – two sectors where one would expect the highest levels of hierarchically organized mass production, particularly in light of Chandler's (1977) argument that mass-produced consumer and producer goods bring forth corporate hierarchies. Furthermore, we have seen that in steel and automobiles, managers selected eventually less-hierarchical forms of governance to avoid, at least in part, the costs and problems associated with unionized labor, environmental regulations, and to respond more quickly to changing demand in the marketplace – factors routinely offered to explain dualism.

However, scholars who are interested in production systems based on flexible specialization and diversified quality production have identified recently several problems with the dualism thesis.[30] For example, Linda Weiss (1988: Chap. 1) criticized adherents to the dualist perspective for adopting an overly society-centered view insofar as they generally attribute dualism to problems and imperatives that stem from civil society – a perspective that systematically neglects how the state, confronting geopolitical and international economic crises, often deliberately promotes different institutional configurations within the economy. She also maintained that dualism tends to slip into functionalist and, at worst, teleological explanations when theorists claim that the traditional sector persists because it serves the needs of large-scale capitalism, such as controlling the demands of organized workers or providing certain special machinery for other mass-production firms, and that such needs and, therefore, traditional sectors develop as inevitably as does large-scale capitalism itself. Recognizing that the state plays an important and autonomous role in helping to determine the institutional forms that capitalism assumes, and rejecting functionalist explanations, she concluded that the process of capitalist development is inherently neutral to the extent that there is no preordained form that will necessarily emerge. Although Weiss cast her argument primarily in terms of the development of flexible specialization in Northern Italy, others, examining a wider range of cases, made similar arguments. Charles Sabel (1989) and Wolfgang Streeck (1989), for instance, also suggested that the

---

30 By flexible specialization, we mean production that utilizes flexible-purpose machines and skilled workers to manufacture special or customized products, a form of production that is quite the opposite of mass production in this sense (e.g., Piore and Sabel 1984). Scholars who prefer the term diversified quality production (e.g., Streeck 1989) refer to the same form of production, but stress that its development may occur gradually through either cooperation among artisanal firms or the decentralization of large hierarchical firms; that this is not a new phenomenon historically in some national economies, such as West Germany; and, thus, that its discovery by scholars does not represent a radically new set of opportunities for organizing industry, as the flexible-specialization literature often suggests.

state plays an important role in fostering or inhibiting the development of different types of production; that firms develop flexible specialization and diversified quality production for a variety of reasons, not just to control or more efficiently exploit labor; and that because the interactions among labor, capital, and the state determine (we would say select) the course of capitalist development, certain structural conditions do not inevitably determine this course through teleological or functionalist processes.[31]

We find some support for this position. First, we have already discussed many cases where the state was responsible for the creation of all sorts of governance arrangements, although not always for reasons having to do with war, economic crises, or the preservation of national security. Society-centered views, as implied before, are often inadequate by themselves. Yet Weiss overstates her case to the extent that she would apparently *abandon* these explanations in favor of a completely state-centered approach. We advocate a more balanced position between these two extremes, as do Sabel and Streeck. After all, we have also seen cases where the state had very little to do with transformations. (Indeed, we see no reason a priori why either perspective must necessarily take precedence over the other with respect to explaining governance transformations.) In addition, as suggested before, the state plays a much more complex set of roles in the transformation process than Weiss recognized – roles that include not only creating pressures for change, the primary thrust of her analysis, but also facilitating in complex ways the selection process. Second, our cases support the claim that there does not appear to be an inherently teleological momentum to the development of capitalism where sectors evolve toward a common governance arrangement, dualist or otherwise. There is simply too much diversity in the examples that we have explored to support such a position. Furthermore, if one takes seriously the proposition that the selection process is largely a collective interaction among many actors, struggling and bargaining with each other, and that the outcomes of these struggles and bargains are never guaranteed in advance, then teleological arguments are even more difficult to sustain.

Weiss (1988: 6) argued that dualist theories tend to fall into the same trap as the convergence theories that they attack, that is, to argue that traditional sectors survive because they are needed to support large-scale capitalism requires an assumption about the inevitability and general direction of economic development in the first place. The same could be said about recent studies that suggest that advanced capitalist societies are

---

31 Weiss's critique of dualism, although insightful in many respects, tends to go a bit overboard. First, some of the dualist theories that Weiss targets are not as society-centered as she claims. Suzanne Berger (Berger and Piore 1980: 144), for example, recognizes the important role the state plays in perpetuating small-firm sectors. Second, although Weiss's concerns about functionalism are generally well-founded, there are exceptions. Again Berger (Berger and Piore 1980: 146–8) rejects functionalist logic.

undergoing a prolonged period of disorganization. For example, in a fascinating and insightful study of five advanced capitalist nations, including the United States, Scott Lash and John Urry (1987) argued that during the late nineteenth and early twentieth centuries, these societies moved through a period of increasing organization, characterized by high levels of union density, industrial concentration, trade association activity, state centralization, and the strengthening of class-based political parties, but that since the Second World War, many of these patterns have started to be reversed. Thus, we are witnessing, they claimed, the end of organized capitalism. However, the disorganization that Lash and Urry saw transpiring across national political economies is much less uniform *within* these societies, at least within the United States. On the one hand, we have seen a degree of disorganization, or at least reorganization in a decentralized and less formally organized direction, with the development of minimills in steel, just-in-time subcontracting in automobiles, increasing competition in meatpacking, and declining union strength in all three – evidence that tends to confirm the disorganization thesis. Yet, on the other hand, automobile manufacturers organized promotional networks during the last twenty years to coordinate research and development aimed at solving engine emission and other industrywide problems, and trade associations became more, not less, active in meatpacking as the market for red meat dwindled. In addition, we have seen increasing levels of vertical and horizontal integration in the hospital sector due to the 1965 Medicare legislation, and a dramatic increase in associative governance in the nuclear sector due to the accident at Three Mile Island. Furthermore, there was a shift from associative to hierarchical governance in the California dairy industry – certainly a reorganization, but not disorganization because the decline in associative activity was accompanied by an increase in hierarchy. What we have, then, is a set of examples, albeit an admittedly small one, that illustrates the *uneven* and *multidirectional* character of institutional development within and across sectors in the United States, rather than a consistent process of disorganization.

The point is that many of the pitfalls that have marked these debates about the trajectory of capitalist development, including functionalist and teleological reasoning, excessively state- or society-centered explanations, and sweeping historical generalizations, could have been avoided if scholars adopted a sectoral analysis and employed an evolutionary theory of governance transformation, as we have, that theorized the causal mechanisms involved in the selection process. Others have also suggested the need for such a theory, but have offered little in the way of empirical evidence to substantiate their theoretical contributions (e.g., Nelson and Winter 1982; Foster 1987). We have started here to fill these gaps by arguing that actors respond to pressures for change by trying to select new governance regimes within a variety of limits, but that they do so in ways that often lead to the eventual transformation of these limits themselves. Thus, we have argued for a theory of governance transformation that neither overemphasizes the actor's free will nor succumbs to excessive institutional determinism. In short, we have offered a theory that takes very seriously Marx and Engels' (1970: 59) famous methodological dictum that "circumstances make men just as much as men make circumstances."

12

THE STATE AND THE ORGANIZATION OF ECONOMIC ACTIVITY

Leon N. Lindberg
Department of Political Science, University of Wisconsin–Madison

John L. Campbell
Department of Sociology, Harvard University

The analytic framework introduced in the previous chapter depicts governance regimes and governance transformations as the products of the strategic actions and institutional structures of private actors and the state.[1] This conception of how the state helps to *constitute* sectors in a national economy differs sharply from the conventional literature on state-economy relations. Economists and non-economists alike typically take the structure of the economy and the direction of economic development as given. In this view, states may help clear the way for accumulation, and distort, retard, or accelerate the accumulation process. But states do not decisively influence the *forms* of economic organization and coordination of economic activities. States may be more or less autonomous, and states may be weak or strong. But they are rarely seen as transformative in this sense (Weiss 1988). Even institutional political economists who have produced so much valuable theory and research on the causes of variations in the forms and effectiveness of state intervention have not come up with good predictions of the *forms of capitalism* that are likely to be promoted by state intervention (Weiss 1988).

The problem lies in the conception of state *intervention* into the economy and the focus of state literature on different types of intervention. The very notion of intervention perpetuates the imagery of a clear separation of state and economy where markets, for example, can, or at least did, once upon a time, exist in a truly laissez-faire condition, completely autonomous of the state's influence. Most orthodox economists, as we have seen, seem to assume this without question or at least treat it as a useful fiction.[2] Yet the historical record does not support this assumption (Polanyi 1944; Lazonick 1986: 2). Rather markets and other forms of economic governance are intimately linked to an ancillary set of institutions and the state (Hall 1986: Chap. 2). Even Oliver Williamson (1975, 1985), who

---

1 Portions of this chapter were published previously as "Property Rights and the Organization of Economic Activity by the State." *American Sociological Review* 5(5): 634–47, adapted by permission of the American Sociological Association.

2 Douglass North (1981) is an obvious exception to this characterization.

argued that alternative forms of economic governance are private responses to market failures, maintained that market transactions are contractually based, which means, we would add, that they are dependent on the state as a result. After all, it is the state that provides the legal framework within which contracts are written and upheld. As Linda Weiss (1988: 162) notes, "politics does not so much 'triumph' over economic forces. It enters into their overall configuration."

Fred Block (1987: 21–2) has suggested that rather than thinking about the state and the economy as potentially autonomous from each other, it is more fruitful to think of them as being permanently connected by a membrane that selectively permits the passage of resources and information back and forth. But of what does this membrane consist and how can we pinpoint the ways in which states help constitute the economy? In order to address these issues, we must specify the *types of policy actions* that are available to states and the *structural features of states* that come into play in governance transformations. The distinction between the state as an actor (or an ensemble of actors) and the state as a political–institutional structure is central to the analysis that follows.

THE STATE AS ACTOR AND AS STRUCTURE

As some of the state literature reminds us (e.g., Krasner 1978b; Stepan 1978; Skowronek 1982; Evans, Rueschemeyer, and Skocpol 1985), the state is comprised of many *actors,* who, for a variety of reasons, deliberately pursue policy options that may have the intended or unintended consequences of contributing to or blocking governance transformations. If we are thinking of the American state, the variety of state actors and the multiple levels at which they operate become a central focus of analysis. Whereas for much of American history, the federal state did not interact closely with the economy, subnational states (the "states" and local authorities) have been continuously involved in the constitution of sectors and industries since the colonial period (Handlin and Handlin 1969; Hughes 1977; Walsh 1978; Eisinger 1988). As important as the distinction between federal, state, and local levels is, the very special role of courts, judges, and the legal profession as distinctive actors in the history of the American economy must not be overlooked (Scheiber 1978, 1980a, 1980b, 1981; Shapiro 1986). For much of American history, the courts were the only state institution that could stand outside of political party domination and claim to perform an integrative statelike function. Courts determined the meaning and effect of laws passed by the legislature, shaped the boundaries of intergovernmental relations, invoked the state's prerogatives over the economy, and became the chief source of economic surveillance. The courts became the American surrogate for the administrative apparatus familiar in European states. Indeed, American judges have adopted a peculiarly aggressive posture toward substantive policy making and an exceptional governing role (Skowronek 1982).

Thus, when we speak of American state actors in the constitution of the economy, we must remember how active subnational governments have been and the distinctiveness of the courts' economic roles. To treat state agencies as important actors in the economy is not to take a position on the relative autonomy of the American state(s), that is, whether state actors have interests and goals of their own or whether state actors merely act on the interests and goals of dominant societal actors. There are ample examples of both in American history, as we will see. Although the pre-ponderant opinion of scholars is to see the American state as thoroughly penetrated, colonized, and dominated by societal interests, the importance of the courts and of legal doctrine, and of war and economic crisis clearly call for more nuanced conclusions. What will be interesting and important to do is to attempt to discern whether distinctive economic structural con-sequences flow from actions driven by "state interests" and those that emerge out of the play of societal interests. We return to this question later.

Important as state actions are in constituting the economy, we should not neglect the structural features of the state. We argue that state struc-tures have entered into the constitution of sectors of the American economy in three distinct ways: as an arena, as an organizational configuration, and as defining distinctive locations for economic activity. As an *arena,* state institutions provide differential access for various societal groups to influ-ence or penetrate the economic policy-making process. It is not necessary to embrace a pluralist theory of policy making to recognize that there are institutional opportunities (not necessarily equally distributed) for those outside the state to engage the policy process in ways that have pertinent effects on policy, including the obstruction of policy formation and imple-mentation, and therefore, governance transformation. In this sense, we follow Peter Gourevitch (1986: 28), who maintained that state structure is much like a prism through which the influence of societal actors is refracted. As a result, although state actors and dominant coalitions may strive for effective economic policy, including the reorganization of economic activ-ity, their efforts are undermined occasionally for structural reasons. Indeed, this condition is often attributed to the United States, particularly in com-parison to other advanced capitalist democracies (e.g., Shonfield 1965; Badaracco 1985).

Structurally speaking, the American state is also a *distinctive organiza-tional configuration* that is peculiarly predisposed to struggles within the state. The roles of the executive, legislature, and judiciary, of executive agencies and independent regulatory commissions, and of federal and state governments have always been and remain sharply contested in the United States. These struggles engage not only competing state actors but also societal interests seeking to capture or insulate parts of the state as a way of advancing a particular economic interest. Therefore, this institutionally fragmented state bears within it a structural propensity for stalemate and for instability that has borne heavily on processes of governance transformation in such sectors as railroads and telecommunications.

On both of these structural dimensions, one can trace a state building trajectory since the nineteenth century that reflects the sway of political competition, and class- and interest-based struggles. Thus, early struggles over economic development took place at a state level and often the balance of power favored agrarian interests. With time, the courts and state legislatures came to protect and promote enterprise and commerce, thereby releasing what Willard Hurst (1964) called "entrepreneurial energies." Defensive mobilizations by agrarian and labor interests in state legislatures were frustrated first by the courts and subsequently by the growing size of firms as their activities spread across state lines. Eventually, the focus of mobilization shifted to the national level as small businessmen, farmers, Progressive reformers, and labor took advantage of the intensive party competition of the time to press their case in Congress. Regulation of the railroads and antitrust legislation reflect this mobilization, but the federal structure of the state facilitated forum shopping, where sectors that were targets of either regulation at a state level or of court-enforced state and federal antitrust laws were able to secure more benign and predictable regulation from the executive branch and Congress. The 1910s through the 1930s saw rear-guard actions by the Supreme Court in defense of efficiency and laissez-faire, thus frustrating populist political mobilizations at both state and federal levels. World War I, the Depression, and World War II accelerated the centralization of power at the national level and the growth of the executive branch. Planning advocates in the federal government encouraged the organization of labor and farmers to establish a system of countervailing power vis-à-vis business that they hoped would foster corporatist-style industrial planning. The New Deal also saw extensive regulation of big business and finance and the creation of more sector-specific regulatory agencies. For a time, the Supreme Court relinquished authority to the executive branch in antitrust and regulatory matters, thus introducing a period in which the property rights of business could be made subject to government manipulation in the interests of other classes or clients of the New Deal. By the end of World War II, Congress had abolished many important New Deal agencies. The Pentagon assumed control of the Reconstruction Finance Corporations' (RFC) assets and the Small Business Association took over the RFC's remaining functions. The national state became a mass of fragmented agencies without unifying institutional mechanisms. The Pentagon and military–industrial complex became arguably the most powerful state actor in the economy with decided consequences for agrarian and labor interests. The early post–War period also marked an initial shift of economic resources toward the south and southwest. A new Pentagon-centered complex emerged linking military bureaucracies, southern and southwestern senators and congressmen, and business interests organized at a state level. Increased competition developed among states and communities to offer favorable investment opportunities through the manipulation of business, corporate, and labor law, tax policies, and the provision of publicly funded infrastructure projects. Through legislation, such as the Taft–Hartley Act, Congress further reinforced the power of conservative coalitions at the state level in the south and the west. Deregulation and continued efforts to subsidize business development in the 1970s and 1980s further demobilized populist interests and strengthened the hand of business against labor. The courts, particularly those presided over by Reagan Administration appointees, reasserted their autonomy and decisively shifted legal doctrine to benefit large corporations on efficiency grounds.

Besides *politically* constituting the economy as an arena reflecting societal forces and as organizational congeries reflecting intrastate struggles, the legal–constitutional structure of the American state has also *defined distinctive locations for economic activity* that shape the strategic choices and relative opportunities of economic actors in their mutual *economic* interactions. Here the federal character of the American state is again important. The existence of constitutionally separate levels of government and of fifty separate state governments has played an important role in the development of regionally distinct economies (Markusen 1985, 1987) as well as important regional cleavages in American politics (Bensel 1984; Sanders 1986).

Harry Scheiber (1978) noted the importance of mercantilist rivalries among the states in American economic history. The fact that labor law and much of incorporation, contract, and regulatory law has remained largely the province of state governments, for example, has permitted some states (notably in the south) to adopt policies that were more favorable to business than those in the north, thus facilitating the migration of industries from the north and upper midwest to the south in pursuit of cheaper labor and less-restrictive environmental regulations (e.g., Goodman 1979; Bluestone and Harrison 1982; Newman 1984). We will see that such opportunities have entered into governance transformations in the dairy, meat, steel and automobile sectors. Given the surge in the 1970s and 1980s in state and local economic development efforts (e.g., Eisinger 1988; Fosler 1988), there is every reason to anticipate that this impact of constitutional structure on economic structure will continue to play an important role in the American economy.

We have seen how the state constitutes the economy instrumentally as a set of actors, and structurally by providing political arenas and organizational configurations through which economic policy is made and deployed, and by defining the spaces within which economic activity occurs. But what types of policy tools does the state use to constitute the economy in these ways?

POLICY ACTIONS THAT CONSTITUTE THE ECONOMY

States decisively constitute the economy by directly or indirectly influencing the selection of governance regimes. Governance regimes arise from the strategic choices and relative power of economic actors. Hence, we must understand how state actions (or inactions) and state institutional forms may condition or structure the strategic choices and power positions of producers (and other economic actors) along the two dimensions of our governance mechanism typology, introduced in Chapter 1: the choice between formal and informal types of organization, and the choice of bilateral or multilateral forms of exchange. Two broad types of policy tools seem important in this regard: production and allocation of resources and information, and regulation of the behavior of parties to exchange through the manipulation and enforcement of property rights.

State agencies participate directly in the economy by providing or producing resources and information, and by manipulating the allocation of resources and information between the state and the economy and within the economy itself. Monetary, fiscal, and exchange-rate policies have these effects, but operate at a macrolevel, that is, they are not targeted at specific industries or sectors. Of more direct relevance to our concern with sectoral or industry-level governance are state procurement, subsidies, tariffs, state borrowing and provision of capital, and direct state investments in the production of education and training, research and development, and transportation and communications infrastructures. This type of policy tool has been the focus of much attention in the study of policy interventions by those who have argued that the state's capacity for intervening effectively into the economy depends largely on its ability to allocate resources, such as finance capital and technology (e.g., Katzenstein 1978; Zysman 1983; Thurow 1984; Skocpol 1985: 18; Cox 1986; Gourevitch 1986; Hall 1986). But for the most part, this work centers on the interaction between different organizational forms of state and civil society, on the one hand, and their effects on state policy and, in turn, economic performance, on the other. Most researchers have not examined how state policy affects the *institutional organization,* that is, the governance, of economic activity. We agree with Richard Samuels (1987) that too often state policy per se, rather than the transformation of economic institutions, has been the dependent variable in political economic research – a serious omission insofar as these transformations have profound and long-lasting consequences for the effectiveness of the state's economic policy and an industry's performance.

In his fine study of energy markets in Japan, Samuels is concerned with determining how state policy either reinforces or displaces the market as the institution primarily responsible for economic governance. Our governance mechanism typology allows us to relate state actions to two critical dimensions of institutional organization at a sectoral or industry level.

The second type of policy tool that influences the selection of governance regimes is one that has been important historically (Horwitz 1977; North 1981; Scheiber 1981), but that has received less sustained theoretical attention in the literature on economic policy and state intervention: the state's capacity to define, enforce, and redefine property rights, the rules which determine the conditions of ownership and control of the means of production.[3] Our understanding of property rights is different from that which is found generally. Property rights often are viewed as defining the relationship between an individual and a commodity, such that someone is said to own or control the means of production to some degree. Yet, for us, property rights also expresses a relationship among people insofar as one person's ownership and control often corresponds with another's absence of ownership and control.[4] Because property rights specify relations among people, not just between people and things, property rights also define the institutional basis of power relations in the processes of production, exchange, and accumulation. This conception of property rights is admittedly a broad one insofar as it incorporates regulatory policies whose effects are to alter rules and relationships of exchange that are rooted in the right to deploy certain kinds of control over property. For example,

---

3 Economists in the so-called new institutional history tradition, such as North, Demsetz, Ekelund, and Tollison, Field, and Libecamp, do explicitly analyze property rights as both dependent and independent variables, departing sharply from standard neoclassical practice. Property rights are defined as rules and laws "governing ownership of, use of, rights of access to, and rights of appropriation of resources, productive factors and output," and include "physical goods, productive factors, and intangible property such as knowledge, music, and specialized technique" (Caporaso 1989: 143). Changes in property rights are typically explained in terms of exogenous changes in endowments, preferences, and technology, with the underlying teleological assumption that efficiency drives the process. Power is rarely incorporated into the analysis and if the state enters in, it is as a producer of inefficient property rights (e.g., North, 1981). For an interesting discussion and critique of the new institutional history, see Caporaso (1989). For an explicit consideration of how states establish property rights, see Thomson and Krasner (1989). The economic theory of regulation (Posner 1974; Stigler 1975; Peltzman 1976) sees regulatory policies as property rights policies to the extent that they seek to limit entry into an industry or profession. Their basic proposition is that such policies are manipulated by economic actors seeking monopoly rents and that the state is "captured" by such interests in a conspiracy against economic efficiency and the public interest.

4 Our thinking here has been influenced by Geoffrey Hodgson's (1988: Chap. 7) extended criticism of the orthodox property rights school in economics. For a review of the orthodox literature, also see Bowles (1984).

labor laws limit or facilitate the power of workers to organize, and antitrust laws limit the exercise of monopoly ownership rights, as do entry and price regulations that are directed against oligopoly and monopoly. Hence, the ability to define and enforce property rights enables the state to determine social relations, and, therefore, the balance of power among a wide variety of economic actors within civil society.[5] It follows that political struggles among actors outside and within the state define property rights policies and that the outcomes of these struggles will vary over time and across sectors.

We do not want to convey the impression that the state always establishes property rights policies, or, for that matter, production and allocation policies, in a carefully conceived or planned manner. Often these actions are devised in an ad hoc and piecemeal fashion in response to particular problems and conflicts that develop in the economy. Nor are we suggesting that the state necessarily creates these policies autonomously from the influence of actors in civil society. Recent state theory suggests that the degree to which autonomy occurs is highly variable (e.g., Skocpol 1985; Block 1987; Samuels 1987), and we agree. In fact, we are making no claims about the state's autonomy in such matters. Our point is simply that state actors, not those in civil society, make the final decisions about which property rights and production and allocation policies to choose, if any – decisions that may well be forced upon them by circumstances in the economy that are beyond their control. Thus, we make no claims to having a theory of *why* the state structures or constitutes the economy. We want to understand the conditions under which the institutional structures of economic governance change, and the roles that the state plays in these transformations, so our focus is on *how* the state influences economic governance. Nevertheless, we will speculate here and there about why the state pursues the policy options that it does, as, for example, when we discuss the economic conditions associated with one or another pattern of state action.

To summarize, we have identified two broad types of policy tools through which state actors or state agencies may constitute the economy. States produce and allocate resources and information, and states define and enforce property rights. But exactly how do these types of policiy action systematically affect the strategic behavior and relative power of economic actors, and thereby the institutional organization of the economy or of economic sectors? We first consider how the state affects strategic choices

5 Neo-Marxists also recognize that state policy may affect property rights, but they tend to focus on the state's influence on the property rights of the capitalist class (e.g., Block 1987: 86). We are equally interested in exploring how the state affects the property rights of other classes and groups.

and relative power along the dimension of informal and formal organization, and then along the dimension of bilateral and multilateral exchange.[6] In so doing, we develop two typologies of state action. Coupled with our understanding of how the state constitutes the economy as both actor and structure, they provide the conceptual tools for analyzing governance transformations in our eight cases.

INFORMAL AND FORMAL ORGANIZATION

As we have seen, most of the literature that explores the transformation of markets into hierarchies relegates the state and state actors to a subordinate position, relative to economic and technological factors, as causes of governance transformations. Yet, many students of American economic and legal history have argued that state actions have, whether intentionally or not, contributed decisively to the generalized impulse to scale and concentration so typical of many sectors of the American economy. Government procurement, subsidies, charters, and borrowing were important stimuli. According to McCraw (1984), tariff policy, the most important policy of the nineteenth-century federal government, accelerated the development of domestic manufacturers in the decades spanning the Civil War. Combined with military demands of Civil War mobilization and the granting of special charters to corporations in order to raise private capital for infrastructure development, these state actions contributed to the decline of entrepreneurial firms and the emergence of large concentrated firms and sectors (see also Galambos and Pratt 1988). Many scholars have pointed to the propulsive effects of federal and state subsidization of the railroads in promoting concentration and laying the foundations for mass-production industry in the United States (Solo 1974; Piore and Sabel 1984; Weiss 1988). Infrastructure investments, such as this, in noncollective or privately appropriable goods played an important part in the nation's early economic development.

Mobilization for World Wars I and II seems to have further reinforced the trend toward economic concentration (away from markets and most forms of obligational networks). Much of the money spent by the War Production Board, the Office of War Mobilization, the RFC, and the military bureaucracies went to the largest firms, such as General Motors, Ford, Alcoa, and U.S. Steel, in the oligopoly, core sectors of the economy (Hooks forthcoming). More competitive, peripheral industries, such as aircraft, shipbuilding, and electronics, also received massive public investments in the war effort, again through the largest firms (Markusen, 1987: Chaps. 5–6; Hooks forthcoming). In the post–World War II demo-

---

6 For a more detailed historical account of how the economy developed generally along these dimensions, see Chapter 2.

bilization, the federal government sold its vast military production facilities to war contractors at very low prices. Using profits earned from sales to the military, the largest firms were able to purchase the most efficient industrial plants in the country, reinforcing their dominant positions in both core and peripheral sectors. In conjunction with the federal government's earlier procurement policies, these sales were the culmination of a massive double subsidy that helped transform the organizational terrain of several important economic sectors by reinforcing oligopolies, such as in steel, where the state spent $770 million on steel plants during the war (Markusen 1985: 83). Continued heavy spending by the much expanded Pentagon bureaucracy in the post–War years led to a quasipermanent link between a new and powerful state actor and dependent sectors or industries, further generalizing the economywide trend toward scale and concentration.

Property rights and regulatory policies seem to have pushed in the same direction. State legislatures and the courts often defined property rights in ways that spawned economic development and the rise of big enterprises (Hurst 1960, 1977; Horwitz 1977; Scheiber 1980b: 1166). State legislatures between 1830 and the 1880s chartered business corporations by the thousands, and eventually passed general incorporation acts that limited entrepreneurial risk and liability (Keller 1981: 57; Hurst 1982: 127). For example, in response to court decisions in New Jersey that had questioned the legality of recently favored trusts, the state legislature adopted laws of incorporation that fostered the rise of big enterprises, mergers, and combinations by permitting firms that were incorporated there to hold stock in both local companies and those beyond its borders, a policy that several other states later adopted (Sanders 1986: 153). Thus, as one prominent legal scholar concluded, laws of incorporation "substantially reduced the volume and importance of resource allocation accomplished wholly by market bargaining, and increased allocations made through the discipline of private organizations" (Hurst 1982: 50).

Morton Horwitz (1977) emphasized the ways in which the legal system, lawyers and the legal profession, and courts and judges contributed to the transformation of the economy in the first half of the nineteenth century. Judges and policy makers in state governments who supported economic development gave enormous assistance to the early development of the American business system, thereby facilitating monopolies, trusts, overinvestment in railroads, and the accumulation of vast fortunes that helped produce oligarchical organization in the rest of the economy. Horwitz stressed the role of private law rather than constitutional law, that is, the judicial promulgation of common law rules in the areas of torts, contracts, property, labor, and corporate law, as the more important vantage point for understanding how law, economics, and society intersected in the United States. Scheiber and Hurst confirmed much of this picture for the post–Civil War period. Hurst showed how law and the courts helped release entrepreneurial energy by favoring what he called dynamic property over static vested rights (Hurst 1964). Scheiber (1981) stressed how property rights have been defined and redefined by legislatures and courts to help stimulate economic development by favoring new technologies and new forms of entrepreneurial organization. He concluded that "the wonderful abstraction called the 'market' had structure and distribution of advantage defined in large part by conscious political decision-making, the investment of public funds, and the shifting purposive allocation of property rights and privileges" (Scheiber 1981: 104).

Other scholars have documented the relationship between the economic regulatory policies and Supreme Court decisions of the late nineteenth and early twentieth centuries and how they facilitated the development of scale and concentration (e.g., Kolko 1963; Solo 1974; Stigler 1975). McCraw (1984, 1986) has argued that, ironically, antitrust law and enforcement also had the same effects. Indeed, he saw antitrust policy as a very successful, if inadvertent, industrial policy that gave an enormous boost to horizontal and vertical integration. The Sherman Act, he pointed out, was a reaction to the trust movement of the 1870s and 1880s, which itself was a product of high tariffs and internal improvements due to infrastructure building policies. But as implemented, antitrust targeted mainly associations of small businessmen and peripheral firms and industries. Large firms and sectors were able to pursue policies of horizontal and vertical integration, thus avoiding direct violation of the antitrust statutes as interpreted by the courts. Martin Shapiro (1986) made a similar argument about the role of the court in recent decades in legitimizing various forms of concentration on efficiency grounds.

This is not to say that all state actions favor the development of industrial strategies that culminate in hierarchical governance. For example, subsidies for research and development, targeted at small firms, infrastructure investment in collective or publicly appropriable goods, such as general education, and legal protections for parts suppliers, subcontractors, and labor have facilitated and supported less formally organized forms of governance, notably markets. Yet the tendency for state action to favor economic concentration and formally organized governance is unmistakable.

To summarize, there is reason to doubt the axiomatic view of so many American economists that the organizational structure and economic performance of the nineteenth- and early twentieth-century American economy can be attributed to the *absence* of significant government interventions. Governments at local, state, and federal levels have contributed through production and allocation and through property rights actions to economic development in ways that were not neutral in terms of either the organizational strategies preferred by economic actors or the relative power positions of small and large firms as well as producers and

Table 12.1. *State actions that constitute the economy: Informal to formal*

Type of policy tool	Type of organizational strategy favored	
	Informal	Formal
Provision and allocation of information and resources	• R&D targeted to small firms • Infrastructure investment in *collective* goods (i.e., education)	• Tariffs • Infrastructure investment in *noncollective* goods (i.e., railroad subsidies) • Defense spending and war mobilization
Property rights and the regulation of the behavior of parties to exchange	• Legal protection for parts suppliers, subcontractors, and labor	• Law facilitating business incorporation and other private law (i.e., tort, contract, corporate) • Antitrust and merger policy • Regulatory policy

suppliers. We have summarized these general points in Table 12.1 in the form of a typology of state actions that constitute the economy by favoring one or another form of organizational strategy. Before using this typology and the historical background on which it is based to analyze the governance transformations that are chronicled in our case studies, we must explain how state actions have affected the strategic choices of economic actors to organize exchange through bilateral or multilateral exchange.

BILATERAL AND MULTILATERAL EXCHANGE

Our reading of American economic and legal history gives support to the broad generalization that in this country state actions have tended to reinforce actor strategies and power distributions among producers, labor, finance, suppliers, and others in ways that favor bilateral over multilateral exchange.[7] This is the case even though the federal government has at one or another time overtly sought to *promote* promotional networks and associational forms of governance! Notable examples of such efforts occurred during World War I (Cuff 1973), the associative era of the 1920s (Kolko 1976: Chap. 4), the early New Deal experiments with the corporatist organization of industries through the National Recovery Administration

7 Agriculture and especially dairying are obvious exceptions.

(NRA) and its codes (Hawley 1966), and in the 1970s and 1980s when the state, for example, has helped to subsidize and grant legal protections to research-and-development consortia in technologically sophisticated industries that are threatened by international competition.

We offer two possible explanations for this lack of symmetry between intention and results. First, as we have seen, policy actions, such as procurement, tariffs, and various subsidies, on the part of different state agencies and at different levels of the American state have tended to reinforce, if not propel, trends toward scale and concentration. One consequence of the domination of hierarchy over market and network forms of organization is an implicit support for the power of large corporate organizations and their managers vis-à-vis labor, parts and resource suppliers, customers and consumers, finance, and the state itself. As many observers have pointed out, the large American corporate hierarchy has become extraordinarily self-sufficient and autonomous from control by, responsibility to, or dependence upon workers and their organizations, financial institutions, or state agencies. This power position would seem to reinforce incentives for self-interested, utilitarian, and opportunistic behavior vis-à-vis other economic actors. Mutual interdependence of interests and power resources and a recognition of the need for coordinated or collective action – the underlying bases for multilateral exchange – is much less likely to characterize firms and industries dominated by large, hierarchically organized producers. Examples of this are the unwillingness of business writers of the early New Deal NRA codes to involve labor or attend to the demands of consumers or small business, and the very limited success of later Depression efforts to foster corporatist-style industrial planning by strengthening the hand of labor in the National Labor Relations Act and the Fair Labor Standards Act (Hawley 1966: 195; Hughes 1977: 173; Galambos and Pratt 1988: Chap. 5).

A second reason for the American state's support or revealed preference for bilateral exchange in spite of deliberate if episodic efforts to promote multilateral exchange has to do with the aforementioned institutional fragmentation of the state and the special role of courts and legal doctrines and ideologies in the American economy (Solo 1974; Scheiber 1980a, 1980b; Skowronek 1982). Although the executive and the legislature have occasionally supported or promoted multilateral forms of economic governance, the courts at federal and state levels, and in constitutional and private law actions, have fairly consistently undermined such efforts in the name of Lockian norms of a radical individualist-normative vision rather than an organicist or communitarian vision that might justify multilateral governance or state planning (Solo 1974). For example, pools, cartels, or the efforts of trade associations to assume extensive coordinating roles typically have been overturned as antitrust violations or have collapsed because courts have been unwilling to enforce what they perceive as being illegal contracts. Ultimately, the NRA itself was declared unconstitutional by the Supreme Court.

Both explanations of the preference for bilateral exchange rely for the most part on state actions with respect to property rights. But the direct participation of state agencies in the production and allocation of information and resources has also militated against multilateral exchange and collective goods. Although there are many examples of state actions that have been designed to produce collective infrastructure goods in technical education and job training, and in research and development, the larger thrust of state procurement, subsidy, and borrowing actions has been in support of private accumulation and privately owned or noncollective infrastructure goods. This was the case with nineteenth-century federal land grants and state and local subsidies to the construction of railroads, and the long-standing practice of state agencies at many levels to issue revenue bonds in private markets to be invested in those public facilities that most closely corresponded to short-term, commercial concerns rather than long-term construction of public goods (Walsh 1978; Horwitz 1977; Scheiber 1980a, 1980b, 1981). Not only were private or noncollective infrastructural goods favored by these types of state actions, but so too was the power of new capital and entrepreneurs vis-à-vis farmers, workers, and old capital. Thus, as David Vogel (1987) has pointed out, it is simply historically incorrect to argue that the state in the United States has not actively promoted industry and industrial modernization. U.S. states have consistently supported the interests of industry and done little to impede the political and economic triumph of large-scale business. No other nation made so few efforts to protect traditional sectors or the interests of labor during periods of transformation or rapid industrial growth. Labor legislation and regulation at the federal level have not accorded the kinds of rights and protections to labor that are commonplace in other advanced capitalist societies. The absence of plant-closing laws and the de facto dominance of state governments in the domain of labor law have further reinforced bilateral strategies on the part of dominant industrial actors. Cooperative relations between labor and business, or among producers and between them and suppliers and finance seem to depend heavily on state coercive regulation, active state encouragements, or explicit exemption from antitrust and other property rights provisions. Where associations and promotional networks, such as research-and-development consortia and cartels, have thrived for a time in the United States, these conditions typically have been met. The dairy industry is a good example.

Table 12.2 summarizes our analysis of how different types of state policy tools may be used to favor bilateral or multilateral exchange. This typology, the previous discussion of how policy tools influence the formal or informal organization of governance, summarized in the typology of Table 12.1, and our understanding of how the state constitutes economic governance

Table 12.2. *State actions that constitute the economy:*
Bilateral to multilateral

Type of policy tool	Type of economic-exchange strategy favored	
	Bilateral	Multilateral
Provision and allocation of information and resources	• Most procurement • Tariffs • Subsidies to individual firms • Infrastructure investment in *noncollective* goods (i.e., railroad subsidies)	• Infrastructure investment in *collective* goods (i.e., education, job training) • Subsidies to networks and associations of firms (i.e., R&D consortia)
Property rights and the regulation of the behavior of parties to exchange	• Legal protection of firm authority (i.e., limiting responsibility to labor, finance, communities) • Antitrust law • Regulatory enforcement of market competition	• Antitrust exemptions • Legal protections for R&D consortia, industrywide and national associations • Legal enforcement of cartels

as an actor and as a structure provide the necessary conceptual foundation and historical background with which to interpret the data that are provided in our eight case studies. We have argued that the central tendency in American economic history has been for state actions to have favored scale and concentration and autonomous bilateral exchange rather than interdependent multilateral exchange. But there are interesting exceptions and sectoral variations, as our subsequent analysis reveals. Thus, there is nothing inevitable (or irreversible) about states constituting economies in these particular ways. In many European countries and in Japan, state actions have tolerated or promoted trade associations, cartels, promotional networks, codetermination with labor, and close institutional links between industrial and finance capital. Furthermore, although these states have also favored concentration, scale, and corporate hierarchies, they have also frequently supported and fostered small firms, networks, and complex subcontracting relationships as an integral part of their industrial economies and as a complement or possible successor to vertically and horizontally integrated hierarchies. In this sense, our two typologies of how state actions constitute the economy can denote a range of strategic possibilities for state actors. Perhaps, where state actors are relatively autonomous or have the organizational capacity to develop a coherent state interest, state actors may be more able to develop strategies in production and allocation and in property rights to favor multilateral exchange and the provision of collective goods, as well as alternatives to hierarchical governance. Promotion by state actors in Europe of corporatist arrangements would seem to be a case in point. Where the state lacks autonomy and institutional capacities, the opposite may be true. Where strong hierarchies with the power to dominate their exchange partners and with little institutionalized dependence on finance are well established and where the state is weak in the previous sense, it may be very difficult for state actors to successfully promote or even decisively support nonhierarchical or multilateral and cooperative strategies, even where technological and competitive conditions may counsel them. Unfortunately, the data to speak confidently on these matters do not exist in our case studies or in the general historical and legal literatures that we have reviewed. Nevertheless, comparisons with other countries are suggestive as are some of our case studies. We return to these issues in what follows.

THE STATE AND THE TRANSFORMATION OF GOVERNANCE REGIMES

How do the actions and structures of the American state help explain the governance transformations that have been described in our case histories? In what specific ways have the successive governance regimes of our eight sectors been constituted by the state? To what extent do our findings confirm the broad central tendencies identified earlier in this chapter? First, we explain how property rights actions have interacted with state structures to shape the selection process and governance outcomes. Second, we do the same thing insofar as production and allocation actions are concerned. Although production and allocation actions have been significant in shaping governance transformations, property rights actions have been much more decisive in our cases, so we discuss them first and more extensively.

In the stylized terms of the evolutionary model offered in Chapter 11, governance transformations are typically initiated by producers responding strategically and opportunistically to a range of possible strategic choices, created by changes in market conditions, technology, and in the institutional and political environment. These *pressures for change* lead producers to adopt new product strategies and perhaps new forms of internal organization that depend for their implementation on producers being able to experiment with, negotiate, or coerce new roles, rules, and rights in their exchange relationships with competitors, labor, suppliers, and sources of finance and innovation. The complex *selection process* that ensues is the product of the interplay among the strategic actions and constraining institutional contexts of economic actors and the state. Selection involves spontaneous trial-and-error experimentation, formal and informal bargaining and negotiation, as well as overt struggle and coercion. Outcomes of selection depend on the ability of various actors to mobilize resources, take advantage of political opportunities, and devise appropriate goals and strategies that break out of existing rules and routines while conforming to new market conditions, and technological, political, and cultural constraints. In turn, the stability and durability of an emergent governance regime depends often on the state's ability and willingness to ratify and help legitimate it. Where the selection process produces a qualitatively different governance regime (which is not at all guaranteed), we describe those outcomes in terms of changes along the dimensions of formal–informal organization and bilateral–multilateral exchange. The state in the United States has played important roles through its property rights actions in all phases of the transformation sequence. However, the state does not necessarily become involved of its own volition. Rather, it often gets pulled into the process by other actors or by the imperatives of new political, economic, or technological circumstances. Hence, we do not suggest that the state necessarily takes an activist role in the transformation process or that this process is necessarily led by the state.

PROPERTY RIGHTS ACTIONS, STATE STRUCTURES, AND GOVERNANCE TRANSFORMATIONS

Pressure for change

The state may crystallize pressures for governance transformations in several ways. As an *actor,* the state may deliberately try to force change on a sector by changing, or threatening to change, property rights. For example, in the commercial nuclear energy sector, Congress passed legislation in 1954 that permitted private firms to own nuclear technology and forbade the federal government from building its own reactors for the purpose of producing electricity commercially. However, it was only after Congress threatened two years later to pass new legislation that redefined property rights so as to mandate the construction of six government-owned commercial plants that utilities began to consider more seriously the construction of nuclear plants. Had this proposed redefinition of property rights been enacted, the government would have competed with the utilities in the commercial electricity market. This threat helped convince utility companies to begin building nuclear plants, thereby creating a market, a new form of governance, for the technology's development. To provide further encouragement for the market's development, Congress passed the Price–Anderson Act in 1957 – legislation that redefined property rights again by restricting a utility's liability in the event of a nuclear accident to $60 million. In turn, this limited the extent to which citizens could assert claims over utility property and reduced the utilities' investment risks (Campbell, Chapter 4 in this volume).

Redefining property rights also helped create a more competitive market in the telecommunications industry. AT&T had been able to establish a monopoly in telephone service during the late nineteenth century, in part because the courts had affirmed the company's right to control the technology through its ownership of hundreds of patents. However, the Federal Communications Commission (FCC) ruled in 1959 that both common carriers, such as AT&T, and private users should be permitted to use microwave frequencies for communication purposes. Eventually, the FCC also granted permission to companies, such as Microwave Communications, Inc., to interconnect their microwave systems with AT&T's telephone grid, thus triggering a dramatic governance transformation whereby a competitive market in long-distance service emerged in place of the old AT&T monopoly (Bickers, Chapter 3 in this volume).

The state may also exert pressure for change as an *organizational configuration* of fragmented and decentralized institutions that often creates property rights policies that are inadequate for solving an industry's dilemmas, occasionally because these policies are contradictory. For instance, scheduling, overcapacity, and other problems plagued the railroad sector during the nineteenth century. In the absence of federal regulation, subnational regulatory agencies were unable to solve these problems because railroads had become an interstate business, thus transcending the jurisdiction of any one state's agency. Industry leaders created associations and pools to improve the situation through self-regulation, but these failed to fully control their members' behavior as cheating on collective agreements became rampant. Congress passed legislation in 1866 that officially permitted associative behavior among railroads, but the collective agreements that these associations crafted proved to be unenforceable because already existing common law held that the agreements were in restraint of trade and, therefore, illegal (McCraw 1984: 49). Two branches of government had developed contradictory property rights policies with respect to the collective control of railroads. The failure of multilateral governance caused the railroads to seek an alternative solution to their problems, a consolidation of companies through a wave of mergers that amounted to a transformation in governance from market to corporate hierarchy (Kennedy, Chapter 5 in this volume).

Finally, by providing *arenas* for public participation in the policy process, the state may create opportunities for outsiders to cause political problems that may trigger searches for new governance regimes due to actual or proposed changes in property rights policies. Cattlemen and ranchers used their access to Federal Trade Commission (FTC) officials during the late 1910s to complain about oligopoly pricing and other unfair practices by the big vertically integrated meat packers, five of whom clearly dominated the purchasing, processing, and distribution of beef within the industry. In response, the FTC recommended government ownership of the stockyards, distribution outlets, and refrigerator cars after which the U.S. Attorney General sought indictments that charged the meat packers with monopoly and collusion. The meat packers believed that changes in policy governing their property rights were immanent, so they quickly agreed to relinquish their stockyard interests voluntarily, a compromise that the government accepted and that reduced the amount of vertical integration upstream, but permitted meat packers to retain control over everything else downstream in processing and distribution (Portz, Chapter 9 in this volume).

More recently, citizen groups and unions worked through Congress and the courts during the 1960s and 1970s to pass and enforce environmental, consumer, and labor legislation that restricted the property rights of manufacturers insofar as the operation of their facilities and quality of their products was concerned (Vogel 1983, 1987). These laws created new problems for industry that led occasionally to the creation of new forms of governance. For example, in the automobile sector, manufacturers responded collectively to new and stricter air-quality regulations by establishing in 1967 an Air Pollution Research Advisory Council and an Inter-Industry Emissions Control Program. These were formally organized, multilateral attempts to develop and cross-license emission-control technologies, and a marked departure from the industry's more typical form of governance, oligopolistic competition (Scherrer, Chapter 7 in this volume; White 1982). In the nuclear sector, after the demise in the mid–1970s of the Atomic Energy Commission and the congressional Joint Committee on Atomic Energy, policy forums responsible for the regulation of commercial nuclear energy became particularly accessible to a wide variety of environmental, antinuclear, and other groups that penetrated the policy process in ways that contributed to the development of new regulations. Regulatory changes contributed to delays in building and licensing nuclear plants, and to the escalation of costs for nuclear plant and radioactive waste-management projects. In turn, this exacerbated capital shortages for utilities that were engaged in nuclear construction and eventually destroyed the market for nuclear plants (Campbell, Chapter 4 in this volume).

The selection process

Once pressures for change have developed, the state may influence the selection process in ways similar to those just discussed. The state may participate in the search process as an *actor,* helping to craft a new governance regime in an industry by manipulating property rights. For example, dairy farmers tried to establish cooperatives and struggled with milk distributors during the 1910s to stabilize milk prices and production levels, but with only limited success. One obstacle was that the U.S. Justice Department opposed the formation of dairy coops and multilateral pricing schemes because officials believed that this violated antitrust law. However, under Herbert Hoover's guidance, the Federal Food Administration convinced the Justice Department not to interfere anymore, and helped organize and institutionalize price bargaining between the two groups, thus ensuring that a more multilateral form of governance would replace the previous, more bilateral and market-based forms. Eventually, Congress passed the Capper–Volstead Act in 1922, which officially exempted the coops from antitrust prosecution by legislating a new set of property rights that permitted collective governance (Young, Chapter 8 in this volume).

Similarly, antitrust exemptions, another example of the selective enforcement of property rights policy, became more frequent during the 1980s in the steel industry and fostered an increase in merger activity, a variety of joint ventures, and further concentration (Scherrer, Chapter 6 in this volume). In automobiles, although the Justice Department had forbidden in 1969 the cross-licensing of emission-control technology, it later reversed its position and permitted this new form of governance, and the Department of Transportation promoted a Cooperative Automotive Research Program in 1978, an industry–government joint venture to improve automobile quality (White 1982). As in the steel example, this was an effort to help the industry overcome its economic malaise. Yet perhaps the most dramatic case of a state-led search through shifts in property rights policies was in the railroad sector, where the federal government created its own rail companies, Amtrak and Conrail, by nationalizing and reorganizing several private railroads in a last-ditch effort to remedy the sector's financial dilemmas (Kennedy, Chapter 5 in this volume). In this case, property rights shifted from private to public control.

Sometimes *state structure* affects the selection process by determining the range of options from which private actors may choose to solve their governance problems. As noted earlier, federalism afforded subnational governments great leeway in devising property rights policies. For example, the Taft–Hartley Act granted state legislatures the right to outlaw union shops, thus making it extremely difficult for labor to organize in conservative regions that were not already predominantly unionized, such as southern and western states that often passed right-to-work laws that helped keep wages relatively low (Newman 1984). Similarly, in the automobile sector, cheap labor, as well as lower operating costs due to more lenient environmental codes, in regions away from Detroit helped encourage the development of just-in-time subcontracting relationships, where independent suppliers in the south and west began to provide parts (just-in-time for assembly) for the large automobile manufacturers. Traditionally, manufacturers had produced these parts within their vertically integrated firms, but when the industry began to suffer a profit squeeze during the 1970s and 1980s, subcontracting offered a way to reduce costs (Scherrer, Chapter 7 in this volume). The same thing happened in the steel industry during the 1960s and 1970s when regional disparities in labor costs due to different subnational property rights policies helped facilitate the development of small, independent minimills in the south that contributed to the development of market competition for specialty steel in a sector that had previously been dominated by an oligopoly (Scherrer, Chapter 6 in this volume). Movement to the south in pursuit of lower costs also helped firms in these and other industries undermine labor unions and, as a result, contributed to the deterioration of multilaterally organized mechanisms for settling labor–management problems, including the establishment of wages and benefits (Bluestone and Harrison 1982). In each of these examples, differences in property rights frameworks among subnational governments helped to encourage the development of new governance regimes by *defining distinctive locations for economic activity,* each offering different economic possibilities to private actors.

The state also influences the selection process by providing *arenas* for outsiders to penetrate the policy process and further limit the range of governance options. In the railroad sector around the turn of the century, small shippers and midwestern farmers gained access to the state through the courts and political parties, pushed for creation of the Interstate Commerce Commission, and convinced regulators to officially prohibit railroad pools, cartels, and associations from setting rates. This restricted the number of governance mechanisms from which the railroads could choose as they tried to stabilize prices, thus contributing further to the creation of large horizontally integrated railroads, perhaps the only alternative left after the gutting of the multilateral forms of governance (Chandler 1977; Kennedy, Chapter 5 in this volume).

As suggested briefly in Chapter 11, one of the most important ways in which the state influences governance selection is through its capacity to ratify or undermine new governance regimes once they have emerged. In this way, the state as an *actor* helps to determine when relative equilibrium returns to an industry. Generally, ratification occurs when, at the insistence of either private or state actors, the government confers legitimacy on a new regime by approving formally either the regime itself, or particular transactions that result from it. This stabilizes the new governance regime and leads to a termination of the selection process, unless it proves to be ineffective in resolving the problems that it was designed to cure. When ratification is not forthcoming, transactions often become difficult and the new regime becomes precarious. As discussed earlier, for example, it was only after 1866, when Congress passed property rights legislation that explicitly permitted administrative pools to coordinate rail traffic, that railroad companies began to use this form of governance with any regularity.

Of course, even when the state is willing, it may be unable to effectively ratify governance regimes, particularly if its legitimacy is in doubt. For instance, concerns developed during the late 1960s that the Atomic Energy Commission had neglected its regulatory responsibilities – concerns that drew into question not only the Commission's legitimacy, but that of the nuclear sector as a whole. Triggered by a legitimation crisis over the Commission's nuclear plant safety policy in the early 1970s, antinuclear activity escalated as groups argued, in effect, that state-regulated corporate and market forms of governance were no longer acceptable, sued to shut plants that they believed utilities were operating unsafely, and lobbied state governments to halt further nuclear plant construction. In effect, the existing structure of governance and property rights was being challenged by those who sought to shift control over utility property in a more public direction. The inability of the Commission to lend legitimacy to corporate activity helped undermine the stability of transactions within the sector as it became more difficult for utilities to purchase and build nuclear plants. Congress eventually replaced the agency with the Nuclear Regulatory Commission to restore legitimacy to the regulatory process, avoid further charges that the sector was operating in ways contrary to the public interest, and stabilize sectoral governance once again (Campbell, Chapter 4 in this volume).

There are also times when the state is unwilling to ratify new governance regimes. Then selection tends to continue. Similarly, if the state refuses to continue ratifying an already established governance regime, then new pressures for change may emerge. Despite the 1866 railroad legislation, when the courts refused to enforce pooling and other collective agreements, railroads continued to search for alternative ways of rationalizing rail service, such as corporate mergers, a governance mechanism with a more legal and legitimate institutional status at the time insofar as such consolidations were legally acceptable. Hence, pools and associations were *transitional* forms of governance precisely because the state never fully ratified them (Kennedy, Chapter 5 in this volume). In the telecommunications sector, the Justice Department refused to continue tolerating many of AT&T's monopolistic practices and, in a deliberate attempt to push the sector in a more market-oriented direction, filed a divestiture suit against the company in 1974, a direct attack on the legitimacy of this sector's long-standing governance regime, which triggered a search for alternatives – a search that culminated in the breakup of AT&T's local service companies in 1984 (Bickers, Chapter 3 in this volume). Elsewhere, the Attorney General attacked meatpacking pools at the turn of the century that were coordinating prices. After the Supreme Court ruled that the pools were illegal in 1905, meatpackers replaced them with a holding company and then, after two more lawsuits challenged the holding company's legitimacy, developed an informal price-leading system (Portz, Chapter 9 in this volume).

Because ratification often involves the delineation and enforcement of property rights, the courts often play a pivotal role in ratifying governance regimes, particularly in the United States, where they are asked frequently to determine, under antitrust statutes, the acceptability of corporate hierarchies and different forms of multilateral governance. Although challengers, including state actors, who object to a particular form of governance often ask judges to rule on these matters, as in the Justice Department's 1974 attack on AT&T's local service monopoly, requests for court ratification occasionally come from dominant actors who benefit from the existing governance regime, and who seek to use the courts and prevailing property rights policies as a *defense* against potential governance transformations. In telecommunications, for instance, the Bell System filed hundreds of patent-infringement suits during the late nineteenth century against would-be competitors – suits that the courts usually upheld, thereby ratifying the corporation's right to monopolize the technology and dominate sectoral governance through a single corporate hierarchy. Indeed, the construction of a patent wall to preserve its monopoly was a deliberate strategy of the Bell System (Bickers, Chapter 3 in this volume).

Ironically, although Douglass North (1981) was one of the few economists to recognize that state officials play a pivotal role in the governance process by altering property rights, he failed to acknowledge their role in ratifying new governance regimes once they have materialized. Instead, he argued that in addition to a theory of the state with which to understand governance transformations, we also need a theory of ideology without which we cannot account for the routine willingness of economic actors to abide by the prevailing governance regime – a commitment, he suggested, that is necessary so that economic activity will be stabilized and not deteriorate into permanent chaos where every transaction becomes subject to legal challenge and dispute. In short, ideology is the key component that is required for stabilizing economic governance. However, as we have seen, it is often the *state* that provides this ideological guidance and stability, particularly through the courts.

After all the law is, among other things, an expression of a society's politically dominant ideology. Insofar as the ratification of governance regimes is concerned, it is the courts' job to determine whether these regimes are ideologically palatable. If they are found to be so, ratification will probably be forthcoming and they will remain intact, as in the Bell patent cases. If not, they will not be ratified, but rather will be undermined and destabilized, as occurred when meatpackers were unable to sustain their pooling agreements. Although courts tend to be conservative and uphold the status quo (Miliband 1969: 138–45; Hurst 1982), occasionally they do veer from precedent. There have been important ideological shifts in the U.S. courts that have precipitated changes in governance regimes (e.g., Solo 1974; Horwitz 1977; Hurst 1982; Hooks forthcoming). Other parts of the state apparatus also provide this ideological judgment, such as regulatory agencies, where officials determine the legality of transactions and governance mechanisms. However, in these other institutional locations, approval is often much more subtle (and politics is often much more important). The Nuclear Regulatory Commission's tacit approval of various multilateral forms of governance after the accident at Three Mile Island is a case of such subtlety (Campbell, Chapter 4 in this volume).

It should be stressed that when the state participates as an actor in the search for a new governance regime, that which emerges usually does not require formal state ratification later. For example, when the Federal Food Administration arranged for price bargaining among producers and distributors in the dairy industry during the 1910s, prices were managed effectively, and nobody challenged this particular form of governance for years. Furthermore, there was no need for overt government ratification beyond that which had already occurred by virtue of the state's participation in the selection process.[8] Similarly, during the search for a commercially viable nuclear energy technology, the state encouraged the formation of several collectively organized research groups that were never challenged and never required formal ratification (Campbell, Chapter 4 in this volume). Furthermore, few objected formally to the creation of the nationalized railroad companies, Amtrak and Conrail, by the Department of Transportation, although acceptance here was probably due as much to the unprofitable nature of these lines as it was to the state's presence in the selection process per se.

On the other hand, when private actors try to select new governance regimes without the state's active participation, demands for ratification will probably be more frequent. For example, in contrast to state-sponsored multilateral governance in the dairy sector, we have seen many privately organized forms of multilateral governance challenged in court and elsewhere such that the state was called upon to determine the legitimacy of the governance mechanisms in question. Railroad pools and associations, automobile research organizations, and meatpacking pools and holding companies were all challenged in ways that required the state to determine the legitimacy of each. Furthermore, in the steel industry, Chicago-area fabricators convinced the Federal Trade Commission to force steel producers to modify their privately organized, oligopolistic pricing systems in 1924, and again in 1938 (Markusen, 1985:82). When independent telephone companies took it upon themselves to form an association in order to compete more effectively with the Bell System in the early 1900s, federal

---

8 This is not to say that once government officials ratify a particular governance arrangement it will *never* be challenged, just that it will be more or less accepted by the actors involved for the immediate future. For example, although milk pricing and other forms of regulation were the norm in the dairy industry for decades, calls for deregulation emerged during the late 1970s and 1980s (Young, Chapter 8 in this volume).

and state authorities ruled that the organization was in violation of antitrust law. The point is that the state's presence in the selection process tends to lend a certain legitimacy and, therefore, stability to the governance regimes that emerge, as long as its own legitimacy is intact.

The examples we have discussed are not unusual. When the state is not actively involved in promoting new governance regimes, those most likely to become subject to ratification challenges in the United States are vertically or horizontally integrated corporate hierarchies, or multilateral forms of governance, such as associations or pools. Wolfgang Streeck and Philippe Schmitter (1985) have argued that associational forms of governance require that the state confer legitimacy and authority on them, as well as occasional help with enforcement, if they are to effectively govern their members. This may be so, but these governance mechanisms also require state legitimacy, at least in the United States, because they are multilateral forms of governance per se. In the United States, such forms of governance are often viewed as being in conflict with the principles of free competition as codified in antitrust law (e.g., Edmonds 1983). The same is often true for large corporate hierarchies, particularly when they have their genesis in mergers that significantly increase market concentration. Hence, it appears that in the United States, when the state is not directly involved as an actor in the creation of governance mechanisms that may appear to undermine the competitive market, actors often will request that the state decide later whether to ratify them.

In contrast, bilaterally organized forms of governance, including markets, limited joint ventures, and subcontracting relationships, are probably less likely to be challenged in this way. Of course, specific transactions that occur *within* these governance mechanisms are often disputed, such as when market contracts are challenged in court. However, the governance mechanisms themselves are not likely to be contested. Similarly, we suspect that collective price-leading arrangements will be subject to state ratification only infrequently but, probably for different reasons, the steel sector's oligopolistic pricing system notwithstanding. Although price leading is a multilateral form of governance, it would be very difficult to prove that participants had violated antitrust law or had otherwise undermined the operation of competitive markets because this form of governance is so underdeveloped in terms of a formal organizational structure, and because participants coordinate each other's behavior in such tacit and soft-spoken ways. This may be one reason why price leading, for example, has operated so successfully in the automobile and steel sectors for decades (e.g., Baran and Sweezy 1966: 60).

Theoretical implications

The central concern of this section has been to demonstrate that through its property rights policies, the state constitutes economic activity on a continuous basis in the United States and that this occurs in a variety of ways, especially during the process of governance transformation. By establishing the rules within which economic activity takes place, the state constantly defines the range of organizational forms through which this activity may occur. Thus, the state is *always* interacting with the economy in important ways, regardless of whether or not it chooses occasionally to influence the behavior of economic actors through the production and allocation of resources and information, activity that we discuss in the next section. This has additional implications for theories that try to specify the relationship between the state and economy in the United States (and in other advanced capitalist countries) and for theories that seek to identify the conditions that precipitate governance transformations.

As noted earlier, many have argued that in the United States, the state is relatively weak because it is generally unable to allocate critical resources and information in ways that influence the organization of economic activity. Others have maintained that an additional source of state strength lies in well-developed administrative bureaucracies that are capable of monopolizing authority within their policy domains, centralized and insulated from the demands of lower levels of government and outside groups, and staffed with people sharing a common esprit de corps (e.g., Katzenstein 1978; Hall 1986). Dietrich Rueschemeyer and Peter Evans (1985: 51), for example, argued that "effective bureaucratic machinery is the key to the state's capacity to intervene" in ways that influence the organization of economic activity. On these dimensions, the U.S. state appears again to be rather weak (Katzenstein 1978; Krasner 1978a), although, as Theda Skocpol (1985) argued, state strength in the United States, as elsewhere, is variable historically and across policy areas, depending in part on the political and institutional arrangements at hand.

However, we have seen that in the United States, the state has derived great *strength* from its ability to define and enforce property rights, at least insofar as we measure strength in terms of the state's ability to orchestrate institutional transformations within the economy – criteria often used in such characterizations (e.g., Krasner 1978b: Chap. 3). FCC decisions to permit independent companies to link their microwave systems to AT&T's telephone grids redefined property rights so as to foster a more competitively structured telecommunications industry. With threats to build government-owned reactors, as well as passage of the Price–Anderson Act, Congress provided definitions of property rights favorable enough to the utilities that a market for nuclear plants began to blossom. Regulatory decisions to permit dairy cooperatives in the late 1910s and early 1920s helped facilitate the development of multilateral forms of governance in that sector.

That the state has done this through various forms of regulatory policy is particularly interesting and ironic. Although much of the prevailing literature attributes relative weakness to states that rely heavily on adopting the regulatory and rule-making policy tools (e.g., Zysman 1983: Chap. 2; Samuels 1987: 17), these tools may actually be sources of great strength for the state. Thus, to focus on the degree to which state actors have the ability to allocate the flow and direction of important resources and information is to offer a rather lopsided analysis of the state's capacity to affect governance transformations. In this sense, we agree with John Ikenberry (1988: 203–8) that there is a much wider range of capacities for state strength then those commonly acknowledged in the literature.[9]

State strength is also derived in a second way from the capacity of government officials to manipulate property rights. Those who have contributed to the debates about weak and strong states recognized that state strength is dependent to a degree upon the organization of actors in society (e.g., Katzenstein 1978; Krasner 1978b; Stepan 1978: 84; Hall 1986; Samuels 1987). We agree with those who argued that state actors will tend to have greater success in forming and implementing the economic policies of their choice if dominant class interests in society are organizationally fragmented, rather than unified and against them (e.g., Rueschemeyer and Evans 1985; Samuels 1987). Yet the state's control over property rights is often an important means of influencing the organization of societal groups in the first place. We are not suggesting that the state alone determines the organizational capacities of private actors. Nevertheless, how government officials manipulate property rights, such as those specified through antitrust and labor law, may facilitate or inhibit the collective organization of business and other groups, and, in turn, affect the degree to which state actors influence the governance process later. For instance, in the meat-packing industry, antitrust policies undermined pools and other multilateral forms of organization that big packers used to try to coordinate their activity during the early 1900s. Later, when the federal government tried to impose beef-grading schemes and enforce a degree of vertical divestiture, to which the big packers had agreed initially, these companies tried to resist, but failed, because they lacked an effective means of interfirm coordination (Portz, Chapter 9 in this volume). Thus, we reiterate Peter Hall's (1986: 266–8) contention that there are reciprocal influences between the state and the organization of groups in society, but add that this reciprocity also influences state strength and is determined in part by the state's ability to develop property rights policies.

Our argument about the importance of property rights also has implications for the recent debates about the conditions under which different types of governance emerge. As suggested in Chapter 11, much of this literature focuses on how the imperatives of economic efficiency (Chandler

---

9 For critical reviews of the literature about strong and weak states, see Skocpol (1985), Samuels (1987: Chap. 7), Wilks and Wright (1987), and Atkinson and Coleman (1989). It is noteworthy that none of these addresses the issue of property rights per se.

1977), technology (Piore and Sabel 1984), profit cycles (Markusen 1985), and other largely *society-centered* conditions create pressures for such change. Ann Markusen (1985), for example, argued that as an industry forms initially and becomes more profitable, subcontracting and competition among many small firms develops, but eventually evolves toward vertically integrated corporate hierarchies. When profitability declines, then vertical disintegration is likely, and will be accompanied by increasing trade association activity and renewed subcontracting. Yet we have seen that governance transformations, such as these, may stem directly from shifts in property rights and, therefore, may be due to changes in *political* as much as economic circumstances.

This is not to say that economic conditions are unimportant, or that they alone never precipitate governance transformations. The point is that there are often times when property rights policy plays a substantial role in these transformations, either alone or in conjunction with economics. Indeed, although a more systematic study is beyond the scope of this chapter, the histories of the industries that we have discussed suggest, however tentatively, that frequently there may be a relationship between shifts in economic conditions, property rights policies, and governance regimes. We hypothesize that during times of economic decline in the United States, the state tends to define and enforce property rights in ways that facilitate the development of more formally and/or multilaterally organized governance mechanisms, such as corporate hierarchies and associations. Conversely, we suspect that during economic prosperity, the state tends to define and enforce property rights in ways that facilitate the development of more informal and less multilaterally organized governance mechanisms, such as the market.

For example, in the automobile sector, the federal government promulgated codes under the National Industrial Recovery Act during the Depression, which encouraged the formation of associations to establish pricing practices, supervise dealer–supplier relations, and set minimum wages throughout the sector (Dyer, Salter, and Webber 1987: 47–8). Furthermore, in 1936, the Automotive Manufacturing Association adopted, without government opposition, a basing-point price quotation system – a form of multilateral price stabilization (Markusen 1985: 169). In contrast, antitrust enforcement became more rigorous during the prosperous 1950s and 1960s as the federal government forced General Motors to relinquish its holdings in Bendix, Greyhound, and Hertz, and required Ford to divest its interests in Autolite (Dyer et al. 1987: 48; Scherrer, Chapter 7 in this volume). Similarly, we saw that as automakers tried to form collective organizations in response to increased regulatory activity after 1965, the federal government blocked these efforts, as well as the cross-licensing activities that followed. Later, however, as the sector began to suffer its decline during the late 1970s and 1980s, the Justice Department agreed to permit cross-licensing, and the Department of Transportation promoted the Cooperative Automotive Research Program.

Furthermore, we have seen that the federal government became more lenient with regard to antitrust when the steel industry began to decline in the 1970s. In the nuclear sector, after a major reactor accident at the Three Mile Island plant in 1979, an accident that many members of the industry feared might kill the nuclear option altogether, the federal government permitted the organization of several multilateral business organizations that were ostensibly designed to help the industry regulate itself more effectively (Campbell, Chapter 4 in this volume). On the other hand, some of the most extreme cases of antitrust enforcement in the industries sampled here occurred in telecommunications, where there was never a major economic decline. After the turn of the century, antitrust suits were filed against AT&T and led to a deal negotiated in 1913 between AT&T and the Attorney General that led to a partial divestiture of the firm's holdings. Of course, this paled in comparison to the federal government's regulatory and legal actions against AT&T since the mid–1960s that deliberately fostered a competitive market for long-distance services, and broke up the company's monopoly over local service (Bickers, Chapter 3 in this volume).

Not only does the state tend to facilitate the development of more multilaterally and formally organized governance mechanisms during downswings in a sector's economic performance *and during wartime,* but, we would further hypothesize, it also tends to define property rights during such times in ways that increase the advantage of business relative to other groups in society. By this we mean that business is not required to make as many concessions to the interests of other groups when making decisions about its use of the means of production. One might say that advantage refers to the *relative autonomy* with which business operates from the constraints of nonbusiness interests, as expressed through the property rights framework.[10] For example, during the declines in the steel and automobile sectors, the federal government loosened its environmental regulations on these sectors in the hope of easing their economic difficulties. Indeed, many of these regulations had been promulgated during the 1960s and early 1970s, when these sectors, not to mention the national economy, were doing well, and when citizen groups were highly mobilized to push for such regulatory policies (Dyer et al 1987; Scherrer, Chapter 7 in this volume). Similarly, it was during a period of expansion in the meatpacking sector in the early twentieth century that the federal government imposed

---

10 The relative autonomy of business is an institutional condition because this autonomy varies in large part according to the institutionalized definitions and enforcement of property rights.

various beef-grading and other regulations (Portz, Chapter 9 in this volume).[11]

Two important caveats are in order. First, and most importantly, although economic conditions may influence the *probability* that changes in property rights will increase or decrease the relative autonomy of business, politics will determine the *specific outcomes* of struggles over property rights policies. The Carter Administration during the late 1970s tried to promote a corporatist solution to the steel sector's economic stagnation, a proposal that provided in part for collective decision making among steel companies, but one that was opposed and defeated politically by organized labor and the steel firms themselves, who preferred a more conservative, protectionist policy (Scherrer, Chapter 6 in this volume). Similarly, intense political pressure from Congress and antinuclear groups caused the Nuclear Regulatory Commission to pass increasingly stringent regulations against utilities during the 1970s although the market for nuclear plants was collapsing (Campbell, Chapter 4 in this volume). Of course, these cases contradict our simple hypotheses about the relationship between economic conditions and the relative autonomy of business (the nuclear case), and about property rights, economic decline, and the type of governance transformations that are likely to emerge (the steel case). However, by doing so, they illustrate the important role that politics plays in mediating how economic conditions influence policy and governance outcomes.

The second caveat refers to Markusen (1985), who found that the relationships between profit cycles and the emergence of different governance forms varied according to the type of sector in question. Although we have not examined a cross section of natural resource, producer goods, and consumer goods sectors, as she did, we have discovered one important sectoral effect. The state promulgated more extreme property rights policies for the infrastructure sectors that we have examined than for others in the sense that these policies have occasionally given the state ownership and control, at least temporarily, over what was once private property. We have seen that nationalization of bankrupt rail companies occurred twice. Furthermore, as of this writing, negotiations are underway wherein the state of New York will purchase the Shoreham nuclear power plant from the Long Island Lighting Company now that political obstacles will prevent the plant from coming on line. Nothing so drastic occurred in the steel, meatpacking, dairy, or automobile sectors during their periods of decline. Even when the Chrysler Corporation was on the verge of bankruptcy in 1979, Congress only provided temporary federal loans and loan

---

11 This does not mean, however, that during economic upswings, property rights fundamentally favor the nonbusiness interests. Property rights in capitalist societies almost always tend to favor business interests. The issue here is simply one of degree.

guarantees (Edmonds 1983: 91–4; Scherrer, Chapter 7 in this volume). Only one other sector that we have studied, telecommunications, another infrastructure sector, experienced nationalization, and that was only for a short time during the First World War (Bickers, Chapter 3 in this volume).[12] Hence, although the economic and political factors, discussed before, are probably more important in explaining the development and effect of property rights policies, there may also be important variations associated with the type of industry or sector in question.

PRODUCTION AND ALLOCATION ACTIONS, STATE STRUCTURES, AND GOVERNANCE TRANSFORMATIONS

As we saw earlier in this chapter, there is no shortage of evidence that state actors in the United States have actively subsidized economic development by providing or allocating resources and information. This has been especially true in periods of economic decline or in boom times when economic actors have been unable to procure the resources and information they needed for continuing or expanding production. Although state governments have historically been most active, the federal government has been prominent during wartime or in periods of high defense spending. On the other hand, with the exception of the general tendency, noted earlier, for government spending to implicitly support scale, concentration, and bilateral exchange, it is much more difficult to identify the effects that both specific production and allocation actions, and the related effects of state structures have had on the transformation of economic governance in our eight sectors. In order to do this, we would have to demonstrate that state actors provided critical resources and information *in ways* and *at times* that actually influenced the organization of economic activity as measured on the two dimensions of our governance mechanism typology.

Why is it more difficult to determine how state production and allocation actions, rather than property rights actions, influenced the strategies of economic actors and, in turn, governance transformations? Although the data are somewhat ambiguous, we hypothesize that there are two reasons for this difficulty. First, in general, this type of state action at the *federal* level has been more politically contested and, therefore, obstructed than has been the case with property rights actions. Property rights and regulatory actions are easily and routinely legitimated by reference to the state's roles of making, interpreting, and enforcing the law. In contrast, produc-

12 The short-lived nationalization in telecommunications and the prolonged debate during the 1950s about building state-owned nuclear power plants for commercial and *military* purposes suggests that the state's role in governance transformations may also be linked to its position in the geopolitical arena, a theme we have not explored here, but which may be worth further study (e.g., Ikenberry 1988).

tion and allocation policies at the federal level tend to benefit some regions of the country more than others (e.g., Markusen 1985). Thus, at this level, these policies often become embroiled in interstate and regional political conflicts, and stalemate often results. Indeed, ever since Alexander Hamilton's Report on Manufactures, federal industrial policies have been blocked and disarmed by interstate and interregional competition as well as by class-based struggles (Zysman 1983; Bensel 1984; Markusen 1985, 1987; Vogel 1987; Eisinger 1988). However, production and allocation actions at the *subnational* level have met far less resistance because they are justified typically on grounds of improving the competitiveness of state-level businesses, and because labor and other challengers to business subsidies have been less well organized in general at the state level than at the national level, at least in the twentieth century. Yet, with the exception of industries that are highly concentrated regionally, such as automobiles in Michigan and dairying in Wisconsin and Minnesota, there is little evidence from our sectors that state-level production and allocation policies have been decisive in the constitution of governance regimes. Why? Because these policies vary so much from one state government to another, it is very difficult to determine the *combined* effect that all of these policies have on a particular sector of the economy. The one possible exception to this generalization is the railroad industry, where lavish state and local government spending in the nineteenth century, and *federal* land grants in excess of 130 million acres, spurred a pattern of railroad development that helped to establish the early monopoly position of the railroad companies.[13] The point is that production and allocation policies at the federal level have relatively little impact on governance transformations because their use is often blocked politically, and at the subnational level, their use is so varied that it is usually impossible to determine what their effects are over all.

Our second hypothesis that suggests why it is difficult to determine the effects of production and allocation actions on the structure of governance has to do with the relationship between the state's production and allocation actions, on the one hand, and the strategies of private economic actors, on the other. Since these state actions have been primarily designed either to directly subsidize private accumulation or to provide public funds to privately appropriable infrastructures, they are likely to *reinforce* already existing *private* production and exchange strategies and power relationships. Thus, it is often very difficult to isolate and determine the *independent* effects that state actions, as opposed to private actions, have on governance transformations. As John Zysman (1983) demonstrated, the United States

---

13 The development of oligopolistic railroads itself helped spur distribution system hierarchies in meatpacking and dairying (see Portz and Young, Chapters 9 and 8, respectively, in this volume).

typically pursues "company-led" industrial adjustment strategies where the state follows and reinforces the strategies that are already preferred by business. Indeed, we have clear examples of this in the preferential loans to steel during the Carter Administration, the Chrysler bailout, and protective tariffs and voluntary restraint agreements in steel and automobiles (Scherrer, Chapters 6 and 7 in this volume).

With these considerations in mind, what patterns seem to emerge from our case histories? In contrast to property rights, we find relatively few clear examples of state production and allocation actions that were explicitly designed to either countervail existing private strategies or power balances, or to promote a specific state interest. Dairying seems to be the most obvious case where federal and state government actors decisively and *deliberately* encouraged governance transformations through production and allocation actions in ways that altered private governance strategies and the existing balance of power among private actors. In the late nineteenth and early twentieth century, the federal government created land-grant colleges, experiment stations, and extension services that provided the institutional base for the later development of an information-sharing network that helped to coordinate economic activity. Again, in the 1930s, state provision of price supports, milk-marketing orders, and technical information explicitly contributed to the emergence of a new multilateral governance regime. Less clear cut are the impacts on governance regimes in the automobile, meat, and steel sectors of state government subsidies, tax provisions, and infrastructures that were dedicated to attracting business to their states or regions. Presumably, these measures were designed to attract companies that were searching for ways to cut labor and other costs, but there is considerable controversy over whether such steps were really decisive in the decision making of firms (Eisinger 1988; Fosler 1988).

Of course, after 1965, in response to political mobilization to implement national health insurance, Congress *unintentionally* triggered transformations in the hospital sector by devising the Medicare program that paid for medical care and increased access for the elderly in ways that absorbed much of the risk of investing in hospitals, and that led to capital market control of new investment and to new organizational forms, such as for-profit chains and contract management (Arnold, Chapter 10 in this volume). Whether the federal government can *deliberately* orchestrate another transformation through production and allocation actions in order to deal with the sector's cost and access problems, embedded in the third-party payment structure of the present regime, is less clear. Promotion of organizational changes, such as health maintenance organizations, and the manipulation of incentives via tax reimbursement policies in order to control soaring healthcare costs could founder because of fragmentation among state authorities, ideological and political opposition to government intrusion, and the structure of financial markets.

Nuclear energy provides the clearest example of a governance transformation that was triggered by state production and allocation actions in order to pursue a coherently articulated *state* interest. In the nuclear sector, the federal government provided technology, information, capital, and uranium enrichment services. It was the federal government that created a variety of multilateral research networks around national laboratories in order to develop a commercially viable reactor technology, and it was the federal government that offered incentives to utility companies to convince them to begin purchasing nuclear plants, thus inaugurating a market for this new technology. However, even in this case, state structures militated against the successful stabilization of the industry. Conflicts between federal and state governments over licensing, safety, radioactive waste storage and disposal, and reprocessing punctuated the short history of the sector. Furthermore, the Joint Committee on Atomic Energy, the Atomic Energy Commission, and the Nuclear Regulatory Commission exercised their mandates in ways that provoked a legitimation crisis and political mobilization using available entry points in other state agencies, both federal and subnational (Campbell, Chapter 4 in this volume).

Several additional points are worth noting. First, where the state's production and allocation tools seem to have had discernible and independent effects on governance transformations, it was usually because state actors used them in ways that exerted *pressures for change,* as occurred in the development of research networks in the dairy and nuclear sectors. To the extent that state-level subsidies, tax benefits, and infrastructure projects were designed to lure auto, steel, and meatpacking companies to different regions of the country, state governments defined economic spaces in ways that may have created pressures for decentralizing these sectors. In contrast, we found relatively few examples of state actors participating in the *selection process* through production and allocation actions, such as when Congress stabilized decentralized coordination in the hospital sector through Hill–Burton grants for hospital construction (Arnold, Chapter 10 in this volume). More often, and this leads to our second point, the structure of the state often fragmented these efforts and stalemated policy making in this regard. For example, although actors in the federal government produced and allocated resources in order to develop a market for waste reprocessing services in the nuclear sector, the state's *organizational configuration* fostered intrastate political stalemates between federal and state governments over waste disposal policy that undermined this market. Similarly, by providing various *arenas,* such as licensing hearings and accessible courts, to outsiders, the state's structure provided these actors with opportunities that contributed further to the reprocessing market's demise (Campbell, Chapter 4 in this volume). Third, insofar as the selection process is concerned, we have not found any examples where the state used production and allocation actions to ratify or legitimize emergent governance regimes. Indeed, legitimation via these tools seems difficult to secure in the American ideological, political, and institutional environment.

Theoretical implications

Our survey of the role of production and allocation tools suggests several theoretical conclusions. For example, the American state has been more aggressive as an *economic player* than much of the literature has recognized. Despite the difficulties associated with discerning the effects of production and allocation tools, we have noted many examples where federal and state governments have provided substantial inputs of resources and information at a sectoral level. There is every sign that this kind of activity will become increasingly prominent, especially at the state level (Eisinger 1988; Fosler 1988) and through various Defense Department projects at the federal level. Scholars who generalize about the relatively passive, noninterventionist, and allegedly weak role of the state in the United States would do well to pay more attention to state policy at the subnational level and to the Pentagon and the defense establishment as perhaps the strongest part of the contemporary American state (Hooks forthcoming). Nevertheless, property rights actions have been much more decisive in governance transformations, at least in our cases – a finding that is broadly consistent with the general observation that the U.S. state tends to prefer, and is better endowed in terms of legitimacy and institutional capabilities, to play the role of a *regulator* or *umpire* of economic activity, rather than the more involved player that actually participates in transactions (e.g., Shonfield 1965; Katzenstein 1978; Dyson 1983; Edmonds 1983:72).

As suggested earlier, our cases also demonstrate the problems of fragmented and decentralized policy making that have frustrated efforts to develop, or even debate, industrial policies (e.g., Shonfield 1965: 323; Edmonds 1983; Zysman 1983; Eisinger 1988). For example, although we saw that the Nuclear Regulatory Commission tried to promote the standardization of nuclear plants as a way to speed licensing and reduce costs of new nuclear facilities, the fear of violating antitrust law was partially responsible for discouraging utility companies from buying standardized plants (Campbell, Chapter 4 in this volume). In railroads, although Congress instructed the Interstate Commerce Commission to rationalize operations in the railroad sector, the courts limited the agency's authority and undermined its capacity to carry out this mandate until Congress passed further legislation between 1903 and 1910 to remedy this problem (Kennedy, Chapter 5 in this volume). Intrastate conflicts have also punctuated the current and prolonged governance regime selection process in telecommunications with Congress, the Federal Communications Commission, and the federal courts taking competing and conflicting stands on the future evolution of the sector. Therefore, there is reason to doubt that *competing* economic development policies at the state level can really add up to a strong thrust for industrial transformation under today's conditions. Often firms appear to play states off against each other as a way of cutting costs rather than reorganizing production or seeking longer-term relations with labor and suppliers, or close and lasting linkages with an industrial district or particular region of the country (Piore and Sabel 1984).

However, we have found instances where those parts of the state apparatus that were involved with sectoral governance were organized very differently and, as a result, had much different effects. The success enjoyed for a time by the very centralized and unified Atomic Energy Commission and the Joint Committee on Atomic Energy in choreographing the initial development of the nuclear sector is a case in point. Another is the Department of Transportation, which revived Conrail so successfully that some in Congress and the Reagan Administration came to believe that the company was capable of surviving on its own and was ready to be returned to the private sector. Thus, we are again impressed by the tremendous variation in the organizational configuration of the state and in the policy tools of federal agencies and subnational governments. These variations can only be detected through comparisons of specific economic sectors.

These findings lend support to the argument that it is difficult to identify a priori which policy instruments and resources a state may utilize in promoting structural change in the economy. It is only when policy tools are mobilized and put to the test that we can properly sort out the contributions of state autonomy, organizational capacities, and political–economic conditions. For example, what was different about the institutional capacities of the French state in 1945 when it succeeded in recasting national capitalism, and the French state in the post–World War I period when it failed in a similar effort? Weiss suggests that it was a greater sense of crisis and decline that enabled the *same state* to outflank segments of business that were associated with collaboration and defeat (Weiss 1988). This should be a caution to those who overgeneralize about the institutional capacities (or lack thereof) of state actors in the United States. Some parts of the federal state are endowed with impressive administrative and bureaucratic capacities and are able to operate within a system of state–society linkages that belie notions of a weak state. Defense and agriculture are well-known examples. Furthermore, the individual subnational governments display wide variations along these dimensions and in their industrial policy strategies (Eisinger 1988; Fosler 1988). Perhaps someday in the United States, a national economic and political crisis will also so discredit dominant economic actors and their preferred organizational and exchange strategies that new state–society coalitions can emerge around more proactive state stategies.

What is important insofar as governance outcomes are concerned is that, for the most part, the kinds of production and allocation actions that are preferred by state actors in the United States have tended to reinforce the relative autonomy of producers, encourage the development and maintenance of hierarchical organization, and discourage the development of multilateral exchange. The *kinds* of state production and allocation actions chosen and the reliance on individual property rights actions, thus, have significant structural consequences for the economy. Our findings, particularly in the diary sector, also lend support to the generalization from comparative studies of corporatism that where clever and coherent state actors with ample resources exist at a sectoral level, producers and other economic actors have stronger incentives to develop strong associations or promotional networks, and that it is out of such multilateral governance regimes that effective industrial policy comes. Indirect intervention via property rights provides little such incentive to economic actors.

GOVERNANCE REGIMES, GOVERNANCE TRANSFORMATIONS, AND PRODUCTIVITY

The foregoing discussion has important implications for policy, particularly insofar as U.S. economic productivity has become a concern during the 1980s. One of the most important recent studies on industrial productivity problems in the United States was conducted by the Massachusetts Institute of Technology Commission on Industrial Productivity, which argued that the nation's productivity problems stemmed from several attitudinal and organizational weaknesses that pervade its production system (Dertouzos, Lester, and Solow 1989). The Commission criticized the preferences of American firms for organizing production hierarchically, their tendency to institutionalize arms-length relationships between firms and finance, thus perpetuating excessively narrow planning horizons, their inability to develop effective *collective* infrastructures for technological development, and their systematic neglect of human resources – a problem, according to the Commission, that arose from the ideological preferences and organizational strategies of firms that favored power imbalances between business and labor, and relatively uncooperative relationships between organizations. The Commission also criticized government policies as having failed systematically to encourage and support truly collective infrastructures, cooperative relations, power sharing, and negotiation and collaboration among participants in the production process. Moreover, they argued that governmental structures undermined efforts to encourage the more rapid development and diffusion of technology, and facilitated fragmentation and conflict rather than coherent, long-term perspectives in policy and regulation.

Whereas these characteristics of industry and the policy environment may not have adversely affected U.S. economic performance in the past, this is no longer the case. The MIT Commission argued that changes in technology, economic conditions, and consumer preferences have created a need throughout the economy for producing and delivering high-quality products and services in more flexible and adaptive ways that require more cooperation within firms, and among firms, workers, suppliers, and customers. In our analytical language, what is required are new governance regimes that tilt more toward multilateral exchange and nonhierarchical organizational strategies.

Despite its many insights, the MIT Commission did not consider *how* these changes might occur or how deeply rooted these behaviors are in existing strategies, structures and power relations. Our case studies and the theoretical perspective on governance transformations that we have developed in these two concluding chapters help rectify this omission by providing insights about how these problematic patterns of behavior and institutionalized relationships emerged historically, and especially how state actions and structures, among other things, have contributed to their development. Hence, we are in a position to at least speculate about the prospects for governance transformations in the directions that the MIT Commission recommended. Of course, in doing so, we recognize that we must be very cautious in generalizing beyond our sample of economic sectors because we find considerable variation within and across them, especially with respect to what we call their evolutionary trajectories.

To review briefly, we stressed in Chapter 11 and in this chapter that state actors and state structures are always part of the process whereby new governance regimes are selected. The state has acted directly in pursuit of its own goals or, more typically in the United States, as a mediator among or a reflection of social pressures. The state has deployed both property rights and production and allocation policy tools in ways that have influenced the strategic choices of private economic actors. In some instances, the state has refrained from doing anything other than enforcing existing property rights and leaving the terrain of economic activity to dominant private actors. Furthermore, the state's structure has influenced significantly the selection process by channeling politics as well as constraining political and economic strategies and struggles in distinctive ways. In this sense, politics also plays an important role in influencing how economic sectors are constituted and how they are transformed (or not) historically.[14] Given the salience we have accorded to the strategic choices of

---

14 Doing full justice to the politics of governance transformations in our sectors is beyond the possibilities of this project. It would have required detailed legislative and legal

private actors and how they are formed, and to the importance of political and institutional factors in shaping the ways in which the state helps constitute the economy, our model of governance selection clearly shuns deterministic accounts in favor of one that recognizes the complexities and contingencies that are involved in the governance transformation process.

Our findings converge generally with those of the MIT Commission with respect to the continued preference in the United States for governance regimes that are dominated by strategies of hierarchical organization and bilateral exchange. We also agree that the state tends to reinforce these tendencies. Of course, our case studies reveal exceptions where the state episodically has favored some forms of multilateral exchange, at least among *producers,* such as in associations or promotional networks. Yet, as we have seen, these efforts have failed frequently to survive due to the fragmented nature of state structures, political conflict and legitimation challenges, and hierarchical traditions that were fostered by state policies that implicitly favored industrial concentration. Indeed, as far as the evolutionary trajectories of our sectors are concerned, there are some cases, most notably automobiles, where obligational networks, multilateral exchange, and other cooperative relationships have emerged recently as a complement to hierarchical governance. However, these forms of governance have not replaced outsourcing and the flight of capital to nonunionized states as strategic options for firms, and state property rights and production and allocation actions have not limited significantly the prerogatives of producers in this sector. In the nuclear energy sector, multilateral forms of governance have emerged, but only in order to cope with what private managers perceived as being failures and contradictions in government regulation and with the effects of antinuclear political mobilizations.

In fact, many of our cases reveal that there has been notable movement recently in the *opposite* direction from that which the MIT Commission recommended. In the meatpacking sector, production is becoming more, not less, concentrated, and relationships between meatpackers and labor, on the one hand, and between meatpackers and other producers, on the other, have been dominated by harsh coercion and disregard for worker health and safety, and intense competition, respectively. The dairy industry, traditionally the epitome of state-supported multilateral governance, seems to be moving in the direction of increasing concentration, regional conflict, and the breakdown of promotional networks as overproduction and rising costs to taxpayers are causing the state to withdraw its support.

histories of each sector, a task that could easily fill eight volumes on its own. The classic example of this genre is Willard Hurst's 700-page history of the nineteenth-century timber industry in Wisconsin. On the problems and promises of doing this kind of research, see Scheiber (1981).

Multilateral forms of governance have never emerged in a significant way in the telecommunications sector, where state-enforced market competition for long-distance service now coexists with the partially regulated regional "Baby Bells," all in a political environment of uncertainty because of conflicts among regulators. In the steel sector, multilateral exchange strategies have weakened as trade associations have lost authority and as relationships with labor have worsened. The hospital sector has experienced increasing concentration and hierarchical organization. Recent efforts have been made to reprivatize and reduce budgets and technological support for Conrail and Amtrak, respectively – two notable examples of successful efforts to organize firms collectively, albeit through public takeover.

The point is that, although each sector has responded to its own set of shifting technological and economic conditions, our cases offer relatively few examples of enduring state support for multilateral exchange and the kind of cooperative relations that the MIT Commission favors. Nor is there much evidence that the preferences of private or state actors are shifting in that direction. To the contrary, our broadest and most consistent finding remains that in times of economic difficulty, such as the present, the state has tended to define property rights and allocate resources and information in ways that tilt to the advantage of producers relative to labor, suppliers, customers, and the public. The state tends to support multilateral exchange among *producers,* but not the development of longer planning horizons on the part of managers or cooperative relations among business, labor, and other participants in the production process. It follows that if changes in governance are to occur, they will apparently come primarily at the initiative of producers. Whether producers in competitive environments will do this without strong incentives or coercive pressure from the state to overcome the inevitable Prisoner's Dilemma constraints remains to be seen. Historical and comparative evidence *and* deductive theory suggest that this is not likely.

REFERENCES

CHAPTER 1

Abercrombie, Nicholas, Stephen Hill, and Bryan Turner. 1980. *The Dominant Ideology Thesis*. London: Allen and Unwin.

Adams, Walter, and James Brock. 1986. *The Bigness Complex*. New York: Pantheon.

Alchian, Armen, and Harold Demsetz. 1972. "Production, Information Costs, and Economic Organization." *American Economic Review* 62 (December): 777–95.

Aldrich, Howard. 1979. *Organizations and Environments*. Englewood Cliffs, NJ: Prentice-Hall.

Aldrich, Howard, and David A. Whetten. 1981. "Organization-Sets, Action-Sets, and Networks: Making the Most of Simplicity." In Paul Nystrom and William Starbuck, eds., *Handbook of Organizations*, Vol. 1. New York: Oxford University Press, pp. 385–408.

Allen, Michael P. 1974. "The Structure of Interorganizational Elite Cooptation: Interlocking Corporate Directorates." *American Sociological Review* 39(3): 393–406.

Alt, James E., and K. Alec Chrystal. 1983. *Political Economics*. Berkeley: University of California Press.

Benson, J. Kenneth. 1975. "The Interorganizational Network as a Political Economy." *Administrative Science Quarterly* 20: 229–49.

Berger, Suzanne. 1981. *Organizing Interests in Western Europe: Pluralism, Corporatism, and the Transformation of Politics*. New York: Cambridge University Press.

Bottomore, Tom. 1980. "Foreword." In Nicholas Abercrombie, Stephen Hill, and Bryan Turner, *The Dominant Ideology Thesis*. London: Allen and Unwin, pp. ix–x.

Bowles, Samuel, David Gordon, and Thomas Weisskopf. 1983. *Beyond the Wasteland: A Democratic Alternative to Economic Decline*. New York: Anchor.

Brock, Gerald. 1975. "Competition, Standards, and Self-Regulation in the Computer Industry." In Richard Caves and Marc Roberts, eds., *Regulating the Product: Quality and Variety*. Cambridge, MA: Ballinger, pp. 75–96.

Burt, Ronald S. 1988. "The Stability of American Markets." *American Journal of Sociology* 94(2): 356–95.

Business Week Team. 1982. *The Reindustrialization of America*. New York: McGraw-Hill.

Buttrick, John. 1952. "The Inside Contracting System." *Journal of Economic History* 12: 205–21.

Chandler, Alfred D. 1966. *Strategy and Structure: Chapters in the History of the Industrial Enterprise*. Garden City, NY: Doubleday.

————. 1977. *The Visible Hand: The Managerial Revolution in American Business.* Cambridge, MA: Harvard University Press.

————. 1980. "The United States: Seedbed of Managerial Capitalism." In Alfred Chandler and Herman Daems, eds., *Managerial Hierarchies: Comparative Perspectives on the Rise of the Modern Industrial Enterprise.* Cambridge, MA: Harvard University Press, pp. 9–40.

Coase, Ronald H. 1937. "The Nature of the Firm." *Economica* 4: 386–405.

Cohen, Joshua, and Joel Rogers. 1983. *On Democracy: Toward a Transformation of American Society.* New York: Penguin.

Commons, John R. 1924. *Legal Foundations of Capitalism.* New York: Macmillan.

Cook, Karen S. 1977. "Exchange and Power in Networks of Interorganizational Relations." *The Sociological Quarterly* 18(1): 62–82.

Cummings, Thomas G. 1984. "Transorganizational Development." In Barry Staw and L. L. Cummings, eds., *Research in Organizational Behavior,* Vol. 6. Greenwich, CN: JAI Press, pp. 367–422.

Daems, Herman. 1980. "The Rise of the Modern Industrial Enterprise: A New Perspective." In Alfred D. Chandler and Herman Daems, eds., *Managerial Hierarchies: Comparative Perspectives on the Rise of the Modern Industrial Enterprise.* Cambridge, MA: Harvard University Press, pp. 203–24.

deVille, Philippe. 1987. *The Coordination of Economic Activities: An Essay on Institutions and Economic Theory.* Unpublished manuscript, S.C.A.S.S. and Catholic University of Louvain, Louvain, Belgium.

Dolbeare, Kenneth. 1984. *Democracy at Risk: The Politics of Economic Renewal.* Chatham, NJ: Chatham House.

Domhoff, G. William. 1974. *The Bohemian Grove and Other Retreats.* New York: Harper and Row.

————. 1983. *Who Rules America Now? A View for the '80s.* Englewood Cliffs, NJ: Prentice–Hall.

Durkheim, Emile. 1933. *The Division of Labor in Society.* New York: The Free Press.

Dye, Thomas. 1976. *Who's Running America? Institutional Leadership in the United States.* Englewood Cliffs, NJ: Prentice-Hall.

Eccles, Robert. 1981. "The Quasifirm in the Construction Industry." *Journal of Economic Behavior and Organization* 2 (December): 335–57.

Elster, Johan. 1978. *Logic and Society: Contradictions and Possible Worlds.* Chichester: Wiley.

Ernst, Dieter. 1987. "New Technologies and Changing Government Relations." Paper presented at the Conference on New Technologies and New Intermediaries; Competition, Intervention, and Cooperation in Europe, America, and Asia, Stanford University, June 4–7.

Etzioni, Amitai. 1988. *The Moral Dimension: Toward A New Economics.* New York: The Free Press.

Foth, Joseph H. 1930. *Trade Associations: Their Services to Industry.* New York: Ronald Press.

Friedland, Roger, Frances Fox Piven, and Robert Alford. 1977. "Political Conflict, Urban Structure, and Fiscal Crisis." *International Journal of Urban and Regional Research* 1(3): 447–71.

Friedman, Milton. 1962. *Capitalism and Freedom.* Chicago: University of Chicago Press.

Galambos, Louis. 1966. *Competition and Cooperation: The Emergence of a National Trade Association.* Baltimore: Johns Hopkins University Press.

Galbraith, John Kenneth. 1967. *The New Industrial State.* New York: Mentor.

Gilder, George. 1981. *Wealth and Poverty.* New York: Bantam Books.

Gordon, Richard. 1987. "Growth and the Relations of Production in High Technology Industry." Unpublished manuscript, University of California, Santa Cruz.

Gottfredson, Linda, and Paul White. 1981. "Interorganizational Agreements." In Paul Nystrom and William Starbuck, eds., *Handbook of Organizational Design*, Vol. 1. New York: Oxford University Press, pp. 471–86.

Granovetter, Mark. 1985. "Economic Action and Social Structure: The Problem of Embeddedness." *American Journal of Sociology* 91(3): 481–510.

Hall, Peter A. 1986. *Governing the Economy: The Politics of State Intervention in Britain and France*. New York: Oxford University Press.

Hannan, Michael, and John Freeman. 1977. "The Production Ecology of Organizations." *American Journal of Sociology* 82(5): 929–64.

Hightower, Jim. 1978. *Hard Times, Hard Tomatoes*. New York: Schenkman.

Himmelberg, Robert F. 1976. *The Origins of the National Recovery Administration: Business, Government, and the Trade Association Issue, 1921–1933*. New York: Fordham University Press.

Hirschman, Albert O. 1970. *Exit, Voice, and Loyalty*. Cambridge, MA: Harvard University Press.

Hodgson, Geoffrey M. 1988. *Economics and Institutions: A Manifesto for a Modern Institutional Economics*. Philadelphia: University of Pennsylvania Press.

Hollingsworth, J. Rogers. 1987. *Controversy About American Hospitals*. Washington, DC: American Enterprise Institute.

Hollingsworth, J. Rogers, and Leon N. Lindberg. 1985. "The Governance of the American Economy: The Role of Markets, Clans, Hierarchies, and Associative Behavior." In Wolfgang Streeck and Philippe Schmitter, eds., *Private Interest Government: Beyond Market and State*. Beverly Hills, CA: Sage, pp. 221–54.

Hurst, James Willard. 1982. *Law and Markets in United States History: Different Modes of Bargaining Among Interests*. Madison, WI: University of Wisconsin Press.

Johanson, Jan, and Lars-Gunnar Mattsson. 1987. "Interorganizational Relations in Industrial Systems: A Network Approach Compared with the Transaction Cost Approach." *International Journal of Management and Organization* 17 (Spring): 34–48.

Knoke, David. 1981, "Commitment and Detachment in Voluntary Associations." *American Sociological Review* 46(2): 141–58.

———. 1985. "The Political Economies of Associations." In Richard Braungart, ed., *Research in Political Sociology*, Vol. 1. Greenwich, CN.: JAI Press, pp. 211–42.

Knoke, David, and David Prensky. 1984. "What Relevance Do Organization Theories Have for Voluntary Associations?" *Social Science Quarterly* 65(1): 3–20.

Knoke, David, and James Wood. 1981. *Organized for Action: Commitment in Voluntary Associations*. New Brunswick, NJ: Rutgers University Press.

Knoke, David, and Christine Wright-Isak. 1982. "Individual Motives and Organizational Incentives Systems." In Samuel Bacharach, ed., *Research in the Sociology of Organizations*, Vol. 1. Greenwich, CN: JAI Press, pp. 209–54.

Knowles, James C. 1973. *The Rockefeller Financial Group*. New York: Warner Modular Publications, Module 343.

Lamoreaux, Naomi R. 1985. *The Great Merger Movement in American Business, 1885–1904*. New York: Cambridge University Press.

Laumann, Edward, and Peter Marsden. 1982. "Microstructural Analysis in Interorganizational Systems." *Social Networks* 4(4): 329–48.

Lazerson, Mark. 1988. "Organizational Growth of Small Firms: An Outcome of Markets and Hierarchies?" *American Sociological Review* 53: 330–42.

Lazonick, William. 1986. "Organizations, Markets, and Productivity." Paper presented at the Economic History Association meeting, Hartford, Connecticut.

Lindberg, Leon N. 1985. "Political Economy, Economic Governance, and the Coordination of Economic Activities." *Jahrbuch 1984/85*, Wissenschaftskolleg zu Berlin, Berlin, West Germany.

Lindblom, Charles. 1977. *Politics and Markets*. New York: Harper and Row.

Macaulay, Stewart. 1963. "Non-contractual Relations in Business: A Preliminary Study." *American Sociological Review* 28(1): 55–67.

McCloskey, Donald N. 1986. *The Rhetoric of Economics*. Madison, WI: University of Wisconsin Press.

McCraw, Thomas K., and Patricia O'Brien. 1986. "Production and Distribution: Competition Policy and Industry Structure." In Thomas McCraw, ed., *America Versus Japan*. Boston: Harvard Business School Press, pp. 77–116.

Macneil, I. R. 1978. "Contracts: Adjustments of Long-Term Economic Relations Under Classical, Neoclassical, and Relational Contract Law." *Northwestern University Law Review* 72: 854–906.

Marglin, Stephen A. 1974. "What Do Bosses Do? The Origins and Functions of Hierarchy in Capitalist Production." *Review of Radical Political Economics* 6(2): 33–60.

Mintz, Beth, and Michael Schwartz. 1985. *The Power Structure of American Business*. Chicago: University of Chicago Press.

Mizruchi, Mark. 1982. *The American Corporate Network*. Beverly Hills, CA: Sage.

Moe, Terry. 1980. *The Organization of Interests and Incentives and the Internal Dynamics of Political Interest Groups*. Chicago: University of Chicago Press.

Naylor, Emmett H. 1921. *Trade Associations: Their Organization and Management*. New York: Ronald Press.

Nelson, Richard R., and Sidney Winter. 1982. *An Evolutionary Theory of Economic Change*. Cambridge, MA: Harvard University Press.

North, Douglass. 1981. *Structure and Change in Economic History*. New York: Norton.

Offe, Claus, and Helmut Wiesenthal. 1985. "Two Logics of Collective Action." In Claus Offe, *Disorganized Capitalism*. Cambridge, MA: The MIT Press, pp. 170–220.

Olson, Mancur. 1965. *The Logic of Collective Action*. Cambridge, MA: Harvard University Press.

Ouchi, William G. 1977. "Review of *Markets and Hierarchies: Analysis and Antitrust Implications* by Oliver E. Williamson." *Administrative Science Quarterly* 22(3): 540–4.

———. 1980. "Markets, Bureaucracies, and Clans." *Administrative Science Quarterly* 25(1): 129–41.

———. 1984. *The M-Form Society*. Reading, MA: Addison-Wesley.

Perrow, Charles. 1981. "Markets, Hierarchies and Hegemony." In Andrew Van de Ven and William Joyce, eds., *Perspectives on Organization, Design, and Behavior*. New York: Wiley, pp. 371–86.

———. 1986. *Complex Organizations: A Critical Essay*, third edition. New York: Random House.

Pfeffer, Jeffrey. 1972. "Size and Composition of Corporate Boards of Directors: The Organization and Its Environment." *Administrative Science Quarterly* 17(2): 218–28.

———. 1987. "A Resource Dependence Perspective on Intercorporate Relations." In Mark Mizruchi and Michael Schwartz, eds., *Intercorporate Relations: The Structural Analysis of Business*. New York: Cambridge University Press, pp. 25–55.

Pfeffer, Jeffrey, and Phillip Nowak. 1976. "Joint Ventures and Interorganizational Interdependence." *Administrative Science Quarterly* 21(3): 398–418.

Pfeffer, Jeffrey, and Gerald Salancik. 1978. *The External Control of Organizations: A Resource Dependence Perspective.* New York: Harper and Row.

Polanyi, Karl. 1944. *The Great Transformation: The Political and Economic Origins of Our Time.* Boston: Beacon Press.

Porter, Michael E. 1986. *Competition in Global Industries.* Boston: Harvard Business School Press.

Powell, Walter W. 1987. "Hybrid Organizational Arrangements: New Form or Transitional Development." *California Management Review* 30(1): 67–87.

Reich, Robert B. 1983. *The Next American Frontier.* New York: Times Books.

Robbins, James A. 1987. "Organizational Economics: Notes on the Use of Transaction-Cost Theory in the Study of Organizations." *Administrative Science Quarterly* 32(1): 68–86.

Sanger, David. 1987. "Trying to Regain the Market in Chips." *The New York Times,* March 8, Section 4, p. 7.

Scherer, Frederic M. 1970. *Industrial Market Structure and Economic Performance.* Chicago: Rand McNally.

Schmitter, Philippe C. 1984. "Neo-Corporatism and the State." EUI Working Paper No. 106. Florence, Italy: Department of Political and Social Sciences, European University Institute.

Schmitter, Philippe C., and Gerhard Lehmbruch, eds. 1979. *Trends Toward Corporatist Intermediation.* Beverly Hills, CA: Sage.

Schmitter, Philippe C., and Wolfgang Streeck. 1981. "The Organization of Business Interests: A Research Design to Study the Associative Action of Business Interests in the Advanced Industrial Societies of Western Europe." Discussion Paper IIM/LMP 81–13. Berlin, West Germany: Wissenschaftszentrum.

Simon, Herbert A. 1961. *Administrative Behavior.* New York: Macmillan.

Skowronek, Stephen. 1982. *Building a New American State: The Expansion of National Administrative Capacities, 1877–1920.* New York: Cambridge University Press.

Staber, Udo, and Howard Aldrich. 1983. "Trade Association Stability and Public Policy." In Richard Hall and Robert Quinn, eds., *Organizational Theory and Public Policy.* Beverly Hills, CA: Sage, pp. 163–78.

Stevenson, Rodney. 1987. "Institutional Economics and the Theory of Production." *Journal of Economic Issues* 21(4): 1471–93.

Stinchcombe, Arthur. 1985. "Contracts as Hierarchical Documents." In Arthur Stinchcombe and Carol Heimer, *Organization Theory and Project Management: Administering Uncertainty in Norwegian Offshore Oil.* Oslo: Norwegian University Press, pp. 121–71.

Stone, Katherine. 1981. "The Origins of Job Structures in the Steel Industry." In Mary Zey-Ferrell and Michael Aiken, eds., *Complex Organizations: Critical Perspectives.* Glenview, IL: Scott, Forseman, pp. 349–81.

Stone, Lawrence. 1981. *The Past and the Present.* Boston: Routledge and Kegan Paul.

Streeck, Wolfgang. 1983. "Between Pluralism and Corporatism: German Business Associations and the State." *Journal of Public Policy* 3(3): 265–83.

Streeck, Wolfgang, and Philippe C. Schmitter. 1985. "Community, Market, State – And Associations? The Prospective Contribution of Interest Governance to Social Order." In Wolfgang Streeck and Philippe C. Schmitter, eds., *Private Interest Government: Beyond Market and State.* Beverly Hills, CA: Sage, pp. 1–29.

Telser, Lester, and H. N. Higinbotham. 1977. "Organized Futures Markets: Costs and Benefits." *Journal of Political Economy* 85(6): 969–1000.

Thurow, Lester C. 1980. *The Zero-Sum Society.* New York: Basic Books.

Useem, Michael. 1984. *The Inner Circle: Large Corporations and the Rise of Business Political Activity in the U.S. and U.K.* New York: Oxford University Press.

Ward, Benjamin. 1972. *What's Wrong with Economics?* New York: Basic Books.

Warner, W. Lloyd, Darab Unwalla, and John Trimm. 1967. *The Emergent American Society: Large Scale Organizations,* Vol. 1. New Haven: Yale University Press.

Warren, Roland. 1967. "The Interorganizational Field as a Focus for Investigation." *Administrative Science Quarterly* 12(3): 396–419.

Weber, Max. 1958. *The Protestant Ethic and the Spirit of Capitalism.* New York: Scribners.

———. 1978. *Economy and Society,* Vols. 1 and 2. Edited and translated by Gunther Roth and Claus Wittich. Berkeley: University of California Press.

White, Harrison. 1981. "Where Do Markets Come From?" *American Journal of Sociology* 87(3): 517–47.

Whitney, Simon. 1934. *Trade Associations and Industrial Control: A Critique of the N.R.A.* New York: Central Book.

Williamson, Oliver E. 1975. *Markets and Hierarchies: Analysis and Antitrust Implications.* New York: The Free Press.

———. 1985. *The Economic Institutions of Capitalism: Firms, Markets, Relational Contracting.* New York: The Free Press.

———. 1986. *Economic Organization: Firms, Markets and Policy Control.* New York: New York University Press.

Williamson, Oliver E., and William G. Ouchi. 1981. "The Markets and Hierarchies Program of Research: Origins, Implications, Prospects." In Andrew Van de Ven and William Joyce, eds., *Perspectives On Organization, Design, and Behavior.* New York: Wiley, pp. 347–70.

Wolfe, Alan. 1977. *The Limits of Legitimacy: Political Contradictions of Contemporary Capitalism.* New York: The Free Press.

Zald, Mayer N. 1970. "Political Economy: A Framework for Comparative Analysis." In Mayer Zald, ed., *Power in Organizations.* Nashville, TN: Vanderbilt University Press, pp. 221–61.

Zeitz, Gerald. 1980. "Interorganizational Dialectics." *Administrative Science Quarterly* 25(1): 72–88.

CHAPTER 2

Ackroyd, S., G. Burell, M. Hughes, and A. Whitaker. 1988. "The Japanization of British Industry," *Industrial Relations Journal* 19: 11–23.

Altshuler, Alan M., D. Anderson, D. Jones, and J. Womack. 1984. *The Future of the Automobile.* London: Allen and Unwin.

Aoki, Masahiko. 1987. "The Japanese Firm in Transition," In Kozo Yamamura and Yasukichi Yasuba, eds., *The Political Economy of Japan,* Vol. 1. Stanford: Stanford University Press.

———. 1988. *Information, Incentives and Bargaining in the Japanese Economy.* Cambridge, MA: Cambridge University Press.

Bain, Joseph S. 1956. *Barriers to New Competition: Their Character and Consequences in Manufacturing Industries.* Cambridge: Harvard University Press.

Becker, William H. 1971. "American Wholesale Hardware Trade Associations, 1870–1900." *Business History Review* 45: 182–5.

Berle, Adolf A., and Gardiner C. Means. 1968. *The Modern Corporation and Private Property.* New York: Harcourt Brace Jovanovich.

Bork, Robert H. 1978. *The Antitrust Paradox: A Policy at War with Itself.* New York: Basic Books.

Braverman, Harry. 1974. *Labor and Monopoly Capital: The Degradation of Work in the Twentieth Century.* New York: Monthly Review Press.

Brooks, Harvey. 1986. "National Science Policy and Technological Innovation." In Ralph Landau and Nathan Rosenberg, eds., *The Positive Sum Strategy: Harnessing Technology for Economic Growth.* Washington, DC: National Academy Press, pp. 119–67.

Burns, Arthur Robert. 1936. *The Decline of Competition: A Study of the Evolution of American Industry.* New York: McGraw-Hill.

Buttrick, John. 1952. "The Inside Contracting System." *Journal of Economic History* 12: 205–21.

Carosso, Vincent P. 1970. *Investment Banking in America: A History.* Cambridge, MA: Harvard University Press.

Caves, Richard, and W. Murphy. 1976. "Franchising: Firms, Markets, and Intangible Assets." *Southern Economics Journal* 42: 572–86.

Chandler, Alfred D. 1956. *Henry Varnum Poor: Business Editor, Analyst, and Reformer.* Cambridge, MA: Harvard University Press.

———. 1962. *Strategy and Structure: Chapters in the History of the American Industrial Enterprise.* Cambridge, MA: The MIT Press.

———. 1977. *The Visible Hand: The Managerial Revolution in American Business.* Cambridge, MA: Harvard University Press.

Coleman, William. 1985. "Analyzing the Association Action of Business." *Canadian Public Administration* 28: 413–33.

Cornish, William R. 1979. "Legal Control Over Cartels and Monopolization, 1880–1914: A Comparison." In Norbert Horn and Jürgen Kocka, eds., *Law and the Formation of the Big Enterprises in the Nineteenth and Early Twentieth Centuries: Studies in the History of Industrialization in Germany, France, Great Britain and the United States.* Göttingen: Vandenhoeck and Ruprecht.

Dankbaar, Ben. 1989. "Sectoral Governance in the Automobile Industries of West Germany, Great Britain, and France." Discussion Paper 89–008. Maastricht, The Netherlands: Maastricht Economic Research Institute on Innovation and Technology.

Davies, Robert B. 1969. "Peacefully Working to Conquer the World: The Singer Manufacturing Company in Foreign Markets, 1854–1889." *Business History Review* 43 (Autumn): 299–346.

Davis, Lance. 1966. "The Capital Markets and Industrial Concentration: The U.S. and the U.K., a Comparative Study." *Economic History Review,* Second Series, 19: 255–72.

Dennison, S.R. 1939. "Vertical Integration and the Iron and Steel Industry." *Economic Journal* 49 (June): 244–58.

Dewing, Arthur S. 1914. *Corporate Promotions and Reorganizations.* Cambridge, MA: Harvard University Press.

DiMaggio, Paul, and Walter W. Powell. 1983. "The Iron Cage Revisited: Institutional Isomorphism and Collective Rationality in Organizational Fields." *American Sociological Review* 48: 147–60.

Dore, Ronald. 1983. "Goodwill and the Spirit of Market Capitalism." *The British Journal of Sociology* 34: 459–82.

Eccles, Robert. 1981. "The Quasifirm in the Construction Industry." *Journal of Economic Behavior and Organization* 2 (December): 355–7.

Edwards, Richard T. 1979. *Contested Terrain*. New York: Basic Books.

Fell, James E. 1979. *Ores to Metals: The Rocky Mountain Smelting Industry*. Lincoln, NE: University of Nebraska Press.

Fox, Eleanor M., and James T. Halverson, eds. 1979. *Industrial Concentration and the Market System: Legal, Economic, Social and Political Perspectives*. Chicago: American Bar Association.

Freeman, Christopher, ed. 1986. *Design, Innovation and Long Cycles in Economic Development*. New York: St. Martin's Press.

Freeman, Christopher, John Clark, and Luc Soete. 1982. *Unemployment and Technical Innovation: A Study of Long Waves and Economic Development*. Westport, CN: Greenwood Press.

Friedel, R., and P. Israel. 1986. *Edison's Electric Light*. New Brunswick, NJ: Rutgers University Press.

Friedman, David. 1988. *The Misunderstood Miracle: Industrial Development and Political Change in Japan*. Ithaca, NY: Cornell University Press.

Galambos, Louis. 1966. *Competition and Cooperation: The Emergence of a National Trade Association*. Baltimore: Johns Hopkins University Press.

Granovetter, Mark. 1985. "Economic Action and Social Structure: The Problem of Embeddedness." *American Journal of Sociology* 91(3): 481–510.

Hawley, Ellis W. 1966. *The New Deal and the Problem of Monopoly*. Princeton: Princeton University Press.

Hennart, Jean-Francois. 1982. *A Theory of Multinational Enterprise*. Ann Arbor, MI: University of Michigan Press.

Herrigel, Gary. 1989. "Industrial Order in the Machine Tool Industry: A Comparison of the United States and Germany." Paper presented at the Conference on Comparing Capitalist Economies, Ballagio, Italy, May 29–June 2.

Hilferding, R. 1968/1910. *Das Finanzkapital*. Frankfurt: Europaische Verlagsanstalt.

Hollingsworth, J. Rogers. 1986. *The Political Economy of Medicine: Great Britain and the United States*. Baltimore: Johns Hopkins University Press.

Hollingsworth, J. Rogers, and Robert Hanneman. 1984. *Centralization and Power in Social Service Delivery Systems*. Boston and The Hague: Kluwer-Nijhoff.

Hollingsworth, J. Rogers, and Leon N. Lindberg. 1985. "The Governance of the American Economy: The Role of Markets, Clans, Hierarchies, and Associative Behavior." In Philippe Schmitter and Wolfgang Streeck, eds., *Private Interest Government: Beyond Market and State*. London and Beverly Hills, CA: Sage, pp. 221–54.

Hyman, Richard. 1988. "Flexible Specialization: Miracle or Myth." In Richard Hyman and Wolfgang Streeck, eds., *New Technology and Industrial Relations*. New York and Oxford: Blackwell, pp. 48–60.

Hyman, Richard, and Wolfgang Streeck, eds. 1988. *New Technology and Industrial Relations*. New York and Oxford: Blackwell.

Jack, Andrew B. 1957. "Channels of Distribution for an Innovation: The Sewing Machine in America." *Explorations in Entrepreneurial History* 9 (February): 113–41.

Katzenstein, Peter J. 1985. *Small States in World Markets: Industrial Policy in Europe*. Ithaca, NY: Cornell University Press.

Keeler, John S. 1987. *The Politics of Neocorporation in France*. New York: Oxford University Press.

Koch, E. 1930. "Methods of Regulating Unfair Competition in Germany, England,

and the United States." *University of Pennsylvania Law Review* 78: 693–712, 854–78.

Kolko, Gabriel. 1963. *The Triumph of Conservatism: A Reinterpretation of American History.* Chicago: Quadrangle.

Kotz, David M. 1978. *Bank Control of Large Corporations in the United States.* Berkeley: University of California Press.

Kramer, Helen M. 1964. "Harvesters and High Finance: Formation of the International Harvester Company." *Business History Review* 38: 284–301.

Kristensen, Peer Hull. 1986. *Industrial Models in the Melting Pot of History and Technological Projects and Organizational Changes.* Roskilde, The Netherlands: Institut for Samfun Dsokonomi.

Kurth, James. 1979. "The Political Consequences of the Product Cycle: Industrial History and Political Outcomes." *International Organization* 33: 1–34.

Lamoreaux, Naomi R. 1985. *The Great Merger Movement in American Business, 1895–1904.* Cambrigde and New York: Cambridge University Press.

Landau, Ralph, and Nathan Rosenberg, eds. 1986. *The Positive Sum Strategy: Harnessing Technology for Economic Growth.* Washington, DC: National Academy Press.

Lawrence, Paul R., and Davis Dyer. 1983. *Renewing American Industry.* New York: Free Press.

Lawrence, Paul R., and Jay Lorsch. 1967. *Organization and Environment.* Boston: Harvard Business School Press.

Lazerson, Mark H. 1988. "Organizational Growth of Small Firms: An Outcome of Markets and Hierarchies." *American Sociological Review* 53: 330–42.

Letwin, William. 1965. *Law and Economic Policy in America: The Evolution of the Sherman Antitrust Act.* New York: Random House.

Levy, Felix. 1930. "A Contrast between the Anti-Trust Laws of Foreign Countries and of the United States." *Annals* 147: 125–37.

Lindberg, Leon N., John L. Campbell, and J. Rogers Hollingsworth. 1989. *Economic Governance and the Analysis of Structural Change in the American Economy.* Cambridge, MA: Harvard University, Center for Research on Politics and Social Organization, Working Papers Series.

McCraw, Thomas K., ed. 1984. *Prophets of Regulation: Charles Francis Adams, Louis D. Brandeis, James M. Landis, Alfred E. Kahn.* Cambridge, MA: Harvard University Press.

———. *America Versus Japan.* Boston: Harvard Business School Press.

McCurdy, Charles W. 1979. "The *Knight* Sugar Decision of 1895 and the Modernization of American Corporate Law, 1869–1903." *Business History Review* 58: 304–6, 314–23.

Moody, John. 1904. *The Truth About Trusts: A Description and Analysis of the American Trust Movement.* New York: Moody.

Mowery, David C. 1983. "The Relationship Between Intrafirm and Contractual Forms of Industrial Research in American Manufacturing, 1900–1940." *Explorations in Economic History* 20: 351–74.

———. 1987. *Alliance Politics and Economics: Multinational Joint Ventures in Commercial Aircraft.* Cambridge, MA: Ballinger.

Navin, Thomas R., and Marian V. Sears. 1955. "The Rise of a Market for Industrial Securities, 1887–1902." *Business History Review* 39: 105–38.

Nelson, Daniel. 1975. *Managers and Workers: Origins of the New Factory System in the United States, 1880–1920.* Madison, WI: University of Wisconsin Press.

Nelson, Ralph. 1959. *Merger Movements in American Industry, 1895–1956.* Princeton: Princeton University Press.

Nelson, Richard R., ed. 1982. *Government and Technical Progress. A Cross Industry Analysis*. New York: Pergamon.

———. *High Technology Policies: A Five Nation Comparison*. Washington, DC: American Enterprise Institute.

Noble, David F. 1977. *America By Design: Science, Technology, and the Rise of Corporate Capitalism*. New York: Oxford University Press.

Oliver, Nick, and Barry Wilkinson. 1988. *The Japanization of British Industry*. Oxford: Blackwell.

Parsons, Donald O., and Edward John Ray. 1975. "The United States Steel Consolidation: The Creation of Market Control." *Journal of Law and Economics* 15 (April): 181–219.

Passer, Harold C. 1953. *The Electrical Manufacturers, 1875–1900: A Study in Competition, Entrepreneurship, Technical Change, and Economic Growth*. Cambridge, MA: Harvard University Press.

Piore, Michael J. 1980. "Dualism as a Response to Flux and Uncertainty" and "The Technological Foundations of Dualism and Discontinuity." In Suzanne Berger and Michael J. Piore, eds., *Dualism and Discontinuity in Industrial Societies*. Cambridge and New York: Cambridge University Press, pp. 13–81.

Piore, Michael J., and Charles F. Sabel. 1984. *The Second Industrial Divide: Possibilities for Prosperity*. New York: Basic Books.

Porter, Glenn, and Harold C. Livesay. 1971. *Merchants and Manufacturers: Studies in the Changing Structure of Nineteenth Century Marketing*. Baltimore: Johns Hopkins University Press.

Porter, Michael. 1986. *Competition in Global Industries*. Boston, MA: Harvard Business School.

Powell, Walter W. 1985. *Getting Into Print: The Decision-Making Process in Scholarly Publishing*. Chicago: University of Chicago Press.

———. 1987. "Hybrid Organizational Arrangements: New Form or Transitional Development?" *California Management Review* 30(1): 67–87.

———. 1988. "The Transformation of Organizational Forms: How Useful Is Organizational Theory in Accounting for Social Change?" In Roger Friedland and Sandy Robertson, eds., *Beyond the Market* (forthcoming).

———. 1989. "Networks and the Governance of Capitalist Economies." Unpublished paper presented at the Conference on the Governance of Capitalist Economies, Rockefeller Foundation Conference Center, Bellagio, Italy, May 29–June 2.

Pratt, Joseph A. 1980. "The Petroleum Industry in Transition: Antitrust and the Decline of Monopoly Control in Oil." *Journal of Economic History* 40: 815–37.

Reich, Leonard S. 1977. "Research, Patents, and the Struggle to Control Radio: A Study of Big Business and the Uses of Industrial Research." *Business History Review* 51: 208–35.

———. 1980. "Industrial Research and the Pursuit of Corporate Stability: The Early Years of Bell Labs." *Business History Review* 54: 504–29.

Riggs, Henry E. 1988. "Innovations: A United States–Japan Perspective." In Daniel I. Okimoto and Thomas P. Rohlen, eds., *Inside the Japanese System*. Stanford: Stanford University Press, pp. 246–520.

Ripley, William Z., ed. 1916. *Trusts, Pools, and Corporations*, revised edition. New York: Ginn.

Sabel, Charles F. 1982. *Work and Politics*. Cambridge: Cambridge University Press.

———. 1987a. "Changing Models of Economic Efficiency and their Implications for Industrialization in the Third World." In Alejandro Foxley, Michael S.

McPherson, and Guillermo O'Donnell, eds., *Development, Democracy, and the Art of Trespassing*. Notre Dame, IN: University of Notre Dame Press.

———. 1987b. "The Reemergence of Regional Economies: Changes in the Scale of Production." Unpublished paper prepared for the Social Science Research Council volume, *Experimenting with Scale*.

Sabel, Charles F., and Jonathan Zeitlin. 1985. "Historical Alternatives to Mass Production: Politics, Markets, and Technology in Nineteenth Century Industrialization." *Past and Present* 108 (August): 133–76.

Scharpf, Fritz W. 1989. "Decision Rules, Decision Styles and Policy Choices." *Journal of Theoretical Politics* 1: 149–76.

Scherer, Frederic M. 1970. *Industrial Market Structure and Economic Performance*. Chicago: Rand McNally.

Schmitter, Philippe C. 1979. "Still the Century of Corporatism?" In Philippe C. Schmitter and G. Lehmbruch, eds., *Trends Towards Corporatist Intermediation*. London and Beverly Hills, CA: Sage, pp. 7–52.

———. 1990. "Sectors in Modern Capitalism: Modes of Governance and Variations in Performance." In J. Rogers Hollingsworth, Wolfgang Streeck, Philippe Schmitter, eds., *The Governance of Capitalist Economies*, (forthcoming).

Schmitter, Philippe C., and D. Brand. 1979. "Organizing Capitalists in the United States: The Advantages and Disadvantages of Exceptionalism." Unpublished paper presented before the American Political Science Association, Chicago, August 1979.

Schmitter, Philippe C., and G. Lehmbruch, eds. 1979. *Trends Towards Corporatist Intermediation*. Beverly Hills, CA: Sage.

Schmitter, Philippe C., and Wolfgang Streeck. 1981. "The Organization of Business Interests: A Research Design to Study the Associative Action of Business Interests in the Advanced Industrial Societies of Western Europe." Discussion Paper IIM/LMP 81–13. Berlin, West Germany: Wissenschaftszentrum.

Schneiberg, Marc, and J. Rogers Hollingsworth. 1989. "Transaction Cost Economics and Trade Associations." In Masahika Aoki, Bo Gustafsson, and Oliver Williamson, eds., *The Firm As a Nexus of Treaties*. London and Beverly Hills, CA: Sage, pp. 320–46.

Schneider, Volker. 1989. "The Governance of Large Technical Systems: The Case of Telecommunications." Unpublished paper presented at the Conference Series on the Dynamics of Large Technical Systems, University of California, Berkeley, October 17–21.

Schroeder, Gertrude G. 1953. *The Growth of Major Steel Companies, 1900–1950*. Baltimore: Johns Hopkins University Press.

Schumpeter, Joseph A. 1939. *Business Cycles: A Theoretical, Historical and Statistical Analysis of the Capitalist Process*. New York: McGraw-Hill.

Smith, David C. 1970. *History of Papermaking in the United States*. New York: Lockwood.

Sorge, Arndt, and Wolfgang Streeck. 1988. "Industrial Relations and Technical Change: The Case for an Extended Perspective." In Richard Hyman and Wolfgang Streeck, eds., *New Technology and Industrial Relations*. New York and Oxford: Blackwell, pp. 19–47.

Stigler, George J. 1951. "The Division of Labor is Limited by the Extent of the Market." *Journal of Political Economy* 59: 185–93.

———. 1968a. "The Dominant Firm and the Inverted Umbrella." In *The Organization of Industry*. Homewood, IL: Irwin, pp. 108–12.

———. 1968b. "Monopoly and Oligopoly by Merger." In *The Organization of Industry*. Homewood, IL: Irwin, pp. 95–107.

Stinchcombe, Arthur, and C. Heimer. 1986. *Organization Theory and Project Management.* Oslo: Norwegian University Press.

Stone, Katherine. 1974. "The Origins of Job Structures in the Steel Industry." *Review of Radical Political Economics* 6: 61–97.

Streeck, Wolfgang. 1981. "Organizational Consequences of Neo-Corporatist Manageability of Industrial Relations." *British Journal of Industrial Relations* 19: 149–69.

———. 1984. "Guaranteed Employment, Flexible Manpower Use, and Cooperative Manpower Management: A Trend Towards Convergence." In Tokunaga Shigeyoshi, ed., *Industrial Relations in Transition: The Cases of Japan and the Federal Republic of Germany.* Tokyo: University of Tokyo Press, pp. 81–116.

———. 1987a. "Industrial Relations and Industrial Change in the Motor Industry: An International View." *Economic and Industrial Democracy* 8: 437–62.

———. 1987b. "The Uncertainties of Management in the Management of Uncertainty: Employers, Labor Relations and Industrial Adjustment in the 1980s." *Work, Employment and Society* 1: 281–308.

———. 1988. "Comment on Ronald Dore, 'Rigidities in the Labor Market.'" *Government and Opposition* 23: 413–23.

Teece, David. 1988. "Technological Change and the Nature of the Firm." In Giovanni Dosi, Christopher Freeman, Richard Nelson, Gerald Silberg, and Luc Soete, eds., *Technical Change and Economic Theory.* London and New York: Pinter, pp. 256–81.

Teece, David, and Gary Pisano. 1987. "Collaborative Arrangements and Technology Strategy." Unpublished paper presented at the Conference on New Technology and New Intermediaries, Center for European Studies, Stanford, June.

Thorelli, Hans B. 1955. *The Federal Antitrust Policy: Origination of an American Tradition.* Baltimore: Johns Hopkins University Press.

U.S. Bureau of the Census. 1960. *Historical Statistics of the United States, Colonial Times to 1957.* Washington, DC: U.S. Government Printing Office.

U.S. Congress, House Banking and Currency Committee. 1913. *Report of the Committee Appointed Pursuant to H.R. 429 and 504 to Investigate the Concentration of Control of Money and Credit,* 62nd Congress, 2nd Session. Washington, DC: U.S. Government Printing Office.

Warren, G. F., and F. A. Pearson. 1932. *Wholesale Prices for 213 Years: 1720–1932.* Memoir 142. Ithaca, NY: New York Agricultural Experiment Station.

———. 1933. *Prices.* New York: Wiley.

Weber, Max. 1978. *Economy and Society,* Vols. 1 and 2. Edited and translated by Guenther Roth and Claus Wittich. Berkeley: University of California Press.

Wilkins, Mira. 1970. *The Emergence of Multinational Enterprise.* Cambridge, MA: Harvard University Press.

Williamson, Harold F., and Arnold R. Daum. 1959. *The American Petroleum Industry: The Age of Illumination, 1859–1899.* Evanston, IL: Northwestern University Press.

Williamson, Oliver E. 1975. *Markets and Hierarchies: Analysis and Antitrust Implications.* New York: The Free Press.

———. 1979. "Transaction Cost Economics: The Governance of Contractual Relations." *Journal of Law and Economics* 22: 233–61.

———. 1985. *The Economic Institutions of Capitalism: Firms, Markets, Relational Contracting.* New York: The Free Press.

Zerbe, Richard. 1969. "The American Sugar Refining Company, 1887–1914: The Story of a Monopoly." *Journal of Law and Economics* 12: 339–76.

Zysman, John. 1983. *Governments, Markets, and Growth.* Ithaca, NY: Cornell University Press.

CHAPTER 3

American Telephone and Telegraph Company. 1907. *AT&T Annual Report for 1907.* New York: AT&T.

Bickers, Kenneth. 1988. *The Politics of Regulatory Design.* Unpublished Ph.D. dissertation, University of Wisconsin–Madison.

Bornholz, Robert, and David Evans. 1983. "The Early History of Competition in the Telephone Industry." In David Evans, ed., *Breaking Up Bell: Essays on Industrial Organization and Regulation.* New York: North-Holland, pp. 7–40.

Brock, Gerald. 1981. *The Telecommunications Industry.* Cambridge, MA: Harvard University Press.

Brooks, John. 1975. *Telephone: The First Hundred Years.* New York: Harper and Row.

Business Week. 1974. November 30, pp. 68–70.

Computer & Communications Ass'n. v. FCC et al. 1981. 693 F2d 198 (D.C.Cir.).

Cushman, Robert. 1941. *The Independent Regulatory Commissions.* New York: Oxford University Press.

Danielian, Noobar R. 1974. *AT&T: The Story of Industrial Conquest.* New York: Arno Press.

Derthick, Martha, and Paul J. Quirk. 1985. *The Politics of Regulation.* Washington, DC: Brookings Institution.

Fainsod, Merle, Lincoln Gordon, and Joseph C. Palamountain, Jr. 1959. *Government and the American Economy,* third edition. New York: Norton.

Gabel, Richard. 1969. "The Early Competitive Era in Telephone Communication, 1893–1920." *Journal of Law and Contemporary Problems* 34(2): 340–59.

Garnet, Robert. 1985. *The Telephone Enterprise: The Evolution of the Bell System's Horizontal Structure, 1876–1909.* Baltimore: Johns Hopkins University Press.

Hurst, James Willard. 1982. *Law and Markets in United States History: Different Modes of Bargaining Among Interests.* Madison, WI: University of Wisconsin Press.

Hush-A-Phone v. U.S. and FCC. 1956. 238 F2d 266 (D.C.Cir).

International Business Machines v. Federal Communications Commission. 1978. 570 F.2d 452 (2d Cir.).

MacMeal, Harry B. 1934. *The Story of Independent Telephony.* Chicago: Independent Pioneer Association.

National Association of Railroad and Utility Commissioners. 1950. *Proceedings.* Phoenix, AZ.

Schiller, Dan. 1982. *Telematics and Government.* Norwood, NJ: Ablex.

Smith, George. 1985. *The Anatomy of a Business Strategy: Bell, Western Electric and the Origins of the American Telephone Industry.* Baltimore: Johns Hopkins University Press.

Stehman, J. Warren. 1967. *The Financial History of the American Telephone Company.* New York: Augustus M. Kelly.

Telephony. 1922a. "Regarding the Bell Memorandum." 83(1): 1.

———. 1922b. "Bell Pledges a Non-Buying Policy." 83(1): 15.

U.S. Department of Justice, Antitrust Division. 1980. *Plaintiffs' Third Statement of Contentions and Proof.* In *U.S. v. A.T.& T. et al.* Civil Action No. 74–1698 (January 10).

U.S. Federal Communications Commission. 1938. *Proposed Report, Telephone Investigation.* Washington, DC: U.S. Government Printing Office.

———. 1959. *Allocation of Frequencies in the Bands Above 890 Mc.* 27 FCC 359. Washington, DC: U.S. Government Printing Office.

———. 1968. *Carterfone.* 13 FCC2d 420. Washington, DC: U.S. Government Printing Office.

———. 1969. *Microwave Communications Inc..* 18 FCC2d 953. Washington, DC: U.S. Government Printing Office.

———. 1970a. *Regulatory & Policy Problems Presented by the Interdependence of Computer and Communications Services & Facilities, Tentative Decision.* 28 FCC2d 291. Washington, DC: U.S. Government Printing Office.

———. 1970b. *Specialized Common Carriers.* 24 FCC2d 318. Washington, DC: U.S. Government Printing Office.

———. 1971a. *Regulatory & Policy Problems Presented by the Interdependence of Computer and Communications Services & Facilities, Final Decision and Order.* 28 FCC2d 267. Washington, DC: U.S. Government Printing Office.

———. 1971b. *Specialized Common Carriers.* 29 FCC2d 870. Washington, DC: U.S. Government Printing Office.

———. 1976. *Second Computer Inquiry, Notice of Inquiry and Proposed Rulemaking.* 61 FCC2d 103. Washington, DC: U.S. Government Printing Office.

———. 1977a. *AT&T Revisions to Tariffs FCC No. 269 and 267 Relating to Dataspeed 40/4.* 62 FCC2d 21. Washington, DC: U.S. Government Printing Office.

———. 1977b. *Second Computer Inquiry, Supplemental Notice.* 64 FCC2d 771. Washington, DC: U.S. Government Printing Office.

———. 1979. *Second Computer Inquiry, Tentative Decision.* 72 FCC2d 358. Washington, DC: U.S. Government Printing Office.

———. 1980a. *Second Computer Inquiry, Final Decision,* 77 FCC2d 384. Washington, DC: U.S. Government Printing Office.

———. 1980b. *Second Computer Inquiry.* 77 FCC2d 384. Washington, DC: U.S. Government Printing Office.

———. 1985. *Third Computer Inquiry.* 104 FCC2d 958. Washington, DC: U.S. Government Printing Office.

———. 1987. *BOC Relief Structural Relief Order.* 2 FCC Rcd 143. Washington, DC: U.S. Government Printing Office.

U.S. House of Representatives. 1934a. *Letter from W. M. W. Splawn.* Committee on Interstate and Foreign Commerce. House Report No. 1273. 73rd Congress, second session. Washington, DC: U.S. Government Printing Office.

———. 1934b. *Secretary of Commerce to the President, Study of Communications by an Interdepartmental Committee.* 73rd Congress, second session. Washington, DC: U.S. Government Printing Office.

———. 1934c. *Statement of Paul Walker, Chairman of the Corporation Commission of the State of Oklahoma.* Committee on Interstate and Foreign Commerce. 73rd Congress, second session. Washington, DC: U.S. Government Printing Office.

———. 1958. *Hearing before the Subcommittee on Antitrust.* Committee on the Judiciary, Subcommittee on Antitrust. 85th Congress, second session. Washington, DC: U.S. Government Printing Office.

———. 1976. House Committee on Interstate and Foreign Commerce, Subcommittee on Communications. Serial No. 94–129. 94th Congress, second session. Washington, DC: U.S. Government Printing Office.

U.S. Senate. 1934. *Document No. 144.* 73rd Congress, second session. Washington, DC: U.S. Government Printing Office.

U.S. v. AT&T et al. 1974 (November 20).

————. 1980. *Defendants' Third Statement of Contentions and Proof.* Civil Action No. 74–1698 (March 10).

————. 1981. 524 F.Supp. 1336 (D.D.C.).

————. 1982. 552 F.Supp. 131 (D.D.C.).

U.S. v. Western Electric Co., Inc., and American Telephone and Telegraph Co. 1949. Civil Action No. 17–49.

————. 1987. ___ F.Supp. ___ (D.D.C., September 10).

von Auw, Alvin. 1983. *Heritage and Destiny: Reflections on the Bell System in Transition.* New York: Praeger.

Wiley, Richard E. 1981. "Competition and Deregulation in Telecommunication: The American Experience." In Leonard Lewin, ed., *Telecommunications in the U.S.: Trends and Policies.* Dedham, MA: Artech House, pp. 37–59.

Williamson, Oliver E. 1985. *The Economic Institutions of Capitalism: Firms, Markets, Relational Contracting.* New York: The Free Press.

CHAPTER 4

Allardice, Corbin, and Edward Trapnell. 1974. *The Atomic Energy Commission.* New York: Praeger.

Allen, Wendy. 1977. *Nuclear Reactors for Generating Electricity: U.S. Development from 1946 to 1963.* Santa Monica, CA: Rand Corporation.

Arnold W. H., and D. R. Grain. 1972. "Standardization of the Nuclear Steam Supply System." *Proceedings of the American Power Conference* 34: 207–15.

Arthur D. Little Inc. 1968. *Competition in the Nuclear Power Industry Part 1, Overview: Summary and Government Policy Implications.* Report to the U.S. Atomic Energy Commission and U.S. Department of Justice. Contract No. AT (30–1)–3853. Washington, DC: U.S. Atomic Energy Commission.

Atomic Industrial Forum. 1982. "State Nuclear Moratoria, 1982." Unpublished report. Washington, DC: Public Affairs and Information Program, Atomic Industrial Forum.

Averch, Harvey, and Leland Johnson. 1962. "Behavior of the Firm under Regulatory Constraint." *American Economic Review* 52(5): 1052–69.

Baran, Paul, and Paul Sweezy. 1966. *Monopoly Capital: An Essay on the American Economic and Social Order.* New York: Monthly Review Press.

Barfield, Claude. 1973. "Broad Campaign Against Nuclear Power Begins with Nader Suit on Reactor Safety." *National Journal* 9(5): 850–1.

Barkenbus, Jack. 1984a. "An Assessment of Institutional Alternatives for Nuclear Power Generation." In *Working Papers: Nuclear Power in an Age of Uncertainty,* Vol. II, Part 3. Washington, DC: U.S. Office of Technology Assessment.

————. 1984b. "Nuclear Power and Government Structure: The Divergent Paths of the United States and France." *Social Science Quarterly* 65(1): 37–47.

Barlett, Donald, and James Steele. 1985. *Forevermore: Nuclear Waste in America.* New York: Norton.

Battelle Memorial Institute. 1978. *An Analysis of Federal Incentives Used to Stimulate Energy Production.* Richland, WA: Pacific Northwest Laboratory.

Beckjord, Eric. 1978. "The Federal Perspective on Spent Fuel Policy." In *American Nuclear Society Executive Conference on Spent Fuel Policy and Its Implications.* LaGrange Park, IL: American Nuclear Society, pp. 16–20.

Benson, J. Kenneth. 1982. "A Framework for Policy Analysis." In David Rogus, David Whettan, and associates, eds., *Interorganizational Coordination.* Ames, IA: Iowa State University Press, pp. 137–201.

Brittan, Samuel. 1975. "The Economic Contradictions of Democracy." *British Journal of Political Science* 5: 129–59.

Bupp, Irvin. C. 1979. "The Nuclear Stalemate." In Robert Stobaugh and Daniel Yergin, eds., *Energy Future: Report of the Energy Project at the Harvard Business School.* New York: Ballantine, pp. 127–66.

Bupp, Irvin. C., and Jean-Claude Derian. 1978. *Light Water: How the Nuclear Dream Dissolved.* New York: Basic Books.

Burn, Duncan. 1967. *The Political Economy of Nuclear Energy.* London: Institute of Economic Affairs.

———. 1978. *Nuclear Power and the Energy Crisis: Politics and the Atomic Industry.* New York: New York University Press.

Campbell, John L. 1986. "The State, Capital Formation, and Industrial Planning: Financing Nuclear Energy in the United States and France." *Social Science Quarterly* 67(4): 707–21.

———. 1987a. "Legitimation Meltdown: Weberian and Neo-Marxist Interpretations of Legitimation Crisis in Advanced Capitalist Society." In Maurice Zeitlin, ed., *Political Power and Social Theory,* Vol. 6. Greenwich, CN: JAI Press, pp. 133–58.

———. 1987b. "The State and the Nuclear Waste Crisis: An Institutional Analysis of Policy Constraints." *Social Problems* 34(1): 18–33.

———. 1988. *Collapse of an Industry: Nuclear Power and the Contradictions of U.S. Policy.* Ithaca, NY: Cornell University Press.

———. 1989. "Corporations, Collective Organization, and the State: Industry Response to the Accident at Three Mile Island." *Social Science Quarterly* 70(3): 650–66.

Catalano, Lee. 1982. "Utilities Cancel Seventeen Powerplants." *Power* 126: 35.

Chandler, Alfred D., and Herman Daems, eds., 1980. *Managerial Hierarchies: Comparative Perspectives on the Rise of the Modern Industrial Enterprise.* Cambridge, MA: Harvard University Press.

Clarke, Lee. 1985. "The Origins of Nuclear Power: A Case of Institutional Conflict." *Social Problems* 32: 474–87.

Cohen, Linda. 1979. *Essays on the Economics of Licensing Nuclear Power Plants.* Unpublished Ph.D. dissertation, California Institute of Technology, Pasadena.

Cook, James. 1986. "INPO's Race Against Time." *Forbes* 137(4): 54–8.

Crozier, Michael J., Samuel P. Huntington, and Joji Watanuki. 1975. *The Crisis of Democracy.* New York: New York University Press.

Dawson, Frank. 1976. *Nuclear Power: Development and Management of a Technology.* Seattle: University of Washington Press.

Del Sesto, Steven L. 1979. *Science, Politics, and Controversy: Civilian Nuclear Power in the United States, 1946–1974.* Boulder, CO: Westview.

Dieckamp, Herman. 1979. "Utility Views on the Nuclear Industry." In *American Nuclear Society Executive Conference on the Economic Viability of the Nuclear Industry.* LaGrange Park, IL: American Nuclear Society, pp. 242–53.

Energy User's Reports. 1974. No. 61. October 10. Washington, DC: Bureau of National Affairs.

EPRI Journal. 1979a. "At the Institute." 4(4): 36.

———. 1979b. "Industry Response to Three Mile Island." 4(9): 33–7.

Ford, Daniel. 1981. *Three Mile Island: Thirty Minutes to Meltdown.* New York: Penguin.

———. 1982. *Cult of the Atom: The Secret Papers of the Atomic Energy Commission.* New York: Simon and Schuster.

Foth, Joseph H. 1930. *Trade Associations: Their Services to Industry.* New York: Ronald Press.

Gandara, Arturo. 1977. *Electric Utility Decisionmaking and the Nuclear Option.* Santa Monica, CA: Rand Corporation.

Gartman, Warren. 1968. "How to Buy a Reactor." *Power Engineering* 72: 47–9.

Gormley, William. 1983. *The Politics of Public Utility Regulation.* Pittsburgh: University of Pittsburgh Press.

Green, Harold, and Alan Rosenthal. 1963. *Government of the Atom: The Integration of Powers.* New York: Atherton.

Gyorgy, Anna, and Friends. 1979. *No Nukes: Everyone's Guide to Nuclear Power.* Boston: South End Press.

Habermas, Jürgen. 1973. *Legitimation Crisis.* Boston: Beacon Press.

Hendrie, J. M. 1976. "Safety of Nuclear Power." In J. M. Hollander and M. K. Simmons, eds., *Annual Review of Energy,* Vol. 1. Palo Alto, CA.: Annual Reviews, pp. 663–83.

Hertsgaard, Mark. 1983. *Nuclear Inc.: The Men and Money Behind Nuclear Energy.* New York: Pantheon.

Hollingsworth, J. Rogers, and Leon N. Lindberg. 1985. "The Governance of the American Economy: The Role of Markets, Clans, Hierarchies, and Associative Behavior." In Wolfgang Streeck and Philippe C. Schmitter, eds., *Private Interest Government: Between Market and State.* Beverly Hills, CA: Sage, pp. 221–54.

Interagency Review Group on Nuclear Waste Management. 1979. *Report to the President by the Interagency Review Group on Nuclear Waste Management.* TID–29442. Washington, DC: U.S. Government Printing Office.

Komanoff, Charles. 1981. *Power Plant Cost Escalation: Nuclear and Coal Capital Costs, Regulation, and Economics.* New York: Van Nostrand Reinhold.

Lawrence, Paul R., and Davis Dyer. 1983. *Renewing American Industry.* New York: The Free Press.

Lester, William. 1970. "Information Requirements and Their Impact on Nuclear Power Plant Design and Construction." *Proceedings of the American Power Conference* 32: 267–75.

Lilienthal, David. 1980. *Atomic Energy: A New Start.* New York: Harper and Row.

Lindberg, Leon N. 1985. "Political Economy, Economic Governance, and the Coordination of Economic Activities." Paper presented at the Wissenschaftskolleg zu Berlin, Berlin, West Germany.

Lucas, N. J. D. 1979. *Energy in France: Planning, Politics, and Policy.* London: Europa.

Mazuzan, George, and Roger Trask. 1979. *An Outline History of Nuclear Regulation and Licensing, 1946–1979.* Unpublished manuscript. Historical Office, Office of the Secretary, U.S. Nuclear Regulatory Commission, Washington DC.

Metzger, Peter. 1972. *The Atomic Establishment.* New York: Simon and Schuster.

Miles, Robert H. 1982. *Coffin Nails and Corporate Strategies.* Englewood Cliffs, NJ: Prentice-Hall.

Mills, Mark, and Donnamarie Mills. 1983. "Activities of Groups Which Influence Public Opinion in Favor of Nuclear Power." In *Working Papers: Nuclear Power in an Age of Uncertainty,* Vol. II, Part 3. Washington, DC: U.S. Office of Technology Assessment.

Montgomery, W. David, and James P. Quirk. 1978. *Cost Escalation in Nuclear Power.* EQL Memo Number 21. Pasadena, CA: Environmental Quality Laboratory, California Institute of Technology.

Musgrave, Richard, and Peggy Musgrave. 1973. *Public Finance in Theory and Practice.* New York: McGraw-Hill.

Nader, Ralph, and John Abbotts. 1979. *The Menace of Atomic Energy.* New York: Norton.

Neese, R.J. 1982. *The Effect of Nuclear Ownership on Utility Bond Ratings and Yields.* PNL–4175. Report prepared for the U.S. Department of Energy. Richland, WA: Pacific Northwest Laboratory.

Nelkin, Dorothy, and Susan Fallows. 1978. "The Evolution of the Nuclear Debate: The Role of Public Participation." In J. Hollander, M. Simmons, and D. Wood, eds., *Annual Review of Energy,* Vol 3. Palo Alto, CA: Annual Reviews, pp. 275–312.

North, Douglass. 1981. *Structure and Change in Economic History.* New York: Norton.

Novick, Sheldon. 1976. *The Electric War.* San Francisco: Sierra Club.

Nuclear Regulatory Commission Special Inquiry Group. 1980. *Three Mile Island: A Report to the Commission and to the Public,* Vol. II, Part I. Washington, DC: U.S. Government Printing Office.

O'Connor, James. 1973. *The Fiscal Crisis of the State.* New York: St. Martin's Press.

Offe, Claus. 1975. "The Theory of the Capitalist State and the Problem of Policy Formation." In Leon Lindberg, Robert Alford, Colin Crouch, and Claus Offe, eds., *Stress and Contradiction in Modern Capitalism.* Lexington, MA: Lexington Books, pp. 125–44.

Orlans, Harold. 1967. *Contracting for Atoms.* Washington, DC: Brookings Institution.

Perrow, Charles. 1981. "Markets, Hierarchies and Hegemony." In Andrew Van de Ven and William Joyce, eds., *Perspectives on Organization, Design, and Behavior.* New York: Wiley, pp. 371–86.

Perry, Robert, A. J. Alexander, W. Allen, P. deLeon, A. Gandara, W. E. Mooz, E. Rolph, S. Siegel, and K. A. Solomon. 1977. *Development and Commercialization of the Light Water Reactor, 1946–1976.* Santa Monica, CA: Rand Corporation.

Piore, Michael J., and Charles Sabel. 1984. *The Second Industrial Divide: Possibilities for Prosperity.* New York: Basic Books.

President's Commission on the Accident at Three Mile Island. 1979. *Report of the President's Commission on the Accident at Three Mile Island, The Need for Change: The Legacy of TMI.* Washington, DC: U.S. Government Printing Office.

Rankin, William, Barbara Melber, Thomas Overcase, and Stanley Nealey. 1981. *Nuclear Power and the Public: An Update of Collected Survey Research on Nuclear Power.* PNL–4048. A report prepared for the U.S. Department of Energy. Seattle: Battelle Memorial Institute.

Rankin, William, Stanley Nealey, and Barbara Melber. 1984. "Overview of National Attitudes Toward Nuclear Energy." In William Freudenberg and Eugene Rosa, eds., *Public Reactions to Nuclear Power.* Boulder, CO: Westview, pp. 41–68.

Salisbury, Robert H. 1979. "Why No Corporatism in America?" In Philippe Schmitter and Gerhard Lehmbruch, eds., *Trends Toward Corporatist Intermediation.* Beverly Hills, CA: Sage, pp. 213–30.

Schmitter, Philippe C. 1984. "Neo-corporatism and the State." EUI Working Paper No. 106. Florence, Italy: Department of Political and Social Sciences, European University Institute.

Shaw, Milton. 1968. "The United States Fast Breeder Reactor Program." *Proceedings of the American Power Conference* 30: 173–88.

S. M. Stoller Corporation. 1980. *Study of Factors Governing U.S. Utility Nuclear Power Decisions.* DOE/ET/34009-TI. Report prepared for the U.S. Department of Energy. New York: S. M. Stoller Corporation.

Starr, Chauncy. 1983. "The Electric Power Research Institute." *Science* 219(4589): 1190–4.

Stich, Robert. 1971. "Financing Problems Facing Electric Utilities." *Public Utilities Fortnightly* 87: 21–8.

Streeck, Wolfgang, and Philippe C. Schmitter. 1985. "Community, Market, State – and Associations? The Prospective Contribution of Interest Governance to Social Order." In Wolfgang Streeck and Philippe C. Schmitter, eds., *Private Interest Government: Beyond Market and State.* Beverly Hills, CA: Sage, pp. 1–29.

Studness, C.M. 1980. "Genesis of the Current Financial Plight of the Electric Utilities." *Public Utilities Fortnightly* 105: 54–6.

Szalay, Robert. A. 1984. "A Nuclear Industry View of the Regulatory Climate." In William Freudenberg and Eugene Rosa, eds., *Public Reactions to Nuclear Power.* Boulder, CO: Westview Press, pp. 295–306.

Tanguy, P. 1980. "French Emphasis on Research to Confirm Margins." *Nuclear Engineering International* 35: 47–50.

Thomas, Morgan. 1956. *Atomic Energy and Congress.* Ann Arbor, MI: University of Michigan Press.

U.S. Atomic Energy Commission. 1967. *Civilian Nuclear Power – The 1967 Supplement to the 1962 Report to the President.* Washington, DC: U.S. Government Printing Office.

———. 1972. "Commission Policy Statement on Standardization of Nuclear Power Plants." Washington, DC: U.S. Atomic Energy Commission.

———. 1973. *The Nuclear Industry, 1973.* WASH–1174–73. Washington, DC: U.S. Government Printing Office.

———. 1974. *Programmatic Information for the Licensing of Standardized Nuclear Power Plants.* Washington, DC: U.S. Government Printing Office.

U.S. Congressional Budget Office. 1982. *Promoting Efficiency in the Electric Utility Sector.* Washington, DC: U.S. Government Printing Office.

U.S. Department of Energy. 1981. *Federal Support for Nuclear Power: Reactor Design and the Fuel Cycle, Energy Policy Study,* Vol. 13. DOE/EIA-0201/13. Washington, DC: U.S. Government Printing Office.

———. 1983a. *Nuclear Power Plant Cancellations: Causes, Costs, and Consequences.* DOE/EIA–0392. Washington, DC: U.S. Government Printing Office.

———. 1983b. *Delays and Cancellations of Coal-Fired Generating Capacity.* DOE/EIA–4046. Washington, DC: U.S. Government Printing Office.

U.S. Federal Energy Administration Interagency Task Force on Nuclear Energy. 1974. *Project Independence Blueprint, Final Task Force Report: Nuclear Energy.* Washington, DC: U.S. Government Printing Office.

U.S. General Accounting Office. 1977. *Nuclear Energy's Dilemma: Disposing of Hazardous Radioactive Waste Safely.* EMD–77–41. Washington, DC: U.S. Government Printing Office.

———. 1980a. *Construction Work in Progress Issues Needs Improved Regulatory Response for Utilities and Consumers.* EMD–80–75. Gaithersburg, MD: U.S. General Accounting Office.

———. 1980b. *Electric Power Plant Cancellations and Delays.* EMD–80–25. Gaithersburg, MD: U.S. General Accounting Office.

———. 1981. *Federal Energy Regulatory Commission Needs to Act on the Con-*

struction Work in Progress Issue. EMD–81–123. Gaithersburg, MD: U.S. General Accounting Office.

U.S. House of Representatives. 1977. *Oversight Hearings on Nuclear Waste Management.* No. 95–15. Committee on Interior and Insular Affairs, Subcommittee on Energy and the Environment. 95th Congress, first session. Washington, DC: U.S. Government Printing Office.

———. 1979a. *Hearings on Plans for Improved Safety of Nuclear Power Plants Following the Three Mile Island Accident.* No. 81. Committee on Science and Technology, Subcommittee on Energy Research and Production. 96th Congress, first session. Washington, DC: U.S. Government Printing Office.

———. 1979b. *Hearings on Industry's Response to the Accident at Three Mile Island.* No. 96–8. Committee on Interior and Insular Affairs, Subcommittee on Energy and the Environment. 96th Congress, first session. Washington, DC: U.S. Government Printing Office.

———. 1980. *Nuclear Economics: Oversight Hearings.* Part VII. No. 96–8. Committee On Interior and Insular Affairs, Subcommittee on Energy and the Environment. 96th Congress, first session. Washington, DC: U.S. Government Printing Office.

———. 1981a. *Utility Financing: The Financial Condition of Utilities and Their Future in the 1980s. Hearings.* No. 97–36. Committee on Energy and Commerce, Subcommittee on Energy Conservation and Power. 97th Congress, first session. Washington, DC: U.S. Government Printing Office.

———. 1981b. *Licensing Speedup, Safety Delay: NRC Oversight.* No. 97–277. Committee on Government Operations. 97th Congress, first session. Washington, DC: U.S. Government Printing Office.

U.S. Joint Committee on Atomic Energy. 1958. *Hearings on Technical Aspects of the Report on the Gas Cooled, Graphite Moderated Reactor.* 85th Congress, second session. Washington, DC: U.S. Government Printing Office.

———. 1974. *Hearings on Development, Growth, and State of the Nuclear Industry.* 93rd Congress, second session. Washington, DC: U.S. Government Printing Office.

U.S. Nuclear Regulatory Commission. 1980. *Program Summary Report.* 4(5). NUREG–0380. Washington, DC: U.S. Government Printing Office.

———. 1981a. *1980 Annual Report.* Washington, DC: U.S. Government Printing Office.

———. 1981b. *Information Report on State Legislation, Special Edition – State Laws: Radioactive Waste Disposal and Management.* Washington, DC: U.S. Nuclear Regulatory Commission.

———. 1982a. *Information Report on State Legislation.* 8(1–6, 8, 10). Washington, DC: U.S. Nuclear Regulatory Commission.

———. 1982b. *Nuclear Property Insurance: Status and Outlook.* NUREG–0891. Washington, DC: U.S. Government Printing Office.

U.S. Office of Technology Assessment. 1975. *An Analysis of the ERDA Plan and Program.* Washington, DC: U.S. Government Printing Office.

———. 1981. *Nuclear Powerplant Standardization: Light Water Reactors,* Vol. II. Appendices. Washington, DC: U.S. Government Printing Office.

———. 1984. *Nuclear Power in an Age of Uncertainty.* OTA-E–217. Washington, DC: U.S. Government Printing Office.

U.S. Senate. 1974. *Financial Problems of the Electric Utilities: Hearings.* No. 93–50. Committee on Interior and Insular Affairs. 93rd Congress, second session. Washington, DC: U.S. Government Printing Office.

———. 1978. *Hearings on Nuclear Siting and Licensing Act of 1978.* Committee on Environment and Public Works, Subcommittee on Nuclear Regulation. 95th Congress, second session. Washington, DC: U.S. Government Printing Office.

———. 1979. *Hearings on Three Mile Island Nuclear Powerplant Accident,* Part 1. No. 96-H12. Committee on Environment and Public Works, Subcommittee on Nuclear Regulation. 96th Congress, first session. Washington, DC: U.S. Government Printing Office.

Van de Ven, Andrew, and W. Grahm Astley. 1981. "Mapping the Field to Create a Dynamic Perspective on Organization Design and Behavior." In Andrew Van de Ven and William Joyce, eds., *Perspectives on Organization, Design, and Behavior.* New York: Wiley, pp. 427–68.

Walsh, John. 1973. "Electric Power Research Institute: A New Formula for Industry." *Science* 182(4109): 263–5.

Ward, John E. 1977. "Nuclear Regulation: The Industry Point of View." *Proceedings of the American Power Conference* 39: 120–6.

Wasserman, Harvey. 1979. *Energy War: Reports From the Front.* Westport, CN: Lawrence Hill.

Westfield, Fred. 1965. "Regulation and Conspiracy." *American Economic Review.* 55(3): 424–43.

Williamson, Oliver. E. 1975. *Markets and Hierarchies: Analysis and Antitrust Implications.* New York: The Free Press.

Williamson, Oliver E., and William G. Ouchi. 1981. "The Markets and Hierarchies Program of Research: Origins, Implications, Prospects." In Andrew Van de Ven and William Joyce, eds., *Perspectives On Organization, Design, and Behavior.* New York: Wiley, pp. 347–70.

Willmott, Hugh C. 1985. "Setting Accounting Standards in the UK: The Emergence of Private Accounting Bodies and Their Role in the Regulation of Public Accounting Practice." In Wolfgang Streeck and Philippe C. Schmitter, eds., *Private Interest Government: Beyond Market and State.* Beverly Hills, CA: Sage, pp. 44–71.

Willrich, Mason. 1975. "The Electric Utility and the Energy Crisis." *Public Utilities Fortnightly* 95: 22–8.

Wolfe, Alan. 1977. *The Limits of Legitimacy: Political Contradictions of Contemporary Capitalism.* New York: The Free Press.

CHAPTER 5

Aldcroft, Derek H. 1974. *British Transport Since 1914: An Economic History.* London: David and Charles.

Alderman, Geofrey. 1973. *The Railway Interest.* Leichester: Leichester University Press.

Armitage, Susan. 1969. *The Politics of Decontrol of Industry, Britain and the United States.* London: Weindenfeld and Nicholson.

Bagwell, Phillip S. 1970. *Britain and America: A Study of Economic Change, 1850–1930.* London: B. T. Batsford.

———. 1974. *The Transport Revolution from 1770.* London: B. T. Batsford.

Benson, Lee. 1955. *Merchants, Farmers and Railroads: Railroad Regulations and New York Politics.* Cambridge, MA: Harvard University Press.

Bogen, Jules I. 1927. *The Anthracite Railroads: A Study in American Railroad Enterprise.* New York: Ronald Press.

Bonnett, Clarence E. 1956. *History of Employer's Associations in the United States.* New York: Vantage Press.

Boyer, Richard O., and Herbert Morais. 1955. *Labor's Untold Story*. New York: United Electrical Radio and Mechanics of America.

Boyle, O. D. 1935. *History of Railroad Strikes*. Washington DC: Brotherhood.

Burtt, Everett Johnson. 1963. *Labor Markets, Unions and Government Policies*. New York: St. Martin's Press.

Campbell, Edward Gross. 1938. *The Reorganization of the American Railroad System, 1893–1900*. New York: Columbia University Press.

Carson, Robert B. 1971. *Main Line to Oblivion: The Disintegration of New York Railroads in the Twentieth Century*. Port Washington, NY: Kennikat Press.

Chandler, Alfred D. 1965. *The Railroads: The Nation's First Big Business*. New York: Harcourt and Brace.

Clark, Charles Hugh. 1966. "The Railroad Safety Movement in the United States: Origins and Development." Unpublished Ph.D. dissertation, University of Illinois, Urbana–Champaign.

Cochran, Thomas C. 1965. *Railroad Leaders 1845–1890: The Business Mind in Action*. New York: Russell and Russell.

Davis, Grant Miller. 1970. *The Department of Transportation*. Lexington, MA: D. C. Heath.

Dearing, Charles, and Wilfred Owen. 1949. *National Transportation Policy*. Washington, DC: Brookings Institution.

Derthick, Martha, and Paul J. Quirk. 1985. *The Politics of Deregulation*. Washington, DC: Brookings Institution.

Eggert, Gerold G. 1967. *Railroad Labor Disputes: The Beginning of Federal Strike Policy*. Ann Arbor, MI: University of Michigan Press.

Encyclopedia of Associations. 1946. First edition. Detroit: Gale.

Frietag, Peter. 1985. "Class Conflict and the Rise of Government Regulation." *The Insurgent Sociologist* 12(4): 55–66:

Godfrey, Aaron Austin. 1974. *Government Operation of the Railroads, 1918–1920*. Austin, TX: Jenkins.

Haney, Lewis H. 1910. *A Congressional History of the Railways in the United States*. Madison, WI: University of Wisconsin Press.

Harbenson, Robert W. 1967. "Railroads and Regulation 1877–1916: Conspiracy of Public Interest?" *Journal of Economic History* 27(2): 230–42.

Hoogenboom, Ari, and Olive Hoogenboom. 1976. *A History of the Interstate Commerce Commission: From Panacea to Palliative*. New York: Norton.

Jagtani, H. M. 1924. *The Role of the State in the Provision of Railways*. London: P. S. King.

Keeler, Theodore E. 1983. *Railroads, Freight and Public Policy*. Washington, DC: Brookings Institution.

Kennedy, Robert Dawson, Jr. 1985. "State Intervention in the Railroads in the United States and Great Britain, 1830–1985: Towards a Theory of Incremental and Stepwise Growth of Statism in Advanced Capitalism." Unpublished Ph.D. dissertation, University of Wisconsin, Madison.

Kerr, K. Austin. 1968. *American Railroad Politics, 1914–1920*. Pittsburgh: University of Pittsburgh Press.

Kolko, Gabriel. 1965. *Railroads and Regulation: 1877–1916*. New York: Norton.

Labor. 1919–. Washington, DC: Plumb Plan League. (Weekly newspaper of the railroad brotherhoods in the United States.)

Locklin, D. P. 1966. *Economics of Transportation*. Homewood, IL: Irwin.

Lyon, Peter. 1968. *To Hell in a Day Coach: An Exasperated Look at American Railroads*. New York: Lippincott.

McNaughton, Wayne L. 1954. *Industrial Relations and the Government*. New York: McGraw-Hill.

McPhearson, Logan G. 1912. *Railroad Freight Rates in Relation to the Industry and Commerce of the United States.* New York: Holt.

Martin, Albro. 1971. *Enterprise Denied: Origins of the Decline of American Railroads, 1897–1917.* New York: Columbia University Press.

Mertins, Herman, Jr. 1972. *National Transportation Policy in Transition.* Lexington, MA: D. C. Heath.

Meyer, Balthasar. 1903. *Railway Legislation in the United States.* New York: Arno Press.

Miller, George H. 1971. *Railroads and Granger Laws.* Madison, WI: University of Wisconsin Press.

Mitchell, B. R. 1971. *Second Abstract of British Historical Statistics.* Cambridge: Cambridge University Press.

Moody's Transportation Manual. 1950. New York: Moody's Investor's Service.

———. 1954. New York: Moody's Investor's Service.

———. 1980. New York: Moody's Investor's Service.

———. 1985. New York: Moody's Investor's Service.

Moulton, Harold Glenn. 1912. *Waterways versus Railways.* Boston: Houghton Mifflin.

Nelson, James. 1959. *Railroad Transportation and Public Policy.* Washington, DC: Brookings Institution.

The New York Times. 1919. "The Demise of the Plan." August 10, p. 10.

Pegrum, Dudley F. 1963. *Transportation Economics and Public Policy.* Homewood, IL: Irwin.

Phillips, Kevin P. 1983. *Staying on Top: The Business Case for a National Industrial Strategy.* New York: Random House.

Rayback, Joseph G. 1966. *A History of American Labor.* New York: The Free Press.

Ripley, William Z. 1920. *Railroads, Finance and Organization – Volume II.* New York: Longmans, Green.

Roberts, Dick. 1980. *American Railroads: The Case for Nationalization.* New York: Pathfinder Press.

Salsbury, Steven. 1982. *No Way to Run a Railroad.* New York: McGraw-Hill.

Sanders, Elizabeth. 1982. *The Roots of Regulation: Economics and Politics Before and During the 1970s.* Paper presented at the annual meeting of the American Science Association, Denver, Colorado.

Saunders, Richard. 1978. *The Railroad Mergers and the Coming of Conrail.* Westport, CN: Greenwood Press.

Savage, Christopher I. 1959. *An Economic History of Transport.* London: Hutchinson.

Schmitter, Phillipe C., and Donald Brand. 1979. "Organizing Capitalism in the United States: The Advantages and the Disadvantages of Exceptionalism." Paper presented at the annual meeting of the American Political Science Association, Washington, DC.

Sharfman, Isaiah Leo. 1936. *Interstate Commerce Commission: A Study in Administrative Law and Procedure.* Oxford: Oxford University Press.

Steigerwalt, Albert K. 1964. *The National Association of Manufacturers, 1895–1914: A Study in Business Leadership.* Ann Arbor, MI: University of Michigan Press.

Tarbell, Ida M. 1936. *The Nationalization of Business, 1878–1898.* New York: Macmillan.

Taylor, William Leonhard. 1970. *A Productive Monopoly: The Effect of Railroad Control on New England Coastal Steamship Lines, 1870–1916.* Providence, RI: Brown University Press.

Uhl, Alexander. 1954. *Trains and the Men Who Run Them.* Washington, DC: Public Affairs Institute.

U.S. House of Representatives. 1919. *Return of the Railroads to Private Ownership. Hearings before the Committee on Interstate and Foreign Commerce,* Vol. 1. 66th Congress, first session. Washington, DC: U.S. Government Printing Office.

Weaver, R. Kent. 1985. *The Politics of Industrial Change: Railway Policy in North America.* Washington, DC: Brookings Institution.

Wiebe, Robert Huddleston. 1962. *Businessmen and Reform: A Study of the Progressive Movement.* Cambridge, MA: Harvard University Press.

Williams, Winston. 1985. "Turning a Railroad Around." *The New York Times Magazine* (January 12): 32–7.

CHAPTER 6

Abel, I. W. 1976. *Collective Bargaining, Labor Relations in Steel: Then and Now.* New York: Columbia University Press.

Acs, Zoltan J. 1984. *The Changing Structure of the U.S. Economy: Lessons from the Steel Industry.* New York: Praeger.

Adams, Walter. 1954. *The Structure of American Industry: Some Case Studies.* New York: Macmillan.

Adams, Walter, and Joel Dirlam. 1964. "Steel Imports and Vertical Oligopoly." *American Economic Review* 54(3): 626–55.

———. 1966. "Big Steel, Invention, and Innovation." *Quarterly Journal of Economics* 80(2): 167–89.

Adams, Walter, and Hans Mueller. 1982. "The Steel Industry." In Walter Adams, ed., *The Structure of American Industry.* New York: Macmillan, pp. 73–135.

Adelman, M.A. 1961. "Steel Administered Prices, and Inflation." *Quarterly Journal of Economics* 75(1): 16–40.

Aglietta, Michel. 1979. *A Theory of Capitalist Regulation: The U.S. Experience.* New York: New Left Books.

———. 1982. "World Capitalism in the Eighties." *New Left Review* 136: 45–72.

Altvater, Elmar. 1987. *Sachzwang Weltmarkt. Verschuldungskrise, blockierte Industrialisierung, ökologische Gefährdung – der Fall Brasilien.* Hamburg: VSA.

Altvater, Elmar, Jürgen Hoffmann, and Willi Semmler. 1980. *Vom Wirtschaftswunder in die Wirtschaftskrise.* Berlin: Olle and Wolter.

American Iron and Steel Institute. Various years. *Annual Statistical Yearbooks.* Washington DC: American Iron and Steel Institute.

———. 1980. *Steel at the Crossroads: The American Steel Industry in the 1980s.* Washington DC: American Iron and Steel Institute.

American Metal Market. 1984. July 20.

Ault, David E. 1973. "The Continued Deterioration of the Competitive Ability of U.S. Steel Industry: The Development of Continuous Casting." *Western Economic Journal* (11): 89–97.

Barnett, Donald. 1977. *The Canadian Steel Industry in a Competitive World Environment.* Ottawa: Resources Industries and Construction Branch, Industry, Trade and Commerce.

Barnett, Donald F., and Robert W. Crandall. 1986. *Up from the Ashes: The Rise of the Steel Minimill in the United States.* Washington DC: Brookings Institution.

Barnett, Donald F., and Louis Schorsch. 1983. *Steel: Upheaval in a Basic Industry.* Cambridge, MA: Ballinger.

Betheil, Richard. 1978. "The ENA in Perspective: The Transformation of Collective Bargaining in the Steel Industry." *Review of Radical Political Economics* 10 (Summer):1–24.

Blough, Roger M. 1975. *The Washington Embrace of Business.* New York: Carnegie Press.

Bluestone, Barry, and Bennett Harrison. 1982. *The Deindustrialization of America: Plant Closings, Community Abandonment, and the Dismanteling of Basic Industries.* New York: Basic Books.

Borrus, Michael. 1982. "Slow Growth and Competition Erosion in the U.S. Steel Industry." In John Zysman and Laura Tyson, eds., *American Industry in International Competition.* Ithaca, NY: Cornell University Press, pp. 60–105.

Brody, David. 1960. *Steelworkers in America – The Nonunion Era.* Cambridge, MA: Harvard University Press.

Burawoy, Michael, and Anne Smith. 1985. "Der Aufstieg der Hegemonialen Despotie in der US-Industrie." *Prokla* Berlin 15(1): 139–53.

Business Week. 1986. August 4, p. 25.

———. 1987. February 2, p. 26.

Chandler, Alfred D. 1977. *The Visible Hand: The Managerial Revolution in American Business.* Cambridge, MA: Harvard University Press.

Christiansen, Jens Peter. 1982. *Labor Productivity in the Steel Industry: A Comparative Study of the Federal Republic of Germany and the United States of America.* Ph.D. dissertation, Stanford University.

Cohen, Stephen, and Ronald I. Meltzer. 1982. *United States International Economic Policy in Action: Diversity of Decision Making.* New York: Praeger.

Cooper, Conrad. 1967. "Collective Bargaining at the Crossroads." *Iron and Steel Engineer* 44(12): 113–16.

Cordtz, Dan. 1967. "Antidisestablishmentarianism at Wheeling Steel." *Fortune* (July): 105–36.

Crandall, Robert W. 1981. *The U.S. Steel Industry in Recurrent Crisis: Policy Options in a Competitive World.* Washington DC: Brookings Institution.

Dilley, David R., and David L. McBride. 1967. "Oxygen Steelmaking – Fact vs. Folklore." *Iron and Steel Engineer* 44(10): 131–53.

Dyson, Kenneth. 1983. "The Cultural, Ideological and Structural Context." In Kenneth Dyson and Stephen Wilks, eds., *Industrial Crisis: A Comparative Study of the State and Industry.* Oxford: Martin Robertson, pp. 26–66.

Eisenhammer, John, and Martin Rhodes. 1986. "The Politics of Public Sector Steel in Italy: From the 'Economic Miracle' to the Crisis of the Eighties." In Yves Mény and Vincent Wright, eds., *The Politics of Steel.* Berlin: W. de Gruyter, pp. 416–75.

Engert, Steffi, and Winfried Wolf. 1983. *Die Krise in der Stahlindustrie.* Frankfurt: ISP.

Fusfeld, Daniel R. 1958. "Joint Subsidiaries in the Iron and Steel Industry." *American Economic Review, Paper and Proceedings* 48 (May): 578–87.

Gray, Peter H., Thomas Pugel, and Ingo Walter. 1982. "International Trade, Employment and Structural Adjustment: The Case of the United States," World Employment Programme Research, Working Paper. Geneva: International Labour Office.

Greer, Edward. 1977. "The Political Economy of the U.S. Steel Prices in the Postwar Period." In Paul Zarembka, ed., *Research in Political Economy: An Annual Compilation of Research.* Greenwich, CN: JAI Press, pp. 59–86.

Hersch, Martin. 1984. *Mini-mill Steelmaking in the U.S.* Cleveland: Predicast.

Hoerr, John. 1988. *And the Wolf Finally Came.* Pittsburgh: University of Pittsburgh Press.

Hogan, William T. 1970/71. *Economic History of the Iron and Steel Industry in the U.S.*, Vol. 5. Lexington, MA: D. C. Heath.

———. 1972. *The 1970's: Critical Years for Steel.* Lexington, MA: Lexington Books.

———. 1983. *World Steel in the 1980s: A Case of Survival.* Lexington, MA: Lexington Books.

———. 1984. *Steel in the United States: Restructuring to Compete.* Lexington, MA: Lexington Books.

Howell, Thomas R., William A. Moellert, Jesse G. Kreier, and Alan W. Wolff. 1988. *Steel and the State. Government Intervention and Steel's Structural Crisis.* Boulder, CO: Westview Press.

Huettner, D. A. 1974. "The Development of Continuous Casting in the Steel Industry." *Economic Inquiry* 12 (June): 267–70.

Hufbauer, Gary Clyde, Diane T. Berliner, and Kimberly Ann Elliott. 1986. *Trade Protection in the United States, 31 Case Studies.* Washington DC: Institute for International Economics.

Hurtienne, Thomas. 1985. "Wirtschaftskrise, internationale Verschuldung und Entwicklungspotentiale in Lateinamerika." *Prokla* Berlin (59): 34–64.

Iron and Steelmaking. 1985. (July): 2–4.

———. 1987. (May): 19–36.

———. 1988. (May): 18–36.

Katz, Harry C. 1985. *Shifting Gears: Changing Labor Relations in the U.S. Automobile Industry.* Cambridge, MA: The MIT Press.

Kurth, James R. 1979. "The Political Consequences of the Product Cycle: Industrial History and Political Outcomes." *International Organization* 33: 1–34.

Lamoreaux, Naomi R. 1985. *The Great Merger Movement in American Business, 1885–1904.* New York: Cambridge University Press.

Leckie, A. H., and A. J. Morris. 1968. "Effect of Plant and Works Scale on Costs in the Iron and Steel Industry." *Journal of the Iron and Steel Institute* 206 (May): 442–52.

Lynd, Staughton. 1984. *The Fight Against Shutdowns: Youngstown's Steel Mill Closings.* San Pedro, CA: Singlejack Books.

Lynn, Leonard H. 1982. *How Japan Innovates: A Comparison with the U.S. in the Case of Oxygen Steelmaking.* Boulder, CO: Westview Press.

McAdams, Alan. 1967. "Big Steel, Invention and Innovation, Reconsidered." *Quarterly Journal of Economics* (August): 457–74.

McColloch, Mark. 1987. "Consolidating Industrial Citizenship: The USWA at War and Peace, 1939–46." In Paul F. Clark, Peter Gottlieb, and Donald Kennedy, eds., *Forging a Union of Steel. Philip Murray, SWOC, and the United Steelworkers.* Ithaca, NY: ILR Press, pp. 45–86.

McConnell, Grant. 1963. *Steel and the Presidency – 1962.* New York: Norton.

McManus, George. 1967. *Inside Story of Steel Wages and Prices, 1959–1967.* Philadelphia: Chilton.

———. 1989. "Mini-Mills: Rising to the Challenge." *Iron Age* (April): 21–31.

MacPhee, Craig R. 1974. *Restrictions on International Trade in Steel.* Toronto: Lexington Books.

Maddala, G., and P. Knight. 1967. "International Diffusion of Technical Change – A Case Study of the Oxygen Steel Making Process." *Economic Journal* 77 (September): 531–58.

Marcus, Peter F., and Karlis M. Kirsis. 1981. *Major Country Carbon Steel Price/ Cost Assessments: 1969–1990.* New York: Paine Webber World Steel Dynamics.

———. 1984. *Economics of the Mini-mill*. New York: Paine Webber World Steel Dynamics.

Markusen, Ann R. 1985. *Profit Cycles, Oligopoly, and Regional Development*. Cambridge, MA: The MIT Press.

Munkirs, John, and James I. Sturgeon. 1985. "Oligopolisitc Cooperation: Conceptual and Empirical Evidence of Market Structure Evolution." *Journal of Economic Issues* 4 (December): 899–921.

Naples, Michele I. 1981. "Industrial Conflict and its Implications for Productivity Growth." *American Economic Review, Paper and Proceedings* 70 (May): 36–41.

The New York Times. 1984a. May 23. Sec. 4, p. 5.

———. 1984b. February 16. Sec. 4, p. 4.

———. 1985. October 22. Sec. 4, p. 11.

———. 1989. July 26. Sec. 1, p. 1.

Old, Bruce S., A. L. Frederic, A. L. Holloway, and Michael Tenenbaum. 1981. *Brief Technology Assessment of the Domestic Steel Industry*. Report to Lehigh University and the U.S. Department of Commerce.

Patton, Wendy. 1985. "Steel Distribution: The Role of the Steel Service Center in the American Steel Industry and in the Chicago Market." Unpublished manuscript for Markusen Economic Research Associates, Chicago.

Piore, Michael J., and Charles Sabel. 1984. *The Second Industrial Divide: Possibilities for Prosperity*. New York: Basic Books.

Piven, Frances, and Richard Cloward. 1972. *Regulating the Poor*. New York: Random House.

Roderick, David. 1983. "Speech before the Congressional Steel Caucus." Committee on the Judiciary, U.S. Senate, 89th Congress, first session. July 1, 1983, Serial No. J–98–51, Hearing, *The Domestic Steel Industry and the Antitrust Laws*. Washington DC: U.S. Government Printing Office.

———. 1984. Statement before the United States Senate, Committee on Finance, Hearings on the U.S. Steel Industry, June 8, 142–50.

Rosegger, Gerhard. 1980. "Exploratory Evaluations of Major Technological Innovations: Basic Oxygen Furnaces and Continuous Casting." In Bela Gold, Gerhard Rosegger, and Myles G. Boylan Jr., eds., *Evaluating Technological Innovations*. Lexington, MA: Lexington Books, pp. 117–210.

Scherer, Frederic M. 1970. *Industrial Market Structure and Economic Performance*. Chicago: Rand McNally.

Scherrer, Christoph. 1987. "Im Alleingang: Die Krisenüberwindungsstrategie des US-Stahlkapitals." *WSI–Mitteilungen* (10): 615–21.

———. 1988a: *Das Akkumulationsregime der USA im Umbruch. Die Suche nach neuen Regulationsformen in der Auto- und Stahlindustrie*. Unpublished dissertation, Fachbereich Gesellschaftswissenschaften, J. W. Goethe Universität, Frankfurt.

———. 1988b. "Mini-Mills – A New Growth Path for the US-Steel Industry." *Journal of Economic Issues* 22(4): 1179–200.

———. 1989. "Die US-Auto- und Stahlindustrie auf der Suche nach dem goldenen Vließ der Wettbewerbsfähigkeit." *Prokla* Berlin, 19(Heft 74): 109–33.

Scheuerman, William. 1975. "Economic Power in the U.S.: The Case of Steel." *Politics and Society* (5): 337–66.

Schorsch, Louis. 1984. "The Abdication of Big Steel." *Challenge* (March–April): 34–44.

Schubert, Alexander. 1985. "Untergräbt die Stärke der USA die Fundamente der Weltwirtschaft?" *Prokla* Berlin (59): 65–77.

Sease, Douglas. 1981. "Little Giants: Mini-mill Steelmakers, No Longer Very Small, Outperform Big Ones." *Wall Street Journal* (January 12): 1.

Shonfield, Andrew. 1965. *Modern Capitalism: The Changing Balance of Public and Private Power.* London: Oxford University Press.

Slaughter, Jane. 1983. *Concessions and How to Beat Them.* Detroit: Labor Education and Research Project.

Steindl, Josef. 1976. *Maturity and Stagnation in American Capitalism.* New York: Monthly Review Press.

Stieber, Jack. 1960. "Company Cooperation in Collective Bargaining in the Basic Steel Industry." *Labor Law Journal* (July): 607–14.

Stocking, George W. 1954. *Basing Point Pricing and Regional Development. A Case Study of the Iron and Steel Industry.* Chapel Hill, NC: University of North Carolina Press.

Stone, Joseph K., and Eduard M. Michaelis. 1985. "Basic Oxygen Steel Making Capacity Continues to Decline." *Iron and Steel Engineer* (September): 48–54.

Stundza, Tom. 1988. "Steel Market Outlook." *Purchasing* (February 11): 38–50.

Sumrall, James B. 1978. *Diffusion of the Basic Oxygen Furnace in the U.S. Steel Industry. A Vintage Capital Model.* Unpublished Ph.D. dissertation, Boston College, Boston.

Thorn, Richard S. 1975. "Changes in the International Cost Competitiveness of American Steel 1966–1973." Working Paper No. 8. Pittsburgh: University of Pittsburgh.

Tilove, Robert. 1948. *Collective Bargaining in the Steel Industry.* Philadelphia: University of Pennsylvania Press.

Tony, W. A. 1987. "Nucor and Yamato Kogyo Join Forces." *Iron & Steelmaker* (July): 15–17.

U.S. Bureau of Labor Statistics. N.d. Unpublished data.

U.S. Congressional Budget Office. 1987. *How Federal Policies Affect the Steel Industry.* Washington, DC: U.S. Government Printing Office.

U.S. Council on Wage and Price Stability. 1977. *Report to the President on Prices and Costs in the U.S. Steel Industry.* Washington, DC: U.S. Government Printing Office.

U.S. Department of Labor. 1980. *The Steel Tripartite Committee Report.* Washington, DC: U.S. Government Printing Office.

U.S. Federal Trade Commission. 1977. *Staff Report on the United States Steel Industry.* Washington, DC: U.S. Government Printing Office.

U.S. General Accounting Office. 1981. *New Strategy Required for Aiding Distressed Steel Industry.* Report to the Congress. Washington, DC: U.S. Government Printing Office.

U.S. International Trade Commission. 1987. *Annual Survey Concerning Competitive Conditions in the Steel Industry and Industry Efforts to Adjust and Modernize.* USITC Publication 2019. Washington, DC: U.S. Government Printing Office.

U.S. Public Law. 1980. *Chrysler Corporation Loan Guarantee Act of 1979.* 96–185-Jan. 7. Washington, D.C.

U.S. Office of Technology Assessment. 1980. *Technology and Steel Industry Competitiveness.* Washington, DC: U.S. Government Printing Office.

U.S. Senate. 1956. *A Study of the Antitrust Laws, Part 7, General Motors.* Committee on the Judiciary, Subcommittee on Antitrust and Monopoly, Hearings. Washington, DC: U.S. Government Printing Office.

———. 1983. *The Domestic Steel Industry and the Antitrust Laws.* No. J–98–51. Committee on the Judiciary. 89th Congress, first session. Washington, DC: U.S. Government Printing Office.

United States Steel Corporation. 1976. *Annual Report 1975*. Pittsburgh: United States Steel Corporation.

Vogel, David. 1978. "Why Businessmen Distrust Their State: The Political Consciousness of American Corporate Executives." *British Journal of Political Science* (8): 45–78.

———. 1984. "A Case Study of the Clean Air Legislation 1967–1981." In Betty Bock, Harvey J. Goldsmid, Ira M. Millstein, and F. M. Scherer, eds., *The Impact of the Modern Corporation*. New York: Columbia University Press, pp. 309–86.

Walter, Ingo. 1982. "Structural Adjustment and Trade Policy in the International Steel Industry." Paper presented at the Conference on Trade Policy in the Eighties, Institute for International Economics, Washington, DC, June 23–25.

Walters, Robert S. 1982. "Industry and Government Approaches to the Crisis in Steel: Protectionism, Structural Shifts and International Economic Peacekeeping." In Harold Jacobsen and Dusan Sidjanski, eds., *The Emerging International Economic Order*. Beverly Hills, CA: Sage, pp. 101–28.

Warren, Kenneth. 1973. *The American Steel Industry, 1850–1970. A Geographical Interpretation*. Oxford: Oxford University Press.

Weiss, Leonard W. 1967. *Case Studies in American Industry*. New York: Wiley.

———. 1971. *Case Studies in American Industry,* second edition. New York: Wiley.

Williamson, Oliver E. 1986. "Transforming Merger Policy: The Pound of New Perspectives." *American Economic Review* (May): 114–19.

Woolcock, Stephen, Jeffrey Hart, and Hans van der Ven. 1985. *Interdependence in the Post-Multilateral Era, Trends in U.S.–European Trade Relations*. Cambridge, MA: University Press of America.

Wyman, Joseph C. 1980. "Mini-mill Outlook." New York: Shearson Loeb Rhoades Inc., Steel Quarterly, Nov. 20.

CHAPTER 7

Abernathy, William J. 1978. *The Productivity Dilemma. Roadblock to Innovation in the Automobile Industry*. Baltimore, MD: Johns Hopkins University Press.

———. 1982. *The Competitive Status of the U.S. Auto Industry. A Study of the Influences of Technology in Determining International Industrial Competitive Advantage*. Washington, DC: National Academy Press.

Abernathy, William J., Joan Dopico, Burton H. Klein, and James M. Utterback. 1981. "A Dynamic Approach to the Problems of the Automobile Industry." Cambridge, MA: Center for Policy Alternatives, Massachusetts Institute of Technology.

Aggarwal, Sumer C. 1985. "MRP, JIT, OPT, FMS? Making Sense of Production Operations Systems." *Harvard Business Review* 63(5): 8–16.

Altshuler, Alan M., D. Anderson, D. Jones, and J. Womack. 1984. *The Future of the Automobile*. London: Allen and Unwin.

American Machinist. 1988. "Less Out-Sourcing in Store for GM?" 132(11): 73.

———. 1989. "Setting Auto-Industry Standards, Interview, with Joseph Phelan and Anthony Zerafa from the AIAG." 133(2): 50–1.

Andrea, David, Mark Everett, and Dan Luria. 1988. "Automobile Company Parts Sourcing: Implications for Michigan Suppliers." Unpublished manuscript.

Andrea, David, Richard Hervey, and Dan Luria. 1986. "The Capacity Explosion: Implications for Michigan Suppliers." *AIM Newsletter* 1(2): 6–8.

Automotive Industries. 1987a. "Ford Demands Cuts." 62 (June): 35.

———. 1987b. "Just-In-Time." 62 (February): 74.

Callahan, Joseph M. 1989. "Tora, Tora, Tora. 232 Japanese Supplier Plants are Gunning for Your Business." *Automotive Industries* 64 (February): 89–112.

Chandler, Alfred D. 1964. *Giant Enterprise. Ford, General Motors, and the Automobile Industry*. New York: Harcourt, Brace and World.

Cole, Robert E., and N. Yakushiji. 1984. *The American and Japanese Auto Industries in Transition*. Ann Arbor, MI: Center for Japanese Studies, University of Michigan.

Conway, McKinley. 1987. " 'Auto Axis' for New Assembly Plants Emerges along Toronto/Detroit/Atlanta Corridor." In *Industrial Development and Site Selection Handbook*. Atlanta: Conway Data, Inc., pp. 236–7.

Doeringer, Peter B., and Michael J. Piore. 1971. *Internal Labor Markets and Manpower Analysis*. Lexington, MA: D. C. Heath.

Dohse, Knut, unter Mitarbeit von Ulrich Jürgens und Harald Russig. 1979. *Bestandsschutz durch Seniorität*. Berlin: International Institute for Comparative Social Research, Labor Policy, IIVG preprint 79–221.

Dohse, Knut, and Ulrich Jürgens. 1985. "Konzernstrategien und internationale Arbeitsteilung in der Automobilindustrie – am Beispiel Ford und General Motors." *Mehrwert* 26 (September): 30–48.

Drucker, Peter F. 1972. *Concept of the Corporation*. New York: John Day.

Dyer, Davis, Malcolm S. Salter, and Alan M. Webber. 1987. *Changing Alliances. The Harvard Business School Project on the Auto Industry and the American Economy*. Boston: Harvard Business School Press.

Epstein, Ralph Cecil. 1972/1928. *The Automobile Industry: Its Economic and Commercial Development*. New York: Arno Press.

Erd, Rainer, and Christoph Scherrer. 1984. "Amerikanische Gewerkschaften – Opfer des Weltmarkts." *Prokla* Berlin 14(1, Heft 54): 78–96.

Ferguson, Thomas, and Joel Rogers. 1979. "Labor Law Reform and Its Enemies." *Nation* (January 6): 1, 20.

Fine, Sidney. 1969. *Sit-down: The GM Strike of 1936–1937*. Ann Arbor, MI: University of Michigan Press.

Flynn, Michael S. 1983. "Comparison of U.S.–Japan Production Costs: An Assessment." In Robert E. Cole, ed., *Automobiles and the Future: Competition, Cooperation, and Change*. Ann Arbor, MI: University of Michigan Press, pp. 81–96.

Flynn, Michael S., and Robert E. Cole. 1988. "Automotive Suppliers: Customer Relationships, Technology, and Global Competition." In Peter J. Arnesen, ed., *Is There Enough Business to Go Around? Overcapacity in the Auto Industry*. Ann Arbor, MI: University of Michigan Press, pp. 91–121.

Friedman, David. 1983. "Beyond the Age of Ford: The Strategic Basis of the Japanese Success in Automobiles." In John Zysman and Laura Tyson, eds., *American Industry in International Competition*. Ithaca, NY: Cornell University Press, pp. 350–90.

Gartman, David. 1986. *Auto Slavery*. New Brunswick, NJ: Rutgers University Press.

Gersuny, Carl. 1982. "Origins of Seniority Provisions in Collective Bargaining." *Labor Law Journal* 33 (August): 518–24.

Gooding, Kenneth. 1987 "When Captive Technology Is a Competitive Advantage." *Financial Times* (September 25): 14.

Hartley, J. 1984. "U.S. Firms Shop for Parts in Japan." *Automotive News* (May 28): 29.

Heaton, George. 1982. "Government Structural Policies and the Automobile Industry." Cambridge, MA: Center for Policy Alternatives, Massachusetts Institute of Technology.

Heckscher, Charles. 1988. *The New Unionism, Employee Involvement in the Changing Corporation*. New York: Basic Books.

Helper, Susan R. 1987. *Supplier Relations and Technical Change: Theory and Application to the US Automobile Industry*. Unpublished Ph.D. dissertation, Department of Economics, Harvard University, Cambridge, Massachusetts.

Herding, Richard. 1980. *Kontrolle am Arbeitsplatz. Kapitalistische Arbeitsorganisation und Gewerkschaften in den USA*. Frankfurt: Campus.

Hounshell, David A. 1984. *From the American System to Mass Production, 1800–1932: The Development of Manufacturing Technology in the United States*. Baltimore, MD: Johns Hopkins University Press.

International Herald Tribune. 1983. "Labor Unrest May Imperil Car Upturn." (November 9): 6.

Jefferys, Steve. 1986. *Management and Managed: Fifty Years of Crisis at Chrysler*. New York: Cambridge University Press.

Jürgens, Ulrich. 1986. "Entwicklungstendenzen in der Weltautomobilindustrie bis in die 90er Jahre." IIVG preprint 86–218. Berlin: International Institute for Comparative Social Research, Labor Policy.

Jürgens, Ulrich, Thomas Malsch, and Knut Dohse. 1989. *Moderne Zeiten in der Automobilifabrik*. Berlin: Springer.

Katz, Harold. 1977. *The Decline in Competition in the Automobile Industry, 1920–1940*. New York: Arno Press.

Katz, Harry 1985. *Shifting Gears: Changing Labor Relations in the U.S. Automobile Industry*. Cambridge, MA: The MIT Press.

———. 1988. "Business and Labor Relations Strategies in the U.S. Automobile Industry: The Case of the General Motors Corporation." In Ben Dankbaar, Ulrich Jürgens, and Thomas Malsch, eds., *Die Zukunft der Arbeit in der Automobilindustrie*. Berlin: Edition Sigma, pp. 149–262.

Katz, Harry, and Charles Sabel. 1985. "Industrial Relations and Industrial Adjustment in the Car Industry." *Industrial Relations* 24(3): 295–315.

Klein, Benjamin. 1980. "Transaction Cost Determinants of 'Unfair' Contract Arrangements." *American Economic Review* 70 (May): 356–62.

Köhler, Christoph, and Werner Sengenberger. 1983. *Konjunktur und Personalanpassung, Betriebliche Beschäftigungspolitik in der deutschen und amerikanischen Automobilindustrie*. Frankfurt: Campus.

Lanzillotti, Robert F. 1971. "The Automobile Industry." In Walter Adams, ed., *The Structure of American Industry*. New York: Macmillan, pp. 256–301.

Lawrence, Paul R., and Davis Dyer. 1983. *Renewing American Industry*. New York: The Free Press.

Macaulay, Stewart. 1966. *Law and the Balance of Power. The Automobile Manufacturers and Their Dealers*. New York: Russell Sage Foundation.

Marx, Thomas G. 1985. "The Development of the Franchise Distribution System in the U.S. Automobile Industry." *Business History Review* 59(3): 465–74.

Meyer, Peter. 1986. "General Motors' Saturn Plant: A Quantum Leap in Technology and its Implications for Labour and Community Organizing." *Capital & Class* 30 (Winter): 74–95.

Mroczkowski, Tomasz. 1984. "Is the American Labour–Management Relationship Changing?" *British Journal of Industrial Relations* 22(1): 47–62.

Nelson, Steven Robert. 1978. *An Economic Analysis of Antitrust Policy in the Automotive Parts Industry*. Unpublished Manuscript, Milwaukee, Wisconsin.

The New York Times. 1984. "Progress in UAW Talks with GM-Canada." October 27, Section I, p. 9.

Nomura, Masami. 1987. "Der japanische 'Produktivismus' am Ende? Die Auswirkungen des Handelskonflikts auf die japanische Arbeitsgesellschaft." *Prokla* Berlin 17(1, Heft 66): 8–30.

Parker, Mike. 1985. *Inside the Circle: A Union Guide to QWL.* Boston: South End Press.

Parker, Mike, and Jane Slaughter. 1988. *Choosing Sides: Unions and the Team Concept.* Boston: South End Press.

Piore, Michael J. 1982. "American Labor and the Industrial Crisis." *Challenge* (March–April): 5–11.

Reich, Robert B., and John D. Donahue. 1985. *New Deals: The Chrysler Revival and The American System.* New York: Times Books.

Ross, George., and Peter Gourevitch. 1984. "Conclusion." In Peter Gourevitch, Andrew Martin, George Ross, Christopher Allen, Stephen Bornstein, and Andrei Markovitz, eds., *Unions and Economic Crisis: Britain, West Germany, and Sweden.* London: Allen and Unwin, pp. 360–86.

Russo, John. 1985. "General Motors Local Votes for Lifetime Job Security and a Three-Tier Wage Plan." *Labor Notes* 71 (January): 5.

Salter, Malcolm S., Alan M. Webber, and Davis Dyer. 1985. "U.S. Competitiveness in Global Industries: Lessons from the Auto Industry." In Bruce R. Scott and G. C. Lodge, eds., *U.S. Competitiveness in the World Economy.* Boston: Harvard Business School Press, pp. 185–229.

Scherrer, Christoph. 1986. "The U.S. Auto Industry: Can It Adapt to Global Competition?" Working Paper No. 4. Freie Universität Berlin, John F. Kennedy-Institut.

———. 1988. *Das Akkumulationsregime der USA im Umbruch. Die Suche nach neuen Regulationsformen in der Auto-und Stahlindustrie.* Unpublished dissertation, Fachbereich Gesellschaftswissenschafter, J. W. Goethe Universität, Frankfurt.

———. 1989. "Umbrüche im Beschaffungswesen der US-Automobilindustrie." In Nobert Altmann and Dieter Sauer, eds., *Systemische Rationalisierung und Zulieferindustrie.* Frankfurt: Campus Verlag, pp. 207–51.

Schonberger, Richard J., and Abdolhossein Ansari. 1984. " 'Just-In-Time' Purchasing Can Improve Quality." *Journal of Purchasing and Materials Management.* (Spring): 2–7.

Shirai, Taishiro, ed. 1983. *Contemporary Industrial Relations in Japan.* Madison, WI: University of Wisconsin Press.

Slaughter, Jane. 1983. *Concessions and How to Beat Them.* Detroit: Labor Education & Research Project.

———. 1988. "UAW Stands Up – And Chrysler Backs Down." *Labor Notes* 109 (April): 1.

Sloan, Alfred P., Jr. 1972. *My Years with General Motors.* Edited by John McDonald with Catharine Stevens. New York: Doubleday.

Smith, Donald N. 1986. "Challenges to Michigan's Automotive Stamping Industry." *AIM Newsletter* 1(3): 1–8.

Snyder, Carl Dean. 1973. *White-Collar Workers and the UAW.* Urbana, IL: University of Illinois Press.

UAW Research Bulletin. 1987. "Maquiladora." July, p. 14. Detroit: United Automobile Workers of America.

United Automobile Workers–General Motors. 1984. "UAW–GM Report." September. Detroit: United Automobile Workers of America.

U.S. Bureau of Labor Statistics. 1976. *Industry Wage Survey: Motor Vehicles and Parts.* Bulletin 1912. Washington, DC: U.S. Government Printing Office.

U.S. Department of Commerce. 1985. *The U.S. Motor Vehicle and Equipment Industry Since 1958.* Washington, DC: U.S. Government Printing Office.

U.S. House of Representatives. 1980. *Auto Situation: 1980.* Committee on Ways and Means, Subcommittee on Trade. Washington DC: U.S. Government Printing Office.

U.S. Office of Technology Assessment. 1979. *Technology Assessment of Changes in the Future Use and Characteristics of the Automobile Transportation System.* Washington, DC: U.S. Government Printing Office.

White, Lawrence J. 1971. *The Automobile Industry Since 1945.* Cambridge, MA: Harvard University Press.

———. 1982a. "The Automobile Industry." In Walter Adams, ed., *The Structure of American Industry.* New York: Macmillan, pp. 136–90.

———. 1982b. "The Motor Vehicle Industry." In Richard Nelson, ed., *Government and Technological Progress: A Cross-Industry Analysis.* New York: Pergamon, pp. 411–50.

Wilkins, Mira, and Frank Ernest Hill. 1964. *American Business Abroad. Ford on Six Continents.* Detroit: Wayne State University Press.

Williams, Harry B. 1985. "Wages at Motor Vehicle Plants Outpaced those at Parts Factories." *Monthly Labor Review* 108(5): 38–40.

Williamson, Oliver E. 1985. *The Economic Institutions of Capitalism: Firms, Markets, Relational Contracting.* New York: The Free Press.

CHAPTER 8

Baker, Gladys L., Wayne D. Rasmussen, Vivian Wiser, and Jane M. Porter. 1963. *Century of Service, The First 100 Years of the U.S. Department of Agriculture.* U.S. Department of Agriculture Economic Research Service, Agricultural History Branch. Washington, DC: U.S. Government Printing Office.

Bartlett, Roland Wiley (1931). *Cooperation in Marketing Dairy Products.* Springfield, IL: Charles C. Thomas.

Cook, Hugh L., Leo Blakley, Robert Jacobson, Ronald Knutson, Robert Milligan, and Robert Strain. 1978. *The Dairy Subsector of American Agriculture: Organization and Vertical Coordination.* N.C. Project 117, Monograph 5. Madison, WI: University of Wisconsin.

Cropp, Robert A., and Hugh L. Cook. 1977a. "What is a Federal Milk Marketing Order?" Madison and Platteville, WI: University of Wisconsin-Extension.

———. 1977b. "What is the M-W Price Series and Why is it Being Questioned?" Madison and Platteville, WI: University of Wisconsin-Extension.

Dyson, Kenneth. 1983. "The Cultural, Ideological, and Structural Context." In Kenneth Dyson and Stephen Wilks, eds., *Industrial Crisis: A Comparative Study of State and Industry.* Oxford: Martin Robertson, pp. 26–66.

Fainsod, Merle, Lincoln Gordon, and Joseph C. Palamountain, Jr. 1959. *Government and the American Economy,* third edition. New York: Norton.

Friedmann, Karen J. 1973. "Victualling Colonial Boston." *Agricultural History* 47(3): 189–205.

Gates, Paul W. 1960. *The Farmer's Age: Agriculture 1815–1860. Vol. III, The Economic History of the United States.* New York: Holt, Rinehart and Winston.

Guth, James L. 1977. "The National Cooperative Council and Farm Relief, 1929–1942." *Agricultural History* 51(2): 441–58.

———. 1980. "Midwestern Dairy Farmers and The New Deal, 1933–1941." Paper presented at the 15th Annual Northern Great Plains History Conference, Duluth, Minnesota.

———. 1981. "Herbert Hoover, The U.S. Food Administration, and the Dairy Industry, 1917–1918." *Business History Review* 55(2): 170–87.

———. 1982. "Farmer Monopolies, Cooperatives, and the Intent of Congress: Origins of the Capper–Volstead Act." *Agricultural History* 56(1): 67–82.

Hartley, Robert M. 1842 (reprinted 1977). *An Essay on Milk.* New York: Arno Press.

Jacobson, Robert E. 1980. "Changing Structure of Dairy Farming in the United States, 1940–79." In *Farm Structure,* U.S. Senate, Committee on Agriculture, Nutrition, and Forestry. 96th Congress, second session. Washington, DC: U.S. Government Printing Office.

Jesse, Edward V. 1984. "The Economics of Government Intervention in Dairy Markets." Agricultural Economics Staff Paper, Series No. 224. Madison, WI: University of Wisconsin.

Key, V. O., Jr. 1947. *Politics, Parties, and Pressure Groups,* second edition. New York: T. Y. Crowell.

Lawrence, Paul R, and Davis Dyer. 1983. *Renewing American Industry.* New York: The Free Press.

MacAvoy, Paul W., ed. 1977. *Federal Milk Marketing Orders and Price Supports.* Washington, DC: American Enterprise Institute for Policy Research.

McCalla, Alex F. 1978. "Politics of the Agricultural Research Establishment." In Don F. Hadwiger and William P. Browne, eds., *The New Politics of Food.* Lexington, MA: Lexington Books, pp. 77–92.

Manchester, Alden C. 1983. *The Public Role in the Dairy Economy. Why and How Governments Intervene in the Milk Business.* Boulder, CO: Westview Press.

National Milk Producers Federation. 1983. *Annual Report.* Washington, DC: National Milk Producers Federation.

Nourse, Edwin G. 1927. *The Legal Status of Agricultural Co-operation.* New York: Macmillan.

Nourse, Edwin G., Joseph S. Davis, and John D. Black. 1937. *Three Years of the Agricultural Adjustment Administration.* Washington, DC: Brookings Institution.

Odom, E. Dale. 1985. "Associated Milk Producers, Incorporated: Testing the Limits of Capper–Volstead." *Agricultural History* 59(1): 40–55.

Parker, Horatio Newton. 1917. *City Milk Supply.* New York: McGraw-Hill.

Pirtle, T. R. 1926. *History of the Dairy Industry.* Chicago, IL: Mojonnier Brothers.

Porter, Kirk, and Arnold B. Johnson. 1966. *National Party Platforms, 1840–1932.* Urbana, IL: University of Illinois Press.

Roadhouse, Chester Linwood, and James Lloyd Henderson. 1941. *The Milk-Market Industry.* New York: McGraw-Hill.

Sheldon, J. P. 1907. *Dairy Farming: Being the Theory, Practice, and Methods of Dairying.* London: Cassell.

Skocpol, Theda, and Kenneth Finegold. 1982. "State Capacity and Economic Intervention in the Early New Deal." *Political Science Quarterly* 97(2): 255–78.

Spencer, Leland, and Charles J. Blanford. 1973. *An Economic History of Milk Marketing and Pricing: A Classified Bibliography with Reviews of Listed Publications, 1840–1970.* Columbus, OH: Grid.

Streeck, Wolfgang, and Philippe C. Schmitter. 1985. "Community, Market, State – and Associations? The Prospective Contribution of Interest Governance to Social Order." In Wolfgang Streeck and Philippe C. Schmitter, eds., *Private Interest Government: Beyond Market and State.* Beverly Hills, CA: Sage, pp. 1–29.

Time. 1985. "The New Grapes of Wrath." January 28, p. 66.

U.S. Department of Agriculture. 1984. *Review of Existing and Federal Dairy Programs.* ERS Staff Report No. AGES840121. Washington, DC: U.S. Government Printing Office.

Vander Schaaf, James F. 1985. "The National Milk Producers Federation." Unpublished paper, University of Wisconsin, Madison.

Washington Post National Weekly Edition. 1985. February 11, p. 23.

Whitaker, George M. 1905. *The Milk Supply of Boston, New York, and Phila-*

delphia. U.S. Department of Agriculture, Bureau of Animal Industry, Bulletin No. 81. Washington, DC: U.S. Government Printing Office.

Williams, Sheldon W., David A. Vose, Charles E. French, Hugh L. Cook, and Alden C. Manchester. 1970. *Organization and Competition in the Midwest Dairy Industries.* Ames, IA: Iowa State University Press.

Young, Brigitte, Leon N. Lindberg, and J. Rogers Hollingsworth. 1989. "The Governance of the American Dairy Industry: From Regional Dominance to Regional Cleavage." In William D. Coleman and Henry J. Jacek, eds., *Regionalism, Business Interests and Public Policy.* London: Sage, pp. 127–52.

CHAPTER 9

Aduddell, Robert. 1971. *The Meat Packing Industry and the Consent Decree: 1920–1956.* Unpublished Ph.D. dissertation, Northwestern University, Evanston, Illinois.

Aduddell, Robert, and Louis Cain. 1981a. "Public Policy Toward 'The Greatest Trust in the World.' " *Business History Review* 55(2): 217–42.

———. 1981b. "The Consent Decree in the Meatpacking Industry, 1920–1956." *Business History Review* 55(3): 359–78.

American Meat Institute. 1985a. *Meatfacts.* Department of Economics and Statistics. Washington, DC: American Meat Institute.

———. 1985b. *Annual Financial Review of the Meat Packing Industry, 1984.* Department of Economics and Statistics. Washington, DC: American Meat Institute.

———. 1985c. *Meat Price Reporting Study and Recommendations for Improvements.* Special Price Reporting Task Force. Washington, DC: American Meat Institute.

Breimeyer, Harold. 1961. *Demand and Prices for Meat.* USDA Economic Research Service. Technical Bulletin No. 1253. Washington, DC: U.S. Government Printing Office.

Business Week. 1983. "The Slaughter of Meatpacking Wages." 2796 (June 27): 70–71.

Butz, Dale, and George Baker. 1960. *The Changing Structure of the Meat Economy.* Cambridge, MA: Harvard University Press.

Cassens, Robert, Charles Cook, and Robert Kauffman. 1984. *The Meat Industry in the 21st Century.* Madison, WI: University of Wisconsin Department of Agricultural Journalism.

Chandler, Alfred. 1977. *The Visible Hand: The Managerial Revolution in American Business.* Cambridge, MA: Harvard University Press.

Clemen, Rudolf. 1923. *The American Livestock and Meat Industry.* New York: Ronald Press (reprinted by Johnson Reprint).

Corey, Lewis. 1950. *Meat and Man: A Study of Monopoly, Unionism, and Food Policy.* New York: Viking.

Duewer, Lawrence. 1984. *Changing Trends in the Red Meat Distribution System.* U.S. Department of Agriculture Economic Research Service. Agricultural Economics Report No. 509. Washington, DC: U.S. Government Printing Office.

Fowler, Stewart. 1961. *The Marketing of Livestock and Meat.* Danville, IL: Interstate.

Greyhound Corporation. 1983. *Annual Report.*

Hayenga, Marvin. 1978. *Vertical Coordination in the Beef Industry: Packer, Retailer and HRI Linkages.* Working Paper No. 22. NC Project 117: Studies of the

Organization and Control of the U.S. Food System. Madison, WI: University of Wisconsin.

Hayenga, Marvin, U. James Rhodes, Jon Brand, and Ronald Deiter. 1985. *The U.S. Pork Sector: Changing Structure and Organization.* Ames, IA: Iowa State University Press.

IBP, Inc. 1975. *IBP Annual Report.*

———. 1977. *IBP Annual Report.*

Kolko, Gabriel. 1963. *The Triumph of Conservatism.* New York: The Free Press.

LTV Corporation. 1981. *Annual Report.*

Marion, Bruce. 1986. *The Organization and Performance of the U.S. Food System.* Lexington, MA: Lexington Books.

Meat Industry. 1981. "Figuring Production Costs." 77(5): 15–16, 60.

Nelson, Kenneth. 1985. *Issues and Developments in the U.S. Meatpacking Industry.* U.S. Department of Agriculture Economics Research Service. Washington DC: U.S. Government Printing Office.

Schnittker Associates. 1980. *An Economic Analysis of the Structure of the U.S. Meat Packing Industry.* Washington, DC: Schnittker Associates.

Shultz, George, and Arnold Weber. 1966. *Strategies for the Displaced Worker.* New York: Harper and Row.

Streeck, Wolfgang, and Philippe Schmitter, eds. 1985. *Private Interest Government: Beyond Market and State.* Beverly Hills, CA: Sage.

United Food and Commercial Workers International Union. 1981a. *1981 Fact Book.* National Packinghouse Conference, Chicago, Illinois, October 1981. Washington, DC: United Food and Commercial Workers International Union.

———. 1981b. *Packinghouse Division Report to UFCW International Executive Board.* Washington, DC: United Food and Commercial Workers International Union.

———. 1984. *Packinghouse Division Report.* March. Washington, DC: United Food and Commercial Workers International Union.

———. 1985. *1985 Meat Packing Industry Fact Book.* National Packinghouse Conference, Denver, Colorado, April 1985. Washington, DC: United Food and Commercial Workers International Union.

U.S. Department of Agriculture. 1983. *Livestock and Meat Statistics.* Washington, DC: U.S. Government Printing Office.

———. 1985. *Economics of the Red Meat Industry.* Food Safety and Inspection Service. Washington, DC: U.S. Government Printing Office.

U.S. Department of Commerce. 1905. *Census of Manufactures.* Washington, DC: U.S. Government Printing Office.

———. 1920. *Statistical Abstract of the U.S.* Washington, DC: U.S. Government Printing Office.

———. 1963. *Census of Manufactures, Industry Series: Meat Products.* Washington, DC: U.S. Government Printing Office.

———. 1982. *Census of Manufactures, Industry Series: Meat Products.* Washington, DC: U.S. Government Printing Office.

U.S. Department of Labor. 1952. *Collective Bargaining in the Meat-Packing Industry.* Bulletin No. 1063. Washington, DC: U.S. Government Printing Office.

U.S. Federal Trade Commission. 1919. *Food Investigation: Meat-Packing Industry, Parts 1–4.* Washington, DC: U.S. Government Printing Office.

U.S. General Accounting Office. 1978. *Beef Marketing: Issues and Concerns.* Washington, DC: U.S. Government Printing Office.

U.S. House of Representatives. 1978. *Small Business Problems in the Marketing of Meat and Other Commodities. Part 1: Meat Marketing.* Subcommittee on SBA and SBIC Authority and General Small Business Problems of the Committee on Small Business. 95th Congress, second session. Washington, DC: U.S. Government Printing Office.

———. 1979a. *Small Business Problems in the Marketing of Meat and Other Commodities. Part 4: Changing Structure of the Beef Packing Industry.* Subcommittee on SBA and SBIC Authority and General Small Business Problems of the Committee on Small Business. 96th Congress, first session. Washington, DC: U.S. Government Printing Office.

———. 1979b. *Small Business Problems in the Marketing of Meat and Other Commodities. Part 5: Anticompetitive Practices in the Meat Industry.* Subcommittee on SBA and SBIC Authority and General Small Business Problems of the Committee on Small Business. 96th Congress, first session. Washington, DC: U.S. Government Printing Office.

———. 1979c. *Small Business Problems in the Marketing of Meat and Other Commodities. Part 6: Electronic Marketing.* Subcommittee on SBA and SBIC Authority and General Small Business Problems of the Committee on Small Business. 96th Congress, first session. Washington, DC: U.S. Government Printing Office.

U.S. National Commission on Food Marketing. 1966. *Organization and Competition in the Livestock and Meat Industry.* Technical Study No. 1. Washington, DC: U.S. Government Printing Office.

Walsh, Margaret. 1982. *The Rise of the Midwestern Meat Packing Industry.* Lexington, KY: University Press of Kentucky.

Williams, Willard, D. B. DeLoach, and G. Engelman. 1959. *Economic Effects of U.S. Grades for Beef.* U.S. Department of Agriculture Marketing Research Report No. 298. Washington, DC: U.S. Government Printing Office.

Williams, Willard, and T. Stout. 1964. *Economics of the Livestock–Meat Industry.* New York: Macmillan.

Williamson, Oliver E. 1975. *Markets and Hierarchies: Analysis and Antitrust Implications.* New York: The Free Press.

———. 1985. *The Economic Institutions of Capitalism: Firms, Markets, Relational Contracting.* New York: The Free Press.

Yeager, Mary. 1981. *Competition and Regulation: The Development of Oligopoly in the Meat Packing Industry.* Greenwich, CN: JAI Press.

CHAPTER 10

Alexander, Jeffrey A., Bonnie L. Lewis, and Michael A. Morrisey. 1985. "Acquisition Strategies of Multihospital Systems." *Health Affairs* 4(3): 49–66.

American Hospital Association. 1975. *Guide to the Health Care Field.* Chicago: American Hospital Association.

———. 1981. *Data Book on Multihospital Systems 1980–1981.* Chicago: American Hospital Association.

———. 1985. *Data Book on Multihospital Systems 1980–1985.* Chicago: American Hospital Association.

———. 1986. *Hospital Statistics.* Chicago: American Hospital Association.

American Medical International. 1980–1985. Annual Form 10-K Filings with the U.S. Securities and Exchange Commission for Fiscal Years Ended 1979–1984.

Arnold, Patricia J. 1987. "Capital Costs, Accounting Choice and Multihospital Systems." Unpublished Ph.D. dissertation, University of Wisconsin, Madison.

Block, Fred. 1980. "Beyond Relative Autonomy: State Managers and Historical Subjects." In Ralph Miliband and John Saville, eds., *Socialist Register.* London: Merlin Press, pp. 227–42.

Blue Cross and Blue Shield Association. 1984. "Questions and Answers About the Blue Cross and Blue Shield Organization." Chicago: Blue Cross and Blue Shield Association.

Brown, Lawrence. 1983. *Politics and Health Care Organization: HMOs as Federal Policy.* Washington, DC: Brookings Institution.

Chandler, Alfred D. 1962. *Strategy and Structure: Chapters in the History of the American Industrial Enterprise.* Cambridge, MA: Harvard University Press.

Enthoven, Alain C., and Roger G. Noll. 1984. "Prospective Payment: Will It Solve Medicare's Financial Problems?" *Issues in Science and Technology* (Fall): 101–16.

Ermann, Dan, and Jon Gabel. 1984. "Multihospital Systems: Issues and Empirical Findings." *Health Affairs* 3(1): 50–64.

Foster, Richard, and Dorothy McNeil. 1971. "How Hospitals Finance Construction." *Hospitals* 45: 47–90.

Health Care Financing Administration. 1986. Provider Reimbursement Manual in *Medicare–Medicaid Guide.* Chicago: Commerce Clearing House.

Herzlinger, Regina, and William S. Krasker. 1987. "Who Profits from the Nonprofits?" *Harvard Business Review* 87(1): 93–106.

Hollingsworth, J. Rogers. 1986. *The Political Economy of Medicine: Great Britain and the United States.* Baltimore: Johns Hopkins University Press.

Hollingsworth, J. Rogers, and Ellen Jane Hollingsworth. 1987. *Controversy About American Hospital: Funding, Ownership and Performance.* Washington, DC: American Enterprise Institute for Public Policy Research.

Hospital Corporation of America. 1980–85. Annual Form 10-K Filings with the U.S. Securities and Exchange Commission for Fiscal Years Ended 1977–1984.

Humana, Inc. 1980–1985. Annual 10-K Filings with the U.S. Securities and Exchange Commission for Fiscal Years Ended 1979–84.

Kennedy, Low Ann. 1986. "Wall Street: The New Health Planning Agency." Unpublished working paper, Department of Health Care Administration, Baruch College, City University, New York.

Kinkead, Brain M. 1984. "Medicare Payment and Hospital Capital: The Evolution of Policy." *Health Affairs* 3: 49–74.

Law, Sylvia. 1974. *Blue Cross: What Went Wrong?* University of Pennsylvania Health Law Project. New Haven: Yale University Press.

Marmor, Theodore R. 1970. *The Politics of Medicare.* London: Routledge and Kegan Paul.

Modern Healthcare. 1977–1985. "Survey on Contract Management." Published annually in *Modern Healthcare,* Vols. 7–17.

North, Douglass. 1981. *Structure and Change in Economic History.* New York: Norton.

O'Connor, James. 1973. *The Fiscal Crisis of the State.* New York: St. Martin's Press.

Offe, Claus. 1975. "The Theory of the Capitalist State and the Problem of Policy Formation." In Leon Lindberg, Robert Alford, Colin Crouch, and Claus Offe, eds., *Stress and Contradiction in Modern Capitalism.* Lexington, MA: D. C. Heath, pp. 125–44.

Peltzman, Sam. 1976. "Toward A More General Theory of Regulation." *Journal of Law and Economics* 19(2): 211–40.

Skocpol, Theda. 1980. "Political Response to Capitalist Crisis: Neo-Marxist Theories of the State and the Case of the New Deal." *Politics and Society* 10(2): 155–201.

Stambaugh, Jeffrey. 1967. "A Study of the Sources of Capital Funds for Hospital Construction in the United States." *Inquiry* 14(2): 3–22.

Starkweather, David B. 1981. *Hospital Mergers in the Making.* Ann Arbor, MI: Health Administration Press.

Starr, Paul. 1982. *The Social Transformation of American Medicine.* New York: Basic Books.

Stigler, George. J. 1971. "The Theory of Economic Regulation." *Bell Journal of Economics and Management Science* 2(1): 3–21.

Taddey, Anthony, and Gordon Gayer. 1982. "Use and Effect of Hospital Tax-Exempt Financing." *Healthcare Financial Management* 12(7): 10–25.

Tillet, J. William, R. Bruce Linklater, and Randy A. Suchen. 1982. "Survey Reveals Trend in Corporate Reorganization." *Healthcare Financial Management* 12(9): 38–9.

U.S. General Accounting Office. 1980. "Hospital's Use of Management Contract Services." June 30. Washington, DC: U.S. General Accounting Office

———. 1983a. "Hospital Merger Increased Medicare and Medicaid Payments for Capital Costs." A Report to the Honorable Willis D. Gradison, Jr., U.S. House of Representatives, HRD–84–10, December 22. Washington, DC: U.S. General Accounting Office.

———. 1983b. "Response to Questions Concerning Percentage Contracts and Limited Service Contracts Under Medicare." February 2. Washington, DC: U.S. General Accounting Office.

———. 1984. "Excessive Respiratory Therapy Costs and Utilization Used in Setting Medicare Prospective Rates." Letter to Margaret M. Heckler, Secretary of Health and Human Services, Sept. 18. Washington, DC: U.S. General Accounting Office.

Williamson, Oliver E. 1975. *Markets and Hierarchies: Analysis and Antitrust Implications.* New York: The Free Press.

Wohl, Stanley. 1984. *The Medical Industrial Complex.* New York: Harmony Books.

Wolkstein, Irwin. 1968. "The Legislative History of Hospital Cost Reimbursement." In *Reimbursement Incentives for Hospital and Medical Care: Objectives and Alternatives.* Department of Health, Education and Welfare, Office of Research and Statistics, Research Report No. 26. Washington, DC: U.S. Government Printing Office.

Zysman, John. 1983. *Governments, Markets and Growth: Financial Systems and the Politics of Industrial Change.* Ithaca, NY: Cornell University Press.

CHAPTER 11

Abolafia, Mitchel, and Nicole Woolsey Biggart. 1989. "Competition and Markets: An Institutional Theory." Paper presented at the First Annual International Conference on Socio-Economics, Harvard Business School, Cambridge, Massachusetts.

Alchian, Armen, and Harold Demsetz. 1972. "Production, Information Costs, and Economic Organization." *American Economic Review* 62 (December): 777–95.

Aldrich, Howard. 1979. *Organizations and Environments.* Englewood Cliffs, NJ: Prentice-Hall.

Baran, Paul, and Paul Sweezy. 1966. *Monopoly Capital: An Essay on the American Economic and Social Order.* New York: Monthly Review Press.

Baumgartner, Thomas, Tom R. Burns, and Philippe DeVille. 1984. *The Shaping of Socioeconomic Systems.* New York: Gordon and Breach.

———. 1985. "Actor and System: Toward a Theory of Social Action and System Structuring." In Tom Burns, Thomas Baumgartner, and Philippe DeVille, *Man, Decisions, Society: The Theory of Actor-System Dynamics for Social Scientists.* New York: Gordon and Breach, pp. 28–49.

Becker, Gary. 1976. *The Economic Approach to Human Behavior.* Chicago: University of Chicago Press.

Berger, Suzanne, and Michael Piore. 1980. *Dualism and Discontinuity in Industrial Societies.* New York: Cambridge University Press.

Bowles, Roger. 1984. "Property and the Legal System." In David Whynes, ed., *What Is Political Economy?* New York: Blackwell, pp. 187–208.

Caves, Richard. 1980. "Industrial Organization, Corporate Strategy, and Structure." *Journal of Economic Literature* 18(1): 64–92.

Chandler, Alfred. 1977. *The Visible Hand: The Managerial Revolution in American Business.* Cambridge, MA: Harvard University Press.

Chandler, Alfred D., and Herman Daems, eds. 1980. *Managerial Hierarchies: Comparative Perspectives on the Rise of the Modern Industrial Enterprise.* Cambridge, MA: Harvard University Press.

Coase, Ronald. 1937. "The Nature of the Firm." *Economica* 4: 386–405.

———. 1988. *The Firm, the Market, and the Law.* Chicago: University of Chicago Press.

Crozier, Michel. 1964. *The Bureaucratic Phenomenon.* Chicago: University of Chicago Press.

Domhoff, G. William. 1974. *The Bohemian Grove and Other Retreats.* New York: Harper.

———. 1983. *Who Rules America Now?* Englewood Cliffs, NJ: Prentice-Hall.

Dosi, Giovanni. 1984. "Technological Paradigms and Technological Trajectories: The Determinants and Directions of Technical Change and the Transformation of the Economy." In Christopher Freeman, ed., *Long Waves in the World Economy.* London: Frances Pinter, pp. 78–101.

Downs, Anthony. 1957. *An Economic Theory of Democracy.* New York: Harper and Row.

Eccles, Robert. 1981. "The Quasifirm in the Construction Industry." *Journal of Economic Behavior and Organization* 2 (December): 335–57.

Elliott, John. 1984. "The Institutional School of Political Economy." In David Whynes, ed., *What is Political Economy?* New York: Blackwell, pp. 59–89.

Etzioni, Amitai. 1988. *The Moral Dimension: Toward a New Economics.* New York: The Free Press.

Foster, John. 1987. *Evolutionary Macroeconomics.* Boston: Allen and Unwin.

Freeman, John. 1984. *Long Waves in the World Economy.* London: Frances Pinter.

———. 1986. *Design, Innovation and Long Cycles in Economic Development.* New York: St. Martin's Press.

Galbraith, John Kenneth. 1967. *The New Industrial State.* New York: Mentor.

Giddens, Anthony. 1984. *The Constitution of Society: Outline of the Theory of Structuration.* Cambridge: Polity Press.

Goldthorpe, John. 1984. "The End of Convergence: Corporatist and Dualist Tendencies in Modern Western Societies." In John Goldthorpe, ed., *Order and Conflict in Contemporary Capitalism: Studies in the Political Economy of Western European Nations.* New York: Oxford University Press, pp. 313–43.

Granovetter, Mark. 1985. "Economic Action and Social Structure: The Problem of Embeddedness." *American Journal of Sociology* 91(3): 481–510.

———. 1989. "Summary and Background of Talk Prepared for the Conference on Socio-Economics." Paper prepared for the First Annual International Conference on Socio-Economics, Harvard Business School, Cambridge, Massachusetts.

Hamilton, Gary, and Nicole Woolsey Biggart. 1988. "Market, Culture, and Authority: A Comparative Analysis of Management and Organization in the Far East." *American Journal of Sociology* 94 (Supplement): 52–94.

Hodgson, Geoffrey M. 1988. *Economics and Institutions: A Manifesto for a Modern Institutional Economics*. Philadelphia: University of Pennsylvania Press.

Ikenberry, G. John. 1988. *Reasons of State: Oil Politics and the Capacities of American Government*. Ithaca, NY: Cornell University Press.

Johanson, Jan, and Lars-Gunnar Mattsson. 1987. "Interorganizational Relations in Industrial Systems: A Network Approach Compared with the Transaction Cost Approach." *International Journal of Management and Organization* 17 (Spring): 34–48.

Knoke, David, and James Wood. 1981. *Organized for Action: Commitment in Voluntary Associations*. New Brunswick, NJ: Rutgers University Press.

Knoke, David, and Christine Wright-Isak. 1982. "Individual Motives and Organizational Incentives Systems." In Samuel Bacharach, ed., *Research in the Sociology of Organizations*, Vol. 1. Greenwich, CN: JAI Press, pp. 209–54.

Kurth, James. 1979. "The Political Consequences of the Product Cycle: Industrial History and Political Outcomes." *International Organization* 33(1): 1–34.

Lash, Scott, and John Urry. 1987. *The End of Organized Capitalism*. Madison, WI: University of Wisconsin Press.

Lazerson, Mark. 1988. "Organizational Growth of Small Firms: An Outcome of Markets and Hierarchies." *American Sociological Review* 53: 330–42.

Lazonick, William. 1986. "Organizations, Markets, and Productivity." Paper presented at the Economic History Association meeting, Hartford, Connecticut.

Lorenz, Edward. 1988. "Neither Friends nor Strangers: Informal Networks of Subcontracting in French Industry." In Diego Gambetta, ed., *Trust: Making and Breaking Cooperative Relations*. New York: Blackwell, pp. 194–210.

Macaulay, Stewart. 1963. "Non-contractual Relations in Business: A Preliminary Study." *American Sociological Review* 28(1): 55–67.

Markusen, Ann R. 1985. *Profit Cycles, Oligopoly, and Regional Development*. Cambridge, MA: The MIT Press.

Marx, Karl, and Frederick Engels. 1970. *The German Ideology*. New York: International Publishers.

Mintz, Beth, and Michael Schwartz. 1985. *The Power Structure of American Business*. Chicago: University of Chicago Press.

Nelson, Richard R., and Sidney Winter. 1982. *An Evolutionary Theory of Economic Change*. Cambridge, MA: Harvard University Press.

Noble, David F. 1977. *America By Design: Science, Technology, and the Rise of Corporate Capitalism*. New York: Oxford University Press.

North, Douglass. 1981. *Structure and Change in Economic History*. New York: Norton.

Offe, Claus, and Helmut Wiesenthal. 1985. "Two Logics of Collective Action." In Claus Offe, *Disorganized Capitalism*. Cambridge, MA: The MIT Press, pp. 170–220.

Olson, Mancur. 1965. *The Logic of Collective Action*. Cambridge, MA: Harvard University Press.

Ouchi, William G. 1977. "Review of *Markets and Hierarchies: Analysis and Antitrust Implications* by Oliver E. Williamson." *Administrative Science Quarterly* 22(3): 540–4.

———. 1980. "Markets, Bureaucracies, and Clans." *Administrative Science Quarterly* 25(1): 129–41.

Perez, Carlota. 1986. "Structural Changes and Assimilation of New Technologies in the Economic and Social System." In Christopher Freeman, ed., *Design, Innovation and Long Cycles in Economic Development*. New York: St. Martin's Press, pp. 27–47.

Perrow, Charles. 1981. "Markets, Hierarchies and Hegemony." In Andrew Van de Ven and William Joyce, eds., *Perspectives on Organization, Design, and Behavior.* New York: Wiley, pp. 371–86.

———. 1986. *Complex Organizations: A Critical Essay,* third edition. New York: Random House.

Pfeffer, Jeffrey. 1987. "A Resource Dependence Perspective on Intercorporate Relations." In Mark Mizruchi and Michael Schwartz, eds., *Intercorporate Relations: The Structural Analysis of Business.* New York: Cambridge University Press, pp. 25–55.

Pfeffer, Jeffrey, and Gerald Salancik. 1978. *The External Control of Organizations: A Resource Dependence Perspective.* New York: Harper and Row.

Piore, Michael J., and Charles Sabel. 1984. *The Second Industrial Divide: Possibilities for Prosperity.* New York: Basic Books.

Polanyi, Karl. 1944. *The Great Transformation: The Political and Economic Origins of Our Time.* Boston: Beacon Press.

Robbins, James A. 1987. "Organizational Economics: Notes on the Use of Transaction-Cost Theory in the Study of Organizations." *Administrative Science Quarterly* 32(1): 68–86.

Sabel, Charles F. 1989. "Flexible Specialization and the Re-emergence of Regional Economies." In Paul Hirst and Jonathan Zeitlin, eds., *Reversing Industrial Decline? Industrial Structure and Policy in Britain and Her Competitors.* New York: Berg, pp. 17–70.

Scherer, Frederic M. 1970. *Industrial Market Structure and Economic Performance.* Chicago: Rand McNally.

Schneiberg, Marc, and Rogers Hollingsworth. 1990. "Transaction Cost Economics and Trade Associations." In Masahika Aoki, Bo Gustafsson, and Oliver Williamson, eds., *The Firm as a Nexus of Treaties.* Beverly Hills, CA: Sage, pp. 320–46.

Schumpeter, Joseph. A. 1983 (1934). *The Theory of Economic Development.* New Brunswick, NJ: Transaction Books.

Sorge, Arndt, and Wolfgang Streeck. 1988. "Industrial Relations and Technical Change: The Case for an Extended Perspective." In Richard Hyman and Wolfgang Streeck, eds., *New Technology and Industrial Relations.* New York and Oxford: Blackwell, pp. 19–47.

Smircich, Linda. 1983. "Concepts of Culture and Organizational Analysis." *Administrative Science Quarterly* 28(3): 339–58.

Stevenson, Rodney. 1987. "Institutional Economics and the Theory of Production." *Journal of Economic Issues* 21(4): 1471–93.

Stinchcombe, Arthur. 1983. *Economic Sociology.* New York: Academic Press.

Stone, Katherine. 1981. "The Origins of Job Structures in the Steel Industry." In Mary Zey-Ferrell and Michael Aiken, eds., *Complex Organizations: Critical Perspectives.* Glenview, IL: Scott, Foresman, pp. 349–81.

Streeck, Wolfgang. 1983. "Between Pluralism and Corporatism: German Business Associations and the State." *Journal of Public Policy* 3(3): 265–83.

———. 1989. "On the Social and Political Conditions of Diversified Quality Production." Paper presented at the International Conference, "No Way to Full Employment?," Wissenschaftszentrum Berlin fuer Socialforschung, Berlin, July 5–7.

Streeck, Wolfgang, and Philippe C. Schmitter. 1985. "Community, Market, State – and Associations? The Prospective Contribution of Interest Governance to Social Order." In Wolfgang Streeck and Philippe C. Schmitter, eds., *Private Interest Government: Beyond Market and State.* Beverly Hills, CA: Sage, pp. 1–29.

Swedberg, Richard. 1989. "Socioeconomics and the New Methodenstreit: On the

Paradigmatic Struggle in Contemporary Economics." Paper presented at the First Annual International Conference on Socio-Economics, Harvard Business School, Cambridge, Massachusetts.

Torstendahl, Rolf. 1984. "Technology in the Development of Society, 1850–1980: Four Phases of Industrial Capitalism in Western Europe." *History and Technology* 1(2): 157–74.

Useem, Michael. 1984. *The Inner Circle: Large Corporations and the Rise of Business Political Activity in the U.S. and U.K.* New York: Oxford University Press.

Weiss, Linda. 1988. *Creating Capitalism: The State and Small Business Since 1945.* New York: Blackwell.

Williamson, Oliver E. 1975. *Markets and Hierarchies: Analysis and Antitrust Implications.* New York: The Free Press.

———. 1981. "The Economics of Organization: The Transaction Cost Approach." *American Journal of Sociology* 87(3): 548–77.

———. 1985. *The Economic Institutions of Capitalism: Firms, Markets, Relational Contracting.* New York: The Free Press.

Young, Oran R. 1989. *International Cooperation: Building Regimes for Natural Resources and the Environment.* Ithaca, NY: Cornell University Press.

CHAPTER 12

Atkinson, Michael, and William Coleman. 1989. "Strong States and Weak States: Sectoral Policy Networks in Advanced Capitalist Economies." *British Journal of Political Science* 19(1): 47–67.

Badaracco, Joseph L. 1985. *Loading the Dice: A Five Country Study of Vinyl Chloride Regulation.* Boston: Harvard Business School Press.

Baran, Paul, and Paul Sweezy. 1966. *Monopoly Capital: An Essay on the American Economic and Social Order.* New York: Monthly Review Press.

Bensel, Richard Franklin. 1984. *Sectionalism and American Political Development, 1880–1980.* Madison, WI: University of Wisconsin Press.

Block, Fred. 1987. *Revising State Theory: Essays in Politics and Postindustrialism.* Philadelphia: Temple University Press.

Bluestone, Barry, and Bennett Harrison. 1982. *The Deindustrialization of America: Plant Closings, Community Abandonment, and the Dismantling of Basic Industry.* New York: Basic Books.

Bowles, Roger. 1984. "Property and the Legal System." In David K. Whynes, ed., *What is Political Economy?* New York: Blackwell, pp. 187–208.

Caporaso, James A. 1989. "Microeconomics and International Political Economy: The Neoclassical Approach to Institutions." In Ernst-Otto Czempiel and James A. Roseman, eds., *Global Changes and Theoretical Challenges.* Lexington, MA: Lexington Books, pp. 135–60.

Chandler, Alfred D. 1977. *The Visible Hand: The Managerial Revolution in American Business.* Cambridge, MA: Harvard University Press.

Cox, Andrew. 1986. *The State, Finance and Industry.* New York: St. Martin's Press.

Cuff, Robert D. 1973. *The War Industries Board: Business–Government Relations During World War I.* Baltimore: Johns Hopkins University Press.

Dertouzos, Michael L., Richard K. Lester, and Robert M. Solow. 1989. *Made in America: Regaining the Productive Edge.* Cambridge, MA: The MIT Press.

Dyer, Davis, Malcolm S. Salter, and Alan M. Webber. 1987. *Changing Alliances.* Boston: Harvard Business School Press.

Dyson, Kenneth. 1983. "The Cultural, Ideological and Structural Context." In

Kenneth Dyson and Stephen Wilks, eds. *Industrial Crisis: A Comparative Study of the State and Industry*. Oxford: Martin Robertson, pp. 26–66.

Edmonds, Martin. 1983. "Market Ideology and Corporate Power: The United States." In Kenneth Dyson and Stephen Wilks, eds., *Industrial Crisis: A Comparative Study of the State and Industry*. Oxford: Martin Robertson, pp. 67–101.

Eisinger, Peter. 1988. *The Rise of the Entrepreneurial State*. Madison, WI: University of Wisconsin Press.

Evans, Peter B., Dietrich Rueschemeyer, and Theda Skocpol, eds. 1985. *Bringing the State Back In*. New York: Cambridge University Press.

Fosler, R. Scott. 1988. *The New Economic Role of American States*. New York: Oxford University Press.

Galambos, Louis, and Joseph Pratt. 1988. *The Rise of the Corporate Commonwealth: U.S. Business and Public Policy in the Twentieth Century*. New York: Basic Books.

Goodman, Robert. 1979. *The Last Entrepreneurs: America's Regional Wars for Jobs and Dollars*. Boston: South End Press.

Gourevitch, Peter. 1986. *Politics in Hard Times: Comparative Responses to International Economic Crises*. Ithaca, NY: Cornell University Press.

Hall, Peter A. 1986. *Governing the Economy: The Politics of State Intervention in Britain and France*. New York: Oxford University Press.

Handlin, Oscar, and Mary Handlin. 1969. *Commonwealth: A Study of the Role of Government in the American Economy: Massachusetts, 1774–1861*. New York: New York University Press.

Hawley, Ellis W. 1966. *The New Deal and the Problem of Monopoly*. Princeton: Princeton University Press.

Hodgson, Geoffrey M. 1988. *Economics and Institutions: A Manifesto for a Modern Institutional Economics*. Philadelphia: University of Pennsylvania Press.

Hooks, Gregory. Forthcoming. *The Battle of the Potomac*. Urbana, IL: University of Illinois Press.

Horwitz, Morton. 1977. *The Transformation of American Law, 1780–1860*. Cambridge, MA: Harvard University Press.

Hughes, Jonathan R. T. 1977. *The Governmental Habit: Economic Controls from Colonial Times to the Present*. New York: Basic Books.

Hurst, James Willard. 1960. *Law and the Conditions of Freedom in the 19th Century United States*. Madison, WI: University of Wisconsin Press.

———. 1964. *Law and Economic Growth: The Legal History of the Lumber Industry in Wisconsin, 1836–1915*. Cambridge, MA: Harvard University Press.

———. 1977. *Law and Social Order in the United States*. Ithaca, NY: Cornell University Press.

———. 1982. *Law and Markets in United States History: Different Modes of Bargaining Among Interests*. Madison, WI: University of Wisconsin Press.

Ikenberry, G. John. 1988. *Reasons of State: Oil Politics and the Capacities of American Government*. Ithaca, NY: Cornell University Press.

Katzenstein, Peter J. 1978. "Conclusion: Domestic Structures and Strategies of Foreign Economic Policy." In Peter Katzenstein, ed., *Between Power and Plenty: Foreign Economic Patterns of Advanced Industrial States*. Madison, WI: University of Wisconsin Press, pp. 295–336.

Keller, Morton. 1981. "The Pluralist State: American Economic Regulation in Comparative Perspective." In Thomas McCraw, ed., *Regulation in Perspective: Historical Essays*. Cambridge, MA: Harvard University Press, pp. 56–94.

Kolko, Gabriel. 1963. *The Triumph of Conservatism: A Reinterpretation of American History, 1900–1916*. Chicago: Quadrangle Books.

———. 1976. *Main Currents in Modern American History.* New York: Harper and Row.

Krasner, Stephen D. 1978a. "United States Commercial and Monetary Policy: Unraveling the Paradox of External Strength and Internal Weakness." In Peter Katzenstein, ed., *Between Power and Plenty: Foreign Economic Policies of Advanced Industrial States.* Madison, WI: University of Wisconsin Press, pp. 51–88.

———. 1978b. *Defending the National Interest: Raw Materials Investments and U.S. Foreign Policy.* Princeton: Princeton University Press.

Lazonick, William. 1986. "Organizations, Markets, and Productivity." Paper presented at the Economic History Association meeting, Hartford, Connecticut.

McCraw, Thomas K. 1984. *Prophets of Regulation: Charles Francis Adams, Louis D. Brandeis, James M. Landis, Alfred E. Kahn.* Cambridge, MA: Harvard University Press.

———. 1986. "Mercantilism and the Market: Antecedents of American Industrial Policy." In Claude E. Barfield, Jr., and William A. Schambra, eds., *The Politics of Industrial Policy.* Washington, DC: American Enterprise Institute, pp. 33–62.

Markusen, Ann R. 1985. *Profit Cycles, Oligopoly, and Regional Development.* Cambridge, MA: The MIT Press.

———. 1987. *Regions: The Economics and Politics of Territory.* Totowa, NJ: Rowman and Littlefield.

Miliband, Ralph. 1969. *The State in Capitalist Society.* New York: Basic Books.

Newman, Robert J. 1984. *Growth in the American South: Changing Regional Employment and Wage Patterns in the 1960s and 1970s.* New York: New York University Press.

North, Douglass. 1981. *Structure and Change in Economic History.* New York: Norton.

Peltzman, Sam. 1976. "Toward a More General Theory of Regulation." *Journal of Law and Economics* 19(2): 211–40.

Piore, Michael J., and Charles Sabel. 1984. *The Second Industrial Divide: Possibilities for Prosperity.* New York: Basic Books.

Polanyi, Karl. 1944. *The Great Transformation: The Political and Economic Origins of Our Time.* Boston: Beacon Press.

Posner, Richard A. 1974. "Theories of Economic Regulation." *Bell Journal of Economics and Management Science* 5 (Autumn): 337–52.

Rueschemeyer, Dietrich, and Peter Evans. 1985. "The State and Economic Transformation: Toward an Analysis of the Conditions Underlying Effective Intervention." In Peter Evans, Dietrich Rueschemeyer, and Theda Skocpol, eds., *Bringing the State Back In.* New York: Cambridge University Press, pp. 44–77.

Samuels, Richard J. 1987. *The Business of the Japanese State: Energy Markets in Comparative and Historical Perspective.* Ithaca, NY: Cornell University Press.

Sanders, Elizabeth. 1986. "Industrial Concentration, Sectional Competition, and Anti-trust Politics in America, 1880–1989." *Studies in American Political Development* 1: 142–214.

Scheiber, Harry N. 1978. "American Federalism and the Diffusion of Power: Historical and Contemporary Perspectives." *University of Toledo Law Review* 9(4): 619–80.

———. 1980a. "Federalism and Legal Process: Historical and Contemporary Analysis of the American System." *Law and Society Review* 14(3): 663–722.

———. 1980b. "Public Economic Policy and the American Legal System: Historical Perspectives." *Wisconsin Law Review* 1980(6): 1159–89.

———. 1981. "Regulation, Property Rights, and Definition of 'the Market': Law and the American Economy." *The Journal of Economic History* 41(1): 103–9.

Shapiro, Martin. 1986. "The Supreme Court's 'Return' to Economic Regulation." *Studies in American Political Development* 1: 91–141.

Shonfield, Andrew. 1965. *Modern Capitalism: The Changing Balance of Public and Private Power.* London: Oxford University Press.

Skocpol, Theda. 1985. "Bringing the State Back In: Strategies of Analysis in Current Research." In Peter Evans, Dietrich Rueschemeyer, and Theda Skocpol, eds., *Bringing the State Back In.* New York: Cambridge University Press, pp. 3–37.

Skowronek, Stephen. 1982. *Building the New American State: The Expansion of National Administrative Capacities, 1877–1920.* New York: Cambridge University Press.

Solo, Robert. 1974. *The Political Authority and the Market System.* Cincinnati, OH: South-Western.

Stepan, Alfred. 1978. *The State and Society: Peru in Comparative Perspective.* Princeton: Princeton University Press.

Stigler, George J. 1975. *The Citizen and the State: Essays on Regulation.* Chicago: University of Chicago Press.

Streeck, Wolfgang, and Philippe C. Schmitter. 1985. "Community, Market, State – And Associations? The Prospective Contribution of Interest Governance to Social Order." In Wolfgang Streeck and Philippe Schmitter, eds., *Private Interest Government: Beyond Market and State.* Beverly Hills, CA: Sage, pp. 1–29.

Thomson, Janice E., and Stephen D. Krasner. 1989. "Global Transactions and the Consolidation of Sovereignty." In Ernst-Otto Czempiel and James A. Roseman, eds., *Global Changes and Theoretical Challenges.* Lexington, MA: Lexington Books, pp. 161–76.

Thurow, Lester C. 1984. "Building a World Class Economy." *Society* 22(1): 16–28.

Vogel, David. 1983. "The Power of Business in America: A Re-appraisal." *British Journal of Political Science* 13: 19–43.

———. 1987. "Government–Industry Relations in the United States: An Overview." In Stephen Wilks and Maurice Wright, eds., *Comparative Government–Industry Relations: Western Europe, the United States, and Japan.* New York: Oxford University Press, pp. 91–116.

Walsh, Annmarie Hauk. 1978. *The Public's Business: The Politics and Practices of Government Corporations.* Cambridge, MA: The MIT Press.

Weiss, Linda. 1988. *Creating Capitalism: The State and Small Business Since 1945.* New York: Blackwell.

White, Lawrence. 1982. "The Motor Vehicle Industry." In Richard Nelson, ed., *Government and Technical Progress: A Cross-Industry Analysis.* New York: Pergamon, pp. 411–50.

Wilks, Stephen, and Maurice Wright. 1987. "Conclusion: Comparing Government–Industry Relations: States, Sectors, and Networks." In Stephen Wilks and Maurice Wright, eds., *Comparative Government–Industry Relations: Western Europe, the United States, and Japan.* New York: Oxford University Press, pp. 274–314.

Williamson, Oliver E. 1975. *Markets and Hierarchies: Analysis and Antitrust Implications.* New York: The Free Press.

———. 1985. *The Economic Institutions of Capitalism: Firms, Markets, Relational Contracting.* New York: The Free Press.

Zysman, John. 1983. *Governments, Markets, and Growth: Financial Systems and the Politics of Industrial Change.* Ithaca, NY: Cornell University Press.

Index